Black Society in Spanish Florida

Blacks in the New World
Edited by August Meier

A list of books in the series appears at the end of this book.

Black Society in Spanish Florida

Jane Landers

Foreword by Peter H. Wood

University of Illinois Press

Urbana and Chicago

To the memory of my parents, Howard C. and Emily Gilmer, and my paternal uncle, Vance Gilmer

Publication of this book has been supported by grants from the Program for Cultural Cooperation between Spain's Ministry of Education and Culture and United States' Universities and from Vanderbilt University.

Manufactured in the United States of America
1 2 3 4 5 C P 9 8 7 6

∞ This book is printed on acid-free paper.

Library of Congress Cataloging-in-Publication Data
Landers, Jane.
Black society in Spanish Florida / Jane Landers.
p. cm. — (Blacks in the new world)
Includes bibliographical references and index.
ISBN 978-0-252-02446-7 (cloth : acid-free paper)
ISBN 978-0-252-06753-2 (pbk. : acid-free paper)
1. Afro-Americans—Florida—History.
2. Afro-Americans—Florida—Social conditions.
3. Slavery—Florida—History. 4. Florida—History—Spanish colony, 1565–1763.
5. Florida—History—Spanish colony, 1784–1821. I. Title. II. Series.
F320.N4L36 1999
975.9'00496073—ddc21
98-25478
CIP

Contents

Foreword

Peter H. Wood

After all these years, how little we know about the black experience in Spanish Florida. At one extreme, in a popular adventure story (*Naufrage et Aventures,* published in 1768 by Pierre Viaud), we read of supposed cannibalism practiced by French shipwreck survivors against an African slave in northwest Florida. At the other extreme, in a prize-winning novel (*Sacred Hunger* by Barry Unsworth, published in 1992), we read of a fictional mixed-race colony founded in southeast Florida at about the same time by the black and white survivors of an Atlantic mutiny aboard an English slave ship. But what of less fictional accounts, lying somewhere between these two extremes? After all, black Floridians in the colonial era were neither victims of cannibalism on the one hand nor participants in a utopian experiment on the other.

It has been more than seventy-five years since Herbert Bolton published several books and articles about colonial Florida, and in the intervening decades other historians intrigued by the Spanish borderlands (including John Tate Lanning, John TePaske, Amy Bushnell, and David Weber) have expanded this scholarly base. Now Jane Landers follows and joins this group, offering us a topical study that makes energetic use of detailed and challenging Spanish documents. These are not easy sources to locate and master, and Landers has done an impressive job in an area where there are few predecessors to lead her. The results are exciting, for in a field such as early Florida history, where the shelf of important books remains small, the impact of a solid and intriguing monograph such as this one can be quite large.

Not only is the history of Spanish Florida thin but the very good work which has been done in recent generations by U.S. scholars remains almost totally cut off from the Anglocentric mainstream. Few of us know much about the nature of life in Florida under Spanish rule, and few have a clear sense of the aggressive expansionism of southern slaveholders at the beginning of the nineteenth century. Similarly, few people have a clear sense of the steady ties between early Florida and the Caribbean, in particular the nearby island of Cuba. One of the largest virtues of this book, therefore, is that it links English and Spanish colonial history, reaching across the southern border in a way that few other historians have been equipped to do. Ethnohistorians and scholars of the Creek and Seminole Indians have made a few successful forays in this direction, but Landers will draw the attention of readers with interests on both sides of the linguistic and cultural border which was so prominent and significant in the centuries before 1820.

Moreover, Landers's work also helps to bridge the gap in understanding which still separates black and white inhabitants of the early Southeast. African American history, much more than early Florida history, has been a growth industry in recent decades, and the black past in such southern cities as Charleston, Savannah, and New Orleans is beginning to be told. But much of the best literature relating to black southerners still concerns the nineteenth and twentieth centuries; there has been very little written by historians with regard to blacks in Spanish Florida. In recent years, for instance, the largest headlines have rightly gone instead to Florida archaeologist Kathy Deagan for her work on Fort Mose, the unique eighteenth-century African American site just north of St. Augustine. So scholars of black history will be especially fascinated, and not a little surprised, by this book.

In short, this book will intrigue a wide audience. It makes careful and extensive use of Spanish-language sources stretching over three centuries. In doing so, it presents a view of early African American life in the Southeast that is unfamiliar and that contrasts sharply with the usual image of the slave in the tobacco patch and the rice field. Many of Professor Landers's subjects are town-dwellers, many are allowed to carry arms, many are Spanish speakers, many are property owners, many profess the Catholic faith, and many are escaped slaves successfully rebuilding their lives. We are in her debt for bringing to life this rich array of individuals and placing them in their historical setting.

Acknowledgments

I am happy, at long last, to be able to thank the many wonderful colleagues and friends who have helped me produce this book, as well as the entities that have supported my research over the years.

At the University of Florida Lyle N. McAlister directed my dissertation and provided a model of scholarship and elegant writing which I still work to emulate. James S. Amelang introduced me to the best in European social and cultural history and has been my mentor and friend ever since, providing endless bibliographic suggestions and reading every page of this work. It takes a true friend to let you know when you've written "drek." I am also indebted to Cheryll A. Cody, whose impressive scholarship on slavery and insightful editing shaped my early research, as well as to the other members of my doctoral committee, David Bushnell, Kathleen A. Deagan, Samuel Proctor, and David R. Colburn. David's subsequent invitation to collaborate with him in editing *The African American Heritage of Florida* was another important step in my professional development and produced a work of which we are both proud. Although he arrived at Florida after my committee was already formed, Murdo J. MacLeod took an interest in my work, attended my early paper presentations, and generously wrote letters of support when I needed them. I value his scholarship as well as his friendship.

Although when I began my dissertation I was warned against doing a Florida topic (for fear of being typecast as a "local" historian), I followed a distinguished group of earlier historians into that field who also did Florida as "international" history. They are an extremely generous and welcoming group who not only set a high standard but supported my research all along the way. I am deeply indebted to John J. TePaske, Eugene Lyon, Amy Turner Bushnell, Michael Gannon, and

John H. Hann, in particular. Susan R. Parker is now expanding upon their fine scholarship on the "first Spanish period" (1565–1763) and has helped me in any number of ways over the years tracking down documents and maps for me, and most importantly, providing feedback on my research from her own deep knowledge of the sources and the period. Florida scholars like Daniel L. Schafer and Canter Brown, Jr., who are elaborating the black history of the British and U.S. territorial periods also provided me with important insights and support.

Another fine scholar of Florida and Caribbean history, Kathleen Deagan, forever changed and immeasurably enriched my work. While I was still her graduate student, Kathy hired me to do the historical research for the Fort Mose Archaeological Project and trained me to look at my documentary evidence in a completely new way, paying more careful attention to material conditions and culture, spatial relationships, ethnicity, topography, and other questions of import to historical archaeologists. She became my role model, mentor, and valued friend. My association with Kathy also led me to other rewarding friendships and collaborations in the world of archaeology. Bonnie G. McEwan, Darcie MacMahon, Donna Ruhl, Kate Hoffman, and James Cusick are still my colleagues on a number of ongoing museum and publication projects.

The historian whose work most influenced my own and who has also critiqued my work from dissertation stage to the present is Peter H. Wood. *Black Majority* was a revelation to me. I read it and felt an immediate connection—not only in the way Peter approached his protagonists but in the historical narrative itself—his Stono rebels were headed to Spanish Florida and I wanted to know why and what their lives were like in that new world. We finally met when Peter became an advisor on the Fort Mose project and I am deeply grateful to him for his work, his support, and his willingness to check me when I veered into the sentimental.

Sitting across the table at the Archive of the Indies I had the good fortune to meet someone who would become another major influence on my work, Gwendolyn Midlo Hall. In Gwen I found someone with whom to share research finds and perspectives and someone whose enthusiasm and love of her work were a real inspiration to me, then and now.

I am most indebted, perhaps, to August Meier, who made this book possible. Augie first noticed my work when he read a panel proposal Theda Purdue had invited me to submit to the OAH. He wrote and asked to see the dissertation, which he promptly covered with red ink. Although he found my writing wanting, he was intrigued by the material, and he encouraged and supported me when I applied to NEH for a fellowship to allow me to revise the dissertation. Later Augie recommended my book for inclusion in the Blacks in the New World series and I am honored to be in the company of the fine authors who have preceded me in this series.

The research for this book took me to a number of fine archives and research institutions, first and foremost of which was the P. K. Yonge Library of Florida History at the University of Florida. It became my second home and I am forever indebted to Elizabeth Alexander and Bruce Chappell for making their rich collections so available to me and for facilitating all my research in Spain. Bruce also trained me in paleography and in the intricacies of the Spanish archives. Robin Lauriault and Pat Payne kindly arranged to photograph maps I needed from the P. K. Yonge Collection and Darcie MacMahon and Pat did the same with artifacts from the Florida Museum of Natural History. My research in the Spanish land grant records was conducted in Tallahassee and I would like to thank David Coles and Joe Knetsch in particular for their generous help to me. I have also been helped over the years by the friendly group at the St. Augustine Historical Society and I would like to thank its director Page Edwards and the great staff including Taryn Rodríguez-Boette, Dorothy Lyon, Charles Tingley, Eddie Joyce Geyer, and Ken Barrett, Jr. The former historian of the Castillo de San Marcos, Luis Arana, generously shared maps, notes, and transcripts collected over many years with me and he is missed.

I am also grateful for the professional and courteous assistance of archivists and librarians at the Archivo General de Indias, Seville; the Archivo General de Simancas; the Biblioteca Nacional and the Archivo Histórico Nacional, Madrid; the Archivo de la Nación, Havana; the Archivo Municipal de Matanzas; and the Archivo de la Nación, Mexico. Many priests and parish archivists patiently assisted me in Cuba at the Cathedral Archives of Havana and Matanzas and in the parish archives of Ceiba Mocha, Regla, Guanabacoa, and Havana. The help and friendship of the scholars at the Escuela de Estudios Hispano-Americanos enriched my stay in Seville and I would like to acknowledge in particular Dra. María Justina Sarrabia Viejo and Dr. Javier Ortiz de la Tabla Ducasse.

Many Gainesville friends provided friendship and support while I was researching this book and I would like to thank Steve and Beverly Noll, Joe and Toni Thompson, Margie and Terry Silverman, Robin Lauriault and Delia McClelland, and Anne Goodwyn Jones for opening their homes to me. Rosemarijn Hoefte has shared my friendship and Caribbean interests since graduate school days and her strength and intellectual standards have been an example to me. Kimberly Hanger and I have also shared detailed discussions on our mutual research interests for many years now and have collaborated on publication projects and shared so many panels that we became a virtual road show. My thanks also to the members of my Ducks softball team for some sorely needed escape, especially Jeremy Stahl.

The friendship, support, and intellectual stimulation provided by my Vanderbilt colleagues have made the last six years joyful and productive. I am particularly indebted to my fellow Latin Americanists, Simon Collier and Marshall Eakin, on whose friendship, support, and advice I have depended heavily. Others of my Vanderbilt colleagues were kind enough to read and comment on parts of this book, and I would like to thank Joel Harrington, Paul Freedman, Joyce Chaplin, J. León Helguera, and Beth Rose for their generous help. Paula Covington's bibliographic expertise, support, and friendship contributed greatly to my work, as did the long, heartfelt discussions with Jimmie L. Franklin on matters of mutual concern. I also thank my good-humored hallmates, Helmut Smith, Michael Bess, and Frank Wcislo for enjoyable distractions from the serious business of writing and my graduate student, Lynne Guitar, for creating a database for my black militias and editing for me. I am also grateful to Russell G. Hamilton, who as dean of graduate studies and research has consistently supported my work.

This work would not have been possible without the critical financial support of many institutions. I would like to acknowledge the generosity of the National Endowment for the Humanities, which gave me a Fellowship for University Teachers in 1991–92 and a summer stipend in 1997, Vanderbilt University and its University Research Council, which funded me for a sabbatical year in 1995–96 and for summer research in 1993 and 1995, and which funded my travel to international conferences in Mexico, Canada, and Brazil. The Program for Cultural Cooperation between Spain's Ministry of Culture and United States' Universities assisted me twice with travel and research grants in 1988 and 1995–96, and the Instituto de Cooperación Iberoamericano supported my initial research in Spain in 1984. The Spain-Florida Alliance and the University of Florida's Department of History also awarded me support for travel and research in Spain and gave me a graduate fellowship in 1982–83.

Chance encounters have also led me to know or have contact with living descendants of some of the historical actors in this book, some of whom retain their connections to St. Augustine and what used to be its hinterlands, and I would like to acknowledge them. St. Augustine's Councilman Henry Twine carried on the tradition of service of his ancestor, Tony Proctor, who served both the Spanish and later the American armies as a linguist to the Seminoles. His widow, Katherine, now carries on without him as a member of the Fort Mose Historical Society. This wonderful group replicates Florida's historical tradition of diversity and now young black men and women from local schools study the history and re-create the roles of documented residents of Mose in public celebrations supported by the community at large.[1]

Another relative of those I now consider my adopted family was a fellow panelist at a conference at the Smithsonian Institution, suitably entitled "Will the

Circle Be Unbroken?" After my presentation Professor Yvonne Daniel asked if I had any information on her ancestor, Jorge J. F. Clarke, who as a surveyor, judge, family member, and patron played such a critical role in advancing and protecting blacks in Spanish Florida. Daniel is a dance anthropologist whose research explores contemporary Afro-Hispanic cultural traditions in Cuba.[2] That chance meeting led to long telephone conversations with Professor Daniel and her brother, Kirby Payne, who attends law school in New York City, and to discussions of the complex genealogy compiled by another family member, Edward Gourdine, a lawyer, the first black judge in Massachusetts, and an Olympic athlete who ran with Jessie Owens. This document tracks both the white and black sides of the Clarke/Garvin/Loften/Gourdine families since Jorge J. F. Clarke's time.

On another occasion while working in the St. Augustine Historical Society library, I was introduced to a couple who were in the midst of their own family research. Roy and Stephanie Myers, of Washington, D.C., were tracking the history of their ancestors, the Holzendorfs. Don Juan Holzendorf was a planter with holdings in Georgia and Florida, but Manuel Holzendorf (also spelled Alcendorf) had French origins and probably came to Florida from Saint Domingue with Jorge Biassou. He served in Spanish Florida's black militia and his son, Tomás, born of a slave mother, remained a slave until he and his wife, Harriet, took advantage of the presence of Union troops along the St. Johns River and made good their escape. Daniel L. Schafer has tracked Tomás Holzendorf's military career with the Union Army and Patricia Kenney has documented his postwar role in helping incorporate the free black town of LaVilla, which was subsequently subsumed by Jacksonville.[3] Another member of this family, Betty Holzendorf, became an educator and later a state senator representing the same area of the state where her ancestors left their historical record. As a member of the Black Caucus of the Florida legislature she has supported historical and archaeological research at Mose and at other important historic sites such as the plantation of Zephaniah Kingsley.

A real highlight was meeting Cornelia Walker Bailey, resident historian of the Hog Hammock Community on Sapelo Island. One stormy night, when the lights went out in the trailer I was sharing with fellow Gullah researchers Tom Stewart, of South Carolina State University, and Emory Campbell, of the Penn Center, our hostess Cornelia came bearing candles. Then, in the flickering light, as lightening crashed around us, this master storyteller regaled us with tales of her ancestors, like Bilali, Thomas Spalding's Muslim overseer.[4] And for that memorable night I was transported to the time in 1788 when Prince and Flora and their two sons and a daughter, and fellow slaves Edmund and Mariana, Cyrus, and March, slipped away from the Spalding plantation and made good their escape to St. Augustine.[5] All of these individuals have enriched me and my work and I acknowledge my heartfelt debt to them.

Finally, I would like to acknowledge the debt I owe my family for years of patient support and encouragement of my academic efforts. My childhood models of achievement and love of learning were my mother and father, my maternal grandmother, my paternal uncle, and my sister. My husband, Jimmy, made this nomadic life possible by helping me raise our son, Vance, in my many absences. Together they shared my worst and best moments and I love them for being able to forgive the former and enjoy the latter. I am also indebted to Jimmy for his unmatched design sense and his meticulous production of my maps. Finally, I would like to thank Richard L. Wentworth, Emily Rogers, and Theresa L. Sears at the University of Illinois Press for their support in producing this book and to express my deep gratitude to Patricia Hollahan for her great care and good-natured guidance in copyediting this massive and complex manuscript.

Black Society in Spanish Florida

Introduction

Frank Tannenbaum's important book, *Slave and Citizen, the Negro in the Americas,* initiated a long historiographic debate about the relative severity of slave systems and the transition from slavery to freedom in the Americas. Many subsequent studies examined these themes in plantation areas, where rapid development of export economies meant resulting deterioration in slave life and reduced opportunities for freedom, and these works clearly demonstrated the flaws in Tannenbaum's analysis.[1] A more appropriate laboratory in which to test Tannenbaum's original thesis would be an area like Spanish Florida and its frontier, where competing slave systems coexisted in a more or less equal level of development prior to the evolution of monoculture and chattel slavery.[2]

The patterns of black society in Florida evolved during Spain's first tenure in the province (1565–1763) and were shaped by complex interethnic relations and international politics. Like other areas in the Spanish Caribbean, Florida suffered from early and dramatic Indian depopulation and a shortage of European manpower, and this demographic imperative created a constant demand for black labor, artisanal, and military skills.

The Barbadian colonization of Carolina in 1670 triggered a century and a half of imperial competition for control of the Southeast and created an international border that enslaved Africans and Native Americans alike negotiated in pursuit of freedom and preservation. The geopolitical pressures exerted by Spain's southeastern and Caribbean rivals created additional leverage for slaves in Florida and even greater Spanish dependence upon free people of color. Great Britain's brief tenure in the colony (1763–84) temporarily eradicated the international border and black freedom became only a remote possibility in Florida. With the restoration of Spanish rule (1784–1821), however, the St. Marys River once again demarcated a political, legal, religious, and cultural divide across which a new group of black and Indian refugees fled southward. They entered a Hispanic frontier colony under almost constant attack, but this turmoil created opportunity as well as danger.[3]

Tannenbaum's critics correctly noted that the institutions that he claimed made Spanish slavery less severe—the church and the law—were not commonly accessible to field hands in remote agricultural settlements. This does not mean, however, that his argument was equally flawed for an urban setting or even for a plantation system whose slaves were still able to connect to the economy and institutions of a city such as St. Augustine.

Michael Mullin's recent study of slavery in the contemporary British Caribbean demonstrates how geographic context and the organization of labor and the slave market, like law and religion, also shaped the institution of slavery. Slavery during the second Spanish Florida period exhibited a number of the features that Mullin contends mitigated its oppressive nature: it was generally organized by the task system, and slaves had free time to engage in their own social and economic activities; slaves were able to utilize the resources of both frontier and coast to advantage; the trade in slaves was never massive, and the paternal model of plantation management prevailed, even on Florida's largest commercial plantation.[4]

Tannenbaum's contention that a lenient attitude toward manumission was crucial in a slave society and foreshadowed the former slave's role in freedom is also borne out in Spanish Florida. As Tannenbaum noted, Spanish law and custom granted the enslaved a moral and juridical personality, as well as certain rights and protections not found in other slave systems. Although legal and social ideals did not always obtain, slaves in Spanish Florida made good on the institutional promises of freedom through creative and persistent individual efforts aided by community support.

This is not to suggest that Spain and its colonies were free of racial prejudice; however, acknowledgement of a slave's humanity and rights and a liberal manumission policy eased the transition from slave to citizen and allowed the formation of a significant free black society throughout the Spanish world.[5]

The exceptionally rich documentary evidence on persons of African descent in Florida demonstrates how, given the proper conditions, both the enslaved and the recently freed could actually "work" the system. Having experienced a much more restrictive form of slavery, the newly emancipated were all the more motivated to test the limits of freedom among the Spaniards.

Soon after the conclusion of the American Revolution, the adolescent government of the United States began testing its strength against its international neighbors. Fueled by reports from Georgian planters, it viewed Spanish Florida with a mixture of fear and desire. The significant, and armed, free black class living in Florida, reputed for both its militancy and its alliance with the Seminoles, set an unacceptable example for plantation slaves of the Anglo South. Thus, the United States government not very covertly supported a number of hostile actions against Spanish Florida, including the Patriot War of 1812, the naval attack on the black fort and settlement at Prospect Bluff on the Apalachicola River in 1815, and Andrew Jackson's devastating raids against black and Seminole villages along the Suwannee River in 1818. The same hostility toward free blacks living among the Seminoles, and the Seminoles' refusal to return their allies and family members to slavery, lay at the heart of the three Seminole Wars from 1818 to 1859.

When, in 1821, Spain finally turned Florida over to the officials of the United States territorial government, it did not abandon its black citizens. As in Louisiana, cession treaties required the incoming government to respect the legal status and property rights of free blacks. Some free blacks, who had acquired property and invested years of hard work in improving it, decided to stay in Florida and risk trusting the newcomers to honor their treaty promises. But most of the free black community, like their predecessors in 1763, joined in a mass exodus to Cuba. Others fought on with the Seminoles and shared their fate.

For more than three centuries, blacks helped shape the geopolitics of the American Southeast and repeatedly created viable communities in Florida when conditions permitted. The institutional framework was in place and sufficient for determined slaves to pursue freedom through legal channels, and Spanish Florida's particular geographic, demographic, economic, and political factors enabled them to do so. Enslaved blacks adeptly manipulated a variety of political contests, as well as the demographic exigencies of the Spaniards in Florida to secure their freedom in ways not anticipated by older Spanish law, or by Tannenbaum. Through their own initiative, persons of African descent expanded the emancipatory potential of Spanish law and reshaped their lives. In effect, they judged Anglo slavery by "voting with their feet" and by risking their lives repeatedly to forestall its advance into Florida, and their political actions seem to confirm at least the basic tenets of Tannenbaum's comparative analysis.[6]

Michael Mullin addresses the historiographical problem of "time compression" in most studies of the African past in the Americas, studies that tend to focus on the more familiar antebellum South or the mature plantation systems of nineteenth-century Latin America. This perspective, he argues, "compromises the African contribution and resistance views generally."[7] Much of the history of the slave trade and the development of antebellum slavery is now general knowledge. On the other hand, the very strength of that narrative tends to subsume and "homogenize" the diversity of the African past in the Americas. For the colonial period at least, Africans in Florida lived not in cotton rows or tobacco patches but in a more complex and international world that linked the Caribbean, Africa, the various competing European powers in North America, and a still vast and powerful, not to mention diverse, Indian hinterland. Pragmatically drawing on African, European, and indigenous models to create a new society in the circum-Atlantic periphery of Florida, they fit Ira Berlin's profile of "Atlantic creoles"; people of "linguistic dexterity, cultural plasticity, and social agility."[8]

In a period when travel, transport, commerce, and communication all flowed more easily across water than land, it is significant that through Florida's small, but cosmopolitan, capital and port city of St. Augustine, where much of this story was recorded, persons of African descent connected to major ports on both sides of the Atlantic and throughout the Caribbean. The foreshortened chronology in the traditional depiction of North American slavery underplays this geographic factor and the international perspective and political awareness that it fostered among persons of African descent, not only in Florida, but along the Atlantic coast in general. Many of the blacks discussed in this volume were at home on the international waters and reshaped their lives by their navigational skills, as pilots, rivermen, sailors, and corsairs. The physical mobility and perspectives of such men and their families were much broader than traditional history commonly allows, and their outlook could be shared even by their enslaved fellows. Finally, if for no other reason than necessity, but, I would argue, for many others as well, persons of African descent in colonial Florida were politicized by imperial contests, Indian wars, and the American, French, and Haitian revolutions. After all, the issues debated in these conflicts—sovereignty, freedom of cultural and religious expression, slavery, political representation, independence, the rights of men, and property rights—were all of central importance to persons of African descent. It is much easier to believe that blacks followed the ideological debates of the era and the course of political events once it is understood that they participated in all of them in one way or another. The lamentably violent history of Spanish Florida is replete with black historical agency.

Contemporary ethnohistorical studies of the colonial southeastern and Gulf regions of North America, such as those of Gwendolyn Midlo Hall, Kimberly S. Hanger, Daniel H. Usner, Jr., and Peter H. Wood, show that Spanish Florida is not an anomaly. Blacks, both free and enslaved, made pragmatic and astute political decisions based on their understanding of a variety of European and Native American political, economic, and social systems. These works also confirm that persons of African descent exercised more important and varied roles on colonial Spanish frontiers of the present-day United States than has previously been appreciated.[9] Complementing these ethnohistorical works are new archaeological studies, such as those of Kathleen Deagan and Leland Ferguson, which are unearthing the lost cultural and material past of Africans and African Americans in colonial Florida. Deagan and Ferguson and their students are confirming the cultural adaptability of blacks in the tri-racial southern frontier, as well as the persistence of certain African material traditions.[10] Together these new and more sensitive inquiries and methodologies tell us that the history of the United States and its race relations is seriously distorted by neglecting the complex and sometimes more empowered past that blacks experienced in Florida and in the colonial Americas.

The Spaniards were meticulous and prolific bureaucrats who recorded their administrative, military, and religious colonial history in detail, including the history of their indigenous and black subjects as well as that of Spaniards. Despite Florida's turbulent past, the records for Spanish Florida miraculously escaped the damage and loss suffered in other colonial sites, and they are preserved in a number of wonderful repositories in Spain, Florida, and Cuba, and other circum-Caribbean locations. Many are now also microfilmed and stored in archives across the United States. Records for the first Spanish period (1565–1763) are less complete than those of the second Spanish period (1784–1821); the most important single subject covered for black history in those earlier records is the gradual evolution of Spain's religious sanctuary policy, which eventually allowed the formation of an important free black community at Gracia Real de Santa Teresa de Mose.[11] The archive for the second Spanish period government known as the East Florida Papers has survived virtually intact. This remarkable source contains a truly vast array of military, criminal, civil, religious, and notarial records, and the history of black Floridians is found throughout, much of it generated in their own words, and often their own hand. Spanning both periods of Spanish rule are the Catholic parish registers for St. Augustine, which record baptisms, marriages, and burials from 1594 forward. These are among the oldest surviving written records for black history generated in the present-day United States. Although originally all records were kept together, in 1738 the visiting bishop of Cuba ordered Florida's clerics to separate the registers by race, as was done in Cuba. After 1738 the Spaniards are registered in one set of books and Indians, Pardos, and Morenos in another set. In some areas Spaniards used the term *pardo* to denote anyone of mixed descent, but in Cuba and Florida it came to mean mulatto, while *moreno* meant someone of pure African lineage. I have used "black" to denote anyone of African descent except in cases where the Spanish term was more significant. Parish registers occasionally referred to persons as *quarterón* (quadroon) or even less frequently, *octarón* (octoroon) but such references are rare and, as R. Douglas Cope, Richard Boyer, and others have pointed out, racial designations were fluid and socially constructed anyway.[12] The other major source for black history in Spanish records is the collection of land grants for the second Spanish period that were deposited in the Florida State Archives in Tallahassee and extracted and translated into a five-volume set by the Works Projects Administration. By tracking across the widest possible range of these original sources one can discern the basic contours of black life in Spanish Florida. What emerges is a picture of the early African past and a black society distinct from contemporary settlements north of the border. Similar records await scholars interested in working other Spanish American frontiers.

Precedents for Afro-Caribbean Society in Florida

Africans in Spain

The patterns of African society in the Spanish Americas including enslavement, manumission, miscegenation, congregation, limited political autonomy, and religious incorporation, all had their institutional and customary origins in medieval Castile but underwent modification in the Caribbean. Africans entered Spain with the Muslims (711–1492) and began to be a noticeable presence in the populations of southern Spain from at least the thirteenth century onward.[1]

During this time Christian kings such as Ferdinand, "King of the Three Religions" (1217–52), and his son, Alfonso X, "the Learned" (1252–84), of Castile, ruled over multicultural and polyglot kingdoms composed of Christian, Muslim, and Jewish subjects. These monarchs promoted royal schools of translation and intellectual exchange and developed legal and social traditions that accommodated difference. Castile's Christian monarchs required large populations of Muslims and Jews who chose to become subjects and remain in their ancient homelands to swear loyalty to the Crown and pay tribute, but otherwise permitted them to practice their own religion, to retain their laws and customs, and to keep their property. Moreover, they would be ruled by their own magistrates.[2] While religious and ethnic prejudice was not absent, and hostility against minorities sometimes flared, they were not encouraged, and diversity was more appreciated than it would be in later centuries.[3]

In the thirteenth century Alfonso X codified Castilian slave codes in the Siete Partidas. This body of law, which was later transplanted to the Americas, acknowledged a slave's moral personality and defined the slave's rights and obligations. Spanish slavery was not exclusively based on race, and Africans joined slaves of other races and ethnicities who had been captured in "just wars," had been condemned, or had sold themselves into slavery.[4] Castilian law considered slavery an unnatural condition and, therefore, provided many avenues out of bondage. The Siete Partidas established mechanisms by which a slave might escape an abusive owner or earn freedom for meritorious service to the state.[5] The medieval ideal of charity toward "miserable classes" also led Spanish owners to manumit favored slaves, often in their wills.[6] Furthermore, Castilian law and custom permitted slaves to hold and transfer property and, with their *peculium* or private property, they could purchase their freedom or that of relatives or friends. Thus, the lenient attitude toward manumission created a free black class in Spain which filled accepted economic and social and, even at the lowest level, political roles.[7]

Just as all slaves in Spain were not Africans, not all Africans were slaves. Some Africans entered Spain as free persons on trade or diplomatic missions.[8] Many others arrived as slaves via the trans-Saharan trade or, later, via the Atlantic trade, but became free. By the fifteenth and sixteenth centuries, free and enslaved Africans formed sizeable populations in southern cities such as Seville, where they worked as stevedores or in the city's public granary, slaughterhouse, gardens, and soap factories. They transported goods and people throughout the city and performed many other menial, but essential, services. Although excluded from Spanish guilds, Africans worked as artisans and petty merchants in the commercial districts and as domestic servants in Spanish households.[9]

One scholar compared early modern Seville to a chessboard with equal numbers of black and white pieces.[10] In the multiracial and multi-ethnic city, miscegenation and common-law unions between Spaniards and Africans were common, and the lower classes entered into mixed-race marriages.[11] Many enslaved Africans lived independently from their owners, and, much as *moriscos* (subject Muslims), *conversos* (converted Jews), and gypsies did, they and the free Africans of Seville congregated together in ethnic enclaves such as San Bernardo, San Roque, and San Idelfonso. While many African *vecinos* (registered citizens) of the lower classes lived "decent" lives, their less fortunate fellows blended into the poor working and unemployed underclass known as the *gente de mal vivir,* becoming beggars, thieves, day-laborers, street vendors, porters, prostitutes, and boatmen.[12]

In an attempt to better regulate the city, officials began to appoint free blacks as *mayorales* (stewards) for the black barrios. The black mayorales arbitrated disputes and defended their charges in court, even against their masters. As Seville's black population grew ever more numerous, Isabella and Ferdinand named a royal servant, Juan de Valladolid, "of noble lineage among blacks" to regulate the city's African community and serve as its "Chief and Judge."[13] This practice followed Reconquest patterns for governing subjugated peoples and foreshadowed Spanish practice in the Americas of establishing dominion through "natural" leaders of alien communities.[14]

Africans also developed their own religious and social institutions in Spain. The Catholic church worked to promote conversions in the rapidly expanding black barrios of southern Spain, and once Africans accepted the "True Faith," they enjoyed both the sacraments and the advocacy of the church. The African incorporation into the Catholic faith was further advanced when, in the fourteenth century, church officials approved the earliest documented religious confraternity or *cofradía* for Africans living in the San Bernardo parish of Seville. This legally constituted and recognized corporation administered the Hospital of Our Lady of the Angels and provided medical care for its members. As Seville's black population grew more numerous, the church established a second black parish of San Roque. San Roque also had its own confraternity, and the members built a church and chapel on the lots they purchased.[15] Gatherings of the confraternity members, which featured African singing and dancing, became known in Spain as *cabildos* and this terminology also crossed to the Americas, where it supplanted *cofradías.*[16]

Spain's African brotherhoods provided fraternal identity for their members and critical social services for their communities in Seville, Cádiz, Jerez, Valencia, El Puerto de Santa María, and Barcelona. Statutes for Barcelona's Cofradía Nigrorum Libertate Datorum Civitatus Barchinionie date to 1455 and outline the organization's mission to attend to the funerals of its members, provide food, alms, and medicine for the needy, and participate in religious observances such as Corpus Christi. In 1472 forty Africans in Valencia established the Cofradía de Santiago Apóstol de Negros Libertos, specifying that they would annually elect four magistrates and a syndic to govern and represent their membership. They also petitioned for their own banner to display in the brotherhood's window and in civic and religious processions such as Semana Santa (Holy Week) and Corpus Christi. More than a century later, Valencia's black cofradía was still in existence and proudly displayed its standard in a parade welcoming King Philip II to the city.[17] Through such civic and religious activity, some Africans created an accepted public sphere for themselves.

Given their numbers and roles in Spanish port cities like Seville, and their generally depressed economic conditions, it is not surprising that both free and enslaved Africans hoped to improve their lots by crossing the Atlantic on the earliest voyages of exploration and conquest. With the Europeans they formed a specialized and limited pool of human resources circulating throughout the circum-Caribbean, and together Africans and Europeans faced extraordinary challenges.

Thirteenth-century Spanish Christians baptizing a black man. Reprinted from *Fueros del Reino de Aragón* (Barcelona, ca. 1260–80). Courtesy of the Florida Museum of Natural History, Fort Mose Exhibition.

Africans in the Era of Exploration

The career of one West African is illustrative of the African experience in the era of exploration. Juan Garrido arrived in Seville (via Lisbon) around 1496 and some time later signed on for a voyage to Hispaniola. In the New World, Garrido encountered other free blacks such as Juan González (Ponce) de León, an interpreter of the Taíno language, whose surname was adopted from his Spanish patron on the island. The two African adventurers no doubt took part in the "pacification" campaigns against the native populations, who were in revolt.[18] They may also have faced other Africans in these battles for Governor Nicolás de Ovando complained in 1503 that some of the island's first African slaves had already run away, thereafter to be known as *cimarrones* (maroons), and that they had found refuge among the Indian rebels.[19] The alliance of rebellious Indians and fugitive slaves haunted the Spaniards, who were still a tiny minority in Hispaniola and only tenuously held power. Ovando charged that the maroons were teaching the Indians "bad customs," a theme that would be reiterated many times in other areas of Hispanic conquest, and he recommended that no more black slaves be sent from Spain.[20]

Despite these fears, however, Spaniards came to regard African slaves as indispensable to successful colonization of the Americas. Warfare, disease, and overwork quickly decimated Indian populations on Hispaniola, and because Spaniards had already benefited from the labor of Africans at home and on their Atlantic island plantations, they thought of them as the logical replacement for the dying Indians. Herbert Klein and others argue that the Atlantic plantation economies fundamentally altered Spanish slavery, stripping the slave of many medieval peninsular protections. As early as 1505, the Crown sent Guinea-born slaves purchased in Lisbon to work in Hispaniola's copper mines, and five years later King Ferdinand authorized the shipment of several hundred Christian and Spanish-speaking African slaves or *ladinos* from Seville for sale to the island's settlers.[21] Still the colonists demanded more slaves, and in 1513 the Crown established the *asiento* system whereby licensed contractors sent an estimated 75–90,000 enslaved Africans to Spanish America by 1600, and approximately 350,000 by the end of the seventeenth century.[22]

Once the Indian wars on Hispaniola waned and settlement was well underway on that island, it became the base from which Spaniards launched new conquests, claiming Puerto Rico in 1508, Jamaica in 1509, Cuba in 1511, and Florida in 1513.[23] Africans took part in all of these expeditions. Juan Garrido and Juan González

African-born explorer Juan Garrido, ca. 1519. Garrido participated in the Indian wars in Hispaniola and Juan Ponce de León's "discovery" of Florida. He is shown here accompanying Hernando Cortés on his Mexican campaign. From Diego Duran's *Historia,* 1581. Courtesy of the Florida Museum of Natural History, Fort Mose Exhibition.

joined Juan Ponce de León's expedition to explore and conquer Puerto Rico (San Juan de Borinquén), and both men settled there briefly to become gold miners. Other free persons of African descent, such as the free mulatto Francisco Mejías, an Indian collector and overseer for the Hacienda del Toa in Puerto Rico, helped establish that island's earliest ranches. Mejías was said to have been killed by Carib Indians while defending the Indian *cacica* (female ruler), Luisa, an ally of the Spaniards. At his death he had 210 pesos of gold, although his annual ranch salary was only fifty pesos, so Mejías, too, may have been involved in gold mining.[24]

Although Queen Isabella had forbidden the enslavement of her new Indian subjects, the alleged ferocity of the Caribs and their reputed cannibalism led her to authorize "just war" against them and, by extension, other hostile groups. Indians who rejected Christianity or Spanish dominion might, henceforth, be legally enslaved.[25] Spaniards swept through the Caribbean islands and then the mainland coasts in search of captives to sell into slavery. From Puerto Rico Ponce de León led slave raids against the Caribs on the islands of Santa Cruz, Guadalupe, and Dominica, and the Africans, Juan Garrido and Juan González Ponce de León, were among the raiders.[26] They also accompanied Ponce de León on his voyages to Florida in 1513 and 1521, where the hostile reception by the indigenes suggests Caribbean-based slavers had already preceded them.

After Ponce de León's death, Garrido enlisted with Hernando Cortés and participated in the bloody battle to conquer the Aztec capital of Tenochtitlán. Garrido's rewards were land and paid positions, including doorman of the Mexico City cabildo and caretaker of one of the city's aqueducts. He also took up gold mining, as he had in Puerto Rico. Several codices depict Garrido at the side of his new patron, Cortés, whom he joined on one final adventure in search of black Amazons in what came to be California. Garrido never became wealthy. In fact, few of the conquerors did, but he lived a free, propertied, and respectable life in the Americas where he raised a free family and made his mark on history.[27]

Africans in the Exploration of La Florida

With the "discovery" of Florida, Africans helped stake Spain's first claim to exclusive sovereignty over an area stretching from the Florida Keys to Newfoundland and west to Mexico, a claim disputed by both the French and the English, who viewed effective occupation as the true measure of sovereignty.[28] To hold Florida, the Spaniards would have to people it.

Five years after Ponce de León's failure and death, Lucas Vázquez de Ayllón departed Hispaniola to attempt a full-scale settlement on La Florida's Atlantic coast at a site believed to have been located near present-day Sapelo Sound in

Georgia. Ayllón named the settlement San Miguel de Gualdape.[29] His expedition included some six hundred Spanish men, women, and children, as well as the first known contingent of African slaves brought to the present-day United States. Paul Hoffman theorized these were probably *ladinos* or Spanish-speaking Catholics who were skilled artisans and domestics, and they may have been. But by the time Ayllón was preparing his expedition a large *bozal* or African-born population performed the mining and agricultural labor on Hispaniola, and it is equally possible that Ayllón brought with him some of those slaves—capable of the hard work of transforming the wilderness into a new settlement. In view of their history in Hispaniola, it seems unlikely that the Spaniards intended to do such demanding labor themselves. Ayllón's ambitious enterprise was quickly undermined by disease, starvation, and his own death. Mutiny ensued, and disaffected elements took control of the failing colony. Then, as winter approached, some African slaves set fire to the compound of the mutineers, an act that raises interesting and as yet unexplored questions about the slaves' political alignments. At the same time, the Guale Indians rose against the Spaniards, completing the settlement's destruction. The surviving Europeans straggled back to Hispaniola, but the escaped Africans took up residence among the Guale, becoming the first maroons in what is today the United States, as many of their counterparts were already doing in Hispaniola, Puerto Rico, Jamaica, Cuba, and Mexico.[30]

Despite the slave arson at Gualdape, the next major colonization effort of La Florida also incorporated Africans. Pánfilo de Narváez landed approximately six hundred Europeans and unknown numbers of Africans somewhere near Tampa Bay in 1528. This colony, too, proved a disastrous failure, undone by hurricanes, supply losses, and separation of the forces. After eight years wandering along the Gulf Coast and westward to the Pacific Ocean, four survivors "came back from the dead." The most famous was the expedition's treasurer, Alvar Núñez Cabeza de Vaca, who left a written account of his trials, but Estévan, the African slave of Andrés Dorantes, also survived. Cabeza de Vaca wrote that Estévan quickly learned the language of indigenous groups and was often the negotiator for the party.[31]

Meanwhile, drawing on lessons learned and fortunes won in Peru (where Africans also fought alongside Spaniards), Hernando de Soto hoped to succeed in Florida where his predecessors had failed. De Soto outfitted ships in Spain and stopped for additional supplies and recruits (including large numbers of Indians) in Cuba. Both free and enslaved Africans joined his 1539 expedition through what is now the southeastern United States.[32] One slave from de Soto's expedition, Gómez, assisted the *cacica* of Cofitachequi in her escape from the Spaniards and returned as her husband to her headquarters near present-day Camden, South Carolina. Along the way other sub-Saharan and Moorish slaves, as well as free Spaniards, also "went over" to the Indians. It is clear that the commingling of the diverse newcomers and indigenous peoples was immediate and continuous in the Americas.[33]

For the next three centuries, the Indian nations of the vast territory of La Florida provided a potential refuge for enslaved Africans. Although the enslaved Africans often tried to ally with the Indians, who might help them to escape, free Africans tended to remain with the Spaniards until the bitter end, hoping to earn their share of the expeditions' fortunes. Among the free Africans in the de Soto force was Bernaldo, a caulker from Vizcaya who was formerly the slave of one of de Soto's captains, Pedro Calderón. Bernaldo survived the many bloody Indian battles, severe hunger, killing marches, and finally a voyage down the Mississippi River in hastily constructed boats. After an epic trek of more than four years, during which the expeditionaries traversed six hundred miles and ten of the present-day United States, he was among those who limped back to Mexico City "dressed only in animal skins." It is unknown if Bernaldo, like other survivors, succumbed to the lure of Peru, returned to Spain as his former master did, or remained in Mexico, where Africans like Juan Garrido and others carved out modest, but free, lives for themselves.[34]

Several more failed attempts preceded the first permanent Spanish settlement of Florida. The province held no great mineral wealth nor major Indian civilizations to justify such effort, and were it not for its strategic location—jutting out into the heart of the Caribbean and the Gulf of Mexico, and astride the Bahama Channel—Spain may have thought Florida not worth holding. However, each fall richly laden treasure fleets had to sail along Florida's long Atlantic coast on their homeward passage, so Spain could not afford to allow the colony to fall into enemy hands.

When French Huguenots established a small settlement near present-day Jacksonville in 1562, Spain was spurred into action. The captain general of the combined Spanish fleets in the Caribbean, Pedro Menéndez de Avilés, embarked on the "enterprise" of Florida, ruthlessly eliminated the French "usurpers," and finally made Florida a permanent outpost of the Spanish empire in 1565.[35] Over the course of the next two centuries, the Spaniards battled Indian and pirate attacks, natural disasters, internal dissension, disease, and foreign invasions to maintain their tenuous sovereignty in Florida.[36]

Africans in the Establishment of Florida

During an exploratory tour of his new province, Menéndez found a shipwrecked mulatto named Luis living among the Calusa Indians south of St. Augustine. Hernando D'Escalante Fontaneda's memoir of his captivity in the same nation described Luis as part owner of a richly laden vessel out of New Spain that wrecked on the Florida coast in 1554. Luis's partnership with Cosme Farfán, famed commander of the Spanish treasure fleets of 1540, 1554, and 1555, suggests that he was a free man of some repute, who had managed to become a client of a most important individual. Luis's knowledge of the Ays language saved other Spanish shipwreck victims, and D'Escalante credited Luis with joining him in exposing a plot against Menéndez's life.[37] It was Menéndez's Christian obligation to try to ransom the shipwrecked captives, and given Luis's linguistic abilities and the trust Chief Carlos placed in him, Luis probably helped in the release negotiations. Chief Carlos released five Spaniards, five *mestiza* women (a person of Amerindian-European parentage) from Peru, and an unnamed black woman. When the rescued group returned to St. Augustine, Menéndez placed Luis and Juanillo, another black captive rescued from Chief Saturiba, on the military rolls as interpreters, a role Africans played often in the encounters throughout the Americas.[38] Menéndez was able to ransom eighteen Christians on his tour of the southern villages. Some of the prisoners Menéndez tried to free, however, chose to stay among their captors, perhaps to avoid separation from Indian families. These included a black woman and a mulatto who had lived among the Calusa since they were children and who could hardly speak Spanish.[39] Such examples may have inspired the slaves whom Menéndez complained later ran to, and intermarried with, the Ays.[40]

The loss of any slaves was significant. Their owners lost not only their original investment but sorely needed labor as well. Slaves were costly, averaging around two hundred pesos for a healthy worker through the sixteenth century, yet demand commonly outstripped supply in many areas. Although Menéndez's charter allowed him to import five hundred African slaves to do the difficult labor required in settling a new colony, he never filled that contract. Probably fewer than fifty slaves accompanied Florida's first settlers, and those probably belonged to the most elite.[41] In the following decades Florida's soldiers began to petition the Crown to pay their back salaries in slave licenses, and it is clear that colonists outside the elite also desired slaves, although more for their labor and profit potential than for the status their ownership implied.[42]

Caribbean Slavery in the Sixteenth Century

It should be remembered that during the sixteenth century slaves of other ethnicities and races still labored alongside Africans throughout the Caribbean. These were often captured or condemned slaves, or *esclavos forzados*. In April 1568 Corporal Alonso Escudero, a Spaniard from Almonte, was condemned to perpetual slavery in the St. Augustine galleys for murdering his wife. Ten years later Escudero surfaced again on a list of king's slaves working as a sawyer.[43] The diverse character of slavery is even more visible in Havana's more ample records. In 1595 officials listed 149 forzados assigned to military service or to the galleys in Havana. Most were Spanish-born; forty-five were identified as Muslims from Tunis, Algiers, Morocco, Fez, Rhodes, Anatolia, and other Mediterranean locations; others were Canary Islanders, Greeks, Portuguese, Mexican, Genoese, and several were listed as gypsies. Only three of the 149 Cuban galley slaves were identified as black or mulatto.[44]

During this period a two-tier system of African slavery developed throughout the Hispanic Americas. As unacculturated bozales did backbreaking labor in the mines, plantations, ranches, and forests, ladino slaves filled a wide range of urban domestic, artisanal, and lower-status economic roles, working in occupations as varied as tailoring and masonry. As a group the urban slaves generally received better treatment than their rural counterparts, based on older metropolitan slave relations, on their access to legal and religious protections, and on their integration into a cash economy.[45]

Following metropolitan practice many slaves in cities such as Havana and St. Augustine labored under a *jornal* (day wage) system that allowed them to work independently and live in their own homes in return for an agreed-upon payment to their owners. In this way owners earned income but avoided many of the responsibilities of feeding, sheltering, clothing, and providing medical care for their slaves. Some slaves were able to make the jornal system work for them. One sixteenth-century Havana official remarked that the slaves "go about as if they were free, working at whatever they choose, and at the end of the week or the month they give their owners the jornal . . . some have houses in which they shelter and feed travelers, and have in those houses, slaves of their own."[46]

The persistent and lucky slaves who acquired freedom soon formed an important sector of Havana's population. They practiced their trades, saved their money, and bought modest homes. Over time, as Havana's population density grew, so did the value of their holdings. Envious Spaniards suggested expelling the "excess" population of free blacks to St. Augustine so that Spaniards might buy their now-valuable properties.[47] Few slaves actually became property owners, however, and many slaves were unable to pay their required jornal, especially in *tiempo muerte* (dead time), when no fleets were in town. To avoid punishments, destitute slaves sometimes fled to join the maroons.[48]

Blacks and Caribbean Piracy

From its earliest days, Florida was threatened by what one scholar called an "epidemic of piracy" growing out of depressed European economies and the religious and political dissent sweeping the Continent.[49] Competing European powers had never recognized the Spanish-born pope's bull of donation granting Castile/León exclusive sovereignty in the Americas (1493) nor the bilateral Treaty of Tordesillas between Portugal and Castile that ratified Spanish claims (1494). Francis I, king of France, purportedly asked to see the will which made Spain's monarchs Adam's sole heirs, and both Francis and Elizabeth I of England supported profitable privateering campaigns against the Spaniards.[50] The waters near Puerto Rico were soon said to be "as full of French as Rochelle," and French and English pirates attacked Spanish ships and settlements with impunity. The raiders became rich on *rescate,* the practice of holding persons or towns for a ransom.[51] Menéndez de Avilés led a naval expedition to the West Indies against a large French fleet in 1566–67, but pirate attacks continued to be a threat to the Florida coasts for more than a century.[52] When the Spanish ambassador complained about the violence "beyond the line," Elizabeth clearly articulated the English position: "The Spaniards by their hard dealing with the English, whom they had prohibited commerce, contrary to the laws of nations, had drawn their mischief upon themselves."[53]

Making matters more treacherous, in Menéndez's view, was the growing racial imbalance in the circum-Caribbean. After 1567 he served simultaneously as governor and captain general of Cuba and Florida, and in that joint capacity Menéndez was responsible for the defense of the entire region. In alarmist tones he informed King Philip II that Hispaniola was populated by 30,000 blacks and fewer than 2,000 Spaniards, while Puerto Rico held 15,000 blacks and only 500 Spaniards. Menéndez claimed the same racial disparity held true in Cuba, Vera Cruz, Puerto Cavallos in Honduras, Cartagena, and Venezuela. He warned that because neither England nor France then allowed slavery, any corsair might, with a few thousand men, take over all Spain's possessions by freeing and arming the grateful slaves, whom he alleged would then slay their Spanish masters.[54]

Menéndez's fears were not groundless. Most of the Spanish colonies had by that time already experienced slave revolts and increasing incidences of marronage.[55] Although the maroons generally attempted to be self-sufficient, they also raided plantations and became notorious roadside bandits. They traded with plantation slaves and with whites for materials they could not obtain in the wild, subverting Spanish efforts to monitor and control the economy. In similar fashion, maroons living near the coasts established a lucrative trade with corsairs and pirates, providing them with cattle and turtle meat, hides, and agricultural products.[56] It was not a great leap from trading partners to military allies, as the cimarrones of Panama proved in 1572 when they helped Sir Francis Drake capture a treasure in silver. The town council of Nombre de Dios (Panama) ominously warned: "This league between the English and the blacks is very detrimental to this kingdom because, being so thoroughly acquainted with the region and so expert in the bush, the blacks will show them methods and means to accomplish any evil design they may wish to carry out."[57]

The numerical superiority of Africans in the circum-Caribbean, combined with foreign challenges to Spanish dominion, created new leverage and opportunities for Africans that they never had in Spain. Like Europeans and Amerindians, Africans carefully evaluated their positions and acted in what they perceived to be in their own best interests. They could and did choose sides and could alter the balance of power in critical ways. Thus, the political engagement of Africans became an increasingly important variable as Europeans formulated their Caribbean policies.

Menéndez, like subsequent administrators, had reason to worry for Florida's security. Although Spain had established a permanent subsidy or *situado* for Florida in 1570 and thereafter committed regular army units to the colony, these were consistently under strength due to death, desertion, and the Spanish custom of allowing widows, orphans, and invalids to hold the *plaza,* or post, of a deceased soldier and receive his pay. Royal officials also padded the military payroll with their slaves, who appeared as drummers, fife players, and flag bearers.[58] The inadequacy of St. Augustine's military force was never more obvious than when Francis Drake's armada of more than twenty large ships and countless corsairs attacked St. Augustine in 1586 in a two-day bombardment. Helpless against such an overwhelming force, the city's defenders abandoned St. Augustine to the looters, who burned it down on their way out of town.[59]

Life in sixteenth-century St. Augustine was precarious for all, but pirate raids, disease, drought, and famine took an especially heavy toll on the overworked slaves. In 1580 the Crown ordered Havana to send royal slaves to supplement the dwindling slave force in Florida, and the following year St. Augustine's treasurer reported the arrival of twenty-three African men and seven African women.[60] By 1583 the new slaves had built several structures, including a church, a blacksmith shop, and a platform for the artillery. They also made repairs on the wooden fort, sawed timber, and cleared land for planting. Soon they were said to be harvesting enough to feed themselves "with no other expense but the oil and the salt."[61] When the work at St. Augustine was completed, officials sent ten of the best slave laborers to help with the construction of the new fort at Santa Elena, Spain's northernmost settlement in the New World at present-day Parris Island, South Carolina.[62]

Blacks in Seventeenth-Century Florida

Their scarcity and their value to the community meant that African laborers were highly prized. Florida's treasury official, Miguel Ybarra, reported in 1603 that there were only thirty-two royal slaves in St. Augustine, five of whom were women, and of the total, he described seven as advanced in years. Ybarra wrote that it was in the community's interest to preserve these valuable workers and that "I see to it that they are well treated in the matter of food and clothing and when they fall sick they are taken to the hospital and cared for as the most valuable soldier." Ybarra promised to maintain this level of care and must have done so, for by 1606 there were one hundred black slaves in Florida, including forty belonging to the Crown.[63]

In his important overview of southeastern racial demography Peter Wood tracked the catastrophic decline of the native population of Florida, which he estimated fell by a factor of ten, from several hundred thousand at first contact with Spaniards, to fewer than twenty thousand in less than two hundred years.[64] The "pests and contagions" which devastated the Florida Indians between 1613 and 1617 must have also affected Florida's black population, for by 1618 there were only eleven aged and infirm slaves left in St. Augustine. Once again, Florida's officials petitioned the Crown for replacements from Havana. The Crown answered, "considering the need existing in Florida for such blacks and the necessity of preserving [sovereignty in] that land," Havana should send as many slaves as it could, "so that for lack of them, royal service does not cease." The order suggested Havana provide thirty men of working age to cut and saw timber for fort and ship repairs, and six women to cook and care for the men in illness. It also noted that the slaves' labor was unceasing, and that Florida's entire situado would not suffice if wages had to be paid for their tasks.[65] Another series of epidemics—typhus or yellow fever in 1649 and smallpox in 1654—took a harsh toll on St. Augustine's limited population, killing many government officials and all the royal slaves.[66]

During these cycles of epidemics, the native population declined most dramatically, leaving the interior of the peninsula almost deserted. The land was vacant and the colony hungry. Records describe this as "the starving time." Although the Crown had hoped to avoid the creation of a landed aristocracy in Florida, the colony's distress finally led it to accede to major land grants and to the introduction of cattle. In 1645 Governor Benito Ruiz de Salazar established the Asile wheat ranch in Apalachee, near present-day Tallahassee, and in violation of a royal prohibition, he employed black slaves to supervise the free Indians working on the ranch. His overseer was a mulatto named Francisco Galindo, who purchased his freedom for six hundred pesos when Ruiz died in 1651. Although it is not known how Galindo accrued that impressive sum on a rather remote Indian frontier (or how long it took him to save it), archaeological evidence from the nearby mission village of San Luis de Tamali demonstrates an unexpected richness of material culture resulting from burgeoning trade with nearby Havana. Galindo may have been a participant in that trade. Another mulatto supervisor at the Asile ranch was Juan de la Cruz. De la Cruz stabbed and almost killed the lieutenant governor of Apalachee province in a dispute but apparently went unpunished, perhaps because good hands by then cost at least five hundred pesos and were difficult to obtain. Witnesses who testified about Ruiz's management of Asile stated that twenty slaves would have been required to work the ranch properly, indicating there were fewer than that actually on site. At least one other African ranch hand is named in the Asile documents—the Angolan named Ambrosio.[67]

Blacks and mestizos, some imported from New Spain, also served as ranch hands on vast cattle estates in north central Florida, such as the La Chua ranch established around 1646 by the Menéndez Márquez family.[68] Such establishments did diversify Florida's economy and made it somewhat more self-sufficient, but much of the surplus production found its way to Havana, rather than to St. Augustine, and the ranches' location in the midst of Indian lands only increased native complaints against the Spaniards.

Black Pirates in the Spanish Lake

By the seventeenth century, the drain of European wars, metropolitan bankruptcies, depopulation in both the metropolis and the colony, and declining mineral revenues left Spain unable adequately to provision or defend her American colonies from foreign encroachment.[69] The weakened condition of both Spain and Florida invited imperial competition, which the English, French, and Dutch were eager to provide. In 1628 the Dutch corsair Piet Heyn captured the New Spain treasure fleet (which included the Florida and Havana situados) for the Dutch West India Company. The proceeds from this haul financed the conquest of Curaçao in 1634. Situated so close to the Spanish Main, the new Dutch colony became an important entrepôt in the smuggling trade. By mid-century French smugglers and buccaneers had also converted the western portion of Hispaniola into a French colony.[70] In 1655 the English took Jamaica, thereby establishing a major economic and military base from which to attack Spain in the Caribbean.[71]

The foreign colonies in the "Spanish lake" menaced Spanish galleons and served as launching bases for attacks against critical Spanish ports. Pirates, including some with African ancestry, found opportunities in the circum-Caribbean chaos. After a career that included many prizes and prisoners taken from Campeche to Veracruz, Capitán Diego Martín, alias Diego el Mulato, offered his service to Spain. In a letter delivered to Spanish officials in Havana in 1638, Martín expressed his great desire to serve as a "valiant soldier of the king, our lord," making appropriate references to the king's championship of the Catholic faith. He promised that if the king agreed, no Dutch ship or any other enemy would any longer stop along Cuba's coasts, "especially knowing that I am here very few would dare pass on to the Indies, for they certainly fear me." Captain Martín's boast must have been well-founded, for Havana officials sent the offer to Spain with a recommendation of royal pardon and a salary equivalent to that of an admiral, making no derogatory mention of his color or class.[72]

The interrogation of another pirate captured in a later raid on St. Augustine adds to our understanding of this little-known black experience. Diego was born in Tortuga and as a young man grew tobacco, which he traded to the buccaneers frequenting the island. Perhaps inspired by his customers, he took up a career in piracy, joining the French corsair named "Sanbo" who sailed for the Mosquito Coast. Diego caught turtles for the crew and participated in the capture of two Spanish prizes from Cartagena, thereby earning a share of the take. Later he joined a Captain Cahrebon on a second corsairing expedition to Cartagena, where he cut wood for some time before canoeing back to the Mosquito Coast. Diego's last captain, the Frenchman Nicholas, sieur de Grammont (Agramón to the Spaniards), sacked Campeche, capturing black slaves, whom he sold at San Jorge (present-day Charleston), and then headed for Florida. Diego and a mulatto interpreter named Tomás joined Agramón in attacking St. Augustine, but after several days of pitched battles against the Spaniards and their black and Indian militias, only Diego and one other pirate survived.[73]

Blacks and the Defense of the Spanish Circum-Caribbean

In response to increased piracy and foreign territorial encroachment, the Spanish Crown belatedly embarked on a major effort to fortify its Caribbean ports. African masonry and metalworking skills eventually helped erect great stone forts at Havana, Santo Domingo, San Juan, Cartagena, Portobelo, Acapulco, and St. Augustine, as well as many minor constructions in lesser ports along the threatened coasts. The Spaniards launched the construction of St. Augustine's massive stone fort, the Castillo de San Marcos, in 1672.[74] Although the construction generated funds and a certain prosperity for the town, the project also increased the labor and food demands on nearby Indians whose numbers had already been "thinned" by recurring epidemics of typhus, yellow fever, smallpox, measles, and unidentified diseases. As a result, the governors elected to import additional Indians from the western provinces of Timucua and Apalachee and Guale Indians from north coastal Florida and Georgia to augment the labor force. Convicts provided another source of labor—among them blacks and mulattoes. From Havana the Crown also sent some of its royal slaves skilled in stonecutting. The polyglot laborers lived and worked in close proximity to one another in St. Augustine.[75]

The Crown required all residents of the Spanish-American colonies to form militias to defend themselves in case of attack. Chronically shorthanded, Spanish officials throughout the circum-Caribbean added free and enslaved Africans to supplement their Spanish forces. Blacks helped the Spanish militias defend Havana in 1555, Puerto Rico in 1557, Cartagena in 1560 and 1572, and Santo Domingo in 1583.[76] Blacks also served as defense forces on plantations and ranches, as coastal sentinels, and as sailors on locally organized patrol boats throughout the Caribbean.[77] By mid-seventeenth century, free blacks and mulattoes were serving throughout the circum-Caribbean in their own formally organized militias. A Central American roster from 1673 listed almost three thousand *pardos* (usually meaning mulattoes, but sometimes referring to non-Europeans of mixed ancestry) serving in infantry units throughout the isthmus.[78] Similar black units served in Hispaniola, Cuba, Mexico, Puerto Rico, Panama, and Cartagena.[79]

A limited number of blacks had served as auxiliaries to white units in Florida since at least 1580, but in 1683 Governor Juan Márquez Cabrera formed a company of free *pardo* (mulatto) and *moreno* (black) militia in St. Augustine.[80] Other than their names, little is known about the forty-two men and six officers who composed this unit. Rosters provide no specific information about them, although Corporal Crispín De Tapia is known from other sources to have been a free mulatto who managed a store in St. Augustine.[81] It is testimony to his need that Governor Márquez would form such a unit because his predecessor and he had been complaining for years that the troops provided from New Spain in the 1670s were "sons of blacks, *chinos* (persons of mixed race), and mulattoes," only good for work as cobblers, tailors, carpenters, blacksmiths, and cattle hands (precisely the kinds of occupations persons of African descent held throughout the Spanish Americas).[82] None of St. Augustine's black militiamen used an African nation for a surname, although several surnames indicate other origins—Catalán, Lima, Mexicano—where Spaniards held sway. These men probably had lived for some time among the Spaniards. Many of the men shared surnames, which may indicate possible kinship ties but might also mean that they were once owned by the same families, among which were some of the oldest in Florida (Menéndez, de Soto, Rutiner, and de Hita). (See appendix 1.)

The black militia members swore before God and the cross their willingness to serve the king. While their pledge may have been formulaic, it was also an effort to define their status as members of the religious and civil community, and as vassals of a monarch from whom they might expect protection or patronage in exchange for armed service. The same year it was organized, the black militia helped to successfully defend St. Augustine against the attack of the pirate Diego's employer, Grammont, whom they fought again in 1686. Conceived of primarily as a defensive force, in the following years the black militia became an effective offensive force as well.

Africans and the Anglo/Spanish Contest for the Southeast

When Barbadian planters, already hostile to Spain, established a new colony at Charles Town, "but ten days journey" from St. Augustine in 1670, the geopolitics of the Southeast were even further destabilized. The Indian nations were now caught in a terrible contest that would ruin most of them. An undermanned Spanish garrison made a feeble attempt to eject the "usurpers" but failed, and almost another century of conflict ensued over the so-called debatable lands.[83]

The Carolinians, in turn, attacked the Spaniards at their weakest point. After 1680 Yamasee Indians allied with the English attacked the chain of Spanish missions of Guale, along the Georgia coast, beginning with its administrative headquarters at Santa Catalina (St. Catherines) Island.[84] Unable to defend their Christian charges, the Spaniards tried to relocate them southward to Santa María (Amelia Island), but some revolted and fled instead to the interior and an English alliance.[85]

The new balance of power in the Southeast required a flexible response, and each side used Indian and African surrogates to do much of their fighting. While fewer in number, blacks were significant for their linguistic and cultural abilities, their knowledge of the frontier, and their military skills.[86] The Spaniards began a campaign of harassment against the new colony which included slave raids by their black and Indian allies.

In 1686 Governor Márquez Cabrera and a combined force of more than 153 Spaniards, Indians, and members of the new pardo militia retaliated against the Carolinians with a raid on the English plantations on Edisto Island, including that of Governor Joseph Morton. The Spanish raiding party killed some of the English settlers and stole thirteen of Governor Morton's slaves before turning southward to burn down the Scottish settlement at Port Royal on their way home to St. Augustine.[87]

The London proprietors held the Carolinians responsible for the hostilities, saying, "[I]t is because those of Carolina notwithstanding the Kings comands and our own repeated orders to the contrary have reced the pyrates and privateers that have unjustly burnt and robbed the houses of the Spainyards." They refused to sanction any designs the Carolinians had on St. Augustine, allowing only that, if invaded, the Carolinians could defend themselves.[88] This did not deter the Carolinians, who began to mount an invasion against St. Augustine, only to be stopped at the last moment by the arrival in Charles Town of the new governor, James Colleton, who was more interested in trade with the Spaniards than in retaliation.[89] A follow-up letter from the proprietors reminded the Carolinians that the Spaniards had acted "in Revenge of those Indians [Yamasee] falling upon, and plundering some Spanish settlements" and warned, "[I]t is not to be expected that the Spanyards should ever let you live peaceably by them if they are soe provoked."[90] Nevertheless, when the Spaniards complained about Yamasee raids on Florida, Colleton disclaimed responsibility, noting that the Yamasee were "a people who live within our bounds after their own manner taking no notice of our Government."[91]

The repeated crosscurrents of raids and migrations across the Southeast acquainted many blacks and Indians with the routes to St. Augustine, as well as with the enmity existing between the English and Spanish colonies.[92] In 1687 Florida's governor, Diego de Quiroga, reported to Spain that eight men, two women, and a nursing child had escaped from Carolina to St. Augustine in a stolen canoe and were requesting baptism into the "True Faith."[93] It is possible that some of the fugitives had been exposed to Roman Catholicism either in Africa or in the Caribbean. Several, such as Gran Domingo and Jacque, had names that indicate such contacts. They may have known of the protections and opportunities the Catholic church offered Africans, possibly even manipulating confessional politics to their own advantage in making a shared request for religious sanctuary.[94]

Governor Quiroga accordingly saw to the runaways' Catholic instruction, baptism, and marriage, but he also took advantage of their skills. The men became ironsmiths and laborers on the Castillo de San Marcos, and the women became domestics in the governor's own household. Florida's authorities claimed to have paid all of them wages; the men earned a peso a day, the wage paid to male Indian laborers, and the women earned half as much.[95]

When an agent from Carolina, William Dunlop, came to St. Augustine to reclaim the runaways the following year, Quiroga refused to return them. Instead he exercised his considerable autonomy and offered to pay the Carolina slaveowners their asking price for the group—1600 pesos—as soon as St. Augustine's annual subsidy arrived. Dunlop also demanded that Samuel de Bordieu's runaway, Mingo, be prosecuted for the murder he committed in the process of freeing himself, his wife, and baby. Quiroga agreed, should the charges be proven. Satisfied with that promise Dunlop returned to Charles Town empty-handed.[96]

The slaves' "telegraph" must have quickly reported the outcome of the negotiations, for soon other fugitives began arriving in St. Augustine. The Spaniards recorded new groups of runaways being received in St. Augustine in 1688, 1689, and 1690, and Carolina's governor, James Colleton, complained that slaves ran "dayly to your towns." Unsure about how to handle the refugees, St. Augustine's officials repeatedly solicited Spain for guidance. Finally, on November 7, 1693, Charles II issued a royal proclamation "giving liberty to all . . . the men as well as the women . . . so that by their example and by my liberality others will do the same."[97] The initiative and determination of eight enslaved Africans who risked their lives to become free thus led to a major policy revision at the Spanish court that would shape the geopolitics of the Southeast and the Caribbean for years to come.[98]

Although in its decree the Spanish Crown emphasized religious and humane considerations for freeing the slaves of the British, political and military motives were equally, if not more, important. In harboring the runaways and eventually settling them in their own town, Florida's governors were following the Spanish policy of *repoblación,* populating and holding territory threatened by foreign encroachment.[99] But if the interests of Spain and Florida were served by this policy, so too were those of the ex-slaves. It offered them a refuge within which they could live free and maintain their families. In the highly politicized context of Spanish Florida, they struggled to maximize their leverage in the community and improve the conditions of their freedom. They made creative use of Spanish institutions to support their corporate identity and concomitant privileges.[100] They adapted to Spanish values where it served them to do so and, thereby, gained autonomy. They reinforced ties within their original community through intermarriage and use of the Spanish institution of godparenthood or *compadrazgo.* And over time, they formed intricate new kin and friendship networks with slaves, free blacks, Indians of various nations, "new" Africans, and whites in St. Augustine that served to stabilize their population and strengthen connections to the Spanish community.[101]

The War of Spanish Succession (known as Queen Anne's War in North America) embroiled Florida and the Southeast in new waves of violence. In 1702 the notorious slave trader and governor, James Moore, led a combined force of about a thousand men, including Carolinians, Yamasee allies, and black slaves, in a series of devastating raids on the Spanish coastal mission sites. The English attackers also burned much of St. Augustine as the townspeople hid within the Castillo walls. In this raid and a follow-up to Apalachee in 1704, Moore's forces slaughtered thousands of mission Indians and carried many more thousands away into slavery. St. Augustine's black and Indian militias fought bravely, but the inability of the Spaniards to protect even the Nombre de Dios mission outside their very walls led many of their once loyal Indian allies to defect to the English. After 1704 only a pitiful group of refugee Indian camps bordered St. Augustine.[102] In 1706 the tri-racial Spanish forces, joined by French allies, struck back at Charles Town, but despite some initial success, this expedition failed.[103]

The provocation inherent in the Spanish sanctuary policy increasingly challenged the Carolinians. Despite the institution of regulatory slave codes, ticket systems, and land and water patrols, Carolina slaves continued to run away—southward to Florida.[104] Not only did each runaway represent an economic loss but planters feared that the success of the few might inspire the many. By the beginning of the eighteenth century, blacks outnumbered whites in Carolina, and in that colony as in all other slave systems, there were chronic fears of slave uprisings. Carolina slaves actually revolted in 1711 and 1714, and the following year many other slaves joined the Yamasee Indian war against the English.[105] This war almost succeeded in eradicating white settlement in Carolina, but after reinforcements from Virginia and North Carolina helped turn the tide, the defeated Yamasees who managed to escape Carolina sought refuge among the very Spaniards they had once harried.[106]

Peter H. Wood asserts that of all the Carolinians' conspiratorial concerns none seemed to worry them more after 1720 than St. Augustine. That year the townspeople of Charles Town uncovered a major slave conspiracy in which at least some of the participants "thought to gett to Augustine." Fourteen got as far as Savannah before being captured and executed.[107] Still slaves continued to take the risk. In 1724, ten more runaways reached St. Augustine, assisted by English-speaking Yamasee Indians. According to their statement, they knew that the Spanish king had offered freedom for those seeking conversion and baptism.[108]

Initially at least, Governor Antonio de Benavides honored the 1693 edict. In 1725 he sent a delegation to Charles Town to negotiate boundary disputes and some agreement on the runaways. Following the precedent set by Governor Diego de Quiroga in 1687, the Spaniards offered to purchase the newly arrived fugitives for two hundred pesos apiece. Angry Carolina slaveowners rejected the offer as insufficient, claimed that their property was worth much more, and added that they should also be compensated for the loss of the slaves' labor since they ran away.[109] Meanwhile, Benavides wrote Spain to inquire whether these fugitives were also to receive sanctuary, entering Florida as they did during a period of truce between England and Spain.[110] As often happened, the governor received no reply, and after the English refused to accept the Spanish offer and threatened to reclaim their lost slaves by force, in 1729 Benavides sold the unlucky fugitives at public auction to the leading creditors of the St. Augustine treasury.[111] Although Benavides handed over the proceeds of that auction to the envoy from Carolina, Arthur Hauk, Carolinians charged that Benavides "Makes Merchandize of all our slaves, and ships them off to Havanah for his own Profit," and they were at least partially correct.[112]

Undeterred, more Carolina slaves continued to flee to Florida. Thomas Elliott and other planters near Stono "had fourteen Slaves Runaway to St. Augustine" in 1726. The acting governor of Carolina, Arthur Middleton, complained to London that the Spaniards not only harbored their runaways but "They have found a New way of sending our own slaves against us, to Rob and Plunder us."[113] Some of the runaways were seasoned warriors who had fought with the Yamasee against the English, and some may have been warriors in their homelands. They became effective additions to the black militia and joined in Spanish raids against their former masters. Governor Middleton claimed that "Six of our Runaway slaves and the rest Indians" in two canoes attacked near Pon Pon in the fall of 1727 and carried away white captives. Another account of the same raid said that "Ten Negroes and fourteen Indians Commanded by those of their own Colour, without any Spaniards in company with them" had taken the action and that they had also brought back to St. Augustine one black man and a mulatto boy. That same year Spanish raiders and Carolina runaways hit again at a plantation on the Edisto River and carried away another seven blacks.[114]

Governor Benavides was enthusiastic about the military abilities of the runaways and, like Pedro Menéndez de Avilés more than a century before, recognized the diplomatic potential of the Africans. English captives in St. Augustine reported that in 1727 Benavides sent a party of four dozen Yamasees northward and offered thirty pieces of eight for every English scalp and one hundred pieces "for every live Negro they should bring."[115] Six years later Governor Benavides advocated sending the runaways north to foment rebellion in Carolina and paying them for English scalps, but the Council of the Indies rejected this plan.[116]

In 1728 the Carolinians and Colonel John Palmer led a retaliatory attack against St. Augustine. The city's black militia was one of its most effective defense forces. The Spanish Crown commended the black militia for its bravery in that action and in 1733 reiterated in a new decree its offer of freedom to runaways from Carolina, although many of those already in St. Augustine remained enslaved.[117]

Over the years the re-enslaved fugitives persisted in their efforts to achieve the freedom promised by the Spanish king. Led by Captain Francisco Menéndez of the slave militia, they presented petitions to the governors and to the auxiliary bishop of Cuba, who toured the province in 1735, but to no avail.[118] When Manuel de Montiano became the new governor in 1737, however, their fortunes changed. Captain Francisco Menéndez once more solicited the group's freedom in a petition that listed thirty-one individuals unjustly enslaved, including some who had been shipped to Havana, and the names of the persons who claimed ownership over them. (See appendix 2.)

This time Menéndez's petition was supported by another from an ally, the Yamasee chief, Jorge, who claimed to be the chief who had initiated the Yamasee War. Jorge stated that Menéndez and three others had fought bravely for him for several years until they were ultimately defeated. When the Yamasees fled southward to St. Augustine, the African warriors joined them, hoping to receive the Christian sanctuary promised by Spain. However, in Florida they had been betrayed and sold into slavery by a "heathen" named Mad Dog.[119] Jorge charged that Mad Dog was not culpable for he knew no better (presumably because he was not Christian). Rather Jorge blamed the Spaniards who bought the unlucky blacks, who in his estimation had been patient and "more than loyal."[120] Montiano was expecting war with England at any moment, and the combined petitions and stated alliance of Africans and Indians must have no doubt made an impression on a governor in need of their services. He wisely chose to investigate.

After reviewing all relevant documentation on the issue of fugitives, Montiano granted unconditional freedom to all fugitives from Carolina on March 15, 1738. Montiano's financially strapped predecessors had satisfied government debts to important citizens by giving them incoming fugitives as slaves. They vehemently protested Montiano's emancipation of their slaves and requested reimbursement for their losses, but Montiano ruled that they had ignored the royal determination expressed in repeated decrees and, therefore, all deals were null and void and all the enslaved were free.[121] When the Crown reviewed Montiano's actions, it approved and ordered that not only all the blacks who had come from Carolina to date "but all those who in the future come as fugitives from the English colonies" should be given prompt and full liberty in the name of the king. Further, so that there be no further pretext for selling them, the royal edict should be publicly posted so that no one could claim ignorance of this ruling.[122]

The Origins of a Florida Sanctuary: Gracia Real de Santa Teresa de Mose

The Foundation

Sometime between March and November of 1738, the runaways from Carolina began new lives as freedmen and women on the Spanish frontier. At a site about two miles north of St. Augustine they established their new town of Gracia Real de Santa Teresa de Mose.[1] The Mandinga captain, Francisco Menéndez, who had initiated the successful suit for freedom and had led the black militia, also governed the new settlement. Governor Montiano referred to the inhabitants of Mose as Menéndez's "subjects," and he probably exercised considerable autonomy over his village.[2] Montiano's successor also stated that the villagers of Mose were "under the dominion of their Captain and Lieutenant," indicating that Antonio Joseph Eligio de la Puente also had an important role in the community, perhaps analogous to that of the war captains found among many maroon groups.[3] Spanish titles and support may have also reinforced these leaders' status. Whatever the nature of their authority, Menéndez commanded the Mose militia for more than forty years, and Eligio de la Puente held his position for at least twenty-six years. Their long careers support Richard Price's contention that eighteenth-century maroon leaders were military figures well-versed in European ways and equipped to negotiate their followers' best interests.[4]

Not all of the original petitioners lived to see the new settlement. Some of the individuals on Menéndez's list had died of smallpox contracted in Carolina and had been buried in Catholic ceremonies at St. Augustine's Tolomato cemetery.[5] And although Governor Montiano formally requested Cuba's captain general to locate and return the eight men on Menéndez's list who had been taken to Havana, only one, Antonio Carvallo, is known to have made it back to join his countrymen at Mose.[6] The founding population of thirty-eight men, "most of them married," would suggest that an estimated total population of about one hundred people made up the first settlement.[7] Menéndez's list of fugitives from Carolina included only five women, and as might be expected, men predominated at the site. Women were often tied to slavery by their children or aged kin, who would not have been able to make the dangerous journey through the swamps to Florida. Only the quick and the strong could escape patrollers, Indian bounty hunters, and the natural predators that lay in wait. Because so few men came with wives, in Florida they formed new unions with local African and Indian women.

The Site

Under the leadership of Francisco Menéndez, the skilled black homesteaders used their talents as carpenters, ironsmiths, and stonecutters to build a walled fort and shelters described by the Spaniards as resembling thatched Indian huts.[8] A royal official, Captain Sebastián Sánchez, supervised the construction of Mose's fort to ensure that it would meet St. Augustine's defense requirements. Later British sources described the fort as constructed of stone, "four square with a flanker at each corner, banked with earth, having a ditch without on all sides lined round with prickly royal and had a well and house within, and a look-out."[9]

Mose was surrounded by fertile lands and forests of hardwoods for building materials. Moreover, a river of salt water "running through it" (Mose Creek, now Robinson Creek) yielded protein-rich fish and shellfish of many types.[10] Buffalo, deer, and fowl of all kinds filled the grassy savannas, piney woods, and marshes around Mose, and there were wild horses for the catching. The freedmen and women broke ground, dug new fields, and planted food crops, but until the newly planted crops could be harvested, the governor provided the homesteaders with corn, biscuits, and beef from the same government stores used to supplement Indian towns.[11] Located at the head of Mose Creek, a tributary of the North River with access to St. Augustine, and lying directly north of St. Augustine, near Indian trails north to the San Nicolás post on the St. Johns River and west to Apalachee, Mose was of great strategic significance. Governor Montiano clearly considered the benefits of a northern outpost against anticipated British attacks. And who better to serve as an advance warning system than grateful ex-slaves carrying Spanish arms? The freedmen apparently understood their expected role for, upon receiving the land, they vowed to be "the most cruel enemies of the English" and to risk their lives and spill their "last drop of blood in defense of the great Crown of Spain and the Holy Faith."[12] The new homesteaders were pragmatists, and their own interests were clearly served by fighting those who would return them to chattel slavery. Mose thus served a vital objective of Spanish imperial policy, and once Governor Montiano justified its establishment, the Council of the Indies and the king supported his actions.[13]

Spanish colonizers throughout the Americas were guided by an urban model. Urban living was believed to facilitate religious conversion, but, beyond that, Spaniards attached a special value to living a *vida política,* believing that people of reason distinguished themselves from nomadic "barbarians" by living in stable urban communities. They depicted theirs as a civilizing mission and sought to create public order and righteous living by creating towns wherever they went. The Crown issued detailed instructions regarding ideal physical layout, location, and functioning of Spanish and Indian towns, but it never made formal provisions for free black towns. Royal legislation reflected a continuing interest, one might say obsession, in reforming and settling so-called vagabonds of all races within the empire. The primary focus of reduction efforts was the Indians, but, as the black and mixed populations grew, so too did Spanish concerns about how these elements would be assimilated into "civilized" society. The theoretical con-

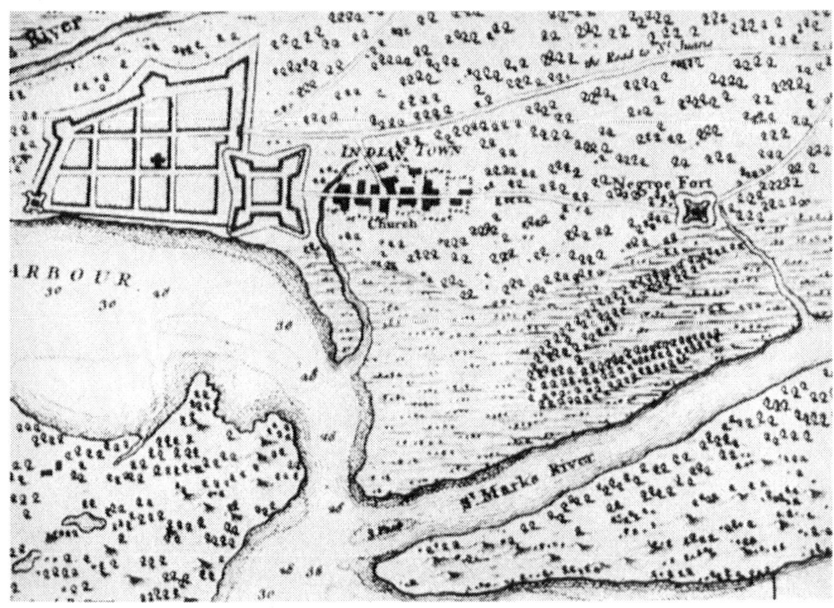

The Thomas Jefferys plan of the town and harbor of St. Augustine, 1762, showing the 1740 location of Gracia Real de Santa Teresa de Mose (labeled Negroe Fort). Courtesy of the P. K. Yonge Library of Florida History, George A. Smathers Libraries, University of Florida, and the Florida Museum of Natural History, Fort Mose Exhibition.

struct of "two republics" of Spaniards and Indians gave way almost immediately to a much more diverse reality.[14] Although the Spanish legal system had always recognized and assimilated a free black class, the Crown assumed that its members would live among the Spaniards, as they had in Spain. But as scholars like Richard Morse have shown, the Spanish administrative system was flexible and adapted to local colonial conditions.[15] By the time Governor Montiano founded Mose, the Council of the Indies had already addressed precedents for approving autonomous black settlements. Earlier free black towns had been created in Panama (1580), Venezuela (1603), New Spain (1609), and Hispaniola (1655), to name a few examples, and all had received royal sanction. Most were legitimized maroon communities, but the Venezuelan example is analogous to Mose, for in that case Spain granted free blacks who would hold the frontier against hostile Indians "perpetual" rights to a town of their own.[16]

Religious Life at Mose

Mose was a village of "new converts" comparable to those of the Christianized Indians, and following that model, Governor Montiano assigned a friar of good character to the settlement to instruct the inhabitants in doctrine and "good customs" and to administer the sacraments.[17] The young Franciscan, Don Joseph de León, lived at Mose with his charges. He quickly baptized children below the age of reason and began teaching the adult villagers the Catholic catechism. As soon as they were able to pass an examination in the basic tenets of the faith, Father de León baptized the adults. Some of the Mose villagers were baptized, married, or buried at Mose, while others celebrated their special sacraments in St. Augustine, presumably because of the more elegant church and the higher status it conveyed, as well as for the visibility. After all, the basis of their freedom was their religious conversion, and it behooved them to be as public as possible about it.[18] On special feast days of the Catholic calendar, such as the feasts of St. Mark, St. Augustine, and Corpus Christi, and the anniversary of deceased soldiers, the villagers at Mose would fire celebratory gunshots and light extra candles, with munitions and wax provided from the government stores.[19]

The Continuing Lure of Mose

News regarding Spain's sanctuary policy in Florida and the existence of Fort Mose spread rapidly northward through the fledgling English colony of Georgia (where race slavery was still prohibited) to the expanding plantations of South Carolina, where roughly thirty thousand blacks were tied to the arduous rice economy by the mid-1730s. Since the 1670s, Spanish raiding parties against Carolina had always included free blacks, whose very presence continually advertised the difference in slave systems. Carolina planters complained that the 1733 edict had been proclaimed publicly (as, in fact, it was), "by Beat of Drum round the Town of St. Augustine (where many Negroes belonging to English vessels that carried thither Supplies of provisions had the Opportunity of hearing it)."[20] They also alluded to secret measures taken by the Spaniards to disseminate their offer among the English slaves and frequently reported suspicious visitors from Spanish Florida. As the word spread, more slaves were emboldened to try for liberty.

On November 21, 1738, twenty-three men, women, and children escaped from Port Royal, Carolina, and made it safely to St. Augustine in a stolen launch. Governor Montiano promptly honored their request for sanctuary, and they joined their countrymen at Mose. Nineteen of the newcomers, eight of them described as workmen, had belonged to Captain Caleb Davis, an English merchant who had been trading merchandise (and intelligence) in St. Augustine for years. Despite his useful relationship with the Spaniards, Governor Montiano refused Davis when he attempted to reclaim his slaves the following month, and Davis reported that his slaves laughed at his fruitless efforts to recover them.[21] Twelve years later, the frustrated Davis submitted a claim to the Spanish government for twenty-seven of his slaves "detained" by Montiano, whom he valued at 7,600 pesos, as well as for the launch in which they escaped and supplies they had taken with them. In the same document, Davis listed debts owed him by citizens of St. Augustine. Among his debtors were Governors Antonio de Benavides, Francisco Moral Sánchez, and Manuel de Montiano, various royal officials and army officers, and even some of the Mose inhabitants, including Captain Francisco Menéndez and Pedro de León.[22]

In February 1739, Carolina authorities captured, but released, several runaways headed for St. Augustine. The following month four slaves and an Irish Catholic servant from Carolina made their escape to Florida on stolen horses. The English angrily reported that although the runaways had killed one man and wounded another, "They were received there [St. Augustine] with great honours, one of them had a Commission given to him, and a Coat faced with Velvet."[23] The same month, another group of envoys from Carolina traveled to St. Augustine to press for the return of the runaways. Governor Montiano was cordial but refused to comply, citing the royal edict of 1733 which reiterated Spain's earlier promise of religious sanctuary. Carolina's governor, William Bull, wrote that the planters were very dissatisfied "to find their property now become so very precarious and uncertain." He added that Carolina's planters feared that "Negroes which were their chief support may in little time become their Enemies, if not their Masters, and that this Government is unable to withstand or prevent it."[24] In April, frustrated members of the South Carolina Commons voted to offer bounties, even for adult scalps "with the two ears," to dissuade other slaves from trying to escape, and for added emphasis staged a public whipping and execution of two newly captured runaways.[25]

Despite the increasingly harsh measures taken against them, the enslaved still sought freedom, and the level of their own desperate violence escalated proportionally. In August, Don Diego Pablo, an Indian ally in Apalachee, sent word to Governor Montiano that the British had attempted to build a fort nearby, but that the hundred black laborers had revolted, killed all the whites, and hamstrung their horses before escaping. Several days later some of the escaped blacks encountered the same Indians in the woods and asked directions to reach the Spaniards, presumably to ask for sanctuary.[26]

The following month, on September 9, 1739, a group of "Angolan" slaves revolted near Stono, South Carolina, where they killed more than twenty whites and sacked and burned homes before heading for St. Augustine.[27] Governor Bull quickly gathered a retaliatory force, which struck the rebels later that day when they stopped along the road for what the white pursuers viewed as a drunken dance, but which John Thornton identifies as a traditional feature of war in Central Africa. Thornton argues that the Stono rebels were probably not actually from Angola, but from the Kongo (which traders generically referred to as the Angola Coast). Kongo had long been a Catholic kingdom with many Portuguese speakers and Thornton contends, as did contemporary Carolinians, that the rebels could well have understood both the offer of Catholic protection and Spanish, a sister language to Portuguese, and have based their flight plans on this knowledge. He attributes the success with which the rebels fought southward down the road for more than a week to their training and service as soldiers in eighteenth-century wars in the Kongo.[28] Eugene Sirmans has argued that the Stono Rebellion was "less an insurrection than an attempt by slaves to fight their way to St. Augustine."[29] Even if this is true, the political nature of the action, as well as the risk taken by participants, remains significant. Those rebels who survived the first day's battle fought on for another week, moving southward toward St. Augustine before a larger white militia force finally caught and killed most of them. However, all reports say that some rebels escaped that battle as well, and if any of them made it to their destination, they would have been sheltered at Mose, like their predecessors.[30]

Peter H. Wood argues that Stono led to a "heightened degree of white repression and a reduced amount of black autonomy" in Carolina. Both factors would have made escape to St. Augustine even more worth the risk. An estimated 150 slaves rebelled near the Ashley River outside Charles Town in June 1740. Like the Stono rebels, they also may have hoped to reach safety at St. Augustine. They chose a dangerous time for their escape since Carolina and Georgia were at that very moment joined in attacking Spanish Florida. It may have been that fact, however, that triggered the revolt. Carolinians captured fifty of the rebels and hanged them at the rate of ten a day, but nothing is known of the fate of the other one hundred. If they made it to St. Augustine, they, too, would have been incorporated into the Mose community, then sheltered in St. Augustine.[31]

Africans and Eighteenth-Century Geopolitics in the Southeast

After fighting in African and Indian wars and deadly insurrections, the men of Mose were hardened veterans and a valuable military resource to the Spaniards as local and international tensions worsened. Their very presence in Florida, however, was also a continuing provocation. When James Oglethorpe founded Georgia in 1733, the sanctuary for escaped slaves in Florida became as much a concern for the Georgians as it had been for the Carolinians. The first point made in the famous Darien antislavery petition of 1739 read, "The Nearness of the Spaniards, who have proclaimed Freedom to all Slaves, who run away from their Masters, makes it impossible for us to keep them, without more Labour in guarding them, than what we would be at to do their Work."[32]

For its part, Spain considered Georgia to be an illegal colony and planned a major invasion from Havana to eradicate it, but the attack was aborted at the last minute to allow for possible diplomatic resolution of contested boundaries. Even as diplomats conferred, however, General Oglethorpe sponsored war parties of Lower Creeks in raids against Florida in 1738 and 1739. With the outbreak of the War of Jenkins' Ear in 1739, Oglethorpe was free to take more direct action. In January he captured Forts Pupo and Picolata on the St. Johns River west of St. Augustine, and these initial victories enabled him to raise a major expeditionary force to oust the Spaniards from St. Augustine. Troops from South Carolina and Georgia, assorted volunteers such as the South Carolina and Georgia Rangers and the Highlanders, approximately six hundred Creek and Uchise allies, and approximately eight hundred black slaves or "pioneers" made up the expedition, and seven warships of the Royal Navy sailed up from Jamaica to join the assault.[33]

The Mose militiamen now had the chance to make good on their pledge to spill their blood for Spain and Catholicism. Governor Montiano relied heavily on his militias to patrol the frontier and report on enemy movements. These guerrilla units were composed in equal numbers of Spaniards, Indians, and free blacks "of those who are fugitives from the English colonies."[34] Indians and troops allied to Oglethorpe roamed the same frontier. "British" Indians scalped a black slave at Fort Diego and later scalped at least one resident of Mose. Jonathan Bryan's Georgia volunteers captured two Mose villagers in their outlying homes.[35] In response Governor Montiano evacuated the black homesteaders to the safety of the Castillo, where he also gathered in over two thousand citizens of St. Augustine.

Part of the English forces quickly occupied the abandoned Fort Mose, dismantling its gate and making several breaches in the walls so that, as Oglethorpe prophetically put it, it would not become "a mouse trap for some of our own people."[36] Oglethorpe and a large force headquartered on Anastasia Island across the inlet from St. Augustine and the South Carolina Regiment, led by Colonel Alexander Vanderdussen, settled at Quartell Point on the mainland. The siege was begun. Royal Navy gunboats bombarded St. Augustine daily for almost a month, and with each blast, the besieged citizenry reportedly offered up a Hail Mary. Governor Montiano wrote frantically to Cuba's captain general begging

"Assault on Fort Mose," a Florida National Guard painting by Jackson Walker. Courtesy of the Florida National Guard.

for assistance and warned that the people were almost out of food. Montiano wrote, "We are thus surrounded by enemies, unable to leave the place without danger. As long as our territory is not peopled, thus driving out the English, the chief cause of all these evils, these Provinces will have no rest."[37] Despite the danger, Captain Menéndez and the Mose militia joined Indian militias in guerrilla operations against the English and also took part in the most significant battle of the invasion, the retaking of Mose.[38]

Just before daybreak on June 14, 1740, Captain Antonio Salgado commanded Spanish forces, Indians, and free blacks led by Francisco Menéndez in a surprise attack on Mose. The Spanish forces killed about seventy-five of the unprepared invaders in bloody hand-to-hand combat, using swords, muskets, and "club work." British accounts refer to the event as "Bloody Mose" or "Fatal Mose" and relate with horror the murder and mutilation (decapitation and castration) of two badly wounded prisoners who were unable to walk.[39] Scholars generally acknowledge that the Spanish victory at Mose demoralized the badly divided British forces, and that it was the significant factor in Oglethorpe's withdrawal. In late June relief forces and supplies from Havana finally reached St. Augustine, and soon after the British warships abandoned Oglethorpe's spent forces, fearful of the approaching hurricane season. Oglethorpe had little choice but to straggle home.[40]

A committee of the South Carolina House of Commons, in a report on the 1740 expedition, not only castigated Oglethorpe for his failure but complained bitterly about slaves lost to the Spanish and blamed the Spanish authorities for the Stono uprising.[41] The report described the "mulattoes of savage dispositions" who had been formed into militias in St. Augustine and estimated that their numbers equaled those of the regular troops. It added:

> Relying wholly on the king's pay for their subsistence, their thoughts never turned to trade or even agriculture, but depending on foreign supplies for the most common necessities of life, they spend their time in universal, perpetual idleness. From such a state, mischievous inclinations naturally spring up in such a people; and having leisure and opportunity, ever since they had a neighbor the fruits of whose industry excited their desires and envy, they have not failed to carry those inclinations into action as often as they could, without the least regard to peace or war subsisting between the two crowns of Great Britain and Spain, or to stipulations agreed upon between the two governments.[42]

Another section of the report attacked all of St. Augustine as a "den of ruffians and thieves" and as the "bane of industry and society," and the character flaws imputed to the mulattoes in the first section are in the latter associated with the entire Spanish settlement. As many scholars have pointed out, it was indeed very difficult by the mid-eighteenth century to distinguish true racial types because miscegenation was so common, and race became more a function of the level of status acquired through wealth, education, and other socioeconomic factors.[43] To the Anglos, and even to many *peninsulares* (persons born in Spain), *criollos* (persons born in the Americas) seemed a lazy, inferior species—the unfortunate byproduct of race mixture and the debilitating effects of the tropics. All the residents of St. Augustine, therefore, might have seemed to the Carolinians "mulattoe-like."

Not surprisingly, Governor Montiano's reports on the invasion took a different tone: "The constancy, valor and glory of the officers here are beyond all praise: the patriotism, courage, and steadiness of the troops, militia, free blacks, and convicts have been great. These last I must say to your Excellency, have born themselves like veteran soldiers. . . . Even among the slaves a particular steadiness has been noticed, and a desire not to await the enemy within the place [the Castillo] but to go out to meet him."[44]

The following summer, under orders from Spain and provisioned from Havana, Governor Montiano mounted a counterattack on Georgia. His force included a flotilla of approximately thirty watercraft of various types; a thousand regular troops, some twenty-four black and mulatto officers, and 468 men of the disciplined pardo and moreno militias from Cuba; and about one hundred blacks from St. Augustine.[45] Governor Montiano hoped, as had Governor Benavides before him, to incite English slaves to rise against their masters, using the example of his free black warriors and promises of land. His war plans called for sending English-speaking blacks of the Mose militia to range the countryside gathering and arming slave recruits. The captain general of Cuba approved that plan and expanded on it, guaranteeing not only liberty but land to slaves who would join the Spaniards:

> After taking possession of Port Royal, it will be proper to send out negroes of all languages (some of which sort accompany the militia of this place for this very purpose) to convoke the slaves of the English in the plantations round about, and offer them, in the name of our king, liberty, if they will deliver themselves up of their own accord, and to say that lands will be assigned them in the territories of Florida, which they may cultivate and use for themselves as owners, under the direction and laws of the kingdom of Spain.[46]

Bad weather, mishaps, and confusion plagued the operation, and the English killed several of the invaders at Bloody Marsh on Saint Simon's island before the Spaniards returned to St. Augustine in defeat. Fifteen free blacks of the Mose militia were among the Spanish forces, but unfortunately, they remain unidentified to date, and there are no specific references to their roles at Bloody Marsh.[47]

General Oglethorpe mounted two more attacks on St. Augustine in 1742 and 1743 and although these were no more successful than Montiano's attack on Saint Simon's, the continuing turmoil may have encouraged more slaves to run southward. In 1743 Carolina authorities alerted Oglethorpe that a group of thirty "sensible Negroes, fifteen of whom had firearms" had escaped and were headed for St. Augustine. It is not known if Oglethorpe was successful in intercepting them.[48] Later that year, however, during a raid against St. Augustine, Oglethorpe's Cowhatie Indian allies returned to camp with a gruesome bounty of "five scalps, one Hand, which was cut off with the Glove on, several Arms, Clothes, and two or three Spades." These they had taken while attacking a boatload of "pioneers" (black laborers) who were digging clay for the royal fortifications.[49] One of the expeditionaries exulted in his journal, "The Siege of Augustine and the continual incursions since made by his Excellency [Oglethorpe], [has] quite render'd the open Country, from St. Mathia's to Augustine, useless to the Spaniards, (and spoil'd their usual Methods of decoying our Negroes from Carolina, and elsewhere; whence, in Numbers, they used to desert to them . . .)."[50] These raids failed to oust the Spaniards, however, and an uneasy stalemate developed on the border, punctuated occasionally by Indian and corsair raids.

Francisco Menéndez, Soldier and Corsair

In the aftermath of the victory at Mose in 1740, Francisco Menéndez directed a petition to the Spanish king in which he outlined his lengthy and loyal service to the Crown and asked for remuneration for "the loyalty, zeal, and love I have always demonstrated in the royal service, in the encounters with the enemies, as well as in the effort and care with which I have worked to repair two bastions on the defense line of this plaza, being pleased to do it, although it advanced my poverty, and I have continually been at arms, and assisted in the maintenance of the bastions, without the least royal expense, despite the scarcity in which this presidio always exists, especially on this occasion."[51]

Menéndez reminded the king that he had served as captain of the black militia since 1726 and said his "sole object was to defend the Holy Gospel and the sovereignty of the Royal Crown." He asked the king to reward him with the proprietorship of the militia captaincy and whatever salary the king saw fit, to enable him to live "decently" (meaning in the style expected of an officer of the militia). He concluded that he hoped to receive "all the consolation of the royal support . . . which Christianity requires and your vassals desire," and closed with the standard, "I kiss the feet of Your Majesty," signing with a flourish.[52]

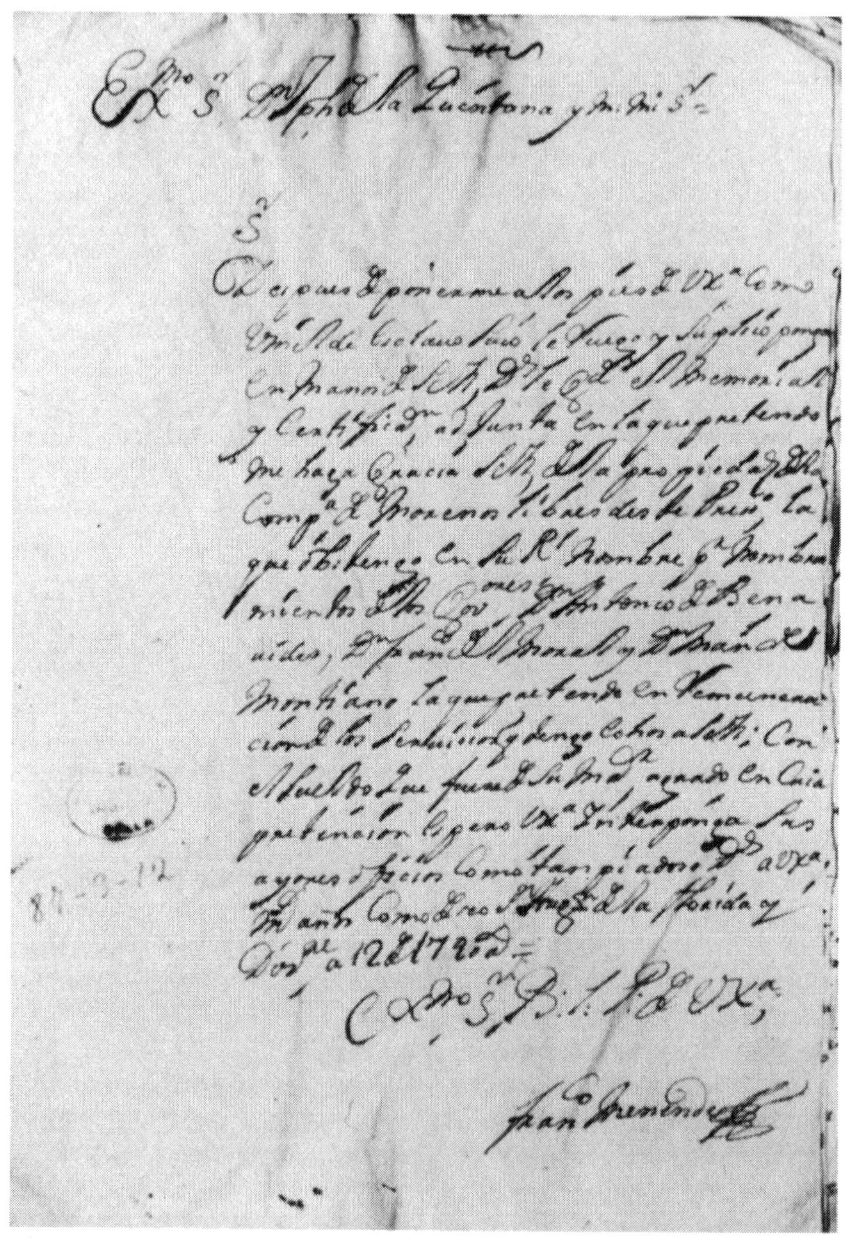

Petition of Francisco Menéndez to King Philip V of Spain asking for a reward for his services during the 1740 invasion of General James Oglethorpe. Courtesy of the P. K. Yonge Library of Florida History and the Florida Museum of Natural History, Fort Mose Exhibition.

Despite Menéndez's good services, and appropriate behavior and rhetoric, there is no evidence of a response, and royal parsimony made such a payment unlikely. Nevertheless, several months later Governor Montiano made the rather unusual gesture of sending the king his own recommendation of Francisco Menéndez. Montiano extolled "the exactitude with which Menéndez had carried out royal service over the three years of their acquaintance" and, particularly, the valor he displayed in the battle of Mose. The governor added that at one point during the siege Menéndez and his men had fired on the enemy until they withdrew from the castle walls, and that Menéndez displayed great zeal during the dangerous reconnaissance missions he undertook against the British and their Indians. In addition Montiano wrote that Menéndez had "distinguished himself in the establishment, and cultivation of Mose, to improve that settlement, doing all he could so that the rest of his subjects, following his example, would apply themselves to work and learn good customs."[53] Three months later Menéndez submitted a second, shorter petition, again asking for the proprietary captaincy and an appropriate salary. When he still did not receive a reply, Menéndez decided to make his way to Spain to press his claims in person, and to accomplish that, he became a corsair.[54]

British, French, and Spanish privateers prowled the Atlantic coasts in the 1740s and 1750s and St. Augustine became a convenient base of operations for Spanish ships. The capture and sale of the prizes they had captured provided badly needed specie and supplies for war-torn Florida, which did not receive its government subsidies in 1739, 1740, 1741, and 1745, and which struggled under the additional burden of maintaining the large number of Cuban reinforcements who arrived to lift Oglethorpe's siege in 1740.[55] Corsairing ships were manned by volunteers, no doubt eager for some employment in the destitute colony, and many of them were drawn from the free black community. Scholars such as Marcus Rediker and W. Jeffrey Bolster have argued that the maritime culture of the eighteenth and nineteenth centuries, "while by no means either color-blind or without internal friction . . . created its own institutions and its own stratifications, which could work to the relative advantage of black men." Bolster contends that merchants recruited crews based on their strength, ability, and experience rather than skin color, with black and white crewmen earning equal pay for equal jobs, and many black sailors, in fact, earning more than whites.[56] Reduced social distinctions and better pay may well have been reasons for Spanish blacks to take to the sea, just as they had to the militias.

Francisco Menéndez and other free blacks sailed with St. Augustine's most successful corsairs. In December 1740, Don Juan de León Fandiño (who ten years earlier had cut off the celebrated Jenkins's ear) selected a crew to man his recently refitted sloop. Francisco Menéndez was aboard Fandiño's expedition to Cape Fear, during which the crew exchanged cannon and musket fire with one English privateer before capturing a schooner and returning to St. Augustine after a month's voyage.[57] Later Menéndez sailed with Captain Pedro de Estrada, whose raids on ports from Vera Cruz, Mexico, to Ocracoke, North Carolina, were cosponsored by Governor Manuel de Montiano. The governor helped arm and provision Estrada's crews and may have recommended Menéndez to Captain Estrada, as he already had to the king. In April 1741, Estrada and thirty men, among them Francisco Menéndez, attacked the British at Ocracoke, "where the Albermarle River comes to the sea." On landing, the Spanish corsairs burned a warehouse full of tar, pitch, and other naval stores, and a partially built sloop. They also captured five frigates and seven sloops. After burning one of the vessels and sinking another, Estrada dispatched eight others, loaded with supplies, to St. Augustine. Of the eight, only two made it safely to St. Augustine, but one carried thirteen hundred tons of badly needed rice.

Estrada's crews made other lucrative captures that summer, but not all expeditions met with success. Some were lost to severe storms and others were captured by the British.[58] On July 28, 1741, the Boston-based *Revenge,* captained by Benjamin Norton, recaptured one of the prizes Estrada had seized on yet another attack on Ocracoke. When the Englishmen interrogated the Spanish crew, one prisoner identified himself as "Signior Capitano Francisco." The captain's quartermaster wrote in the ship's journal that Francisco was "Capt. of a Comp'y of Indians, Mollattos, and Negroes that was att the Retaking of the Fort [Mose] att St. Augus'ne formerly taken Under the Command of that worthless G—— O——pe who by his trechory suffered so many brave fellows to be mangled by those barbarians."[59]

Under questioning, Menéndez stated that he became a privateer in hopes of getting to Havana, and from there to "Old Spain," where he hoped to "get the reward of his brave actions" at Mose.[60] The combination of his titles, admitted war role, and the pride he took in his "brave actions" must have infuriated his captors, who tied Francisco Menéndez to a gun and ordered the ship's physician to pretend to castrate him (as Englishmen had been castrated at Mose). But while Menéndez "frankly owned" that he was captain of the company that retook Mose, he denied ordering any atrocities, which he said the Florida Indians had committed. The English interrogated three other mulattoes found on board, whom they named as Pedro Sancho, And'w Estavie, and Augustine (also abbreviated as Aug'ne). Augustine seems to have shared Menéndez's room and presumably was closer to him, and for that the Englishmen gave him twelve lashes. Despite this punishment, all his men substantiated Menéndez's account. Captain Norton was still not satisfied and, "to make Sure and to make him remember that he bore such a Commission," he ordered Menéndez given two hundred lashes and then "pickled him and left him to the Doctor to take Care of his Sore A-se."[61]

Norton and his crew may have had some sympathetic connection to the Carolinians mauled in Oglethorpe's 1740 invasion of Florida. However, the source of their violent antipathy toward Menéndez and other black "barbarians" might have originated closer to home. Only months before, a series of suspicious fires swept New York, which the terror-stricken whites attributed to a slave conspiracy—"The Great Negro Plot." Mobs focused in particular on the menace of the "Spanish negroes," such as "Jacob Sarly's Juan," who had been seized aboard a Spanish sloop in 1740 and who, like eighteen other of his fellow crewmen, insisted they were "free men in their own country." "Captain Sarly's Juan" had been heard to say that he would set fires and "William, Captain Lush's Spanish negro," threatened to "ruin the city" if he were not returned to his homeland. Juan and William were not referring to some African locale but rather to their adopted Spanish homeland. The conspirators were said to have been waiting on an expected Spanish/French attack against New York, but when it did not materialize, the slaves took action. One suspect was reported to have said, "Those Spaniards know better than York negroes. . . . They're more used to war, but we must begin first to set the houses on fire." After a lengthy investigation and a series of trials, New York authorities burned thirteen black men at the stake and hanged seventeen others, along with four white co-conspirators, including two white women.[62]

As fate would have it, Captain Norton had stopped in New York to try to recruit sailors in the midst of the hysteria, and on Friday, June 12, three of the crewmen of the *Revenge* were in the crowd that watched four of the convicted conspirators burn to death at the stake, including the Spanish black, Francis. Several months later, "Jacob Sarly's Juan" went to the gallows and was said to have "prayed in Spanish, kissed the crucifix and insisted on his innocence to the last."[63] Francis and Juan represented to the crowds before them three dreaded and despised elements—the internal enemy or disloyal slave, a foreign, particularly a Spanish, threat, and fervent Catholicism.

In August, the *Revenge* landed at New Providence, in the Bahamas, and the captain's quartermaster vehemently argued before the Admiralty Court that Menéndez and his men should be condemned as slaves. "Does not their Complexion and features tell all the world that they are of the blood of Negroes and have suckt Slavery and Cruelty from their Infancy? Can any one think when we Call to mind that barbarous Action Committed to his Majestys Brave Subjects att the Retaken of the fort att St. Augustine, Occasioned by the treachery of their vile Gen'l who sacrificed them to that Barbarous Colour, that it was done by any that had the Least drop of blood Either of Liberty or Christianity in them?"

Answering his own question in the negative, he went on to describe Menéndez as "this Francisco that Cursed Seed of Cain, Curst from the foundation of the world, who has the Impudence to Come into Court and plead that he is free. Slavery is too Good for such a Savage, nay all the Cruelty invented by man . . . the torments of the World to Come will not suffice."[64]

The quartermaster again identified the three mulattoes as being members of the company commanded by Francisco Menéndez at the Battle of Mose, and he argued that "by the old Law of Nations . . . all prisoners of War, nay even their posterity are Slaves."[65] Unfortunately, no record of Francisco Menéndez's testimony appears in this account, but his earlier petitions to Governor Montiano and to the Spanish king prove that he was equipped to plead his own case. Not surprisingly, however, the Admiralty Court ruled against him, and on August 21, 1741, after Captain Norton sold the prize cargo of corn, pork, beef, tar, pitch and oil, he "then Sett up Seignior Capt. Francisco Under the Name of Don Blass," and sold him to a Mr. Stone, "according to the Laws of the plantation."[66]

Menéndez's torture and the vitriolic slurs of the quartermaster illustrate the extreme racial hatred that some British felt for Spain's black subjects, as well as the grave dangers the freedmen faced in taking up Spanish arms. Oglethorpe's forces had denied any quarter to the fugitives from Carolina, and when free blacks were captured at sea, the British presumed them by their color to be slaves, thus eligible for sale. In 1746 New York's Admiralty Court considered the fate of twenty "Indians Mollattoes & Negroes" captured aboard two Spanish prizes the year before. Although Spanish officials from Havana presented proof that seventeen were, in fact, free men, by the time the New York court finally met and ordered freedom for four of the men, only three could be located.[67]

Nor was this an isolated incident. On August 16, 1748, the British corsair, *Ester,* captained by Robert Troup, seized the *Nuestra Señora del Carmen* after it left Havana and claimed as part of the prize forty-five black privateers. However, the recently concluded Treaty of Aix-la-Chapelle guaranteed that all captures after August 9 of that year would be returned, so Florida's governor, Melchor de Navarrete, permitted the *Carmen*'s captain, Francisco de Laguna, to travel to New York and try to recover his ship and crew.[68] Governor Navarrete asked Cuba's captain general to gather information about the captives and to complain to England that the New Yorkers were using the Spanish crewmen "like slaves."[69] Despite the treaty provisions, Laguna met with failure, so in 1752 Governor Fulgencio García de Solís allowed him to try again, noting "without those of 'broken' color [a term for anyone of mixed race, usually meaning mulatto], blacks, and Indians, which abound in our towns in America, I do not know if we could arm a single corsair solely with Spaniards."[70]

This Spanish dependence upon men of color made it imperative that they try to recover their captured black crewmen from the British, and García de Solís wrote letters to the governors of Havana, Cartagena, Santa Marta, and Margarita, and to the lieutenant of the Cuban village of Bayamo, asking their prompt assistance in determining the free status of the captives. García de Solís fulminated that the English were tyrants for enslaving Spanish vassals, simply "for the accident of their broken color," adding that no Spanish owner would allow a slave to enlist as a corsair for fear of losing him, nor would the Spaniards use them, for "free people of color abound in the Spanish Dominions." He believed that the English policy was designed to terrorize black corsairs and keep them from serving on Spanish ships in the "next war," and he may well have been correct. According to the governor, Spaniards generally accepted the testimonies of fellow corsairs that a man was free, while the English asked for such proofs as were almost impossible to produce; they wanted certificates which gave age, stature, complexion, occupation, dates of departure from Havana, names of the ships on which they sailed and the captains' names, the date and location of their capture, and the name of the British corsair that captured them. When Laguna went before the Admiralty Court once again, this time armed with baptismal and militia records as well as notarized depositions about the free status of the captives, New York's governor, George Clinton, reheard the case and freed two of the forty-five men in question. Some four years after they were first captured, the free mulattoes Francisco Pérez and Antonio Raymundo de Ortega finally returned to their homes in Havana.[71]

Given this dismal recovery rate, Francisco Menéndez might well have been among the "disappeared" of the era; however, as he proved many times, Menéndez was a man of unusual abilities. Whether Menéndez successfully appealed for his freedom in British courts as he had in the Spanish, was ransomed back by the Spanish officials of Florida, or escaped is unknown, but by at least 1759 he was once again in command at Mose.[72]

The St. Augustine Interlude, 1739–52

While some free blacks, like Menéndez, went to sea, others remained in the city of St. Augustine, struggling to rebuild lives after the devastation wrought by Oglethorpe's invasion. After months of raids, siege, and battles, Governor Montiano described the colony as "a Hospital." Mose and the outlying forts had been destroyed, along with many of the crops and almost all of the animals on which the community subsisted. Surveying the wreckage, the governor wrote Havana to request "300 armed men more, mulattoes and free blacks from the militia of Cuba" as military reinforcements and to assist in all the rebuilding that would be necessary.[73]

Hunger plagued the small colony in these years. Many of the royally chartered Havana Company ships that were to provision Florida were seized by corsairs, and residents complained that the few food shipments that reached St. Augustine were usually ruined. Continual attacks by Uchizes and other Indians loyal to the British kept the citizenry close to the Castillo's defensive walls. Fields went untilled as the countryside was abandoned.

Spain addressed the dangerous depopulation of Florida by devising a plan to import impoverished farmers recruited from the Canary Islands. The Crown also offered frontier lands to retired military men and even to deserters, who would also receive pardons if they would become homesteaders.[74] Like many Spanish plans, however, this belated effort to fill the territorial vacuum took years to enact, and the first Canary families (only sixteen families totaling seventy-five individuals) arrived only in the late 1750s.[75]

Meanwhile, despite the danger and privation, new runaways continued to filter into Florida. A Carolinian complained in 1749: "[T]he Spaniards, at St. Augustine, who during the war, seduced and encouraged our negroes [or slaves] to desert from this province, and gave them their freedom, continue that practice, now in peace, notwithstanding all the remonstrances made on that subject. And there is hardly a week but a dozen of them go off at a time in canoes."[76]

Such estimates by anxious planters may have exaggerated departures, and not all who attempted the long and dangerous journey made it safely, but Spanish officials welcomed any black refugees from South Carolina—and, during the 1750s, from Georgia as well. Each newcomer to St. Augustine represented one more mouth to feed, but the community needed skilled hands, willing homesteaders, and persons deeply hostile toward the English slaveholders who could help hold the threatened frontier.

Some of the original founders of Mose had already lived among the Spaniards for years prior to their emancipation in 1738 and were, by this time, fully acquainted with Spanish customs and law. For relatively recent immigrants, however, this urban interlude was critical to their integration into Spanish St. Augustine.[77] A primary goal of the Spanish governors was the religious incorporation of the foreign blacks, which was seen as necessary to the harmony and order of the community. Governor Montiano's successor, Melchor de Navarrete, saw to the religious instruction of the refugees, and in 1752 he boasted of the conversion of fourteen adults from Carolina, adding that "all the others" were still undergoing Christian instruction. Navarrete promised certificates of freedom once the catechumens had been successfully examined and baptized.[78]

As they learned their catechism, the newcomers probably lived much like free blacks in other Spanish colonial ports, engaging in craft production, artisanry, and the provision of services. Although certain racial restrictions existed on paper, they were rarely enforced in a frontier settlement such as St. Augustine, where more relaxed personal relations were the norm. Everyone knew everyone else, and this familiarity could be a source of assistance and protection for the free blacks of Mose, who had acquired at least a measure of acceptability.[79] Susan R. Parker's study of contemporary "urban Indians" living in St. Augustine shows they also used church and military connections and interpersonal relations such as godparentage to break through supposed racial barriers in the "tri-racial" town.[80] Wage lists in treasury accounts and military reports from this urban interlude show that the free blacks of Mose and St. Augustine worked on government building projects, were sailors and privateers, tracked escaped prisoners, and helped forage for food, wood, and fodder. In the spring, the men, some of whom had tended herds of cattle in Carolina, rounded up wild cattle for slaughter and wild horses for cavalry mounts. Men with military ability joined the urban black militia, which continued to patrol the frontier. Up to eighty men served when needed, and according to a 1756 report, they were armed and provisioned at the expense of the royal treasury.[81] (For a later militia list, see appendix 3.)

Mose Resettled, 1752–63

As noted, the vacated frontier between St. Augustine and the English colonies to the north invited hostile incursions, and as the number of runaways entering the city grew, Governor Navarrete decided to fill the void by reestablishing Gracia Real de Santa Teresa de Mose. He was unable to do so because "persistent illnesses" of an unknown nature among the blacks made such a homesteading effort impossible. By the time the next governor, Fulgencio García de Solís, picked up the plan to reestablish Mose in 1752, the former residents had become accustomed to an urban life and were not eager to submit themselves to further British and Indian attacks on the frontier. García faced unexpected, and stubborn, resistance. He complained that it was not fear of the enemy but "the desire to live in complete liberty" that motivated the rebels, and so he resorted to force. He "lightly" punished the two unnamed leaders of the resistance and threatened worse to those who continued to fight his resettlement plan. In a familiar litany,

García alluded to "bad customs," "spiritual backwardness," and "pernicious consequences" and condemned not only the original Mose settlers but also "those who have since fled the English colonies to join them."[82]

The Franciscan missionary Pedro Lorenzo de Asevedo used similar pejoratives in describing Indians who attempted to maintain tradition in their outlying villages. Father Asevedo claimed their lack of Spanish, "evil superstitions," and "the unfaithfulness to which their nature inclines them" were responsible for their continuing abuses (religious errors). In an interesting linguistic conflation, the priest referred to such Indians as "Indios bozales," a term usually reserved for unacculturated Africans.[83]

Governor García may well have been disturbed by the presence and influence of unacculturated Africans among the latecomers. Slave imports increased into South Carolina in the 1740s and, after Georgia legalized African slavery in 1750, into that even-closer locale as well. The "bad customs" that the governor alleged had so troubled his predecessor and himself may have been African cultural retentions. In 1744 St. Augustine's parish priest, Father Francisco Xavier Arturo, had baptized Domingo, a Carabalí slave, on his deathbed, with the comment that his "crudeness" prevented his understanding of Christian doctrine. On two other occasions, Father Arturo gave the Congo slave Miguel and the Congo slave Francisco conditional baptisms because each told the priest he had been baptized by a priest in his homeland and taught to pray in his own language. As Miguel was baptized, he blessed himself in that unidentified language. In 1748 Father Arturo gave the same conditional baptism to Miguel Domingo, also a Congo slave who had been baptized in Africa and continued to pray in his native language.[84]

Governor García was required by repeated royal edicts to grant sanctuary to slave refugees who converted to Catholicism, but he was not required to accommodate them in St. Augustine and he could fulfill dual objectives by resettling them at Mose: isolate the townspeople from possible religious contamination and defend the frontier. To give the reluctant settlers "no pretext which could excuse them" from living at Mose, the governor paid them daily wages from the government treasury to build themselves a new and more fortified town. The governor also assigned a permanent detachment of regular Spanish cavalry to Mose, to supplement the settlers' own reorganized militia, which as before would be captained by Francisco Menéndez.[85]

The settlers erected a new fort, slightly north of the first village, on the banks of Mose Creek. Built of earthen or sod walls, faced in clay and topped with prickly pear, it was a larger, three-sided structure, lacking a wall on the creek side. A dry moat surrounded the fort, which had mounted on its bastions six small cannons provided by the governor.[86] Within the fort walls, the homesteaders also built guard and storage houses, a board church, and a sacristy that doubled as a house for the priest.[87] Despite protests by St. Augustine's secular priest, Juan Joseph de Solana, who ministered to the people of Mose when they first arrived and who had been both owner and godfather to some, Governor García treated Mose as any other *doctrina,* or mission, and he and his successors thereafter assigned a series of Franciscans to minister to the rebuilt black town.[88] The first Franciscan priest assigned to the rebuilt town, Father Andrés de Vilches, came to Mose from the Indian village of Nuestra Señora de la Puríssima Concepción de Pocotalaca where he had established a school for Yamasee children. At Mose Vilches assisted in building the platforms for artillery and mortars to better fortify the town and he also specified that he worked "one year, one month, and a few more days" in helping build Mose's church.[89] Franciscan histories also credit Vilches with establishing a school at Mose, as he had done at Pocotalaca.[90] When Father Vilches was reassigned to Apalachee province in 1753 another Franciscan, Father Juan de la Vía, replaced him. Father Vía served the Mose Catholics for the next four years, and in 1757 Father Ginés Sánchez came from Havana to assume the pastoral position at Mose.[91] By 1759 Father Agustín Gerónimo Resio was Mose's resident priest, and he was also its last, evacuating to Cuba with his charges in 1763.[92]

A map of Mose drawn by a Spanish engineer in the year of the evacuation shows the village's public structures but not the homes of the twenty households listed on a village census in 1759. (See appendix 4.)[93] It must be assumed that the houses of the sixty-seven villagers recorded in that census were scattered outside the fort, among planted fields, as had been the case at the first Mose settlement.

In 1759 Mose had more than twice as many males as female occupants (thirty-seven men and fifteen women), and almost a quarter of its population consisted of children under the age of fifteen (seven boys and eight girls). Thirteen of the twenty-two households belonged to nuclear families, and fifty villagers, or 75 percent of the total population, lived with immediate members of their families. There were no female-headed households at this outpost, but there were nine households composed entirely of males, many of whom had slave wives or children in St. Augustine. (See appendix 4.)[94]

The parish registers reflect the great ethnic and racial diversity at Mose, which was also true of Spanish Florida in general. Among the African "nations" specifically identified for the original population at Mose were the Mandinga, Fara, and Arará. Later additions further diversified the group, incorporating Congo, Carabalí (Calabarí), and Mina into the mix. In the larger community of St. Augustine were also found Gambas, Sambas, Gangás, Laras, and some persons identified only as Guineans. Interracial relationships were common, and families were restructured frequently when death struck and widowed men and women remarried. The core group of Carolina fugitives formed intricate ties among themselves that can be tracked through the parish records for up to three generations. They married within their group and served as witnesses at each other's weddings and as godparents for each other's children, sometimes many times over. They also entered into relationships with Indians, free blacks, and slaves from other locations. Some of these slaves later became free, which suggests mutual assistance efforts by the nascent black community.[95]

Ethnic identifications became more complex when couples of different nations intermarried. It seems likely that although children of these mixtures would have known their parents' ethnicities, they may have identified themselves in new ways. Even the first-generation Africans at Mose must have drawn on several sources when constructing new identities for themselves. Their freedom was dependent upon Catholic conversion and political enmity toward the English; the privilege to live autonomously under their own leaders was tied to Spanish corporatism and concepts of social organization; and the ability to protect both was guaranteed by Spanish legal constructs of community and citizenship, and the expectations of military vassalage. West and Central Africans would have been familiar with many of these ideas and systems and could certainly have adapted to them as needed. A few examples should suffice to illustrate the complex nature of frontier relationships.

The African Francisco Garzía and his Indian wife of unstated nation, Ana, fled together from Carolina. In St. Augustine Ana and Francisco became the slaves of the royal treasurer, Don Salvador Garzía. Like most Spaniards of status, Garzía observed the church requirement to have his slaves baptized and properly married, for the couple's children are listed as legitimate in the parish records. Their daughter, Francisca Xaviera, was born and baptized in St. Augustine in 1736, while her parents were still enslaved. Francisca's godfather was a free mulatto, Francisco Rexidor, who also served as godfather for Francisco and Ana's son, Calixto, born two years later, soon after the family moved to Mose. Francisco Garzía died sometime before 1759, for in that year the widowed Ana married a black slave named Diego, whose nation was not given. Calixto disappeared from the historical record and presumably died, but Francisca Xaviera grew up to marry Francisco Díaz, a later slave runaway from Carolina, and the couple raised their own children, Miguel Francisco and María, at Mose.[96]

Also among the first Carolina homesteaders at Mose were Juan Jazinto Rodríguez and his wife, Ana María Menéndez. Shortly after Mose was founded, their son, Juan Rodríguez, married Cecilia, a Mandinga from Carolina who was the slave of Juan's former owner, cavalry captain Don Pedro Lamberto Horruytiner. As a member of the Mose militia, Juan joined his former owner in guerrilla op-

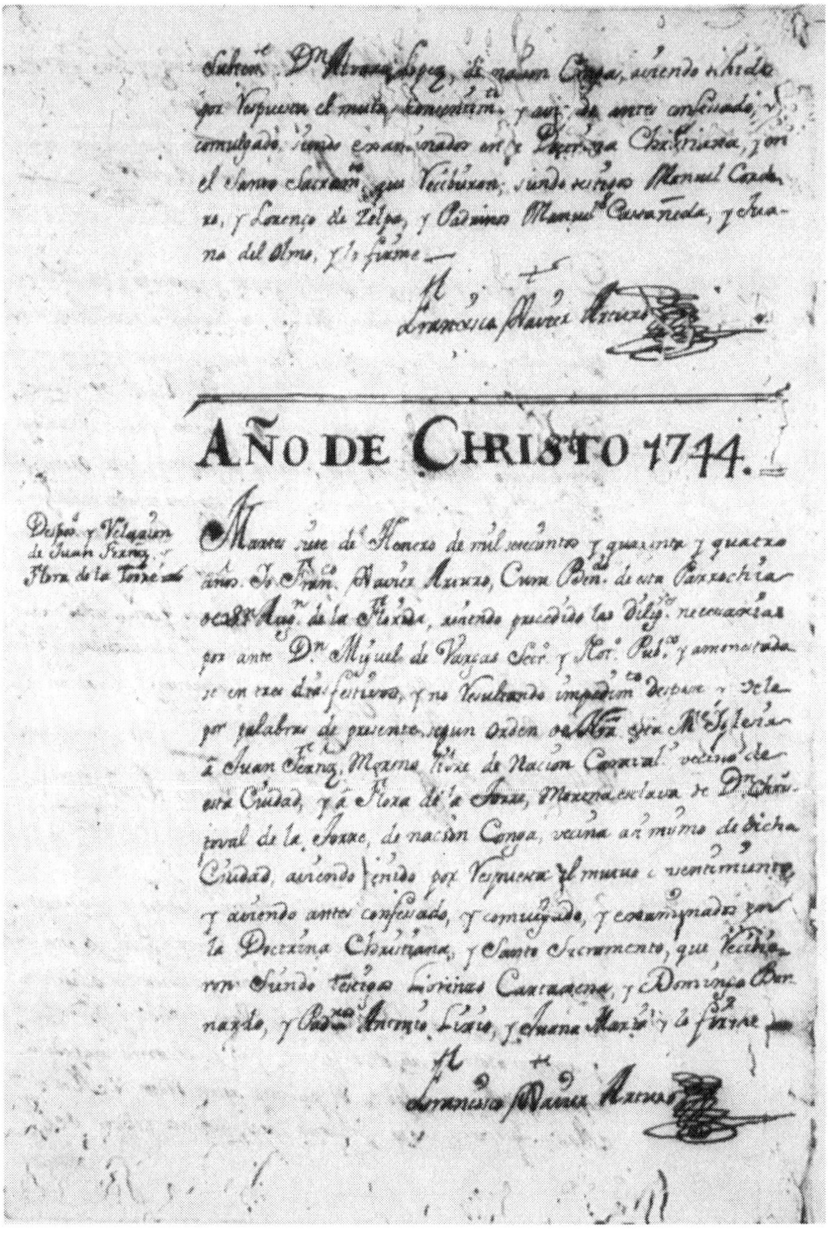

AÑO DE CHRISTO 1744.

St. Augustine parish record of the 1744 marriage of the free African Juan Fernández, of the Carabalí nation, and the enslaved Flora de la Torre, of the Congo nation. Fernández was a resident of Gracia Real de Santa Teresa de Mose, while Flora lived in her owner's home in St. Augustine. Black Marriages, CPR, microfilm reel 284 C, PKY. Courtesy of the P. K. Yonge Library of Florida History and the Florida Museum of Natural History, Fort Mose Exhibition.

erations on the frontier. Juan's sister, María Francisca, had been godmother at Cecilia's baptism two years earlier. While the Mose homesteaders lived in St. Augustine, María Francisca married Marcos de Torres, a "free and legitimate" black from Cartagena, Colombia. The couple had three children born in town, and María Francisca's brother, Juan, and sister-in-law, Cecilia, served as the children's godparents. After Marcos de Torres died, María Francisca and her three orphaned children lived with her parents at the second Mose, and in 1760 the widowed María Francisca married a widower, Tomás Chrisóstomo, and they formed their own household at Mose.[97]

Tomás Chrisóstomo and his first wife, Ana María Ronquillo, were Congos. When they married in 1744, Tomás was the slave of Don Francisco Chrisóstomo and Ana María was the slave of Juan Nicolás Ronquillo. Pedro Graxales, another Congo slave, and his legitimate wife, María de la Concepción Hita, a Carabalí slave, who had married the year before, served as the couple's marriage sponsors. By 1759, Tomás Chrisóstomo was a free widower living at Mose and the following year, he and the widowed María Francisca were wed. By that time Tomás Chrisóstomo's godfather, Pedro Graxales, was free, and serving as sergeant of the Mose militia, but Graxales's wife and at least six children remained enslaved in St. Augustine.[98]

Many other examples of ethnically complex families appear in the records. When María Luisa Balthazar, an Indian from the village of Nuestra Señora de la Asumpción de Palica (northwest of Mose and east of the St. Johns River, in the Diego Plains), married Juan Chrisóstomo, of the Carabalí nation, he was a slave living in St. Augustine.[99] The couple's daughters, María Magdalena and Josepha Candelaria, were born free at their mother's village of Palica. One daughter, María Magdalena, was already the widow of Juan Margarita (who may have been an Indian) when she married Pablo Prezilla, a free mulatto from Cumaná, Venezuela. After Prezilla died, María Magdalena married for a third time. Her third husband, Phelipe Gutiérres, was a free man whose race was not given in the record, and thus he can be assumed to be white. In 1747, María Luisa and Juan's second daughter, Josepha Candelaria, married an Indian widower in the village of Nuestra Señora del Rosario de la Punta (south of St. Augustine, near the Atlantic coast) and made her home there.[100] After María Luisa Balthazar died, the widowed Juan Chrisóstomo married María Antonia, a slave of his Carabalí nation, and that couple had children together. While María Antonia and the children remained enslaved, Juan Chrisóstomo gained his freedom and joined the Mose militia.[101]

These examples also illustrate the extensive cultural adaptation that went into the formation of this Afro-Indo-Hispanic community. Many of its members were born in West or Central Africa and then spent at least some time in a British slave society before risking their lives to escape. At least some had spent years among the Yamasee Indians and fought other Indian nations before reaching Spanish Florida. At least thirty-one became slaves of the Spaniards before litigating their way to freedom. Once free, they associated closely with the remnants of the seven different Indian nations aggregated into the two outlying Indian villages, where some of their children even lived. From 1740 to 1752 the Mose group lived exclusively in the ethnically diverse city of St. Augustine, after which time they were removed to the second Mose. Meanwhile, new infusions of Africans of different nations continued to be incorporated into the original Mose community. And by 1759, at least, many of the Mose residents had returned to the safety of St. Augustine.

The Material Culture of Mose

Archaeological research has also provided evidence for the cultural adaptations at Mose. An interdisciplinary team of researchers led by Kathleen Deagan, of the Florida State Museum of Natural History at the University of Florida, conducted two seasons of fieldwork at the second Mose site in 1987 and 1988.[102] The team located the fort which, due to changes in the water table, now sits on a small marsh island approximately two and half miles north of the Castillo de San Marcos. Over two seasons they were able to excavate portions of the moat, the earthen fort wall, and foundations of some of the interior structures.

Researchers sought to determine what mixture of customs and material culture residents adopted and what in their own traditions might have influenced Spanish culture. Recovered artifacts included military objects such as gunflints, strikers, and musket balls; and domestic articles such as metal buckles, metal and bone buttons, including one still in the process of manufacture, thimbles, pins, clay pipe bowls and stems—of both local and European design—nails, and a variety of glass bottles and ceramic wares—of English, Spanish, and indigenous types. The archaeologists also excavated religious artifacts, including amber rosary beads, and metal rosary pendants and chains, and perhaps the most interesting find of all—a handmade pewter St. Christopher's medal.[103] The iconography on this medal may be read many ways. St. Christopher is the Catholic patron of travelers and an appropriate choice for a person born in West or Central Africa, transported across the water to Carolina or Georgia, who then relocated to Florida. St. Christopher is also the patron saint of Havana, Cuba, and the person who made this medal may have traveled to Cuba and adopted that devotion, or been sent from Cuba as some of the Spanish priests and cavalrymen posted at Mose had been. On the reverse side of the medallion is a compass

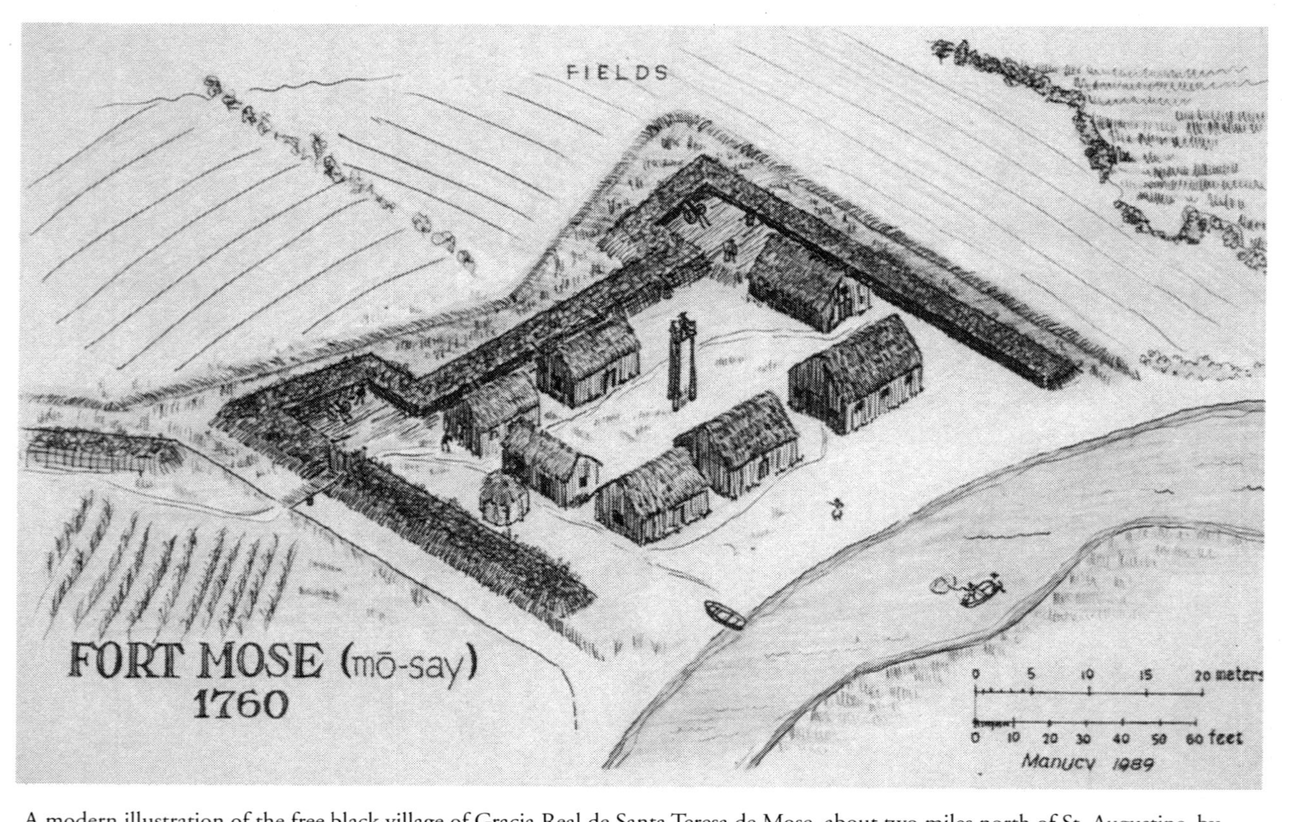

A modern illustration of the free black village of Gracia Real de Santa Teresa de Mose, about two miles north of St. Augustine, by Albert Manucy. Courtesy of the Florida Museum of Natural History, Fort Mose Exhibition.

rose—also an appropriate symbol for these world travelers, and possibly an indication that the maker was a sailor or pilot in Spain's maritime system.[104]

The team zooarchaeologist, Elizabeth Reitz, analyzed faunal remains from the site and found that the Mose villagers had much the same diet as nearby Indian villagers, relying heavily on estuarine resources and wild foods. In addition to fish (primarily Atlantic croaker, sea catfishes and sea trout, drums, silver perch, spots, mullet, and sheepsheads, but also sharks and rays) and shellfish, the Mose villagers consumed deer, rabbits, squirrels, raccoons, and turtles (pond and chicken turtles and diamondback terrapin) to supplement the occasional government gifts of beef and corn. These findings suggest a high degree of self-sufficiency at Mose. Interestingly, many resources available in the Mose estuary, for example the gopher tortoise, were exploited by neither Indians nor Africans, indicating that the Africans and creoles of Mose may have adapted to Indian traditions of food ac-

Handmade St. Christopher's medal found at Gracia Real de Santa Teresa de Mose. St. Christopher is the patron saint of travelers and of Havana. He is typically depicted as carrying Jesus over the water. The affinity with St. Christopher may reflect a possible reference to the belief in transmigration to Africa after death. Courtesy of the Florida Museum of Natural History, Fort Mose Exhibition.

quisition. Reitz compared faunal collections from Mose and from the mission Indian village of Nombre de Dios (the village closest to Mose) and found almost identical use of estuarine resources, especially in the levels of consumption of Atlantic croaker and fingerling mullets. On the basis of cross-cultural analysis of faunal remains from multiple archaeological sites in and around St. Augustine, Reitz argues that resource use by both Spaniards and Africans reflects "the local setting rather than previous ethnic traditions."[105]

Mose's Final Years

According to a detailed report of Father Juan Joseph de Solana in the summer of 1759, Spain's belated efforts to repopulate and rebuild Florida failed. After receiving numerous complaints about the colony's misery, the Crown appointed Father Solana to conduct an official investigation of Governor Lucas Fernando de Palacio's administration. Solana described the colony as still destitute despite its natural resources, primarily due to the unceasing Indian attacks and to Governor Palacio's inactivity, mismanagement, and corruption. When the Canary Island families finally arrived, the governor gave them homesteading lands located between St. Augustine and the northernmost settlement of Mose, but little else in the way of support. Hostile Indians killed one of the Isleños almost directly in front of the fort at Mose and kidnapped another. Father Solana complained that when the settlers of Mose requested more munitions (having only four pounds of gunpowder remaining), the governor told them to cut sticks for clubs with which to defend themselves. In fairness, the governor was actually unable to offer the homesteaders any other support because he had only two boxes of gunpowder left for the defense of the Castillo and could spare none of it.[106]

All reports indicate that the colony, in general, and the Canary Islanders and the residents of Mose, in particular, suffered extreme poverty in the latter years of Spanish Florida.[107] Both Governors Alonzo Fernández de Heredia (1755–58) and Lucas Fernando de Palacio (1758–61) asked the Crown to assign special subsidies for Mose, but they received no more than noncommittal replies.[108] Meanwhile, provisioning St. Augustine remained an ongoing nightmare. The Havana Company never improved its service to Florida, and Solana stated that because British goods were still cheaper and better, the governor and the citizenry were forced to depend on enemy suppliers for their most critical needs.[109] The misery was heightened when hostile Indians killed more than twelve hundred head of cattle and many horses on the San Diego ranch north of town.[110]

Although the colony was in a desperate state, Father Solana reported that Governor Palacio was dangerously rude to once-friendly Indians from the town of Salacaliche, who came to St. Augustine to sell furs and whom the governor denied entrance at sword point. The same Indians later stopped the mail courier and ripped up all the correspondence coming from the post at San Marcos de Apalachee, threatening to do the same to the governor if they caught him. The Indians said they did not blame the "pobrecitos españoles" (poor little Spaniards), but that they would nonetheless pay for the insults of the governor and none would leave Florida alive.[111] The extreme danger on the frontier drove allied Indians, Isleños, and free blacks alike to seek nightly protection within the walls of St. Augustine. Father Solana's report of 1759 states that although six men from the Mose militia served weekly tours at the fort (apparently night duty), when daylight came, the freedmen returned to "their labors," leaving only a corporal, four soldiers, and two artillerymen from the regular Spanish army who were permanently posted at the fort. Solana reported that the "rest" of the Mose residents by that time had returned to live in the city, with official permission.[112]

Despite the chronic reports of poverty, at least some members of the Mose militia somehow managed to purchase homes in St. Augustine; among them were Lieutenant Antonio Joseph Eligio, Ensign Francisco Escovedo, and the soldiers Ignacio Roso, Tomás Chrisóstomo, Francisco Gómez Escovedo, Juan Tomás de Castilla, and Antonio Gallardo. Other members of the Mose community maintained *solares* or town lots, on which they may have planted crops or raised animals.[113]

Given Father Solana's report and the numerous complaints that prompted it, Governor Palacio's sudden death at the end of 1761 could not have been deeply or widely mourned. An interim governor served briefly until the installation in 1762 of Melchor Feliú, Florida's last governor of the first Spanish tenure. Feliú worked energetically to repair the damage wrought by Palacio. He tried to restore relations with the alienated Indians while, at the same time, refortifying the colony. War with England was, once again, imminent, and the governor rushed to prepare. Because the thick forests between St. Augustine and Mose provided cover for raiding Indians, Feliú had them felled, culling five thousand stakes for use in major defense projects. He described the forestry effort as huge, and there is no doubt that the Mose militiamen were among the lumberjacks recruited for the task. They also must have helped build the new defense line that stretched from Fort Mose on the eastern coast across the land bridge west to the San Sebastián River. The line consisted of a raised earthen wall topped with prickly pear, on the northern side of which ran a tidal-fed moat. The Mose militiamen and members of the disciplined pardo and moreno troops of Havana assigned to help defend St. Augustine worked together to build a stockaded fort at the line's juncture with the San Sebastián River, where Indians frequently crossed to attack St.

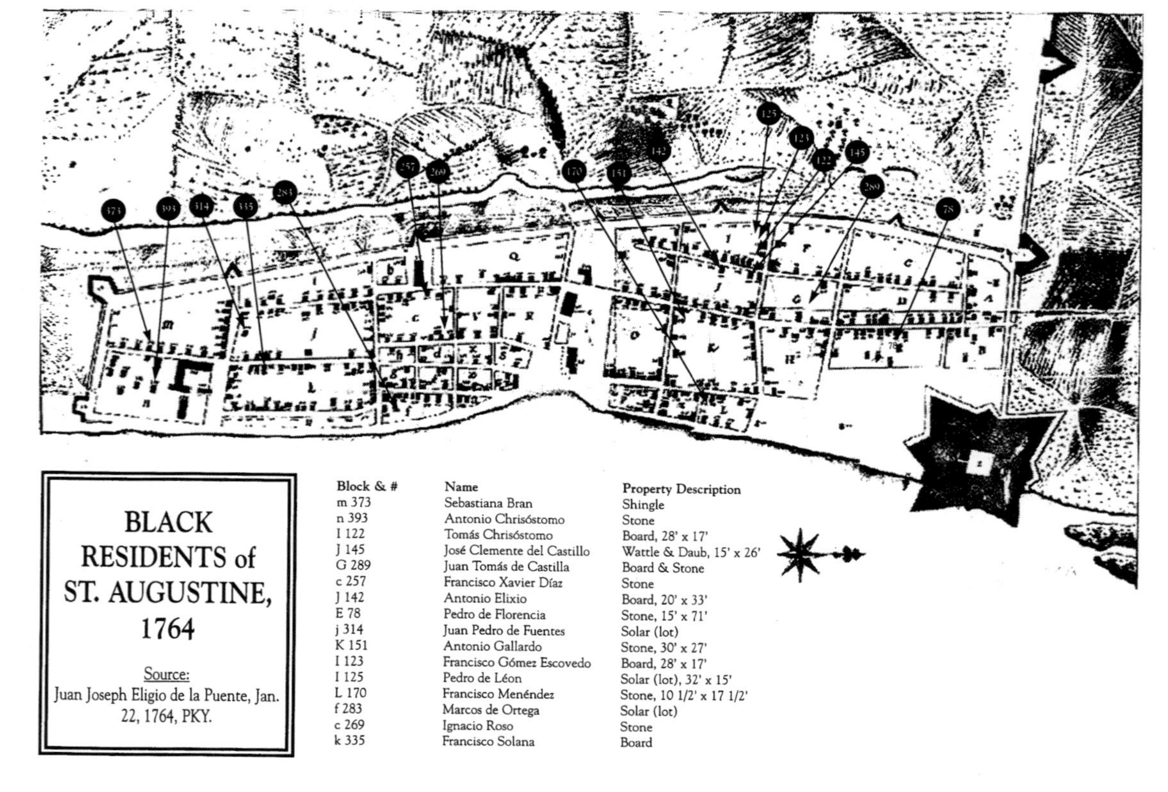

Block & #	Name	Property Description
m 373	Sebastiana Bran	Shingle
n 393	Antonio Chrisóstomo	Stone
I 122	Tomás Chrisóstomo	Board, 28' x 17'
J 145	José Clemente del Castillo	Wattle & Daub, 15' x 26'
G 289	Juan Tomás de Castilla	Board & Stone
c 257	Francisco Xavier Díaz	Stone
J 142	Antonio Elixio	Board, 20' x 33'
E 78	Pedro de Florencia	Stone, 15' x 71'
j 314	Juan Pedro de Fuentes	Solar (lot)
K 151	Antonio Gallardo	Stone, 30' x 27'
I 123	Francisco Gómez Escovedo	Board, 28' x 17'
I 125	Pedro de Léon	Solar (lot), 32' x 15'
L 170	Francisco Menéndez	Stone, 10 1/2' x 17 1/2'
f 283	Marcos de Ortega	Solar (lot)
c 269	Ignacio Roso	Stone
k 335	Francisco Solana	Board

Map of St. Augustine showing city residences of the free blacks evacuated from Gracia Real de Santa Teresa de Mose after the invasion of General James Oglethorpe in 1740. Adapted from the 1764 map of Juan Joseph Eligio de la Puente by James R. Landers.

Augustine.[114] Patrols of the disciplined unit from Havana, the Mose militia, and the Indian militia, captained by Antonio Matichaiche of the village of Toloma-to, worked jointly to protect the frontier in these years.[115]

Evacuation

During the Anglo-French Seven Years' War, Great Britain captured Cuba, Spain's heavily fortified and prized hub of trans-Atlantic commerce. Governor Manuel de Montiano had once described the island as "the beautiful woman whom all nations are wooing," and when the Treaty of Paris concluded the war in 1763, Spain did not hesitate to ransom Cuba with Florida, despite the consequences for its forsaken colonists.[116] In an evacuation staggered over the course of ten months, more than three thousand individuals packed their personal belongings and emptied the Spanish colony. Europeans, Africans, and Amerindians from Spanish Florida sailed off to uncertain futures.[117]

The freedmen of Mose had vowed to be "the most cruel enemies of the English" and to shed their "last drop of blood in defense of the Great Crown of Spain and the Holy Faith," and many did so during nearly thirty years of armed service.[118] Over the course of the first Spanish tenure the black militia of Mose had acquired distinction and privileges for themselves. Their military service had earned them freedom, homesteads, titles, and salaries. They clearly identified their interests with those of Spain and even another dislocation was far preferable to once again coming under the control of their former masters. Like the rest of the Spanish community, the people of Mose abandoned homes and belongings to comply with the royal evacuation order.[119]

The Significance of Mose

Located on the periphery of St. Augustine, between the Spanish city and its aggressive northern neighbors, Mose's interstitial location paralleled the social status of its inhabitants—people who straddled cultures, pursued their own advantage, and in the process took part in the colonial history of the circum-Caribbean and helped shape the beginnings of a new creole culture in North America. Although there were other towns like Mose in Spanish America, Mose was the only eighteenth-century example of a free black town in what is today the United States. It provides an important, and heretofore unstudied, variant in the experience of African-born peoples in North America. Mose's inhabitants were able to parlay their initiative, determination, and military and labor skills into free status, autonomy at least equivalent to that of Spain's Indian allies, and a town of their own. These gains were partially offset by the constant danger and deprivation to which the townspeople of Mose were subjected, but they stayed, making informed decisions about their best options. Despite the adversities of slavery, flight, wars, and repeated displacements, the freedmen and women of Mose managed to maintain intricate family relationships over time and to shape a viable community under extremely difficult conditions. They became an example and, on occasion, a source of assistance to unfree blacks from neighboring British colonies, as well as to those within Spanish Florida, some of whom they helped become free. The Spanish Crown subsequently extended the religious sanctuary policy first confirmed at Mose to other areas of the circum-Caribbean and applied it to the disadvantage of Dutch and French slaveholders, as well as the British.[120] The lives and sacrifices of the people of Mose, thus, took on a long-term international political significance that they could not have foreseen.

Transitions

Floridians in Cuba

On August 7, 1763, Captain Francisco Menéndez, Lieutenant Antonio Eligio de la Puente, Ensign Francisco Escovedo, and forty-eight men, women, and children from Mose boarded the appropriately named schooner *Nuestra Señora de los Dolores* (Our Lady of the Sorrows) and sailed away from Florida.[1] While the evacuation must have been difficult for all, the already marginalized Indians and Africans from Florida had fewer resources and less institutional or social support to call upon in time of need than the Spaniards. Although the Spanish Crown recognized its responsibility to resettle and temporarily support all citizens dislocated through the fortunes of war, Havana was not prepared to receive such a large influx of immigrants, and the exiled Floridians experienced severe hardships in Cuba. Most of Florida's administrative and military personnel remained on royal payrolls and could at least count on some income, but civilians had to rely on charity until they could get reestablished. There were no facilities for housing the incoming homeless, so Floridians had to be quartered among the homes of private Cuban citizens living in Havana and outlying towns. Cuban officials never intended for all the Floridians to be permanently housed in and around Havana. That burden certainly would have been unwelcome and might have produced unneeded social tensions.[2]

By the time of the evacuation, most of the people of Mose were fully acculturated into Spanish society and would have found Havana not drastically different than St. Augustine. Havana was already the domicile of a large population of free blacks and mulattoes, who dominated many skilled craft occupations such as shoemaker, tailor, carpenter, mason, and goldsmith. Moreover, by midpoint in the eighteenth century, more than one-fourth of the military force of Cuba was black or mulatto.[3] Free pardos and morenos from Florida with military and navigational training, and skills in carpentry, masonry, and ironsmithing, probably would have been able to find useful employment in the city. Sherry Johnson has described the intensive fortification campaign Spanish officials initiated in Havana after they regained Cuba and skilled black laborers from Florida may have worked on those constructions.[4] They also may have found support networks through the Catholic church or their African brotherhoods.[5]

Free blacks from Florida whose wives and children were enslaved probably remained in Havana to be near their families. Others who were married or linked to Indian women or families may have chosen to go with them to Guanabacoa, since at least one free black from the Mose militia, Manuel Rivera, died there.[6] However, at least thirteen free families, including those of Captain Francisco Menéndez and Lieutenant Antonio Eligio de la Puente of the Mose militia, and Captain Manuel de Soto and Adjutant Juan Fermín de Quixas of the disciplined pardo militia from Havana, went to live in Regla, a suburb southeast of Havana.

Cuban authorities may have sought to prevent their assimilation in Havana, since they were destined elsewhere, but not all of Florida's black families followed the government's resettlement plans. Ana María de León, daughter of the Mose militiaman Pedro de León, was married in the Regla church seven years after her evacuation from St. Augustine, and her son was baptized in the same church the following year.[7]

In 1764 a wealthy landowner reputed to have Florida ancestry donated 108 *caballerías* of land located southeast of Havana and about twenty-four leagues from the provincial capital of San Carlos de Matanzas as homesteads for the displaced Floridians. Following medieval precedents the Floridians were to become *nuevos pobladores* and make a just and ordered community out of a vacant land. Eighty-four Florida families eventually relocated to a new settlement they called San Agustín de la Nueva Florida popularly known as Ceiba Mocha, in Matanzas province.[8]

The new San Agustín was, like the original, a multi-ethnic and multi-racial community formed of the homeless Floridians from many different backgrounds. The dominant population at the new community, however, consisted of forty-three families (197 individuals) from the Canary Islands.[9] They were probably a fairly cohesive group, united by their origins, language, shared hardships, and relatively recent arrival in the New World. The rest of the new settlement at San Agustín was composed of thirteen Spanish families, four German Catholic families, and the four free pardo families and nine families of free blacks who had been living at Regla.

Cuba's governor and captain general assigned responsibility for the relocation project to the royal treasury in Matanzas and ordered that each head of household receive one *caballería* of uncultivated land, which they were forbidden to sell to non-Floridians or even to another of their group without official consent. The Floridians also received a stipend of sixty pesos, foodstuffs (meat, flour, rice, and cassava), and tools (machetes, axes, hoes). Each head of household was also given a newly imported African slave to assist in the hard work of building the new frontier settlement.[10]

These minimal provisions and the total lack of infrastructure at the site made conditions extremely difficult for the new homesteaders. They struggled to clear the land, plant fields, and build new structures in an untamed wilderness, all the while pleading for additional assistance from Havana. After two years of effort, the settlement was in pitiful condition. Although the area was thickly wooded, the Floridians lacked sufficient tools to harvest the timber and had built "sad shacks" of *yagua,* the impermeable and pliable bark that joins a palm frond to the trunk of the palm. They could not afford oxen and had to cultivate their land with hoes, but managed to grow some maize, yucca, beans, yams, and squashes. Another serious defect in the settlement was the lack of water. The homesteaders complained that they could not drill wells in the hard land, and the closest water source was the river, which was one-half to three-quarters of a league distant. Disease also plagued the settlement. An epidemic of measles killed four of the African slaves, and eight free persons died of unstated illnesses. These deaths increased the workload on the weakened survivors, and desperation led to violence in the struggling community. The slave of one of the Canary Islanders killed his owner. The man's pregnant wife died of fright, and because the homesteads were spread far apart from one another, their orphaned isolated child then starved to death. Another slave killed the wife of his owner.[11] The fate of the slaves who murdered their owners is unknown, but because there is no mention of trials or punishment, they may have escaped to one of the maroon communities that dotted Matanzas province.[12]

Despite the many problems, some Cubans actually attempted to move to the Floridano community. The free black, María de Jesus de Justiz, asked Matanzas authorities for a donation at San Agustín, since she had no other land. She volunteered to cultivate it and take possession under the terms outlined, and based her request on her marriage to a free black from Florida, Joseph Bentura, of the Mose militia.[13] Captain Manuel de Soto, of the free pardo militia, also seems to have thought the place suitable to his needs. He worked his land at San Agustín, and after the death of his Florida-born wife, he married a Canary Island woman with whom he had a daughter. Several years later, Captain de Soto had his Carabalí slave baptized in the Matanzas Cathedral, evidence that de Soto at least seemed to have prospered.[14]

On the whole, however, the Floridians believed that they were due better for their sacrifices and they considered life at San Agustín unbearable. By 1766, only sixteen of the original families remained on their assigned lands, and they stayed, allegedly, because they were too poor to move away. The poverty-trapped included Lieutenant Antonio Eligio de la Puente, of the Mose militia, his wife, and five children. Eligio de la Puente resorted to selling pieces of his allotted land to help support his family.[15] Seven other families remained in the general area of San Agustín but rented better lands on which to sustain their families. Among those who were farming elsewhere were the Congo militiaman from Mose, Tomás Chrisóstomo, his wife, and three children. Chrisóstomo died a widower in 1798 and was buried in the new San Agustín. His wife Francisca, a freed slave from Carolina and daughter of one of the founding families of Mose, preceded him in death.[16]

The rest of Florida's black and mulatto community eventually quit the frontier. Five families moved into the provincial capital of Matanzas to find work. Included in this group were seventeen persons from Mose: the Carolina runaways, Antonio Gallardo, his wife and two children; Domingo de Jesus, his wife, and seven children; Joseph Ricardo and his wife; and Juan Fernández and his wife. Joachim de Orozco, formerly of the Havana pardo militia, also moved his Florida-born wife and four children to Matanzas. Forty-five other settler families moved back to Havana, assisted by private charity. Among these were two pardo families and three families from Mose, including that of the Mandinga captain, Francisco Menéndez. Before leaving, some had managed to pay back some of the start-up money loaned to them by the Crown and returned their slaves to the royal accountants, but other debts remained on the Matanzas books for years after their departures.[17] The departing families sold their San Agustín de la Nueva Florida properties to the Canary Island families, who thereby enlarged their own holdings at rock-bottom prices and consolidated their control on the community.[18]

Old networks in Havana may have served to cushion some of the hardships of yet another dispersal, but the least skilled, the elderly, and the ill probably suffered. Many poignant petitions went to the king reminding him of the loyal military service of the Floridians and of the royal order of 1763 that promised aid to the obedient evacuees. The 1731 *limosna* (a charitable pension) of two reales daily was minimal, but white women and orphans of Floridian servicemen were guaranteed at least that support for the rest of their lives, unless they married. Many of these women continued to receive pensions well into the nineteenth

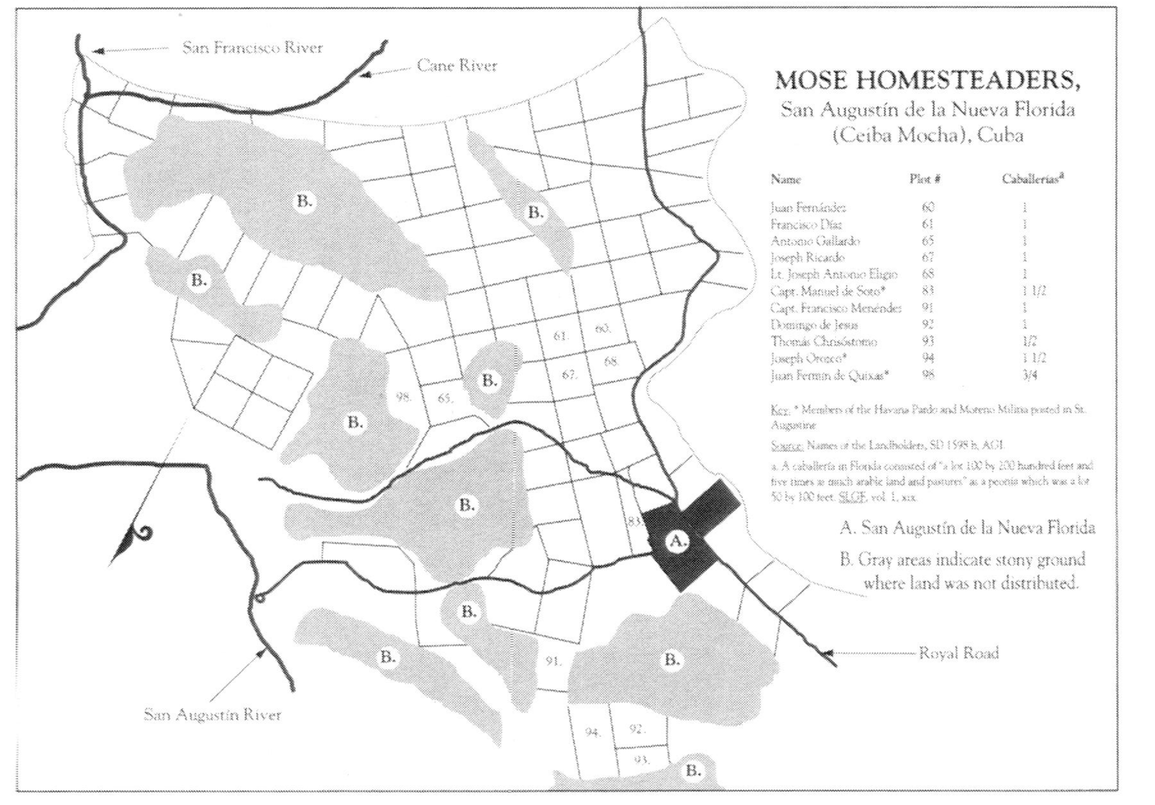

Land grants to the free black refugees from Florida at Ceiba Mocha, Cuba. Adapted from Juan Joseph Eligio de la Puente's map of San Agustín de le Nueva Florida, SD 1598, AGI, by James R. Landers.

century. Because many men from Florida had absolutely no other means of support, their wives and daughters were also made eligible for assistance. In effect, the whole family was assisted. Several of the free pardo and moreno men were also retained on the dole granted them for relocating to the new San Agustín. But at least one black widow was repeatedly denied any support. In 1763 the thirty-one-year-old María Gertrudis Roso, widow of the Mose militiaman Ignacio Roso, applied for the Floridana pension for herself and her orphaned daughter. She stated that the family left a hard-earned house, lands, and furniture in Florida, only being allowed to bring out their clothing and bedding, and that they were in need of assistance. Tellingly, she asked for only one real daily, or half what the white Floridanas received. Cuban authorities repeatedly rejected Roso's requests for a pension, despite her proofs of a legitimate marriage and of her husband's government service. Nevertheless, María Gertrudis Roso persisted with her suit for twenty-nine years, by which time she was old and ill, and asking for all the years of back *limosnas* due her as well. Cuban officials finally referred the case to Spain for royal review, but Spanish law placed heavy emphasis on precedent, and *negras y pardas* had never been awarded such assistance, so the women were ultimately denied the Floridana pension.[19]

The British Interregnum

While black exiles from Mose struggled on new homesteads on the Matanzas frontier, Great Britain worked to develop Florida along the lines of successful Anglo/Caribbean and southern plantations. The new British governor of Florida, James Grant, tried to promote colonial development by offering political offices and generous land grants to prominent Carolina planters.[20] Wildly enthusiastic promotional literature on Florida also may have encouraged such men to take a chance on the new colony. Early settlers transferred already skilled "country-born" slaves from South Carolina and Georgia to break in their extensive new estates in Florida. John Moultrie transferred 180 slaves from South Carolina to Florida to build the Bella Vista estate on the Matanzas River. Robert Bissett and his son, Alexander, brought in more than one hundred slaves, who built Mount Plenty.[21] These seasoned hands and hundreds of African slaves imported by Richard Oswald and other traders cleared and fenced land, planted crops, erected buildings, built dams and drains, and transformed vast stretches of inhospitable swamp and hammocks (well-drained and higher lands scattered throughout the marshes) into profitable fields.[22] Within a few years, slave labor enabled British Florida planters to develop large and flourishing plantations along the St. Marys and St. Johns Rivers on which their slaves grew rice, cotton, indigo, oranges, and sugar cane. Slaves also harvested lumber from Florida's thick forests, sawed timber, and prepared naval stores for export. While official policy called for white Protestant settlement, Governor Grant encouraged slave imports for strenuous work, stating that "Africans are the only people to do the work in warm climates." Grant also noted that white laborers were unsatisfactory because "Upon their landing they are immediately seized with the pride which every man is possessed of who wears a white face in America, and they say they won't be slaves and so they make their escape."[23] When British Loyalists were forced by the course of the American Revolution to evacuate Charleston and Savannah, East Florida provided a last haven, and the refugees brought more than eight thousand slaves with them. Until that exodus, blacks had outnumbered whites two to one in East Florida. The new influx raised that ratio closer to three to one.[24] The labor force in British East Florida, then, was predominantly black and African-born.

The usual problems of slave control were exacerbated by the chaos of war, continual immigration of new Loyalist refugees, and the confusion accompanying the British evacuation of the new republic of the United States.[25] Slave resistance persisted, and untold numbers of slaves escaped British plantations to live among the Seminole in the hinterlands. The British eventually sought security in slave codes and by severely curtailing black freedom, eventually requiring the few who were free to wear silver armbands engraved "free." Many of the newly stigmatized were ex-slaves who had earned their freedom by fighting for the English in Virginia, South Carolina, Georgia, and finally in East Florida's provincial militia and Rangers. This small group supported themselves selling produce, fish, game, and crafts in the public market, or by their skills as ironsmiths, butchers, and masons.[26]

Rise of the Seminole Nation

The exodus or extinction of Florida's indigenous nations created a vacuum in middle Florida, and in the later eighteenth century, Lower Creek groups who came to be the Seminoles established flourishing villages in the interior savannas.[27] When the Pennsylvania naturalist William Bartram visited Cuscowilla, the capital of the Alachua Seminoles in the 1770s, he described a prosperous settlement, based upon agriculture, "innumerable droves of cattle" and "squadrons of the beautiful fleet Seminole horse." Bartram found a population which already had been "tinctured with Spanish civilization." Some of the Seminoles wore "little silver crucifixes, affixed to a wampum collar around their necks, or suspended by a small chain upon their breast." But although Bartram claimed most spoke and understood Spanish, under Chief Cowkeeper's rule they were "the most bitter and formidable Indian enemies the Spaniards ever had." Bartram noted that the Seminoles' slaves were then defeated Yamasee Indians who kept their slave status for the rest of their lives. Although Bartram claimed they served Cowkeeper in "the most abject fear" he also noted they were permitted to marry Seminoles and that their children were born free and "considered in all respects equal" to the Seminoles.[28]

Over the next decades, many runaway slaves found refuge among the Seminoles led by Cowkeeper's successor, Chief Payne, and Payne's successors, Micanopy and Bowlegs. Unlike the Yamasee slaves who preceded them, the runaway slaves lived in a sort of feudal arrangement with the Seminoles, residing in their own villages and providing their "masters" with annual tribute and military service. They also intermarried with the Seminoles and became their trusted interpreters and advisors in war councils. These "village Negroes," as they were sometimes called in English sources, recognized that Anglo rule would return them to slavery, so they became fierce enemies of any seeking to remove Spain from Florida. Under their influence, the Seminoles would become allies rather than enemies of the Spaniards.[29]

Spain Regains Florida

In 1784 the fortunes of war once again altered Florida history and, by the Treaty of Paris, Spain reclaimed the province from the British.[30] As distraught Loyalists proceeded with their removal arrangements, the Spanish Crown began to organize a new government for East Florida. On October 31, 1783, it appointed Vicente Manuel de Zéspedes governor and captain general of the city of St. Augustine and the provinces of Florida. Although the captain generals of both East and West Florida and Louisiana were all technically subordinate to the captain general of Cuba, in practice they enjoyed considerable autonomy.[31] After extensive preparations the new governor, his administration, a military garrison of more than five hundred men, and various civilian employees and private families sailed out of Havana's harbor for Florida. The main body of the entourage arrived in St. Augustine on June 26, 1784, and a formal transfer of the province took place on July 12, 1784. Amidst much pomp and ceremony, the second Spanish occupation of East Florida began.[32]

To speed Florida's development, a royal order of 1789 required Cuban authorities to "take all measures to see that the families of Florida return to their country."[33] Incentives included new pensions for those who would emigrate and the return of formerly held properties, if possible, or if not, properties of comparable value. For those who had no homes to go to, Cuban officials modeled a plan like the one that failed at San Agustín la Nueva. Each new homesteader would receive land to cultivate, a black slave, and tools, advances for which they would be liable in ten years.[34] Many Floridano families chose to return to their former homeland, but reclaiming lost properties proved to be a tangled affair.[35] There is no evidence that any of the Florida Indians ever returned to their ancestral homes; most had perished quickly after evacuation or had been absorbed into the mestizo population of Guanabacoa. Nor is there any clear evidence that any of the free blacks of Mose returned to Florida.[36]

Traditional studies portray eighteenth-century Florida as a backwater of the Spanish empire, characterized by a military structure and a stagnating economy. Certain elements of that depiction are accurate, but the province was more than a garrison, if less than a thriving metropolis.[37] Despite a restrictive mercantilist policy and political instability, ordinary people of various ethnicities lived and worked and sometimes even improved their lot in St. Augustine. They cleared the land and coaxed forth a wide range of agricultural products; they harvested the plentiful forest and coastal resources; and they did both well enough to produce surplus for export. They built homes and raised families and occupied themselves with small businesses and trade. And because Spanish Florida had the misfortune to be the southern desire of a "nation, as ambitious as it is industrious," and because it had an important Atlantic port, the people participated, more fully than many would have wished, in the dramatic political and military events of the era.[38]

The Province

Soon after his arrival, Governor Zéspedes undertook a review of the province and its resources. The capital, St. Augustine, lay on an inlet sheltered from the open sea by Anastasia Island. Dominating the city landscape was the Castillo San Marcos, the *coquina* (native shellrock) fort on the northern perimeter, which withstood attacks by pirates and English and Indian raiders in the first Spanish period. St. Augustine was laid out on the traditional Spanish grid pattern, with a central plaza onto which faced the government houses and the Catholic church. The public market stood between the plaza and the harbor, and merchants congregated in a commercial area of shops and docking one block north of the harbor, on the waterfront. Wealthier citizens had homes near the plaza, while the poorer elements, including most persons of color, made their homes on the periphery.

St. Augustine's houses were built of a variety of materials, including coquina, timber, and tabby (a mixture of limeshell mortar, sand, and oyster shells devised by Africans). Although many homes were little more than shacks, some were two-

View of the governor's house, St. Augustine, Nov. 1764. Original watercolor sketch, British Library, London. Courtesy of the St. Augustine Historical Society Collection.

story structures that held shops and storage areas on the first floor and family living space on the second. Many displayed typical Spanish features such as side entrances, loggias and patios, which enclosed a variety of fruit trees, vegetable plots, and grape arbors.[39] The English had failed to maintain their Florida properties, knowing evacuation was imminent, and even the governor's home was close to ruin.[40]

St. Augustine was a city surrounded by water. The Matanzas River formed the eastern edge of the city, the San Sebastián River the southern and western perimeters, and running parallel to the harbor was the María Sánchez Creek. Although a shifting sand bar in the harbor blocked the passage of larger vessels, supplies could easily be brought in at the deeper harbor to the north, at the mouth of the St. Marys River.

The Northern Frontier

The St. Marys River demarcated the international border separating Spanish Florida from the United States of America, but it proved to be an easily penetrated barrier. For that reason, the northern frontier would claim the governors' closest attention throughout the second Spanish period. Susan R. Parker has called the region an "Anglo suburb," almost exclusively Protestant, and culturally dis-

View from the governor's window of the counting house and royal treasury, St. Augustine, Nov. 1764. Original watercolor sketch, British Library, London. Courtesy of the St. Augustine Historical Society Collection.

tinct from the Spanish capital at St. Augustine. To emphasize this cultural difference, a Spanish official described the Anglo settlers living there as men "without God or king."[41]

Two islands lay on either side of the St. Marys Bar—Cumberland, the American possession to the north, and Amelia, belonging to the Spanish Crown on the south. Noted for its fertile soil and abundant pines, cedars, and oaks, Amelia was home to approximately twenty families and also a Spanish military and customs post. The St. Marys River was navigable for forty miles inland, and an interior passage, although shallow, connected it to the St. Johns River, which cut through the western portion of the peninsula. Approximately sixty families lived along the L-shaped course of these two rivers on some of the province's richest plantations. Lying in the passage between the rivers were several small islands which also held fine stands of timber and important plantations.

In addition to the two main rivers, the Nassau River and its branches, and the Matanzas and North Rivers also allowed small boats and skillful pilots access to the colony. Ferries operated at the south end of the Camino Real, or royal highway, which ran from Coleraine, Georgia, to St. Augustine, at King's Ferry on the St. Marys River, and at Cowford on the St. Johns.[42] Although Spain attempted to enforce its borders with military patrols and to control trade and immigration with passport and customs regulations, the province was almost impossible to police and raiding Indians and Georgians could enter almost at will.

From the announcement of the cession, a group of former Loyalists had taken to raiding Florida's riverine plantations for slaves and other "moveable property." The outgoing English government had declared the men outlaws, and even the new Spanish regime's offer of clemency did little to end the raids. Governor Zéspedes was finally forced to arrest or deport those "banditti" who did not leave of their own accord, but in the interim many slaves and probably some free persons of color were taken from Florida.[43] Residents considered themselves "victims of the many ambitious characters that infest the major part of the United States, especially Georgia."[44]

Nor did Indians respect the international border that whites had negotiated and imposed. Like the Georgians, they were attracted by slaves, cattle, and horses and found the settlements along the St. Marys and St. Johns Rivers easy targets. Settlers complained to Governor Zéspedes that they lived "in great dread" of both Americans and Indian raiders and in a subsequent appeal for protection they named Young Warrior as a leader of one of the attacks.[45] A Spanish commander noted that although the northern Indians were "uncivilized in their actions," they showed a sophisticated understanding of their own geopolitical interests.[46]

The Seminole Interior

The Spaniards enjoyed better relations with the Seminoles whose settlements lay west of the St. Johns River. Viewing the Seminoles as a buffer against Anglo encroachment, the Spanish government attempted to ensure their friendship by regularly hosting and gifting them in St. Augustine. The Crown allotted six thousand pesos annually for their gifts, which included items such as cloth and clothing, hats, thread and needles, thimbles, scissors, beads, pipes, knives, axes, razors, mirrors, tin pots, spurs, munitions, tobacco, *aguardiente* (rum), and food. Women received gingham and chintz cloth, children received red paper, and luxury items such as saddles went to head men like Perryman, Long Warrior, Filatuche, and Tupane. On at least four occasions groups identified specifically as cimarrones came to St. Augustine, always in the company of Seminoles, and they too, were presented with gifts.[47] The Spaniards stood to lose their colony, the blacks their freedom, and the Seminoles their rich lands and cattle herds, and Spanish officials capitalized on this convergence of interests often during their second tenure in Florida.[48]

The Economy

Financial and material resources were an immediate and pressing problem for the incoming administration. Banditry and political chaos had taken a toll on the economy of Florida, and the once flourishing estates along the rivers, like the city homes, public properties, and defense works, had fallen into great disrepair.[49] Governor Zéspedes noted that in 1785 only the cattle ranch of the Spaniard Francisco Xavier Sánchez and the plantation of the Swiss Francis Phelipe Fatio still operated.[50] Although the Sánchez and Fatio plantations provided "exquisite" fresh meat, it was costly, and Zéspedes complained that the forty thousand pesos with which he had arrived were insufficient.[51]

By 1785 Governor Zéspedes had exhausted his original funds and had made little progress in the rebuilding of the colony. He remarked that even the trade at the local market had totally stalled for lack of currency. The government was in debt to foreigners, and he sought immediate financial relief to "lend spirit, energy and encouragement to this very weak republic."[52] Citizens of note loaned the government various sums in order to meet its most basic obligations.[53] As it had been in the first Spanish period, Florida was supported by a government subsidy called the situado derived from the taxation of Puebla, a province in the Viceroyalty of New Spain. However, the money came to St. Augustine by way of Havana, where Florida officials spent approximately two-thirds of the 350,000 peso allotment on needed supplies, and receipt of the remaining situado was never certain. Unforeseen catastrophes, such as piracy or natural disasters, sometimes interrupted or diverted the regular financing of the province. The complaint of insolvency was a leitmotif running through the correspondence of each of the second-period governors. In the fashion of good bureaucrats, they may have exaggerated the deterioration of their facilities and the scope of their economic needs in order to increase financial support. However, Florida was very irregularly supported throughout the second Spanish period, as the Crown struggled simultaneously to finance a series of disastrous European wars and to maintain its far-flung empire against foreign and domestic challengers.[54]

Spain sought to eliminate economic competitors and ensure control of its colonies through its mercantile policies. These required all cargo to be carried on Spanish ships manned by Spanish crews and prohibited the introduction of foreign goods.[55] However, the network of waterways lacing Florida, and the shortage of government personnel, made strict enforcement impractical. Moreover, when approved supplies failed to arrive from Cuba, or proved to be of poor quality, the governors took the initiative to purchase flour and other foodstuffs in Philadelphia and New York, or cattle from Georgia, banking on post facto royal dispensation on the basis of the colonists' dire need. Many American merchants and traders were eager to supply Florida the goods Spain could not, and they often extended credit and offered cheaper prices than their Cuban counterparts.[56]

The governors recognized that poor provisioning led to hardships and promoted illicit trade. They warned that the colony would be lost for want of population, enterprise, and adequate metropolitan support. After Zéspedes left office in 1790, the Crown renewed efforts to restrict illicit trade to Florida, and while the new governor, Juan Nepomuceno de Quesada, promised to obey, the poverty he encountered and the impossibility of enforcing restrictions led him to the same conclusions as his predecessor. Aware that illicit trade was being conducted in the colony, "because of the universal misery of its inhabitants, I refrained from making a rigorous investigation into the matter for, without benefiting the royal treasury, this would have destroyed the community."[57] The Crown finally bowed to the inevitable and liberalized trade in Florida in 1793.[58] While the concessions were most welcome, recovery was still slow and difficult.

Land Policy and Provincial Development

Like other Spanish administrators on contested frontiers, Florida's administrators believed that "to govern is to populate." Inadequate and declining populations worried the early governors of East Florida almost as much as lack of money. Governor Zéspedes urged the Crown to grant lands to Roman Catholic foreigners and those who desired to convert to that faith, and the Crown acceded. It formulated a policy designed to encourage settlement and the development of the colony through land grants and other supports including royal subsidies of critical industries, such as shipbuilding, exemption of the required *diezmos* tithe, free tools from the royal factories in Vizcaya, and cattle paid for by the royal accounts. The Crown also granted the colony the unlimited introduction of black slaves. Despite these attempts to encourage immigration, uncertainty about land tenure frustrated efforts to maintain a stable population in Florida. The governors repeatedly advised that some provision be made to clarify land titles of the non-Spanish residents so that those already living in East Florida would not depart and so that new settlers might be attracted. In 1790 Spain finally revised Florida's land policy, modeling the new plan on the English headright system. Foreigners who wished to settle in East Florida were required to swear an oath of allegiance but were no longer required to convert to Catholicism. Each head of household received one hundred acres for himself and fifty for every person, white or nonwhite, attached to the household. Recipients had ten years to hold and develop the land and could not sell it within that time, but after ten years they were granted a full title to the land. By custom the governors also granted land as rewards for meritorious service to the Crown. Both measures served to encourage foreigners to settle permanently in East Florida, and these newcomers were classified as *nuevos pobladores* or new settlers.[59]

Within a few months after the declaration of the new land policy, approximately 300 whites moved into the province, bringing with them about 1,000 slaves.[60] By 1804, 750 new Anglo immigrants had sworn loyalty oaths in St. Augustine and claimed homesteading land for their families. The new colonists brought an additional 4,000 slaves with them, 2,270 of whom were transported into Florida in 1803 alone.[61] Daniel L. Schafer has described the resulting population and economic boom. Planter optimism ran high as their slaves began the grueling work of carving new plantations out of the swamps and harvesting timber from Florida's thick hardwood forests. Some of the enslaved laborers escaped the killing work regime by running to the Seminole nation west of the St. Johns River, just as they had done during the British tenure and as they would continue to do when Americans succeeded the Spaniards in Florida.[62] The sweat and blood of the less fortunate slaves who stayed behind eventually yielded harvests of rice, indigo, oranges, tobacco, several types of cotton, hemp, and foodstuffs such as corn, beans, chickpeas, squashes, and potatoes. Florida's new homesteaders exported cotton, sour oranges, lumber (oak, cedar, cypress, laurel, and pine), and naval stores (turpentine, tar, rosin, and pitch), as well as great quantities of cattle, deer, otter, bear, and antelope hides.[63]

Florida's Population

The heterogeneous nature of the population of East Florida presented a unique and constant challenge to the Spanish administrators of the second period. The commander of the northern frontier, Captain Carlos Howard, reported that in 1790 the natural Spaniards, including troops and dependents, accounted for only about one-sixth of the total population of thirty-five hundred, making Florida unlike any of the other Spanish possessions in the New World.[64]

The largest group of non-Spaniards consisted of approximately 460 Italians, Greeks, and Minorcans, remnants of Dr. Andrew Turnbull's ill-fated attempt to establish an indigo plantation at New Smyrna. They were, in the main, Roman Catholics, and although they spoke a variety of languages—Catalán, Italian,

Greek, and assorted dialects—they were Mediterranean people and could easily assimilate into the Spanish culture. In St. Augustine they became fishermen and merchants or raised produce on rented lands to sell at the public market. Intimately tied to the urban economy, the Minorcans clustered near St. Augustine and along the North and Matanzas Rivers.[65]

As noted above, many "British" also remained in Florida—a designation the Spaniards used to identify English-speaking people of many ethnic backgrounds—English, Irish, Scotch, even Swiss.[66] In general they were welcomed by Spanish administrators, for they operated large plantations that helped supply the colony and were a source of credit to the oft-impoverished government. The group included people with useful skills and connections to the American state and national governments, but some of its members also became involved in assorted plots to wrest control of the area from their hosts.

The other main group of non-Spaniards to inhabit the province were those of African descent, most of whom were enslaved. However, hundreds of slaves ran away from evacuating British owners rather than face unknown places and climes or forced separation from loved ones.[67] Spain's seventeenth-century sanctuary policy remained in effect, and Governor Zéspedes was forced to honor it, although he doubted the religious motivation of the latter-day supplicants.[68] It was his appraisal, and undoubtedly an accurate one, that the fugitives sought liberty or escape from a cruel master. Zéspedes charged that "not one of them has manifested once here the least inclination to be instructed in and converted to our Holy Faith."[69] Although he may have doubted the sincerity of their motives, Zéspedes would not tolerate continued theft and conflicts, and he acted to curtail both. The governor required anyone wishing to remove a slave from the province to obtain a license bearing his signature. He also wanted an accounting of all persons of color remaining in the province. Any whites "having in their control" blacks or mulattoes, either free or slave, were to register them and "every vagrant black without a known owner or else a document that attests to his freedom" was to report to the authorities within twenty days to clarify his or her status and obtain a work contract. Those failing to report would forfeit their freedom and be enslaved by the king.[70] The outgoing governor, Patrick Tonyn, protested that these requirements violated the provisions of the peace treaty that allowed any who wished to leave the province, and further observed that many slaves were held without title and that many free blacks did not have legal documents to prove this status.[71]

Despite Tonyn's objections, Zéspedes enforced his decree, and more than 250 blacks hoping to legitimate their free status came forward to be registered. Most of their declarations simply stated the name and race of the petitioner, who showed the Spanish notary documents signed by British military authorities attesting to his or her free status.[72] More complete declarations gave information on previous owners, family composition, occupations, reasons for escaping, and employment in St. Augustine. As might be expected, almost twice as many males as females (165 to 84) presented themselves and the majority (206) were described as blacks. More than half of the petitioners (128) presented themselves in thirty-six family groupings. Thirteen families consisted of childless husbands and wives, and ten families were formed of a father, mother, and children. Seven families were female-headed and five were headed by single fathers. One sister and brother appeared together and several other units were formed by apparently unrelated runaways from the same owner. The numerous groupings demonstrate that the fugitives sought to maintain family and friendship ties even in flight.

The largest family consisted of Bacchus and Betty Camel and their seven children. Notaries listed three of the children, Andrew, Isaac, and Sally, as field hands, like their parents; hence, although their ages were not given, they were probably adolescents. The family also included Bacchus, age nine; Betsy, age seven or eight; Kitty, age five or six; and Grace, age two. Bacchus Camel stated that the family fled to escape the bad treatment of their owner, Mr. Jameson, of Savannah. In St. Augustine the adults of the family, with the exception of Isaac, lived with and worked for Don Roque Leonardy, an Italian wine merchant. Isaac hired out to an innkeeper, James Clarke.[73]

In 1786, after several failed attempts, Prince Witten, his wife, Judy, and their children, Polly and Glasgow, also escaped from slavery in Georgia and requested sanctuary in St. Augustine.[74] Witten had belonged to Lt. Col. Jacob Weed of the Georgia Assembly, who advertised to try to recover his valuable property. The notice described Prince as "6 feet high, strong built and brawny, a carpenter by trade, 30 years of age . . . talkative," Judy as a "smart, active wench," and their children, Glasgow "about 8 years of age, a well looking boy of an open countenance and obliging disposition," and Polly "6 years old, lively eyes and gently pitted with the small pox." Weed had been arranging to return the family to former owners from whom they had been stolen by the British, and he believed that Prince had "carried them off with him to Florida to avoid a separation from his family to which he is much attached."[75] What transpired in the next three years is unknown, but in 1789 Prince presented himself to the Spanish notary as required by Governor Zéspedes's decree and hired himself out to the Minorcan Francisco Pellicer, who was also a carpenter.[76]

It appears that Governor Zéspedes followed precedent and, as previous Florida and Cuban governors had done, set an example by taking some of the refugees into his own home. The rest he parceled out among townspeople and plantation owners able to shelter them, at least temporarily. This was the beginning of many subsequent connections between the townspeople and the former slaves. Because the black freedmen and women lived and worked among them daily, it was almost inevitable in this community that other social relations would follow. Ira Berlin, Steven F. Miller, and Leslie S. Rowland have argued that British slaves understood their society "in the idiom of kinship" and that, for slaves, "familial and communal relations were one."[77] The Spaniards also viewed society as an extension of family structures. The institutions of the extended kinship group (*parentela*), which included blood relations, fictive kin, and even household servants and slaves, and the *clientela,* which bound more powerful patrons and their personal dependents into a network of mutual obligations, were so deeply rooted that, according to Lyle N. McAlister, they might have been the "primary structure of Hispanic society."[78] Thus, African and Spanish views of family and society were highly compatible, and each group surely recognized the value the other placed on kinship.

Undoubtedly aided by their early contacts and patrons, refugees from the United States like the Wittens and Camels became the most important component of the free black community in second-Spanish-period Florida. Bacchus Camel and his sons worked hard, defended their community when called upon, and made free lives for themselves, acquiring property and intermarrying with other successful runaways. The Witten family became even more prosperous and Prince went on to have an important military career in St. Augustine.[79] As in the earlier Spanish period, these freedmen proved to be a valuable source of skilled labor and military reserves for the Spanish community, and despite attempts by some of their former owners to recover their chattel through legal channels, Governor Zéspedes consistently supported the blacks' right to liberty.

The Loyalist brothers Major Henry Williams and William Williams tried for many years to reclaim three of their runaway slaves who escaped on the day after Christmas of 1784, as the Williamses prepared to evacuate their slaves to New Providence in the Bahamas. The brothers' 1785 advertisement described "Reynor [Reyna], wife to Hector, and Sam, for they both have her to wife."[80] In 1788, the trio of runaways presented themselves to Spanish authorities and disputed the Williamses' account. Hector stated that they had accompanied Major William Williams to East Florida in Hector's own boat, and that they had all lived as free persons as a consequence of the men's military service. Sam's statement confirmed their free status and military service, adding the information that he had once belonged to Henry Alexander of South Carolina and that Hector and Reyna had belonged to Diego Devaux. Hector and Sam both identified Reyna as Hector's wife.[81] By the time the Williams brothers initiated a suit to recover

Hector, Sam, and Reyna in 1788, all three had hired themselves as free laborers to Don Francis Phelipe Fatio, whose Nueva Suiza (New Switzerland) plantation was near their former workplace. Governor Zéspedes upheld the freed slaves' claims to freedom despite numerous appeals by the Williams brothers.[82]

Diplomatic Pressure and the End of Sanctuary

Once again Florida became a haven for runaways, and Georgia planters renewed the complaint that their very livelihood was threatened by the continued loss of slaves. When the refugees came by water, Spanish authorities usually inventoried the contents of their canoes. Two slaves who escaped from Charleston in 1788 had with them only two blankets, a hand axe, and a small cauldron. The ruddered canoe in which another group escaped from Savannah in 1789 was better equipped and carried four oars, a mast and sail, five iron pots, a cauldron, two wooden plates, a small cask for water, and two boxes of clothing.[83]

The route to Florida, however, was not always direct. Remnants of Lord Dunmore's "Ethiopians" formed maroon communities along the Savannah River, which also attracted slave runaways. In 1787 a joint force of South Carolina and Georgia militias, accompanied by Catawba Indian allies, searched Patton's Swamp determined to eradicate the menace. Chancing upon some blacks in canoes, they exchanged gunfire and gleefully reported having killed the band's leader, Sharper, but their exultation was premature. The force finally stumbled upon the maroons' hideout, killed the lookout, and proceeded with their attack upon the stockaded settlement. They killed six of the unlucky maroons outright, and more were supposed injured, because of the "blankets . . . clotted with blood" that they left behind. The attackers destroyed some twenty-one houses and took seven "boats" before heading home with the women and children they had taken prisoner. The next day, they encountered Sharper and eighteen members of his community headed for the Indian nation, and another fight ensued. Once again, Sharper and some of the others were able to escape, although nine more women and children were captured. Shortly thereafter a fugitive named Sharper and his wife, Nancy, were among those petitioning for sanctuary in St. Augustine.[84]

Such provocations led to renewed complaints against Florida's sanctuary policy. Finally, in 1790, the Spanish government yielded to the strong persuasions of Thomas Jefferson, the secretary of state for the new government of the United States, and abrogated the century-old sanctuary policy.[85] In a letter to Governor Quesada, Jefferson expressed his pleasure with Spain's policy shift, calling it "essential" to the good relations between their two nations.[86] Despite the diplomatic agreements ending sanctuary, tangled disputes over slave property continued for many years because the United States sought the return of all escaped slaves who entered Florida after 1783, while the Spanish Crown offered up only those who entered after the notice ending sanctuary had been posted in 1790. The United States government appointed James Seagrove to solicit the return of American slaves, or their comparable value, from the Spaniards, and Georgia's governor appointed his own representative, Thomas King, to assist in that effort.[87]

Each side prepared lists of missing slaves, and while the English lists offer little more than the names and owners of the missing slaves, the Spanish lists offer interesting insights into the makeup of the slave community in East Florida. Most of the descriptions remarked on the slaves' "country marks," such as scars on the cheeks and missing top front teeth, and on their supposed age, physical build, height, and skin color. Although some were specifically described as being natives of Angola and Guinea, even they were still said to be able to speak a variety of languages, and most spoke English. One woman, Gega, born in Georgia, spoke "regular Spanish" and very good English and "Mexican." The slaves included field hands and servants, as well as skilled craftsmen such as sawyers and carpenters, and none was valued at under three hundred pesos. Don Francis Phelipe Fatio refused to set a price on his missing slave, Nero, because he did not want reimbursement. Fatio stated that Nero's parents had a large family on his plantation, and he sought to reunite them.[88]

Among the Georgia runaways whom Commissioners Seagrove and King hoped to retrieve from Spanish Florida was Titus, who had led twelve runaways in a successful group escape from Georgian planter John Morell but unfortunately entered Florida too late to be protected by religious sanctuary. Governor Enrique White placed Titus and the others in the temporary care of the influential planter Juan McQueen, and in May 1797 was preparing to return them all to United States, when Titus ran again.[89] From Point Petre Commissioner James Seagrove wrote the Spanish governor that in July "The notorious fellow, Titus, with some negroes from Florida, made their way along the seacoast until they got into the Savannah River and among the rice plantations where he was well acquainted. There Titus formed a party with some other outlaying negroes who became very troublesome to the people by plunder and as a receptacle for runaways."[90]

Once again, an American armed force went in search of maroons, with orders to kill those who did not surrender. Although they discovered and fired upon Titus's band, most of the maroons escaped, "it being a very thick swamp." Trackers captured some and took them to the Savannah prison, but none were found dead, although the correspondent reported "a quantity of blood found on the ground." He added, "parties are constantly after them and there is little doubt they will be taken or killed."[91]

As it struggled with economic problems, frontier violence, and diplomatic pressures from the United States, Florida was further destabilized by the effects of the French Revolution and its Haitian counterpart.[92] Alarmed by republican ideology emanating from France, the governors of Spanish Florida, like their counterparts throughout the greater Caribbean, attempted to quarantine the colony by forbidding the introduction of French ideas, books, and citizens, or of slaves originating from French possessions.[93] Despite these efforts, Florida was unable to avoid the contagion, and in 1795 it experienced a French-inspired invasion that resulted in the destruction of valuable plantations, the dislocation of landholders and slaves, political dissension created by sedition trials, and a weakened frontier which, thereafter, was subject to chronic encroachment.[94]

New Additions to the Black Population

After the conclusion of a peace treaty between Spain and the Directory of the French Republic in 1795, Spain ceded its eastern portion of Hispaniola to the French, and the Black Auxiliaries of Charles IV were disbanded and evacuated from the island. In January 1796, one of the main figures in the slave revolt against the French, General Jorge (i.e., Georges) Biassou, caudillo of the Black Auxiliaries of Charles IV in Santo Domingo, took up residence in Florida with some twenty-five of his followers.[95] Most of the newcomers were from Guarico, Marmelade, and Granada, on the northern coast of Saint Domingue, but at least one man came from San Miguel on the Guinea Coast. The men were seasoned by war against French planters, French and British troops, and their own countrymen, and were well acquainted with "dangerous notions" of liberty, equality, and fraternity.[96] The black auxiliaries caused consternation not only among the Spanish governors who reluctantly received them but also among the Anglo planters on Florida's borders, who were already disturbed by Spain's racial policies and its reliance on black militias.[97] At a time when slave conspiracies and rebellions, maroon settlements, and Indian war unsettled the southeastern frontier, this new black presence seemed particularly threatening. Ultimately the Spaniards' dependence upon armed black forces contributed to a series of invasions sponsored by the United States and to the acquisition of Florida by the United States.

After 1800 Floridians also imported slaves directly from Africa. As described in chapter 7, cargoes arrived from Sierra Leone, Guinea, and Mozambique, among other areas, and the shipments were composed of a wide array of "castas" or "nations."[98] Thus, Florida's black population not only incorporated different legal statuses but was as ethnically diverse as the larger population.

It may never be possible to determine the exact size of the black population of

Table 1. Population Figures for Second Spanish Period, 1784–1821

Year	White	Black[a]	Total	Black as a Percentage of the Total
1784[b]	1,418	574	1,992	28.8
1786[c]	1,231	461	1,692	27.2
1788[d]	1,078	651	1,729	37.6
1793[e]	1,607	1,653	3,260	50.7
1797[f]	1,007	585	1,592	36.7
1814[g]	1,302	1,779	3,081	57.7

a. Includes both free and enslaved persons and those listed either as pardo or moreno.

b. Report of Vicente Manuel de Zéspedes, Oct. 20, 1784, SD 2587, AGI.

c. Hassett made minor errors in addition which when corrected show 167 black males (rather than 156) and 137 black females. Foreigners or Anglos owned 72 male slaves and 56 female slaves, Minorcan settlers owned 45 male slaves and 37 female slaves, Floridanos (of Spanish extraction born in Florida) owned 42 male slaves and 40 female slaves and Spaniards owned 8 male slaves and 4 female slaves. Hassett estimated a garrison force of 450, which is quite a bit higher than later figures. He also estimated a rural population of 130 whites and 170 blacks (Census of Father Thomas Hassett, 1786, Census Returns, 1784–1814, EFP, microfilm reel 148, PKY). For an analysis of this census see Joseph B. Lockey, "The St. Augustine Census of 1786, Translated from the Spanish with an Introduction and Notes," *Florida Historical Quarterly* 18 (July 1939): 11–31.

d. This count excluded the garrison and specified that 281 blacks lived in the city while 367 lived in the countryside. Of the total number of blacks, Anglos owned 354 slaves and Zéspedes counted 63 fugitives from the American areas as free (Vicente Manuel de Zéspedes to Joseph de Ezpeleta, Oct. 2, 1788, Cuba 1395, AGI). The following year Zéspedes reported the arrival of 57 more fugitive slaves. For a comparative analysis of the 1788, 1793, and 1814 censuses see Pablo Tornero Tinajero, *Relaciones de dependencia entre Florida y Estados Unidos: 1783–1820* (Madrid, 1979), 35–45.

e. This census included St. Augustine, 430 men of the garrison, and plantations along the St. Marys, North, Nassau, St. Johns, and Matanzas Rivers. Of the total black population of 1653, only 126 were free, or slightly less than one-tenth (Report of Juan Nepomuceno de Quesada, Nov. 30, 1793, Cuba 1437, AGI).

f. This census included St. Augustine (excluding the garrison) and plantations along the North and Matanzas Rivers. In a total black population of 585, 483 were slaves and 102 were free.

g. This count does not include the garrison, which was reduced to only 209 men this year, or the disciplined pardo and moreno militias, which then numbered 259 men. Of the total black population of 1779, 128 were free (Sebastián Kindelán, Census of Oct. 5, 1814, Plans and Papers on Public Buildings, Fortifications, and Defense, 1779–1815, EFP, microfilm reel 76, PKY).

the second Spanish period. Censuses notoriously undercount the poorer elements of society, and because many blacks lived outside the city on remote plantations or farmsteads, they may have escaped the notice of government or ecclesiastical officials charged with enumerating the inhabitants of the province. The accounts will sometimes admit that the figures for the countryside are estimates. Nevertheless, the censuses clearly show that Florida's black population grew progressively over the course of the second Spanish regime.[99] (See table 1.)

These censuses show that blacks, free and slave, constituted between slightly over one-quarter to more than one-half of the total population of St. Augustine and its environs in the census years. After Spain abrogated the religious sanctuary policy in 1790, the free black population remained fairly stable, while the slave population steadily increased. Rumors of a French-inspired invasion led to an increase in garrison strength in 1793, and the 430 soldiers account for part of that year's population growth. The apparent decline in black population as a percentage of the whole in 1797 is also deceptive, for that year's census did not include the St. Johns, St. Marys, or Nassau River areas included in 1793. Taking those factors into account, the general population shows moderate growth, despite the political turmoil of later years.

Black Entrepreneurs and Property-Holders

Spanish Precedents

Although freedom was the primary goal that enslaved blacks may have aspired to in Spanish Florida, they also managed to acquire significant amounts of property under successive Spanish regimes. Many of Florida's black residents had once been considered property themselves, and in the English-speaking areas from which they fled, they had had few opportunities to hold property. But Castilian law and custom (which was grounded in Roman law) guaranteed even slaves the right to a *peculium,* or personal property.[1]

Sevillian notarial registers of the fifteenth and sixteenth centuries record enslaved blacks lending money to their freed counterparts.[2] And despite the generally depressed economic and social position of free blacks in early modern Spain, the same registers show at least some black property owners renting houses to other free blacks, as well as to Europeans. Early examples of propertied blacks in Seville include Ana Fernández, who rented a house to Catalina Gutiérrez, race unknown, in 1498, and the free black Leonór Rodríguez, who rented a house to the free black Juan García, in 1501. Two years later García rented a house on the corridor of the Lonja (the present-day Archive of the Indies) to the Genoese Silvestre Vento.[3] Because Castile transferred its legal institutions and socioeconomic customs, first to the Atlantic Islands, and then across the Atlantic to the Americas, free persons of African descent could also become propertied in the "New World."

In theory, all land in the Americas belonged to Castile, and its monarch might grant usufruct of it to faithful vassals or to corporate groups. Spanish political, religious, and social values all promoted the creation of ordered and well-governed communities that would redound to the prestige of the state. The Crown granted land to its vassals in proportion to their perceived social standing, making sure that even the least noteworthy received sufficient arable land to sustain family and animals. Moreover, persons of other ethnic and racial backgrounds might, under specified conditions, become Spanish vassals and, once incorporated into the Spanish community, would have the same property rights as free Spaniards.[4] Just as did others who contributed to the conquest of new lands, free blacks (and even some slaves) received rewards of land, of government posts, and occasionally of commended Indians.[5]

Believing that "to govern is to populate" and drawing on medieval Reconquista patterns, Spain followed a policy of *repoblación.* Lands vacated by war, conquest, or epidemic created a dangerous vacuum into which enemies might filter. The Crown, therefore, filled these *tierras baldías* with loyal settlers who, in gratitude, were to defend royal interest as, indeed, their own. In addition to land grants, incentives for relocation included municipal *fueros* (charters specifying exemptions and privileges), royal subsidies, and tax relief. During the reconquest of Spain from the Moslems (718–1492), the Crown resettled Spaniards into the newly won areas. In the Americas, the Crown often relocated loyal Indian allies, like the Tlaxcalans, to threatened areas it wished to hold, and after the Indian population was diminished, the Crown also transported Galician and Canary Island populations across the Atlantic to fill critical voids.[6]

Early Florida Property Patterns

With these understandings of property and frontier expansion, Spanish citizens had settled Florida since 1565, concentrating themselves near the walled city of St. Augustine but eventually establishing large cattle and wheat ranches in the rich lands of the Apalachee Indians near present-day Tallahassee and in the north central savannahs near present-day Gainesville. These seventeenth-century Florida estates were owned by important families connected to the royal government, and while free blacks worked on them as overseers and ranch hands, it is doubtful that in the seventeenth century any persons of African descent acquired substantial rural property.[7] One exception might have been Diego de Espinosa, described in various documents as mulatto, who built a sizeable cattle ranch complete with fortified house in the Diego Plains, twenty miles north of St. Augustine, and whose economic success may have been made possible by a white father.[8] In general, however, the free population of African descent was small in Spanish Florida's early years and had less leverage, and property, than it later would.

Notarial records for the so-called first Spanish period (1565–1763) are scattered and fragmentary, so it is impossible to determine whether property patterns visible in the eighteenth century had earlier origins. Occasional references to free black property ownership in St. Augustine surface from other types of documents. In the late seventeenth century, the free black Isabel de los Ríos sold sweets and baked goods from her St. Augustine home, and a free black militia member, Captain Crispín de Tapia, operated a grocery store/tavern in his home.[9] It seems probable that free blacks concentrated in, or near, the city of St. Augustine, where employment and community life were possible, rather than disperse themselves across a dangerous frontier. Indian and pirate attacks threatened even the large spreads with resident workforces to protect them, and smaller family farmsteads would have been all the more vulnerable.[10]

In 1670 the frontier was made even more dangerous when the English established Charles Town in Carolina, triggering almost a century of Anglo/Spanish imperial conflict over what is today the southeastern United States. Repeated attacks by the English and their Indian allies devastated many Indian nations as well as the Spanish mission system and most productive enterprises in Florida.[11] The geopolitical turmoil had important demographic repercussions. Not only were most of the southeastern Indian nations destabilized or forced to migrate from traditional homelands but, as discussed in chapter 2, runaway slaves from Carolina and later Georgia began to escape to St. Augustine and eventually founded the free community of Gracia Real de Santa Teresa de Mose in 1738.[12] This is the first reference to free blacks living autonomously outside the urban context of St. Augustine, but in creating Mose, the governor drew on an approved model—the mission village or *reducción.* This Caribbean institution had been approved by Queen Isabella on the grounds that congregating the Indians into villages near Spanish settlements would facilitate the religious instruction of the residents, while making sure that they provided required labor or tribute. Refugee Indian villages already encircled St. Augustine following the British raids of 1700–1704 and until an epidemic in 1727 killed all but six of them, Apalachee and Yamasee Indians had once populated Mose. The strategic location of the site, north of St. Augustine and blocking both land and water access to the city, made it imperative to hold, and Governor Montiano assigned the vacant lands to the newly freed blacks. Thereafter, governors administered Mose as they did the allied Indian villages, providing the black villagers with the same subsidies and goods and some of the same Franciscan priests.[13] Its settlers abandoned Mose in the mass evacuation of Florida at the end of the Seven Years' War, and none of the descendants of the original townspeople seems to have returned to reclaim their homesteads when Spain returned to power in 1784.[14]

Spain worried about its weakness in the face of the territorial ambitions of the United States and also about the failure of the United States to control its citizens on the turbulent southern frontier. For several years after the cession, assorted "banditti" stole cattle, slaves, and other moveable property from planters and farmers who were thinly spread south of the St. Marys River. In an effort to stabilize the province, Florida's new governor, Manuel de Zéspedes, offered amnesty to those who would desist and deported those who would not, but opined that "the best fortification would be a living wall of industrious citizens."[15]

Spain tried to increase Catholic immigration into Florida by offering tax exemptions and royal subsidies to critical industries and by approving the unlimited introduction of slaves. Despite these encouragements, uncertainty about land tenure frustrated Spanish efforts to maintain a stable population in Florida.[16]

Free Black Labor

Spain's failures to repopulate the frontier created an opportunity for the fugitive slaves of the Loyalists who, during the chaos of the American Revolution and the subsequent retrocession of Florida to the Spanish government, escaped from bondage and fled to St. Augustine to claim religious sanctuary until 1790. As discussed in chapter 3, Governor Zéspedes required the incoming fugitives to register with the government notary and present proof of gainful employment. With this act the governor sought to supervise the "strolling vagrant blacks with which this province abounds . . . a pest to the public tranquility" and generate a pool of sorely needed skilled labor.[17] Although not all registrants gave their occupations, those who did indicated a wide variety of work skills. Most described themselves as field hands, but four skilled carpenters, three sawyers, two hostlers, three domestics, two cooks, two laundresses, and two menservants also registered. Five men reported that they had been soldiers or sailors for the British. One hunter and one fishermen, one overseer, and one ranch foreman also registered. At least two men were entrepreneurs. One owned an *aguardiente* shop, or tavern, and another was a butcher.[18]

Work contracts, which offer little detail, appear to have been for a year's duration. The contracts of Small and Morris simply stipulated that those who "rented" them should dress and feed them and "in all else treat them as free."[19] Numerous notations on the census forms indicate that the fugitives changed employment frequently and, apparently, of their own volition. Prince Witten first took work at the plantation of Ambrosio Nelson on the St. Johns River, but when it was reported that Witten's former owner, Major Weed, had vowed to recapture him by force if necessary, Nelson asked the governor to allow the family to move into town and the governor agreed.[20] Witten later signed a yearlong contract to work for Jayme McGirtt on his North River plantation. Witten's work contract stipulated that his wife, Judy, would cook and do domestic work. When Witten's employer tried to put Judy to work in the fields, in violation of their agreement, Witten took him to court and stated "he could not permit" Judy to do field labor, and he asked release from his contract and payment for the nine and a half months of labor he had already performed for McGirtt.[21]

Prominent members of the community such as the governor, his secretary, Don Carlos Howard, Juan Leslie of the firm of Panton, Leslie and Company, and the wealthy planters Don Francis Phelipe Fatio and Don Juan McQueen, hired the ex-slaves. Less affluent citizens, primarily Minorcans, also hired the registrants. The Minorcan carpenter Francisco Pellicer hired the skilled carpenter Prince Witten, as well as several other of the runaways, whose occupations were not given. Those who hired the black newcomers signed documents attesting to the good behavior of their employees and were required to notify authorities of any problems. But work contracts specified that all the men were free, as were their wives and children.[22] By 1789, Governor Zéspedes reported with satisfaction that almost all the fugitives were rented out and earning a living, either in the countryside or in town.[23]

Free black men who did not secure annual contracts sometimes made short-term agreements with less reputable individuals and then found it necessary to sue to be paid. After working for two months at the bakery of Juan Studres, the free black Juan Villalonga sued to be paid the twelve pesos he said was due him. However, his employer told the court that he had only agreed to feed and shelter Villalonga, and since Villalonga could produce no written contract, he went unpaid.[24]

Blacks in Spanish Florida created economic opportunities for themselves where few existed and often had to work at several jobs to make ends meet. The tailor Antonio Coleman augmented his income by playing the fiddle at dances.[25] Felipe Edimboro earned money butchering, raising pigs for sale, gathering and selling firewood, and transporting rations to the outlying military posts at San Nicolás and Buena Vista. As described in chapter 6, he and his wife Filis also earned income hosting parties and masked balls for which members of the black community paid admission.[26] Manuel Alzendorf and Juan Baptista hired on to help Miguel Chapuz and his son fish for turtles, although Alzendorf was nominally a barber. Juan Baptista fished for turtles but, like many others who had to declare their occupation, often replied "working at whatever presents itself."[27] Black hucksters carrying strings of fresh fish or balancing baskets of shrimp, oysters, stone crabs, and fruits and vegetables on their heads could usually do good business walking the St. Augustine streets.[28]

Such men provided a ready pool of workers for the government, which regularly called on them, especially members of the free black militia, for demanding physical labor, including work on government fortifications projects or unloading ships at the wharf. Fathers and sons, and interrelated members of the black militia, worked side by side for months at a time on government projects. When they had the funds, administrators paid the standard daily wage, or jornal, of four reales (half a peso) for these general employments. More skilled laborers, such as the masons Pedro Miguel and Benjamín Seguí, earned twelve reales daily from the government. In later years, as the situado arrived more irregularly, the men worked for food allotments from the royal storehouses, providing valuable skilled labor as carpenters, masons, cartwrights, and lumberjacks. Free black militiamen like Sambo Pevet, Tomás Pelliser, Juan Antonio Florencia, Jorge Brus, Pedro Pons, Benjamín Seguí, Estévan Cheves and his son Francisco performed regular maintenance on the Castillo de San Marcos, the fortified lines, and the María Sánchez redoubt in return for barrels of wheat flour, beef, and pork.[29]

Some free blacks were able to secure more permanent positions on the government payroll. Antonio, a free black, worked in the royal armory from approximately 1794 to at least 1797, cleaning weapons. Antonio was also credited with making "Indian rifles," indicating he was capable of more skilled labor, but he received the same wage paid to unskilled laborers. This may have been the same Antonio who earned money by capturing and returning a black prisoner who had escaped from jail.[30] Occasionally skilled black craftsmen worked for themselves and marketed their products to the government. The carpenter Juan Wright earned 252 reales in 1788 for the carts he built for the king's service.[31]

The government also employed free blacks for rural assignments. The militiaman Carlos Hall cut timber from royal land and hauled it to specified locations. José Bonom, also of the free black militia, was a courier who carried official communications from the Plaza to Commandant Carlos Howard on the northern frontier. Pedro Berta gathered fodder for the cavalry mounts. Other free blacks earned wages as oarsmen on government boats on the St. Johns River.[32]

Black Entrepreneurs

Free mulattoes dominated trades such as shoemaking and tailoring in St. Augustine, although free blacks also participated in smaller numbers. The free mulattoes Pedro Casali and José Rivas were shoemakers, as was the free black Jorge Jacobo. Another free mulatto, Juan Peterson, was a master tailor to whom parents who could afford to apprenticed their children. The free mulatto María Guadalupe Rubio and her white husband Juan Mañé, a cook at the royal hospital, apprenticed their thirteen-year-old son, Nicolás Mañé, to Peterson, who agreed to admit the boy into his household and train him for five years. Eva Fish and Andrés Bacas apprenticed their son to a master tailor under the same arrangement.[33]

One of Florida's most enterprising free black entrepreneurs was Juan Bautista Collins. A free mulatto born in Nagitoches, Louisiana, Collins was a literate man of initiative and apparently at least modest means (perhaps a bequest from his white father). He entered Florida in 1770 during the British occupation and stayed on through the second Spanish regime, during which time he bought and traded items ranging from butter to cattle and horses to slaves in locations as diverse as Charleston, Havana, New Orleans, Pensacola, and the Indian nations in the interior. In 1792 Collins petitioned the Spanish government for a new settlers' headright grant of three hundred acres for himself, his mother and daughter, and two slaves, and the governor granted his request.[34] The same year Collins asked permission to go to Havana for business, describing himself as a "man of known good behavior" and stating that his mother would be "in the care of someone who will be like her son." Collins's accounts showed a favorable balance and Governor Quesada approved his passport.[35] By the next year, Collins had bought a town home on Marine Street three houses away from the new troops' barracks and three away from the large household of the well-to-do Espinosa-Sánchez family. In his household he supported his sixty-two-year-old mother, Juliana Cecilia Bobi, a free black laundress from Cabo Francés, Santo Domingo, and his two-year-old daughter, María Rosa Collins, a free mulatto.[36] María's mother was a black slave whom Collins never married, and their child would have also been a slave had not Collins purchased his daughter's freedom.[37]

Collins neither freed nor married the mother of his child, but in 1798 he married María de la Concepción Tunno, the free quadroon daughter of Don Tomás Tunno. At the couple's wedding, Don Manuel Solana, a white army officer, and his wife Doña María Mestre served as sponsors, and two years later Don Felipe Solana and Doña Luisa Canto served as godparents to the couple's newborn son, Tomás Felipe Collins.[38] Collins's legitimate marriage, his marriage partner, and the choice of sponsors at his wedding and for the baptism of his legitimate child reflect his relatively high status in the community. In many ways Collins acted and lived as a Spaniard. Like a proper master, he saw to it that his slaves and their children received baptism and when the priest collected donations to build a new church, Collins gave ten pesos, equivalent to the gift of many "dons" and higher than that of others.[39]

Assisted by the $500 dowry her father gave his bride, Collins opened a store in his mother's home and transacted business with a wide assortment of people in St. Augustine. Sometimes these dealings went sour, and Collins sought relief in the courts. The same year he was married, Collins sued a ship's captain who had failed to deliver twenty-eight dollars worth of butter Collins ordered from Charleston. He also sued Nansi Wiggins (also known as Ana Gallum), the free Senegalese widow of the planter Job Wiggins, for 108 dollars, the price of a horse and three cattle the deceased owed him. In both cases Collins recovered at least part of his losses.[40]

But like other merchants in the beleaguered colony, Collins lived on the edge of bankruptcy. In 1801 his debts became so numerous that he temporarily fled his responsibilities, and his abandoned wife initiated a lawsuit to try to reclaim her dowry out of Collins's remaining goods. When court officials inventoried Collins's store, they found small quantities of *aguardiente,* syrup, rum, salt, sugar, oil, soap, butter, and starch. They also reviewed the store accounts, which Collins kept in Spanish, English, and French; these records showed that in better days Collins once dealt in more valuable merchandise, including gold and silver watches of French manufacture and household furniture. Collins carried on his books the debts of influential members of the community, such as Don Francis Phelipe Fatio, Don Jesse Fish, and Don Juan McClery, each of whom owed Collins more than one hundred pesos. Not only was Collins buying and selling merchandise, he was lending money and buying notes from others. Collins floated many loans to soldiers of the Third Battalion and to members of the black militia, such as General Jorge Biassou, Estévan Cheves, Antonio Sandy Edimboro, and José Bonom. Their notes often promised payment "when the silver [government payroll] arrives." The chronic shortage of currency led Collins also to engage in barter. In one such transaction he gave the black militiaman Carlos Hill a horse for a promise to deliver 225 feet of lumber.[41]

Collins eventually returned from hiding in Georgia to face his legal obligations. He told the court he had never intended to default on his debts but that he was desperate because others would not pay him, "Whether because of his color or some other motive." In fact, the money owed to Collins exceeded his debts to others and he began to file suits to try to collect and clear his own past due accounts.[42]

Collins resumed store-keeping but also began supplementing his income through Indian trade. In 1808 the royal treasury commissioned Collins to travel to the Seminole nation in La Chua (Alachua, near present-day Gainesville) to buy cattle. This was a significant responsibility, for it required Collins to travel great distances on a difficult journey of five to eight months, to trade independently and tactfully among his Indian suppliers, and to bring back herds of several hundred head of cattle for the sustenance of St. Augustine. Benjamín Wiggins took part in one of these cattle drives and may have been along as a translator and advocate for Collins.

The Seminoles had threatened to sell their stock to the United States instead of to the Spaniards and some artful negotiations were in order. Collins made several trips to establish relations with Chief Bowlegs, during which he distributed gifts of cloth, handkerchiefs, belts, beads, sugar, tobacco, *aguardiente,* knives, and powder and shot among his Seminole hosts. Only after several of these visits did Collins actually conduct business; he showed a diplomat's skill in preparing the sale.

Collins was able to purchase a herd of 125 cattle at Chiscochate, eighteen of which were sold to him by the black woman named Molly, but he lost seventeen on the trail back to St. Augustine. He presented a bill for the remaining 108 cattle and returned to Seminole country to secure more. When Collins returned the second time to St. Augustine, the interim treasurer, Don Antonio Yguíniz, refused to pay him for the cattle that had already been slaughtered. After two years had passed without payment, Collins filed suit to press his claims, and Yguíniz countered that Collins asked too high a price at nine pesos a head. Collins demonstrated his knowledge of Seminole customs when he explained that the Indians valued their cattle by age, and that they considered a two-year-old cow to be three because in that time they made three harvests. He called witnesses who testified that the cattle he had delivered were worth up to fifteen pesos a head and that the goods Yguíniz had supplied for the Indian gifts had been vastly overpriced. Moreover, Collins presented witnesses to the abusive behavior with which Yguíniz answered his efforts to collect payment. Collins testified that Yguíniz swore at him and called him a "mulatto dog," to which he responded that no dog had ever received holy baptism as he had nor been entrusted with a government contract. At another witnessed encounter Yguíniz attacked Collins with the horns of a slaughtered cow, and "out of respect for the office of the treasurer," Collins retreated.

Collins was in a vulnerable position. He was a man of color challenging a royal official, and, as he pointed out to the court, Yguíniz was the commander of his militia unit and might at the slightest excuse extract his revenge. But Collins asserted that he was not a slave of the treasurer who might be expected to work for no pay. As the suit and countersuit progressed, Chief Bowlegs's sister, Simency, came to St. Augustine to testify on Collins's behalf. Simency charged that Yguíniz had not kept his word and threatened that, henceforth, the tribe would sell their cattle to the United States.

The evidence clearly weighed in Collins's favor, but the dilatory nature of Spanish justice was ruining him. While the matter was in court, other debtors who owed Collins money refused to pay him. At the end of 1813, Collins asked Governor Kindelán for a passport to go to Havana, "due to the necessity I suffer here," and the governor finally ordered Yguíniz to pay Collins the 853 pesos he owed him, but Yguíniz continued to stall. The case was only settled in 1816, eight years after Collins first went for the cattle, and by that time Collins had to pay 271 pesos in court costs.[43]

In the interim, Panton, Leslie and Company employed Collins to take a large herd from St. Augustine all the way to their Pensacola store. This contract indicates that Collins's reputation was left intact and his services were still in demand, despite the interim treasurer's attempt to defame him.[44]

Black Leisure

Free and enslaved blacks spent at least some of their hard-earned income and free time on leisure activities. A Catholic calendar full of feast days and the mandatory observation of royal accessions, births, marriages, and other festive occasions

The Villalonga house on St. George Street, St. Augustine. Filis and Felipe Edimboro hosted dances for the black community on the top floor. © 1998, Ken Barrett, Jr. Courtesy of Ken Barrett, Jr.

provided general public amusements such as serenades, presentations of popular comedies such as *Amigo, Amante y Leal,* military parades, religious processions, and bonfires. During Carnival musicians strolled the streets playing guitar and violin for costumed revelers and the midsummer celebrations for St. John brought another round of festivities. At other times Minorcans entertained the rest of the community with charivaris, fromajardis serenades, and posey dances.[45] Black men joined in the gambling and card games such as *naipes* in local taverns, and men and women, free and enslaved, attended dances and dress balls.[46] The upper floor of Juan Villalonga's house on St. George's Street (now part of the restored Spanish Quarter in St. Augustine) proved a popular venue for these dances for more than twenty years. Filis and Felipe Edimboro hosted dances there in the 1790s and although periodic legislation attempted to prohibit late night dances for "people of color," in 1813 the government sentenced Villalonga, who had by then become a barrio commissioner, to eight days' house arrest for violating the useless ban.[47] Given that dances had been part of the Afro-Hispanic tradition recorded since at least the fourteenth century, it is not surprising that attempts to restrict them proved ineffective.[48]

Black Slaveowners

A number of Florida's free blacks invested some of their income in slaves, among them Juan Bautista Collins, Prince (Juan Bautista) Witten, Felipe Edimboro, Jorge Biassou, Anna Kingsley, and members of the extended Clarke, Wiggins, and Sánchez families. It does not appear that black slaveowners had a relationship with their slaves that was significantly different than that between a white owner and a slave. They rented out and sold slaves and posted them as bonds. Like white slaveowners, black masters sometimes assisted slaves to become free and sometimes opposed their manumission. In 1812 the free black Juan Papy bought a recently imported African boy of about thirteen years of age whom he named Santiago. Five years later the aged Papy signed a notarized document which would free Santiago on Papy's death, in payment for his "good services and help in my infirmities."[49] However, the free black Jorge Sanco had to sue the former slave Nansi Wiggins to accomplish the manumission of his wife, Rosa. Sanco told the court he had agreed to pay Nansi Wiggins 350 pesos to free his wife and that he had already paid Wiggins 47 pesos, a statement Nansi later refuted. Depositing another 233 pesos with the court, Sanco initiated a *coartación* suit and asked the court to grant Rosa's freedom once she had paid the remaining 70 pesos from her earnings or jornales. Nansi Wiggins testified she had agreed to free Rosa for 400 pesos and denied Sanco had paid her anything, although she admitted that Rosa had been paying her 6 pesos monthly for the past four months. Governor Enrique White ruled in favor of his militiaman and Rosa became a free woman.[50]

Another *coartación* case of special irony involved Felipe Edimboro, who was this time the slaveowner. Juan Zamorano, a free black, told the court he had loaned an aged slave by the name of Holbran one hundred pesos, interest free, with which to buy his freedom from a Mr. Hall. The notarized instrument Zamorano presented as evidence showed that Holbran had agreed to repay his loan in three months' time.[51] However, two days after borrowing the money from Zamorano, Holbran loaned it to Felipe Edimboro, who promised to repay the full sum in two months (thereby allowing Holbran to repay his debt to Zamorano as scheduled). Edimboro apparently used the money to purchase Holbran from Mr. Hall. Holbran may well have initiated this change of owner, as other slaves often did in Spanish Florida, but that is never specified. Several weeks later Holbran paid his new owner, Edimboro, fifty pesos, as partial payment for his freedom. Somewhere along the line, the chain or repayments broke down, and in October Zamorano sued Edimboro and asked the court's intercession to help Holbran "escape from the yoke of servitude." However, because neither Edimboro or Holbran could repay Zamorano, Governor White ordered the unlucky Holbran sold at public auction where Don Rafael Días purchased him for 170 pesos. Zamorano finally recovered the money he loaned Holbran, but his good intentions were unfulfilled. Holbran remained a slave, of yet another owner, and Edimboro lost his half share in the slave.[52] As noted in chapter 9, Edimboro had earlier owned another slave named Jack, who was briefly captured by the Seminoles while doing fieldwork for Edimboro.[53]

Black Homesteaders

In 1790, as noted in chapter 3, Spain finally adopted a revised land policy based on the British "headrights" system, and free blacks quickly tested their rights. The new policy required foreigners who wished to move to Florida to swear allegiance to the Spanish Crown, but eliminated previous requirements to convert to Catholicism. Each incoming head of household would receive one hundred acres for himself and fifty for every person attached to his household, of whatever race. The *nuevo poblador,* or new homesteader, had ten years in which to hold and develop the land, after which time he received full title.[54]

As soon as they could, free blacks petitioned for land as new settlers. In general, the need to hold the frontier and make it productive overrode any racial qualms the governors may have had, and all legitimate land requests were approved unless the land in question was already occupied. Petitioners carefully described the land that they wanted, and the governor would then request a recommendation from the royal engineer. The engineer would investigate whether the land was available and would offer an opinion on the industry of the applicant and the benefits to the Plaza of having the land settled, whereupon the governor would grant the request. If problems later arose, and the land became unproductive or uninhabitable due to danger from Indian attacks, for example, the owners appeared to request exchanges for new land, and these, too, would usually be granted. Among the recipients of land were Estévan Cheves, who received 200 acres; Tory Travers and Felipe Edimboro, who each received 100 acres; Antonio Williams and Abraham Hannahan, who received 50 acres; and Scipio, who received 25 acres.[55]

In 1792, the free English-speaking mulatto Juan Moore petitioned for and received 350 acres near Trout Creek for himself, his wife, and four grown sons; however, Governor Enrique White later required that land to pasture cattle herds belonging to Panton, Leslie and Company. In place of the original grant, which he reclaimed, the governor granted Moore an equal amount of acreage on the St. Johns River, about six miles south of the Buena Vista fort where Moore served militia duty. Moore and his family began anew and improved their claim by building a home on it, fencing the land, and cultivating fields. The family also raised cattle and seemed to be on an upward trajectory when the Indian raids of 1800–1803 intervened. Although Moore and his wife remained on the dangerous frontier to defend their homestead, their grown sons reported for militia service in St. Augustine. After the trouble subsided, the sons returned to the farm, enabling the Moore family to hold the land until after the end of the Spanish regime, when in 1823 Moore sold it for $1,200 to the American Elihu Woodruff.[57] While his sons worked the country homestead, Juan Moore relocated to Fernandina on Amelia Island. In 1814, Governor Coppinger granted Moore's request for a town lot, Jorge J. F. Clarke surveyed and recorded the property, and Moore built his family a new town house.[58]

In 1806 a new homesteader, Thomas Primus, and his family became farmers on a government grant of fifty acres located west of the North River at Mose, where over half a century before, their predecessors had established the first free black colonial town in the present-day United States.[59] Primus had escaped from slavery in Georgia eight years earlier and then had to fight reenslavement when his former owner, Lucia Braddock Fitzgerald, also became a new homesteader in Florida and tried to reclaim Primus and his family as her property. Initially uncertain of their rights under Spanish law, the Primus family once again worked as slaves for Fitzgerald until Primus went into St. Augustine and initiated a suit for their freedom.[60] Successful in that effort, Primus went on to use the system to acquire property on which to support his newly freed family.

By 1793, the Witten family lived in a house in St. Augustine which was probably rented. Witten's neighbors included his marriage sponsor, Don Manuel Fernández Bendicho, Don Juan Leslie, head of the Panton, Leslie and Company Indian trading house, and Don Juan McQueen, of American revolutionary fame, who was also a major landholder and later judge in Spanish Florida.[61] Two years later Witten petitioned the government for land outside the city walls on which to build houses for himself and the other free blacks of the community. He also asked permission to cut timber so as to be self-employed and support his family. The new governor, Juan Nepomuceno de Quesada, agreed to the request, but as fate would have it, the French-inspired invasion from Charleston rocked the province that year, and the panicked governor ordered all the northern settlements evacuated and burned to deny them to the enemy.[62] Three years later, Witten's son, Francisco, signed a petition "for my father who does not know how to write," asking for land to cultivate south of the city, which the governor granted.[63]

In 1796, black refugees from Santo Domingo arrived in Spanish Florida and, despite some initial concerns about their recent involvement in a slave revolt, they quickly blended into the free black community and began to work the Spanish system. General Jorge Biassou and his "family" of some twenty-six followers and their families were welcome additions to the free black militia and the labor force, and some offered the community skilled labor as well. For example, Jorge Jacobo was a shoemaker, Pedro Miguel a mason, and León Duvigneau and Benjamín Seguí were bakers. Seguí also found employment at various times as a hairdresser and as a cook.[64] Soon the exiles from Santo Domingo also began to claim rights as "new homesteaders." Although General Biassou took up residence in a fine house in town, he also began clearing a plantation seven miles north of St. Augustine, lending the place the names of Plantation of the Black General or Bayou Mulatto. When Biassou applied for that land, he stated that many of his countrymen would soon be establishing themselves nearby.[65]

Both Biassou and Witten had indicated in their requests that their countrymen hoped to live near them and, indeed, free black homesteaders clustered around several rural locations. Some, like Thomas Primus, took land at the previous site of Gracia Real de Santa Teresa de Mose. Another group clustered within the vicinity of the Buena Vista outpost on the St. Johns River. Still a third group homesteaded south of St. Augustine near the Matanzas outpost. The men may have grouped together for companionship, but also because they could assist one another in collaborative work arrangements such as that between Felipe Edimboro and Tommy Moore. In 1798 the men entered into an agreement to jointly work Edimboro's land along the St. Johns. When their partnership broke down, Moore took Edimboro to court to collect wages he claimed were due him for nine

Petition of the free African Prince Witten (a.k.a. Juan Bautista Witten or Wiet), 1795. Witten asks the Spanish governor to grant him and other free blacks land on the basis of their citizenship, and Governor Juan Nepomuceno de Quesada grants his request. SFLR, record group 599, series 992, box 12, folder 35. Courtesy of the Florida State Archives.

months' labor. Edimboro testified that he had never promised Moore wages but rather that they had agreed to split a harvest and the animals produced during their partnership. Edimboro also claimed to have built a house for Moore and his family and to have sustained them during nine months. He also charged that Moore had only worked for two months, causing their cultivation to lag and forcing Edimboro to put two other men to work on the land. Edimboro complained that Moore was impertinent and that his suit had no legal merit, but he offered to end the controversy by giving Moore more than sixty bushels of corn from their nine months' harvest.[66] Edimboro apparently enjoyed a more harmonious partnership with his son-in-law, Benjamín Wiggins.

Free women of color also became homesteaders and the government granted them acreage based on the number of their children and slaves. Flora Leslie, the consort of St. Augustine's white surveyor Jorge J. F. Clarke, did so and received five hundred acres, and Isabella Wiggins, the consort of his brother, Carlos Clarke, was granted three hundred acres. While even the poorest women could appeal to the government, connections with important whites in the community helped many free black women acquire substantial property holdings. Isabella Wiggins's mother Nansi Wiggins managed the 1200-acre estate of her deceased consort Job Wiggins, as well as the seventeen slaves who worked it, and her children shared in their father's property. Seminole raids of the early 1800s forced the widow and her children to leave the estate and move to the new city of Fernandina on Amelia Island. In Fernandina, Nansi and her daughters petitioned for, and received, town lots on which they had new homes built. After the Indian threat subsided, Isabella Wiggins petitioned for her own land. Governor Coppinger granted her three hundred acres on the east side of Lake George based on her family of five children and the five slaves she owned, and her brother-in-law, Jorge J. F. Clarke, surveyed and recorded her new property. When Florida became a territory of the United States in 1821, a board of commissioners determined that conditions of Isabella Wiggins's grant on the east side of Lake George had not been met and denied the claim. Isabella's sons and heirs, Job W. Clarke, James W. Clarke, and Thomas W. Clarke, fought the determination through the Supreme Court of the United States, but eventually lost the case and the land.[67]

One of Florida's most successful black female property owners was the Wolof Anna Magigine Jai, known in Florida as Anna Kingsley. Daniel L. Schafer has tracked her remarkable life from Senegal to Cuba, Florida, Haiti, and back to Florida, where she died a wealthy widow in her seventies on the eve of the United States Civil War. Raised in a slave-holding family, Anna was captured and sold into slavery as a young girl and taken to the slave markets of Havana, where the Scottish Quaker Zephaniah Kingsley bought her at age thirteen. Kingsley made Anna his wife and established her as the mistress of his sizeable Florida estate, Laurel Grove. In 1812 Anna Kingsley petitioned for, and received, her own land grant from the Spanish government and began a new homestead at Mandarin, across the St. Johns River from her husband's plantation. She took her children and twelve slaves with her. Before long, her slaves had built their mistress a two-story home of stone and logs, and her fields and farm animals were flourishing. Unfortunately, the timing could not have been worse, for the so-called Patriot Rebellion broke out the same year. In 1813, Georgia slave catchers attacked her farm, and a Spanish commander later described her bravery under fire: "Anna Kingsley deserves any favor the governor can grant her. Rather than afford shelter and provisions to the enemies of his Majesty . . . [she] burned it all up and remained unsheltered."[68] Anna subsequently sued the United States government for $1694 in damages resulting from the Patriot invasion. The losses she listed included a burned house and storehouse, six hundred bushels of corn, five hundred pounds of nails and spikes, cart chains, axes, tools, spinning wheels, and furniture, ten dozen ducks, four dozen fowl, ten hogs, and three "Negro houses."[69]

Anna Kingsley eventually resettled on her husband's new estate on nearby Fort George Island, but the Spanish government awarded her a 350-acre grant at Dunn's Creek to compensate for her war losses.[70] Her personal estate grew even

The main house at the Kingsley plantation, Fort George Island. Zephaniah Kingsley and his African-born wife Anna Magigine Jai moved into this home in 1814. Courtesy of the Florida State Archives.

larger when her husband also deeded her title to a 1,000-acre estate at Deep Creek on the St. Johns River, for "wages and faithful services during twenty-five years together."[71]

Military Service Grants

Membership in the militia enabled free black males to acquire property. As representatives of the Crown, governors could grant lands for meritorious service to the state, which included military service. By the early nineteenth century, Spain was fighting invasions at home and revolutionary movements throughout the empire, so could devote very few resources of any kind to Florida. Unfortunately, Florida was also under siege much of that time. As discussed in chapters 9 and 10, Florida suffered through the Genêt-inspired invasion (1794–95), repeated Indian attacks during the State of Muskogee's war against Spain (1800–1803), another invasion during the so-called Patriot Rebellion (1812), in which the United States government supported Georgians attempting to take the province, and repeated violations of Spanish sovereignty by the United States, such as the United States Navy's attack on the Negro Fort on the Apalachicola River (1816) and General Andrew Jackson's raids on the black and Seminole villages along the Suwannee River (1818). In its final years, Spanish Florida also suffered the seizure of Amelia Island by revolutionaries, pirates, and, lastly, the United States Navy. Given Spain's inability to protect Florida, desperate governors had to make do with the resources at hand, and their necessity created leverage for free blacks who saw service in all those crises.[72]

The men had compelling reasons to serve. Most importantly, their interests lay with Spain, the nation that had freed them. They knew full well what would come of a United States' takeover. Moreover, their service underscored their loyalty and citizenship and won them pay, titles, recognition, and the gratitude of the beleaguered Spanish community. In 1812, Sergeant Juan Bautista (Prince) Witten's black and Indian troops attacked the United States Marines who were supporting the Patriot siege of St. Augustine, thus liberating vitally needed food supplies for the starving Spanish citizens.[73] Spain declared that it was "well satisfied with the noble and loyal spirit which animates all the individuals of this company" and promised that "each one's merit shall be magnanimously attended to and compensated with all the advantages the state can assign."[74] Despite the rhetoric, actual cash rewards were minimal; however, such guerrilla operations provided free blacks with the opportunity to enrich themselves at the expense of the enemy. Witten and the other black officers received orders that specified that they could appropriate any guns, powder, and provisions they might need from the rebels' sizeable plantations. In addition, horses, cattle, equipment, supplies, clothing, and household goods went to the takers, and these spoils of war no doubt were put to good use by the militiamen.[75] More importantly, as a result of their service in 1812, a royal order of 1815 made black militiamen eligible for service-related land grants, and many thereby acquired land for the first time or added to their existing holdings. Among those receiving service grants were Antonio Proctor, 185 acres; Pedro Sivelly, 150 acres; Prince Patton, 300 acres; Aysick Travers, 115 acres; and Tory Travers, 125 acres.[76]

Florida's military dependence upon free blacks presented the militiamen with opportunities, but the ever-present danger also took its toll on black families and farmsteads. As we have seen, some black homesteaders lost their original homesteads during the invasion of 1794–95. During the Indian raids of 1800–1803, others were forced to flee for their lives to the shelter of the city, and a decade later the Patriot Rebellion drove others from their land. On these occasions the black homesteaders reported their losses to Spanish authorities, who made an attempt to relocate them to new properties. (See appendix 5.)

Some years after the fact, blacks also made claims against the United States government, which reviewed and paid for part of the damages for which it was liable as a result of its sponsorship of the Patriot Rebellion. At least twenty-six free blacks pressed claims against the United States. Their claims ranged from a high of $3,062 for well-connected free blacks such as Harry McQueen, to a low of $320 for "Seguí, a free black." The average claim of the black claimants was approximately $2,000. Their claims describe black homesteads and the value of the losses sustained and also indicate how the free property holders worked their lands.[77]

One of the homesteads described on these claims was that of the carpenter Lewis Sánchez and his wife Diana, who were once the slaves of Don Francisco Xavier Sánchez.[78] They owned a "plantation" four miles north of St. Augustine on which they planted eight to ten acres of corn as well as peas, potatoes, peanuts, pumpkins, and melons in fenced fields. They also owned a herd of sixty cattle, twenty-six hogs, six work horses, and a large number of poultry. Lewis had built two log dwelling houses, corn cribs, four poultry coops, and a cookhouse on the place. He owned considerable farm equipment and carpentry tools, and the plantation was said to be "in a flourishing state" when the family was forced to abandon all they had worked for. Sánchez's primary witness was Col. Joseph Sánchez, the son of his former master, who attested that Sánchez was an "honest and hard-working man" and a "good farmer" and supported his claims to losses worth $2,625.75. When driven from his land, Lewis Sánchez joined the black militia and served against the invaders who ruined him.[79]

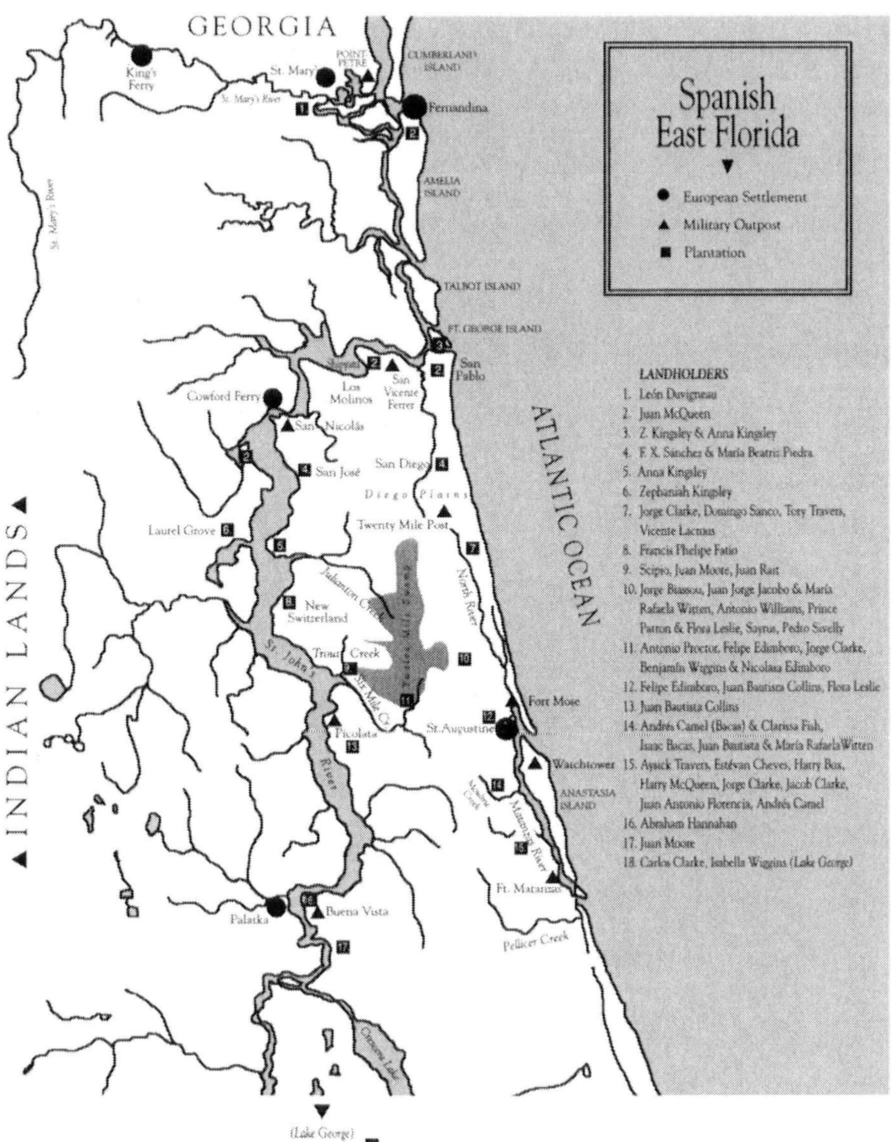

Map of major plantations and black homesteads during the second Spanish period (1784–1821). Adapted by James R. Landers with the assistance of Daniel L. Schafer from original maps.

The Patriots also struck the homestead of the black pilot, Indian language interpreter, and militiaman Benjamín Wiggins, who served repeatedly in the many disturbances which shook Florida.[80] Wiggins was the mulatto son of Job Wiggins and of the free Senegalese Nansi Wiggins, and through his sister, Isabella Wiggins, was the brother-in-law of the powerful Clarke brothers. Wiggins, his wife, Nicolasa, and their three children homesteaded a government grant adjacent to that of his father-in-law, Felipe Edimboro, three miles west of St. Augustine, near Pevet Swamp. The eldest Wiggins child lived with his grandparents, and the families worked their holdings cooperatively. Wiggins owned a herd of thirty-eight cattle, two yokes of oxen, six milk cows with calves, eight horses, a dozen sheep, and numerous turkeys, ducks, chickens, and pigeons. Wiggins had planted crops of corn, potatoes, peas, and pumpkins. While maintaining his homestead, Wiggins also earned an average of $500 to $600 annually as a stock keeper, part of which he received in cash and part in cattle. When he piloted for someone, Wiggins earned $2 a day and another $1 daily for the use of his horse.[81] His brother-in-law, Carlos Clarke, testified to support Wiggins's compensation claims for $1,196.50, stating that "the circumstances of the claimant were very good for a person of color before the rebellion," but that the family was "entirely reduced" immediately afterward. Clarke reported that Benjamín Wiggins was a man "who always had money . . . but kept it private" and that "he must have expended it for the support of his family during the siege . . . for he was actually very poor directly afterwards." Despite his losses, Wiggins's industry sustained the family in town. In addition to the pay he received as a pilot, he earned money fishing and oystering, and Nicolasa added to their income by unspecified work. Clarke also remarked that Wiggins had inherited some income from his (white) father's estate and "is again getting up in the world."[82]

The insurgents had also ruined Wiggins's father-in-law, Felipe Edimboro, burning his contiguous farm and robbing him of cattle, horses, and hogs. On April 28, 1815, Edimboro asked for and received new lands and began to rebuild his life. He later filed claims against the United States for damages in the amount of $1,624 and received the full amount for his losses.[83]

Wiggins's claims point to another means by which free blacks acquired property. He and others in St. Augustine commonly inherited from their fathers, who may not have married their mothers but who recognized their children at baptism and provided for the mothers and their children in their wills. José Sánchez, the natural son of the wealthy cattle rancher Don Francisco Xavier Sánchez, married Lucía Ysnardy, the natural daughter of the royal accountant Don Miguel Ysnardy. Wiggins and Sánchez both left their children property, including houses,

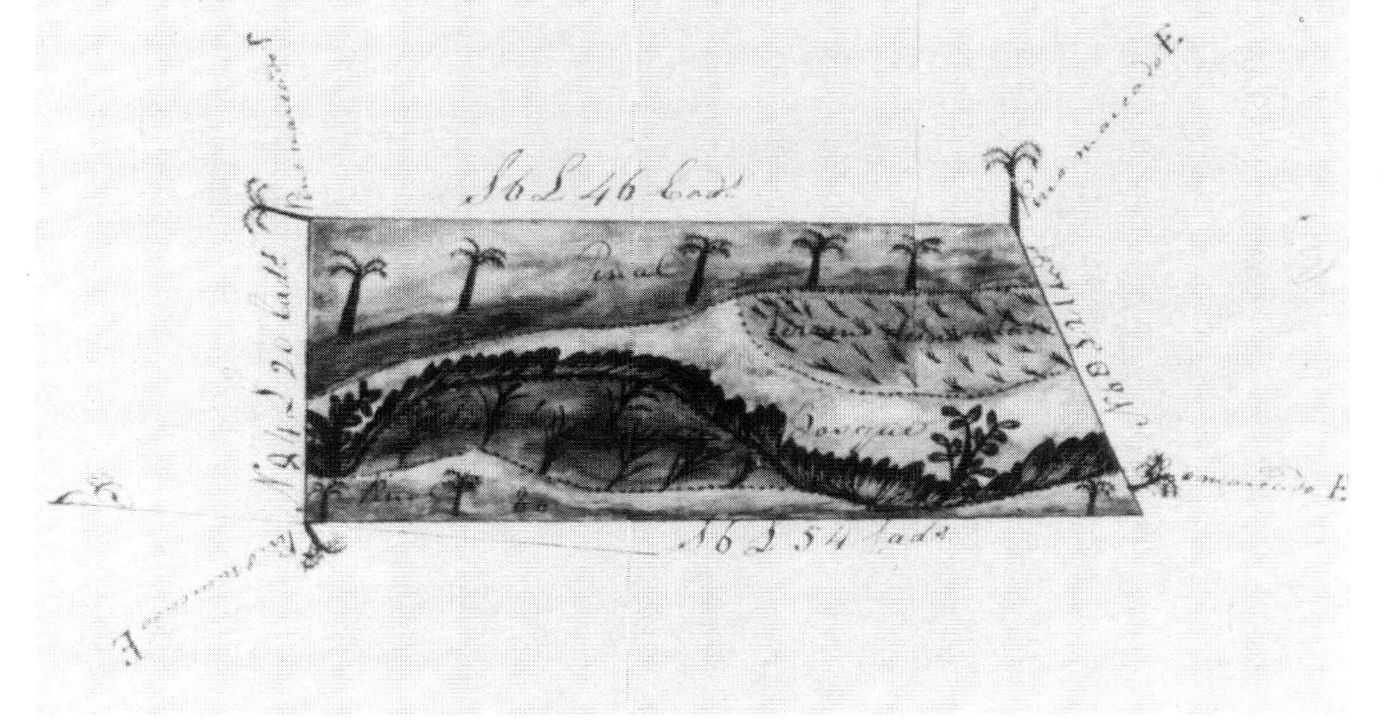

Watercolor survey Felipe Edimboro's land grant. SFLR, record group 599, series 990, Confirmed Spanish Land Claims, box 11, folder E-4. Courtesy of the Florida State Archives.

land, and slaves of considerable value.[84] Finally, free blacks, like any other *vecinos,* or citizens, could buy property, had they the resources.

Several factors combined to facilitate the growth of a free black property-holding class in Florida, including law, custom, and Spain's geopolitical necessity to hold a frontier under constant threat. The American and French revolutions created havoc in Spanish Florida, but they also made it possible for some former slaves of the southern colonies and of Spanish Santo Domingo to claim sanctuary and freedom in Florida.[85] Blacks who had once been counted as chattel themselves must have valued more than most the right to be free citizens, to own and dispose of property, and to take up arms in defense of their families and homes. Given the opportunity, the freedmen and women worked hard and made good lives for themselves and their families on Florida land, and as some of the case studies above illustrate, many prospered until factors beyond their control ruined their efforts. As long as it could, and for its own purposes, the Spanish Crown continued to reward loyal black citizens with land grants and subsidies, and with that commitment in place, free black Floridians repeatedly rebuilt their lives and their homesteads.

Black Religious Life

Early Patterns of African Religious Incorporation

It is difficult to overestimate the significance of the Roman Catholic church as a vehicle for African assimilation and social acceptance and advancement in Spanish communities. In a sense it was the one true equalizer, for within the church all were "brothers in Christ." Medieval Spaniards worried more about religious difference than they did about racial or ethnic or color differences, and the Catholic church incorporated Africans centuries before Spain's expansion into the Americas.[1] Although the Spanish monarchs permitted the private observance of other faiths within its realms, non-Catholics were distrusted and periodically became the target of persecution. Muslims, Jews, and Africans who converted to Catholicism found more acceptance in Spanish society, although even they were not totally free of suspicion.[2] This medieval pattern of incorporating (but never fully) the converted "other" shaped Spanish society in the Americas and had important implications for Africans in what is today the southeastern United States.

Contemporaries and historians alike have viewed the Spanish expansion into the New World as an extension of the religious Reconquest of Spain, with both territories and souls at stake. Pope Alexander VI granted the Catholic monarchs Isabella and Ferdinand sovereignty in the "New World" in exchange for evangelization of the indigenous populations. As a result, Spain expended tremendous resources on contacting and learning the culture of native peoples in order to convert them. After centuries-long religious wars against the Muslims (718–1492), Spain also tried to ensure that all Africans who traveled to the Americas, whether free or enslaved, were good Catholics. As sugar production was transplanted from the Atlantic Islands to Hispaniola and other circum-Caribbean sites, however, and the demand for African slaves increased exponentially, this became a losing battle.[3]

Partially in fear that bozales, or unacculturated slaves from Africa, might introduce the dread "contamination" of Islam or other "heathen" practices, the New World church began to try to assimilate Africans. Beginning in the sixteenth century, royal decrees ordered slaveowners to allow slaves to hear Mass, to provide chapels on their estates for such purposes, and to baptize all newly introduced slaves. Although Spain made no large-scale missionary outreach among enslaved Africans, royal officials believed that Christianizing slaves might safeguard against rebellion and promote social order.[4]

Black Religious Corporations in the Circum-Caribbean

The Catholic evangelization effort among Africans may have appeared minimal, but the corporate structure that the church established in the Americas had important cultural implications for both free and enslaved Africans. By the sixteenth century, the church had adapted Spanish patterns and institutionalized African religious brotherhoods along national lines throughout the circum-Caribbean.[5] Within the framework of Spanish Catholicism, cabildos provided a place where Africans of like language and culture could congregate freely, exchange information, pool resources, define corporate interests, and promote corporate goals.[6]

In Santo Domingo, Hispaniola, Africans belonging to the Biafra and Mandinga nations formed the cabildo of Nuestra Señora de la Candelaria, while criollos born on the island formed themselves into a separate brotherhood, La Virgen de los Remedios. In Havana, the Mandinga, Carabalí, Lucumí, Arará, Gangá, and Congo nations proliferated and also organized important brotherhoods. These organizations devoted themselves to a patron saint whom they honored on his or her feast day and dues-paying members supported an array of mutual aid functions, including caring for the ill, freeing the aged, and burying the dead. Members defined their devotions as well as rules of conduct in charters or constitutions. Elected officers promised to monitor their own members and expel any miscreants, and because the organizations promoted positive social values and good order, Spanish officials usually approved their requests to organize and granted them licenses. Eighteenth-century cabildo officers in Cuba carried military titles, but the cabildos also still elected kings and courts for Carnival, whom Spanish officials informally recognized as representatives of their people, much as they had the black barrio mayorales in Andalusia.[7] John Thornton has suggested that through such elections national groups "adopted the idiom of the state" and thereby raised suspicions among some colonial officials about their purposes.[8] Havana's existing cabildo charters list only male officers and members by name, but free and enslaved women also belonged. Havana's Carabalí brotherhood, Nuestra Señora de Belen, which recorded sixty-one named male members in 1771, also claimed 240 unnamed female members.[9]

Despite the low economic status of most members, many of Havana's eighteenth-century cabildos were able through loans, bequests, and savings to buy their own buildings, which could not be sold without the unanimous vote of the membership. These were usually connected to and located near Catholic churches in the city center. The Royal Congo cabildo, also known as the Cabildo Rey Mago San Melchor, from whom members claimed to be descended, owned a property on Florida Street. The Mandingas owned one on the corner of Habana and Merced, and the Ararás, whose earliest known license dated to 1691, owned a house on Compostela Street.[10]

The activities and observances of the black brotherhoods blended European and African cultural elements. Perhaps the most popular celebration for Africans in the circum-Caribbean was the Día de Reyes, celebrated on the sixth of January (Epiphany), and possibly chosen for the reason that one of the three Magi (variously Gaspar, Melchior, or Baltasar) was reputedly black.[11] This was a day of license and role-reversal on which the nations paraded through the streets of Havana, led by their newly elected kings and queens. Participants performed African songs and dances accompanied by drums, scrapers, and hollowed gourd rattles, while wearing elaborate costumes of raffia, peacock feathers, animal skins and horns, and beads. Stilt-walkers, lantern-bearers, masked figures, and gymnasts added to the merriment. Throughout the day, the Africans paraded under balconies or into courtyards requesting *aguinaldos* or gratuity for the entertainment they provided onlookers.[12] Guided by an intricate vocabulary of color, artifacts, and symbols, black and white observers read the cabildo processions for syncretic references to their African deity of choice. For example, Cubans still recognize the patron saint of the Lucumís, Santa Bárbara, as Shangó, the Virgin of Cobre as Ochún, and San Lázaro as Baba-lú-Ayé.[13]

But as Fernando Ortiz put it, "if not the souls of the cabildos, dances were the heart." National groups congregated at the cabildo houses every Sunday and on the numerous other feast days to sing and dance during specified hours, which in theory were not to extend beyond eight in the evening. Members sold food and drink at their well-attended dances and the music and crowds eventually so disturbed the "honored" citizenry of Havana that a 1792 edict gave the cabildos one year to relocate outside the city walls. The same edict ordered cabildos to take the bodies of deceased members to the public mortuary rather than staging celebratory and "disorderly" wakes in their meeting houses. It would seem from

"El Día de los Reyes," by Federico Miahle. This nineteenth-century painting shows African cabildo members in Havana dancing in peacock feather and horn headdresses, raffia hoop skirts, and woven hoods.

the frequency of the pronouncements that early efforts to limit cabildos were no more successful than sumptuary and other sorts of restrictive legislation.[14] While there are no specific references to black cabildos in Florida, other informal associations along tribal, geographic, and kinship lines are noted, and the long-lived religious associations so well documented in Cuba probably had at least an informal Florida counterpart.[15]

The Early Church in Florida

Like the rest of the Caribbean, Florida suffered dramatic Indian depopulation, but the indigenous population was still significant, and Spain devoted great effort to its conversion. Although Jesuit missionaries made little progress in the sixteenth century, the Franciscans who succeeded them founded a string of Indian missions along the southeastern coasts into South Carolina and westward across the panhandle.[16] During this so-called Golden Age of Catholicism in Florida, friars "converted," or at least baptized, thousands of Florida Indians. At the same time the secular clergy, under the direction of the bishop of Cuba, dedicated itself to the spiritual lives of the townspeople of St. Augustine, where most of Florida's small black population lived.[17]

St. Augustine's Catholic church records date back to 1594 and are the oldest extant for what is now the United States. Black Catholics appear scattered throughout these earliest marriage, baptism, and burial registers. The volumes provide evidence about early black families, including in many cases their African "nations," and also document miscegenation among Spaniards, Indians, and blacks in Florida, a pattern that can also be traced in the rest of the Spanish circum-Caribbean. While official Spanish policy discouraged race mixture, it preferred marriage between partners of different races to cohabitation.[18]

Although missionaries described the religious practices of the indigenous populations they worked among, especially the practices they sought to extirpate, such as ball games and polygamy, they recorded hardly anything about African religious practices.[19] It seems likely that in the face of the ever-present official religion, blacks were pragmatically syncretic and blended their own beliefs with those of the Catholic faith.[20]

The Protestant Challenge in the First Spanish Period

As Philip II waged the Counter-Reformation in Spain, Pedro Menéndez de Avilés massacred French Huguenots and eliminated the Protestant faith in Florida. After Barbadians established plantations in Carolina in the 1670s, however, the Anglican church once again challenged Catholic hegemony on the southeastern frontier, and the old religious and territorial struggle for supremacy was rejoined.[21]

Spanish officials in Florida worried not only about the political and military but also the religious consequences of the English Protestant presence. As discussed in chapter 1, by at least 1687, fugitive slaves, who probably had little exposure to Protestantism, began seeking sanctuary among the Spaniards and requesting baptism in the "True Faith," which they claimed their English owners had denied them.[22] Florida's governor, Diego de Quiroga, gave them the refuge they sought, housing the newcomers with local Catholics, who were charged with seeing to their religious instruction. As soon as the priest decided that the catechumens had a basic understanding of the Catholic doctrines, he baptized them and consecrated their marriages in the church. Lest it appear that this system of farming the catechumens out was a disguised form of slavery, it should be noted that in exchange for room, board, and religious training, guardians paid the fugitives the going rate for their work, and white Protestant orphans received the same treatment. Metropolitan officials periodically reminded the Florida governors to be sure that the fugitives were not simulating their religious motivation, nor falling back into old errors, a warning they did not seem to feel the need to issue in reference to white Protestants.[23] Still, at least some blacks obviously considered this arrangement preferable to their former conditions, for new groups of fugitive slaves periodically attempted the same exchange. In 1693 the Crown formally offered religious sanctuary to all slaves fleeing the English enemy and repeated the offer in various later edicts.[24]

This provocative policy further strained Anglo/Spanish relations and heightened conflict on the frontier. As noted in chapter 2, in the early eighteenth century the English and their Indian allies repeatedly raided and effectively destroyed the extensive Franciscan missions, killing and enslaving thousands of Florida's "Christian" Indians.[25] The pitiful remnants of once powerful nations either fled westward or moved closer to St. Augustine, forming refugee villages a stone's throw from the walls of the Castillo. Often recongregated more than once, these villages took on a linguistic and cultural diversity reminiscent of St. Augustine.[26]

The disruption caused by the English raids demoralized Spanish Floridians, and when the auxiliary bishop of Cuba, Francisco de San Buenaventura y Tejada, arrived in the province in 1735, he was horrified by what he felt was the resultant spiritual decadence. For the next ten years, he worked to revive the threatened Catholic faith in Florida and sparked a religious revival of sorts. Buenaventura initiated a daily procession of the rosary through the town, tried to root out "indecent" and "forbidden" games and dances (possibly like those of Cuba?), rebuilt the church, opened a school for the religious instruction of the town's young boys, and confirmed 630 Spaniards and 143 blacks, free and slave.[27]

Of all the challenges facing the church in St. Augustine, the bishop was most concerned about the influence of Protestantism. George Whitefield's tour of the southern colonies in 1740 had "awakened" an evangelical fervor in the region, and Bishop Buenaventura charged that English traders openly preached their Protestant beliefs in the streets of St. Augustine, while conducting commerce forbidden by Spain. Moreover, in Carolina, enthusiastic proselytizers like Hugh and Jonathan Bryan gathered "great Bodies of Negroes" and before them prophesied about the "Destruction of Charles-Town, and deliverance of the Negroes from their Servitude." Coming on the heels of the Stono Rebellion (1739), during which Angolan slaves killed many whites and headed for St. Augustine, such messages were alarming to all slave regimes.[28] Many of the Africans then living in St. Augustine had once lived among the Protestants and, therefore, may have been "infected" by both the religious heresies of Protestantism and by the radical social message of men like Whitefield and the Bryans. This double threat also may have encouraged Governor Manuel de Montiano to establish the African village of "new Christians" at Gracia Real de Santa Teresa de Mose, thereby protecting his frontiers and the purity of the church with one move.

Early Black Catholicism

After the Stono Rebellion South Carolina authorities levied punitive taxes on slaves which in Governor James Glen's words "amounted to a prohibition," and indeed, no slaves were legally imported in 1741, 1742, or 1743. Before long, however, the slave trade to South Carolina resumed with a new intensity.[29] No other colonial city imported more slaves than Charleston, and a vast majority of those slaves were imported directly from Africa. As before, some of the newly arrived Africans learned of the religious sanctuary available in St. Augustine and escaped southward. After Georgia legalized slavery in 1749, enslaved Africans began to enter Savannah, which also received the largest number of slaves transshipped from Charleston, so it is probable that many of the runaways from either of those locations had been born in Africa.[30] In the 1750s Governor Fulgencio García de Solís complained of the "bad customs" and "backwardness" exhibited by blacks from Carolina. Parish priests also noted that some Africans had to receive conditional baptisms "in extremis" because they could not understand the Catholic doctrine or because they had been baptized in their nation and still prayed in their native tongue.[31]

Despite Governor García's concerns about backwardness, black Catholicism flourished in Florida. The black homesteaders who resettled Mose in 1752 built themselves a new chapel that was larger than the church in St. Augustine, as well as a sacristy in which their resident Franciscan priests slept. These priests gave religious instruction and oversaw daily observance of Catholicism at Mose, as they did at nearby Indian villages, but the black residents of Mose also joined the black townspeople of St. Augustine in celebrating their baptisms, marriages, and burials in the parish church, reconfirming their Catholicism with that more public act.[32]

When Great Britain acquired Florida in 1763, black Catholics joined the general exodus to Cuba. Once the Church of England replaced the Catholic church, it is not surprising that Protestantism made inroads among the African slaves whom the English introduced into the colony. Nevertheless, as Daniel L. Schafer has shown, the "Africanization" of Florida continued throughout the British period and with it, most probably, the importation of various African religions.[33] This Africanization was probably heightened at the end of the British period when thousands of Loyalists fled Charleston and Savannah to resettle in East Florida with many more thousands of their slaves, although it is unknown how many of those may have been "country-born."[34] Blacks first established their own Baptist churches in Georgia and South Carolina in the 1770s, and many slaves who entered Florida with Loyalist settlers from those areas may have brought their Protestant faiths with them.[35] A German traveler who visited St. Augustine in 1784 noted that "an association of negroes have a cabin, in which one of their own countrymen, who has set himself up to be their teacher, holds services," and he added that they were of the Anabaptist sect.[36] Nevertheless, despite this countervailing influence and the alleged British repressions of African religious practices, one free African, Jacob Steward, declared on his evacuation from St. Augustine in 1784 that he owned a house where his countrymen practiced "rites in the style of Guinea."[37]

The Catholic Church in the Second Spanish Period

When the Spaniards returned in 1784, they reestablished Catholicism in Florida. From first arrival the Florida clergy struggled to expand their flock, while operating a physically inadequate and underfunded church. The former Catholic chapel had been reduced to a "pile of useless masonry," and Father Thomas Hassett and his congregation had to take up temporary quarters in the house formerly occupied by the Anglican bishop. Although the Crown provided regular subsidies for Florida's church, in large part it was supported from rents of eleven church-owned properties in Havana, three of which were rented to black *cabildos.* So, in addition to their local confraternal activities, the Carabalí nation, the Bambara nation, and the Ganga nation in Cuba contributed to the maintenance of the Florida church.[38]

In 1793 Catholics of all ethnicities and races joined in the effort to construct a new church in St. Augustine, a hopeful sign after a rather poor and unstable beginning. A public display of civic and religious philanthropy at such a time was well noted and appreciated. A prominent planter, Don Francisco Sánchez, donated one hundred pesos toward its construction, and Don Francis Phelipe Fatio and Don Miguel Ysnardy each donated one thousand feet of boards. Other elite whites gave much less. The governor's secretary, Don Carlos Howard, for example, donated six pesos. Given this opportunity to reinforce their membership in the community, free blacks also contributed to the church construction fund. The merchant Juan Bautista Collins donated ten pesos and Juan Bacas donated five pesos, while other free blacks donated smaller sums or contributed in kind.[39] Still others contributed skilled labor over the five-year construction period, and in December, 1797, Father Miguel O'Reilly dedicated St. Augustine's impressive new cathedral.[40]

St. Augustine Cathedral, built in 1790. Courtesy of the St. Augustine Historical Society Collection.

The Catholic church in St. Augustine, as it was throughout the Hispanic world, was a central element in the city, both physically and metaphorically.[41] Occupying a highly trafficked location on the north side of the plaza, across from the governor's quarters, the church was a hub of community activity where parishioners celebrated a wide array of regular and special feast days and the various religious rites of passage. As a deputy of the church, the governor usually staged important civil ceremonies, such as those marking the marriages, deaths, and accessions of monarchs, or the birth of children to the royal household, in front of the church, where more common events, such as plays, were also performed. Officials also posted royal edicts and any other important declarations and news on the church doors, where they would be sure to be seen.[42]

St. Augustine's church was deliberately a colorful and enticing place, attractive to all the senses. Clergy and wealthy members of the congregation decorated it with a wide array of silver candelabra, chalices, incense burners, crosses, bowls and cups, and an ornate silver canopy that sheltered the image of St. Augustine. Less affluent members of the church added flowers and ribbons to the silver objects and altars. At services the governor occupied a special chair in the front of the church, men sat on benches on either side, and women sat on carpets laid on the tabby floor. While the churchgoers appreciated the visual spectacle, they also enjoyed music provided by an organist and singers, which floated down from the gallery above. The scent and smoke of wax candles and incense added drama to the experience that Catholics of all backgrounds enjoyed together.

St. Augustine's second-period church was as polyglot and diverse as the community itself. Fathers Thomas Hassett and Miguel O'Reilly, the pastor and associate pastor of St. Augustine's parish church, were Irish priests educated at the Irish College at Salamanca. Hassett and O'Reilly were assisted by Francisco Troconis and Pedro Camps, the longtime pastor of the Minorcan colony, who alone among them spoke the Minorcan dialect of Catalán.[43] Congregants included Spaniards speaking various regional dialects, Italians, Greeks, Minorcans, English-speakers of various national backgrounds, Africans coming from a wide variety of linguistic, cultural, and religious backgrounds, and even, on occasion, Seminole Indians accompanied by their black slaves.[44]

Catholic Education

Remarking on the special need to educate children in Catholic precepts in a colony populated by so many foreigners, Governor Manuel de Zéspedes enacted a royal order to establish a school for boys in St. Augustine in 1786. The governor required St. Augustine's priests to enumerate all the boys living in town and to visit their parents and explain the importance of educating their children. Fathers Hassett, O'Reilly, and Troconis shared duties teaching the children reading, writing, arithmetic, and Christian doctrine. Black boys could attend the new school, but had to sit next to the door. Despite this attempt at segregation, the governor required the priests to give the black pupils the same spiritual and temporal instruction as white students. The teachers were not to permit any student to call another a name or "remind them of the faults of their fathers," rather all were to be treated alike as faithful Christians with "love and impartial charity." School rules also fostered a corporate identity among the schoolboys, requiring group attendance at such functions as Sunday Mass, religious processions, and the funerals of classmates.[45]

It may not have been easy for blacks to avail themselves of this educational opportunity, even if they lived in town. Although the government assumed the costs of the school, other necessities may have prevented attendance. Not only were children required to be clean and well-groomed but they were to have shined shoes. Father Hassett described the colony in 1788 as "miserable" and "dying" for lack of money, trade, and population, and even poor white parents may not have been able to afford the luxury of withdrawing children from work to attend school.[46] Nevertheless, the only known enrollment list shows that ten years after its inception, the school seemed to be doing well, with eighty-one students attending. Among the students of African descent were Antonio and Mateo Sánchez, the quadroon sons of Don Francisco Xavier Sánchez and his mulatto consort, María Beatrice de Piedra. They joined their half-brothers, Román and Domingo Sánchez, sons of Don Francisco and his white wife, Doña María del Carmen Hill. Attending with the half-brothers was their former slave, who had spent time in both those households, Mariano Ambara, the son of Felipe and Filis Edimboro. Families who had escaped from slavery in the north and availed themselves of religious sanctuary also took advantage of educating their sons. Students with those origins included Antonio Capo, whose father, Antonio, was Guinea-born and whose mother, Ester, was born in Virginia, and Antonio Florencio, the mulatto son of Mariana Bisit, of New York.[47]

Black Religious Activity

In 1788 Fray Cyril de Barcelona, the bishop of Tricaly and auxiliary bishop of Cuba, conducted an ecclesiastical visitation of the recovered colony. In his seventy-one-page report on that visit, Cyril praised the work of Hassett, O'Reilly, and Camps, but he had several concerns about the religious environment in the province. He charged that even the Minorcans, Greeks, and Italians had become lax in their Catholicism as a result of their contact with all the English living in Florida. Although Catholicism was the official religion, Spanish officials permitted Protestant colonists and slaves to practice their faith privately, and many did so. Cyril made great efforts to convert the English and their slaves, but found the English unmotivated. Only ninety-eight English had adopted the Catholic faith by 1789. The bishop attributed this failing to the fact that they could not feel secure in the province until they received some sure title to their lands. The bishop also observed with "great pain" that almost all the slaves, or the majority of all blacks living in the province, lived without the sacrament of baptism, and were thus denied the happiness of being Christians. He conducted a census of the slaves and counted 284 residing in the city and 367 in the countryside, 354 of which belonged to English owners (in the main, Protestants). Cyril reminded Catholic slaveowners that diocesan statutes as well as royal *cédulas* required them to instruct their slaves and have them baptized, and he gave them two months to see to it. Those buying new slaves had six months to comply or suffer the penalty of excommunication and fines of ten ducats. In order to accomplish this goal, the bishop required the clergy to ring the church bells every Sunday to call the slaves to lessons and ordered owners to allow them leisure on Sundays and holy days.[48] However, blacks who lived most of their lives on the outlying plantations of Protestants tended either to remain outside any Christian church or to be Protestants.

When rural slaves testified in court proceedings, as they commonly did, most were sworn on the Holy Bible, "in the name of the Protestant sect which they profess," and they had to use translators, never having learned Spanish.[49]

Conversion and Baptism

Done properly, it took time and effort to convert slaves. Adults could not be baptized until they had successfully passed the priest's examination on the basic tenets of the Catholic church. One eighteenth-century Cuban example of this *doctrina* exam consisted of twenty-six questions with set answers on the nature of the Trinity, creation, immaculate conception, Christ's death and Resurrection, sin, confession, and salvation.[50] The Cuban church oversaw Florida's church, and it is probable that urban slaves in St. Augustine, at least, were instructed on the Cuban model. Just as they did in Havana, leading members of the Catholic community complied with church requirements to have their slaves baptized. Governor Zéspedes set a public example by having four of his slaves baptized, and all later governors and state officials also made sure their slaves were Christians. Military officers such as Artillery Commandant Don Pedro Josef Salcedo and Distinguished Sergeant Don Miguel Marcos de Torres also brought at least some of their slaves into the church, as did St. Augustine's leading merchant, Don Juan Leslie, of the trading firm of Panton, Leslie and Company. One of St. Augustine's foremost planters, Don Francisco Xavier Sánchez, baptized only a few of his slaves, who may have been the favored urban slaves, but he and his brother made sure that their natural children by black and mulatto consorts were baptized. And the church leaders Thomas Hassett, Miguel O'Reilly, Francisco Troconis, and Bishop Cyril himself all baptized each others' slaves. The same slaveowners made sure that slaves living in their households married and did not live in what was commonly referred to as a "scandalous connection."[51]

Despite the bishop's critical report, Fathers Hassett and O'Reilly had made some progress in religious conversions. A five-year summary of the religious activity in the province showed that whites and blacks alike were participating in the church. (See table 2.)

The fact that more black adults than white were converted probably reflects the efforts of fugitives from the United States to secure and protect their freedom. Unlike some whites, the fugitives had no intention of returning to a land of slavery and thus had more to gain by the conversion that guaranteed them sanctuary.

Over the course of the second Spanish regime (1784–1821), priests recorded a total of 1,605 Catholic baptisms in the black parish registers of St. Augustine,

Table 2. Religious Activity in St. Augustine, 1784–89

	Black	White	Total
Conversions	52	46	98
Baptisms	72	227	299
Marriages	2	50	52
Burials	25	73	98

Source: Report of Thomas Hassett, May 20, 1789, To and from the Bishop and Curate, 1786–1824, EFP, microfilm reel 38, PKY.

compared to 2,016 entries in the white registers. They classified almost three-quarters of the individuals baptized as black and the remainder as mulatto, *quarterón,* or *octarón.* The ratio of black to other baptisms approximated that of slave and free baptisms. (See table 3.)

Approximately a third of all baptisms (33.7 percent) took place in the months of April, May, and June, when epidemics were known to have occurred and when the priests would have taken special care to reach the unbaptized, especially the young. Nearly 90 percent of the baptisms were of children under six, who were considered under the "age of reason" and eligible for automatic baptism.[52]

Freedmen and women usually had their children baptized as soon as possible. Prince Paten and Flora Spole had six of their children baptized in the five-year period covered in the bishop's report. In the same period, Juan and Mila Right baptized four children, Antonio and Anna Overstreet baptized five, and Antonio and Ester Capo also baptized five children. Prince and Judy Witten had their children, Glasgow (Francisco Domingo) and Polly (María Rafaela), baptized shortly after presenting themselves to Spanish authorities in 1788, and four years later the parents themselves were baptized.[53]

Blacks who lived within the town limits or nearby no doubt had easier access to the church and whatever comforts, protections, entertainments, or opportunities it offered. But even those living in the countryside were not beyond its reach.

Table 3. Black Baptisms, 1784–1821

Race	Slave	Free	Total	Percentage of All Baptisms
Black	1,008	193	1,201	74.2
Mulatto	190	148	338	21.2
Quarterón	3	33	36	2.3
Octarón	0	16	16	1.0
	1,201 (74.2%)	390 (24.5%)	1,591	98.7

N = 1,605 (827 males; 778 females)

Source: Black Baptisms, CPR, 3 vols., microfilm reel 284 J, PKY. Either race or legal status was not given on fourteen cases.

The clergy made visits to the outlying plantations in times of emergency, such as when epidemics raged. It is doubtful that many rural planters actually transported their slaves into St. Augustine for the religious instruction required by the Cuban synods, and only adults on death's door were baptized without it.

After the celebration of Semana Santa (Holy Week) and Easter in 1790, Father Hassett toured the rugged northern frontier, spending a day at each of the major plantations. Many estates had to be reached by water, and Hassett was accompanied by Antonio Suárez, the owner and pilot of a small launch. Hassett's trip took approximately a month, but he wrote that the effort was very little when compared with "the salvation of so many souls."[54] Hassett registered a total of forty-seven slave children and two free black children receiving "non solemne" baptisms, a classification denoting those not conducted in the church, and in each case he advised the godparents (often members of the planter families or their neighbors) to bring the children in to St. Augustine to be anointed with holy oils and properly baptized as soon as possible. Hassett conducted twenty-four baptisms along the St. Johns River at the plantations of Francis Phelipe Fatio, Hannah Moore, Angus Clarke, Guillermo Barnaby, Guillermo Pengree, and Joseph Mills. On Talbot Island he baptized six more children belonging to Spicer Christopher and Guillermo Henerix. He baptized the same number at the estates of Thomas Crier, Juan Houston, and Juan Bealy on the St. Marys River, and baptized eleven children on the Nassau River plantations of Guillermo Bogen, Ruben Hogan, and Jorge Erron. Before returning to the city, Hassett stopped back at the Fatio estate to baptize one more child.[55] Fatio was the only one of the slaveowners who followed the priest's admonition to have the children properly baptized. Approximately a year and a half after Hassett's visit, Fatio's slaves were all anointed and baptized in St. Augustine's church.[56]

Hassett made another tour in 1793 because measles had spread from St. Augustine out to the countryside and "it would be a great shame to leave so many poor innocents exposed to the fatal consequences of the contagion without the necessary assistance for their eternal salvation."[57] Don Juan McQueen, himself a convert to Catholicism, owned forty-four of the fifty slave children who were baptized during this tour. At McQueen's plantation Hassett baptized twenty-nine black boys, fourteen black girls, and one mulatto girl six years or younger. McQueen eventually had 110 of his enslaved workers baptized—more than any other single planter. St. Augustine's priests made two other visitation tours of the riverside plantations during May of 1794 and June of 1799 and on each occasion conducted more mass baptisms of slave children.[58]

Some slaves moved between plantations and town houses, and in town, if not always in the countryside, they would surely have noticed the dominance of religion in the daily affairs of the Spaniards. They would certainly have become aware that the ex-slaves from North America had gained freedom by conversion and that their children were all baptized. They would have known that even the public school functioned as an agent of religious conversion. They would have recognized the priests as potential advocates whose intervention might assist them in manumission suits.

Felipe Edimboro and his wife, Filis, were such a couple. As slaves of Don Francisco Xavier Sánchez, they probably spent most of their time in the country, but Sánchez sent both of them to live in the city when he required their services there. During one of these sojourns, Filis and Felipe Edimboro had their three-year-old son baptized on the same day that their master and his mulatto consort, María Beatriz Piedra, were baptizing their natural son. María Beatriz often had Felipe and Filis Edimboro in her service and she was godmother to two of their sons, who died shortly after birth. Felipe and Filis Edimboro eventually had ten more children baptized in St. Augustine's church, and in July of 1794, they were themselves baptized and married there. Their baptism and marriage coincided with their suit to buy their freedom, and may have contributed to the successful outcome of the litigation.[59] (See appendix 6.)

Godparentage

Baptism into the Catholic faith served several important functions for black converts. Most important in the view of the priests was the religious function of removing the stain of original sin and bringing the baptized into the brotherhood of the church. Perhaps equally important for black converts, however, was the social function of establishing a system of reciprocal obligations between the *ahijado,* the baptized, and his or her godparents, and between the *compadres,* or parents and godparents. From the earliest days of the Christian church, it had been customary to select sponsors not only for baptisms but for other important religious events such as confirmations and marriages. Godparents or *padrinos* were expected to provide for the spiritual and material care of the child in the event of the parents' death. The act of sponsoring a child at baptism established spiritual paternity of that individual. Such fictive kinship may have had even stronger significance for adult converts, many of whom were uprooted and kinless bozales. Godparents typically gave gifts at the baptism, but more important were the ties that bound the members of the newly linked "family." All parties could expect trust, confidence, respect, and mutual assistance from the relationship.[60]

In Spanish Florida it was common for white planters or members of their families to serve as godparents for their slaves or those of their neighbors. During

Father Hassett's tour of the province in 1790, the elite whites Don Jorge Fleming and Doña María Magdalena Crespel sponsored a dozen of the slaves of Don Francis Phelipe Fatio. When Fatio brought the children into town for proper baptism the next year, Doña María sponsored three more slaves and Fatio, himself, sponsored seven. Doña Sophia Philipina María Fatio later was godmother to three more Fatio slaves. Doña Honoria Cummings y Clarke, Doña Catalina de los Hijuelos, and Doña Isabel Perpal also sponsored slaves that they owned.[61]

When slaves had a choice, they chose godparents of a higher status for their children, who might be expected to help them in some way. This might mean whites, free persons of color, or even slaves who were well connected. The three black males who most often served as godfathers were Luis Almansa, who sponsored forty-one children, Juan Bautista (Prince) Witten, who sponsored twenty-three children, and Felipe Edimboro, who sponsored twenty-one children. All of these men were once slaves but had achieved freedom in St. Augustine—Almansa and Edimboro through litigation and self-purchase and Witten through the religious sanctuary provision. They all were baptized and legally married, and their children were, therefore, legitimate. Witten rose to lieutenant in the black militia and was a hero in the 1812 rebellion, and Edimboro became a sergeant of the militia. Black parents may have considered them good role models, or they may have hoped for more tangible aid for their children. All three men were also born in Guinea, thus retaining African identity within their Catholicism—a fact which may have also made them desirable choices.[62]

Parents may have prized godparents of higher status for their children, but the priest's assistant sponsored more slave children than did the planter class. Church sacristan Lorenzo Capo was the godfather for 102 black children. In such instances of mass service it was unlikely that Capo actually assumed a responsibility for the godchildren, or a relationship with the parents. Despite the probable absence of a close relationship between the sacristan and those he served as a godparent, black parents must have considered the inclusion into the church community important for themselves and for their children.

Black parents also selected certain godmothers more commonly than others. Luis Almansa's legitimate wife, María Belen de Sayas, was a Carabalí slave who became free and served as godmother to thirty-two individuals. María de la Luz Blanco, a black slave from Campeche who was legitimately married to José Rivas, a free mulatto shoemaker from Havana, also became free and sponsored thirty-one persons. Juan Bautista (Prince) Witten's free "country-born" wife, María Rafaela (Judy) Kenty, served as godmother for thirty-one persons. And Josefa Fernández, another Carabalí slave married to a free black from Kingston, was godmother to twenty-four individuals. Josefa Fernández was the only one of these women who did not become free, but as the slave of Father Miguel O'Reilly, she also may have been considered a good role model and was easily available to more parents.[63]

The racial designation of 62 percent of godfathers sponsoring black children can be determined and of the 1,009 cases nearly 35 percent of the sponsors were white, slightly over 20 percent were black, and almost another 6 percent were identified as mulatto. Over 63 percent of the godfathers were free. Parents did not appear to place the same premium on white or free godmothers. Thirty-two percent of the godmothers were black, slightly more than 20 percent were white, and a little over 6 percent were mulattoes. Only about half of the godmothers enjoyed free status. (See table 4.) In his analysis of chapel registers for the Engenho Sergipe in Brazil, Stuart B. Schwartz finds a similar pattern of endogamy in godparent selection. Schwartz argues that while a white godfather offered potentially more protection and aid for the child, should the biological mother die, parents wanted a surrogate mother from the same racial category.[64]

Marriage

Although vertical ties may have been the goal in godparentage choices, it seems that horizontal ties also served to reinforce links among black members of the community. This pattern is most visible in the marriages of free blacks, whose lives were more fully documented by the Spaniards.

Many compadrazgo links connected the two large families of Don Francisco Xavier Sánchez, the first of which was created with his mulatto consort, María Beatriz Piedra, and the second with his white wife, María del Carmen Hill. (See appendix 7.) These links publicly confirmed the amicable relations between the families and strengthened the social positions of the natural children of color. When Don Francisco died intestate, his legal widow, Doña María del Carmen, protected the inheritance of his mixed-race children, as their father had wished.[65]

Table 4. Godparents at Black Baptisms, 1784–1821

	Race			Status	
	White	Black	Mulatto[a]	Free	Slave
Godfathers	563 (34.8%)	345 (21.3%)	101 (6.2%)	1,024 (63.2%)	199 (12.3%)
Godmothers	335 (20.7%)	518 (32.0%)	104 (6.4%)	799 (49.4%)	332 (20.5%)

Source: Black Baptisms, CPR, 3 vols., microfilm reel 284 J, PKY.

a. Includes *quarteróns,* with one mulatto and one white parent, and *octaróns,* with one *quarterón* and one white parent. Data on race and/or legal status is missing in some cases.

While the bishop's inspection tour of Florida may have encouraged black baptisms, it seems to have had little effect on black marriage rates. Only fifty-one black couples registered legal marriages during the second Spanish regime.[66] The church exempted blacks from paying for church sacraments on the grounds of their poverty, so financial considerations do not seem to have affected this pattern. However, the fact that more blacks lived as slaves in the countryside and only had occasional access to priests may account for the lower number of black church ceremonies of all kinds—baptisms, marriages, and burials.[67]

Perhaps because of the logistical difficulties, many couples, free or slave, simply lived in long-term stable unions. Concubinage and illegitimacy did not carry the disadvantages in this frontier society that they may have elsewhere, but studies of Spanish capitals such as Mexico show that marriage was not the norm for any racial group, even in urban settings.[68] Even if men did not marry the mothers of their children, they frequently recognized the children at baptisms and in their wills, and the illegitimate status of the children did not normally interfere with their inheritance. Nor did illegitimacy in itself hinder employment or educational opportunities, such as they were. Spaniards and blacks living in Spanish communities appear to have valued membership in the church more than legitimacy. It does appear, however, that some owners felt an obligation to see that their slaves were married, as required by the church, and that the free blacks who married had social or legal reasons for doing so. A church marriage conveyed respectability and status, and would have been expected of leaders of the free black community, as it was of important whites.[69]

Black Catholic marriages were celebrated in the same manner as those of whites. The priests posted and read the bans at three consecutive high Masses to notify the community of the couple's intention to wed. Because the sacrament of marriage was based upon the mutual consent of the partners, the couples had to affirm that they were entering into the institution voluntarily. If both partners had been baptized, and no impediments existed, the church ceremony could proceed. Unfortunately, we have no descriptions of festivities that also may have been celebrated in the homes of the individuals marrying, although it is likely that black Catholics, like others in the community, would have observed this practice.

Two witnesses or sponsors usually attended the bridal couple, but in some instances a single witness served. As was true for baptisms, certain sponsors appear more frequently than others. Luis Almansa and his wife María de Belen served as witnesses for eleven of the fifty-one marriages, and in nine of those cases, at least one spouse was African-born, as Luis and María were.[70] José Rivas and María de la Luz Blanco sponsored four couples, and María de la Luz served without her husband at two other ceremonies.[71]

Whites also served as witnesses at the marriages of blacks and mulattoes. When the natural quadroon daughter of Don José Sánchez married another free mulatto, her paternal uncle, Don Francisco Xavier Sánchez, and her father's wife, Doña Christina Hill, were her sponsors. Don Manuel Solana and Doña María Mestre served as witnesses at the marriage of the mulatto merchant Juan Bautista Collins and María de la Concepción Tunno, the quadroon daughter of Dr. Tomás Travers. After Josefa Fernández died, the widowed Juan Mayes married the slave Ana Saunders, and the marriage witnesses were Ana's owner, Doña Ana Saunders and Don Santos Rodriguez.[72]

Within the small number of recorded black marriages, some patterns may be discerned. More than 90 percent of the individuals married persons of the same race, and almost 87 percent married persons of the same legal status. Twenty-nine slave couples and fifteen free couples wed, while six slave brides married free men, and at least three of these women later became free. Only one free woman married a slave. The choice of spouses, like that of godmothers, shows a clear pattern of endogamy. (See table 5.)

The church insisted that married couples, free or enslaved, had the right to a conjugal life, but it did not argue that all persons had a right to wed. In order for slaves to marry they had to secure their owner's permission, and if the partners lived in separate locations, both owners had to agree. Don Francisco Xavier Sánchez no doubt regretted allowing his slave, Francisco, to marry the slave Catalina, who belonged to St. Augustine's military commander, Bartolomé Morales. When Morales was about to be shipped back to Havana in 1802, two years after the marriage, Francisco filed a petition asking the governor's tribunal

Table 5. Characteristics of Black Marriages, 1784–1821

	Race		Legal Status		Birthplace	
	Black	Mulatto	Free	Slave	Africa	St. Augustine
Grooms	39 (76.5%)	11 (21.6%)	21 (41.2%)	30 (58.8%)	17 (33.4%)	15 (15.7%)
Brides	42 (82.4%)	8 (15.7%)	16 (31.4%)	35 (68.6%)	16 (31.4%)	13 (25.5%)

Both partners black = 39 (76.5%)
Both partners mulatto = 7 (13.7%)
Black brides married to mulatto grooms = 3 (5.9%)
Both partners free = 15 (29.4%)
Both partners slave = 29 (56.9%)
Slave bride/free groom = 6 (11.8%)
Free bride/slave groom = 1 (2%)

Source: Black Marriages, CPR, microfilm reel 284 L, PKY.

to require Sánchez to sell him to Morales so that the slave couple would not be separated. In his petition he argued: "uniting a family has always been the most equitable maxim practiced by states in which slavery exists. This custom has always been followed in this [province] and as it does not contravene the principles of *derecho* [what is just] it appears to have taken the force of *ley* [law]."[73]

Morales had already bought the couple's young daughter and agreed to buy Francisco for five hundred pesos. The commandant filed a petition supporting Francisco's request and also argued that Sánchez should not be allowed to "dissolve forever a marriage authorized and performed according to the rites of our Sainted Mother the Catholic Church whose religion the supplicant and his wife both profess."

The tribunal began its deliberations and solicited statements from all the parties. Sánchez claimed that Morales was the author of a plot to defraud him of his valuable mason and offered, instead, to buy Catalina, but she refused to be sold to him. According to Morales, Catalina objected to the corn diet that Sánchez fed his slaves, the hard work he expected of his field hands, and the fact that Sánchez took all of her husband's jornales (wages earned on his own time). The parish priest also gave a statement and reiterated that "one of the obligations of marriage is cohabitation" and that if slaves were deprived of that through separations, there would be "bad spiritual consequences." After Sánchez stalled, Morales filed another petition on the couple's behalf, and finally, was able to use public humiliation to shame Sánchez into the sale. Francisco, Catalina, and their daughter sailed to Havana together.[74] Owners might impede, or attempt to impede, marriages of their slaves, but if slaves managed to appeal to the ecclesiastical courts, they found, in the words of Frederick P. Bowser, "a consistent champion."[75]

Although it was technically forbidden, the community recognized cohabitation among slaves and generally tried to keep families united, but only a legal marriage could guarantee that couples would stay together. When Moses Travers's owner, Don Tomás Travers, died, Pablo Sabate bought Moses from the estate, but Moses's wife and daughter remained the property of the widow. Moses convinced Sabate to buy his family "so that they could live together because they never wanted to be separated," but the widow stated she would agree to the sale only reluctantly and only if ordered to do so by the governor's tribunal. Before the hearing could proceed, the widow moved Moses's wife and daughter to the countryside and planned to remove them from the province. Moses asked the court's intervention to prevent the separation, and Governor Enrique White issued an immediate order to that effect. In earlier times, official efforts to maintain harmony and traditional community support for slave families would have probably worked in Moses's favor. However, when the widow's lawyer argued that no legal matrimony had ever been celebrated and that the law in such cases favored the property owner, White suspended his original order and imposed "perpetual silence on the matter." He added that if any other slaves asked the tribunal to protect their unapproved cohabitation they would be severely punished. He had obviously been embarrassed by this incident, which must have had a chilling effect on any future attempts by unmarried slaves to appeal to the court. The Anglo emphasis on property rights was beginning to supersede more traditional and flexible Spanish interpretations of "family."[76]

Legal marriage not only served to protect slaves and convey respectability on free blacks, it was yet another mechanism for strengthening ties within the black community.[77] Parish registers from St. Augustine show that free militia families commonly intermarried and served as marriage sponsors and godparents for one another. Once again the large Edimboro family can be illustrative. Felipe and Filis Edimboro's daughter, Nicolasa, married Benjamín Wiggins, the free mulatto son of Don Joseph (Job) Wiggins and a member of the black militia to which three of the Edimboro men also belonged. When Nicolasa and Benjamín had a son, his maternal grandparents, Felipe and Filis Edimboro, served as baptismal sponsors. Four years later, when Nicolasa Edimboro had a child fathered by Don Francisco Díaz, elite whites sponsored the child.[78] Three other Edimboro children, Eusebia, Isabel, and Antonio, had children without benefit of marriage. Eusebia Edimboro and the free black Antonio Proctor, an Indian translator for the military, had a son, for whom the paternal uncle and aunt served as godparents.[79] Isabel Edimboro's son was fathered by Pedro Casali, a free mulatto shoemaker who was the half-brother of her sister's husband, Benjamín Wiggins. Casali was also a member of the black militia and another of its members, Fermín Fernández, was their child's godfather.[80] Antonio Edimboro and the free black Isabel Bacas had a daughter, for whom María Belen was godmother. Isabel's father and brother served with Antonio Edimboro in the free black militia.[81]

Within the black militia, the choice of marriage and baptismal sponsors seemed to follow geographic lines, and this pattern may have held true in the larger black population. The ex-slaves who availed themselves of religious sanctuary often selected religious sponsors from their place of origin. Juan Bautista Witten, his wife María Rafaela, and their children were frequent choices as godparents for ex-slaves from South Carolina and Georgia, such as Estévan Cheves, Bacas Camel, Andrés Camel, and Sayrus Thompson, all members of the black militia. Juan Bautista and María Rafaela were also baptismal sponsors for slaves from these areas, including the child of their own slave.[82]

In 1796, members of the disbanded Black Auxiliaries of Charles IV from Santo Domingo were exiled with their families to Florida. Despite major differences in language and culture, the Dominican blacks quickly blended into St. Augustine's free black community.[83] Within four months of the auxiliaries' arrival in Florida, Jorge Jacobo, the brother-in-law and military heir to Jorge Biassou, married Rafaela (formerly Polly) Witten, the daughter of Juan Bautista Witten, the acknowledged military leader among the free blacks from North America.[84] Their wedding in the cathedral joined the two leading free black families of St. Augustine and must have been well attended by members of the black community. Either this was a whirlwind romance or it may have been an effort by the Dominican and American groups to combine forces and consolidate status. Rafaela's brother, Francisco (formerly Glasgow) Witten, and Jorge's sister and Biassou's wife, Romana Jacobo, were the couple's marriage sponsors, and they also became the godparents to the couple's children. Jorge's sister, Barbara (Gran Pres) Jacobo, and his mother, Ana Gran Pres, also served as godmothers for several of the couple's children.[85] When, two years later, Juan Bautista (Prince) Witten formally married María Rafaela (Judy) Kenty, after a union of twenty-one years, Felipe Edimboro and Romana Jacobo served as sponsors, and the following year they were also sponsors at the marriage of Francisco Witten, the couple's son.[86] (See appendix 8.) The overlapping relationships and creation of extended fictive families among blacks can be traced up to the evacuation of Florida and may well have continued thereafter in Cuba.

If there was a difference in the race or legal status of the betrothed, or if there might be any opposition to a marriage, regulations required the couple to solicit a marriage license from a tribunal that included the governor, a notary, and, in cases involving military men, the auditor of war. Of 144 licenses requested between 1786 and 1803, only seven involved mixed-race marriages. When José Rivas, a free mulatto shoemaker, requested permission to marry the black slave María de la Luz, he sought official approval. Rivas's aunt had no objections, María's owner stated that he was "very pleased about the marriage," and the tribunal approved the marriage. When the white Indian interpreter Antonio Huertas wanted to marry Rivas's aunt the following year, he asked for, and was also granted, a license.

Most of the cases involved simple inquiries into the background of the couple. Acquaintances testified about what they knew of the racial and class origins of the individuals, and if no objections were presented, the governor granted permission to marry.[87] When white Spaniards sought to marry the three quadroon daughters of Don Francisco Xavier Sánchez, the declarations were more detailed. In 1795 Francisco Pérez, a practitioner in the royal hospital, petitioned to wed Beatriz Sánchez. Pérez was from Castile, but as he himself stated, he "did not enjoy such sublime exemptions that the marriage could be criticized, for his parents were humble, although Spaniards." Pérez had promised to wed Beatriz and reminded the governor that "one of the strictest precepts of the church was to keep a promise to a maiden and guard her honor, to avoid the gossip of the town."[88] Although he acknowledged that Beatriz was a bastard, Pérez asked the tribunal to declare her "free of the stain of a vile race as she was very light and no one would suspect her origins." Further, he argued that when an *hidalgo* in Spain fathered a child by a common woman, the child enjoyed the status of the father. St. Augustine's tribunal referred this case to an ecclesiastical tribunal, which must have approved, for the couple wed.[89]

Within a week a Spanish sailor, José Manuel Fernández, asked to marry another of Sánchez's daughters, Ana. Fernández was from Galicia and had no relatives present to object to the marriage. Sánchez led off the proceedings by declaring his permission for his daughter to marry Fernández. Three of Fernández's fellow crew members from the *San Pablo* next attested to his character, and the governor's tribunal approved the marriage license.[90]

Seven years later Francisco Sánchez, a Spanish soldier from Granada, asked to marry Catalina, another of Sánchez's natural daughters. Three Spaniards of the Third Battalion of Cuba testified that they had known Francisco for many years and that he was honorable and honest. They also testified that Catalina was "honest, modest, and of good heritage," and once again the wedding proceeded.[91] The marriages of Sánchez's daughters do not appear in the register of black marriages, and because the women were apparently so light-skinned, had wed Spaniards, enjoyed the recognition of their wealthy and influential father and, if witnesses are to be believed, of the townspeople as well, they apparently were accepted as white.[92] However, the subsequent baptisms of their children, who were even further "whitened," were recorded in the black registers, as was the marriage of Don Francisco's quadroon son, José, to Lucía Ysnardy, the quadroon daughter of St. Augustine's official interpreter.[93] This changing and more rigid perception of race may reflect the growing influence of Anglo/southerners in the province.

Burials

While marriage and baptismal records are rich sources of black history in Spanish Florida, the black burial records for the second Spanish period are disappointing.[94] Florida's clergy recorded very few church burials for black Catholics—only 221 for the entire second Spanish period (1784–1821). It is obvious that not all black Catholics received church burials, but problems of record-keeping in years of recurrent crisis also must have affected this pattern. The first burial was not recorded until 1785, and none were recorded for the years 1794–95 and 1810–11, or if they were recorded, the books have been lost.[95] During the 1795 rebellion, the fierce Indian attacks of the early 1800s, and the Patriot Rebellion of 1812, ecclesiastical tours of the outlying areas were impossible, and many blacks may have died without benefit of any church sacraments.

Florida's priests made every effort to attend the dying and, if time permitted, the priest would baptize those in need, hear their confession, and give them last rites. In emergencies lay persons, such as an attending midwife, could also baptize a dying person. Few of the black burial entries give cause of death, but frequent references to rapid demise might reflect epidemic catastrophes. Three persons drowned, including two slave children whose mother Juana jumped with them into a well and one woman who died during a river crossing. One man was found hanged under unexplained circumstances, and another, as described in chapter 8, was executed by hanging for an axe murder. Before the executioner carried out Tomás's sentence, a priest baptized the twenty-nine-year-old slave, who confessed and received communion. The lay brothers of the Misericordia consoled the condemned in prison, helped him make his confession, prayed for his soul, and escorted him to the gallows where he was dressed in confraternal robes (symbolically making him a brother). The confraternity later lowered Tomás's body and buried him the following day in the church cemetery, redeemed by his conversion.[96] Between 1812 and 1819, sixteen soldiers of the Companies of Pardos and Morenos of Havana were killed in action in Florida and members of their military corporation escorted them to their graves in St. Augustine.[97]

Florida's tropical climate required prompt interments, and urban black Catholics were usually buried the day after they died at the Tolomato cemetery on the edge of town. Officials reserved one-quarter of this church graveyard for blacks at a cost of three pesos for a plot, but burial was free to "paupers without a casket."[98] Not all of Florida's black Catholics were buried in the Tolomato graveyard, however. Some were buried at battle sites or on the rural plantations where they died. Slaves professing Protestant beliefs (which included most of the plantation slaves) could not be buried in holy ground and were, instead, usually interred in plantation graveyards. Although a number of his slaves were baptized Catholics, Don Francis Phelipe Fatio also demarcated a cemetery area on his impressive Nueva Suiza (New Switzerland) plantation for Protestant slaves. Fatio's Protestant burial ground was said to be located on the "banks" ("a la orilla") of the St. Johns River.[99]

It is interesting to speculate if, in those areas remote from Catholic influence, blacks also may have practiced other forms of honoring their dead, especially on plantations owned or operated by African-born persons. Among West Africans, burial had great importance as a ritual designed to placate the spirit of the departed, who in turn would guard the interests of surviving family members. Throughout the eighteenth century, repeated waves of West and Central Africans entered Florida via Charleston or Savannah. The coastal Atlantic from South Carolina, through Georgia, to St. Augustine came to form a fairly similar demographic niche that was heavily African. Many rich ethnographic studies of the Africans of coastal Carolina and Georgia (the Gullah and Geechee) describe customs, traditions, and even linguistic remnants that were carried to new settlements in Florida (and later to Oklahoma, Texas, and Mexico).[100] Photographers and writers from the Works Projects Administration, historians such as Peter H. Wood, Daniel C. Littlefield, Charles Joyner, anthropologists and folklorists such as Patricia Jones-Jackson and Zora Neale Hurston, art historian Robert Farris Thompson, and linguistic scholars such as Lorenzo Dow Turner, Ian Hancock, and others, all document common traditions practiced throughout that African littoral, many of which focus on death.[101] Along that Atlantic coast (as in the Caribbean), blacks often decorated graves with the last objects touched by the deceased, in the manner of the Congo. Sometimes the bereaved placed symbolic objects such as a white chicken, seashells, lamps or bottles, or even the skull of a bottle-nosed dolphin on the grave, or planted a tree at the head. Some graves had anthropomorphic wooden cutouts at foot and head, while other graves were

Some modern graves in the black section of the Bosque Bello cemetery at Fernandina on Amelia Island are still outlined with white conch shells or are decorated with white conch shells and white porcelain chickens. Photograph by the author.

marked with tall wooden sculptures. Modern graves in the black section of the old cemetery at Fernandina are still decorated with white conch shells and white porcelain chickens. Until plantation archaeology has been conducted in Florida, we will not know if African grave goods accompanied the dead, or if the dead were buried in cemeteries or under house floors, and unfortunately, many sites may have already been lost.[102]

Blacks may have observed other non-Catholic rites in private in Spanish Florida. Building on the work of Allan D. Austin, Michael A. Gomez has documented a small but influential group of enslaved Muslims living in the coastal plantations of colonial and antebellum South Carolina and Georgia. However, given the mutual antipathy between Catholics and Muslims, it would seem unlikely any of the faithful would have entered Florida.[103] Although the deathbed confession of General Jorge Biassou indicates that he died a Catholic, no record of his baptism or, for that matter, the baptismal records of any of the adult members of his party from Santo Domingo can be found. We must assume that at least Juan Luis Menar, Plácido Asil, and Jorge Jacobo, all of whom were officially married in the Catholic church, must have received baptism and been received into the church prior to those ceremonies. But the others from Santo Domingo were not to be found among the baptized, and Biassou's extended "family" of some thirty individuals had certainly been exposed to yet another competing religious system, *vodun.* Historians of Haiti often repeat Thomas Madiou's lurid description of Biassou's war tent "filled with kittens of all shades, with snakes, with dead men's bones and other African fetishes. At night huge campfires were lit with naked women dancing horrible dances around them, chanting words understood only on the coast of Africa. When the excitement reached its climax, Biassou would appear with his *boccors* [religious specialists] to proclaim in the name of God that every slave killed in battle would re-awaken in his homeland of Africa."[104]

Whether or not such a scene ever took place, the contemporary suspicion was that all participants in Saint Domingue's slave revolt were primitive and dangerous, by virtue of their war conduct as well as by their religious practice, and planters throughout the circum-Caribbean feared their influence as a plague.[105] Given the atmosphere, it is not surprising that no overt practice of *vodun* was recorded in Spanish Florida, or that Biassou and others of his troop, who had cast their political lot with the Spaniards, saw the wisdom in observing at least a syncretic Catholicism. An examination of Biassou's accounts conducted at his death showed that he had borrowed money to be able to properly observe Catholic religious celebrations such as the Day of Kings (Epiphany, January 6).[106] As John Thornton and others have pointed out, hosting entertainments and redistributing wealth were a way an aspirant might attain noble status in some African societies. Biassou's patronage of events such as the Day of Kings no doubt reinforced his position as the most important figure in the black community.[107] Given earlier allegations about Biassou's practice of *vodun,* this celebration may have been observed for its African, rather than Catholic, significance. In the 1790s, when Biassou's entourage had left for Florida, the adult slave population of Saint Domingue was 60–70 percent African-born and a majority of the slaves had arrived within the previous ten years from the lower Guinea coast or the coast of Angola.[108]

When Biassou died in July of 1801, his bereaved family and followers arranged a wake, and the following day he was buried with full honors. After Mass, which included songs, tolling bells, candles, and burning incense, Governor Enrique White and other persons of distinction in the community accompanied Biassou's cortege to the graveyard. Drummers and an honor guard of twenty members of the black militia completed the procession, and these troops discharged a volley at the gravesite. The obligations of military corporatism outweighed any racial distinctions in this ceremony, the public notary attesting that "every effort was made to accord him the decency due an officer Spain had recognized for military heroism."[109]

Such public ceremonies were much appreciated in St. Augustine. Festivities marked royal weddings and births and the inaugurations of new governors. Plays, military and religious processions, balls, and visits by Indian delegations all were occasions of enthusiastic and general participation. But Biassou's elaborate burial, carefully staged to honor Florida's only black *caudillo,* was something new for St. Augustine. Despite rumors about Biassou's bloody past and his heretical religious practices in Santo Domingo, in his last years he apparently became a Catholic and, as such, he deserved and received a full Catholic burial.

Black Evangelicalism

As Catholic outreach declined, and as more Anglos entered the province during the 1800s, black evangelicals seem to have gathered a following among outlying plantations, and the numbers of slaves practicing some variant of Protestantism grew. Once again, the traditional Catholic paranoia was activated by the dual threat of heresy and subversion. In 1815 anxious authorities investigated the free black cooper and militia member Antonio Williams for preaching Methodism among the slaves on plantations south of St. Augustine in the Mosquitos region. Planters who testified said that Williams's teachings incited slaves to disobedience and prompted many of them to run away to the Indian nations. Williams denied the allegations against him and attributed the preaching to another Antonio, a slave belonging to Don Juan Bunch. Williams confirmed that both he and the other Antonio were Anabaptists but said that the other Antonio only exhorted slaves to be "faithful to their owners and serve them with love." Antonio Williams had lived for thirteen years in the Mosquito region, making fishing canoes and other useful items for sale and serving in the militia when called. This history somewhat protected him, for the court ruled that there was insufficient proof for a formal process against him. Nonetheless, the court ordered Williams to leave the province for good. It also ordered the owner of the other Antonio to sell him out of the province. The court intended both expulsions to "warn of the bad results of this sect."[110]

Even planters of known toleration, such as Zephaniah Kingsley, were fearful of evangelical Protestants. After Indians killed or stole away many of his slaves in the 1812 invasion, however, Kingsley had to purchase new slaves and "a man, calling himself, a minister, got among them. It was now sinful to dance, work their corn or catch fish, on a Sunday; or to eat cat fish, because they had no scales; and if they did they were to go to a place where they would be tormented with fire and brimstone for all eternity."[111]

Kingsley said that the new slaves formed "private societies under church regulations, where all were brothers and sisters," that had night meetings several times a week, "with an abundance of preaching and praying (for they all exhorted, men as well as women) with an ample entertainment from my hogs, as it was no sin to steal for the church." Kingsley despaired that neither he nor his overseer, nor severity, made any difference and all order broke down. He also described a change for the worse in the slaves' material conditions with the advent of this "hurtful tendency of superstition (by some called religion) among negroes." Kingsley described the slaves as become "poor, ragged, hungry and disconsolate," hoping for death, and he believed that "in some instances, sick children were allowed to die, because the parents thought conscientiously that it was meritorious to transfer their offspring from a miserable and wicked world to a happy country, where they were in hopes of soon joining them!"[112]

Such religiously induced despair and disorder could lead to more severe trouble, Kingsley felt, for he also connected the slave insurrections in Barbados and Demerara to "influential preachers of the gospel."[113] Having been present during the slave revolt in Saint Domingue, Kingsley had firsthand evidence of the potentially dangerous connection between religion and rebellion.

The Final Years

The combination of official support and sponsorship of black Catholicism and growing antagonism toward evangelical black Protestants was marked in Spain's last turbulent years in Florida. In St. Augustine black Catholics continued to celebrate a full liturgical calendar of religious observances, attended school, and were baptized, married, and buried in the Catholic church. In all these events, they reiterated their ties to each other and to the Spanish community. When the Adams-Onís treaty ceded Florida to the United States of America in 1819, Florida blacks, free and enslaved, faced great changes. In anticipation of the political transition, free blacks solicited legal titles to their lands and properties, documented their manumissions, and made sure that their Catholic baptisms and marriages were recorded in parish registers.[114]

Slaves also tried to secure their lives by seeking changes of owners if necessary, or by appealing to authorities not to be separated from kin. Sometimes slaves asked specifically not to be sold to Protestant owners, a request that might have been based on true religious considerations or that could have been motivated by the pragmatic desire not to be left to the mercy of the incoming system. Although both the Catholic and Protestant faiths sanctioned slavery, the former permitted more frequent and open African cultural expression throughout the circum-Caribbean. Black Catholic marriages, baptisms, and burials received the full support of the church and the community, and the custom of marriage and baptismal sponsors was a useful mechanism for linking the black community horizontally to important patrons. Catholicism also offered significant tangible rewards, such as educational opportunities for free blacks and legal protections of their family lives for married slave couples. Few, if any, of these advantages accrued to black Protestants in the United States, nor would they in its new territory of Florida.

The Lives of Black Women

The Comparative Context

Women of African descent have long been depicted as doubly "victimized" by their race and gender and "without voice" in the Anglo South where, if enslaved, they were legally oppressed as well.[1] However, across the linguistic, political, and cultural divide that separated Florida from its northern neighbors, black women, whether free or enslaved, acquired a legal personality and social opportunities significantly better than those of their counterparts in Anglo settlements.[2] This is not to suggest an absence of racial prejudice in Florida or other Spanish settlements or to minimize the often horrific conditions of Hispanic slavery; however, black women in Spanish Florida made active use of the Spanish legal, religious, and social systems to ameliorate their conditions and achieve a variety of goals.

Free women reported their needs, complained against neighbors, asked for land grants, pensions, licenses, and passports, posted bonds, mortgaged, bought and sold properties, assumed debt, and stated their dying wishes in testaments. Enslaved women also appealed frequently to the Spanish civil and religious authorities and made their voices heard. They reported or responded to complaints, negotiated to change owners or to improve their enslaved conditions, and petitioned for freedom. In some cases they even sued their owners for restoration of property or to achieve another end.[3] Their verbatim testimony appears in a wide range of records of daily life, allowing a sense of the creativity of these women, even within a patriarchal and conservative society such as Spanish St. Augustine.[4]

Spanish Constructions of Gender

Spaniards constructed particular political and social identities for women that drew on a variety of sources, including Roman and Visigothic law, Aristotelian philosophy, Catholic theology, and centuries of customary law and practice in a racially and ethnically diverse metropolis.[5] Castile's thirteenth-century legal code, the Siete Partidas, classified women along with children, invalids, and delinquents as in need of supervision but also deserving of familial and societal protection. Such juridical categorization obviously limited, at least temporarily, a woman's legal autonomy and economic power. A woman in Spanish society was subject to the will of her father or brothers until they died or until she reached twenty-five years of age or married.[6]

Behavioral prescriptions and normative rules also circumscribed women in Spanish society. Spanish prescriptive literature which blamed Eve for man's fall from grace shared much with that of the rest of early modern Europe. In a famous Spanish example women were described as "the limbs of Satan, the fountainhead of sin, and the destroyers of Paradise."[7] As a corrective for their inherent weaknesses, women were encouraged to emulate the chaste, passive, and long-suffering mother of Christ, a standard against which most women would be deviant. It was even more difficult for dark-skinned women to approach this standard since another Spanish stereotype, a remnant from Spain's Muslim rule, emphasized their sensuality.[8] Women in Spanish communities were constrained in many ways, but because their social and legal status was lower than that of men, women could sometimes use the images of gender weakness and motherhood for their own benefit.[9]

Paradoxically, women also enjoyed specific protections based in the same medieval Spanish law and customs which limited them. For example, women could inherit, hold, and disperse property left to them by either parent, including real property, and it could not be seized for the debt of their husbands. Moreover, by law, women and men inherited equally from their parents, except in very notable exceptions. A husband could not alienate the dowry or *arras* (the groom's marriage gift) of his wife, and upon the husband's death, the widow was also eligible for one-half of the *bienes gananciales,* or monies earned jointly over the course of the marriage. With her husband's written license or power of attorney, a woman could, and did, enter into a wide variety of legal transactions, and women could also testify in secular courts and seek redress for grievances.[10]

As already noted, Spanish law and custom also guaranteed slaves a legal personality and voice. In theory, slave women had rights to personal security and legal mechanisms by which to escape a cruel master, conjugal rights and the right not to be separated from children, and the right to hold and transfer property and initiate legal suits.[11] Castilian legal institutions and customs were transferred to the Americas, where they underwent some modifications, codified as the Recopilación de Leyes de los Reynos de Las Indias, but their core principles remained remarkably durable. One of the most basic principles was the right to *buen gobierno,* or good government and justice within the vast Spanish empire, which required access to the courts or a voice for all vassals, including women and slaves.[12]

Black Women Litigants in Spanish Florida

Women of all ethnicities, backgrounds, and legal conditions, including free and enslaved women of African descent, took advantage of their access to law in Spanish Florida. The clearly understood significance of law in Spanish society, the intimate nature of the tribunal, which consisted of the governor, his legal counsel, and the royal notary, and the small size and interrelatedness of the community may have minimized petitioners' fears about approaching the court. When they did so, they followed long-established formulae of procedures and behaviors. Whether male or female, they usually identified themselves by name, race, and legal condition and opened with phrases such as, "with all due respect" or "with the utmost submission." The memorialist then specified the complaint, charge, or request as well as the action they wished the court to take. Petitions typically closed with a phrase such as "humbly trusting in the merciful charity and noted wisdom of the justice administered by Your Excellency." Although by modern standards the language might sound obsequious, in its own time, such flowery and flattering phrases were considered a mark of civility and, in that context, graceful language might conceivably improve the outcome of a petition.

Although men and women employed the same formulaic openings and closings, women and slaves might also include within their memorials and petitions references to their weakness, poverty, or lack of other sources of assistance in order to elicit the proper sympathetic responses from the court. In a community which operated within the idiom of family, women frequently referred to themselves as mothers and made references to their children. If they were sick, widowed, or abandoned, they made sure to mention it. The court was, then, held accountable for the same acts of charity and justice that a patriarch would be expected to render to family members or those of the "miserable classes."[13]

If the women who approached the court were illiterate, as they often were, they could use the services of a friend or of the government notary. In those cases, the women's "Xs" would be accompanied by the signature of the person assisting and by the notation "at the request of——— who cannot write." But literate women of all races and ethnicities wrote and signed many of their own memorials and petitions. Women sometimes required the assistance of translators when they produced texts, and this fact, too, was duly noted in the documents. Many women in colonial Florida, however, were multilingual, especially women of African descent.

Black Women Become Free

Just as they learned new languages, women of African descent learned to manipulate Spanish law, customs, and gender conventions to their advantage. Due to Spanish custom and law, and to the particular economic and political circumstances of Spanish Florida, a greater percentage of women of African descent became free in that colony than in the Anglo colonies to the north. Until 1790, hundreds of women became free in Florida by the provisions of Spain's religious sanctuary policy, and their children were, then, born free.[14] As in other areas of the circum-Caribbean, Spanish law and custom permitted slave women to hire out their own time, to manage their own property and economy, and even to seek more beneficent owners who would agree to purchase them.[15] Enslaved women could also purchase themselves or family members through the institution of *coartación* or gain their freedom or that of their children through uncompensated manumission, which sometimes, but not always, involved a sexual relationship with their owners.[16] Don Tomás Tunno freed his slave, Catarina Cecilia, and her young daughters, Cecilia Francisca, age three, and Catalina Joaquina, age one, without acknowledging paternity. This relationship can be determined, however, from the children's baptismal records, where he was listed as their father.[17] Although men like Tunno may not have married the mothers of their children, they usually took parental responsibilities more seriously. As seen below, Tunno also provided a sizeable dowry for another of his natural daughters. Don Guillermo Johnston also freed his mulatto slave, Mary Beard, and her seven children, which were probably also his, acknowledging Mary's "good services and other circumstances." Two of the boys were adolescents so this family group represented a considerable property. It was 1818 and Johnston must have feared that his Anglo family or Anglo law might someday threaten Mary and the children. To prevent that possibility, he included in their manumission document a provision that neither he nor any of his heirs could ever reclaim this family.[18]

One of the most common ways in which female slaves "worked" the Spanish legal system was in petitioning for manumission. If the slaveowner and slave amicably agreed upon a price, and the slave secured the money through wages earned in his or her free time, gifts, or loans, the owner would appear before the government notary to have manumission papers prepared. If no agreement could be reached, however, or if an agreement broke down, slaves were quick to use the institutional structures available to them.

By the mechanism of *coartación* slaves could petition the courts to set their just purchase price.[19] Each party, owner and slave, then chose an assessor to evaluate the slave's value. If wide disagreement arose, the court appointed a third assessor and then made its decision. In cases involving children, a special advocate was appointed to protect the children's interests. Once the court established a slave's "just" price, owners had to honor it. If slaves could not afford their immediate freedom, they could make payments and move slowly out of slavery, or they could seek out new owners willing to pay the price and effect a change in their conditions that way.[20]

To illustrate—the mulatto slave Margarita Saunders was born and raised in the St. Augustine home of her owner Don Juan Saunders.[21] In 1794, Margarita asked the court to set her purchase price, alleging that Saunders was trying to take her out of the city so that she could not earn a daily wage with which to buy her freedom. In St. Augustine, as in many other Spanish colonial cities, owners permitted slaves to work for themselves or for others in exchange for an agreed-upon return to the owner called a jornal. Any money earned above that amount was the slaves' to keep. This system gave slaves an autonomy that, in some cases, simulated freedom, but in reality it was a privilege the owner could easily revoke.

In his required response, Saunders stated that he could not afford to free Margarita or all his other slaves would follow suit. Another mulatto woman had just fled his home, and he told the court resignedly that she would probably petition, too. He refused to name his choice of assessor, but this tactic did not interrupt the process. The governor's tribunal ruled that Saunders's excuses were "insufficient reasons to impede her solicitation of liberty," and Margarita's price was set at 300 pesos (approximately equivalent to 300 U.S. dollars at the time). Saunders claimed that he had been offered 600 pesos for her and argued that, since he was being forced to free Margarita against his wishes, he should be paid at least 500 pesos. The governor refused this request, and after paying 300 pesos and court costs, Margarita obtained her certificate of freedom.

Although Margarita was nominally married to Juan Gray, the mulatto overseer of Hannah Moore's St. Johns River plantation, and had borne him several children, at some point she became the consort of Hannah's son, Don Eduardo Mills Wanton. Margarita was pregnant with Wanton's child when she initiated her manumission suit and it is possible that Wanton helped Margarita become free. The couple had ten children together over the next twenty-five years, all of whom Wanton recognized and named as his "sole and universal heirs."[22]

As Saunders had predicted, another of his slaves, Lucía (also born and raised in his home), appeared before the court the following year petitioning for freedom. Saunders asked 350 pesos for her, but Lucía claimed this was an exorbitant price and, after three assessments, she was able to buy her freedom for 275 pesos. In telling the court that both women had been born and raised in his home, Saunders made a sort of dual claim over them, as owner and as "father." Ordinarily, both those images were powerful sources of authority; however, Spanish justice recognized the women's natural right to "liberty" as even stronger.[23]

Sometimes women of African descent sought influential allies in their manumission suits. The slave Andaina charged in a handwritten petition, which she signed with a flourish, that her owner, Catalina Acosta, had continually mistreated her. Andaina asked the court's permission to seek another owner, as was her right, but she also wanted to pursue *coartación.* She asked the court to intervene because her owner's asking price for her freedom (350 pesos) was too high, and at that rate, Andaina charged, she could find no other owner.[24]

Andaina reported she had been paying her mistress seven to ten pesos monthly from earned income over a three-year period. She estimated she had paid Catalina a total of 250 pesos and was, nevertheless, forced to buy her own clothing and that of her infant. "The few clothes with which I cover my flesh cost my said owner nothing, for what I earn from my labor I spend on my clothing and that of my little son." Andaina complained that, on one occasion, Catalina had ripped her hard-earned clothing.[25]

Catalina, an illiterate shopkeeper of Minorcan descent, was unable to sign her required response to Andaina's petition, and a government scribe recorded it for her, verbatim. Catalina protested that she did not understand how a slave could complain. Denying any abuse, she conceded in colorful fashion that she yelled a lot but added, "Shouts do not hurt anyone." Catalina portrayed herself to the court as a compassionate person, who although "weighted down with small children and my husband absent," allowed Andaina to work as a wet nurse in the home of the widowed Don Domingo Reyes because he "begged with tears in his eyes." Catalina stated that she had pity on a "widowed father surrounded by little ones." With these descriptions, Catalina attempted to make the court also pity the grieving and widowed father and orphans and, perhaps, deflect some of the criticism Andaina had aimed at her.

After a short time in Don Domingo's employ, Andaina became pregnant and returned to Catalina's home to deliver her baby, which was presumably also Don Domingo's since the widower tried to buy the mulatto child's freedom for twenty-five pesos. At first Catalina rejected the offer and refused to allow Andaina to return to Reyes's home, motivated, she said, by her desire to "end a scandalous connection." Seeing that Don Domingo was unwilling to detach himself from Andaina and their daughter, however, Catalina agreed to the child's manumission for twenty-five pesos and let Andaina return to work for ten pesos monthly, rather than the seven Catalina had previously charged Don Domingo.[26]

At that point, Andaina took charge of the situation. According to Catalina, Andaina announced that she would hang herself rather than work, so Catalina finally agreed that her slave could be assessed and seek another owner. When Catalina agreed to this arrangement in another dictated document, she could not resist adding an extended comment on Andaina's unseemly behavior. She said that Andaina went to masked balls (those hosted by Filis and Felipe Edimboro) in clothing so fancy that her owner worried people would talk.[27] When Catalina challenged her slave on that issue, Andaina retorted, "So what? Weren't the governor's own slaves there?" At that, Catalina admitted she had ripped Andaina's ruffles from her skirt, prompting Andaina, yet again, to threaten suicide and leave the house. Within moments, Don Domingo stormed in "like a wild beast," shouting that Catalina had no rights to Andaina beyond the money she was due. In effect, Catalina did not, for once the court agreed to a just price, her slave moved inexorably toward freedom.[28] Catalina lost the dispute and her slave, but she closed with the final commentary that "passion blinds one" and discounted the statements of Don Domingo and of his friend, the commissioner of their barrio, because everyone knew they were "as close as fingernail and finger."[29]

From the safety of Don Domingo's household, it took Andaina four more years to accrue sufficient funds, but she finally secured her manumission papers, and within months of becoming totally free, Andaina was back in court with another handwritten petition. After describing how her former owner continued to abuse and insult her, events that she stated were witnessed by many cited dons, Andaina demanded that Catalina sell Andaina's two children, whose mistreatment was also witnessed. Witnesses to Catalina's abusive behavior included Don Francis Phelipe Fatio, Don Pedro Cosifacio, and Don José Peso de Burgo, among others. The men who had sheltered Andaina's son included "the soldier Luna" and "the convict laborer Arturo." When Don Domingo Martinely found the bruised and starving boy in his kitchen he first took him to Don Domingo Reyes's house, but because of the ongoing dispute, Reyes was reluctant to harbor the boy. Martinely then deposited the boy with the priest to await the court's determination. Catalina countered that Andaina repeatedly harbored her nine-year-old runaway son. Andaina denied that charge and specified which members of the community had sheltered her son until Father Miguel O'Reilly finally took him in.[30]

Andaina used powerful imagery when she asked the court "Do you think that even for hiding a son a mother deserves the martyrdom [and here she used the metaphor of being whipped by a lash] I continually suffer? . . . It is impossible to believe the inhumanity and rigor with which they treat my two children." Andaina reported that her son had been beaten so badly that his back bled and that he had been found almost dying of cold and hunger after running in the countryside. She also charged that her younger daughter was regularly beaten and that her body was covered in bruises, as the neighbors could testify. When the governor's tribunal threatened a hearing to investigate the alleged mistreatment of Andaina's children, Catalina agreed to their sale. Once again, Andaina successfully employed a combination of personal connections, determined resistance, and traditionally accepted justifications, in this case, motherly grief and concern over witnessed mistreatment and neglect of her children, to "work the system." She won the freedom of her children.[31]

Not all slave women, of course, were as successful in their quest for freedom as those already discussed. Nancy McQueen, alias Ysabel McCully, went to court in 1792 when she found that she, her husband, and her two children had been sold by Don Juan McQueen, one of Spanish Florida's most prominent planters. Although unable to read or write in any language, Nancy told the notary that McQueen had no right to sell them since she and her family had been freed by their former owners in Charleston and she had written proof of this manumission. Nancy further claimed that her family members were *nuevo pobladores* or homesteaders, not slaves. She challenged McQueen to show proof of their purchase.[32]

As required, McQueen answered Nancy's charge with his own memorial and told the court that following the British evacuation of Charleston during the American Revolution, the governor of South Carolina deposited with him a number of unclaimed slaves. McQueen cared for the slaves, including Nancy and her husband, for more than six months, during which time no one reclaimed them. In consideration of his services, expenses, and war losses, South Carolina's governor rewarded McQueen with the remaining slaves. McQueen and other witnesses stated that they had read the paper Nancy believed was her manumission and that it seemed, instead, to be some sort of soldier's certification. McQueen stated that as he was preparing to move the slaves to St. Augustine, Nancy showed the papers to the magistrate on Sapelo Island, who also felt the paper was "useless."[33]

Informed by the court of McQueen's testimony, Nancy responded and verified that she and her husband had been deposited with McQueen, but said they only agreed to stay because she was pregnant, sick, and starving. Had she better understood Spanish conventions about the protections due to women and mothers and those of the "miserable classes," Nancy might have phrased this information more powerfully to elicit sympathy from the court. Instead, she understated her family's suffering and proceeded to what she considered to be more important—legal property requirements. How, she asked could deceased owners have reclaimed them? She charged that the overseers to whom she showed her paper must have altered it and discounted the testimony of these witnesses, since they were all dependents of McQueen. Again she challenged McQueen or his representatives to show proof of ownership. She also asked that the court solicit testimony from witnesses in Philadelphia, where her former owners had lived.[34]

Nancy first took her case to court in 1792 and fought for the next seven years to win freedom for herself and her husband, whose name never appeared in the records. Although by this time McQueen had become even more prominent in the community, acquiring vast properties as well as military and judicial appointments from the Spaniards, he was repeatedly required, nevertheless, to respond to her petitions. Finally, a new governor ruled that it was unfair to McQueen to leave the case unresolved and continually require him to appear in court. He said Nancy had repeatedly shown poor proofs of liberty and that she had fifteen days to produce better, or forever hold her peace.[35]

Although Nancy's determination equaled Andaina's, Nancy suffered many handicaps that contributed to her ultimate failure. She was an illiterate field hand, with, apparently, limited access to St. Augustine and a flawed understanding of Spanish institutions. There is no evidence that Nancy or her husband pursued the available option of *coartación,* for example. They may have had no way to earn extra money in the countryside. Instead, Nancy staked her claims on a piece of paper issued by a foreign government in a hand she could not even read. Although Nancy understood the concepts of property and contract and repeatedly demanded written proof of sale and ownership, she seemed unable to grasp the important influence that social relations had on determinations in the Spanish courts. Nancy had no important connections or allies in the community nor witnesses to any abuse from her owner. Furthermore, there is no evidence that she sought the intercession of the church or any other legal representatives. Her case rested solely on her own testimony and on a text that ultimately betrayed her. Although Nancy lost her long battle, the fact that she was able to fight such a long delaying action against one of its own officers indicates the seriousness with which the Spanish court reviewed claims to freedom. Her case also underscores Spanish commitment to the principle of access; even an illiterate slave woman could get repeated hearings and engage the court and her powerful and wealthy owner in a case lasting more than seven years.

Citizenship and Rights

Once free, women of African descent in Florida enjoyed full citizenship and the legal and customary rights enjoyed by Spanish women. They managed plantations, operated small businesses, litigated in the courts, and bought and sold property, including slaves. Free black women also went to court, if necessary, to protect their financial interests. The free mulatto María Tunno requested an embargo and inventory of her absent husband's general store, telling the court that the business was opened with the $500 given to her as a dowry by her father Don Tomás Tunno.

María reported that her husband Juan Bautista Collins had fled his creditors and she charged that neither Collins's elderly mother nor his daughter (by another woman) were competent to manage the store. She also charged that they were defrauding her interests. As noted, Spanish law protected both a woman's dowry and her *bienes gananciales,* so the court was required to investigate María Tunno's charges. Collins's mother told the officials sent to conduct the required inventory that the store, which was located in her home, was her only source of income since her son had left the province. The investigators located a signed power of attorney by Collins which charged that his wife María had misspent and wasted the better part of his property, worth beyond the $500 she brought to the marriage. Collins asked that the court collect the debts owed him (more than $1,000), pay his creditors, and divide the remainder equally between his two children, Rosa and Tomás.

Informed of Collins's written charges, María countered with another complaint saying she was bedridden from injuries suffered at the hands of her husband, and again asked for what she felt her mother-in-law owed her. She also notified the court that Collins kept cattle in the countryside—further assets to which she might lay claim.

The court was faced with conflicting claims by two women who were due its protection; María, the abandoned wife, who represented herself as defrauded and beaten, and Juliana, the elderly mother dependent upon an absent son for her survival. Although he was not present, by his notarized statement Collins had in effect testified that his wife was wasteful. When he instructed the court to pay creditors and provide for his children as an honorable man would do, he added to his credibility. All parties were well known to the court, which may have considered Collins's portrayal more accurate and the widowed and elderly Juliana and the children more deserving of protection than the younger María. Ultimately, however, the court decided that, in the absence of legal proofs, it could not enforce María's demand, ruling that "even if her husband were guilty of injuring her as she claimed, she was not by those injuries entitled to his goods, since she had never presented documentation about her dowry."[36]

Although María's efforts to reclaim her dowry were unsuccessful, women of African descent clearly recognized the possible remedies available to them under Spanish law and were willing to use the law even to protest mistreatment by elite Spaniards. María Rafaela Witten (the former Judy Kenty, who escaped from South Carolina and received religious sanctuary in Florida) filed suit against members of one of the wealthiest Spanish families in the community, whom she claimed had insulted and physically mistreated her. When María Rafaela was waiting in a doorway for a young slave apprenticed to her, the wife of Don José Sánchez asked her repeatedly about her business there. María Rafaela told the court that on the third query she had responded, "Madam, I have not come to rob anyone of anything." Both María Rafaela's failure to respond immediately to the elite woman and the sarcastic response she finally gave would have clearly been read as insolence, given her lower socioeconomic status and her race. But such a challenge would have been almost inconceivable in the Carolinas. María Rafaela told the court that, on hearing the exchange, Don José Sánchez began to berate and beat her until her mouth and nose bled. She added that she was undeserving of such treatment since she was doing no harm and was in the neighborhood on business, and she asked the court to admonish her abusers. María Rafaela was illiterate but her son Francisco, who was educated in St. Augustine, produced the petition for her and signed beside her "X." In this document, María Rafaela identified herself as a *vecina,* a term signifying a property-holding member of the community, but she made no reference to her race or legal status. The omission is anomalous and seems a deliberate attempt by the black woman to put herself on equal footing with those whom she was suing. María Rafaela seems to have internalized at least some of the egalitarian rhetoric circulating through the circum-Caribbean in this age of revolutions.[37]

Don José Sánchez responded to María Rafaela's suit by admitting that he had beaten her, but he claimed that the plaintiff had used English to answer his wife, saying "I'm not doing anything, you damned bitch." Although María Rafaela had filed the suit and had her hearing, the governor found that "The latter statement having more verisimilitude . . . María Rafaela should abstain in the future from lack of due respect to white persons." Spanish justice may have guaranteed access, but as this example or others between persons of the same race might equally illustrate, courts deferred to the person of higher status—in this case the elite Spanish woman.[38]

Black Women's Work and Economy: The Urban Context

Although the judicial system was relatively effective and might even be regarded as sympathetic to the goal of liberty, slaves like Margarita Saunders knew that access to the cash economy of the city was almost a prerequisite for successful self-purchase. Even slaves who lived in the city would have found it an arduous process to save several hundred pesos when the average day's pay for a man was a half peso.[39]

Very little is known about how slave women earned money to buy such a costly and precious commodity as freedom, but fascinating glimpses of their entrepreneurial activities occasionally surface in manumission suits. For example, Filis Edimboro and her husband Felipe Edimboro, both Guinea-born, saved for many years before winning their freedom in a court battle against their wealthy and influential owner Don Francisco Xavier Sánchez, the largest cattle rancher in Florida and a government creditor. While Felipe Edimboro used his free time to ply his trade as a butcher and gathered and sold firewood, Filis, who was a laundress in the Sánchez household, took in washing on the side. Filis also made and sold toys, of unknown description, and baked and sold "tortes of flour and honey, called *queques* [cakes?] which only blacks and poor boys eat." Filis and Felipe Edimboro's entrepreneurial drive also led them to rent the top floor of a home in St. Augustine, where they hosted dances for the African American community—a sort of colonial forerunner of the rent party. The attendants contributed money for the music and "refreshments," and Felipe and Filis Edimboro earned between one and a half to two pesos a night at these gatherings after paying for the rent of the place and the party fare. When they had saved enough money, Filis and Felipe Edimboro successfully worked their way through the courts to achieve freedom, despite the heated opposition of Sánchez.[40]

Many free black women like Filis Edimboro, María Rafaela Witten, and Cecilia Tunno took in washing for soldiers, prisoners, and other single males in St. Augustine. It was not a profitable business because men frequently reneged on payment to the women. For nine years the free black woman Rafaela Lluly did the laundry of Daniel McGirtt, a rebel who was jailed in the Castillo de San Marcos. When McGirtt was freed, his brother, with whom she had contracted for her services, had only paid her seven pesos, despite her repeated requests for payment. Rafaela finally resorted to a lawsuit, and the court ordered McGirtt to pay her within eight days. Cecilia Tunno also had to sue to recover wages the barrio commissioner Mariano de Lasaga owed her for doing his laundry for eight months.[41] Another free black laundress, Judy (surname not given), contracted with Mariana Tudory to work at unspecified labor for four days monthly in exchange for the rent of twelve reales on a house on Calle de la Marina. At this rate, Judy earned three reales a day, or less than a half peso. When Judy defaulted on her rental agreement, her landlady referred the matter to the commissioner of their barrio, the same Lasaga who failed to pay the laundress Cecilia Tunno. Judy agreed to start paying off her back rent, but another year went by, and Judy still had not paid as promised, so her landlady took her to court. This time, in addition to complaining about nonpayment, the landlady charged that Judy was "negative and untrustworthy" and that the neighbors considered her presence a

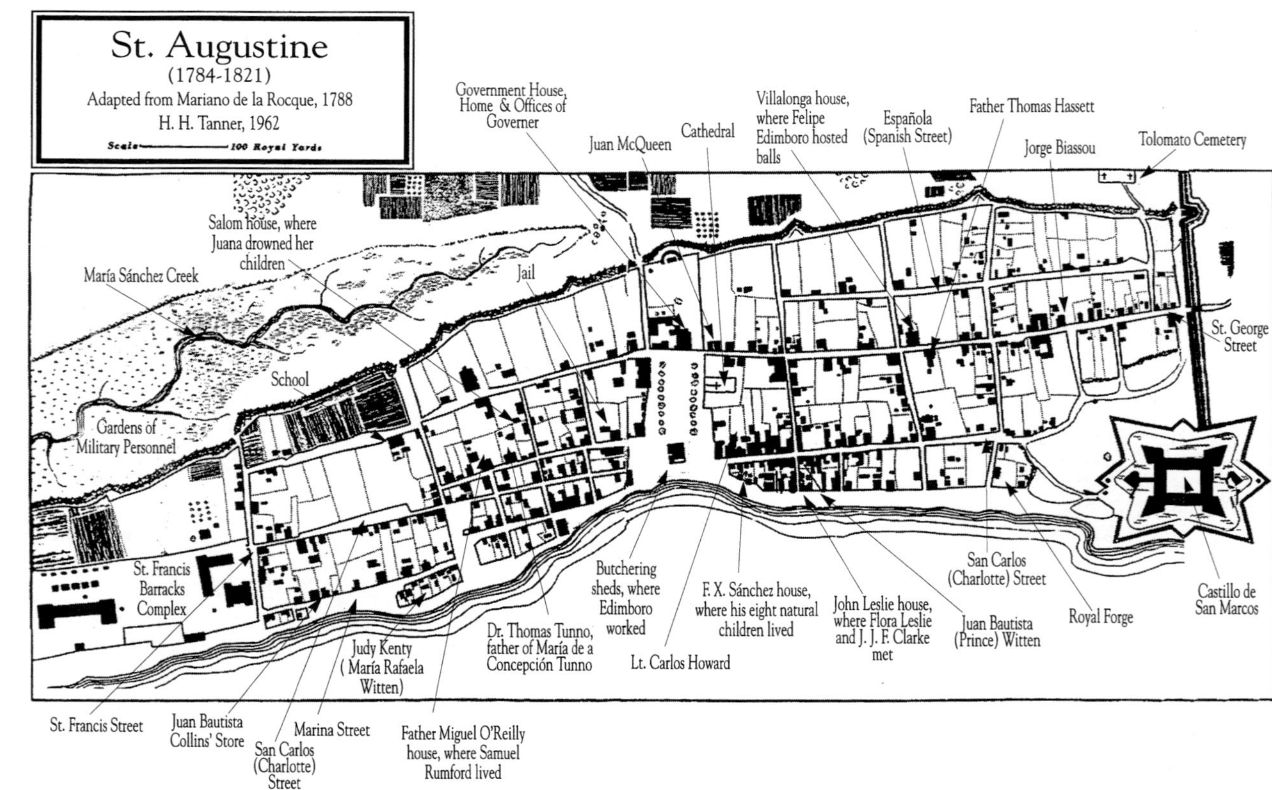

Map of St. Augustine in the second Spanish period (1784–1821), showing locations of black residences and businesses. Adapted from the 1788 map of Mariano de la Roque by James R. Landers.

scandal because she continually entertained "troops, blacks, and other subjects." The governor ordered a report from commissioner Lasaga, who denied the landlady's allegations of a neighborhood scandal (which would have reflected badly on his own supervision) but admitted that Judy had not paid because the troops would not pay her for their laundry.[42]

Free black women, like black men, usually had to work at several jobs in order to help sustain themselves and their families. Filis Sánchez laundered, baked, and made and sold toys. The free black María Rafaela Witten laundered, cooked, and took in young slave apprentices to train them as domestics, for which she was paid by their owners. The free black women Rafaela and Vara bred and raised pigs for sale.[43] Since many of the community women had emigrated from Carolina and Georgia, they may well have made versions of the famous lowcountry baskets to sell at public markets.[44] Other women earned income as midwives and wet nurses, or they operated small businesses or were storekeepers. Juan Fernández left the free woman Juana, "with whom he has lived many years and who has helped him to make his fortune," a half share in his estate, consisting of two houses, seven horses, a canoe, a cart, and a tavern, which Juana probably helped manage.[45]

Slave Women's Work and Economy

Most of Florida's enslaved women lived in rural settings ranging from small farms on which they might work with their husband and children to large estates worked by large numbers of bozales and criollos. They worked at a wide variety of tasks—including agricultural field labor and animal husbandry, domestic work such as child care, cooking, cleaning, and laundering, and skilled labor such as weaving, sewing, and midwifery. Slave women with special skills could make them pay. The slave midwife Betty earned three pesos when she assisted her fellow slaves deliver their children on the Sánchez plantation.[46]

Some slave women were able to take advantage of the Spanish jornal system and work off the plantation. By this arrangement they paid a determined sum to their owners but could retain and dispose of any surplus. After the planter Don Juan Saunders died in debt, his executor hired out some of Saunders's slaves to help satisfy his many creditors. Of ten adult slaves hired out in 1800, seven were women, and the women earned enough to pay monthly jornales of six to seven pesos each. The executor's accounts show that the women's jornal payments remained relatively stable through at least 1803. At least one of the women, the mulatto Richel, used some of her earnings to pay the executor twenty-five pesos for the freedom of the child she was carrying.[47]

Plantation inventories show that most slave women in Spanish Florida lived in nuclear families with husbands and children or in extended families which sometimes included three generations of women.[48] This held true even on commercial plantations such as San Pablo, owned by Panton, Leslie and Company. The relatively even sex and age distribution and the recognition and grouping together of nuclear families, even on an Anglo-managed, commercial plantation under stress, would seem to indicate a deliberate effort to maintain stable family relationships among slaves. Thus, young girls and working-age mothers often had the moral support, training, and other sorts of assistance of other women in the household or nearby. Women of a common age group, nation, or shared experience also supported one another in important ways. When Diana McGirtt's owner sent her to collect oyster shells for making lime, she deposited her daughter Clarissa with a female friend who was a slave on the McGirtt plantation because she did not think that Clarissa would be safe left alone at home.[49]

Interracial Families

Some of the black women living on rural plantations were not slaves but mistresses of the estates. European-African unions were common and accepted in Florida, much as they were on the African coast and in other areas of Latin America. Many of Florida's wealthiest ranchers, planters, government officials, and merchants had large mulatto families (sometimes in addition to their white families) and recognized their mulatto children, educated them, and provided for them in their wills. Among the prominent planters, merchants, and government officials with African wives and consorts and mixed-race children were Joseph (Job) Wiggins, Zephaniah Kingsley, James Erwin, John Fraser, Francis Richard, Luis Mattier, Francisco Xavier Sánchez, John Sammis, Oran Baxter, Juan Leslie, Miguel Ysnardy, Eduardo Wanton, the brothers Jorge J. F. Clarke and Carlos Clarke, and the physicians Tomás Tunno and Tomás Sterling. Even in cases involving concubinage, the law and community consensus protected their widows and heirs, and the church often interceded "paternally" on behalf of mothers of African descent. Many men left substantial property to their common-law wives and natural children, and the community respected the desires of the deceased, as well as the rights of the bereaved.[50]

Women also made full use of the powerful institutions of the extended kinship group *parentela* and *clientela,* or clientelism, to advance their interests and those of their children.[51] Spaniards viewed society as an extension of family structures, as did members of many African nations, and women of African descent developed important connections in St. Augustine through marriage, concubinage, and godparent choices that could produce tangible benefits.

Don Francisco Xavier Sánchez (who unsuccessfully challenged Filis and Felipe Edimboro's *coartación* suit) was the patriarch of two large families. Sánchez and his common-law wife María Beatriz Piedra, a free mulatto born in Charleston, lived together for almost twenty years on his San Diego plantation. There they raised Sánchez's first family—three sons and five daughters. Sánchez recognized all these children when they were baptized in the Catholic church, and his influential Spanish friends served as their godparents.[52]

Sánchez's extensive landholdings and wealth made him a respected and powerful member of the Spanish community. His cattle empire stretched along the Diego Plains north of St. Augustine almost to the St. Marys River and west to the St. Johns River. His main plantation, San José, comprised over eleven hundred acres. To the south of that plantation lay another, Ashley, of about half that size, and to the east lay his original homestead, San Diego, of another one thousand acres. Below San Diego lay the smaller homesteads of Capuaca and Santa Bárbara. All around these were other Sánchez holdings devoted to pasturage and forests, and like all large Spanish landholders, he maintained a variety of town properties as well.[53] Sánchez was an associate in the important Florida merchant house of Miranda y Sánchez, which operated a general store in the lower floor of the house on San Carlos (Charlotte) Street and whose ships plied an important trade with Havana, Charleston, St. Marys, and Savannah.[54]

Sánchez's status devolved upon his natural children, who were also considered to be respectable members of the Spanish community. When they grew older, Sánchez moved his quadroon children into town and they lived in St. Augustine attended by slaves of their own (including the enterprising laundress Filis). Sánchez's sons attended the public school in St. Augustine, and his daughters also received an education, perhaps from a home tutor, for they were literate.[55] As noted in chapter 5, with their father's blessings and official dispensation from the bishop of Havana, three of Sánchez's quadroon daughters married peninsular Spanish soldiers, further enhancing their standing in the community.[56] Sánchez's twin daughters remained unmarried and lived together in the town house provided by their father.[57] Sánchez's surviving natural son, Joseph, named after his paternal grandfather, eventually married Lucía Ysnardy, the free and propertied quadroon daughter of St. Augustine's royal treasurer.[58]

In 1787, the fifty-one-year-old Sánchez married María del Carmen Hill, the seventeen-year-old daughter of a wealthy South Carolina family from the 96 District. This marriage meant new commercial connections and social elevation for Sánchez, whose common-law wife, María Beatriz Piedra, died three years later. María Beatriz's testament recorded that she left no property "due to her poverty," but this formulaic phrase denoted her legal rather than actual condition, for as his treatment of his illegitimate children substantiates, Sánchez would have been shamed by such a failure of community-sanctioned responsibility. Moreover, during her lifetime, María Beatriz was listed as the owner of a number of slaves for whom she served as godmother.[59] Sánchez's marriage to María del Carmen produced four legitimate sons and six daughters, the last of whom was born days before her father's death in 1807. María del Carmen and her children apparently enjoyed a close relationship with the children of Sánchez's first union and served as godparents for their children.[60]

Although Sánchez died intestate, he had expressed his wishes that his natural children inherit, and his legitimate widow and children supported the inheritance of his first family in court. María del Carmen Hill wrote to the court, "It is well known . . . that my deceased husband always recognized them as his natural children . . . and as proof he provided for their food, education, and everything else necessary for their station." Moreover, María del Carmen stated that shortly before he died she had heard her husband say that he wanted to give each of his natural children several slaves each for their support. She added, "I should not oppose their petition, on the contrary I wish them to receive what by law they are due." The two families were closely intertwined in multiple godparent relationships, and the legitimate family was bound by that obligation as well as by Sánchez's desires. The widow could afford to be generous. The court carefully inventoried Sánchez's five plantations, other land holdings, and town properties before making the division in which the six natural children divided one-sixth of his estate. Sánchez's five natural daughters inherited a house, lots, and slaves worth about $7,000.[61]

Perhaps the most successful of Florida's black plantation mistresses was the former Wolof slave Anna Magigine Jai, who wed her owner Zephaniah Kingsley in a marriage "celebrated and solemnized by her native African custom, altho' never celebrated according to the forms of Christian usage." Despite any irregularities, the Spanish community never questioned Anna Kingsley's obvious status, and Kingsley wrote, "She has always been respected as my wife and such I acknowledge her, nor do I think that her truth, honor, integrity, moral conduct and good sense will lose in comparison with anyone."[62] In 1811 Kingsley freed Anna and their children, George, Martha, and Mary, and he did the same for other African co-wives and their children including Flora Hannahan, who bore his son, Charles. Flora was the daughter of the Wolof Sophie Chigigine and of Kingsley's mulatto overseer, Abraham Hannahan, all of whom Kingsley freed.

Kingsley also freed another co-wife, Munsilna McGundo, and their daughter, Fatimah Kingsley.[63]

Few of Florida's black plantation mistresses approached Anna Kingsley's success. For example, the Senegalese Ana Gallum (alias Nansi Wiggins) first appears in Florida documents as a slave of the English planter and one-time Indian trader Don Joseph or Job Wiggins. At some unknown point, Wiggins freed Nansi and married her in a Protestant ceremony in Rollestown, Florida, a marriage which would not have been legally recognized by the Spaniards. Nansi and Wiggins lived together for approximately eighteen years before his death and had six children, all of whom were baptized in the Catholic church.[64] When Wiggins died in 1797, Nansi was left in charge of their minor children and an estate that included a furnished plantation house, fourteen hundred acres of land, farm equipment, almost one hundred head of cattle, and fourteen slaves living in six cabins. She continued to manage the estate, probably with the help of her grown sons, and appeared frequently in the legal records of the day, buying and selling horses and slaves.[65]

But Nansi's life on the plantation was not an easy one. Two years after her husband's death, Nansi reported to the governor's tribunal that she had been raped by Pedro Casaly, who had come to her plantation to get a horse. On his way back to town, Casaly was drowned, but Nansi was left pregnant. She appealed to the court for financial assistance for the son that was born of the rape, as she claimed to have no money. The governor, and everyone else in the community, knew Nansi held substantial property and had important and wealthy "family" on whom she could depend, namely the white consorts of her daughters, so no government assistance was forthcoming.[66]

In 1811, Nansi petitioned the government for lands on which to work four slaves and live with her twelve-year-old son, but the acting governor replied that she already owned lands on the St. Johns and ordered her to get that acreage into cultivation or lose it.[67] Instead, Nansi moved to the newly developing town of Fernandina, to live near her daughters and their families, and she eventually acquired two lots and two half-lots in the booming town.[68]

Sexual Violence against Black Women

As Nansi's story illustrates, despite the protections of a fairly responsive legal and religious system, and community surveillance, even free women of African descent were vulnerable to sexual depredation and violence in St. Augustine, as they were in other societies based on race slavery. Enslaved women were even more at risk.[69]

Spanish legal and religious authorities viewed public morality as their legitimate responsibility and tried to monitor St. Augustine closely. When the free black militiaman Tony Capo challenged the white tailor Duncan Noble for entering his house uninvited, Noble told authorities that Tony had threatened him with a saber, and Tony was jailed. As the investigation of Noble's charges proceeded, however, Tony's wife, Ester, and other free blacks testified that Noble had come in search of a black slave woman named Binas, belonging to Juan Quevedo. Quevedo denied that his slave had a "friendship" with Noble, but Binas admitted it, although she said she "did not enjoy the visits of the Englishman." Binas told the court that Noble gave her and other black slave women living near his house stockings for their favors. Having heard the various testimonies, the court freed Tony. It also ruled that Noble was guilty of soliciting Quevedo's slave and of "scandals to the republic" and sentenced him to pay the court costs.[70]

Authorities also heard and adjudicated cases of black domestic violence. Authorities jailed Carlos Gil after he injured his wife, the free black woman Lucía, in a domestic dispute. Several days later, however, Lucía went to court to declare that she had hurt her head while running away and that her husband had "sufficient motives to have reprimanded her." Luzia told the court that she needed Carlos and asked that her imprisoned husband be released. Lucía probably did need whatever income Gil might provide, so the governor freed Gil with a warning to behave.[71] As noted in chapter 8, the court was not so lenient in more obvious and extreme cases of violence.

The violence Thomas visited on Sara had origins in their flight from the South Carolina plantation of Isaac Wied.[72] Although two other men also accompanied them in the escape, only Thomas required Sara to enter a sexual relationship in return for protection. Sara reluctantly agreed to Thomas's demands, on the condition that when they got to Florida, the arrangement would cease.

In Florida, Thomas and Sara registered as slaves seeking religious sanctuary and went to work at the plantation of Don Jorge J. F. Clark. After almost three months of bad treatment from Thomas, Sara left the plantation and moved to town, but Thomas refused to return her clothes. When she returned to the country to try to retrieve them, Thomas once again solicited her. Sara refused his advances and told him she loved another, infuriating Thomas. In a pathological reenactment of the most brutal slave/master relationship, Thomas stripped Sara, tied her to a tree, and beat her "until she could no longer scream." Another slave tried to intercede on Sara's behalf, but Thomas was bigger and stronger. Once Thomas went to work in the fields the next morning, Sara escaped from his cabin and found shelter at the nearby house of Fernando Falany. At day's end, Thomas found her and, as a number of witnesses reported, shouted angrily, "You've hidden in a white's house where I can't remove you—so the white's horse will pay." At this Falany confronted Thomas, who finally fled, later to be arrested.

During his interrogation, Thomas told the court that "he found himself with rights and dominion over the said woman, because he had helped her flight and she had agreed to be his woman." Moreover, Thomas alleged Sara had taunted him, saying if he were a man he'd punish her, so he did. It is clear that by virtue of his sexual relationship with Sara, and in response to her sexual taunt, Thomas felt he was within his rights to "discipline" her; however, he denied he had threatened Falany's horse (a white man's property). Indeed, the court may not have been involved if this had been private and marital violence, but because the violence had been so severe and had been witnessed by so many, and "because they were not married," the court sentenced Thomas to be whipped one hundred lashes at a public venue and then to work on public works in shackles and chains.[73]

Women's Health

By law and tradition, slave women were not only due certain protections against abuse, they were also supposed to have access to medical treatment, if needed, and there is evidence that at least some owners complied with this requirement. Plantation records and estate inventories, as well as civil and criminal proceedings, all yield scattered references to health care provision and some evidence about the health of black women in Spanish Florida. Expense records indicate slaves shipped from the African coast probably received at least some medicines and care en route, and when their ship anchored off the Florida coast, a physician gave them at least a cursory examination to ensure that they carried no contagious diseases. Once slaves were unloaded and transported to rural plantations their care was probably entrusted to other slave women knowledgeable in herbal medicines. One traveler along the St. Johns described a black woman treating a wounded guide with "some herbs, the sovereign remedy for every sore among the negroes."[74] At the dangerous moment of childbirth, slave midwives routinely attended their fellow slaves. But if a slave's condition seemed grave, planters often paid for the services of white male practitioners and physicians in St. Augustine. Practitioners from the royal hospital administered common treatments such as blood-letting for undiagnosed illnesses and generalized complaints, but well-qualified physicians also attended free blacks, slaves, and their owners.[75]

When a slave's health was at question in a criminal investigation, as discussed in chapter 7, the government solicited medical testimony. The senior surgeon of the royal hospital, Dr. Valentine Fitzpatrick, attended the free black woman Salee, who complained that her menstrual period had ceased, but who displayed no other symptoms of illness. After several weeks, Salee returned to see the doctor, complaining of insufferable pain in the left groin, headaches, thirst, vomiting, and difficulty in urinating and sleeping. Fitzpatrick ordered "appropriate general remedies" for her inflammatory symptoms and reexamined her several times over the next several days. She seemed to improve and he prescribed medication, but Salee refused the treatment, saying she did not need it. Because she would not follow his recommendations, the physician stopped treating her and Salee died fifteen days later. Her unexplained death led to the suspicion that she had been poisoned and a free black man was charged with the crime. This time Dr. Fitzpatrick conducted an autopsy on Salee's cadaver to provide evidence for the criminal inquiry. Fitzpatrick found "the peritoneum . . . was entirely destroyed . . . the mesentery inflamed . . . the right ovary the size of a chicken's egg and the left [ovary] entirely suppurated . . . the fallopian tube gangrenous . . . and a copious amount of white and fetid pus spilled throughout the abdominal cavity." Fitzpatrick stated that poison could not have caused the damage he described and that Salee's death was attributable only to the pus which destroyed the principal organs of digestion. Don Bernardo Nicolás de la Madrid, a professor of medicine and the chief medical officer at the hospital, reviewed the case and confirmed his colleague's opinion that poison had not killed Salee. The suspect was freed and Salee was buried in the cemetery the following day.[76]

Several important institutional, political, and social factors protected black women in Spanish Florida, even those enslaved. One was the observance of a legal code that upheld the rights of slaves and the property rights of women generally and that supported the access of both to the courts. In this litigious society, all could generate texts and make their voices heard. The courts in Spanish Florida regularly supported the inheritance rights of women and children of African descent if their relationship to the deceased had been publicly acknowledged, even when the mothers were not legally married to the fathers of their children. After centuries of experience, Spaniards were accustomed to Africans in their communities, and miscegenation was common in Florida. While racism was not absent, racial categorization was less rigid than in Anglo areas and more important were personal connections and behavior. Another factor was the particular political circumstance of Spanish Florida. Bordered by a competing nation that practiced chattel slavery, Florida sought to weaken the enemy by attracting and then freeing its slaves, and this policy worked to the advantage of women as well as men. Also important were the family-based religious and social systems and the gender conventions operating in Spanish Florida, which held that women, including women of African descent, free or enslaved, were due certain protections, particularly against sexual violation and excessive physical mistreatment.

Slaves and the Slave Trade

Slave Imports during First Spanish Period Florida

Spanish Florida was first established and sustained by enslaved laborers belonging either to the king or to a few wealthy individuals. But slave importations were modest for most of the first Spanish tenure, and most slaves belonging to Floridian owners were either criollos, born in other parts of the Southeast or the Caribbean, or ladinos, acculturated Africans. Toward the end of the first Spanish period, however, Floridians began to introduce more bozales, or African-born slaves. The New York merchant resident in Spanish Florida, Jesse Fish, introduced most of the African-born slaves registered in the decade preceding Spain's loss of Florida (1752–63). Fish was partners with the Charleston merchant and slave trader John Gordon, who was also connected to the Florida Indian traders Panton, Leslie and Company. Other English-speaking residents such as John Jones and Samuel Piles, originally from Georgia, Thomas Rogers, and Jacob Kip of New York were relatively smaller players in the Florida slave trade in this period.[1]

Anyone wishing to admit and/or to sell a slave legally in Florida had to register the transaction before a tribunal consisting of the Spanish governor, the royal treasurer, and the royal accountant. These officials examined the slaves, recorded information about their apparent age, stated nation, and physical appearance—including information on color, detailed scarification patterns, body, face, eye, nose, and ear shape, and any visible deformities. They then assigned each slave a name and, on the basis of age, primarily, but also physical size, declared the slave either a whole *pieza* (usually reserved for adult males, but often assigned to robust adolescents as well), two-thirds, one-half, or one-third a *pieza*. The owner then paid the required duty—which was set at thirty-three pesos, three reales for one *pieza*. This may have been an incentive to introduce younger slaves (or to claim them as younger), for 123 of the 204 slaves were registered as one-third pieza. The final act was to brand the slave with an "RF", usually on the left shoulder. This was proof that the royal duty had been paid and the slave was legally registered. It is unclear who actually did the branding, but they burned even the youngest slave listed, the five-year-old Mandinga whom they named Melchora. Some of the numerous children registered showed signs of abuse, such as broken noses. Ten-year-old Antonio, of the Musinbata nation, had a "very broken" nose. Nine-year-old Vizente, of the Mozindi nation, had a broken nose and had already been branded before with an "R" and a crown over the right nipple. Eighteen-year-old Thorivio, of the Mungundu nation, also bore the "R" and crown brand over his right nipple.[2]

The slavers legally imported 203 slaves into Florida from 1752 to 1763 (ninety-four of them in 1763), and the slaves represented a surprising variety of ethnic nations. The Congo nation formed the largest single group (thirty-eight). Criollos (meaning those born on the American side of the Atlantic) ranked next (twenty-eight), with Mandingas close behind (twenty-seven), Carabalís fourth (fourteen), and Gold Coast fifth (ten). The Congo, Mandinga, and Carabalí nations were also heavily represented in Cuba at the same time, but the Florida tax lists document the presence of less commonly encountered groups such as the Bara, Besi, Dudrian, Fai, Femi, Filina, Limba, Moyo, and Pati, to name only a few. (See appendixes 9 and 10.)

With the English capture of Havana in 1762 and the remarkable increase in slave importations into Cuba in the eleven months that Great Britain held the island, bozales suddenly became more available to Florida.[3] Given the sharp increase in Florida imports in 1763, it appears that Fish may have been trying to stockpile slaves for ready sale to the incoming English planters, who were sure to need them.[4]

Slave Imports into British Florida

As Daniel L. Schafer and David Hancock have shown, during Florida's British period (1763–84), planter/slave traders imported thousands of slaves directly from Africa to work the large rice and indigo plantations they established in the new colony. Schafer has shown that 66 percent of the slaves on Governor James Grant's model plantation were "new Negroes." Another early investor in British Florida, Richard Oswald, received a parliamentary grant of twenty thousand acres in the Mosquito district south of St. Augustine. In 1767 Oswald imported a shipment of 106 slaves from his slaving factory on Bance Island in the middle of the Sierra Leone River. He brought in two similar shiploads in 1771 and 1772.[5] South of Oswald's estate, James Penman established a plantation on his ten thousand acre grant, and with credit from Henry Laurens, Penman also established a slave-trading company based in East Florida. Penman's partners in Penman and Company were two other Florida planters, Robert Bissett and William Mackdougall. Henry Laurens of Charleston and John Graham of Savannah also supplied many African slaves to British planters in Florida. One contemporary estimated that as many as one thousand African slaves were imported into Florida in 1771 alone, a peak year of the Africa/Florida trade. As a result, the labor force in British East Florida came to be predominantly black and African-born. British Florida planters described their "new Negroes" as being from the Windward, Grain, Gold, and Guinea Coasts of West Africa, from Gambia, and from Angola, and they sometimes identified them by specific "nations" such as the Sulundie or Ibo.[6] The "Africanization" of Florida continued throughout the British period and with it the importation of a variety of African cultural practices.[7]

Toward the end of the American Revolution, Loyalists fled Charleston and Savannah to resettle in East Florida with over eight thousand slaves, an influx that brought the black population to three times that of the white.[8] Elias Ball transferred 175 slaves from South Carolina to set up a plantation on the west side of the St. Johns River. James Graham sent his brother, John, ahead from Georgia with fifty-three slaves to clear and plant 500 acres in East Florida, and then sent another 215 slaves to join them. James Hume also brought 105 slaves from Georgia to work on the Oak Forest plantation he purchased from Panton, Leslie and Company. These seasoned hands cleared and fenced land, planted crops, erected buildings, built dams and drains, and transformed vast stretches of inhospitable swamp and hammocks into profitable fields.[9]

Schafer vividly described the turmoil associated with the final years of British control in Florida. Georgian marauders attacked plantations and stole slaves, other slaves ran away to the interior Seminole villages, and planters formed slaves into militias to fight the multiple enemies. Some planters relocated to safer locations, requiring their slaves to start anew the backbreaking process of plantation building. Finally, on hearing that Florida was to be retroceded to Spain in 1784, major British planters like James Grant, John Moultrie, and Richard Oswald shipped their slaves back across the northern border to South Carolina or Georgia or southward to the Bahamas, Dominica, and other Caribbean sites where they might still own slave property.[10]

Slave Imports during Early Second Spanish Period Florida

Some Loyalist planters accepted Spain's offer to remain in the colony, and for their slaves, work and life proceeded much as it had before the change in governments.

As described in chapter 3, other slaves of British owners seized the opportune moment and fled from evacuating owners rather than face unknown places and climes or forced separation from loved ones, changing their lives dramatically. Twenty-eight of Alexander Patterson's slaves "eloped" during the evacuation, making their escape in a large six-oared canoe and a boat from Patterson's plantation for which he also made claims. Robert Robinson's slave, Jack, ran away on the day of Robinson's departure for Halifax "for his dread of encountering so cold a climate."[11]

Florida's economy was slow in recovering from the damage of the war years and the uncertainty of the change in regimes, and because incoming Spanish homesteaders brought few slaves with them Florida suffered a chronic shortage of manpower. The deficit was most notable in the early years, as the government struggled to restore plantations fallen into ruin and public properties and defense works in a state of great disrepair.[12]

After the transition was finally completed and as the colony began to stabilize, Florida's economic prospects appeared somewhat brighter and planters began to import small lots of slaves from Charleston and Savannah. Although the data on slave taxation are incomplete, only sixty-six slaves were legally imported during the thirteen years for which there are tax records (1785–97), and those were usually country-born.[13] Florida's treasurer, Don Gonzalo Zamorano, repeatedly urged the Crown to permit the free introduction of slaves in Spanish ships, arguing that slave labor was indispensable to the development of the province, and in 1789 the Crown conceded to a tax moratorium for two years from the date of the publication of its edict.[14] The government repeated the tax moratorium on slaves from mid-1793 through 1796 and this encouraged some owners to bring in African-born slaves purchased in Cuba. Sebastián Berazaluze brought an African woman from Cuba for whom he had paid 230 pesos, despite the seller's usual disclaimer that she was sold "soul in mouth, skin and bones, as the market allows, without checking for defects, illnesses, heart trouble, epilepsy or leprosy, or any other diseases which humans could suffer."[15]

At the same time, the government officially encouraged new settlers to bring their slaves into Florida by allotting land on the basis of headrights and by liberalizing trade. No exact figures exist for the numbers of slaves imported from 1789 to 1791 (or from 1794 to 1796), but by 1793 there were 1,185 slaves on the rural plantations outlying St. Augustine, indicating that the government's incentive program was beginning to work.[16] Although the government once again began to tax slave imports in 1793, Floridians legally imported twenty slaves that year.[17]

Demographic Profile: Growing Slave Populations

After Spain abrogated the religious sanctuary policy in 1790, the free black population remained fairly stable, while the slave population steadily increased. Spanish census data, which only tracked the patterns through 1814, show the increasing significance of the slave population, rising from 29 percent of the total population in 1784 to 53 percent in 1814.[18] Most of the enslaved people lived and worked on the large plantations along the St. Johns River area, and by 1813 the black/white ratio along the lower St. Johns River was four to one, with fairly equal sex ratios among each population.[19] (See table 6.)

Spanish Florida was atypical of many slave systems in that sex ratios were fairly evenly balanced, at least for the first forty years of the second Spanish period. This is probably due to the general absence of labor-intensive industries and the pattern of maintaining family units even on large-scale plantation operations. However, as more Anglo planters moved into Florida with their slave forces, the black population grew proportionally larger and more male. By 1813, the slave population of Amelia Island was more than double that of the white, and while the white population showed a fairly even sexual division, the enslaved population was two-thirds males.[20]

Table 6. Census, 1813, Upper and Lower St. Johns River

			Mulatto				Black			
Age	White		Free		Slave		Free		Slave	
(Years)	M	F	M	F	M	F	M	F	M	F
Upper St. Johns River										
0–7	7	5	2	3	0	0	—	—	5	5
7–16	5	3	4	—	0	0	—	—	4	4
16–25	4	1	—	—	0	0	—	—	3	6
25–40	19	10	1	1	0	0	—	1	15	2
40–50	3	2	—	—	0	0	—	—	4	6
50+	5	1	—	—	0	0	—	—	2	—
	43	22	7	4	0	0	0	1	33	23
Lower St. Johns River										
0–7	8	11	—	—	0	0	—	—	26	29
7–16	7	5	—	—	0	0	—	—	38	24
16–25	6	9	—	—	0	0	—	—	42	35
25–40	12	10	—	—	0	0	—	—	43	40
40–50	4	1	—	—	0	0	—	—	11	8
50+	3	3	—	—	0	0	—	—	12	11
	40	39	0	0	0	0	0	0	172	147

Source: Census for St. Johns River, June 1, 1813, Census Returns, 1784–1814, EFP, microfilm reel 148, PKY.

Slave Labor: The Urban Context

While free laborers and convicts were important components of Florida's labor pool, by far the largest part of the workforce was enslaved. The more "fortunate" slaves lived in the city and served as domestics to middle- and upper-class families. The women cleaned their homes and were their maids, cooks, wet nurses, nursemaids, and laundresses. Male slaves cared for their animals and were their gardeners, guards, and messengers. Testimony from the vast array of civil and criminal records for St. Augustine demonstrates that urban slaves moved relatively freely throughout the city and interacted closely with the sizeable free black population—in their homes, in the market, in local stores and taverns, in church, and during the frequent public gatherings on the central plaza. The access to information, civil and religious institutions, a cash economy, and both black and white patrons all moderated urban slavery in St. Augustine and helped some enslaved people to become free. Slaves understood the advantage of their urban location and resisted attempts to move them to country plantations.

Some of St. Augustine's slaves belonged to the Crown. These royal slaves served in a wide range of urban occupations—as auctioneers, interpreters, night watchmen, and executioners. The Crown's slaves included skilled lumberjacks, carpenters, masons, and ironsmiths employed in St. Augustine's ongoing efforts to repair and maintain defense works such as the Castillo de San Marcos and other smaller outlying forts, on government buildings, wharves, and seawalls. They quarried coquina on Anastasia Island, harvested timber, rowed the king's galleys, or tended royal gardens and stables. A line item in the government budget covered these slaves' annual food and clothing expenses as well as the pay for officials charged with their supervision. Setting an example for its citizenry, the Crown ensured that its royal slaves were baptized, married, and buried with full sacraments and also allotted occasional monies to allow the slaves to observe important religious and civic festivities.[21]

Plantation Slavery in Spanish Florida

By the late eighteenth century, Spanish Florida held some very large plantations with sizeable slave populations. Daniel L. Schafer has described the deliberate attempt by British planters to model their plantations after those of South Carolina, which themselves carried the imprint of their Barbadian antecedents. It is not surprising, then, that Florida's late-eighteenth-century plantation system resembled the more-studied Anglo-Caribbean/lowcountry model. Planters employed slaves on the task system, and the slaves often provisioned themselves.

Florida's system tolerated slave mobility, free market and feast days, and an internal slave economy, and permitted the slaves relatively free cultural expression. Slaves lived in fairly durable families and developed extensive and long-term networks of kin, shipmates, and friends across plantations and in the city.[22] A significant difference, however, was that Florida's plantation owners actually lived on their estates for most of the year and had close contact and sometimes personal relationships with many of their slaves. More importantly, Florida slaves knew that the power of their owners was limited in key respects by the Spanish legal and religious institutions, which were never far away. Emancipation was always a tangible possibility—via legal and extralegal pathways. The proximity of the Seminole nation, trackless forests and swamps, and rivers and oceans provided alternatives for those who would take them. Selected case studies can illustrate the contours of plantation slavery in Spanish Florida.

One of the largest plantations in the colony belonged to a holdover from the British period, Francis Phelipe Fatio. Fatio lived in baronial splendor on his 10,000-acre Nueva Suiza (New Switzerland) plantation stretching along two miles of the eastern bank of the Saint John's River. The complex featured Fatio's plantation manor, numerous storage buildings, two stables, and twenty-seven slave cabins, which housed a workforce of eighty-six slaves and four free blacks. Together, free and enslaved workers herded and slaughtered cattle, pigs, and sheep, and tended groves of sweet and sour oranges, citrons, and lemons, and fields of cotton, corn, and other crops. Fatio's slaves also harvested lumber and made tar, resin, and turpentine for export to circum-Caribbean and Atlantic ports.[23]

Fatio's plantation lay west of St. Augustine on the frontier of the Indian Nation, and although he normally maintained cordial relations with the Seminoles, during the State of Muskogee's War against Spain, Indians raided the plantation several times. On June 7, 1800, Mithlogy and his warriors stole the slave Simon and his wife Susy from a new plantation that Fatio was developing on an island facing Nueva Suiza. Fatio's informants related that the couple was taken to a place called Red Ground near the Chattahoochee River, where they became the property of the Indian Eswolgie. Fatio sent envoys to try to redeem his missing chattel, which in some cases he was able to do. In 1801 sixteen warriors stole, or enticed away, thirty-eight slaves, whom Fatio later enumerated. The raiders took several children away from parents, but also entire family groups of up to three generations. Old Tom, age sixty, Artemesia, his wife, their four children, Rose, Sarah, Lawrence, and John, and Rose's children, Primus (a grown boy), Peter, and Cuffee (an infant) made up one sizeable group. The Seminoles also carried off ten people over the age of fifty, including Old Harry (above sixty) and his wife, Old Peggy (above sixty-two), whose value as workers must have been negligible.

Perhaps those "captives" joined the risky flight voluntarily, to stay among family members or to find the freedom that Seminoles typically granted their black vassals in the nation.[24]

Don Francisco Xavier Sánchez operated the only other private plantation still functioning when Spain returned to Florida. Sánchez "rose from a state of obscure poverty to a degree of wealth seldom attained," amassing vast land holdings as the meat and firewood contractor for three successive regimes in Florida (first Spanish, British, and second Spanish).[25] In 1784 his main estate, the San Diego, encompassed more than one thousand acres, on which Sánchez kept a herd of eight to nine hundred cattle, thirty to forty horses, and thirty-four slaves.[26] When Sánchez was away on business in Havana and other ports, his trusted Guinea-born slave and the skilled butcher of his cattle, Felipe Edimboro, acted as overseer of the San Diego. It was much to oversee. The San Diego encompassed the main dwelling, assorted ranch buildings such as a cookhouse, stables, granaries, storehouses, houses for the overseer and hands, carpentry and ironworking shops, a millhouse, and a slaughterhouse. Like other plantations, this was a largely self-sufficient operation on which Sánchez's slaves also raised and processed corn and other garden crops.

At Sánchez's death in 1807, he owned nine separate plantations and several hundred slaves. Thirty-eight slaves on the San José worked primarily in agricultural production, but also managed a herd of one hundred cattle.[27] Other slaves fulfilled Sánchez's lumber and firewood contracts, cutting timber, hauling it to riverbanks, and then canoeing it into St. Augustine. Still others worked in Sánchez's commercial ventures, which included a store in St. Augustine, a circum-Caribbean trade in goods and slaves with Havana and the Bahamas, and an interior trade with the Indian nations of the hinterland.[28] Some slaves from the Sánchez plantations also worked periodically at his various town residences. Sánchez's extensive and far-flung enterprises allowed at least some of his slaves access to a cash economy and a knowledge of institutions and mechanisms that may have ameliorated their bondage. For some, like Filis and Felipe Edimboro and their children, it led to freedom, despite the opposition of their owner.[29]

After 1790 Spain enticed foreign planters to enter Florida by offering generous land grants based on a British headrights system. Don Juan McQueen was among the most distinguished takers. McQueen escaped creditors by moving many of his slaves from Georgia plantations south to St. Augustine and in Florida became a trusted advisor, militia commander, and judge for the Spanish governors. For his services McQueen acquired huge tracts of land, totaling over twenty-six thousand acres.[30] McQueen brought seventy-seven slaves, including thirty-three men, twenty-one women, and twenty-three children of both sexes, with him to Florida, and they cleared and planted the virgin lands, and built dwellings and plantation structures on his five plantations.[31] McQueen's slaves grew cotton, rice, and indigo for export and subsistence crops for their own maintenance. Other slaves developed his forest industries and erected sawmills to process the valuable timber on McQueen's vast holdings.[32]

McQueen's letters back to family members in Georgia reflect the patriarchal relationship he seems to have fostered among his slaves. McQueen reported on the health and occupations of "my people" and passed messages along to the slaves' family members. Two years after moving to Florida, McQueen wrote his daughter Eliza and asked her to "tell Gran that Will is well and is here helping to make Indigo vats." Many years later McQueen lamented to Eliza: "[E]very young person in Florida is laid up with the hooping cough all my young Negroes have it to a violent degree—about ten days ago Negers wife Sofy fell dead in an appoplectic [*sic*] fit—all the old people are well and often enquire when I last heard from you."[33]

McQueen's son, John Jr., also reported from Florida on the health of "the people," and once wrote his sister never to marry "a hard Negro master, it shows a little mind & bad disposition."[34] McQueen Sr. followed the same dictum in hiring his overseers. He described the new overseer of his San Pablo plantation, Joseph Fenwick, as a "sober well informed active mild & well meaning Man—his Wife exceedingly attentive to my Negroes." McQueen also reported that his people were much better pleased (under that overseer's administration) than they had ever been.[35]

Inventories of McQueen's property show that with few exceptions, McQueen's slaves lived in family units, that most lived in nuclear families, and that some households included three generations. McQueen also maintained a fairly evenly balanced sex ratio on most of the estates. (See table 7.) At Los Molinos, an estate of 2,633 acres, ninety-three slaves lived in family units in seventeen wooden cab-

Table 7. Household Size, Age, and Sex Distribution of Los Molinos Slaves

Household size	1	2	3	4	5	6	7	8 . . . 19
No. of households	6	4	0	2	2	3	1	2 . . . 1

Age (Years)	Male	Female
1–14	20	20
15–49	25	15
50+	6	7
	51	42

Source: Testamentary Proceedings of Don Juan McQueen, Oct. 14, 1807, Records of Testamentary Proceedings, 1756–1821, EFP, microfilm reel 141, PKY.

ins. The plantation complex also included McQueen's own house, several other wooden houses, including one for McQueen's white carpenter, two cotton gins, a water-driven saw, a smithy, a separate kitchen, a mortuary, stables, and animal pens for oxen, mules, horses, pigs, and sheep.

At the time of McQueen's death, his slaves seem to have been in the process of developing the smaller Shipyard plantation, because the overseer's house was still a simple palm structure. But McQueen's workers had already built a wooden cookhouse, granary, and storehouses for corn and wood, and had cultivated two hundred acres. Fifty-eight slaves lived in nine cabins, and as at Los Molinos, the slaves lived in family units based on nuclear families. One couple, Cupid and Chloe, were both said to be ninety years old and "inutil," meaning beyond working age. Another woman in the same category, María, was said to be 105. If they were not at the new site to work, they may have been living there to be with younger family members. Otherwise, the population was fairly young.[36] (See table 8.)

Two slaves left the slave cabins to become McQueen's trusted menservants, and they ranged far beyond the plantations with him. Strephon and Harry (Enrique) McQueen accompanied McQueen on a trip of several weeks through the Lower Creek nation to Tampa in 1793. From there, Strephon and McQueen returned overland to St. Augustine, but Harry boarded a royal ship for Havana with McQueen's baggage, which he subsequently conveyed back to St. Augustine.[37] Years later Harry McQueen testified that he enjoyed his owner's full confidence, having "been with" him since age twelve and having accompanied him throughout his many travels. Harry served McQueen one last time when he supervised his burial at his Los Molinos plantation. A cortege of twelve blacks carried McQueen's coffin to the prepared site and then covered the grave with mounded earth as the plantation slaves gathered and, according to Harry, wept over "the loss of such a good owner." On McQueen's death, Harry McQueen became a free man and began a homestead on a government land grant, but like many others, was driven off his property during the Patriot Rebellion. He relocated to Fernandina

Table 8. Age and Sex Distribution of Shipyard Slaves

Age (Years)	Male	Female
1–14	10	10
15–49	15	15
50+	4	4
	29	29

Source: Testamentary Proceedings of Don Juan McQueen, Oct. 14, 1807, Records of Testamentary Proceedings, 1756–1821, EFP, microfilm reel 141, PKY.

(where he joined the free black militia) and later filed claims against the United States government for damages to his homestead.[38]

Despite McQueen's best efforts, he was never able to clear his debts in Georgia, yet he resisted advice to sell his slaves north in order to do so. Instead he sold off pieces of Florida property and rented his surplus slaves to the purchasers of the land. Conventional wisdom weighed against renting slaves to those who had no vested interest in them, but McQueen had "little or no provisions" for them and preferred renting to selling his slaves. McQueen sold his Fort George Island plantation to John Houston McIntosh in 1804 and rented him a number of working hands for one year at $10.00 a month per slave. McQueen obviously hoped to recover the slaves at year's end and wrote his son, "I hope yet to leave my poor Negroes to my family."[39]

The "Africanization" of the Slave Force

Daniel L. Schafer and David Hancock have clearly demonstrated the Africanization of Florida during the British tenure (1763–84). A similar demographic process occurred in the early years of the nineteenth century, driven first by the African connections, commercial and familial, of many of Florida's planters, and then later by the demand from across the United States border for forbidden African slaves.

Like Henry Laurens had earlier, Florida planters/slave traders like Zephaniah Kingsley imported their own laborers directly from Africa. Kingsley moved to St. Augustine from Charleston in 1803, with approximately sixty-four "new African negroes," some of whom he had personally brought from the coast of Africa. His large workforce of Africans included Ibo and Susu and Sereer people from West Africa, but he also imported slaves from Zanzibar on the East African coast.[40] By 1808 Kingsley's slave force had grown to seventy-four, and over the years he acquired thousands of acres of land, including both Fort George and Drayton Islands, and more slaves to work them.[41]

Working on the task system, Kingsley slaves planted cash crops such as corn, cotton, sugar cane, tobacco, and oranges, as well as potatoes, peas, and other subsistence crops. Other slaves worked ginning cotton, in the blacksmith or carpenter's shop, or in the shipyards, putting up cypress fences, tending the chickens, hogs, cattle, and horses, spinning cotton, and making clothing. Once their tasks were completed, slaves were free to manage their own homes, animals, and gardens, or to hunt and fish to supplement their diet.

Patriot troops and Seminole raiders plundered Kingsley's various plantations on the St. Johns River during the so-called Patriot Rebellion of 1812, and he filed a claim against the United States government for damages. The Seminoles raided and killed slaves at Kingsley's Drayton Island plantation on Lake George, including the African-born slave driver, Peter, "a mechanic and a most valuable manager" valued at $1,000. They also burned twelve "negro houses" and stole or killed forty-one slaves at Laurel Grove. Among the stolen slaves were African-born slaves whom Kingsley identified as Ibos, and individuals from the Rio Pongo, New Calabar, and Zanzibar. Some of them retained African names, or chose them for their children. Kingsley's lists included Quamila, a woman from the Rio Pongo, and the carpenter Jack Tinguebari and his wife Tamassa, from Zanzibar. Three of Jack and Tamassa's children bore English names, but another was named M-toto (Swahili for small child). Among the slaves killed at Laurel Grove was Morton, the blacksmith, "a very prime young man," valued at $1,000.[42] Kingsley described how the Seminoles tied up Morton's wife and prepared to carry her away, thinking that Morton, who carried their child in his arms, would follow. Instead Morton gave up the child to its mother and refused to go, "not wanting to be thought a runaway." The raiders promptly shot him, and Morton died the next day.[43]

Although Kingsley believed slavery was a necessary state of control for labor, he recognized the talents of his slave force, felt slaves could be trained to any skill, and that they could, if profit demanded, be moved out of the fields and into manufacturing. An eyewitness to the destruction on Saint Domingue, Kingsley was convinced that free blacks enjoying property and protection under the law, and having common interests with white slaveowners, would be "a barrier to insurrection" and, therefore, the key to the maintenance of a stable slave system.[44] Kingsley practiced what he preached. As discussed in chapter 6, Kingsley freed the Wolof woman Anna Magigine Jai Kingsley, whom he recognized as his primary wife, as well as his other African co-wives and his numerous mulatto children. He also freed favored slaves such as Abraham Hannahan, his mulatto overseer, and their families. In his will, Kingsley urged his executors not to separate slave families by sale and ordered that any slave be permitted to purchase freedom at half their declared value. He also created a profit-sharing/indenture plan for the slaves he took with him to Haiti in his later years.[45]

Kingsley considered himself to be an enlightened capitalist and drew on his long experience in Africa, the Caribbean, Brazil, and the southern states in formulating paternal management principles for what he called "the co-operative system of society." In his own interest, Kingsley made the lives of his slaves as pleasant as possible, and on his plantations they had autonomy and time enough to produce surplus for their own families as well as for sale. Slaves thereby gained both choice in their own foodways and cash, and Kingsley was relieved of fully provisioning them, thereby reducing his plantation expenses. Kingsley also permitted his slaves autonomy in areas such as personal relations, cultural expression, and religious belief and advocated these management principles in a treatise published in 1829. Describing the slaves on his Fort George plantation he wrote:

> They were mostly fine young men and women, and nearly in equal numbers. I never interfered with their connubial concerns, nor domestic affairs, but let them regulate these after their own manner. I taught them nothing but what was useful, and what I thought would add to their physical and moral happiness. I encouraged as much as possible dancing, merriment and dress, for which Saturday afternoon and night, and Sunday morning were dedicated; and, after allowance, their time was usually employed in hoeing their corn, and getting a supply of fish for the week. Both men and women were very industrious. Many of them made twenty bushels of corn to sell, and they vied with each other in dress and dancing, and as to whose woman was the finest and prettiest. They were perfectly honest and obedient. . . . I never allowed them to visit, for fear of bad example, but encouraged the decent neighboring people to participate in their weekly festivity, for which they always provided an ample entertainment themselves, as they had an abundance of hogs, fowls, corn and all kinds of vegetables and fruit.[46]

Life on the Kingsley plantations, in many ways, followed the Caribbean model with which Kingsley was already familiar. As long as tasks were completed and the plantation prospered, Saturday entertainments and dances and Sunday "market day and jubilees" were nothing to be feared or prohibited; in fact, in Kingsley's view they contributed to his own success. Neither did Kingsley see any harm in allowing African cultural expression such as music and dancing, which he also felt promoted harmony and good order on his plantations.[47]

Kingsley's toleration extended even to Gullah Jack, later made notorious in the Denmark Vesey revolt of 1822. Kingsley imported Gullah Jack from Mozambique to Charleston in 1806, probably in the same shipment that brought Jack Tinguebari and his family. Both men belonged to a caste of skilled wood-carvers and became carpenters in the Americas—Jack Tinguebari on Kingsley's Laurel Grove estate in Spanish Florida and Gullah Jack on the Carolina plantation of Paul Pritchard.[48] Kingsley described Gullah Jack as a "conjurer" or "priest in his own country, M'Choolay Morcema," whom he purchased "as a prisoner of war at Zinguebar [*sic*]," and he wrote that Jack "had his conjuring implements with him in a bag which he brought on board the ship and always retained them."[49] Kingsley found traditional African religious practices less disruptive than those of the Protestant sects he tried to root out among his workers, for he never confiscated Jack's "implements" nor complained of his behavior.[50]

Kingsley claimed that he rarely had any need to correct his slaves except by "shaming them" and that, if ever he exceeded that, the punishment was slight, for "they hardly ever failed in doing their work well." "My object," he said, "was to excite their ambition and attachment by kindness; not to depress their spirits by fear and punishment." As proof of his success in managing his slaves, Kingsley pointed to their rapid natural increase.[51]

Although the picture Kingsley paints may seem suspiciously idyllic, much of the detail he included about the daily life of his slaves can be confirmed from other sources. Archaeologist Charles Fairbanks conducted investigations of two of the twenty-six extant slave cabins at the Kingsley plantation on Fort George Island. These dwellings are believed to be those of the overseers and skilled and domestic slaves—the elite of Kingsley's slave force. The two-room tabby buildings measure 24.5 feet by 18.6 feet. The cabins had plastered walls, interior brick

Slave cabins at the Kingsley plantation, Fort George Island. The two-room tabby structures with brick fireplaces were still inhabited by African American families when this photograph was taken, ca. 1870. Courtesy of the Florida State Archives.

fireplaces more than eight feet wide, poured tabby floors, and wooden window closings and doors. Material evidence also supports Kingsley's contention that the slaves had plenty to eat. Fairbanks excavated shot and casting net weights, as well as bones of fish, cattle, pigs, raccoons, chickens, turtles, and shells of both clams and oyster, which the slaves roasted in their fireplaces. Resource exploitation on the tidal salt marsh of Fort George Island was relatively simple and produced a high calorie yield per acre to supplement the plantation provisions. The ample quantity of such varied food remains also suggests that the slaves had considerable spare time to secure them, as Kingsley alleged. Domestic equipment and clothing articles excavated at the cabins were varied and probably represent items donated from the plantation house.[52]

John Fraser was another of several important planters in Spanish Florida whose African connections contributed to their success. Fraser's wife, Fenda, was a free African slave trader and the widow of Thomas Hughes Jackson when she married Fraser in 1799, "according to the customs of the Rio Pongo." Fenda and John Fraser filled their coastal baracoons with slaves purchased from native chiefs such as Mongo Barkey, chief of Bashia Branch, and Mongo Besenty, chief of Bahia, "Principal Merchants of the Rio Pongo."[53] Perhaps encouraged by Zephaniah Kingsley's example, in 1810 Fraser petitioned the Spanish government for, and received, hundreds of acres along the St. Marys River on which he established flourishing rice and cotton plantations.[54] Fraser imported the 370 Africans who worked the Greenfield and Roundabout plantations from his own slave pens at Bangra on the Rio Pongo.[55] When he drowned in 1814, three of Fraser's daughters still lived at Bangra, but Fraser's will decreed that his five children should share equally in his sizeable estate, which included 158 African-born slaves.[56]

A significant number of Florida slaves belonged not to a single planter but to Panton, Leslie and Company, the mercantile firm that had enjoyed a special monopoly in the Indian trade since the earliest days of the second Spanish government. At the time of the 1786 census, Panton, Leslie and Company owned 250 slaves and nineteen separate land grants totaling 12,820 acres. Most of the Panton, Leslie and Company slaves worked on its various plantations and ranches, but some had specialized functions. The company hired Langueste to the government as an interpreter for the Indians and collected his wages.[57] Panton Leslie slaves traveled to and from the Indian nations regularly, bringing back cattle and trains of packhorses loaded with deerskins. At trading stores like the Almacén de Nuestra Señora de la Concepción, located about six miles south of Palatka on the west bank of the St. Johns River, fifty to sixty slaves worked tending fields of corn and vegetables, herding cattle, and curing and tanning the deerskins their compatriots brought in from the Indian settlements.[58] In the company's St. Augustine warehouse, slaves processed the hides and prepared them for export.

As Spain's grip on the province weakened and assorted plots and invasions wreaked havoc on the outlying ranches, stores, and plantations, Panton, Leslie and Company decided to transfer some of its holdings to Matanzas, Cuba. In 1815 the company filed an inventory of its San Pablo plantation, on which 117 slaves lived and worked. This exit inventory listed the names, sex, ages, and sometimes the occupations and health of the slaves. The able workforce between the ages of ten and seventy-five consisted of forty-four men and thirty-two women. No specific occupational information was given for the women, but among the men were one fisherman, one carpenter, and a first and second foreman. The slaves were fairly evenly matched in age and sex, with a slight preponderance of males between the ages of fifteen and fifty. Several of the slaves were quite old. One woman was listed simply as very old, and a man described the same way was seventy-five years old, while twelve others were over fifty. At the other end of the age spectrum were eight nursing children. Several of the slaves were incapacitated. One fifty-five-year-old male was listed as useless, one woman was blind, and another crippled. Yet even these "useless" slaves were being transferred to Matanzas.

Enumerators grouped the San Pablo slaves into thirty-three units, which probably represented households, and they recorded the relationships within those groupings. Seven slave households were composed of single men, but the rest consisted of nuclear and stem families. Females headed three households. The largest family included ten members, but the most common household (of which there were nine) was composed of a man and his wife. (See table 9.)

The relatively even sex and age distribution, the recognition and grouping together of nuclear families, and the decision to relocate disabled or superannuated slaves would seem to indicate some effort to maintain stable family relationships among the slaves.[59] Even this commercial operation, then, seems to have followed a "paternal" model of plantation management in Spanish Florida.

Table 9. Household Size, Age, and Sex Distribution of San Pablo Slaves

Household size	1	2	3	4	5	6	7	8	9	10
No. of households	7	9	4	4	1	3	2	1	1	1

Age (Years)	Male	Female
1–14	25	22
15–49	33	25
50+	6	6
	64	53

Source: Plantation List, Feb. 8, 1815, Cuba 419 A, AGI.

The Internal Slave Trade

From the beginning of the second Spanish period, local planter/merchants like Don Francisco Xavier Sánchez carried on a slave trade between Havana and St. Augustine. That trade derived from the turmoil of the political transition and consisted primarily of stolen criollo slaves shipped out from Florida for sale in Havana or across the northern boundary with the United States.[60] The extent of that illicit trade is hard to document, but Cuban officials complained that the slaves introduced from the American colonies to the north were criollos "of advanced age and full of vices and other defects" and so of little use for agriculture.[61]

Notarial records of slave sales offer only a partial picture of the internal slave trade in St. Augustine. Many sales were routine exchanges involving a single slave or a small family group. However, when slaveowners died in debt, the government ordered judicial sales of their property, including their slaves, and on some of those occasions many more slaves were sold. In 1790 the estate of John and María Hudson went on the auction block to satisfy creditors, and in 1794 so too did the estates of William Hall and Jesse Fish. With each auction a number of slaves changed hands.[62]

Also evident in the Spanish records is the degree to which the periodic episodes of political turmoil during the second Spanish period stimulated the internal trade in slaves as the government seized and resold property. Many of the major Anglo planters in the northern regions of the province were implicated in the 1795 rebellion, and Governor Quesada charged them with treason. Those who did not flee were imprisoned. The government embargoed the rebels' property, including ninety-one slaves. As trials dragged on, the wives of several of the sentenced rebels recovered slaves if they could prove ownership or prove that the slaves constituted their half of goods earned during marriage, in accordance with Spanish law. But other embargoed slaves languished in government custody for years. At the beginning of 1797, the supervising official, Don Miguel Ysnardy, reported that many of the unfortunates were entirely nude and that several adults and a newborn infant had died. Ysnardy complained that he had no more funds nor any way to feed his charges, and urged that they be sold "before they become useless." As a result of the deteriorating condition of the slaves, as well as of the royal finances, in 1799 sixty-seven individuals were sold at public auction to loyal Spanish citizens. Francisco Xavier Sánchez paid 650 pesos to acquire one slave seized from George Knolls and three who once belonged to William Jones. The four had originally been appraised at 780 pesos, so Sánchez made a good bargain. Other would-be slaveowners could not afford to pay cash but were allowed to take the slaves out of custody if they could post a bond guaranteeing payment of the slave's appraised price. In some cases, third parties posted the bonds.[63] After insurgents, pirates, and, later, United States troops seized Amelia Island, many more slaves changed hands. Again the Spanish government conducted treason trials. Carlos Seton was among those convicted in absentia, and in 1819 his slaves were sold at another public auction.[64]

Increased United States intervention had another effect on the last years of the internal slave trade. In 1812 the Seminole Indians harbored fugitive slaves and fought invaders from the United States who sought to reclaim them, but after the devastation visited on them in 1818 by Andrew Jackson, they, too, became the sellers of slaves. Indian owners sold thirty of the sixty-six slaves sold in 1821.[65] In some cases the Indians were only selling back to their former owners, or to other whites, slaves they had captured from them. It is possible that the Seminoles may have considered the recently captured as outsiders, rather than vassals. In 1819 Pincali, a Seminole from Mikasuki sold to Don Manuel Solana "my slave Kelty with two of her children, one a boy of six named Davy and the other a girl of two named Manuela whom I have brought from said town and whom I sell as captives." Two months later, Simancy, sister of the Seminole chief, Bowlegs, and a resident of Gaucafole, sold Solana an unnamed adult male slave, and another Seminole, Pafosafacho, sold him a mother and her three children. In all cases Solana was assisted by the interpreter of Indian languages Antonio Huertas, and the pair may have been on an official mission to recover missing slaves from the various Seminole towns.[66]

The African Slave Trade

By at least 1793, Floridians began to import cargoes of slaves directly from Africa, and the pace of the trade increased after Congress theoretically ended importations into the United States in 1808. Early shipments were small and the slaves were destined for Florida's riverine plantations. Fifty slaves imported on the brigantine *Ida* in 1800 were sold individually or in small groups to Spanish planters living along the St. Johns and St. Marys Rivers. Although their sales contracts contained the standard disclaimer that they were sold "with soul in mouth and like bones in a sack," the slaves must have been healthy for adult males sold for 425 pesos and a young boy for 250 pesos.[67]

Over time, the pace and scope of imports increased. Established planters such as Zephaniah Kingsley had an early advantage because they already had ships, African contacts, and experience in the slave trade. In 1802 Kingsley carried 250 bozales of unknown African origins to Havana on the *Superior.* His cargo represented approximately one-quarter of the total slave imports to Havana that month. Some of those slaves may have been destined for his own Florida plantations, as perhaps were the sixteen slaves he imported from Mozambique several years later.[68]

Panton, Leslie and Company also had ships, Caribbean connections, goods, and credit with which to enter the slave trade, and in 1802 one of their employees, William Lawrence, introduced 114 slaves from the African coast into Florida. Panton, Leslie and Company took sixty of the slaves, and the remainder were the consignment of Fernando de la Maza y Arredondo, who later became a major importer of African slaves.[69]

Independent traders also saw the potential in the Florida slave trade and found Spanish officials accommodating. In 1802 William Northrup imported 117 slaves from the Bahia de San Carlos, Sierra Leone, and William Cook imported a cargo of thirty-nine slaves, whom he had purchased in Guinea. Cook's slaves may have been loaded together at Guinea, but they were described as "being each of a distinct *casta,*" or nation. Royal officials inspecting the slaves, as required prior to sale, had difficulty questioning the polyglot group. The public interpreter, Don Miguel Ysnardy, passed down the line of Cook's thirty-nine slaves, asking questions in several European languages. The slaves only responded to English, but answered "yes" to everything, without understanding. Black interpreters next attempted to interrogate the captives and passed down the line asking questions in their own native languages. Only seven of the thirty-nine slaves could communicate with the black interpreters. The rest spoke other unknown languages. Those slaves who could confirmed that they set out from the coast of Guinea in a large ship and that they were loaded onto the ship in which they were interviewed, the schooner *Cristiana,* at another port (probably Havana). After the physician examined them and declared that the slaves were healthy, authorities gave Cook permission to unload and sell them.[70]

As the congressional prohibition of the importation of Africans, due to take effect in January of 1808, approached, even reputable figures such as Don Juan McQueen were tempted by the potential for illicit profits. He wrote to his son-in-law, Robert Mackay: "do not you think great matters may be done in the african trade from the island of Amelia in this province when the door shall be shut next year by Congress to the importation of slaves tho we are at war with great Britain they may be imported here in danish bottoms."[71] Death took McQueen before his plan went into effect; however, the embargo did stimulate slave imports and sales in Spanish Florida.

The embargo also led to the spectacular growth of Fernandina, the Spanish port city on Amelia Island, which quickly became a major slaving center. After 1808 traders registered, had inspected, unloaded, and sold their slave imports at Fernandina rather than St. Augustine. The Africanization of Florida began in earnest in 1810. In January Florida's treasurer licensed Captain José Chaple to sail the Spanish schooner *Cirila* to the African coast and the same month he licensed the brigantine *Don Alonso* to sail for Liverpool with 10,000 pounds of cleaned cotton, 25,000 pounds of rice, and thousands of casks on board. This ship, too, was probably involved in the African trade.[72] In March of 1810 Captain Daniel Hurlbert imported thirty-nine slaves from the African coast on the *Enterprise,* only ten of whom were adult males.[73] John Fraser's factors on the Rio Pongo did a brisk business with Florida-bound ships that year. In April, Fraser's captain, Francisco Ferreyra, imported 126 Africans aboard the *Aguila de San Agustin.*[74] The following July, James Cashen, owner of the *Amanda,* also imported twenty-eight slaves from the Rio Pongo. Cashen's captain, Lorenzo Segui, had died on the African coast and although no mortality figures were given for the return voyage, Cashen stated that the slaves had also suffered greatly.[75] In December of 1810 another of Fraser's captains, Captain Bartolomé Mestre, brought 140 new Africans in on the *Joana.*[76]

The mercantile firm of Hibberson and Yonge, a partnership of Joseph Hibberson and brothers Henry and Philip Robert Yonge, also became a major player in the Africa/Florida slave trade. The company purchased ships in Liverpool and in 1811 Governor Estrada granted Hibberson and Yonge free land in Fernandina on which the firm built a wharf and warehouse.[77]

In their long-term quantitative study of the Cuban slave market, Laird W. Bergad, Fe Iglesias García, and María del Carmen Barcia found that the sharp rise in the international prices for tropical products resulting from the Haitian Revolution and the Napoleonic Wars also drove Cuban slave prices sharply upward from 1790 to 1800. The authors found relative stability for Cuban slave prices during the period from 1800 to 1820, however, and it is during this period that the growing Florida slave market attracted the interest of Cuban slave merchants such as Fernando de la Maza y Arredondo.[78]

Fernando de la Maza y Arredondo was already well known to Spanish officials, having replaced Panton, Leslie and Company in providing Florida's annual gifts to the Indians. His ships brought imported muskets, saddles, tools, and even fine waistcoats from Havana for the interior Indian trade.[79] As noted above, Arredondo was investing in the African/Florida slave trade by at least 1802, when William Lawrence of Panton, Leslie and Company served as his agent in selling fifty-four slaves at Amelia Island. At some later date, Arredondo's son, Juan, joined his father's business and replaced Lawrence as factor for Arredondo and Son, and the company established its headquarters in Fernandina on a government land grant.

In August of 1810 Arredondo and Son imported a major shipment of 174 African slaves into Fernandina on the *Sevilla.*[80] The sixteen-man crew, their captain, and pilot made the round-trip voyage from Florida to the coast of Africa in ten months. Although the *Sevilla* carried rice, salted pork, and fresh and salted beef, and at least some medicines, by the time the frigate reached Amelia Island, twenty-eight slaves had died, for a mortality rate of almost 17 percent. Fifty-five slaves were so ill that Arredondo sold them for between fifty and one hundred pesos, and nine more may have been even more unhealthy, for they went unsold. The company was able to sell only 110 slaves for prices ranging from a high of four hundred pesos to a low of fifty. Most of the buyers bought one to three slaves, but several bought more. Hibberson and Yonge bought twenty-six sick slaves for 2,600 pesos. Jorge Atkinson, a local planter, bought another twenty-three prime hands, none of whom was valued at less than 210 pesos, and eight of whom sold for 400 pesos apiece. A new resident of the province, a Mr. McHardy, bought thirty slaves, including twenty-five sick and young, for whom he paid 3,515 pesos. With the proceeds from these sales, Arredondo and Son purchased Florida cotton, which the company shipped on the English brig *Thetis* to Glasgow, and on piraguas to the United States, and cotton and pine, which it shipped on the English galleon *Swift* to Nassau.[81]

Slaving Profits in Spanish Florida

Arredondo and Son must have found the Florida slave trade lucrative, for the following year the company imported 343 slaves from the coast of Africa on the *Doña Juana.* On that consignment, the sales totaled 39,765 pesos and expenses came to 17,916 pesos, 4 reales, for a profit of 21,848 pesos, 4 reales—more than five times the annual salary of the governor and about one-seventh of the annual situado for East Florida. Once again, although the company charged a medic's wages and medicines to expenses, 103 slaves, or almost a third of the shipment, died on the voyage. Another 110 slaves were transshipped from Florida to Havana for sale, and the remaining 130 were sold at Fernandina, but ten were ill, so were sold at a discount. Twenty-one of the thirty buyers were Anglos, and they bought all but fifteen of the slaves. John McIntosh, who had fled the province for Georgia when his Patriot Rebellion failed, was still welcome as a buyer. He and a Talbot Island planter, Spicer Christopher, bought the largest number of slaves, thirty and twenty, respectively.[82]

The Spanish government saw slave traders as men who would help develop the underdeveloped colony, therefore as worth supporting. Some traders had more status than others, provided more services to the Spanish government, and reaped major rewards. During the Patriot Rebellion of 1812, Fernando de la Maza y

Arredondo served in the militia and as aide-de-camp to Governor Estrada, transported government correspondence and supplies to and from Havana, and served as contractor for the royal military hospital—all for no pay. It is no surprise that when Arredondo proposed a settlement in the interior of Florida, the grateful governor granted him what he had to give—free land. Seeing in Arredondo's plan to settle Alachua "the Prosperity of the Province for which our government has longed," with a decree confirmed by Cuba's intendant, Alejandro Ramírez, Governor Coppinger in 1817 awarded Arredondo and his partners absolute property in almost 290,000 acres (in the heart of Seminole- and Creek-held lands).[83]

After the Patriot-inflicted damage to Fernandina, Arredondo and Son relocated their Florida slaving operations to Havana in 1815, and Horatio Dexter served as the company's agent to sell the slaves they left in Florida. The death of Zephaniah Kingsley and the departure of Arredondo and Son for Cuba allowed less influential or prosperous Anglo captains such as Dexter and Daniel Hurlbert thereafter to dominate the St. Augustine slave trade.[84] Like Arredondo, Dexter, Hurlbert, and other Anglos associated with the slave trade took advantage of the Spanish government's policy on land grants. After declaring their intentions to settle in the province and become *nuevo pobladores,* these men petitioned for and usually received sizeable grants of land. Several governors granted Daniel Hurlbert land. Governor Enrique White awarded him a small 125-acre headright grant on Pevet Swamp in 1805 and Governor Sebastián Kindelán awarded him another 200 acres at Casacola in 1814. Hurlbert also purchased several small plantations, including the Five Mile Plantation in 1814. In 1818 Governor Coppinger granted Horatio Dexter more than 2,000 acres in Volusia, and the following year Dexter acquired even more acreage from the Seminole Indians with whom he traded. Dexter moved slaves onto the property and began to cultivate rice, cotton, and sugarcane. Dexter and his wife Abbey also purchased acreage from other grant recipients.[85] Spanish governors still hoped to attract permanent settlers whose loyalty they could ensure by their generosity, and they also hoped for the development that slaves seemed to guarantee.

Although Spanish slave importation into Florida declined after 1814, the trade continued even after Spain and Great Britain signed the 1817 treaty that, in theory, prohibited the slave trade north of the Equator. In March of 1819 Spanish officials approved the request of one *nuevo poblador* to sail for Puerto Rico and on to the coast of Africa to buy bozales for sale in Florida. They stipulated that two-thirds of Captain Benjamin Pearson's crew be Spaniards and that all purchases be conducted "south of the line," as required by the Anglo/Spanish treaty.

Pearson's voyage was a disaster. His second pilot died on the African coast, two crewmen deserted, and the remainder allegedly conspired to kill their captain on the return voyage, but Pearson came back with thirty-nine slaves to sell, which he stated were acquired in Cabo López, "south of the line." Unfortunately for Pearson, one of his unhappy crew charged that while they were docked in Africa, an African slave trader was heard to say, in good English, that they were docked in Cabo Monte, which was, in fact, fifty miles north of the Equator. As required by treaty, Spanish officials investigated—inventorying the *Florida*'s contents, checking the ship's log, and deposing all the crew and investors. After considering all the evidence, officials ruled that because the Anglo/Spanish treaty banned the slave traffic, the boat should be confiscated and sold for the government's benefit and that the enslaved cargo should be declared emancipated. With that, Pearson, who had declared his intention to homestead in Florida, hijacked his share of the slaves and departed the province, heading for the Cape of Good Hope, according to the boastful note he left behind. Several other bozales from Pearson's shipment escaped into the hinterland, never to be seen again, and the remainder were warehoused for four months at the expense of the consignees, Santiago (James) Darley and Ysaac Wickes.[86]

Despite the problems experienced on board the *Florida,* Darley sent a sloop, *Los Tres Amigos,* back to the African coast in July of 1819. Like the previous expedition, this one was a debacle. The slaves revolted and killed some of Captain Juan Llufrio's crew before being subdued. The sloop finally made it to Santo Domingo, where Darley had to sell most of the slaves just to cover costs. He returned to Florida with only nine bozales, whom he sent to join the twenty-three he had working his 500-acre grant on Turnbull's Swamp, south of St. Augustine.[87]

The Continuing African Presence

As described above, Spaniards continued to legally import new Africans into Florida well into 1819; it is, therefore, not surprising to find evidence of the African presence in Spanish Florida scattered throughout the notarial archives of the colony. Civil and criminal records also verify the entry of Africans and the introduction of African languages and cultural practices into Florida. For example, when turtle fishermen found five blacks shipwrecked on the Mosquito bar in 1799, two of the men were *criollos* from St. Christopher, but the other three were natives of Guinea. One, who could speak some Spanish, said he was of the Congo nation and he reported the other two identified themselves as Carabalís Suam. The officials called in the slave Antonia María, who was also Carabalí Suam, and she translated into Spanish what they told her.[88]

Africans imported together on the same ships maintained contact with one another and, years later, as owners sold or freed them, they referred to the ships on which their slaves originally entered the province. In 1819 Felipe (Philip Robert) Yonge sold Juan Atkinson six young slaves (ages 19–25), all of whom Fernando de la Maza Arredondo brought from Africa to Florida on the *Sevilla* in 1810. As children they had shared the trauma of the middle passage and had been together at least nine years before being sold as a group, so their relationship continued under a new owner.[89]

The Trade Northward

Not all of Florida's newly imported Africans remained in Florida, however. Untold numbers of enslaved captives found themselves shipped northward despite congressional prohibitions. Even the highly regarded Don Juan McQueen had hoped to profit from such a business and less reputable investors actually did. Historians such as W. E. B. Du Bois and Ulrich B. Phillips estimated illicit imports of slaves into the United State between 1808 and 1860 at between 250,000 and 270,000, while Kenneth Stamp estimated the imports in just the decade from 1810 to 1820 at 60,000. Philip Curtin and others subsequently revised those estimates downward, as did Kenneth F. Kiple, who argued against a Cuba-Florida slave trade in the nineteenth century, without referring to any Spanish Florida sources.[90] While there may never be a definitive count, the Spanish notarial records, which may be presumed to undercount them, clearly show that Africans were being imported into Spanish Florida in increasing numbers after 1802 and until the Spanish departed in 1821. They further show that citizens of the United States were involved in this trade as investors, ship captains, sales agents, and purchasers, despite the intentions of the United States Congress.

As discussed in chapter 10, the illegal evasion of the United States embargo reached new heights in 1817, when privateers claiming to represent various Spanish American nations "liberated" Amelia Island from the Spanish empire. On Amelia these erstwhile "Republicans" began a brisk business in the sale of captured prizes and their cargoes, which often included slaves. One unsuspecting Spanish ship returned from the African coast carrying 290 enslaved Africans whom the privateers promptly sold to eager buyers on the docks. The *Nile's Weekly Register* charged that "the Negroes will certainly be smuggled into the United States, as many others have been lately." The writer added, "This trade in human flesh is so profitable, that if that island [Amelia] is not taken possession of by the United States, we shall hear of many slave vessels sent as prizes that have very conveniently laid off the port to be captured."[91] Customs agents posted across the Florida border estimated that the French pirate, Luis Aury, sold more than one thousand Africans in less than two months, most of whom were "spirited" northward to Georgia or other southern states where importation was forbidden.[92]

After satisfying himself that the Amelia privateers acted independently of "any organized government whatever," President Monroe ordered a United States naval force southward to seize the unruly island and, hopefully, end the illicit trade.[93] Noting that United States revenue laws applied only to vessels larger than five tons, Captain John Elton of the USS *Saranac* despaired. He described African rowers ferrying slaves from ship to shore almost continuously and even after United States forces occupied Amelia in late November 1817, the misery continued.[94] When Elton intercepted the Spanish slaver *Savina* in 1818, he was shocked by the suffering he witnessed. The ship had been swept by "coast fever" and only twenty-five of the 118 Africans who were taken from the Guinea Coast remained alive. Elton described the weakened and shivering slaves as "all very young, not exceeding fifteen years of age." He distributed blankets among them, but several people died during the night and Elton estimated that "a number more . . . will, in all probability, terminate their miserable existence before another sun." Elton added, "It is enough to make the stoutest heart sicken."[95] Later that year (and a decade after the embargo was enacted) the *Savannah Republican* reported the *Saranac*'s seizure of a "small schooner of about sixty tons" which held "130 souls . . . packed into a small space." Had the captain managed to evade capture the paper suggested how he would have disposed of his cargo. "[A] regular chain of posts is established from the head of St. Marys River to the upper country, and through the Indian nation, by means of which, these emaciated wretches are hurried and transferred to every part of the country."[96]

Ironically, the very attempt to end the slave trade actually increased the pace of African importations into Spanish Florida, and also probably exacerbated the conditions under which the Africans entrapped in the trade suffered. Most of the Africans entering Florida in these decades were destined for slavery across the northern border. The smaller number of slaves who were absorbed into Spanish Florida's plantation and urban workforces lived through years of frontier violence before some owners left with them for Cuba. Once Spain and the United States signed the Adams-Onís Treaty in 1819, the pace of the exodus to Cuba increased.

Postscript

Even after Spain formally ceded Florida to the United States in 1819, slave traders made a mockery of the inadequately supported slave trade embargo. In 1820 a United States Treasury cutter patrolling off the coast of St. Augustine captured the *Antelope,* a slaver incoming from Cabinda and carrying 280 Africans aboard.

During eight years of litigation, by the Spanish, Portuguese, and United States governments, and a decision by the Supreme Court, treasury officials hired out the surviving Africans to Georgia planters. Finally, sixteen fortunate men were freed (by a lottery system), and more than one hundred men, women, and children were resettled in Liberia by the American Society for Colonizing the Free People of Color of the United States, commonly known as the Colonization Society. The remaining thirty-nine slaves became the property Congressman Richard Wilde of Georgia, who sent them to labor on his plantation in Monticello, Florida.[97]

The same year the Africans from the *Antelope* were being dispersed to Liberia and Florida, a British gunboat chased the Spanish slaver *Guerrero* onto the Florida Reef. The *Guerrero* carried on board 350 Africans, most of whom were taken to Cuba. Another 114 went to Key West, suffering from dysentery and ophthalmia. Finding himself unable to provide for the Africans while British, Spanish, and American interests fought through the tangled legal debates surrounding the cargo, the United States revenue agent in Key West shipped the slaves to St. Augustine and hired them out to none other than Zephaniah Kingsley. Kingsley availed himself of thirty-nine new Africans from the *Guerrero* at a cost of only $2.00 a month and upkeep for each of the slaves.[98] After a ruling by John Quincy Adams, the secretary of the navy recalled Kingsley's new Africans in order to repatriate them to Cape Mesurado, Liberia.[99] Kingsley argued that his workers were "free men and could not be sent to Africa contrary to their wishes," but eventually all but three of the men in Kingsley's charge boarded the schooner *Washington's Barge* for a return voyage across the Atlantic, where they may have encountered the survivors of the *Antelope*.[100] As a result of cases such as the *Antelope* and the *Guerrero,* new Africans continued to enter territorial Florida decades after their supposed introduction had been outlawed. (See appendix 11.)

Crime and Punishment

Historian Charles Cutter has described a distinct legal culture found in even the most peripheral areas of the Spanish empire as "the touchstone by which Spanish subjects understood and negotiated their relationship to the rest of society."[1] Black subjects in Spanish Florida operated within this distinct culture and clearly appreciated the possibilities that it held for them. As we have seen, persons of African descent regularly used the law to their own advantage in pursuing manumission, justice, and economic advance in the Spanish colony. It is also true, however, that black subjects suffered harsh penalties for serious crimes, such as murder or infanticide (as any other subject also would), and that they often suffered more punitive treatment than others did for lesser crimes. The Spanish legal culture, which was, like the rest of the society, hierarchical and corporatist, worked to curb behaviors defined as inappropriate or threatening and targeted blacks, like other "outsiders," for special supervision. Repeated incidents of insubordination or notorious behavior, could, in a sense, be considered status crimes in Spanish communities, and governors usually responded by sentencing the convicted "nuisance" to hard labor or banishment. Nevertheless, in a culture that believed that the prime directive of a good government was justice, even frontier administrators strove to administer the law equitably. The care with which Spanish officials in Florida adjudicated cases involving black slaves, the "least among them," demonstrated this commitment and must have made a powerful impression on the many "foreign" blacks in Spanish Florida, who would never have had access to the courts in their previous settings.[2]

In Spanish colonies any accusation or report of a crime by any member of the community, free or enslaved, triggered an immediate *sumaria,* or fact-finding inquiry, in which the court solicited testimony from all witnesses regardless of race, class, gender, or legal status. Because so many residents of Spanish Florida did not speak Spanish, the court employed translators of English, Spanish, and African languages. Once testimony was given, authorities read the statements back to those who gave them and allowed changes or corrections, additions or deletions. The court followed the same judicial procedures in each case, expending just as much time and expense on crimes against slaves as it would against more elite members of the community. In addition to taking testimony from witnesses, the court made full examinations of crime scenes, weapons, and other physical evidence, and even conducted autopsies to help arrive at justice.[3] Selected case studies illustrate the meticulous nature of the criminal inquiry in Spanish Florida.

Black-on-Black Crime

In his classic work, Frederick P. Bowser found that in colonial Peru black violence was most often directed against other blacks, and that pattern seems to hold true in Spanish Florida as well.[4] Commissioners appointed from the Spanish community were responsible for maintaining order in their barrios and responded to and attempted to resolve minor complaints without involving higher authorities. If blacks attacked other blacks in the streets, where the violence was witnessed and threatened community order, however, or if the violence resulted in death, the governor's tribunal investigated and adjudicated. The criminal records offer insights into the workings of Spanish law, but also into the complex relationships among members of the free and enslaved black communities and their interactions with the nonblack community.

Shortly before Christmas, 1795, the slave Bob entered the cabin of his fellow slave Cesar and knifed him as he slept next to his wife. Their overseer ordered the Bambara slave Prince and the free laborer Liberty to capture Bob, "without harming him," but in the process Liberty shot Bob in the back with Cesar's loaded gun.[5] During the investigation which followed, authorities discovered a long-running feud among the slaves on Don Francis Phelipe Fatio's Nueva Suiza plantation. Cesar related that it had its origins in a disagreement between his own father-in-law and a brother of Bob's. As Bob had attacked the sleeping Cesar, he had declared that anyone who offended his brother offended him. Cesar felt, however, that Bob's main motive was to "fool around" with Cesar's wife, whom Cesar said had spurned Bob.

Authorities jailed Liberty, an escaped slave from South Carolina who was working for Fatio as a free wage laborer. As his employer, Fatio was responsible for his good behavior and sent his son to town to represent Liberty in court. The younger Fatio testified that Liberty had not acted in malice and he asked for compassion for "his client." He also charged that Bob's death was "a punishment of the Almighty for his wickedness and dishonesty." Governor White ruled that a death required punishment and condemned Liberty to one year of hard labor on the public works. The sentence was actually a light one for homicide, and that may reflect the influence of Liberty's defender as well as the character of the governor.[6]

In a second example, the sentence for murder was death. The second homicide case involved the axe murder of Benito by his co-worker, Roberto Linse.[7] With the help of an appointed public defender and translators, Roberto told the court he was from Pennsylvania, but later said he came from South Carolina. He had been the slave of Don Francisco Antonio Urrutia in Havana but escaped slavery by sailing with a corsair from Providence Island, who took him to the St. Marys River. There Roberto jumped ship and requested and received sanctuary in Florida, where he found employment as a free laborer on the plantation of Don José Antonio Yguíniz. Three other freed fugitives from Georgia also worked on the plantation, and when Roberto accused Benito of stealing his jornales (wages), Benito's friends, black fugitives from Georgia named Luis and David Hall, held Roberto to allow Benito to beat him. Roberto reported the beating to Yguíniz, who told him to return to work, where the quarrel resumed. Roberto said that although Benito challenged him, he refused to fight until Roberto came after him with an axe. Roberto tried to make the case for self-defense, but the fact that he axed Benito as he was halfway out a window and that he admitted sharpening the murder weapon prior to the fight made that claim unbelievable. Despite the seeming premeditation, the St. Augustine court made further inquiries about Roberto in Havana before ultimately declaring him guilty and condemning him to death. Although sentenced in 1796, he was not finally executed until six years later.[8]

Women and Crime

On the night of October 6, 1787, the St. Augustine slaveowner Juan Salom awoke to find that his slave Juana and her two children were missing from their usual sleeping place on the floor next to his bed. He assumed that they had fled. Before returning to sleep, he went out to the patio well to get a drink and discovered the two small bodies of Juan Baptista Salom, age five, and Isabel Anna Salom, age two, floating in the dark water. Salom ran to inform the sergeant major, and at 9:00 the next morning the governor's tribunal opened an investigation into the deaths of Juana's children.[9]

Three days after the murders, Juana was captured and jailed in the Castillo de San Marcos, where she gave her testimony about the children's deaths. The court's detailed attempts to assess the truth of Juana's story and its willingness to accept the testimony of female slaves against a white male owner stand in sharp contrast to legal procedures in the Anglo South. The verbatim statements that the slave women gave in this case are also an extremely rare and valuable window into the sensitive issues of race, sexuality, and gender. Juana's final punishment and the resolution of the case are classic examples of Spanish efforts to achieve compromise and restore community order through a combination of *derecho* (customary law) and *ley* (written law).[10]

Despite Juana's slave status and the horror of her "unnatural" crime of infanticide, meticulous Spanish bureaucrats conducted her investigation as they would any other.[11] They followed all legal requirements and took great care to gather available physical evidence as well as lengthy testimony from the involved parties. They tried to be sure that Juana understood the charges against her, as well as the religious and legal implications of her acts. And when Juana revealed important mitigating circumstances for her crime, the St. Augustine court referred the case to a higher court, seeking its guidance on her punishment. This careful prosecution was extended to someone who could well have been considered an "outsider" and who lacked important personal connections within the community. Juana had been born in New York and raised among Protestants. She was illiterate and spoke only English, so a bilingual interpreter recorded Juana's testimony and although he directed the testimony by his questions, he also allowed Juana to add any statements that she wished to make.

Upon discovery of the crime, Governor Vicente Manuel de Zéspedes had ordered an investigation of the murder site. The man who had retrieved the children's bodies from the well had been unable to get out without assistance, and so Juana's contention that she jumped into the well with a child under each arm, was kept afloat by her clothes, and got out unassisted, and in some unknown manner, raised questions. Upon examining the crime scene St. Augustine's master carpenter and one other appointed official reported that it would have been impossible for Juana to have committed the crime as she described, and that she would not have been able to get out of the well unassisted because it was too deep and narrow. This would seem to indicate that either Juana threw the children in and did not jump in herself, or that someone whom Juana was protecting by her silence had helped her to get out. Although interrogators voiced their opinion that the story was unlikely, Juana stuck to it.[12] When the interpreter asked Juana's motive for drowning her own children, her story began to unfold.

Juana related that on the night of the crime her owner had instructed her to say a final farewell to her children because she had been sold as a wet nurse and would be sailing for Havana the next day.[13] The translator inquired why she had not gone to the priest for help, as was her right. Juana said she would have, but Salom told her he had already spoken to the priest and that the clergyman had signed papers allowing her sale. This was untrue, but Juana had no way of knowing that, and seeing no way out, she admitted that she had attempted to end all their lives.

Juana was listed in the records as an "infidel" because although she had been baptized into the New Light sect in New York, she said she never had been taught any prayers. Given this lack of religious instruction, the translator attempted to determine if Juana understood that killing her children and attempting suicide were wrong and deserving of punishment. Juana replied in the affirmative, but said she was beside herself ("fuera de sí").

When the translator asked if she had ever tried to find another owner, as was also her right, Juana stated that two persons had offered to buy her, but Salom would not allow her to bring the prospective buyers to his house.

Even before Juana began telling her story, her owner, Juan Salom, appeared before the governor to voluntarily give up custody of his slave, "in consideration of her enormous crime," and leave her "in the hands of Justice." A female slave of Juana's age and condition would have been valued at several hundred pesos, or the equivalent of several hundred dollars, so this was an expensive gesture for Salom. As it soon became clear, there were reasons for his largesse.

During Juana's interrogation she described a pattern of regular sexual solicitation by her owner. Solicitation was a serious charge under Spanish law and if proven, the Siete Partidas required the court to remove Juana from the owner's household. Juana said that on many occasions when Salom propositioned her, his wife, with whom he also had sexual relations, was asleep in the bed next to which Juana slept. Asked if there were any witnesses to the solicitations, Juana replied that many times these took place when she was working in the fields alone, but that occasionally her owner also harassed her in the house. One time her protests attracted another slave whom Juana stated overheard Salom threaten to beat her if she did not comply and who also heard Juana's resistance. Sadly, Juana added that on many occasions Salom had his way, "by force of blows." Only a few nights before the crime, her owner had chained Juana to his bed. As soon as his wife was asleep, Salom awoke Juana with a kick and promised that if she would have sex with him, he would remove her chains. Asked why she did not tell Salom's wife of these multiple offenses, Juana said she had, but the woman only called her a liar and helped to punish her. At this point the translator interjected that it was unlikely a wife would not do something about her husband's misdeeds if she knew the circumstances; but Salom's wife, Margarita Neto, was the mother of two small children and may not have felt it wise to confront this situation directly. The wife must have been suspicious, however, for she repeatedly questioned her husband about his behavior with Juana. Each time, Salom denied Juana's accusations, and his wife accepted his denials.[14]

But the mulatto slave María had overheard the solicitation. Like Juana, María had been raised in the Anglo north and was not a Catholic. She was forty-six years old and illiterate, but certainly not without "voice." María knew of Juana's plight because she lived in the adjoining house and "would have had to stuff my ears not to hear what I did." María testified that she heard Salom instruct the distraught mother to look one last time at the children which were not hers, but his, and that he taunted, "every ounce of flesh and each bone in your body belongs to that woman [Juana's new owner]." Asked about Juana's response, María said she heard Juana agree that her owner had a right to sell her, but that Juana had also reminded him he was obliged to sell her children with her. It is clear from this that, although Juana was not a Catholic, she understood elements of the church requirements that were critical to her welfare.

The court asked María if Salom had starved or punished Juana frequently, mistreatment which the Siete Partidas forbade of slaveowners.[15] María answered that Juana got abundant food, but that once when Salom discovered Juana had spent the night elsewhere, he gave her "about a dozen lashes" and locked her up. She also testified that Juana complained that Salom would not allow her to see the black man with whom she had a relationship (possibly the father of the children) and that Salom's motive was to have Juana to himself.

On that note, María testified that one afternoon the previous summer she was in the street and saw Salom's wife leave the house. Approaching an open window, María had stuck her head in to talk with Juana when she heard Salom call for his slave to get in bed with him. She heard Juana refuse and tell her owner that he had "his own woman." When Salom's wife came back suddenly, María got away from the window, briefly. As soon as the coast was clear, however, she returned to her listening post to hear Salom's wife query Juana about what she was doing at the top of the stairs. Juana answered that she was there at Salom's order and when the wife asked her why, Juana replied, "If I tell you you'll whip me." That time the wife encouraged her to confess, saying she had overheard all anyway. Here María interjected that it was untrue that Salom's wife had overheard, but that she only wanted to get the story. Trapped, Juana told the wife the truth, and this time Salom's wife marched to the bedroom and proceeded to slap her husband repeatedly. To further discredit Salom, and as if to emphasize his guilt, María testified that when his wife was attacking him, he never said a word, nor did he try to stop the physical abuse.

María's lively and verbatim testimony caused the court to question how she understood the Catalán exchanges among the three. María stated that she knew that language after living with two different Minorcan families for the past eight or nine years. She was also asked if the Saloms spoke English, which she confirmed they did. The court did not question the veracity of her statement; however, it wanted the legal record to be clear that María had, indeed, been able to understand and faithfully report the conversations that she overheard.[16]

María had not spoken with Juana since the night of the murders, so the court had no reason to believe that she may have conspired to support Juana's version of the crime. Given the open windows, close proximity of the houses, and relatively unrestricted movement of slaves throughout the city, the court simply assumed that María would have knowledge of Juana's treatment by her owner. As noted in earlier chapters, Spanish justice, like Spanish society of the time, suffered from class bias and commonly gave greater credit to testimony by elite witnesses.[17] Had María been telling such tales about members of the governor's circle, she may have had a more difficult time being believed. But Salom was not of that social standing, was not even Spanish, and had once been an indentured servant himself, transported to New Smyrna, Florida, in 1768 to work on Andrew Turnbull's indigo plantations. Salom and the others suffered such horrible conditions there that in 1777 they rebelled and escaped to St. Augustine, where Governor Patrick Tonyn freed them. Salom's background meant he was due no assumed superiority in the case.[18]

The following day, the thirty-six-year-old, illiterate Juan Salom appeared in court to give his version of events. Salom acknowledged that Juana had killed her children because she was about to be separated from them, but he said she had heard the news from her new owner, not from him. Salom said he told Juana she should be happy to be going to the prosperous city of Havana, where she would be able to earn money with which to buy her liberty and return to Florida to see her children.

From the various testimonies, Juana is known to have worked in the fields, in domestic service, and as a wet nurse, but she had no highly valued skills, and Salom's statement implied that Juana had little chance in St. Augustine of earning the funds required to buy herself and her children. Since the average price for a healthy woman of Juana's age was approximately 250–300 pesos, and the cost of her children's freedom would have added another 100–200 pesos, and since the average day's pay for a man was a half peso, and women commonly earned less, Salom may have been right. Buying freedom was an arduous process, no doubt; however, other of Juana's contemporaries managed it, as she well knew. The unnamed father of Juana's children, or friends in the community, might have also been able to help her work toward that goal. The fact that Salom introduced the idea of *coartación* into his testimony may signify that Juana had been discussing the possibility.

The court signaled some sympathy for Juana when it asked Salom if the "true and sole" motive for Juana's actions was "the pain she felt to find herself sold to a country across the water, leaving behind her children." Given the opportunity to paint a darker picture of Juana, even Salom had to agree that it seemed her grief was to blame.

The court also asked Salom to say how and why he punished Juana. He answered that in the two years he had owned Juana, he had once given her a few slaps (*bofetones*) and only on two other occasions had he struck her—once for refusing to get dressed on time to go to a wet-nursing appointment and once for leaving the house. However, Salom's version of why Juana left his house differed from the story that Juana told María, and that María told the court. Salom said that Juana ran to the governor's house (once again illustrating that she understood where to seek protection) because his wife was going to punish her, and that Juana refused to allow it, biting the wife on the arm before running away. The angered wife followed Juana and proceeded to punish her on the spot, until the governor intervened and chided Salom's wife for disrespecting his house. It is significant that Governor Zéspedes, who was hearing the case, had witnessed some of Juana's mistreatment and had interceded for her on at least one occasion.

The court then proceeded to the more serious charges made by Juana and asked if Salom had solicited his slave or ever had carnal knowledge of her. Salom said he never had and, in an eerily contemporary vein, said that the charges were incredible because "my wife is pretty." The court asked Salom to better refresh his memory on this matter since several previous testimonies had alleged otherwise, but Salom repeated his denials. He was asked specifically about the afternoon solicitation and, once again, denied it.

Although Governor Zéspedes had full authority to decide this case, the severity of the crime and of the allegations Juana made against her owner led him to refer the case to the next level of justice—the royal *audiencia* (court of appeal) in Havana. By the following January, that court had rendered a decision that "there were not conclusive or clear enough proofs of the malice" required to hang Juana, which would have been the normal sentence for a capital crime. It added that the crime may have been involuntary or impetuous on the mother's part since she was driven almost mad by the pain of leaving her children forever in the custody of a feared owner. Rather than execution, therefore, the audiencia recommended a severe punishment, to be left to the discretion of the governor. The higher court suggested lashes in the pillory and that "the delinquent" be made to wear an iron collar for six years to satisfy her punishment and, at the same time, "cleanse" the community of the evil of infanticide. No mention was made of Juana's charges of sexual harassment because Salom had already given up custody of Juana. Had he not, the court would have been required to remove her from his home. Lastly, the court ordered Juana's sale at public auction to defray the court costs in Florida and Havana.

On receipt of the dictate from Havana, Florida's governor sentenced Juana to two hundred lashes at the public pillory and to wear an iron collar as recommended. On February 14, 1788, the free black, July, administered Juana's sentence, and although such a brutal whipping would seem impossible to survive, the castigated Juana returned to the Castillo to await her sale. Perhaps because of her physical condition, bidders offered very little for Juana at two public auctions, causing the governor to suspend the sales. Finally, after Juana had spent almost five months in prison (recuperating?), Pablo Villa paid 135 pesos for her at a third auction, and Juana's historical trail disappears.[19]

Juana escaped execution due to the extenuating circumstances of the crime, which she and her friend, the slave María, were able to present to the court in their unconstrained testimonies. Nevertheless, she was severely whipped and humiliated in a staged morality play, and if the rest of Havana's sentence was enforced, she displayed the iron reminder of her crime every day for six years. More horribly still, she lived with the knowledge that she had killed her children in the mistaken belief that the priest had authorized her separation from them. Juana remained a slave, but she was free of Salom's harassment, and it seems doubtful that her new owner would attempt similar mistreatment given the serious attention the governor's tribunal had paid to Juana and María's testimonies.

Salom and his wife escaped any punishment other than the public scandal that surrounded them. Not only were the details of their intimate relations made public but the story of Salom's physical abuse by his wife (an inversion of the "natural order" of Spanish gender conventions) would surely have been the stock of popular jokes in that day. In addition to their disgrace, they also suffered the economic loss of Juana and her services, and the potential profits they may have made on the later sale or services of her children. Their downfall, too, was a lesson to be read by the community.[20]

Masters Who Murdered Slaves

Although masters killing slaves was an extraordinary event in Spanish Florida, within one fatal month in 1811, slaves accused two masters of murder.[21] On March 12, 1811, the Mandinga slave Yra ran to the nearby Amelia Island plantation of Don Santiago Cashen, where a slave woman "of his nation" translated his terrible report that his owner Don Domingo Fernández had just beaten a fellow slave to death. Although Fernández was one of the area's important planters and enjoyed a distinguished military reputation as a gunboat commander, as justice of the peace for Amelia Island and the "American frontier" Cashen was required by law to launch an immediate investigation.[22] He ordered the arrest of the accused planter, embargoed his property, and appointed bilingual (Spanish and English) *testigos de asistencia* (court assistants), who began taking the testimony of witnesses.[23]

After swearing on the Holy Cross, the slave Bely, a native of South Carolina, testified that when he returned from field labor for a midday meal, Yare told him that Fernández had beaten him with a stick and because of the beating he was feeling ill. Three hours later Yare was dead. The slave Coffe, "a native of the African coast," was not sworn because he "professed no religion," but he confirmed Bely's account. Neither slave thought Fernández had ever beaten Yare before, and Bely added that Fernández usually assigned him the task of punishing other slaves. The slaves described the stick with which Fernández beat Yare as a walking stick he carried on his rounds, about an inch thick.

Next, Don Domingo Fernández gave his account. He testified that he had discovered the Africans Yare and Somer idle, and that as he marched them before him to a designated workplace, they began to converse in their own language. Fernández described Yare as "enteramente bozal," meaning he could speak no European languages, but Somer could speak some English and he told his owner that Yare was sick. Thinking the pair unwilling to work because of the cold, Fernández was unsympathetic and set them to work. When he checked on them later, however, he found them sitting at a fire. Fernández admitted striking their backs and heads with his walking stick before they all returned to the plantation to eat lunch. Fernández testified that he had decided to allow Yare to stay out of the fields, but that the slave returned to work before the owner could excuse him. A few hours later, Somer and Coffer brought their dead compatriot back to the house.

Fernández immediately sent for the physician, Don Francisco Sontag, who testified that he found no marks on the body, but he knew that various slaves from the same *armazón* (shipment) had been sick and that some had died of inflammation of the liver, ruptured arteries, and excessive phlegm. To satisfy himself of the cause of death, Sontag conducted an autopsy on Yare and found his stomach full of warm air and his abdominal cavity putrefied and "destroyed." Sontag declared that the blows by Fernández had not caused Yare's death.[24]

Despite this finding, the governor found fault with the investigation because Yra reported the crime and should have been the first to be interviewed. The governor also wanted Fernández's walking stick. Further, he ordered an immediate embargo and inventory of all Fernández's goods. And so the investigation continued.

As ordered, Cashen interviewed Yra, using Coffe as his translator. Yra testified that when he heard their owner had killed Yare, he feared he planned to kill all his slaves, and so he ran to Cashen's house, where he found a slave woman of his nation who could understand him. Yra was not an eyewitness and knew only what his friend Somer had told him about the death, but Cashen sent the governor the new testimony and the walking stick, which was made of rattan and weighed only about four ounces.

After Fernández paid a 300-peso fine, the governor lifted the embargo on his goods, but there was still the matter of whether he had dressed the slaves properly for the weather. The governor ordered Fernández jailed in the Castillo de San Marcos and pursued this new area of questioning. Fernández testified that he gave his slaves four sets of clothing annually, two each summer and two each winter. He admitted that Yare's winter pants were "somewhat torn" but attributed his death to his advanced age and illness.

The governor required one final legal review by his prosecutor, who ruled that although Fernández had not baptized his slaves, he did promise in the future to make religious instruction available to those who wanted it and were capable of understanding (presumably the language). The prosecutor found that Fernández had provided his slaves with sufficient clothing and food, and that Yare's illness was more than sufficient to "cut the thread" of the old man's life. After paying court costs and posting a bond, the slaveowner Fernández was finally set free in June 1811.[25]

Even as Cashen was investigating Yare's death, the African-born slave Rayna ran to Magnolia, the plantation of Don Enrique Yonge, to report that she had witnessed Don Guillermo Braddock horribly beat the slave Duncan, who died as a result. Yonge immediately informed authorities of "the horrid news" that Braddock had flogged Duncan "in such an inhuman manner as to occasion his death." As he was writing, a second slave arrived to report the death. Yonge urged a party to come the same night to arrest Braddock so that he could not escape "the punishment so abominable a piece of cruelty loudly calls for." Both Yonge and Braddock were recent immigrants from Georgia and might have been expected to hold similar attitudes toward slaves, but class may account for the difference. While Yonge was a merchant of some means, Braddock was a small farmer who described himself as "poor." Yonge's descriptions of Braddock as cruel, inhumane, and abominable may have been designed to differentiate between them and to demonstrate that Yonge understood Spanish Florida's conventions related to slavery.[26]

Justice Cashen named two interrogators and a translator, who must have arrived the same night to arrest the accused. Braddock's attitude under interrogation, unlike that of Don Fernández, was totally unrepentant. Braddock said that it was not the beating that killed Duncan but his "arrogant and haughty character," which was demonstrated by his knife attack on Braddock's white overseer (who after the slave's death had fled the province). Braddock said that he had to punish Duncan as an example and to maintain the subordination of the other slaves, but the inventory of Braddock's embargoed goods listed only six slaves, three of whom were women. Braddock only belatedly added that he knew harsh treatment was forbidden and said he did not mean to kill the slave.

A number of Anglo character witnesses testified that Braddock was an "indulgent" master who gave his slaves plots of land on which to grow crops and raise animals and spent a great deal of money on slave maintenance. They also added remarks about Duncan's bad character, and some of their slaves supported Braddock's contention that Duncan had told the kitchen slaves "if that white man puts his hands on me I'll kill him with this knife."[27]

Other slave witnesses gave a different version of events. Rayna was visiting the Braddock plantation and witnessed the master and his overseer beat Duncan until he fell to the ground. Braddock's slave Sally added that after the first beating, her owner locked Duncan up for the night. The next morning Braddock and his overseer both beat Duncan again before placing him in a pillory. Sally testified that Duncan was weak and fainting and that she brought him a cup of coffee and some porridge, but he was able to eat very little. By midday he was dead.

Don Eben O'Neill, who owned the contiguous New Hope plantation, testified that, after the incident with the overseer, Duncan had hidden for two weeks but then came to his house asking his intercession with Braddock.[28] O'Neill delivered Duncan back to Braddock and asked him to forgive his slave. Braddock promised to wait until the morning to punish Duncan, and O'Neill had planned to be present. By the time O'Neill arrived, however, Duncan had already been beaten twice, and Braddock even told O'Neill that he planned to give him twenty-five additional lashes each of the next six days.

Although Braddock had buried his slave shortly after his death, Cashen ordered the body exhumed, and the physician and surgeon Don José Gantt conducted the required autopsy. Gantt opened Duncan's chest and made a second incision through his ribs, and in both locations the surgeon found coagulated blood beneath the skin, which he attributed to the blows. Gantt did not find sufficient damage to believe the blows had been mortal, however, and stated that he had seen much worse on slaves who had not died.[29]

Authorities continued to question Braddock in prison and specifically asked if he had intended to kill Duncan. This time the less arrogant (if no more contrite) master said that he would not have beaten Duncan so much if he had known it would kill him, because he was a poor man and could not afford the loss of his purchase price. Braddock stated that it was the white overseer who gave Duncan 250 blows with a walnut cudgel and suggested that Duncan had strangled himself to death rather than face further beatings. Although that possibility seems ludicrous, the surgeon's testimony that the blows were insufficient to have caused death exonerated Braddock of murder. Instead, authorities charged him with excessive and cruel treatment of his slaves and charged him court costs. The inquiry and imprisonment may have ruined Braddock because his name does not appear on territorial land review claims.[30]

Status Crimes

In Spanish communities such as St. Augustine, reputation carried tremendous importance. A person of honor and good character, no matter how poor and even if a slave, could count on the support of a wide network of family, friends, and patrons, including that of the highest government officials and, by extension, even the monarch. Examples of the tangible benefits of such a "good" reputation are scattered throughout these chapters. On the other hand, someone who repeatedly violated social norms, exhibited violent or unruly behavior, or frequently disrupted the peace of the community was soon labeled a troublemaker and could count on little support.

The carpenter Samuel Rumford, his wife, and his mother were once slaves of the English owner Juan Coddington. In 1785 they claimed religious sanctuary in Spanish Florida, were emancipated, and went to live in the home of the parish priest, Miguel O'Reilly. The couple performed free labor for O'Reilly for some time—Rumford building a fence and doing general carpentry and repairs, and his wife tending O'Reilly's garden, cooking, and doing his laundry—but Rumford's mother was ill and unable to work.

Rumford also plied his trade in the community and deposited his jornales, or earnings, with Father O'Reilly for safekeeping, hoping to save enough for the family to be able to live independently. In the meantime, the priest charged the family two reales daily for food (about a quarter in U.S. currency) and also charged Rumford's "account" twenty-five pesos for the purchase of a canoe Rumford used to do business. Father O'Reilly also reported that he had spent money on medicine and medical care for Rumford's mother, which he also must have charged to the son's debt.

Becoming disgruntled with his lack of economic progress, Rumford tried to move, but O'Reilly held his tools hostage. So Rumford took the clergyman to court. O'Reilly had to respond to Rumford's charges, and took the opportunity to level some of his own. He reminded the court that Rumford had been involved in an incidence of "mutiny" at the Nueva Suiza plantation of Don Francis Phelipe Fatio, for which he had been imprisoned and forced to wear shackles. O'Reilly described Rumford as "false and malicious," "impudent," "of bad conduct," and as possessing a "bad heart." He also reported that Rumford had sworn vengeance on all who mistreated him, and O'Reilly considered his life in danger were Rumford not exiled.[31]

Not cowed, Rumford came back to court two months later to sue Captain Eduardo Nugent for twenty-five pesos that he said Nugent owed him for roof repairs. He asked Governor Zéspedes to order payment or have Nugent explain why he should not pay. The governor asked for Nugent's response, which was that O'Reilly had asked him to withhold Rumford's payment to satisfy his debt to the priest.[32]

Two years later, Rumford was in trouble again. This time he stood accused of trying to poison the free black carpenter Juan Wright. At this inquiry Father O'Reilly reminded the court of Rumford's prior incarcerations under both the British and Spanish legal systems, his "bad reputation," and his "perverse" and "indomitable character." Governor Zéspedes finally exiled Rumford to Havana with strict instructions to Cuban authorities that he never be allowed to return, admitting that he was exiling Rumford, not so much for attempted poisoning as for his perverse character. The governor ordered that Rumford's common-law wife be allowed to follow him to Cuba some time later.[33]

Blacks and Military Justice

In the spring of 1805, authorities arrested the urban black militia member Sandi Edimboro for attacking a white grenadier from the Cuban Third Battalion, José Rosas. The two men had vied for the affection of the free black Fany, and Rosas lost. When he returned to see Fany, a scuffle broke out, and Sandi gave Rosas several blows to the head. Sandi ran from the scene but was captured by members of the garrison. Because both Rosas and Sandi were covered by the *fuero militar* (a corporate exemption from prosecution in civilian courts), the case was settled in a military hearing. The *auditor de guerra* gathered testimony from all witnesses in the case and found that the accounts followed racial lines. Black witnesses contended that Sandi employed self-defense when Rosas went after him with a knife, and the whites averred that Sandi surprised and injured the defenseless grenadier. It is interesting to note that the court assigned Sandi's father, Felipe Edimboro, the task of gathering the conflicting declarations. The *auditor* explained that Edimboro was "known for his honesty" and that he had tried to correct the "wicked ways" of his son, going so far as to have Sandi jailed once.

Edimboro's reputation did not save Sandi. Although much uncertainty about the facts in the case remained, the *auditor* concluded that there was no doubt that Sandi had indeed given Rosas several blows, that the incident, while not premeditated, had its origins in the color differences of the contestants for Fany's favor, and that Sandi was "impudent and insulting and without respect for whites." He recommended, and the governor approved, a sentence for Sandi of one year at hard labor in chains and fetters. This harsh sentence was meant to "serve as a warning to others of his class, as well as a correction."[34]

This case illustrates the unwritten limits that free blacks faced. Edimboro was reputed to be honest and hardworking, and he conformed to the community's standards. When he challenged, as he did often, it was through litigation, an acceptable course of action. Sandi, on the other hand, was considered to be wild and impudent. Not even his father could correct him, and he represented an intolerable threat to St. Augustine's white, patriarchal society. His loss of control could not be excused.

A military court also punished the free black militiaman Carlos Francisco Travers (also known as Tory) for unseemly and threatening public behavior. Travers was beating a dog in the street when several bystanders intervened—two of them whites and another a black slave. Travers angrily threatened one of the whites and told another who was trying to get him to leave the scene that "the street belongs to all." He reserved his physical retaliation for the slave Jorge Arredondo. White witnesses alleged Travers chased Jorge through the streets threatening for all to hear that "even if he were the slave of God Almighty, he'd kill him." Although Travers denied such blasphemy, he admitted that he had told Jorge since they were both blacks he would beat him. The subtext of this threat was that since the other men were white he could not beat them and get away with it. Three days later, Travers waylaid Jorge in the streets, but again witnesses intervened, and this time they filed formal complaints. Travers had to return from his river post to face a military inquiry. An array of important white witnesses, most of whom were recent Anglo immigrants connected to trade and slaving, accused Travers of being "a bad citizen, insubordinate, rowdy." Travers denied this and claimed to be a person of "tranquil character who had always lived within the law."

Like most of his accusers, Travers was an Anglo immigrant. Born in North Carolina, he and his three brothers had entered Florida with their parents, Aysick and Tara Travers, when Tory was only about fourteen years old. The family of runaway slaves became Catholics and were among the last recipients of religious sanctuary. Travers and his father served in the free black militia and worked the homestead which the government granted Aysick Travers.[35] Although Travers had lived in the community for over two decades, the combined weight of the white testimonies against him proved too much—at least temporarily.

Although Sandi Edimboro and Tory Travers were accused of similar incidents, a decade had passed since Sandi's trial. In the interim, as discussed in chapter 9, the United States embargo and the resulting economic boom in Fernandina, the Patriot invasion, and immigration had greatly strengthened Anglo influence in Florida. In this case, the Spanish court deferred to slave-trading and commercial interests and sentenced Travers to permanent exile from Florida. It gave him three days to depart or face the full rigor of the law.[36] However, the sentence must have been commuted, for less than a year later Governor José Coppinger awarded Travers, his wife, and eight-year-old daughter a military service grant of 125 acres of land.[37] Tory Travers stayed in Florida even after his parents and siblings evacuated to Cuba in 1821.[38]

Black Convict Labor in Florida

Ruth Pike's important study of penal servitude in Spain documents the escalating use of state prisoners during the eighteenth century, when Bourbon reformers put thousands of *presidarios* to work on massive public works projects in Spain, North Africa, and the Caribbean.[39] Following Spain's losses to England during the Seven Years War (1756–63), and the especially shocking British seizure of Havana in 1762, Spanish bureaucrats clamored for convicts to build and repair circum-Caribbean fortifications. In Florida, too, Spanish governors found *presidarios* to be a cheap labor supply for critical public works.

Convicts from Havana had always proved a handy, if insufficient, source of labor for Florida, and Governor Vicente Manuel de Zéspedes tapped this pool as well. Many of Florida's imported convict laborers were members of Havana's free black militias who had been convicted of "bad conduct," "disordered living," "incorrigible vices," or "insubordination." Josef Gallovera, age seventeen, was a shoemaker and a volunteer of the Pardo Battalion of Havana. As a youth of thirteen, he had served at the siege of Pensacola and, the following year, was part of the Spanish expedition against Providence in the Bahamas. Despite his years of service, he was sentenced to five years of forced labor on the fort at St. Augustine for bad conduct and living the "low life." Another shoemaker, Antonio Escobar, age sixteen, received the same sentence after his mother complained about his bad conduct and requested his exile. According to his criminal sentence, the carpenter Manuel Josef de la Luz was only eleven when he served in the Spanish expedition against Mobile, and he passed his next two birthdays in the siege of Pensacola and the expedition against Providence. By the age of seventeen, he was sentenced to four years of labor at St. Augustine for "a disordered life, bad customs, incorrigible vices, and insubordination, accompanied by the crime of theft."[40]

The captain generals of Cuba rid themselves of "undesirables" by shipping them off to St. Augustine, but since these free men had useful skills and received no more than rations for their hard work, they were a cheap and valued fixed labor force for Florida. Their sentences ranged from two to six years, and the men were generally young, which made them prime hands. Nevertheless, the terms of these young convicts eventually expired, and the governors complained that they never had enough convicts to accomplish the necessary work on the Plaza.[41]

Despite such complaints about supply, convict laborers always appeared on Florida rolls. These included the Cuban convicts destined to return home and local convicts. While the governors could appropriate their unpaid labor, they had to maintain the convicts, providing their food and clothing and medical care, including hospitalizations when necessary.[42] The governors also had to observe certain restrictions on convict use. During the Indian wars in 1802, the royal engineer was repairing defenses on the St. Johns and asked the governor to send him the free black carpenter Prince who was a convict at the time. Governor White denied the request because regulations forbade assigning convicts to hazardous duty. Instead, he assigned Prince to work repairing the church in St. Augustine. The governor's legal counsel, however, noticed Prince working on the church roof in shackles and chains, which he considered dangerous, and he ordered the royal engineer to remove them. The engineer refused, saying that he could not allow Prince privileges that the white prisoners did not enjoy. The counsel persisted, stating that there was too much risk to Prince, and he gave the engineer an ultimatum to remove Prince's chains or chain all the white prisoners as well.[43]

Some of Florida's convict laborers had been convicted of more serious crimes. In 1812 and 1813, Cuban officials began exporting blacks charged with rebellion and sedition to St. Augustine. The Havana court sentenced José María Balmaceda and José Joaquín Placeres to six years of labor on the public works of St. Augustine and to perpetual exile for having participated with thirteen others in an insurrection in San Juan de los Remedios, during which Spaniards were killed. A royal decree of 1814 reduced all prisoners' sentences by two years and so, in 1817, after working for four years in Florida, Balmaceda and Placeres appealed for their liberty.

Because of the severity of their crime, however, the Cuban court had also required that upon completion of their sentences the men be sold as slaves, with the proceeds assigned to the state. The Cuban courts had long since stopped sentencing free whites and Indians to slavery and, as in other contemporary societies, it had become a condition associated only with blacks. This element of the men's sentence clearly reflects the heightened fear of race war throughout the Caribbean following the Haitian slave revolt as well as growing racial tensions in Cuba.[44]

Discriminatory Aspects of Spanish Law

Every study of slave societies has included detailed discussions of the discriminatory aspects of law, and Spanish law contained many of the typical prohibitions for blacks who were not to carry arms, gather in large numbers, ride horses, or dress in manner above their station, among others. If one looked only at the periodic Bandos de Buen Gobierno issued by various governors of Spanish Florida one would also find such attempts to limit blacks. Governor Manuel Vicente de Zéspedes's edict of 1787 forbade blacks in St. Augustine to carry arms "except in prescribed circumstances," and this prohibition was repeated by Governor Enrique White in 1807, who stated that earlier prohibitions were being ignored. White specified that unless a free black carried his signed license or a certificate of good conduct signed by a reputable citizen, his weapons would be confiscated and used for Indian gifts. Slaves had to have their owner's permission to carry weapons or they could be sentenced to two months' unpaid labor in chains on the public works.[45] However, civil and criminal records yield many examples of slaves and free blacks owning fine clothing and horses and carrying arms of different descriptions. This evidence records actual practice and shows that sumptuary laws were ignored altogether and weapons restrictions were applied only on occasion.

The Spanish law did regulate black citizens of Florida more closely than it did whites. When Governor Juan Nepomuceno de Quesada reviewed his province in 1790 he despaired that "a voluminous code would not be sufficient" to address all that needed reforming. Fortunately, he satisfied himself with thirty-seven articles, the second of which was aimed at "the multitude of foreign blacks who as a result of their flights have obtained liberty." Quesada ordered such persons to find employment or find someone who would post a bond guaranteeing their good behavior. While race was part of the governor's concern, the "foreignness" of the refugees was just as worrisome, for article eleven requires the expulsion of all unknown men, of whatever condition or *calidad* (quality).[46] Censuses and other periodic lists track the whereabouts of free black males, but also those of all white immigrants and males over fourteen years of age who could serve at arms.[47] All men were expected to defend the colony, but free blacks in Florida were also required on some occasions to present themselves for paid work on critical public works projects, a requirement not expected of white citizens.[48] Similarly, curfews limited all citizens, but blacks were required to vacate the streets at an earlier hour than whites. Army patrols caught the slave brothers Santiago and Benjamín out at 11:00 P.M. and delivered them to jail when the patrols found that the brothers also carried forbidden knives. Santiago explained they were out to visit their girlfriends, but Benjamín claimed that they were headed to gather wood in Moultrie swamp and carried the weapons as protection against wild animals. Neither answer satisfied the governor and his legal counsel. To emphasize the warning to "this class of people," they sentenced the brothers to one hundred lashes at the public whipping stand with their knives hung around their necks.[49]

As the cited cases have shown, the actual implementation of law and its punishments depended on the local conditions, the persons involved, and the degree of their assimilation into the community. As many other scholars have also determined, many discriminatory regulations were more often breached than observed. Spain's written law could be appealed to, even by the lowest members of the society, and Spanish administrators took meticulous care to adjudicate properly. Moreover, because of attention to local concepts of fairness, the legal culture could be "customized" to reflect the society in which it operated. Spanish Florida was a society of densely interlaced networks of kin, friends, clients, and corporations that helped shape the law. Blacks who were part of these interlocking systems generally received less harsh treatment under the law, but even "foreign" and non-Catholic slaves had their day and their say in court.[50]

Black Military Service

Precedents for Black Militias in the Circum-Caribbean

Free blacks had been organizing themselves into militia units under their own leaders in Florida since the seventeenth century, just as they had in other circum-Caribbean locales—in exposed coastal areas and contested territories.[1] Although often employed in low-status labor on construction projects and guard duties, blacks also served in important military campaigns. Military service won blacks the appreciation of the Crown and recognition as vassals of the king. Meritorious service could also mean emancipation, often over the objections of owners who resisted not only the blurring of racial and social stratification but the loss of their slaves.[2]

In the eighteenth century, Spain's Bourbon reformers embarked on a campaign to shore up the defenses of their far-flung empire and reduce the naval advantage of the British. The Spanish Crown strengthened its colonial armies by establishing a formal rotation for Spanish-based battalions, adding new officers and personnel to regular units recruited in and permanently garrisoned in the colonies, and creating "disciplined" militias for the Americas. In contrast to older provincial and urban militias, which were supported by private or corporate sponsors and called up only in emergencies, these were regular units with regular officers, systematic training, and state-supplied pay, equipment, arms, and uniforms. Pardos (mulattoes) and morenos (blacks) composed many of the new disciplined units.[3]

Florida's military structure was technically subordinate to Cuba, where officials devised a dual command and staff group—one of white regulars and one of volunteers of color—and although black officers enjoyed prestige among their fellows, ultimate authority resided in the white sub-inspector. Nevertheless, the Crown continued to promote improved racial attitudes and community respect for its new black militia companies. In 1714 the king commended the loyal and efficient service of the Cuban black militias and ordered Havana's officials to see that his black "vassals" were well treated. He also forbade anyone from making racial slurs against them, indicating that those were common enough in Cuba. Prejudice and ranking inequalities did not dissuade blacks from enlisting, however, and by 1770 more than three thousand men had joined Cuba's black militia.[4]

The Crown, for pragmatic reasons, if for no other, was often more liberal racially than its colonists, and to encourage recruitment in the new units, it exempted black militia members from tribute payments and certain municipal taxes or levies. Tribute payment was a mark of conquest and subjugation and was so deeply resented by blacks in the Hispanic colonies that the monies were rarely collected, so the exemption cost the Crown little and gained it the goodwill of the militiamen.

Two other changes were also socially significant. The reforms allowed blacks formally to elect their own officers (a practice already observed in the provincial militias) and, most importantly, the Crown extended the *fuero militar* to pardo and moreno units. The *fuero* was a corporate charter with important implications. By its provisions, blacks were exempt from prosecution in civilian courts and gained equal juridical status with white militiamen. The juridical and social benefits of militia membership were clearly appreciated by men of African descent in the Spanish circum-Caribbean who developed traditions of long-term family service. By the late eighteenth century, blacks made up more than one-fourth of the total Spanish army on the island.[5]

Black military service in Florida must be examined in this broader Caribbean context. Like their counterparts in Spanish Louisiana, Florida's black militias drew on Caribbean antecedents and formed an integral part of Spain's eighteenth-century Caribbean defense system. Free blacks had a vested interest in maintaining Spanish sovereignty in Florida, and formed into an urban militia company, they proved a valuable addition to Florida's military structure.

Problems of Defense in the Second Spanish Period

Most historians have failed to appreciate the important role of local militias and in particular that of the black militias which patrolled the frontier. Occasionally the Crown granted Florida's governors emergency funds, and in response to imminent attack, the Crown might dispatch additional troops from Cuba, Mexico, or Catalonia. But in the interim, hard-pressed administrators had to use imagination and local resources to do the job.[6] Blacks in second Spanish period

Florida continued a long tradition of military service begun in the seventeenth century, and they had ample opportunity for it. The Spaniards returned to Florida in an era of intense imperial competition and revolution and colonial provinces were often battlegrounds. Black militias saw action in a French-inspired invasion (1795), in Indian wars (1800–1803), in the so-called Patriot Rebellion (1812–13), and in the various seizures of Amelia Island by Patriots, South American revolutionaries, pirates, and the United States Navy (1812–17).

The returning Spaniards found themselves a minority in their own colony. The loyalty of the Mediterranean Catholics among them was not a serious concern, but Spanish administrators were less sure of the Anglo Protestants. Those planters had too many connections to Florida's aggressive and unhappy northern neighbors who bitterly contested Florida's fugitive slave policy and resented its friendship with the Seminole and Creek nations, whose lands they coveted.[7] The Spaniards rightly feared the Anglos' territorial ambitions and hoped the Indian nations would serve as a buffer to Florida. Well aware of the colony's vulnerable position, Governor Vicente Manuel de Zéspedes complained incessantly to Spain about crumbling defenses, irregular receipt of the government subsidy, and the poor quality of his troops.[8] Florida and Louisiana, and even Mexico, received the dregs of the Spanish army and assignment to Florida was often a punishment for earlier misbehavior. From all accounts even severe discipline failed to produce any significant improvement in the character of the Florida troops.[9] Even had the men been of the best caliber, however, there were too few of them to adequately patrol Florida's great expanse. Long stretches of coastline lay beyond the control of the government located in St. Augustine, and even the sparsely populated areas surrounding the capital were laced with waterways which provided easy access into the province by assorted "banditti" and invaders. Florida's settlers, their haciendas, harvests, and slaves were always at risk.

In 1786 Spain stopped rotating Spanish battalions to America, and thereafter the Third Battalion of the Infantry Regiment of Santiago and the Hibernia Regiment from Cuba provided detachments for Florida. The Crown allotted St. Augustine a total of between 350 and 390 *plazas,* or troop positions, but in actuality, effective troop strength usually fell below three hundred men.[10] Although the manpower for this battalion was mainly Spanish-born, a group defined in the Spanish caste system as innately superior to Spaniards born in the Americas, Governor Zéspedes complained that the battalion consisted of deserters, incorrigibles, and other ne'er-do-wells. He described these troops as full of "vicious habits, from which it is hopeless to reform them, especially their perverted inclinations to steal, to get intoxicated, and to desert. Right from the start, they began deserting by gangs, becoming scandalously intoxicated and stealing from the gardens of the unfortunate settlers. . . . These men have been rejected by every other corps in the army and should not be sent to this province, especially since we are surrounded on all sides by foreigners who are in the majority."[11]

It is not surprising, given this characterization, that when danger threatened, as it so often did, the desperate governors of the second Spanish period depended heavily upon local militias to supplement their regular forces. On orders from the governors and their white commanders, black Floridians served as scouts, pilots, sailors, messengers, foot soldiers, and cavalrymen. They manned the frontier and river posts outside the city as well as the batteries and the lines of Florida's main fort, the Castillo de San Marcos. In the eighteenth and nineteenth centuries, governors also posted black units among the Seminoles to encourage their continued loyalty to Spain. In their military correspondence, Florida's governors commented frequently on the excellent contributions of the black militia.

Impact of the French Revolution in Florida

Florida was still struggling to stabilize after the turmoil of the American Revolution and, alarmed by republican ideology emanating from France, Spain ordered administrators throughout the greater Caribbean to screen carefully materials and persons entering the province and to forbid the importation of slaves from French possessions. Zéspedes's successor, Juan Nepomuceno de Quesada, who took office in 1790, attempted to quarantine the colony, as required, but the unstable frontier and heterogeneous population made the task almost impossible. In 1793 Edmond Charles Genêt, the first minister of the French Republic to the United States, arrived in Charleston and Spain's consul, Diego Murphy, informed Governor Quesada of Genêt's plan to revolutionize Spanish and English North America, from Canada to Mexico. Genêt and other revolutionaries attempted to stir up the Creek Indians and raised an army of American backwoodsmen with promises of money, commissions, and land. Apprised of all the rumors of invasion, Quesada informed Spain's representatives in Philadelphia and his immediate superior, the captain general of Cuba, Luis de Las Casas.[12] Quesada had reason to be alarmed. Florida's garrison was chronically undermanned, and, as noted earlier, the Cuban Third Battalion which provided detachments for Florida consisted largely of deserters, incorrigibles, and other ne'er-do-wells. Quesada depicted his dilemma graphically when he wrote to Las Casas that "half of the soldiers of the Third Battalion are capable of lending a hand to any misdeed and of uniting to flee the province . . . and . . . together with the black fugitives from the United States, who are very detrimental here, and many discontented slaves, convert the province into a theater of horrors."[13]

The troops were not only less than first rate, they had also gone more than a year without pay and desertions were common. Colonel Carlos Howard, the commandant of the American frontier on the St. Marys River, learned that Genêt's planned invasion would be led by traders Samuel and Abner Hammond from Camden County, Georgia. As the Spaniards would later learn, the Hammonds were supported by influential, but disloyal, Anglo planters such as John McIntosh, Richard Lang, William Plowden, and John Peter Wagnon, who had availed themselves of the generous Spanish land policies to establish plantations in northern Florida.[14]

Governor Quesada convened a special war council in St. Augustine and ordered the arrest of the plotters and a series of defensive preparations. He called on all white males over the age of fourteen to report for militia duty and organized three companies of white urban militia organized more or less along ethnic lines—the Spanish, the Irish (Anglos of Irish, Scottish, and British backgrounds), and the Mahonese (Minorcans, Italians, and Greeks). These men patrolled the outlying river areas and the islands where their own plantations were located.[15]

Despite the governor's stated horror of "detrimental" fugitive and "discontented" slaves, he needed all hands in this emergency so he began arming all the free blacks and mulattoes of the province and at Colonel Howard's request assigned Indian and black scouts to help patrol the northern frontier.[16] Most of the blacks who reported for duty were freed slaves from the former British colonies. The free black militia of about fifty men operated land and river patrols on the northern frontier and proved to be a most effective force for the Spaniards. They elected their own sergeants, but ultimate command remained with white officers, who were linked to the African community in a number of ways, including kinship.[17] These interracial community connections and the sanctuary available to fugitive slaves in Florida deprived the invaders of support that French Jacobins successfully employed in other areas of the Caribbean, such as Grenada and Saint Vincent.[18]

As the militias were being organized, Governor Quesada required all citizens with slaves to present them for government construction projects for which the slaves would be paid four reales (half a peso) a day. Slaveowners such as Don Juan McQueen, María McIntosh, and Andrew Dewees contributed slaves to labor on the public works and to serve as sailors and rowers in transporting government supplies.[19] To the great disgust of Governor Quesada, Don Francisco Xavier Sánchez, who had grandly offered twenty armed blacks for government service, reneged when black militias were actually organized, claiming that his slaves were too busy planting corn.[20] To make up the shortage Governor Quesada required all free blacks not in military service to work on the same projects for the same pay. If they failed to report within three days of the issuance of Quesada's decree, free blacks were subject to three months of unpaid labor on public works in shackles.[21]

One propertied member of the free community of color, the merchant Juan Bautista Collins, failed to report on time and even though he was the first sergeant of the free black militia, he was imprisoned on the governor's orders. His mother appealed to the governor's mercy, claiming her son had been away and did not read the notice to report for duty. Although the imprisoned Collins asked permission to enlist, the governor instead sentenced him to hard (and menial) labor on the fortifications as an example to the "rest of his class."[22]

By April, Florida's new company of free black militia was fully operational and consisted of about fifty men under the command of Don Juan Leslie of Panton, Leslie and Company. Leslie may have volunteered or may have been chosen for his ability to underwrite the company expenses. He might also have been selected because he had a black consort and mulatto children. Unfortunately no rosters have been located for this unit and so the composition and racial makeup of the members is unknown, but payments were made to black sergeants, corporals, and soldiers.[23] A separate unit of slaves was attached to the artillery and trained to man the canons and in other ways relieve the regular military. The governor donated one of his own slaves to this unit and the commandant of the Third Battalion, Bartolomé de Morales, donated two, but other planters offered "only a thousand excuses."[24]

The Revolutionary Legion of the Floridas finally attacked in the summer of 1795, capturing two outlying batteries north of St. Augustine. With resources stretched thin, Quesada ordered all citizens to remove south of the St. Johns River. Then, to their great dismay and anger and against the recommendations of his advisors, the governor resorted to a scorched-earth policy, ordering that all the plantations north of that perimeter be burned. As a result he alienated Florida's most important landowners and ruined the most productive plantations in the colony.

In July the outpost of San Nicolás (present-day Jacksonville) fell to the invaders, and Colonel Howard ordered the small batteries at Santa Ysabel and Dos Hermanas further down river abandoned, but the following month he led a water assault to retake San Nicolás. Howard's brig carried forty-two men of the free black militia, forty Cuban infantrymen, and thirteen members of the urban white militia. The Spaniards and their black and Indian allies successfully dislodged the invaders, who retreated to Amelia Island, not to return. A small mounted party of free blacks followed to scout the routed rebels. They also rounded up eighteen "stray" horses which were later inventoried with other of the rebels' property. Other black militiamen patrolled the southern frontier near Matanzas, allowing Spanish troops to remain near the city.[25]

The relative independence and mobility of Florida's black troops seems even more remarkable in light of the contemporary paranoia regarding slave revolts.

David Geggus called 1795 "the planters' darkest hour in the Caribbean," notable for the second Maroon War in Jamaica, slave revolts in Demerara and Coro, Venezuela, the Pointe Coupee slave conspiracy in Spanish Louisiana, and the Morales conspiracy in Cuba, to name only the best-known examples.[26] Apparently Governor Quesada had no fear that these men might conspire, or might desert as the regular troops were so wont to do. In light of their military conduct, the black troops must have put some of the regulars to shame. The community could not fail to be aware of the contributions blacks had made to its successful defense. In addition to performing valuable labor on the new outposts, the free black militia had proved themselves more than capable in the naval offensive against the Georgians and had operated independently in scouting and roundup operations on the frontier. Payments to the black militia continued through December of 1795, indicating they continued their patrols well after the plot was put down.[27]

As Florida's earlier governors had discovered, the freed black allies, who had the most to lose should an invasion of unhappy slaveholders succeed, proved to be among Spain's most effective troops. Quesada later commended all the militias and even noted the contributions of "the excellent company of free blacks."[28] The governor's conflicting opinions about the free blacks of Florida reflected the dilemma faced by Spaniards throughout the Caribbean. Although they frequently disparaged blacks, Spanish administrators depended upon them to maintain a tenuous sovereignty which was under almost constant attack in the eighteenth century. Faced with a chronic shortage of worthy regular troops and inadequate financial and material resources, governors in Spanish Florida repeatedly relied on their black forces. Spain's necessity created opportunities for blacks, who parlayed initiative and military skills into free status. As Africans did throughout the Caribbean, black Floridians became adept at reading the political tides, and they pursued pragmatically their best options during international conflicts. Royalism suited them when the threat of rebel slaveholders loomed.

The 1795 invasion proved a short-lived fiasco. After a series of trials, some of the leaders were imprisoned in the Castillo de San Marcos at St. Augustine and others served time in Cuba's Morro Castle. All were ultimately pardoned. Despite its comic-opera overtones, however, this episode left lasting scars on Florida. The community had endured almost two years of tense anticipation. In that highly charged atmosphere, suspicion and distrust flourished. Neighbor turned on neighbor; race relations were poisoned; the government suffered a leadership crisis during the invasion; flourishing plantations were burned; pitiful gangs of slaves belonging to sentenced rebels languished and died in embargo; embittered Anglos departed the province with everything they could take; and misery and hardship were widespread. A series of investigations and sedition trials went on for three more years, during which the government confiscated and sold at public auction ten plantations and much property seized from sentenced rebels. While this enabled some Spanish citizens to acquire holdings they may not otherwise have been able to afford, it also discouraged any further capital investment in the colony, and Florida's recovery from the debacle proved to be painfully slow. Moreover, the weakened frontier was thereafter subject to chronic encroachment.[29]

Once the immediate crisis passed, Spain drew off supplemental troops from Mexico and Catalonia and the military situation of the colony reverted to its previous pathetic condition. The interim governor, Bartolomé Morales, echoed a familiar complaint about his regular recruits: "those that enter are sentenced vagabonds and deserters from the Mexican Regiments equal in property and customs to the prisoners and as desirous as those are of obtaining their liberty through flight."[30]

Many of the better troops had completed their tours or been lost to illness and once again the garrison was short 106 *plazas.*[31] The chronic deficit meant continued reliance on black troops in the coming troubles.

Jorge Biassou and the Black Auxiliaries of Charles IV in Florida

Only a year after the failed invasion and to the great consternation of Governor Quesada, Jorge Biassou and his disbanded Black Auxiliaries of Charles IV arrived in Florida.[32] Born to slave parents at Cap Français in Saint Domingue, Biassou rose from slavery to become the self-titled "Viceroy of the Conquered Territories," outranking the more famous Toussaint L'Ouverture, who was his aide and physician to the army Biassou commanded. Biassou was infamous for his alleged fondness for drink and use of *vodun,* as well as his ferocity in battle, but he was also a skilled commander who maintained strict discipline in his untrained and polyglot army, which at its peak numbered forty thousand men.[33] He and his comrades had early realized their material limitations and, in what C. L. R. James described as "Judas work," offered peace in exchange for their own freedom and the recognition of political rights promised by the French Assembly. The reactionary planters of Saint Domingue rudely rejected their offer, so angering Biassou that he ordered the execution of all his white prisoners, vowing that they would pay "for the insolence of the [Colonial] Assembly which has dared to write to me with so little respect."[34] And so the bloody fighting continued. After England and Spain declared war on France, both powers courted the black rebels and Biassou and his co-commander Jean-François accepted the Spanish offer of alliance. When Commissioner Sonthonax tried to win back them Jean-François and Biassou allegedly responded, "Since the beginning of the world we have obeyed the will of a king. We have lost the king of France but we are dear to him of Spain who constantly shows us reward and assistance. We therefore cannot recognize you until you have enthroned a king." Spain designated their armies the Black Auxiliaries of Charles IV, decorated the three primary leaders with gold medals bearing the likeness of the king, and presented them with documents expressing the gratitude and confidence of the Spanish government.[35] Toussaint's followers in Dondon allegedly warned prophetically, "You have received commissions and you have guarantees. Guard your liveries and your parchments. One day they will serve you as the fastidious titles of our former aristocrats served them."[36] Newly supplied and under a Spanish flag, Biassou's forces fought many bloody battles against the French. When the French Assembly abolished slavery, however, Toussaint broke with the Spaniards to offer his services and loyalty to the French Republic. Biassou remained loyal to Spain, thereby losing his chance at a more significant place in history. Before long, Biassou was losing battles against his former aide.[37]

The Treaty of Basle required Spain to disband and evacuate the Black Auxiliaries from Hispaniola, and the Spanish governor of Bayajá, site of a bloody massacre of French civilians, recommended that the Crown abolish black military employment and titles immediately.[38] Bothered by the auxiliaries' "pretensions to superiority," he argued that he had seen evidence of their fury, and "although they paint themselves with other colors, they are the same who murdered their owners, violated their wives, and destroyed all those with property." He told Biassou and the other leaders they would have to evacuate because the French Republic did not find their presence "compatible," but he urged the "simple soldiers" to remain, as they had been offered freedom by both the French Republic and Spain. The black armies wanted, instead, to maintain their units, ranks, salaries, and rations and to embark together for some designated place where they should be given lands to cultivate and be permitted to form a town. They argued that they would then constitute a ready force, able to fight for the king wherever he should care to send them. There was, in fact, royal precedent for this; the town of Gracia Real de Santa Teresa de Mose, also composed of former slaves, was evacuated en masse to Cuba, granted homesteads together, and allowed to retain their militia titles.[39]

Despite the governor's opposition, "a considerable number" of soldiers embarked with their leaders for Havana, where he predicted they would expect "the same distinctions, prerogatives, luxury, and excessive tolerance" they had in Bayajá. He assured the captain general of Cuba that he never promised the "venomous vipers" they would be allowed to remain in Havana.[40] Other Spaniards echoed his racial biases. The governor of Santo Domingo, Joaquín García, had once written glowing reports about the exploits of the "valiant warriors" he decorated in the king's name, but as soon as the fighting ceased, he, too, shipped them to Havana. García knew full well their capabilities. The unfortunate black troops were not even given time to dispose of their property or settle family affairs.[41] Before leaving Santo Domingo, however, the embittered Biassou lodged a formal complaint against García and urged his dismissal.[42]

Cuba's captain general, Luis de Las Casas, was no more anxious than the governors of Bayajá and Santo Domingo to have a large number of unemployed, armed, and experienced "wolves," as they were now referred to, on his hands. Havana's hastily convoked war council decided to deport the black armies, using as their authority the royal order forbidding the introduction of blacks from French areas. No matter that these particular people had fought against the Republic; they were well acquainted with its ideology and thus represented a threat. Jean-François and twelve other leaders, along with their extended families, sailed for Cádiz, Spain. Other groups were dispersed to Trinidad, Guatemala, and the Yucatán. When Biassou's entourage arrived in Havana, they were not even permitted to disembark and Biassou was given only a night to make a choice between the Isle of Pines, just south of Cuba, and St. Augustine, Florida, as a place of exile. He chose the latter.[43] It is possible that he had heard about St. Augustine from the Florida merchants and sailors who frequented Cap Français before the revolt and that he hoped to make use of those personal connections.

Spain transported Biassou and his dependents to St. Augustine at government expense in January of 1796. Biassou's immediate household included his wife, Romana Jacobo, Romana's mother, sisters, and brother, and a slave belonging to Biassou. Also with Biassou were at least twenty-five followers whom he referred to as "family" because they paid him allegiance and because he claimed responsibility for them. However, Biassou was forced to leave behind his own mother, whom he had allegedly rescued from slavery in the early years of the revolt.[44] Several months after arriving in St. Augustine, Biassou petitioned to be allowed to return to Hispaniola and search for his "beloved mother" and for other members of his "family." Spanish authorities on that island had promised Biassou that any of his dependents left behind would soon be sent to join him, but when he asked them to honor that pledge, the bureaucrats stalled, noting that Biassou's petition did not specify how many "troops" he sought to recover or exactly where they might be located. They were hardly inclined to reunite a force they had gone to such lengths to disperse.[45]

Later that summer, by serendipity, another smaller contingent of Black Auxiliaries arrived in St. Augustine. Commandant Luis Boeff and eight of his men, all of whom had served under Jean-François at Bayajá, were being evacuated from Hispaniola when their ship's rudder broke. The men drifted for months and their Spanish captain died before the survivors finally wrecked on Cumberland Island. Georgia officials interrogated the black men and then sent them on to St. Augustine, where authorities also investigated them for the possible murder of the ship's captain. As the investigation proceeded, Boeff paid a visit to Biassou, who later testified that he had known Boeff in Hispaniola and for that reason gave him assistance. St. Augustine's tribunal refused to prosecute the auxiliaries for lack of evidence, but neither did they want to allow them to stay in the province which was "loaded with prisoners, blacks, free and enslaved, and refugees from the United States." Following the precedent from Hispaniola, they dispersed the men to different Caribbean locales, and only Roman, a Guinea-born man of the Lachi nation, was allowed to remain in Florida.[46]

Biassou had enjoyed a position of command for five years before he settled in Florida, and his haughty demeanor had immediately alienated Governor Quesada, who arranged lodging for Biassou and his immediate family and sent two nights' supper to the house when they arrived, only to have Biassou complain that he had not been invited to dine at the governor's home. Quesada reported this in amazement to his Cuban superior, warning, "I very much fear the proud and vain character he displays. . . . it is a great problem to decide how to deal with him."[47]

If Quesada had misgivings about Biassou, the white citizenry apparently displayed a mixture of curiosity and dismay about the unusual newcomers. According to Quesada, who may have been projecting his own concerns, "The slaveowners have viewed his arrival with great disgust, for they fear he will set a bad example for the rest of his class."[48] The garrison soldiers, attracted by the novelty,!0ook to gathering at Biassou's house to ogle him, and Quesada maintained that they, too, expressed disgust. Biassou must have been equally displeased, because he petitioned that the soldiers be forbidden this pastime.[49] No record exists of the reaction of the large population of slaves and free blacks to the arrival of the decorated black military figure and his retinue, but surely all were aware of Biassou's slave origins and his rise above them.

Quesada soon had more to complain about than Biassou's unsuitable pride. Biassou apparently also became a financial burden. Quesada complained that although Biassou had been paid his salary in advance, he spent large sums of money and always asked for more. When Quesada was not forthcoming, Biassou wrote directly to the governor's superior—the captain general of Cuba. To do so, Biassou, who did not write or speak Spanish, used an interpreter from the

The Salcedo house on St. George Street, St. Augustine. Jorge Biassou, the former slave rebel and black general from Saint Domingue, lived in this house. © 1998, Ken Barrett, Jr. Courtesy of Ken Barrett, Jr.

Cuban Third Battalion whom Quesada had assigned him. Quesada must have regretted his assistance to Biassou when he read the letter to Las Casas:

> The many and valuable services which I have received from your Excellency oblige me to disturb you although you are so importantly occupied. I render all due thanks, although these are never sufficient; neither I nor my family could ever repay you with more than gratitude, which is constant in us; and as proof of it I happily inform you of my arrival at this [port] where I have been paid respects by the governors, the nobles, and the people. I owe this fine reception to the kindness of your Excellency, whom I beg not to fail to forward your desires and orders, which I eagerly look forward to, in order to have the honor of being your most unworthy servant. . . . Sir, I hope to deserve your kindness and that you will order that I be advanced money to buy a house. If I am to subsist in this province I would not be able to manage the costs of rent.[50]

This flowery letter is a masterpiece of veiled sarcasm. Biassou alluded to the supposed favors he had received from Las Casas, whose hospitality, it will be remembered, had not even allowed Biassou to debark in Havana. Biassou also contrasted the implied inconstancy of the Spaniards with his own unceasing gratitude. When he described the way the governor honored him in St. Augustine (a reception with which Quesada had already reported Biassou was not satisfied), he reminded Las Casas that he was due homage. In begging to be allowed to discharge the captain general's orders, he made an effort to shame Las Casas into some reciprocal feelings of obligation, and perhaps circumvent the local authority of the governor. The effort was in vain. Nor was Biassou advanced money to buy a house, a request which was not illogical because he and the others had abandoned property in Saint Domingue and the Crown customarily provided for evacuated citizens.

Undaunted, Biassou peppered Governor Quesada and his successor, Enrique White, with complaints.[51] He and his officers were promised that their salaries would continue and that they would be provided with rations and an annual clothing allowance in Florida. However, the Crown made no provision to augment St. Augustine's subsidy to cover these costs, and the governors' appeals to the viceroy of New Spain for extra funds were denied. After the disasters of the 1795 invasion, the Florida treasury could barely support its regular troops, so the additional burden of supporting Biassou and his band was most unwelcome. Biassou's annual salary (based on that paid in Hispaniola) was 3,840 pesos—not an inconsiderable sum and only 120 pesos less than the annual salary of Florida's governor. After much wrangling, the treasury officials of St. Augustine finally agreed to pay Biassou an annual salary of three thousand pesos, but Quesada warily noted, "since the certificate that he has presented verified the black's claims [to the higher 3,000-peso salary], he is very dissatisfied, and this added to his high temper and taste for drink, although it has not caused any harm to date, I feel will present a problem."[52]

Indeed, Biassou and the other Black Auxiliaries were quick to protest any grievances, which usually involved their reduced incomes and status in St. Augustine. In their first year in the colony, both Biassou and one of his followers, Pedro Miguel, complained directly to the captain general of Cuba, who returned the appeals to Florida's new governor, Enrique White. The embarrassed White stiffly admonished all involved that future correspondence be directed through proper channels, meaning himself.[53] One memorialist, Jorge, who identified himself as the sergeant and adjutant to the auxiliary troops of the Spanish island of Santo Domingo, petitioned to receive the salary he had customarily received in Hispaniola, because the single ration he was allowed was insufficient to support his large family. He recalled his service to the king in the war against France, naming five battles in which he took part, but there is no record of the captain general's response.[54]

Despite his reduced circumstances, Biassou attempted to maintain the lifestyle expected of a *caudillo* in St. Augustine. He wore fine clothes trimmed in gold, a silver-trimmed saber, and a fancy ivory and silver dagger. The gold medal of Charles IV must also have impressed the townspeople of St. Augustine, unaccustomed to seeing such finery on a black man. Biassou was forced to borrow money to pay the "salary" of dependents for whom he was responsible, such as his brother-in-law and military heir, Juan Jorge Jacobo. Although Biassou struggled to retain the privileges and position he once enjoyed in Hispaniola, his prestige suffered when he could no longer provide well for his troops and once they found they could apply to alternative authorities.

When Biassou ordered the arrest of Juan Bautista for fighting, the man appealed to the governor. He argued he was now a civilian, not a soldier, and as Biassou had told them to apply to the governor for rations, he considered that he was no longer subject to the general's (Biassou's) orders. Biassou felt compelled to address the governor about this challenge, always referring to Juan Bautista as a soldier under his command. Biassou stated that he had repeatedly admonished Juan Bautista about his drunkenness. He had warned Juan Bautista that he would arrest him should he succumb again, but when Biassou gave the order for his arrest, Juan Bautista insolently denied Biassou's authority. Biassou reminded the governor that the Catholic monarch gave him "full powers" to punish and reward those in his service, as Juan Bautista knew full well. Biassou added that even though Juan Bautista may have been ignorant of that fact, he would never before have dared argue with Biassou as he had now done twice. Biassou's honor was clearly at stake in this dispute. He told the governor that he had been too ill to handle the insult previously, but as he did not want to give the town more to talk about, he hoped the governor would support his authority. The governor must have avoided this thicket, for there is no evidence of a response.[55]

Biassou's patronage powers and control may have been reduced, but he was still able to exercise other forms of influence as the titular head of an ever-expanding "family." Despite major language and cultural differences and at least a few incidents of conflict, marriage and godparental ties soon linked the former Black Auxiliaries with members of the black community in St. Augustine, many of whom were former fugitives from the United States. As described in chapter 5, only three months after arriving, Biassou's brother-in-law, Sergeant Juan Jorge Jacobo, married Rafaela Witten.[56] This union, which may have followed a whirlwind courtship, was important politically. The bride was the daughter of Juan

Bautista Witten, the skilled carpenter and property owner who by then had lived in Florida for a decade and whose status in the black community was marked by the frequency with which he was chosen as godfather or marriage sponsor. Like Biassou and Jorge Jacobo, Witten was a member of the free black militia and had served well against the Genêt-inspired invaders of 1795. The marriage of Biassou's heir, Jorge, and Witten's daughter, Rafaela, thus united the leading families of both groups of blacks who had allied with the cause of the Spanish king against the forces of French republicanism. Subsequent marriages and baptisms added new layers of connection, and the refugees consistently used the structures of the Catholic church to strengthen their blended community.[57] For example, Juan Bautista Witten and his wife, María Rafaela, served as godparents for the children of the black militiamen Estévan Cheves, Bacas Camel, his son Andrés Camel, and Sayrus Thompson. The younger Wittens, Francisco and Rafaela, served as marriage sponsors at the wedding of the black militiaman Tomás Herrera, and when Francisco Witten married his marriage sponsors were Felipe Edimboro and Romana Jacobo (a.k.a. Biassou), who had also served the same roles at his parents' wedding the previous year. Three of Felipe Edimboro's daughters married members of the black militia and his son married a woman whose father and brothers also served in the black militia. When children were born of these unions family members and other black militiamen served as godparents in each case.[58]

The men of these two communities were also blended into a single militia unit under the command of Jorge Biassou, who by virtue of his service in Santo Domingo used the title of general. Until that time, the highest rank ever achieved by a black militiaman in Florida had been sergeant. Biassou's elevated title thus raised the status of Florida's black militia.[59] Although there may have been some objections to such social promotion, Biassou's perquisites came from the king and were beyond challenge. Spanish governors and captains general, no matter what their personal sentiments, forwarded even Biassou's most controversial memorials through proper channels to the minister of war in Spain.

Biassou understood the importance of this critical access and exercised it. In 1799 he asked to be allowed to go to Spain and fight for the king in his European wars, since he had no way to demonstrate his military services in Florida. Governor White's cover letter assured Cuba's captain general of his good conduct and "total obedience to the government although at times he has been harassed by some Frenchmen, and even by those of his own color, he has endured it without requiring any other justice than that he asked of me."[60] Despite this reference, Biassou's request was denied. The following year he asked simply for any other destination. When that request was also rejected, Biassou sent his ailing wife and four members of her family to Havana and asked that they receive the daily subsidy other blacks from Santo Domingo were receiving in Cuba. Finally, Biassou asked to be able to reorganize two separate companies of pardo and moreno militias, to be placed under his command, and to have equal footing with the white militias.[61] Biassou's efforts seem designed to improve both his social and his always overextended financial positions.

Blacks in the Indian Wars

Florida had not yet fully recovered from the destitution following the 1795 invasion, and metropolitan support was becoming increasingly irregular as Spain's power declined. This meant that like the hard-pressed governors before him, Governor White had to depend heavily on his black guerrilla forces when British governmental and commercial interests backed the political pretensions and filibustering raids of William Augustus Bowles in Florida. Formerly a soldier with the British army in Pensacola, Bowles had married a Creek princess and been "adopted" by that nation. From the 1780s onward he used those connections to agitate against Spanish interests in the Southeast. Bowles eventually won support from Quebec, London, and the Bahamas for recognition of a separate Indian state (with which the British would establish trade alliances).[62] In 1800 the Seminole and Lower Creek nations "elected" Bowles director of their new state of Muskogee, which promptly declared war against Spain. Director Bowles raised an army (and navy) of ambitious and land-hungry Anglos, southeastern Indians, and blacks—both fugitive slaves and slaves of the Seminoles—and for the next three years his polyglot forces wreaked havoc on Florida. One party composed of "from twenty-five to thirty Indians, Negroes, and infamous whites all of them direct from Bowles headquarters" had orders to "plunder and break up all the settlements in Florida."[63] Major East Florida planters such as Don Juan McQueen and Don Francis Phelipe Fatio were among those who lost slaves and property to Bowles and his raiders, but black homesteaders also suffered losses in the raids. At dawn on June 24, 1800, three of Bowles's Indians attacked the homestead of the free black militiaman, Felipe Edimboro, and stole his slave, Jack, who was already at work in the fields. Edimboro saw the Indians take Jack away in their canoe and he quickly loaded his own family and that of his free black neighbor, Juan Moore, into another canoe to take them to safety. Edimboro unloaded the group up river at Don Francis Phelipe Fatio's Nueva Suisa estate and returned to his homestead only to find the Indians had returned. Edimboro saw that they had taken additional captives—the wife and seven children of the free black militiaman Tony. Meanwhile, Fatio had sent five of his own armed slaves in a canoe to assist Edimboro. En route, Fatio's slaves found and rescued Edimboro's slave, Jack, who had escaped from his captors, and Edimboro found and assisted Tony's eldest son, who had also managed an escape.[64] The *Nassau Gazette* reported "the Muskogee Army has marched to plunder, pillage & lay waste Augustine, from whence they have already brought a number of Prime Slaves & some considerable share of very valuable property, & will entirely lay waste & ravage that Country ere they withdraw from thence nor can Spain send any Troops to act against them unless she wishes to sacrifice them which would be the case with any Troops who would enter their Country as they must bush fight it with them, which no Troops are equal to the doing with success."[65]

Perhaps the only troops "equal to the doing" were St. Augustine's free black militia who, like their opponents, were effective frontier guerrillas. While twenty-two free black militia helped garrison Fort Picolata on the western frontier, Biassou and the rest of the free black troops guarded St. Augustine's southern frontier, near the Matanzas River. Governor White instructed Biassou to detain all Indians seeking to come to the city and allow to pass only those who were friendly—such as those who brought hogs and cattle to sell. White's orders called on Biassou to treat the Indians with "humanity and kindness" and use force only when required, but in other matters to employ his own judgment.[66]

In July of 1801, after leading several expeditions against the marauding Seminoles, Biassou fell ill, returned to St. Augustine, and on the fourteenth, died quietly in his home. The parish priest entered Biassou in the death register as "the renowned *caudillo* of the black royalists of Santo Domingo."[67]

Biassou had fought his way out of slavery in the hemisphere's bloodiest revolution. Indeed, he continued to wage war until death overtook him and was, no doubt, capable of some of the violent acts attributed to him in Saint Domingue. Moreover, he was a proud and difficult man who caused Spanish administrators much annoyance.[68] But the very pride which irritated the Spaniards whom he challenged must also have been a source of comfort to those he led, and perhaps to the larger black community, for in demanding respect for himself, he sought it by extension for all.

Because Biassou and his men were seasoned by war against French planters, French and British troops, and their own countrymen and were well acquainted with "dangerous notions" of liberty, equality, and fraternity, they caused consternation not only among the Spanish governors who reluctantly received them but also among the Anglo planters on Florida's borders, who were already disturbed by Spain's racial policies and its reliance on black militias.[69] At a time when slave conspiracies and rebellions, maroon settlements, and Indian war unsettled the southeastern frontier, this black presence seemed particularly threatening. Ultimately the Spaniards' dependence upon armed black forces contributed to a series of invasions sponsored by the United States and to United States acquisition of Florida.

In January, 1802, the Indians staged a particularly violent attack on the plantation of Josiah Dupont, the site of Biassou's former headquarters south of St. Augustine. They abducted a white woman and her five young children, killing the oldest boy, and stealing ten slaves. The governor's war council feared Spain might lose the province and futilely appealed to the captain general of Cuba for more regular troops. When these were not forthcoming, the hapless settlement called once again upon the black militia.[70]

Forty-seven free blacks reported by mid-February and served at arms through November under the general command of Biassou's heir and military successor, his brother-in-law Jorge Jacobo. The black militia was by now a blend of former fugitives from North America, who had served so competently in 1795, and of the former auxiliaries of Charles IV in Santo Domingo. All were experienced warriors but they were also described as "artisans and field hands." Among the group were several carpenters, a butcher, several hostlers, and several skilled guides and navigators.[71] Many family, marriage, and godparent ties now linked the two groups. For example, Jacobo's captains were his father-in-law, Juan Bautista Witten, and Benjamín Seguí, his fellow pensioner from Guarico, Santo Domingo (and godfather to his daughter).[72] A pattern of family service had also emerged as sons followed fathers into the unit and often to the same posts.

The governor posted free black militia members at Amelia Island, at the river forts of Picolata and San Nicolás on the St. Johns River, at the fortified houses of Buena Vista and Pellicer, and at the second battery of Leslie. From these posts they went out on daily patrols in search of the enemy. Other members of the black militia served on government launches patrolling the rivers.[73] As before, the men were given arms and paid two reales (a quarter of a peso) and a ration daily and each time they left St. Augustine they presented themselves for review and to receive their rations.[74]

Prior to joining one of these expeditions to the banks of the St. Johns, Sergeant Jorge Jacobo petitioned for a promotion to the rank of lieutenant and for the full salary he had received in Santo Domingo—equal to that of a sergeant first class in the royal army. Jacobo argued that two reales and a ration daily was no better pay than that accorded the most infirm soldier in his command and that he should be paid "in accordance with his class, and the charge and responsibility he exercised in command of his troops." Jacobo reminded the governor that in all previous expeditions out of St. Augustine he had been paid the salary of a sergeant. There is no record of the response but since Cuban support was so minimal and the situado so irregular from 1800 to 1803, and since Jacobo had declared himself disappointed but "nonetheless . . . willing and ready to serve his king and country", there is a strong probability he had to settle for the two reales and a ration a day.[75] The issue was not money, although surely the black militiamen could have used it. Rather, such requests reflect a desire to be validated in a society preoccupied with questions of honor and status.

Throughout the spring and summer the black militias pursued the Indians. In June Juan Bautista Witten led two separate expeditions which engaged the enemy and killed several of them. Two months later he led his men to the aid of the detachment of white dragoons who were besieged by Indians at the Joaneda post. These successes may have been instrumental in the Seminole decision to sign a peace treaty with Spain in August 1802. Still, the depredations continued until Bowles was arrested at an Indian congress the following May and shipped in chains to Cuba, where he died.[76] During this Indian threat to Spanish rule, as during the Genêt-inspired invasion of 1795, the black militia had proved invaluable in frontier service. They volunteered for hazardous duty at very little pay, and became ill during the fever months in the desolate river posts. Many were injured. The black militiaman Tomás Herrera was badly injured fighting the Seminoles and spent almost a month in the royal hospital before he recovered sufficiently to rejoin the unit. Some even gave their lives in defense of Spanish interests. It is doubtful that the whites could have pacified the frontier without their help.

After Bowles's arrest, life in St. Augustine returned to "normal." The situado was, as usual, in arrears and military reports for these years are filled with complaints about nonpayment and lack of clothing and short rations. The colony was becoming more dependent than ever on United States goods, legal or otherwise, and on the credit of merchants in Charleston and Savannah. Even the uniforms for the Third Battalion were now made in the United States. When the situation became most desperate, Governor Enrique White resorted to writing certificates against the treasuries of Havana and Vera Cruz, but local merchants discounted these greatly and government dependents, including the military, were cheated of the full value of their government pay.[77] Sometime during this period Biassou's suggestion to divide the black militias along color lines was enacted, thus bringing Florida's black militia into conformity with those in other of Spain's circum-Caribbean colonies. What this change may have meant for relationships among the men is unknown.[78]

Blacks and the Defeat of the Patriot Rebellion

In 1812 the juxtaposition of a number of factors—European turmoil, revolutions in other parts of the Spanish empire, the poverty and instability of the Spanish interim junta, an acting governor with a poorly defended and supplied position in East Florida, and an administration in the United States that favored acquisition of the Floridas—made possible the initial success of a revolution against Spanish rule.[79] President James Madison and his influential advisors, Secretary of State James Monroe and former president Thomas Jefferson, secretly sanctioned a plan to pressure Spain to cede the Floridas to the United States. A hero of the American Revolution and a former governor of Georgia, George Matthews, led the expansionist plot. His second-in-command was a member of another prominent Georgia family, and a wealthy, if ungrateful, East Florida planter, John Houston McIntosh.[80] In March, 1812, with an army of several hundred volunteers and seven United States Navy gunboats, the Patriots, as they referred to themselves, captured the port of Fernandina and then all of Amelia Island. They declared an independent "Republic of Florida," complete with a constitution and flag, and the new republic's director, John Houston McIntosh, promptly delivered Amelia Island up to the United States. Next, the Patriots moved on to lay siege to St. Augustine, from a camp located at the former black fort of Mose. Lieutenant Colonel Smith described his predicament as commander of the United States regular troops supporting the Patriots: "With a weak detachment, but badly provided, laying before one of the strongest fortified places on the Continent, containing a garrison five times our numbers, what can be expected from me? I shall endeavor to do my duty, but the consequences I am apprehensive will reflect dishonor on the Arms of the United States."[81]

The Georgia invaders had hoped for an easy victory, but the Spaniards refused to surrender. Although forced to abandon Amelia Island, Florida's acting governor, José de Estrada, mounted a defense of the mainland. He sent a schooner and four launches up Mose Creek to bombard Fort Mose and forced the invaders to retreat temporarily.

Estrada's replacement, Sebastián Kindelán, arrived from Spain in mid-June only to find his new post besieged by rebels supported by a nation with which Spain was not at war. Nor could it afford to be. As Rembert Patrick pointed out, the United States Congress had never openly sanctioned the administration's action and Spain did not want to force Congress to change its position as Spain waged war against Napoleon.[82] Governor Kindelán immediately began a diplomatic campaign to pressure the United States abandon the rebel cause. He offered an amnesty for all participants in the rebellion, but also sought and received reinforcements from Cuba.

Much to the consternation of the Georgians, two companies of morenos and one company of pardos belonging to the Cuban Disciplined Black Militia arrived in Florida in mid-1812. The 270 fresh troops should have been a welcome addition, but Kindelán had little confidence in them and preferred his local black troops, as he alleged the colonists did also. Kindelán complained to the captain general that most of the Cuban troops had been convicts, were full of "vices," and, moreover, were incompetent soldiers. He charged that as soon as they faced any danger or heard any shots they threw themselves to the ground, or even into the water, and he assured his superior that "there is not one among them that does not shut his eyes when he fires his rifle."[83]

Although Kindelán was dubious about their utility, the introduction of such a large force of armed blacks inspired sanctimonious outrage among the Georgia invaders who already worried about the dangerous example of armed blacks in the neighboring province. McIntosh, as director of the Patriots, wrote Secretary of State Monroe: "Our slaves are excited to rebel, and we have an army of negroes raked up in this country, and brought from Cuba to be contended with. . . . St. Augustine, the whole province will be the refuge of fugitive slaves; and from thence emissaries . . . will be detached to bring about the revolt of the black population of the United States."[84]

Georgia's governor, David Mitchell, who replaced Matthews as Madison's commissioner, also warned Monroe: "They have armed every able-bodied negro within their power, and they have also received from the Havana a reinforcement of nearly two companies of black troops! [If these blacks] . . . are suffered to remain in the province, our southern country will soon be in a state of insurrection."[85]

The Patriots repeated assorted rumors about imported black troops from Jamaica, the Bahamas, or various other West Indian sites, made direct allusions to Santo Domingo, and promised no quarter to any black captured under arms.[86] Other pronouncements by the rebels decried the backwardness of the region, which they attributed to Spanish lethargy and neglect and which they contrasted with the prosperity that would surely be achieved in Florida by republican government. The horror of Saint Domingue's race war was, however, clearly the more powerful image to the invaders. Governor Mitchell even had the gall to reprimand Kindelán for using black troops. "Your certain knowledge of the peculiar situation of the southern section of the Union in regard to that description of people would have induced you to abstain from introducing them into the province, or from organizing such as were already in it."[87]

Kindelán responded that blacks served equally with whites in militias in all Spanish provinces and sarcastically compared Mitchell's protest to that of a burglar who complains that the householder had a blunderbuss and the burglar only pistols.[88] Nevertheless, the Spanish governor also realized that the provocative use of black troops might cost him greater trouble ahead and he and his spokesmen downplayed the numbers of Cuban troops in the province and promised not to use them north of the St. Johns River.[89]

Within the province, however, Kindelán made regular use of his urban black militia. Jorge Jacobo commanded the local black militia and once again, Juan Bautista Witten of South Carolina and Benjamín Seguí of Santo Domingo were his captains. In July Kindelán ordered Captains Jacobo, Witten, and Seguí to proceed with their men to Julianton and surprise a guard of ten to fifteen rebels at the plantation of Fernando Quinby. Although their war orders specifically granted them the latitude to deal as they saw fit with circumstances not otherwise addressed, an oblique reference to their prior experience in Hispaniola enjoined the black commanders not to be "excessively sanguinary" or exceed the limits of "civilized" nations. They were ordered to destroy the rebels' cannons and bury or render useless any other large pieces. Any guns, powder, and provisions the unit needed were theirs for the taking. After supplying their own needs they were to burn the houses, storehouses, machinery, seeds, and boats found at the plantation and to take any slaves into custody. A small group of men were to remain at Julianton to intercept any rebel communications with the St. Johns posts, but the rest of the black militia members were then to cross the St. Johns River and surprise another rebel outpost of about the same strength at Picolata. Their orders for Picolata were the same—take what they needed and destroy the rest. All slaves belonging to the rebels or any free blacks they encountered might be armed and added to the force so long as they were carefully supervised. The orders reminded the black commanders that all prisoners were to be taken alive and well treated and that force should be used only against those resisting. The black militia carried only eight days' rations for the expedition and had to live off the land or the rebels' spoils when those ran out, which everyone assumed (correctly) they could do. Their war orders also specified the division of the spoils between the Crown and the black troops; horses, cattle, equipment, supplies, clothing, and household goods went to the takers, while artillery, arms, munitions, and slaves belonged to the king.[90] In view of the general poverty of the province and the minimal pay and support the administration gave its militia, these expeditions, while hazardous, were also a way by which blacks could acquire potentially valuable moveable property.

By the summer of 1812 the siege of St. Augustine had become costly for the Patriots. Supplies were running short and typhus fever, dysentery, and other diseases had depleted their ranks while the Spaniards had received Cuban reinforcements.[91] While the governor maintained Spanish neutrality by remaining in St. Augustine, black militias and Seminole Indians and their black "slaves" success-

Abraham, leader of the Alachua blacks living at Pilaklikaha and interpreter and advisor for Seminole chief Micanopy. Abraham was a member of the Seminole delegation to Washington, D.C., in 1826. From Joshua R. Giddings, *The Exiles of Florida* (Columbus, Ohio, 1858), courtesy of the Florida State Archives.

fully harried the Patriots—raiding their camps, burning and sacking their plantations, and stealing away their slaves. The multiracial guerrillas also engaged in scalpings and mutilations which took a psychological toll on the Georgians. One Patriot soldier wrote anxiously to his mother and brother that Florida was "pregnant with sickness and death" and "but a fit receptacle for savages and wild beasts." He graphically described the torture, death, and mutilation of a mail carrier by the "dreadful lurking Indian" and the black troops who were "strangers to fear."[92]

Governor Kindelán took skillful advantage of the hostility of the Seminole

Indians toward the land-hungry interlopers from Georgia. Many fugitive slaves from Georgia had found sanctuary in the villages of Payne, Bowlegs, and other Seminole chiefs, where they lived in a sort of feudal arrangement with their Indian overlords. These village Negroes, as they were sometimes called in English sources, recognized that Georgian rule would return them to slavery, and so they were among the fiercest enemies of the Patriot forces. The Spaniards capitalized on this convergence of interests. Governor Kindelán posted some of the local black militia among the Indians and Payne and Bowlegs reciprocated by sending some of their own black vassals to fight alongside the Spaniards as a gesture of good faith.[93] Governor Kindelán was pleased when Chief Bowlegs brought two hundred warriors to fight for the Spaniards on the St. Johns River, but he complained that anytime the Seminoles captured a slave, a horse, or any other valuable they left the field to secure it in their towns and so their advantage was only momentary.[94] Kindelán also employed black translators, like Benjamín Wiggins and Tony Proctor, "the best translator of the Indian languages in the province," to promote the Spanish-black-Indian alliance.[95] Tony Proctor went to the Seminole village of La Chua (near present-day Gainesville) in July and recruited several hundred warriors for the Spanish side. When the Patriots recognized Proctor's utility, they captured him and tried to employ him in the same capacity. Proctor, however, told the Seminoles that he was speaking for the rebels under duress and all that he told them was false. He later managed to escape from the Patriots and returned to St. Augustine, where the grateful Kindelán felt "obligated to reward the service and loyalty of this miserable slave." In the name of the government he paid Proctor's owner 350 pesos and granted the translator his liberty.[96]

Governor Kindelán demonstrated his appreciation and regard for his provincial black militia when he nominated the leaders for promotion—Jorge Jacobo for captain, Juan Bautista Witten for lieutenant, and Benjamín Seguí for second lieutenant. The formulaic nominations instruct the men of the company, as well as the rest of the officers and soldiers of the Plaza, to recognize and respect these men in their new positions and grant them all honors, favors, exemptions, and preeminences due them.[97] These promotions raised the pay and status of the black militia to levels equal to those of the black militia of Cuba.

A promotion from sergeant first-class to captain represented a salary raise of 75 percent for Jorge Jacobo. Witten earned a 73 percent raise. However, these gains must be considered in the context of paper script, inflated prices, and inadequate supplies. Moreover, as it did for white officers, the government deducted sums from the black officers' salaries to pay for their coverage in a military pension fund, the *Montepío militar,* and for an insurance program, *Ynvalidos.* The black unit, like the white, also had to pay for its own hospitalizations.[98] As these three officers moved up the ladder, however, other men moved into their vacant positions and advanced as well. Eventually the unit included three sergeants, and twelve corporals. The increase in pay and status may have encouraged recruitment, for by January 1813 Jacobo's militia numbered eighty-seven men. However, one corporal (who later rose to sergeant second-class), León Duvigneau, a literate storeowner and baker originally from San Marcos, Santo Domingo, declined any pay for his militia service. Instead, he made it a "donation in favor of the mother country."[99]

This gesture came at a time of severe deprivation in Florida. The situado had not arrived in seven years, a hurricane had ruined the barracks, and the troops were on half-rations. Kindelán fired off almost a continuous barrage of urgent requests for supplies from Cuba, describing the misery of his troops and predicting the loss of the colony if aid were not forthcoming. The starving citizenry were largely fed by the free black militia who at great risk roamed the countryside rounding up and herding back cattle to pasture at Anastasia Island, across from the Castillo de San Marcos.[100]

The turning point of the Patriot siege came in September of 1812, when Lieutenant Juan Bautista Witten led a band of twenty-five black militia men, thirty-two of Chief Payne's blacks, and a handful of Seminoles in a well-executed ambush of twenty United States Marines and approximately sixty to seventy Patriots escorting a supply convoy through Twelve Mile Swamp at night. Witten's forces took down Marine Captain John Williams, his sergeant, and the wagon horses in the first volley. For two hours afterward they battled the more numerous rebel forces, killing many but suffering several casualties as well. That night Witten's men destroyed one wagon and the next morning used the second to transport their own wounded back to St. Augustine. This action lifted the Patriot siege and allowed badly needed supplies to reach St. Augustine. Its importance can be compared to the surprise night attack on Mose which broke the spirit of Oglethorpe's invaders in 1740. Seven of Witten's troops were wounded at Twelve Mile Swamp—five Indians and two blacks—and one Indian subsequently died.[101] The Patriot accounts (and therefore, most historical treatments based on the English-language sources) reported that the ambush at Twelve Mile Swamp was the work of the Indians, but Kindelán wrote that the "Indians" were actually "our parties of blacks, whom they [the rebels] think are Indians because they wear the same clothing and go painted."[102] Bereft of supplies, the demoralized Patriot and United States forces began to pull back. When later that month a force led by Georgia volunteer Colonel Daniel Newnan failed to break up the Indian towns near La Chua/Lotchaway (present-day Alachua) and was mauled by Payne's polyglot warriors, the invasion was spent.[103]

Disease, the ferocity of the black and Indian militias, and weakening United States enthusiasm for the land grab when war with England threatened, the combination eventually ruined the Patriots. In the name of the captive king Fernando VII, the Spanish Junta offered the insurgents a general amnesty. Looking for a graceful out, the United States asked Kindelán to honor the offer, and he did, granting rebels three months within which to register for pardon.[104] In May of 1813, Spanish troops marched back into Fernandina and all foreign forces were withdrawn from Florida, but the full restoration of Spanish rule was only to be temporary. Florida was saved for a few more years, but the province was a shambles due to constant political turmoil, and Spain, which had suffered invasions and political turmoil of its own, was in no position to assist its needy colony. The Crown expressed both its gratitude to the black militias and its poverty:

> Although this government is well satisfied with the noble and loyal spirit which animates all the individuals of this company, and although their zeal for service to their country and our august monarch, Señor Don Fernando VII does not require other stimulus than the glory of doing their duty; they are assured, nonetheless, in the name of His Majesty, that each one's merit will be magnanimously attended to and compensated with all the advantages the state can assign, and the national supreme government can support for their good services to the country.[105]

The fighting may have ended but, as described in chapter 10, Floridians of all classes and colors suffered greatly during the invasion. Only five years earlier the province had been flourishing, but now "Everything was thrown into disorder, the houses all burned . . . fields ravished; the cattle stolen or driven away . . . [the country] was left by the patriots a perfect desert."[106] Bad feelings did not easily subside. When Patriot collaborators presented themselves before government notaries to claim pardon, St. Augustine's young men and blacks gathered to insult and mistreat them and Kindelán had to issue a decree forbidding these "excesses." He noted that since he had promised pardon, these acts discredited his authority, and he called on parents and family heads to use their own authority to correct their children and domestics or they would suffer the consequences.[107]

Despite these "excesses," Kindelán recognized St. Augustine's debt to the urban black militia. "To this company and their repeated sallies, we have owed our subsistence in the provision of fresh meat, and they have allowed me to lift the fortified camp of the enemies." Noting that most of the men were family men as well as bitter enemies of the Americans, he suggested the Crown grant them sufficient contiguous land to form several settlements on the northern frontier. The governor argued that such settlements would be of great benefit. Not only would St. Augustine have a vigilant advance guard but the city would have readier access to corn, vegetables, fowl, and other foodstuffs it so badly needed. Governor Manuel de Montiano had made the same general arguments when he established Gracia Real de Santa Teresa de Mose seventy-five years earlier on the same northern frontier.[108] Thus, earlier precedents were being followed when in 1815 the Spanish Crown began to award thousands of acres of land to its black militiamen. As discussed in chapters 4 and 10, the recipients exploited those military service grants and became successful farmers and small businessmen as well as fighters.

Racial Geopolitics and the Demise of Spanish Florida

Spain's black guerrillas and their Seminole allies undid the half-hearted Patriot Rebellion, but the United States remained firmly committed to an expansionist foreign policy in the Southeast and repeatedly violated Spanish sovereignty in Florida. The United States' interventions were motivated by territorial ambition, by the lingering fear that Britain would displace the weakened Spanish regimes in the Southeast, and by racial politics. The very success of the Spanish/African/Indian alliance, in effect, ensured further intervention by Americans who could not tolerate such dangerous collaboration on their frontier. Americans were determined to drive the Spaniards (whom they deprecatingly lumped together with mulattoes) and their "savage" black troops back to the Caribbean. At the same time, they hoped to defeat the British and eradicate or remove the Indians who stood in the way of "civilization" and prosperity for the region. The War of 1812 and the simultaneous Creek War of 1813–14 evolved into a long-term effort to push the Creeks, Seminoles, and blacks out of their settlements in western and central Florida, and eventually to drive out the Spaniards as well.[1] In a desperate series of battles, American forces pushed blacks and Indians ever farther south down the peninsula. Meanwhile, in the northeastern peninsula, free blacks allied to the Spaniards helped defend St. Augustine and its environs against a series of bizarre filibustering expeditions.

"The Seductive . . . Promise of Liberty"

During the War of 1812, as during the American Revolution, the British deliberately encouraged slaves of the enemy to desert plantations, enlist in royal military service, and be recognized as free. The British also promised that after war's end the blacks would receive land. Many ambitious slaves (belonging to both American and Spanish owners) availed themselves of the British offer and, just as before, they found themselves on the losing side. In the summer of 1814, Colonel Edward Nicolls and his aide, Captain George Woodbine, established a large number of fugitive slaves from Mobile, Pensacola, Georgia, and St. Augustine, as well as beleaguered Red Stick Indian allies, at a small but well-armed fort at Prospect Bluff on the Apalachicola River, within Spanish territory and about twenty-five miles north of the Gulf of Mexico. They gave the escaped slaves uniforms and arms, drilled them, and formed the men into three companies of Negro Colonial Marines. In almost all respects, the British policy followed the Spanish, including finally giving their black recruits an armed fort—although that at Prospect Bluff was much more threatening than Mose, established almost a century earlier. The provocation was too much, and Americans, Lower Creeks, Spaniards, and the powerful West Florida trading firm of John Forbes and Company all considered eliminating the fort to be a necessary objective.[2]

The Treaty of Ghent ended the war in 1815, and shortly thereafter General Andrew Jackson defeated the British forces at New Orleans. British intrigues in the Southeast, however, continued. News of the peace took some time to disseminate across the frontier, and meanwhile, Admiral George Cockburn deployed ships off Cumberland Island just north of Amelia Island and reiterated the British offer of freedom to runaway slaves. By late January Cockburn had gathered 450 blacks on Cumberland Island and held approximately 350 more aboard ships.[3] For more than two centuries slave runaways had fled from Anglo planters, southward to Spanish Florida. Now, the British lured slaves away from Spanish owners with similar promises of freedom and homesteads. Floridians Jorge Atkinson and Pedro Capo crossed the quarter-mile sound separating Amelia and Cumberland Islands to try to retrieve their escaped slaves, but British officials told them that British law did not recognize slavery, and runaways could not be forced to return. At the end of February, seventy-seven slaves from John Forbes's San Pablo Plantation on the St. Johns River escaped to Cumberland Island, and Forbes warned Spanish officials that "not one of this class" would remain if English policy were not altered. From St. Augustine Governor Sebastián Kindelán fired off repeated complaints to Admiral Cockburn that slaves were being induced to flee by "the seductive . . . promise of liberty."[4] Zephaniah Kingsley described the sentiments of many Georgians and Floridians who lost slaves to the British recruiters. Such a man was, he said, "so unlucky as to see, on Cumberland Island, last war, the magical transformation of his own negroes, whom he left in the field but a few hours before, into regular soldiers, of good discipline and appearance."[5]

In January, Cockburn's black recruits landed on Cumberland Island, helped attack the village of St. Marys in Georgia, and forced the retreat of the American force at Fort Point Petre. After occupying Cumberland briefly, Cockburn sailed away to Bermuda with the freedmen and all attempts by Spanish citizens to recover their lost property were in vain. John Forbes found and tried to recover thirty-six of his slaves in Bermuda. Forbes also learned that other of his slaves had joined a black regiment bound for Halifax. Forbes filed a formal protest through Spanish diplomats and initiated a lengthy, but ultimately unsuccessful, suit in London courts to recover his lost chattel.[6]

Destruction of the Negro Fort at Prospect Bluff

During the spring of 1815, escaped slaves and refugee Indians continued to filter into Prospect Bluff. By summer an estimated force of 1,100 warriors, including several hundred blacks, garrisoned the so-called Negro Fort. The former slaves built a village behind the fort and planted extensive cornfields, which were said to stretch along the river for more than forty-five miles.[7] Nearby, advancing Georgians were also establishing settlements, and as commander of the Southern Military Division of the United States, General Andrew Jackson demanded the "immediate and prompt interference of the Spanish authority to destroy or remove from our frontier this banditti."[8] Pensacola's governor, Mauricio de Zúñiga, agreed to solicit specific orders from Spain, but he was in no position to actually send any troops against the fort. Instead, he sent Captain Vicente Sebastián Pintado to investigate the matter and to retrieve any runaway slaves belonging to Spanish owners in East and West Florida.

After first securing promises of assistance from British admiral Alexander Cochrane, Pintado headed for the fort on the Apalachicola. Spaniards living in Pensacola gave Pintado lists of 136 runaway slaves, including seventy-eight men, twenty-three women, eight boys, four girls, and twenty-three whose gender was not given. Pintado's lists gave the age, color (black or mulatto), and family status of the runaways, and in some cases the circumstances by which they arrived at Prospect Bluff, their occupations, and their stated value. Don Antonio Montero claimed to be the owner of the black commander at the fort, Garçon, who was a thirty-year-old carpenter, as well as four other men and three women. Pensacola's former governor, Vicente Folch, also claimed two of the runaways—the thirty-year-old carpenter Tom, valued at seven hundred pesos, and twenty-three-year-old Agustín, valued at five hundred pesos.[9]

The Pensacola merchant house, John Forbes and Company, claimed that forty-five of its slaves had also escaped to the settlement at Prospect Bluff. In April of 1816, the company's agent, Edmund Doyle, reported to his employers "the following Negroes, who are now on the Bluff, the restoration of them appears doubtful, to Wit—Billy & Lally & their children, Cressy, Flora, Beek, Cynthia & Nero—Stephen & his wife Cynthia—Tom a House servant."[10] Also among the Forbes and Company slave runaways were Congo Tom, Carlos Congo, and Carlos Mayumbe, presumably African-born men. Among the most highly valued of the Forbes and Company runaways were Ambrosio, a shoemaker valued at nine hundred pesos, and Harry, a caulker and navigator who knew how to read and write and was valued at two thousand pesos.[11] The runaways also included

African-inspired mahogany drum found in the bank of Little Manatee River, Florida. Courtesy of the Florida Museum of Natural History.

sailors, master carpenters, coopers, ironsmiths, bakers, servants, laundresses, cooks, sawyers, masons, cartwrights, and field hands. If this group is representative, and there is no reason that it should not be, the blacks who lived at this settlement were certainly equipped to be self-sufficient. While they may not have been "black Robin Hoods," as Herbert Aptheker called them, neither were they the parasitical "villains" described by the Americans.[12]

Doyle believed the English sponsors of the fort, Nicolls and Woodbine, to be motivated by self-interest. He charged that Captain Woodbine seduced away "not more than ten" slaves belonging to the Americans, whose retaliation he feared, but that instead with the "help of their [Nicolls and Woodbine's] agents and black spies, corrupted the negroes of their friends and Spanish allies." Woodbine had traveled to East Florida to aid Admiral Cockburn at Cumberland and, along the way, he gathered slave recruits wherever he could. Doyle charged that Woodbine returned to Prospect Bluff with approximately twenty men and women from St. Augustine, the St. Johns River, and Alachua.[13] Woodbine later admitted that Spanish owners from St. Augustine recognized and claimed some of the blacks in his forty-man escort when he was in St. Augustine, but he claimed that he was not authorized to return them as they had already become free by virtue of their escape to the Indians. While Woodbine was in East Florida, Colonel Edward Nicolls, as a self-appointed British agent to the independent Creek Nation, directed letters of remonstrance to the U.S. Indian agent, Benjamin Hawkins, for attacks he said Americans had committed against Creek and Seminole towns there. Hawkins responded that the Indians could appeal for redress to either legitimate Spanish or American officials, but he charged that Nicolls had no authority to speak for the Indians and likened him to William Augustus Bowles, "that Prince of Liars."[14]

When Captain Pintado finally arrived at Prospect Bluff, his escort, Royal Navy captain R. C. Spencer, would not allow the slaves to be forcibly returned to the Spanish representative. In Pintado's presence Spencer disarmed the men, paid them for their service, and gave each a discharge from the British service. He told the blacks that new orders precluded him from transporting them to British possessions as promised earlier by Admiral Cochrane and he warned them (correctly) that when the English departed, the blacks would be preyed upon by the Americans and their Indian allies.[15]

Only twenty-eight of the 128 runaways interviewed by Pintado agreed to return with him, and overnight several of those ran away or changed their minds. Pintado was able to convince only ten interviewees to return voluntarily, and all of those were women. Pintado estimated that the total number of runaways at the fort approached 250 and he reported that a number of them planned to remove themselves to black Seminole settlements at Tampa Bay. Pintado confronted Captain Woodbine about the slaves he allegedly lured from East Florida, and Woodbine stated that seventy-eight slaves belonging to the Indians accompanied him to Prospect Bluff, but that none came directly from St. Augustine.[16]

Meanwhile, General Jackson had already ordered Major General Edmund Pendleton Gaines to destroy the fort that was "stealing and enticing away our negroes" and that had "been established by some villain for the purpose of murder, rapine, and plunder." Gaines assigned the job to Lieutenant Colonel Duncan L. Clinch, who was reinforced by the Coweta Creeks, led by the wealthy Chief William McIntosh, son of a British Indian agent. Two gunboats of the United States Navy sailed upriver to join in the attack. The fort's black commander, Garçon, defiantly informed a Creek delegation that "he had been left in command of the fort by the British government and that he would sink any American vessels that should attempt to pass it."[17] He vowed to blow up the fort rather than surrender. Given that Garçon and the Choctaw chief who jointly commanded the fort had at their disposal ten cannon, several thousand muskets and sidearms, ammunition, and military stores, in addition to their well-trained and determined warriors, it portended to be a costly siege.

When the battle actually began on July 27, 1816, the blacks in the fort hoisted a red flag under the Union Jack and hurled insults as well as cannon shots at the Americans. One of the attacking officers noted with some admiration the "spirited opposition" of the blacks, who made it clear that they would neither ask for, or give, quarter and that they would fight to the death. The blacks led several sorties against McIntosh's warriors but were driven back into the fort, and on the second day a "miraculous" American shot hit the powder magazine, blowing up the fort with a blast that shook Pensacola, sixty miles away.[18] Colonel Clinch described the action in graphic, yet exculpatory, terms

> The explosion was awful, and the scene horrible beyond description. Our first care, on arriving at the scene of the destruction, was to rescue and relieve the unfortunate beings who survived the explosion. The war yells of the Indians, the cries and lamentations of the wounded, compelled the soldier to pause in the midst of victory, to drop a tear for the sufferings of his fellow beings, and to acknowledge that the great Ruler of the Universe must have used us as his instruments in chastising the blood-thirsty and murderous wretches that defended the fort.[19]

It is possible, but seems unlikely, that Garçon would have blown up the fort without first giving the attackers a good fight. On July 17 he and others had engaged in a riverine battle with five U.S. Navy men. They killed three outright and captured a fourth, whom they later tarred and burned to death. A fifth escaped to tell the tale, and may have helped incite the murder of Garçon and the Choctaw chief on their capture.

Only forty individuals survived the explosion and few of those lived long. The Americans handed Garçon and the Choctaw chief over to the Creeks, who "passed sentence of death" and promptly executed them. The victors returned the few live captives to owners, who claimed them and paid the costs of their retrieval. With the "banditti" exterminated, the American naval forces set fire to the fort and sailed away with approximately $200,000 worth of arms and supplies.[20]

"Laying Waste" the Seminole Heartland

Having routed the nativist Upper Creeks or Red Sticks at Horseshoe Bend, Alabama (1814), and the British at New Orleans (1815), and with the Negro Fort at Prospect Bluff destroyed (1816), in April of 1818 General Andrew Jackson and more than three thousand troops launched a three-week campaign against the Seminole heartland in what came to be called the First Seminole War. The doomed trader Arbuthnot, in a last letter to his son, alleged "The main drift of the Americans is to destroy the black population of Suwany."[21] General Gaines confirmed this when he wrote the Seminoles, "You harbor a great many of my black people among you, at Sahwahnee. If you give me leave to go by you against them, I shall not hurt anything belonging to you." King Hachy (Heijah) responded that some blacks may have taken refuge among the English during their war with the Americans, but "it is for you, white people, to settle those things among yourselves. . . . I shall use force to stop any armed Americans from passing my towns or my lands."[22]

General Jackson began by forcing the surrender of the Spanish garrison at San Marcos de Apalachee, where he arrested and executed the Red Stick prophet Francis (Hillis Hadjo). He also arrested the Bahamian Indian trader Alexander Arbuthnot and Colonel Nicolls's surrogate in the Southeast, Robert Ambrister. A court later convicted the Bahamians of inciting and arming the Indians and blacks and executed them both. Evidence at Ambrister's trial included a letter he had written Nicolls from the Suwannee stating that the three hundred blacks there "beg me to say, they depend on your promises, and expect you are the way out. They have stuck to the *cause,* and will always believe in the faith of you."[23] Joined by the Coweta Creek leader William McIntosh, who had besieged the Negro Fort, on April 16, 1818, Jackson's troops burned almost four hundred black and Seminole homes at Bowlegs Town on the Suwannee River, destroyed large quantities of food supplies, and spirited away herds of cattle and horses.[24] Blacks and Seminoles, who had been forewarned by Arbuthnot, put up a desperate fight, with three hundred black warriors holding back a greatly superior force at the Suwannee to give the women and children time to cross over to safety. Although the Seminole's northern settlements were ruined, their desperate resistance continued. Black and Indian refugees dispersed to the west and south of Florida, join-

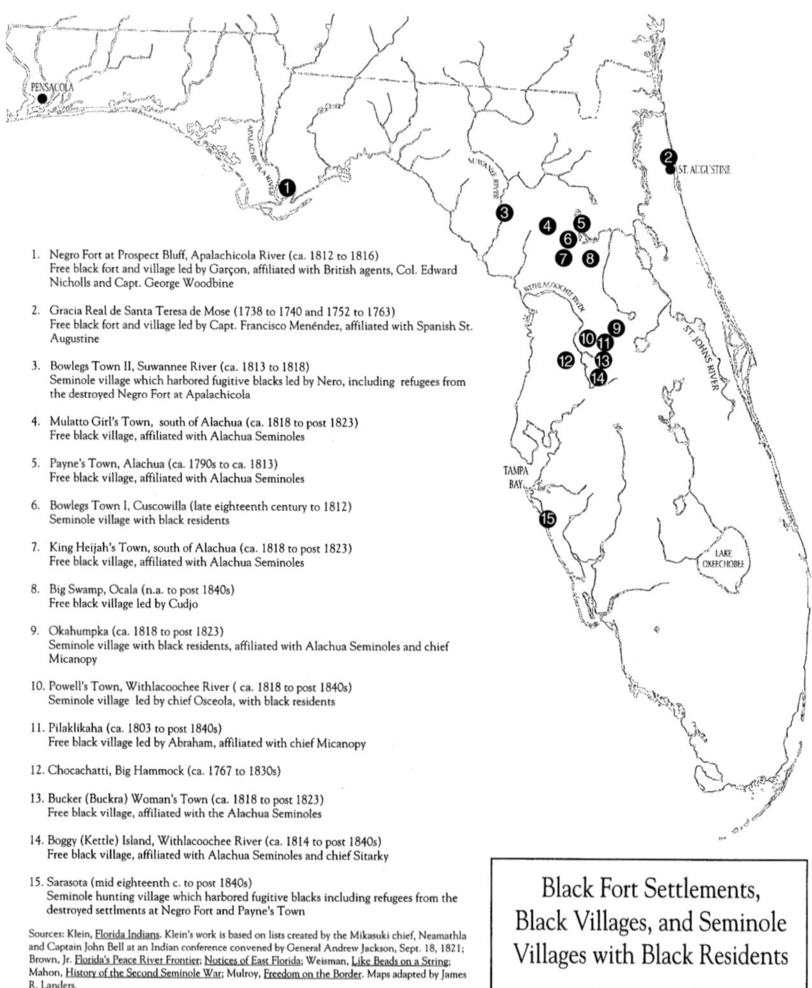

Nineteenth-century black fort settlements, black villages, and Seminole villages with black residents. Adapted by James R. Landers from Howard F. Cline, *Florida Indians,* vol. 2: *Provisional Historical Gazeteer with Locational Notes on Florida Colonial Communities* (New York, 1974).

ing others who had anticipated the attacks at Prospect Bluff and at the Suwannee and had already resettled in traditional hunting villages near Tampa Bay.[25]

Refugee Villages

Captain James Gadsden described Tampa Bay as "The last rallying spot of the disaffected negroes and Indians and the only favorable point from whence a communication can be had with Spanish and European emissaries."[26] From Tampa the desperate Seminoles and their black allies sent repeated diplomatic missions to the British in the Bahamas and the Spaniards in Cuba. Although the Spaniards in St. Augustine managed to provide them with substantial food supplies and muskets, the British sent only nominal gifts, not wanting to alienate the Americans who, by the Adams-Onís Treaty, were soon to take possession of Florida.[27]

In 1821 General Andrew Jackson became governor of the new United States territorial government of Florida and recommended removing the fugitive Creeks, Seminoles, and free blacks from the peninsula. As he awaited a response, powerful proponents of the Indian removal policy acted through intermediaries. In 1821 several hundred Coweta warriors sponsored by Georgia speculators raided the Tampa Bay and Sarasota Bay settlements and carried northward a number of blacks, cattle, and horses. Once again escaping Seminoles and blacks were forced to flee—this time to the tip of the peninsula at Cape Florida. There, Cuban fishermen and Bahamian wreckers with whom they had long conducted trade carried hundreds "in a famishing state" to safety in Cuba and to Andros Island and Bimini.[28] One sizeable group of black and Seminole exiles built a permanent settlement at Red Bays, on Andros Island, where they sustained themselves by "felling timber, cutting Dye woods, gathering sponges and picking up wrecked property." Within ten years some had managed "through their industry and good management" to purchase their own fishing smacks.[29]

Amelia Island

As blacks and Seminoles waged their desperate struggle to survive in the hinterlands, blacks living in St. Augustine, on St. Johns River homesteads, and on Amelia Island faced a different set of challenges and enemies. Lying just south of the United States border and blessed with a good harbor, the city of Fernandina boomed as a result of the U.S. Embargo Act of 1807, shipping large amounts of Florida cotton and lumber to eager customers. With the congressional ban on the African slave trade in 1808, slave traders and their customers found Fernandina a convenient market. Fernandina became a free port the same year and soon was attracting smugglers from every Atlantic port and many Caribbean ones.

Georgia slaveowners complained that their slaves were also "dayly passing to that province." Although the practice had been abrogated in 1790, Georgia planters always feared the possible revival of Spain's religious sanctuary policy for escaped slaves, and one Amelia Island resident warned "in all probability one half the negroes of your sea coast would be over the St. Marys river in less than one month."[30] One runaway, John, escaped from Darien with several other slaves in the summer of 1811 but was recaptured at St. Mary's, Georgia. He managed to break jail and finally made it to Florida the same year, where he assumed the name John Spaniard. Two years later, John's owner wrote Spanish authorities and offered a reward for John's recovery. He thought it significant to note in his correspondence that his escaped slave wore "something in a small bag suspended by a string around his neck." This may have been a *nkisi* or Congo charm bag such as that worn by Gullah Jack. Because many black Floridians were Congos or had family members who were, it is probable that John found not only employment but a community in Fernandina. John spoke English, Spanish, and French, and his former owner described him as "very plausible and artful . . . a good boat hand and something of a sailor." With such a résumé, John would surely have found quick employment in bustling Fernandina, where few questions were asked and where a man's talents counted more than his skin color.[31]

Uncertain government revenues in St. Augustine and the flurry of commercial activity on the island also drew population away from the Florida mainland. Local planters like Samuel Harrison and John Rushing established new plantations on the western side of Amelia to which they transferred large slave forces. As Jorge J. F. Clarke later testified to the United States Supreme Court, "The condition of the country was most prosperous. Every man was making money hand over hand as fast as he could, and in consequence of the restrictive measures of the American government, the trade of the United States with all the world, except Spain, centered in Fernandina."[32]

By 1813, 902 blacks lived on Amelia Island, accounting for 67 percent of the total population of 1,330. (See table 10.) Most of the persons of color labored on plantations beyond the neat town squares, but thirty-seven of the forty-one free blacks and mulattoes lived in Fernandina.[33] (See appendix 12.)

The haphazard growth of Fernandina disturbed Governor Enrique White, who appointed his surveyor, Don Jorge J. F. Clarke, to design an urban renewal plan that would bring Fernandina into line with the Spanish urban model. Clarke laid out a model city along rectilinear lines of thirteen squares, four lots wide and four

Table 10. Census, 1813, Fernandina

Age (Years)	White		Mulatto Free		Mulatto Slave		Black Free		Black Slave	
	M	F	M	F	M	F	M	F	M	F
0–7	57	68	3	4	5	4	—	—	97	58
7–16	31	36	6	1	4	2	—	—	77	52
16–25	27	44	2	3	—	6	4	2	110	74
25–40	64	40	3	1	1	1	2	5	167	112
40–50	17	15	1	1	—	—	1	1	58	23
50+	21	8	—	1	—	—	—	—	5	5
	217	211	15	11	10	13	7	8	514	324

Source: Fernandina Census, June 1, 1813, Census Returns, 1784–1814, EFP, microfilm reel 148, PKY.

long. To encourage the beautification program, all residents who already held land and had built homes were guaranteed reimbursement for any moves or required changes to their homes, as well as title to their lots. One former resident recalled: "The town consists of about forty houses, built of wood, in six streets, regularly intersecting each other at right angles, having rows of trees (Pride of India) and a square, with a small fort of eight guns, fronting the water. Several of these houses are two stories high, with galleries, and form a handsome appearance."[34] The town also featured a Catholic church, which no proper Spanish town would do without, a hospital, inns, stores, and warehouses to serve the growing population.[35]

Fernandina's prosperity attracted ambitious free blacks who applied for, and received, land grants in the new town. In the census of 1814, Fernandina's free blacks were grouped into sixteen households, seven of which were female-headed. Although listed as the heads of their households, the women were not always without partners. Some of them women were the consorts of wealthy white men, who helped them acquire property in Fernandina. An examination of block eight shows that Don Jorge J. F. Clarke's consort, Flora, occupied a house that backed up to that of their daughter, Felicia Garvin. Flora's neighbor, Anna Wiggins, the Senegalese consort of the English planter Job Wiggins, and one daughter, Isabella Wiggins, lived on the same block. Two other of the Wiggins daughters owned property on block two, and one of them, Jennie, also owned a lot on block three. The women, thereby, gained potential support and companionship from one another.[36]

If a free black couple was legally married, the household was usually listed under the man's name, as in the case of José Sánchez, the natural quadroon son of the planter Don Francisco Xavier Sánchez, and his wife, Lucía Ysnardy, the natural quadroon daughter of Don Miguel Ysnardy. Both spouses received inheritances

BLACK RESIDENTS OF FERNANDINA

Adapted from Florida State Archives
Map of Fernandina, 1811

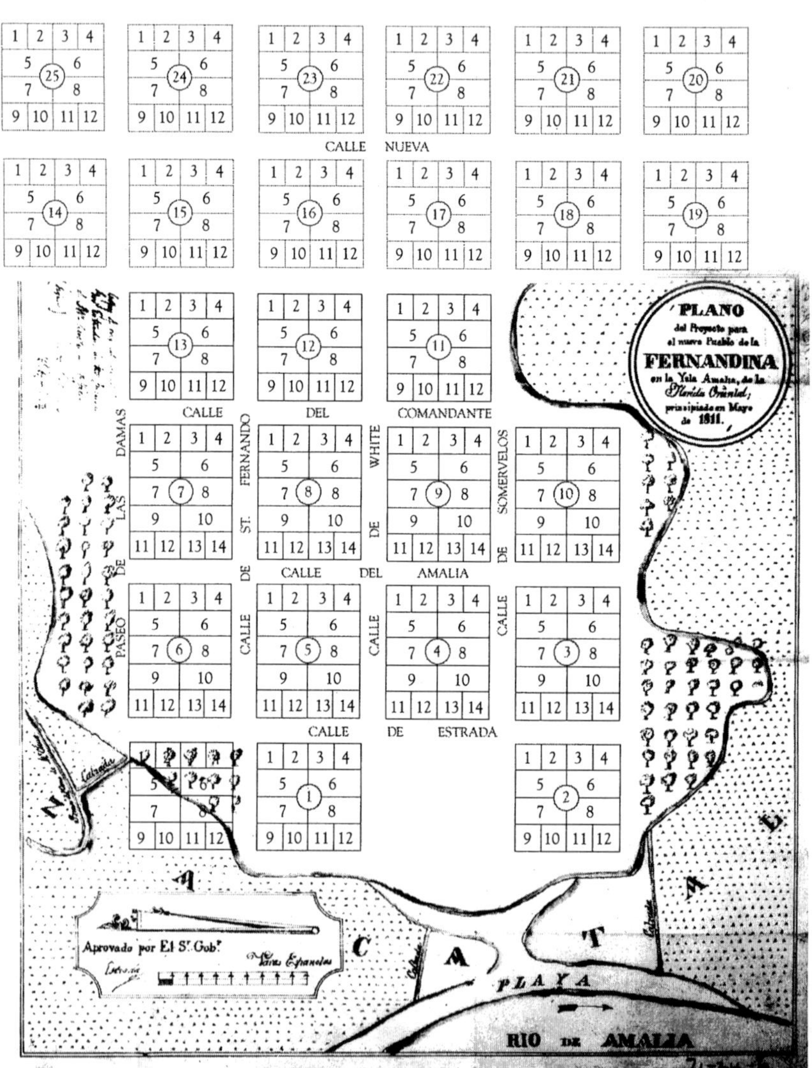

Black residents of Fernandina, Amelia Island. Adapted by James R. Landers from Fernandina map of 1811 adapted by Frank Dollheimer (Dollheimer map courtesy of the Florida State Archives).

BLOCK #2

Lot # 5 Juana Wiggins
Lot # 6 Jenny Wiggins
Lot # 10 Don Jorge J. F. Clarke
Flora Leslie Clarke
Juan Nepomuceno Diego Clarke b. 5/16/1806
Guillermo Roman Clarke b. 3/5/1808
Jorge Felipe Clarke b. 6/6/1814

BLOCK #3

Lot # 1 & 2 Jorge Brus
María Carlota m. 6/8/1797
Juan Matias b. 2/17/1798
Felipe b. 9/26/1803
Rosa b. 8/25/1806
José b. 1809
Apolonia b. 1816
Carlito b. 1818
Lot # 8 David Garvin
Felicia Clarke Garvin (dtr. Jorge & Flora Clarke)
Lot # 10 Jenny Wiggins
Lot # 13 Jenny Wiggins

BLOCK #4

Lot#
3 Juan Jorge Santiago Jacobo (after 1806, Biassou)
María Rafaela Witten, m. 4/12/1796
María del Carmen, b. 7/16/1797, d. 6/17/1799
Julian Santiago, b. 6/19/1801
Josef Baltazar, b. 9/18/1803
Rafaela Biasu (sic), b. 6/19/1806
Catalina Melchora Santiago, b. 1/6/1808

BLOCK #8

Lot#
1 (1/2 lot) Harry (Enrique) McQueen & wife
María Reyes, agregada
2 Diana Domingo
4 Rob Rivas
5 Flora Clarke
6 Felicia Clarke Garvin
9 Nansi Wiggins (aka Anna Gallum),(mother of Ysabel Wiggins)
10 Don Carlos Clarke
Ysabel Wiggins (aka Patty)
Anna Josefa Clarke b. 1/12/1799
Carlos Manuel Clarke b. 1/24/1802
María Leonor Clarke b. 4/7/1804
José Clarke b. 8/25/1805
Ysabel Josefa Leona María Wiggins b. 4/11/1809
Jayme Francisco Clarke b. 7/16/1812
Jayme Francisco Clarke, b. 7/16/1812
12 (1/2 lot) Ysabel Wiggins (aka Patty)
14 Ysabel Wiggins (aka Patty)
15 Patricio Moore

BLOCK #12

Lot#
1 María Sivelly & daughter
Tina Diana, Agregada
3 Abraham Hudson
4 Tory Travers

BLOCK #13

Lot#
2 Felipa
3 Felipa
4 (1/2 lot) Juan Peterson (property originally ceded to María Dolores, free black who sold it to Peterson)

BLOCK #14

(New Lots Added after 1816 on Calle Nueva)
Lot#
4 Benjamin Seguí
María Juana Francisca Bacas (aka) Camel
Luis Seguí b. 6/21/1816
Jorge Aniceto Seguí b. 3/16/1818
Pedro Alexander Seguí, b. 4/24/1820
8 Nansi Wiggins
11 Joe Richo

BLOCK #15

Lot#
1 Jacobo Moore

BLOCK #16

Lot#
1 (1/2 lot) León Duvigneau (his bakery)
2 (1/2 lot) León Duvigneau (his residence)
Margarita Simonette
Pedro Camilo de Solis b. 1803
María Luisa b. 1/6/1808
Juan José b. 6/16/1810
Juan Margarita b. 1/12/1812
Justo Leon b. 9/6/1814
Clara Elena b. 12/24/1816
Orora Angela b. 12/27/1818
Manuel Simon Edmundo b. 12/24/1820
6 Nansi Wiggins
8 María Rafaela Scott
9 & 10 José Gres (Grey)
11 (1/2 lot) Jorge Brus
12 (1/2 lot) Free black, unnamed
13 (1/2 lot) Free black, unnamed
14 (1/2 lot) José Bonam

BLOCK #17

Lot#
4 Juan Rait (Wright)

BLOCK #21

(New Lots Added after 1816 on Calle Nueva)
Lot#
1 & 2 Abraham Hannahan

BLOCK #23

(New Lots Added after 1816 on Calle Nueva)
Lot#
1 Juan Moore & wife
Juan Moore, Jr.
Tomas Moore
Jacobo Moore
one other son

BLOCK #24

(New Lots Added after 1816 on Calle Nueva)
Lot#
10 (1/2 lot) León Duvigneau
11 (1/2 lot) León Duvigneau

BLOCK #25

((New Lots Added after 1816 on Calle Nueva)
Lot#
3 Nansi Wiggins
William Garvin

BLOCK #32

(New Lots Added after 1816 on Calle Nueva)
Lot#
1 Domingo (aka Mingo) Sanco & wife

Sources: Free Blacks and Mulattos of Fernadina and Amelia Island, 1814 and 1814 Census of Fernandina, EFP, microfilm reel 148, PKY; SLGF, vol. 1; Series 996, Memorials for City Lots in Fernandina, 1809-1821, SFLR; Landers Data Base.

from their deceased fathers, and their household included three slaves. Unfortunately, most of the free black householders would lose their property when the United States acquired Florida.[37]

Fernandina's black residents included many members of St. Augustine's urban militia. Jorge Jacobo moved his family to Fernandina and opened a store to take advantage of the commercial and population growth. His countryman León Duvigneau and his family opened a bakery.[38] Other members of St. Augustine's militia who relocated to Fernandina were Jorge Brus, Tory Travers, Juan Moore, Juan Peterson, Felix Castoral, and Domingo Sanco. The men organized themselves into a new urban militia, the Company of Pardos and Morenos of the National Urban Militia of Fernandina, led by Lieutenant Juan Jorge Jacobo, who had inherited the command of his deceased brother-in-law, Jorge Biassou. The unit was comprised of twenty-six men, exactly half the strength of the white militia unit, and was nominally under the authority of Don Carlos Clarke.[39] In their civilian lives, the men were shopkeepers, bakers, and butchers, among other occupations. They prided themselves on their citizenship, their property, and their loyalty to Spain. When enemies threatened, they were among the first to contribute money and service. In 1810, Jorge Jacobo, Felipe Edimboro, and other members of this militia made ten-peso contributions to a fund known as "the war effort to capture French emissaries," equivalent to the donations of many Spanish dons.[40]

Two of those dons, the surveyor and judge Jorge J. F. Clarke, and his brother Carlos, commander of the Company of Pardos and Morenos, both of whom had black consorts and many natural children whom they recognized, educated, and named in their wills, moved their extended families to the new city of Fernandina in 1808 and contributed to its rapid development. Jorge J. F. Clarke's consort Flora Leslie had once belonged to the merchant Juan Leslie, of Panton, Leslie and Company, for whom Jorge J. F. Clarke was an apprentice and in whose household he lived. In 1794, Jorge bought Flora for four hundred pesos and their daughter Felicia (Philis) for sixty pesos, and he freed them both in 1797. Although Clarke never married Flora, the Fernandina census of 1814 identified her as his "esposa" (wife) rather than just his "mujer" (woman), and by that time the couple had four children. Clarke established a tanyard, a horse-powered sawmill, and a lumber warehouse in Fernandina, and his extended family members also owned town houses and a number of slaves.[41]

After Flora died, Jorge J. F. Clarke began a second family with the slave Hannah Benet, and in his will, dated 1834, he provided for both families (as many of his associates also did). Clarke divided his estate evenly among the eight children he fathered by Flora and provided a separate legacy of fifteen hundred acres of land for Hannah Benet and their four children. Clarke instructed his executors to sell the land and buy the family's freedom as the owner, Catalina Benet, had agreed to purchase a home and lot for the family. They were to "leave the mother in hand (who is very industrious and saving) the beginning of a moderate independency toward raising and educating these children." Any money remaining should be used to purchase "well grown and well disposed slaves," and Hannah's brother, Antonio, was to be the first purchased. Clarke wrote, "I consider the hire of negroes in these southern countries the most lucrative, sane and simple investment that can be found." Clarke later added $2000 for Hannah and the children from any payments he might collect from the United States government on Patriot War claims.[42]

Jorge J. F. Clarke's brother, Carlos Clarke, was also the patriarch of a large quadroon family of six children whose mother was Beatriz María Wiggins (also known as Ysabel, Eliza, and Patty), the free mulatto daughter of Don Joseph (Job) Wiggins and the Senegalese Nansi Wiggins. Carlos and Beatriz shared English ancestry and a common birthplace and background, as well as many children. In 1820, Carlos Clarke sold Beatriz María Wiggins land, probably to document her claim and ownership, and in 1836, he deeded Thomas Clarke 250 acres of land on the Indian River, "in consideration of the natural love and affection I bear my son."[43] An interesting commentary on the relative influence of the brothers is the fact that despite her well-known father, the Fernandina census lists Beatriz María (Patty) as an "agregada" or lodger in Carlos Clarke's household, rather than as his wife.

Jorge J. F. Clarke served as *capitan de partido* or *juez pedaneo* for Fernandina in 1812, a position that combined the functions of conciliator, policeman, and judge. In 1816, Clarke assumed an expanded role of *capitan* for the larger Upper and Lower St. Marys district, with "superintending jurisdiction for the whole," in effect becoming "deputy governor." Meanwhile, he continued to serve as the royal surveyor, in which capacity he facilitated and documented claims for most of the property owned by free blacks.[44] Carlos Clarke served as lieutenant of the Provincial and Urban Militias of Florida, commanding one hundred men of the Pardos and Morenos units from Havana as well as Fernandina's local black militia unit.[45] Thus, both Clarke brothers held influential positions from which to protect the extended black community in which they had many kin and friends and they functioned as their patrons, sponsors, and supporters. These connections were often critical, especially during Florida's territorial transition. Jorge Clarke surveyed many land grants for free blacks and he and his brother helped them document and retain these grants when the United States finally took Florida in 1821.[46]

The last years of Spanish tenure in Florida were especially hard on the free black communities of Fernandina and St. Augustine. The violence of multiple invasions repeatedly threatened their families and their hard-won property, which the men of both communities fought to defend.[47] Florida's government was in dire financial straits, and officers repeatedly complained that their naked men were suffering in the elements, on half rations and without supplies. The local black militia patrolling the banks of the St. Johns River and those posted at Buena Vista fort were said to be "totally nude," and in need of blankets to get through the approaching winter.[48]

Florida Filibusters

On June 29, 1817, Gregor MacGregor, a veteran of the Napoleonic wars and of the South American revolutions, seized Fernandina as a launching pad from which to free all of Florida from monarchy. Following the lead of his former mentor, Simón Bolívar, MacGregor planned also to emancipate East Florida's slaves. However, when MacGregor's "Republic of the Floridas" failed to gain the official United States support he hoped for, he abandoned his early idealism and supported his forces by selling slaves captured as prizes by commissioned privateers. Within months MacGregor was gone, reportedly uniting with Captain George Woodbine and heading for New Providence.[49]

Following MacGregor's departure, on September 9, 1817, "about 350 Spanish troops, principally negroes," attacked the remaining Florida "republicans" outside Fernandina but failed to dislodge them in two battles. An unidentified British officer described the battle, the courage of the black troops, and what he perceived as the incompetence of their Spanish commander who, after being fired upon by gunboats and land guns, ordered a retreat. The black troops "reluctantly obeyed," although "it is well known [they] may be perfectly relied upon for steadiness and courage."[50]

Spanish reports offer a somewhat different picture. In a letter to the governor, Jorge J. F. Clarke, commander of the St. Marys district militia, who also took part in the attack, wrote that one "poor" commander "found himself in an inferno, with the enemy in front and behind, abandoned by the population and surrounded by characters who know no other obligation than self-interest and they did nothing but try to distract or confuse him."[51]

Lt. Col. Tomás Llorente, who commanded the Spanish regulars and militiamen, described the scene as a "sea of confusion." Llorente ordered his troops to dismantle Fernandina's fortifications and set fire to the fort, and as flames consumed the buildings, the men retreated. Their forty-two-mile march back to St.

Augustine was accomplished in a torrential storm in which the soldiers waded through knee-deep water most of the way. In places the water reached their chests. During the two-day march, they lost most of their ammunition and ruined shoes, clothes, and supplies, but they arrived safely at St. Augustine.[52] Unable to pay them adequately for their efforts, Governor José Coppinger followed the lead of his predecessor, Sebastián Kindelán, and offered them military service land grants. Such royal grants were absolute and, unlike those granted to new settlers, conveyed immediate title.[53]

After MacGregor came "Commodore" Luis Aury, a former Napoleonic officer/opportunist/revolutionary from Santo Domingo, who also claimed to be advancing the causes of liberty and republicanism. Aury had fought in the insurgent movements of Cartagena and Mexico and, in 1816, he seized Galveston Island in the name of the Mexican Republic. Aury set up an admiralty court and began a brisk business in condemned prizes with his associate, the notorious pirate Jean Laffite. On September 21, 1817, Aury formally claimed Fernandina for the "Republic of Mexico." As he had at Galveston, Aury set up a nominal government and pronounced eloquently his goal to "plant the tree of liberty" and to "foster free institutions" in Fernandina. He was aided in this effort by more than one hundred black Haitians. Like the Spaniards, Aury planned to use land to reward loyalty, promising a private who would serve the republican cause for six months 320 acres of Florida land; those with longer service or higher rank would earn even more generous bounties.[54]

Despite Aury's liberal rhetoric, his main effort seems to have been dedicated to personal enrichment, and privateering and smuggling grew to epic proportions on Amelia Island. In two months prize goods reputedly worth $500,000 were sold at Fernandina, and newspapers compared Amelia Island to Barataria, the notorious lair of Laffite.[55] Much of the profit came from slave sales. In November, 1817, Aury's privateers captured a Spanish ship returning from the African coast and promptly sold off the shipload of 290 enslaved Africans found on board. The *Niles Weekly Register* charged that once sold at Amelia "the Negroes will certainly be smuggled into the United States, as many others have been lately." The writer added, "This trade in human flesh is so profitable, that if that island [Amelia] is not taken possession of by the United States, we shall hear of many slave vessels sent as prizes that have very conveniently laid off the port to be captured."[56] An eyewitness account by Captain John Elton of the USS *Saranac* described African rowers ferrying slaves from ship to shore almost continuously and contemporaries estimated that Aury sold more than one thousand Africans in less than two months, most of whom were "spirited" northward to Georgia or other southern states where importation was forbidden.[57]

The fact that most of Aury's troops came from the first black republic in the hemisphere also raised alarms. The *Savannah Republican* described the black troops as "brigands who had participated in the horrors of St. Domingo," and the former director of the Patriots, John Houston McIntosh, warned, "His great dependence however, is upon about one hundred and thirty brigand negroes—a set of desperate bloody dogs. . . . Aury's blacks make their neighborhood extremely dangerous to a population like ours and I fear if they are not expelled from that place [Fernandina] some unhappy consequence might fall on our country. It is said they have declared that if they are in danger they will call to their aid every negro within reach. Indeed, I am told that the language of the slaves is already such as to be extremely alarming."[58]

The fear of lost customs' profit and potential slave flight from the southern states inspired another United States intervention (based as was the Patriot Rebellion on the secret law of 1811). President Monroe told Congress that Amelia was "made a channel for the illicit introduction of slaves from Africa into the United States, an asylum for fugitive slaves from the neighboring states, and a port for smuggling of all kinds." A United States naval squadron soon arrived to clear out the "pirate's den," and one of the first acts of the commander was to take on board and disperse to other locations all of Aury's black troops. On December 23, 1817, United States forces occupied Amelia Island and held it until the Spaniards finally departed Florida for good. These troops caused almost as much damage to Spanish properties as the previous pirates. Jorge J. F. Clarke described American soldiers dismantling his valuable tanyard and sawmill for the timber, but the protests that he and other influential property owners lodged went unanswered. The property rights of free blacks were even less significant to the troops.[59]

Blacks in the Second Exodus to Cuba

In its weakened state, Spain ultimately lost Florida to the territorial ambitions of the United States. In the final days of Spanish tenure, Cuba's captain general ordered Governor José Coppinger to encourage East Floridians to emigrate to Cuba, Texas, and Mexico. Spanish officials hoped, too, that the beleaguered Seminoles might be enticed to form a buffer community along the Texas border, replicating their position in East Florida.[60] Governor Coppinger dutifully played for time, but American officials were impatient to take possession, and he was finally forced to initiate Spain's second full-scale evacuation to Cuba. Although all Floridians had struggled to the best of their abilities to stave off the inevitable, Spanish sovereignty in Florida ended on July 10, 1821. In a public address explaining the terms of the transfer Coppinger expressed his appreciation to the citizenry: "I hope that with this change all the vicissitudes which circumstances have made you suffer with heroic resignation may cease! As witness whereof to the sacrifices that you have made for the country, I shall testify to those things which are known to me of each one, if occasion offers. . . . I flatter myself with the idea that you will be happy, which is the greatest desire of your friend and fellow citizen."[61]

All of Florida's Spanish citizens had, indeed, suffered and sacrificed. But it might be argued that the black families and their soldiers so often exposed on the frontier and so frequently targeted for capture, punishment, or reenslavement by the plague of invaders that swept over Florida may have endured the heaviest toll. They knew, too well, the racial attitudes and legal systems entering the colony with the newcomers and prepared to leave their homes for safer, if unknown, territories. The first and largest contingent of free black Floridians associated with the black militia sailed out of St. Augustine on August 22, 1821, with smaller groups following. Some did not leave until as late as 1827, but eventually forty black militiamen, twenty-seven women, and seventy-eight children were resettled in Cuba at the expense of the royal treasury. Spanish officials granted them homesteading lands and a pension of a daily ration each and kept records on the exiled group for some time thereafter, recording deaths and reducing allotments accordingly.[62]

Some younger members of the group joined the militias in Cuba, but many like Juan Bautista Witten, who was sixty-two, and Benjamín Seguí, who was fifty-one, had already devoted well over twenty years of service to the Spanish Crown fighting against French, British, North American, and Indian enemies. Despite broken promises and sometimes shabby treatment from colonial authorities, the black militiamen were steadfastly loyal to Spain. They were unable to stem the tide of North American expansion, but in slowing its advance, the black soldiers enabled the weak and neglected Spanish administration in Florida to endure longer than it might otherwise have done. Many of the men who composed the black militia were remarkable for their ability to "take the tide." Having risen out of the chaos of two revolutions and fought their way out of slavery, they proved formidable and loyal allies of the Spaniards who freed them.[63] In Florida they gained renown as self-sufficient and enterprising guerrilla fighters. Although the conditions under which they served were abysmal at best, the military status they acquired served their larger interests, and they artfully employed it to maximum advantage. It provided them (and by extension their families) with a corporate identity in which they were juridically equal to whites, it offered them a useful occupation and a source of income which was minimal but legal, and it must also have been the source of intangible but very significant rewards such as pride and community recognition—none of which had been theirs under slavery.

Several large families traveled to Cuba together. Sixteen members of the Zamorano family, fourteen members of the Bacas family, eight Pellicers, seven Morells, and nine Aisiks (Travers) were among the largest family groups. Other families were separated by their decisions. Although Felipe Edimboro stayed behind, perhaps to secure his hard-won property, his thirty-year-old son Antonio Embara moved his wife Ysabel Andros and their daughter Teresa Embara to Cuba. Other families were divided by death. Within a year of the exodus the forty-year-old Domingo Sanco was dead, leaving behind a widow, Ysabel, and three young sons. Domingo's brother Jorge, who might have been expected to help that family, followed his brother to the grave the next year. Jorge Sanco left his widow María Rosa to raise five sons, including his brother's nine-year-old namesake.[64]

The few free blacks who trusted cession treaties and remained in the new territorial Florida found the white supremacist planters who immigrated into the area unable to tolerate such a challenge to the myth of black inadequacy. The Americans were determined to install a two-caste racial system and eliminate Florida's intermediate free black class. Over the next years these immigrants pressured many free blacks into selling what remained of their property at rock-bottom prices; and in the years leading up to the United States Civil War, some free blacks joined later exiles going to Cuba, Haiti, and Mexico, where their histories are only beginning to be traced.[65]

Afterword

The Afro-Hispanic past of Florida is marked by amazing cultural diversity and adaptation. It was probably so in other colonies as well, but in the distinct tradition of Spanish record-keeping it is more possible to discern the imprint of specific African national, cultural, and linguistic groups and to know about the many cultural transformations Africans mastered on this side of the Atlantic. Reshaping various African, Indian, and European cultures, they worked through differences to create a viable, interest-based community. These highly politicized people, shaped by wars and revolutions, were keenly attuned to the political winds which might once again disperse them. One can only imagine the discussions generated by survivors of the slave revolt in Haiti and of the American Revolution such as Jorge Biassou, Jorge Jacobo, and Juan Bautista Witten and their constituents as increasing Anglo pressure threatened to undo their hard-won gains in Florida.

Real people such as they generated this history and I have attempted to piece together as many of their stories as I could to illustrate specific principles and episodes throughout this book. It was a deliberate, if in places anecdotal, effort to make the simple point that the history of colonial Africans is neither anonymous, lost, nor irretrievable. But over time it has become dimmed.

During the Spanish history of Florida, if one were to imagine three interlocking circles representing Indian, African, and Spanish worlds, there were always overlapping areas the three groups inhabited together. Assisted by the corporate nature of Spanish society and Spain's medieval tradition of integration and assimilation, and by the almost constant threat to Spanish sovereignty in Florida, multiple generations of Africans leveraged linguistic, military, diplomatic, and artisanal skills into citizenship and property rights. Although other Africans and their descendants remained enslaved, they enjoyed more legal and social protection in this Spanish colony than they would again until almost two hundred years of Anglo history had passed in Florida.

Once Florida became a territory of the United States the Indian, African, and white worlds that had once coexisted and shared space were deliberately separated. The social and legal system introduced by southern planters, wed to concepts of white supremacy, chattel slavery, and Indian removal, might be imagined as one dominant circle of whites with two associated, but unshared, circles of much diminished size in its shadow. With the loss of legal personality, access, and voice, Florida's Indians and Africans saw their shared pasts largely written out of subsequent Florida, American, Cuban, and Indian histories.

I hope that this volume will partially address that erasure and stimulate further research. One of the most heartening aspects of this long project has been the interest of lay audiences and students in recovering this past and finding out more. My innumerable talks to historical societies, museum audiences, and teacher workshops have always encouraged and stimulated me.

Although the book has taken much longer than I imagined to research and write, some of the public history work in which I have been engaged in the meantime has born earlier fruit. The level of general and scholarly attention to the history of Gracia Real de Santa Teresa de Mose has led to several important developments. In 1990 the governor and the Florida legislature acknowledged Mose and created the Study Commission on African American History in Florida. That commission established the Black Heritage Trail, on which a number of the sites discussed in this book are now featured. The National Park Service also initiated a National Register of Historic Places review for Mose. In 1994 the Department of the Interior designated the site as a National Historic Landmark, thereby protecting it from development and degradation, and in 1995 the community looked on as park officials placed a bronze plaque where Francisco Menéndez and his community once built and defended their free homesteads. Recognizing that the first fugitives from slavery ran southward to Florida, the National Park Service has also incorporated Mose's history into their research programs and educational materials on the historic Underground Railroad.

The museum exhibit entitled "Fort Mose: Black Fortress of Freedom" recently concluded a national tour which lasted over six years. At last count over seven million visitors had seen the exhibit. Kathleen Deagan and Darcie McMahon's award-winning catalogue for the exhibit is also guaranteed to reach a wide audience. Numbers of Florida teachers have told me that they have already incorporated Mose into their fourth-grade Florida history curriculums and I also featured it and other parts of my research in a fourth-grade Florida social studies text.[1] Young students of Florida history now grow up reading and learning about a more diverse and multicultural past than once was presented.

Working with Vinnie Jones and Denise Matthews, producers of the award-winning television documentary, *Black Warriors of the Seminoles* for WUFT, at the University of Florida was also rewarding. In assisting their research, I advanced my own and took it in new directions. At a symposium organized by Broward Community College in Fort Lauderdale, Denise Matthews and I were able to meet with Seminole educators and reestablish some links between black and Seminole histories. Almost all the research on the black Seminoles and Seminoles has relied on English-language records, most of them generated by enemy military figures—hardly an unbiased or accurate source on which to depend.[2] Much more remains to be done in the rich Spanish records for that chapter of Florida history. And Brent Weisman has pointed us to the need for historical archaeology of black Seminole villages.

Two other projects have allowed me to follow my protagonists to Cuba. In 1991, Ralph Johnson, associate dean of the University of Florida's College of Architecture, organized a trip to look for evidence of the resettlement of Mose refugees in Cuba. We found that the story of the black emigrations from Florida to Cuba was unknown in Havana, Matanzas, or Ceiba Mocha, but scholars and lay persons alike were eager to know more about that history. A subsequent trip in 1993, with Latin American Microform Project (LAMP) teammates Eugene Lyon, Beth Lyon, and Jim Craig, allowed a more intensive search through eighteenth-century church records in Havana, Regla, and Guanabacoa and produced more important fragments of the past. A full search for the refugees from Mose remains to be done. And although there has been some historical and archaeological work done on the black Seminole settlements in the Bahamas, no one has yet begun to track the black Seminoles whom the Cubans rescued from the Florida coasts following Andrew Jackson's devastating raids, nor those who emigrated to Cuba with the Spaniards when Florida became a territory of the United States.[3]

These varied historical trails which I have followed remind us again that the colonial Africans about whom I write were also international travelers. Some freely crossed the Atlantic with Spaniards and accompanied them throughout the Americas on almost unbelievable journeys of exploration and conquest. Others were forcibly transported across the Middle Passage as slaves bound for Carolina or Georgia. Almost immediately, some escaped and traveled through the southeastern and Florida Indian nations, where some stayed to create new lives. Others moved on to Florida, where they became part of the Caribbean and Atlantic worlds. From the port of St. Augustine Africans roamed the Atlantic on corsairing commissions that took them northward as far as North Carolina, and if they were unlucky, to New York. Others moved via Spanish commercial, military, and diplomatic missions to and from the Bahamas, the Dominican Republic, Haiti, Mexico, and Cuba.

However, when Florida became part of the United States, blacks lost physical and social mobility as well as citizenship. The shock waves of the slave revolt in Saint Domingue and subsequent violence in Haiti, combined with two more costly and deadly wars against the Seminoles and their black allies led to increasing repression of both the enslaved Africans and their earlier more empowered history.[4]

The loss of the international border and the black and Spanish military allies who had fought alongside them also badly weakened the Seminoles, but influential black Seminole leaders such as Abraham, Harry, and Juan Cavallo resisted removal westward as long as they practically could.[5]

Meanwhile the United States territorial government enacted restrictive legislation designed to create a two-caste system in Florida and bring it in line with the rest of the South. Canter Brown, Jr., and Daniel L. Schafer have traced how in quick succession free blacks were barred from entering the territory, forbidden to assemble, carry arms, serve on juries, testify in courts, or vote. New laws also prohibited interracial marriages and sexual relations between whites and blacks and ended the inheritance rights of children of interracial unions. Finally, manumission was made almost impossible and free blacks had to post bonds guaranteeing good behavior and acquire guardians. Although free blacks, assisted by their white kin and patrons, struggled to retain property and citizenship rights and a more flexible system of race relations, the tide was against them. Only those who had the most influential protectors managed to retain some of their customary privileges.[6] It is not surprising that in the decades leading to the Civil War Florida newspapers document the emigration of various groups of free blacks to Haiti and Mexico and a continuing pattern of slave flight to the Indian hinterlands or via water to the Bahamas and Cuba. Ironically, a brig named *America* transported 113 free blacks from the St. Johns River area to Puerto Plata, Haiti, arriving there August 8, 1839. These were probably people related or connected to Anna and Zephaniah Kingsley. In 1843, the *St. Augustine News* carried a running account of the exploits of seven men who stole a boat and headed for the Bahamas. Two of the men were sailors and they took with them a compass, spyglass, lead line, food, and four hundred rounds of ammunition.[7] For the rest of the enslaved black majority life took on the severely reduced, fixed, and dehumanized contours of the Cotton Kingdom.

As the landscape, economy, and racial and social systems were being reshaped, so was the historical production. Florida's past was bleached and homogenized until it looked less disturbingly Caribbean and more comfortably southern. But immigration has once again made Florida a part of the Afro-Hispanic Caribbean, changing the way it looks and sounds. From my admittedly skewed perspective, this reblending of peoples who will have to shape livable interest-based communities out of great diversity is both a return to a more historically "normal" state of affairs, and a move toward the future.

Appendix 1

Pardo and Moreno Militia of St. Augustine, 1683

Commanded by Ensign Domingo Masías	Toribio Rodrígues
Sergeant Juan Estévan	Juan Ramos
Second Lieutenant Juan Merino	Nicolás Ponse
Corporal Juan de Medina	Juan Mexicano
Corporal Crispín De Tapia	Juan Rutiner
Corporal Juan Cuello	Matheo Rutiner
Corporal Antonio Baruosa	Lucas de Fuentes
Thomás de Santiago	Christóbal Meléndez
Marcos de Estrada	Antonio Canisares
Manuel Jorxe	García Ruis
Juan de Osorio	Felipe Meléndes
Christóval de los Santos	Nicolás Riberos
Juan del Ruis	Pedro de Hita
Juan Borroso	Antonio Manrique
Cosme Catalán	Pasqual de Soto
Domingo de la Ruis	Marcos de Soto
Francisco Baruosa	Francisco de los Reyes
Francisco Barrionuebo	Bentura de Casas
Juan de Milibia	Pedro Días
Antonio de Sigarroa	Domingo Días
Matías Hixan	Antonio Chrisóstomo
Juan de Sigarroa	Diego Chrisóstomo
Manuel de Lima	Joseph Chrisóstomo
Manuel Meléndez	Manuel Chrisóstomo
Antonio Meléndez	

Source: SD 226, AGI

Appendix 2

Slaves Petitioning for Freedom, 1738

Petitioner	Owner
Francisco Menéndez	Don Francisco Menéndez, royal accountant
Juan Gaspar	Don Melchor González
Sebastián Rexidor	Don Antonio Rexidor, cattle rancher
Manuel de Canto	In Havana, owner unknown
Pedro Menéndez	In Havana, Don Juan Ygnacio de Herrera
Luis Menéndez	In Havana, Don Antonio Urbano
Ana María Garzía	Don Salvador Garzía, royal treasurer
Francisco Borne	In Havana, owner unknown
Antonio Carvallo	In Havana, owner unknown
Francisco el chino[1]	Don Pedro de Escobedo
Juan Mandinga	In Havana, owner unknown
Andrés Pueyo	In Havana, owner unknown
Juan Lamberto	Don Pedro Lamberto, army Captain
Francisco Garzía	Don Salvador Garzía, royal treasurer
Juan Solana	Don Juan Solana, priest
Francisca Solana	Don Juan Solana, priest
Ana María Menéndez	Petronila Pérez
Theresa Garzía	Don Salvador Garzía, royal treasurer
Pedro Joseph	Diego de Espinosa, cattle rancher
Juan Rodriguez	Petronila Pérez
Pedro Fuentes	Don Francisco de Fuentes
Clemente Peinero	In Havana, Nicolás Peinero, army Captain
Bartólome Elixio	In Havana, owner unknown
Dionisio Rutiner	In Havana, Manuel de la Vega

Petitioner	Owner
María Dueñas	Juan Dueñas
Juan Garzía	Don Salvador Garzía, royal treasurer
Francisco Prieto	King's slave
Antonio, sawyer	King's slave
Pedro, sawyer	King's slave
Juan Antonio Congo	King's slave
Pedro Rexidor	Don Antonio Rexidor, cattle rancher

Source: SD 844, microfilm reel 15, PKY.

1. *Chino* denotes a person of mixed African and European ancestry, usually of a yellowish cast.

Appendix 3

Black Militia Company of Gracia Real de Santa Teresa de Mose, 1764

Commandant Don Geronimo de Hita y Salazar	Joseph Bentura
Chaplain Don Agustín Geronimo Resio	Manuel Rivera
Capt. Francisco Menéndez, Mandinga	Joseph de Peña, Carabalí
Lt. Antonio Joseph Eligio, Carolina	Nicolás Briones, Congo
Ensign Francisco Escobedo, Carolina*	Francisco Suri
Sgt. Pedro Graxales, Congo	Joseph Fernández, Mandinga
Antonio Gallardo, Virginia	Santiago Solís
Tomás Chrisóstomo, Congo	Francisco de Torres, Mandinga
Pedro de León, Congo	Juan Rodríguez
Pedro de Fuentes	Antonio Carballo
Francisco Roso, Carabalí	Juan Lamberto, Carolina
Juan Fernández, Carabalí	Antonio García
Juan de la Torre	Julian Bulero, Criollo
Francisco Joseph Meléndez, Mina	Pedro Martínes, Caracas
Joseph Escobedo	Nicolás de Cesar, Havana
Francisco Graxales, Congo	Ignacio Roso, Carabalí
Antonio Blanco, Carolina	Juan Chrisóstomo, Mandinga
Francisco Díaz, Carolina	Juan Tomás Castilla, Jamaica

Source: Pie de Lista, Jan. 22, 1764, SD 2595, AGI.

Note: African-born persons are identified by nation. Persons born in the Americas are designated as *criollos,* but if the entries specified a place of birth, I listed that instead. Persons specifically identified as mulatto are noted by an asterisk.

Appendix 4

Land Grants to Free Blacks, 1784–1821

Holder	Date(s) Granted	Acres
Jorge Biassou	07/27/1797	n.a.
Luis Bills	10/05/1802	n.a.
Hary Box	11/18/1799	200
Andrés Camel	02/08/1799	town lot
	1805	135
Bacas Camel	06/11/1800	
Estévan Cheves	11/14/1797	200
Carlos Clarke	03/22/1821	300
Jacobo Clarke	11/18/1799	200
Jorge Clarke	02/1800	200
	01/26/1809	150
Juan Bautista Collins	02/06/1792	300
	06/18/1799	town lot
León Duvigneau	09/28/1803	290
	1820	town lots
Felipe Edimboro	01/05/1807	100
	04/28/1815	150
Juan Ant. Florencia	01/09/1808	50
	02/03/1808	n.a.
Juan Gres (Gray)	06/25/1805	50
Abraham Hannahan	09/18/1816	50; town lot
Abraham Hudson	09/05/1803	n.a.
Jorge Jacobo	07/15/1807	n.a.
Vicente Lacrous	09/13/1815	50

Holder	Date(s) Granted	Acres
Flora Leslie	04/12/1810	500
Enrique (Harry) McQueen	03/01/1800	200
Juan Moore	11/16/1792	300
	11/09/1805	350
Prince Patton	11/28/1801	300
	03/09/1816	170
Antonio Proctor	03/08/1816	185
Juan Rait (Wright)	12/1803	145
Domingo Sanco	11/26/1808	50
	1815	town lot
Sairus	12/18/1801	300
Scipio	10/09/1809	25
Pedro Sivelly	07/08/1819	150
Aysick Travers	1801	town lot
	11/10/1803	115
Tory Travers	06/19/1816	125; town lot
Antonio Williams	12/01/1801	300
Juan Bautista Witten	11/27/1795	n.a.
	09/26/1798	n.a.
Isabella Wiggins	11/30/1817	300

Source: Data compiled by author from *SLGF* and SFLR.

Appendix 5

Census of Gracia Real de Santa Teresa de Mose, 1759

House	Name	Age	Birth/Baptism	Nation
1	Francisco Menéndez	55		Mandinga
	Ana María de Escovar	39		Mandinga
2	Antonio Eligio	45		
	Juana María Eligio	40		
	Andrés	24		
	María	20	bapt. 1/31/1740	
3	Francisco Escovedo	55		
	Francisca Roso	50		
4	Pedro Graxales	44	bapt. 12/9/1738	Congo
	María de la Concepción			
	Joseph Ynisario		b. 4/10/1755, bapt. 4/13/55	
	María		b. 11/4/1744, bapt. 11/8/44	
	Manuela de los Angeles		b. 1/1/1747, bapt. 1/6/47	
	Ysidora de los Angeles		b. 12/22/1748, bapt. 12/25/48	
	Manuel Rivera	33		
5	Salvador Cinquero	60	bapt. 2/3/1741	
	Antonia del Rosario	20		
	Juan		bapt. 7/16/1742	
	Manuela		bapt. 4/25/1740	
	Antonio de la Paz		b. 5/16/1743, bapt. 5/17/43	
	Antonio Gallardo	20		
	María Quintero	18		
	Antonio	1		
6	Pedro de Fuentes	60		

House	Name	Age	Birth/Baptism	Nation
	Juana de Araujo	78	bapt. 4/3/1725	
	Manuel Tan	45		
7	Francisco X. Menéndez	50		Mina
	María de los Angeles	30		Carabalí
	Juan Gaspar	18	bapt. 2/14/1748	
	María Margarita	14		
8	Joseph Escovedo	28		
	María Loreto	25		
9	Francisco Roso	54		Carabalí
	María Cruz Brison			Carabalí
	Carlos Ros		b. 11/4/1743, bapt. 11/7/43	
10	Francisco Xari	45		
	María Flora	50		
11	Antonio Caravallo	50		
12	Pedro Joseph de León	30	bapt. 2/12/1739	Congo
	Manuela Gaviño	35		Carabalí
	María	11		
	Micaela	8		
	Joseph María	6		
13	Tomás Chrisóstomo	40		Congo
14	Francisco Díaz	35		
	Francisca García	20		
	Miguel Francisco	7	b. 1/29/1753	
	María	1		
15	Antonio Blanco	35		
16	Domingo de Jesus	50	bapt. 1/26/1740	Criollo
	María del Rosario	35	bapt. 4/2/1725	Criollo
	Francisco	11		
	Rosa	9		
	Mariana	7	b. 11/20/1752, bapt.11/22/52	
	Pedro	4		
	Joseph	1	bapt. 2/6/1758	
17	Santiago Solís	50		
	María de los Dolores	40		
18	Juan Jacinto Rodríguez	78		
	Ana María Rodríguez	60		
	Juan Lamberto	35		
	María Francisca Solana	25		
	Juan Antonio	7		
	Ana María	4		
	Francisco Joseph	1		

House	Name	Age	Birth/Baptism	Nation
19	Francisco X. Torres	55		Mandinga
	Ana María Torres			Mandinga
	Juan Arranzate, son	30		Mandinga
20	Joseph de Peña	55		Carabalí
	Ana María Yzquierdo			Congo
	Juan Francisco Torres	40		
	Nicolás de Briones	30		Congo
	María de Leche		bapt. 11/16/1738	
21	Joseph Fernández	30		Mandinga
	Ana María			Carabalí
	Francisco Grandeman	55		
	Juan Antonio de Jesus	25		
22	Francisco Sori	55		
	Juan de Jesus	30		
	Juan Baptista	28		
	María de Jesus			
	Bentura Hernández	25		
	Francisco de Meza	40		

Source: Adapted from Census of Ginés Sánchez, Feb. 11, 1759, SD 2604, AGI, with supplementary information compiled by the author from CPR.

Appendix 6

Baptismal Sponsors for the Edimboro Family

Baptized	Birthdate	Baptism Date	Sponsors
Edimboro	1749	07/15/1794	Tomás Alvarez (a)
			María de la Luz Blanco (a)
Filis	1760	07/15/1794	Tomás Alvarez (a)
			María de la Luz Blanco (a)
Juana	1778	01/13/1788	Lorenzo Capo (b)
			Barbara Strasburg (b)
Mariano	1784	07/12/1787	Lorenzo Capo (b)
			Mariana Quevedo (b)
Antonio	12/15/1787	01/13/1788	Lorenzo Capo (b)
			Barbara Strasburg (b)
Tiburcio	08/11/1788	08/17/1788	Lorenzo Capo (b)
			María Beatriz Piedra (c)
Placido	10/05/1789	10/15/1789	Luis Almansa (a)
			María de la Luz Blanco (a)
Pablo	01/25/1791	02/01/1791	José Rivas (c)
			María Beatriz Piedra (c)
Nicolasa	09/10/1793	09/14/1793	José Rivas (c)
			María de la Luz Blanco (d)
Francisca	10/04/1797	10/08/1797	José Rivas (c)
			María de la Luz Blanco (d)
Florentino	11/07/1798	02/17/1799	José Rivas (c)
			María de la Luz Blanco (d)
Eusebia	03/15/1801	03/11/1801	José Rivas (c)
			María de la Luz Blanco (d)

Baptized	Birthdate	Baptism Date	Sponsors
Isabel	11/14/1802	11/28/1802	Manuel González (b) Juana Sánchez (d)
Clímaco	03/30/1805	04/13/1805	Marcelino Espinosa (c)

Key: (a) black slave, (b) free white, (c) free mulatto, (d) free black
Source: Black Baptisms, vols. 1–3, CPR, microfilm reel 284 J, PKY.

Appendix 7

Baptismal Sponsors for the *Quarterón* Children of F. X. Sánchez and María Beatriz Piedra

Children of Beatriz María Sánchez and Francisco Pérez
- Estéban José Fernando Pérez, b. 12/26/1797, bapt. 1/2/1798
  - Sponsors: Don Francisco Xavier Sánchez (Beatriz's white father)
    Doña María del Carmen Hill (Beatriz's white stepmother)
- Francisco Xavier Pérez, b. 12/3/1799, bapt. 12/7/1799
  - Sponsors: Don Francisco Xavier Sánchez (Beatriz's white father)
    Doña María del Carmen Hill (Beatriz's white stepmother)
- Fulgencio Pérez, b. 1/16/1802, bapt. 1/23/1802
  - Sponsors: Don Francisco Xavier Sánchez (Beatriz's white father)
    Doña María del Carmen Hill (Beatriz's white stepmother)
- Tomás de Cosca Zerapio Sánchez Pérez, b. 2/29/1803, bapt. 3/16/1804
  - Sponsor: Francisco Agapito Pérez
- Miguel Pérez, b. 10/29/1811, bapt. 11/11/1811
  - Sponsors: Catalina Sánchez (Beatriz's sister)
    Francisco Sánchez (Beatriz's white half-brother)

Children of Ana Sánchez and José Fernández
- Estévan Fernández, b. 1799
- Damiana Marcos Josefa Fernández, b. 9/27/1799, bapt. 10/12/1799
  - Sponsors: José Sánchez (Ana's brother)
    Catalina Sánchez (Ana's sister)
- Juan Rafael Ulatia Fernández, b. 1/14/1802, bapt. 1/23/1802
  - Sponsors: Manuel Domingo Sánchez (Ana's white half-brother)
    Teresa Sánchez (Ana's white half-sister)
- Faustina Fernández, b. 2/15/1803, bapt. 2/16/1803
  - Sponsors: Francisco Xavier Roman Sánchez (Ana's white half-brother)
    María de la Concepción Sánchez (Ana's sister)

Estanislao Manuel Basilio Fernández, b. 5/7/1804
Sponsors: Manuel Domingo Sánchez (Ana's white half-brother)
Rafaela Teresa Basilia Sánchez (Ana's white half-sister)
Francisco Vidal Fernández, b. 4/28/1814, bapt. 8/1/1814
Sponsors: Francisco Pérez (Ana's white brother-in-law)
Gabriela Sánchez

Children of Catalina Rosa María Sánchez and Francisco Sánchez
Gabriela Marcelina Sánchez, b. 6/18/1803, bapt. 6/25/1803
Sponsors: Manuel Domingo Sánchez (Catalina's white half-brother)
María Beatriz Sánchez (Catalina's sister)
Benito Ysidoro Sánchez, b. 4/3/1806, bapt. 4/10/1806
Sponsors: Don Santiago Gonzalez
María Beatriz Sánchez (Catalina's sister)
María de la Concepción Dolores Sánchez, b. 9/18/1808, bapt. 10/12/1808
Sponsor: María de la Concepción Dolores Sánchez (Catalina's sister)
Gerónimo Socorro Sánchez, b. 9/25/1810, bapt. 10/15/1810
Sponsor: Don Santiago Gonzalez
Casimiro Francisco Sánchez, b. 3/4/1812, bapt. 4/21/1812
Sponsors: Don Gregorio Suarez
Doña María Pellicer
Elena María Sánchez, b. 8/8/1813, bapt. 8/16/18
Sponsors: Don Santiago Gonzalez
Doña Francisca de Agui
Josef Hipolito Casiano Sánchez, b. 8/19/1815, bapt. 8/26/1815
Sponsors: Don Santiago Gonzalez
María Fernández

Source: Black Baptisms, vols. 2 and 3, CPR, microfilm reel 284 J, PKY.

Appendix 8

Baptismal and Marriage Sponsors for the Witten Family

	Date	Sponsors
Baptisms		
María Rafaela (daughter)	08/16/1788	Pedro Cosifacio (b)
Francisco Domingo Mariano	08/16/1788	Domingo Martinoli (b)
		Mariana Quevedo (b)
Juan Bautista	01/11/1792	Don Manuel Fernández Bendicho[1] (b)
		Doña Rafaela Rodríguez (b)
María Rafaela (wife)	01/11/1792	Don Manuel Fernández Bendicho (b)
		Doña Rafaela Rodríguez (b)
Marriages		
Jorge Jacobo and		Francisco Witten (d)
María Rafaela Witten	04/12/1796	Romana Jacobo (d)
Juan Bautista and		Felipe Edimboro (d)
María Rafaela	07/07/1798	Romana Jacobo (d)
Francisco Witten and		Felipe Edimboro (d)
María Francisca Fatio	01/26/1799	Romana Jacobo (d)

Key: (a) black slave, (b) free white, (c) free mulatto, (d) free black

Sources: Black Baptisms, vol. 1, CPR, microfilm reel 284 J, PKY; Black Marriages, CPR, microfilm reel 284 L, PKY.

1. The 1793 census shows that Don Manuel Fernández Bendicho and his wife Doña Rafaela Rodríguez lived next door to the Wittens.

Appendix 9

Slave Imports into Florida, 1752–63

Date	Owner	Sex	Nation	Age	Given Name	Pieza
07/18/52	Jesse Fish	M	Congo	8	Gerbaccio	1/3
07/18/52	Jesse Fish	M	Congo	10	Juan Antonio	1/3
07/18/52	Jesse Fish	M	Criollo	11	Francisco Ant.	1/3
07/18/52	Jesse Fish	F	Congo	10	María Isabel	1/3
07/18/52	Jesse Fish	M	Dudrian	9	Miguel	1/3
07/18/52	Jesse Fish	M	Dudrian	12	Raphael	1/3
05/09/53	Jesse Fish	M	Congo	28	Miguel	1
05/09/53	Jesse Fish	M	Congo	10	Francisco	1/3
05/17/53	John Hume	M	Criollo	30	Francisco Xav.	1
05/17/53	John Hume	M	Criollo	20	Agustin	1
10/02/53	Jesse Fish	M	Carabalí	12	Juan Estévan	1/3
10/02/53	Jesse Fish	F	Calamanti	8	María Dolores	1/3
02/14/54	John Hume	M	Carabalí	15	Carlos	1
02/14/54	John Hume	M	Congo	16	Antonio	1/3
07/11/54	Juana Mecoay	F	Criolla	16	Barbara	1/3
07/11/54	Juana Mecoay	F	Criolla	5	María Carmen	1/3
07/11/54	Juana Mecoay	M	Criollo	7	Joseph	1/3
07/11/54	Juana Mecoay	M	Carabalí	23	Joseph Antonio	2/3
07/11/54	Juana Mecoay	M	Congo	45	Antonio	1
08/05/54	Jesse Fish	M	Guinea	9	Hades	1/3
04/10/55	Jesse Fish	M	Carabalí	30	Thomas	2/3
04/24/55	Juana Mecoay	F	Congo	45	Thomasa	1/2
04/24/55	Juana Mecoay	M	Criollo	12	Francisco Xav.	1/3
05/12/55	Jesse Fish	M	Ibo	8	Francisco	1/3

Date	Owner	Sex	Nation	Age	Given Name	Pieza
05/27/55	Jesse Fish	M	Congo	22	Joseph	1
02/20/56	Jesse Fish	F	Congo	12	María de la Luz	1/3
02/20/56	Jesse Fish	M	Congo	12	Juan Joseph	1/3
12/15/56	Juan Deasplitar	M	Criollo	30	Juan Antonio	1
01/14/57	Antonio Fern/z	M	Criollo	16	Joseph	1/3
04/15/57	Jesse Fish	F	Criolla	18	María Gertrudis	1/2
04/16/57	Jesse Fish	M	Mandinga	30	Francisco Xav.	1
04/16/57	Jesse Fish	M	Mandinga	30	Juan	1
04/16/57	Jesse Fish	M	Bambara	31	Agustin	1
05/06/57	Jesse Fish	M	Mandinga	40	Pedro	1
05/06/57	Jesse Fish	M	Carabalí	25	Joseph	1
05/16/57	Jesse Fish	M	Criollo	40	Diego	1
05/16/57	Jesse Fish	M	Criollo	26	Felix	1
05/16/57	Jesse Fish	M	Criollo	38	Joseph Juan	1
06/20/57	Jesse Fish	M	Carabalí	28	Juan	1
06/20/57	Jesse Fish	M	Criollo	35	Francisco	1
06/21/57	Jesse Fish	F	Mandinga	14	Francisca Teresa	1/3
06/21/57	Jesse Fish	M	Mandinga	14	Joseph Miguel	1/3
08/18/57	Jesse Fish	F	Mandinga	12	Ysidora	1/3
08/18/57	Jesse Fish	F	Ibo	12	María Antonia	1/3
08/18/57	Jesse Fish	F	Mandinga	12	Theresa	1/3
08/18/57	Jesse Fish	F	Mandinga	9	María Dolores	1/3
08/19/57	Jesse Fish	F	Criolla	10	Barbara	1/3
08/19/57	Jesse Fish	M	Congo	14	Pedro	1/3
11/04/58	Juan Jones	M	Congo	12	Francisco Xav.	1/3
11/04/58	Juan Jones	F	Ganga	15	María Dolores	1/2
11/04/58	Juan Jones	F	Mandinga	10	María Theresa	1/3
11/04/58	Juan Jones	M	Mina	10	Joseph Miguel	1/3
11/04/58	Juan Jones	F	Bamba	15	María Rosario	1/2
11/04/58	Juan Jones	M	Criollo	10	Thomás	1/3
11/04/58	Juan Jones	M	Mina	18	Francisco Xav.	1/2
05/08/59	Jesse Fish	F	Mandinga	10	María Ana	1/3
05/08/59	Jesse Fish	M	Mandinga	10	Thomás	1/3
12/17/59	Jesse Fish	M	Mandinga	10	Pedro	1/3
12/17/59	Jesse Fish	M	Yalongo	12	Joseph Antonio	1/3
12/17/59	Jesse Fish	M	Yalongo	12	Domingo	1/3
12/17/59	Jesse Fish	F	Mandinga	12	María Rosa	1/3
05/17/60	Jesse Fish	M	Congo	14	Antonio	1/3
05/17/60	Jesse Fish	M	Criollo	12	Joseph María	1/3
07/02/60	Juan Jones	F	Criolla	9	María Asención	1/3

Date	Owner	Sex	Nation	Age	Given Name	Pieza
08/16/60	Juan Jones	M	Criollo	20	Antonio Joseph	2/3
09/01/60	Juan Jones	M	Congo	13	Joseph Rafael	1/3
09/01/60	Juan Jones	M	Criollo	20	Manuel Trinidad	2/3
09/01/60	Samuel Piles	M	Criollo	12	Joseph Bonifacio	1/3
12/05/60	Juan Jones	M	Mandinga	10	Buenaventura	1/3
02/03/61	Samuel Piles	M	Criollo	12	Joseph Bonifacio	1/3
02/23/61	Samuel Piles	M	Criollo	20	Diego	2/3
02/23/61	Jesse Fish	M	Congo	18	Pedro	1/2
06/18/61	Jesse Fish	M	Criollo	14	Santiago	1/3
08/03/61	Jesse Fish	M	Mandinga	12	Cayetano	1/3
08/07/61	Jesse Fish	M	Guisi	9	Joseph Bentura	1/3
08/07/61	Jesse Fish	M	Mandinga	9	Buenaventura	1/3
08/07/61	Jesse Fish	M	Mandinga	10	Joseph Miguel	1/3
08/07/61	Jesse Fish	M	Mandinga	10	Antonio María	1/3
08/07/61	Jesse Fish	F	Mandinga	13	Antonia Jesus	1/3
08/07/61	Jesse Fish	F	Carabalí	13	María Antonia	1/3
08/07/61	Jesse Fish	M	Besi	18	Juan Francisco	1/2
08/07/61	Jesse Fish	M	Besi	15	Manuel	1/2
08/07/61	Jesse Fish	M	Fai	18	Cayetano	1/2
08/07/61	Jesse Fish	M	Guasi	9	Francisco	1/3
08/07/61	Jcssc Fish	M	Mandinga	10	Joseph	1/3
08/07/61	Jesse Fish	M	Fai	9	Antonio	1/3
08/07/61	Jesse Fish	M	Mandinga	20	Francisco Xav.	1
08/07/61	Jesse Fish	M	Mandinga	20	Antonio Joseph	1
08/07/61	Jesse Fish	M	Timini	20	Pedro	1
08/07/61	Jesse Fish	F	Limba	11	Theresa	1/3
08/07/61	Jesse Fish	F	Fula	11	Cathalina	1/3
01/07/62	Juan Jones	F	Criolla	24	Rita	1
01/12/62	Juan Jones	M	Criollo	12	Antonio Joseph	1/3
01/17/62	Jesse Fish	M	Meni	12	Pedro Jesus	1/3
01/17/62	Jesse Fish	F	Yalongo	12	María de Jesus	1/3
01/17/62	Samuel Piles	M	Gold Coast	10	Juan Baptista	1/3
01/17/62	Samuel Piles	M	Gold Coast	10	Juan	1/3
01/17/62	Samuel Piles	M	Gold Coast	9	Antonio	1/3
01/17/62	Samuel Piles	M	Gold Coast	11	Buenaventura	1/3
01/17/62	Samuel Piles	M	Gold Coast	10	Estévan	1/3
01/17/62	Samuel Piles	M	Gold Coast	9	Pedro	1/3
01/17/62	Samuel Piles	M	Gold Coast	12	Francisco	1/3
01/17/62	Samuel Piles	F	Gold Coast	9	María Dolores	1/3
01/17/62	Samuel Piles	F	Gold Coast	9	María Concepción	1/3

Date	Owner	Sex	Nation	Age	Given Name	Pieza
01/17/62	Samuel Piles	F	Gold Coast	8	María Rosario	1/3
01/17/62	Jesse Fish	M	Congo	20	Nicolás	2/3
02/17/62	Jesse Fish	F	Meni	14	María Ysavel	1/3
02/17/62	Jesse Fish	F	Criolla	18	María Dolores	1/3
02/17/62	Juan Jones	M	Mandinga	25	Joaquin	1
02/17/62	Juan Jones	F	Yalongo	12	Josepha Leche	1/3
02/01/63	Jesse Fish	M	Timini	18	Felix	1/2
07/01/63	Jesse Fish	M	Mandinga	20	Francisco	2/3
09/01/63	Jesse Fish	M	Mungundu	15	Tadeo	1/2
09/01/63	Jesse Fish	M	Mondongo	20	Casimiro	2/3
09/01/63	Jesse Fish	M	Mungundu	14	Bernardo	1/2
09/01/63	Jacob Kip	M	Guinea	10	Fernando	1/3
09/01/63	Jessie[1] Fish	M	Mungundu	15	Pablo	1/3
09/01/63	Jessie Fish	M	Mungundu	20	Fernando	2/3
09/01/63	Jessie Fish	M	Mungundu	9	Vizente	1/3
09/01/63	Jessie Fish	M	Mozindi	20	Geronimo	2/3
09/01/63	Jessie Fish	M	Pati	16	Gaspar	1/2
09/01/63	Jessie Fish	M	Mungundu	15	Hipolito	1/2
09/01/63	Jessie Fish	M	Mondongo	16	Alonso	1/2
09/01/63	Jessie Fish	M	Sozongo	20	Andrés	2/3
09/01/63	Jessie Fish	M	Musulcamba	24	Gabriel	2/3
09/01/63	Jessie Fish	M	Mumboma	20	Fulgencio	1/2
09/01/63	Jessie Fish	M	Mungundu	18	Thorivio	1/2
09/01/63	Jessie Fish	M	Yololo	18	Luis	1/2
09/01/63	Jessie Fish	M	Mondongo	12	Patricio	1/3
09/01/63	Jessie Fish	M	Moyo	12	Balthazar	1/3
09/01/63	Jessie Fish	M	Mumbata	12	Ambrosio	1/3
09/01/63	Jessie Fish	M	Musundi	24	Melchor	2/3
09/01/63	Jessie Fish	M	Sanai	15	Lorenzo	1/2
09/01/63	Jessie Fish	M	Sozongo	20	Benito	1/2
09/01/63	Jessie Fish	M	Mumbat	12	Joachim	1/3
09/01/63	Jessie Fish	M	Meni	15	Mauricio	1/2
09/01/63	Jessie Fish	M	Gianes	14	Dionisio	1/3
09/01/63	Jessie Fish	M	Mungoma	18	Pasqual	1/2
09/01/63	Jessie Fish	M	Mondongo	18	Raphael	1/3
09/01/63	Samuel Piles	M	Congo	12	Francisco	1/3
09/01/63	Samuel Piles	M	Congo	10	Antonio	1/3
09/01/63	Samuel Piles	M	Congo	11	Joseph	1/3
09/01/63	Jessie Fish	F	Musicongo	9	Catharina	1/3
09/01/63	Jessie Fish	M	Musinbata	10	Antonio	1/3

Date	Owner	Sex	Nation	Age	Given Name	Pieza
09/01/63	Jessie Fish	M	Munque	8	Joseph Rafael	1/3
09/01/63	Jessie Fish	M	Congo	9	Buenaventura	1/3
09/01/63	Jessie Fish	M	Congo	10	Francisco	1/3
09/01/63	Jessie Fish	F	Congo	10	Rita	1/3
09/01/63	Jessie Fish	F	Congo	10	Rosa	1/3
09/01/63	Jessie Fish	M	Congo	11	Antonio María	1/3
09/01/63	Thomas Rogers	F	Congo	9	Barbara	1/3
09/01/63	Jessie Fish	F	Congo	10	Augustina Jesus	1/3
09/01/63	Samuel Piles	F	Congo	10	Rosa María	1/3
09/01/63	Jessie Fish	M	Congo	10	Vizente Joseph	1/3
09/01/63	Thomas Rogers	F	Congo	10	María Dolores	1/3
09/01/63	Thomas Rogers	M	Congo	12	Diego	1/3
09/01/63	Thomas Rogers	F	Moyo	8	Rosa María	1/3
09/01/63	Thomas Rogers	M	Bara	10	Joseph	1/3
09/01/63	Thomas Rogers	M	Ymundo	9	Antonio	1/3
09/01/63	Thomas Rogers	M	Guinea	10	Joseph	1/3
09/01/63	Thomas Rogers	F	Congo	9	María Buen Viaje	1/3
09/01/63	Juan Jones	F	Criolla	27	María	1
09/01/63	Samuel Piles	M	Congo	16	Augustin	1/3
09/01/63	Thomas Rogers	M	Guinea	10	Jazinto	1/3
09/01/63	Jessie Fish	F	Congo	9	María del Carmen	1/3
09/01/63	Jessie Fish	F	Mandinga	7	María Anna	1/3
09/06/63	Samuel Piles	M	Guinea	9	Nicolás	1/3
09/06/63	Thomas Rogers	F	Mosonbo	12	Rosa María	1/3
09/06/63	Thomas Rogers	M	Carabalí	9	Luis	1/3
09/06/63	Thomas Rogers	M	Carabalí	9	Antonio	1/3
09/06/63	Thomas Rogers	M	Carabalí	12	Miguel Joseph	1/3
09/06/63	Thomas Rogers	F	Carabalí	9	Ana	1/3
09/06/63	Thomas Rogers	F	Carabalí	9	Rosa María	1/3
09/06/63	Thomas Rogers	F	Carabalí	12	María Ysavel	1/3
11/03/63	Thomas Rogers	M	Ibo	9	Joseph Leche	1/3
11/03/63	Thomas Rogers	F	Ibo	13	María de la Luz	1/3
11/03/63	Thomas Rogers	F	Ibo	10	María de Regla	1/3
11/03/63	Thomas Rogers	F	Congo	12	Barbara Antonia	1/3
11/03/63	Thomas Rogers	M	Congo	9	Juan de Dios	1/3
11/18/63	Jessie Fish	M	Guolofo	20	Felix	2/3
11/18/63	Jessie Fish	M	Pul	16	Joseph	1/2
11/18/63	Jessie Fish	M	Yngar	15	Mariano	1/2
11/18/63	Jessie Fish	M	Congo	25	Christóval	1
11/18/63	Jessie Fish	M	Mondongo	16	Vizente	1/2

Date	Owner	Sex	Nation	Age	Given Name	Pieza
11/18/63	Jessie Fish	M	Mondongo	16	Pablo	1/2
11/18/63	Jessie Fish	M	Manuguri	18	Luis	1/2
11/18/63	Jessie Fish	M	Coromanti	25	Buenaventura	1
11/18/63	Jessie Fish	M	Mondongo	16	Antonio	1/2
11/18/63	Jessie Fish	F	Mandinga	5	Melchora	1/3
11/18/63	Jessie Fish	F	Pul	16	María Angeles	1/2
11/18/63	Jessie Fish	F	Golofo	16	Rita	1/2
11/18/63	Jessie Fish	F	Mondongo	28	Barbara	1
11/18/63	Jessie Fish	F	Meni	20	Victorina	2/3
11/18/63	Jessie Fish	F	Ganga	16	Francisca	1/2
11/18/63	Jessie Fish	F	Ynca	28	María Candelaria	1
11/18/63	Jessie Fish	F	Femi	28	Geronima	1
11/18/63	Jessie Fish	F	Coromanti	28	Josepha	1
11/18/63	Jessie Fish	F	Nucumi	18	Manuela	1/2
11/18/63	Jessie Fish	F	Mandinga	20	María Ysavel	2/3
11/18/63	Jessie Fish	F	Soso	18	Clara	2/3
11/18/63	Jessie Fish	M	Soso	13	Joseph	1/2
11/18/63	Jessie Fish	M	Filina	18	Antonio	1/2
11/18/63	Jessie Fish	F	Congo	12	María Rosario	1/3
11/18/63	Jessie Fish	M	Carabalí	18	Andrés	2/3

Source: Books of Indultos, 1752–62, Cuba 472, AGI.

1. Spelling of this name varies.

Appendix 10

Slave Imports into Florida by Nation, 1752–63

Bamba	1	Guinea	5	Munque	1
Bambara	1	Guisi	1	Musicongo	1
Bara	1	Guolofo	2	Musinbata	1
Besi	2	Ibo	5	Musulcamba	1
Calamantí	1	Limba	1	Musundi	1
Carabalí	14	Mandinga	27	Nucumi	1
Congo	38	Manuguri	1	Pati	1
Coromanti	2	Meni	4	Pul	2
Criollo	28	Mina	2	Sanai	1
Dudrian	2	Mondongo	8	Soso	2
Fai	2	Mosconbo	1	Sozongo	2
Femi	1	Moyo	2	Timini	2
Filini	1	Mozindi	1	Yalongo	4
Fula	1	Mumbat	1	Ymnudo	1
Ganga	2	Mumbata	1	Ynca	1
Gianes	1	Mumboma	1	Yngar	1
Gold Coast	10	Mungoma	1	Yololo	1
Guasi	1	Mungundu	7		204

Source: Books of Indultos, 1752–62, Cuba 472, AGI.

Appendix II

AFRICAN IMPORTS INTO SPANISH FLORIDA, 1784–1821

Date	Ship	Type	Captain (C) or Owner (O)	Origin	Number of Slaves
1793	*La Diana*	n.a.	G. Forrester	Africa	n.a.
1800	*Ida*	brig	S. Newton (C)	n.a.	50
1802	n.a.	n.a.	Wm. Lawrence (C) Panton, Leslie & Co. (O)	Guinea	60
1802	*Superior*	n.a.	Z. Kingsley (O)	Africa/Havana	250
1802	*Christiana*	schooner	William Cook (C)	Guinea	39
1802	*James*	brig	Wm. Northrup (C) Panton, Leslie & Co. (O)	S.Carlos Sierra Leone	117
1803	*Tamez*	n.a.	John Mason (C) Gabriel Perpal (O)	Africa	n.a.
1804	*Amistad*	n.a.	Juan Vermonet (O) William Cook (O) Luis Gleuse (O)	n.a.	n.a.
1806	*Peje*	n.a.	Joel Dunn (C) Zephaniah Kingsley (O)	Mozambique	16
1810	*Cirila*	schooner	José Chaple (C)	Africa	n.a.
1810	*Enterprise*	n.a.	Daniel Hurlbert (C/O)	Africa	39
1810	*Amanda*	schooner	Lorenzo Seguí (C) James Cashen (O)	Rio Pongo	28
1810	*Sevilla*	frigate	Manuel Ruíz (C) Arredondo & Son (O)	Africa	205
1810	*Aguila*	n.a.	Francisco Ferreyra (C) John Fraser (O)	Rio Pongo	126

Date	Ship	Type	Captain (C) or Owner (O)	Origin	Number of Slaves
1810	*Joana*	frigate	Bartolomé Mestre (C) John Fraser (O)	Rio Pongo	140
1810	*Doña Juana*	frigate	Leonard Joaquin dos Reis Velloso (C) Arredondo & Son (O)	Africa	343
1812	*Topacio*	schooner	Bernardino Sánchez (C/O)	Africa	n.a.
1814	*Dolores*	schooner	Joaquin Zorrilla (C)	Africa	n.a.
1817	*La Fé*	schooner	Pedro del Valle (C)	Africa	n.a.
1817	*Nueva Intentativa*	schooner	Sebastián Aguirre (C)	Africa	n.a.
1817	*Piragua*	schooner	Tomás Billosa (C)	Africa	n.a.
1817	*Mariana*	bilander	Daniel Hurlbert (C)	Havana	n.a.
1817	*Española*	n.a.	Antonio Giraldo (C) Arredondo & Son (O)	Havana	n.a.
1817	*Baladora*	n.a.	Francisco Sánchez (C)	Havana	56
1818	*Nuestra Señora de la Pineda*	n.a.	n.a.	Africa	n.a.
1818	*Eugenia*	n.a.	Horatio Dexter (C)	n.a.	n.a.
1818	*Monserrate*	n.a.	Arredondo & Son (O)	Africa/Havana	38
1818	*Gov. Coppinger*	n.a.	Daniel Hurlbert (C)	Havana	29
1819	*Tres Amigos*	sloop	Juan Llufrio (C)	Africa	n.a.
1820	*Florida*[1]	schooner	Benjamin Pearson (C)	C.Lopez or C.Monte, Africa	39
1821	*San Juan*	schooner	Villar y Aprisa (C)	Africa	n.a.
1821	*San José*	schooner	Villar y Aprisa (C)	Africa	n.a.

Sources: Passport for Lorenzo Seguí, Oct. 9, 1809; Relación de venta de negros, July 9, Aug. 6 and 12, 1810, Mar. 1 and 30, 1811, Nov. 21, 1810, Cuba 419A and Cuba 470, AGI; Petition of William Cook, Feb. 3, 1802, and Petition of William Northrup, July 20, 1802, Miscellaneous Legal Instruments and Proceedings, 1784–1814, EFP, microfilm reel 113, PKY; Petition of Daniel Hurlbert, Mar. 1, 1810, Miscellaneous Legal Instruments and Proceedings, 1784–1819, EFP, microfilm reel 115, PKY; Petition of Guillermo Travers, Mar. 26, 1819, Exchequer Proceedings, 1787–1819, EFP, microfilm reel 134, PKY; Papers on the District of Amelia Island, 1813–17, EFP, microfilm reel 66, PKY; Escrituras [Notarized Instruments], 1784–1821, EFP, microfilm reels 167–73, PKY; Accounts of the Royal Treasury, 1784–95, SD 2635, and 1796–1819, SD 2636, AGI; To and from the Collector of Amelia Island, 1803–17, EFP, microfilm reels 63–64; *SLGF,* vol. 1, 54–55.

1. Formerly the *Enterprise.*

Appendix 12

Free Blacks and Mulattos of Fernandina and Amelia Island, 1814

Mariana Rile, 60, and two sons, between 7 and 14
attached to the household: Vicenta de la Cruz, 20
Margarita Hill, 20

Jorge Brus, 34, his wife, 30, and two sons, between 7 and 14

Tory Travers, 45, and his wife, 25

Felix Castoral, 42, and his wife, 25
attached to the household: Rita Marian, 15

Juan Peterson, 34

María Sively, 25, and her daughter, between 1 and 6
attached to the household: Tina Diana, 32

Juan Moore, 50, and his wife, 39

Domingo Sanco, 50, and his wife, 30

Lucía Volantin, 25, and her daughter, between 7 and 14

Harry McQueen, 36, and his wife, 34
attached to the household: María Reyes, 25

Jaime Ríos, 25, and his wife, 24

Isabel Rivas, 46

Nancy Rivas, 20

Nicolasa Edimboro, 22

José Sánchez, 45, and his wife, 35
  one male slave, between 15 and 25
  two female slaves, between 7 and 14

Juana Wiggins, 25
  attached to the household: William Lely
    female child, between 1 and 6

Source: Census for Fernandina and Amelia Island, 1814, Census Returns, 1784–1814, EFP, microfilm reel 148, PKY.

Notes

Acknowledgments

1. The members are raising site improvement funds to help mark the site and provide on-site education. For information contact Fort Mose Historical Society, P.O. Box 4230, St. Augustine, Fla. 32085-4230.

2. Yvonne Daniel, *Rumba: Dance and Social Change in Contemporary Cuba* (Bloomington, Ind., 1995).

3. Daniel L. Schafer, "Freedom Was as Close as the River: African Americans and the Civil War in Northeast Florida," in *The African American Heritage of Florida,* ed. David R. Colburn and Jane L. Landers (Gainesville, Fla., 1995), 157–84, and Patricia L. Kenney, "LaVilla, Florida, 1886–1887: Reconstruction Dreams and the Formation of a Black Community," ibid., 185–206.

4. Michael A. Gomez, "Muslims in Early America," *Journal of Southern History* 60 (1994): 671–710.

5. Census Records, 1784–1814, East Florida Papers (hereafter cited as EFP), microfilm reel 148, P. K. Yonge Library of Florida History, University of Florida, Gainesville, Fla. (hereafter cited as PKY).

Introduction

1. Frank Tannenbaum, *Slave and Citizen, the Negro in the Americas* (New York, 1947); Eugene D. Genovese, "The Treatment of Slaves in Different Countries: Problems in the Application of the Comparative Method," in *Slavery in the New World: A Reader in Comparative History,* ed. Laura Boner and Eugene D. Genovese (Englewood Cliffs, N.J., 1969), 202–10; *Slavery and Race Relations in Latin America,* ed. Robert Brent Toplin (Westport, Conn., 1974); Rebecca J. Scott, *Slave Emancipation in Cuba: The Transition to Free Labor, 1860–1890* (Princeton, 1985).

2. For a most impressive synthesis of the Hispanic frontier experience, focusing on the themes of contention and transformation, see David J. Weber, *The Spanish Frontier in North America* (New Haven, Conn., 1992).

3. I am indebted to Susan R. Parker for our many fruitful discussions on the significance of international borders for Florida.

4. Michael Mullin, *Africa in America: Slave Acculturation and Resistance in the American South and the British Caribbean, 1736–1831* (Urbana, Ill., 1992).

5. David W. Cohen and Jack P. Greene, eds., *Neither Slave nor Free: The Freedmen of African Descent in the Slave Societies of the New World* (Baltimore, Md., 1972); Gwendolyn Midlo Hall, *Africans in Colonial Louisiana: The Development of Afro-Creole Culture in the Eighteenth Century* (Baton Rouge, La., 1992); Kimberly S. Hanger, *Bounded Lives, Bounded Places: Free Black Society in Colonial New Orleans, 1769–1803* (Durham, N.C., 1997); *Against the Odds: Free Blacks in the Slave Societies of the Americas,* ed. Jane G. Landers (London, 1996).

6. Jane Landers, "Traditions of African American Freedom and Community in Spanish Colonial Florida," in *The African American Heritage of Florida,* ed. David R. Colburn and Jane L. Landers (Gainesville, Fla., 1995), 17–41.

7. Mullin, *Africa in America,* 3.

8. Berlin argues that many New World planters feared and rejected Atlantic creoles for their dangerous knowledge and skills, but such assets were welcomed in a marginal slave society such as Spanish Florida (Ira Berlin, "From Creole to African: Atlantic Creoles and the Origins of African-American Society in Mainland North America," *William and Mary Quarterly,* 3d ser., 53 [Apr. 1996]: 251–88).

9. Hall, *Africans in Colonial Louisiana;* Hanger, *Bounded Lives, Bounded Places;* Daniel H. Usner, Jr., *Indians, Settlers, and Slaves in a Frontier Exchange Economy: The Lower Mississippi Valley before 1783* (Chapel Hill, N.C., 1992); Peter H. Wood, *Black Majority: Negroes in Colonial South Carolina from 1670 through the Stono Rebellion* (New York, 1974).

10. Unfortunately, many of the sites discussed in this volume have yet to be investigated. See Kathleen A. Deagan and Darcie MacMahon, *Ft. Mose: Colonial America's Black Fortress of Freedom* (Gainesville, Fla., 1995); Kathleen A. Deagan and Jane Landers, "Excavating Fort Mose: A Free Black Town in Spanish Florida," in *I, Too, Am America: Studies in African American Archaeology* (Charlottesville, Va., forthcoming); Leland Ferguson, *Uncommon Ground: Archaeology and Early African America, 1650–1800* (Washington, D.C., 1992).

11. Jane Landers, "Gracia Real de Santa Teresa de Mose: A Free Black Town in Spanish Colonial Florida," *American Historical Review* 95 (Feb. 1990): 9–30.

12. A sort of "racial drift" allowed persons to move through racial categories by birth, by self-designation, by community approbation, and even, in the late eighteenth century, by purchase of a document called "gracias al sacar," which legally dispensed one from "taints" such as illegitimacy or "vile" race (R. Douglas Cope, *The Limits of Racial Domination: Plebeian Society in Colonial Mexico, 1660–1720* [Madison, Wis., 1994]); Richard Boyer, "Negotiating 'Calidad': The Everyday Struggle for Status in 17th Century Mexico," *Historical Archaeology* 31 [1997]: 64–73).

Chapter 1
Precedents for Afro-Caribbean Society in Florida

1. The Muslim armies that invaded and occupied Spain and Portugal beginning in 711 included sub-Saharan soldiers (José Luis Cortés López, *Los orígenes de la esclavitud negra en España* [Madrid, 1986]; William D. Phillips, Jr., *Slavery from Roman Times to the Early Transatlantic Trade* [Minneapolis, 1985], 138–39, 155, 160–63; Herbert S. Klein, *African Slavery in Latin America and the Caribbean* [New York, 1986], 1–43).

An excellent study of black society in Portugal is A. C. de C. M. Saunders, *A Social History of Black Slaves and Freedmen in Portugal, 1441–1555* (Cambridge, 1982).

2. J. H. Elliott, *Imperial Spain, 1469–1716* (New York, 1963), 48–49; Amerigo Castro, *España en su historia: christianos, moros y judíos,* 2d ed. (Barcelona, 1983); Lyle N. McAlister, *Spain and Portugal in the New World, 1492–1700* (Minneapolis, 1984), 32; Patricia Seed, *Ceremonies of Possession in Europe's Conquest of the New World, 1492–1640* (Cambridge, 1995), chap. 3; Felipe Fernández-Armesto, *Before Columbus: Exploration and Colonization from the Mediterranean to the Atlantic, 1229–1492* (Philadelphia, 1987), 51.

3. In the fourteenth century, Jews became the scapegoat throughout Europe, and in Seville a pogrom killed thousands. The fifteenth-century state-building of Isabella and Ferdinand further heightened religious xenophobia with the institution of the Holy Office of the Inquisition and the eventual expulsion of Jews and Muslims who refused to convert. Fortunately for many of the now despised "other," at that moment the way to a "New World" opened. See David Nirenberg, "Muslim-Jewish Relations in the Fourteenth-Century Crown of Aragón," *Viator* 24 (1993): 249–68, and *Communities of Violence: Persecution of Minorities in the Middle Ages* (Princeton, 1996); McAlister, *Spain and Portugal,* 43–45; Elliott, *Imperial Spain,* 51–60. The sixteenth century witnessed further expulsions of Moriscos (Ruth Pike, *Aristocrats and Traders: Sevillian Society in the Sixteenth Century* [Ithaca, N.Y., 1972], 154–70).

4. Cortés López, *Orígenes de la esclavitud,* 23–44, 121–32; Phillips, *Slavery from Roman Times,* 162; Pike, *Aristocrats and Traders,* 170–92. Other enslaved groups in fifteenth-century Spain included Jews, Moors, Turks (actually Egyptians, Syria, Lebanese), white Christians (Sardinians, Greeks, Russians, and Spaniards), and Guanches from the Canary Islands (Leslie Rout, *The African Experience in Spanish America, 1502 to the Present Day* [London, 1976], 17). Even Amerindians sometimes were sold as slaves in Seville, despite royal prohibitions against their enslavement (Alfonso Franco Silva, *Regesto documental sobre la esclavitud Sevillana (1453–1513)* [Seville, 1979]).

5. McAlister, *Spain and Portugal,* 24–26; Cortés López, *Orígenes de la esclavitud,* 133–50.

6. Maureen Flynn, "Charitable Ritual in Late Medieval and Early Modern Spain," *Sixteenth-Century Journal* 16, no. 3 (1985): 335–48, and *Sacred Charity: Confraternities and Social Welfare in Spain, 1400–1700* (Ithaca, N.Y., 1989).

7. Cortés López, *Orígenes de la esclavitud,* 151–76; Rout, *African Experience,* 3–12; Pike, *Aristocrats and Traders,* 173, 188. For numerous examples of self-purchase or gratis manumission see Franco Silva, *Regesto documental.*

8. John Thornton, *Africa and Africans in the Making of the Atlantic World, 1400–1680* (Cambridge, 1992), 25; Berlin, "Creole to African," 255, 272; Ricardo E. Alegría, *Juan Garrido, el Conquistador Negro en Las Antillas, Florida, México y California, C. 1503–1540* (San Juan de Puerto Rico, 1990), 20.

9. Antonio Domínguez Ortiz, *The Golden Age of Spain, 1516–1659* (New York, 1971), 162–72. Notarial records from Seville (1501–1525) counted 5271 slaves, almost 4000 of whom were listed as blacks or mulattoes (Phillips, *Slavery from Roman Times,* 161; Ruth Pike, "Sevillian Society in the Sixteenth Century: Slaves and Freedmen," *Hispanic American Historical Review* 47 [Aug. 1967]: 344–59, and *Aristocrats and Traders,* 171–92).

10. Antonio Domínguez Ortiz, "La esclavitud en Castilla durante la Edad Moderna," *Estudios de historia social de España* 2 (1952): 377–78.

11.Pike, *Aristocrats and Traders,* 188.

12. Mary Elizabeth Perry, *Crime and Society in Early Modern Seville* (Hanover, N.H., 1980), 12–32; Pike, *Aristocrats and Traders,* 181, 192–214. Free and enslaved blacks in Portugal had comparable experiences (Saunders, *Black Slaves and Freedmen in Portugal,* chaps. 4–6).

13. Pike, *Aristocrats and Traders,* 173–74; Diego Ortiz de Zúñiga, *Anales eclesiásticos y seculars de la muy noble y leal ciudad de Sevilla, metrópoli de la Andalucía,* 3 vols. (Madrid, 1796), 3:78.

14. Seed, *Ceremonies of Possession,* chap. 3.

15. Pike, *Aristocrats and Traders,* 173–74, 186, and "Sevillian Society," 357–58; Rout, *African Experience,* 18.

16. Fernando Ortiz, *Los cabildos y la fiesta afrocubana del Día de Reyes* (Havana, 1992), 4.

17. Vicenta Cortés Alonso, *La esclavitud en Valencia durante el reinado de los Reyes católicos (1479–1516)* (Valencia, 1964); Cortés López, *Orígenes de la esclavitud,* 175–76; Phillips, *Slavery from Roman Times,* 163, 168. Corpus Christi became one of the most popular religious and civic celebrations in the Americas, where it also served to incorporate multiracial elements into the Spanish community (Linda A. Curcio-Nagy, "Giants and Gypsies: Corpus Christi in Colonial Mexico City," in *Rituals of Rule, Rituals of Resistance,* ed. William H. Beezley, Cheryl English Martin, William E. French [Wilmington, Del., 1994], 1–26).

18. Alegría, *Juan Garrido,* 17, 20, 30. Alegría located other persons of African descent on the passenger lists and other unedited documents for Puerto Rico, including "Francisco Melgarejo, black servant of Jerónimo de Mendoza," "the black Antonio," "Juan, the black slave of Juan Martínez," "Piñon's wife, black," and "Gaspar, free black." On the wars in Hispaniola see Samuel M. Wilson, *Hispaniola: Caribbean Chiefdoms in the Age of Columbus* (Tuscaloosa, Ala., 1990), 74–109.

19. Crown to Nicolás de Ovando, Mar. 29, 1503, in *Colección de documentos inéditos para la historia de Hispaniola-América,* vol. 6, ed. José María Chacón y Calvo (Madrid, 1929), 73. It used to be thought that Ovando's fleet brought the first Africans to Hispaniola in 1502, and that these became the first maroons (Richard Price, *Maroon Societies: Rebel Slave Communities in the Americas* [Baltimore, Md., 1973], 1–2).

20. Carlos Esteban Deive, *Los guerrilleros negros* (Santo Domingo, 1989), 20; Carlos Larrazábal Blanco, *Los negros y la esclavitud en Santo Domingo* (Santo Domingo, 1967), chaps. 5 and 6; José Juan Arrom and Manuel A. García Arévalo, *Cimarrón* (Santo Domingo, 1986).

21. Deive, *Guerrilleros negros,* 22. Officials sent the seventeen African slaves to work in the mines of Puerto Real on the north coast (*Puerto Real: The Archaeology of a Sixteenth-Century Spanish Town in Hispaniola,* ed. Kathleen A. Deagan [Gainesville, Fla., 1995], 96; Pike, *Aristocrats and Traders,* 175).

22. Because contraband trade in slaves was endemic, these are probably conservative figures (Phillips, *Slavery from Roman Times,* 184–94; Klein, *African Slavery in Latin America,* 16–20).

23. Alegría, *Juan Garrido,* 17, 20, 30.

24. Ibid., 30; Services of Francisco Mexía [*sic*], Contaduría 1072, Archivo General de Indias, Seville, Spain (hereafter cited as AGI), cited in Jalil Sued-Badillo, *La mujer indígena y su sociedad* (San Juan de Puerto Rico, 1989), 59.

25. Royal decree, Dec. 24, 1511, *Colección de documentos inéditos,* vol. 6, 411–14.

26. McAlister, *Spain and Portugal,* 153–54; Alegría, *Juan Garrido,* 20, 27–36.

27. Peter Gerhard, "A Black Conquistador in Mexico," *Hispanic American Historical Review* 58 (1978): 451–59; Alegría, *Juan Garrido,* 114, 116, 119, 127–38.

28. Eugene Lyon, *The Enterprise of Florida: Pedro Menéndez de Avilés and the Spanish Conquest of 1565–1568* (Gainesville, Fla., 1974), 1–10.

29. For an overview of this and subsequent explorations by "the intruders" and their impact upon "the original Southerners" see J. Leitch Wright, Jr., *The Only Land They Knew: The Tragic Story of the American Indians in the Old South* (New York, 1981), chap. 2.

30. At Christmas time in 1521, Wolof slaves from Diego Colón's sugar plantation on Hispaniola led the first major slave revolt in the Americas. The following month the Crown issued the first slave codes for the Americas (royal decree, Jan. 6, 1522, Patronato 295, AGI, in Deive, *Guerrilleros negros,* 33, 281–89). It seems logical that the Spaniards would have carefully screened any Africans from that island they were taking with them. Although the slaves seem to have initially sided with Spanish authorities in the mutiny, at least some of them finally chose to join the Guale (Paul E. Hoffman, *A New Andalucia and a Way to the Orient: The American Southeast during the Sixteenth Century* [Baton Rouge, La., 1990], 73–79).

31. The Indians of West Texas came to regard Estévan as a shaman and gave him a sacred gourd rattle that he carried to his death in the southwestern expedition of Hernando Coronado (*Castaways: The Narrative of Alvar Núñez Cabeza de Vaca,* ed. Enrique Pupo-Walker [Berkeley, 1993], 51, 56, 64–66, 72–73, 100, 104–5, 111, 127; Herbert E. Bolton, *Coronado, Knight of Pueblos and Plains* [Albuquerque, N.Mex., 1949], 10–16, 25–35). The Indians at Piachi later told de Soto that when the Narváez expedition was skirting the coast in homemade boats somewhere between Pensacola and Mobile, an unnamed black who came ashore for water was killed (*The Journey of Alvar Núñez Cabeza de Vaca* trans. Fanny Bandelier [New York, 1973], 38–40).

32. I am indebted to Peter H. Wood for a reference to the Capitulations between Charles V and Hernando de Soto, dated Apr. 20, 1537, which permitted de Soto to take to Florida "other fifty black slaves, the third part of them females, free from all duties" (D. B. Quinn, *New American World: A Documentary History of North America to 1612,* ed. David B. Quinn, with the assistance of Alison M. Quinn and Susan Hillier [New York, 1978], 2:94). Like later expeditionaries he may not have taken full advantage of this permit. On the impact of the Spanish expeditions on indigenous populations see Marvin T. Smith, "Aboriginal Population Movements in the Early Historic Period Interior Southeast," in *Powhatan's Mantle: Indians in the Colonial Southeast,* ed. Peter H. Wood, Gregory A. Waselkov, and M. Thomas Hatley (Lincoln, Nebr., 1989), 21–34.

33. *Narratives of the Career of Hernando de Soto,* ed. Edward Gaylord Bourne (New York, 1904), 72. The de Soto expedition left a black slave named Robles at Coosa because he was too ill to walk. He was described as a "very fine Christian and a good slave," and the chief promised personally to nurse him back to health. The Indians later told Spaniards from the Tristán de Luna expedition of 1560 that Robles lived another eleven or twelve years among them before finally dying (Garcilaso de la Vega, *The Florida of the Inca,* trans. John Varner and Jeanette Varner [London, 1951], 347). In September 1540, another black slave, Johan Biscayan, was left at Ulibahali (near present-day Rome, Ga.). He may have been trying to escape because his master, Juan Lobillo, later returned to Ulibahali without permission to try to find him (Chester B. DePratter, Charles M. Hudson, and Marvin T. Smith, "The Hernando de Soto Expedition," in *Alabama and the Borderlands from Prehistory to Statehood,* ed. R. Reid Badger and Lawrence A. Clayton [University, Ala., 1985], 108–27, esp. 118–19).

34. Another free African, Luis Moreno, accompanied one of the chroniclers of the de Soto expedition, Luis Hernández de Biedma. Spaniards Baltasar de Gallegos and Juan de Añasco also took African slaves to Florida with them, some of whom survived with Bernaldo (Ignacio Avellaneda, *Los Sobrevivientes de la Florida: The Survivors of the De Soto Expedition* [Gainesville, Fla., 1990], 17, 29, 34, 47, 56, 63). Other expeditionaries of African descent identified with de Soto include Alonso de Pereda, Pedro de la Torre, and Juan Martín (Antonio de Solar y Taboada and José de Rújula y Ochotorna, *El adelantado Hernando de Soto* [Badajoz, 1929], 293, 305, 333; see also Pike, *Aristocrats and Traders,* 189). On the prominence of Africans in early Peru, where de Soto and others in his expedition had also seen action see Frederick P. Bowser, *The African Slave in Colonial Peru: 1524–1650* (Stanford, 1974).

35. Amy Turner Bushnell, *Situado and Sabana: Spain's Support System for the Presidio and Mission Provinces of Florida* (Athens, Ga., 1994), 29, 36–48. The failed expeditions included Tristán de Luna's attempt to settle at Pensacola and Angel de Villafañe's attempt at Port Royal Sound, S.C. (1559–61) (Verne E. Chatelain, *The Defenses of Spanish Florida, 1565–1763* [Washington, D.C., 1941], 6; Lyon, *Enterprise of Florida,* 20–23, 100–130).

36. Eugene Lyon estimates that from 1565 to 1568 Philip II spent roughly 275,735 pesos to support Florida, while Menéndez spent an additional 103,401 pesos of his own money (*Enterprise of Florida,* 183).

37. "Memoria de las cosas y costa y indios de la Florida," *Colección de documentos inéditos relativos al descubrimiento,* vol. 5, ed. Luis Torres de Mendoza (Madrid, 1866), 540–45.

38. D'Escalante and another survivor, Alonso de Rojas, also became interpreters (Florida ration list, 1566–67, Florida Accounts, Contaduría, 941, AGI, reproduced in Lyon, *Enterprise of Florida,* 186). Juanillo served as a Florida linguist until taken to Puerto Plata, Hispaniola, in 1567 (Lista de la gente de guerra, Contaduría 941, AGI). Also see Eugene Lyon, "Cultural Brokers in Sixteenth-Century Spanish Florida," in *Spanish Borderlands Sourcebooks 24: Pedro Menéndez de Avilés,* ed. Eugene Lyon (New York, 1995), 329–36.

39. The Jesuit missionary Father Juan Rogel complained that he could not trust the interpretive skills of this black woman and mulatto, saying they knew little Castilian. Betraying his prejudice, he added that they were not very intelligent because of their race (Father Juan Rogel to Father Didacus Avellaneda, Nov. 1566 to Jan. 1577, cited in *Missions to the Calusa,* ed. John H. Hann [Gainesville, Fla., 1991], 281).

40. In 1603 the Ays nation again gave refuge to seven black slaves from St. Augustine. Five were later recaptured but two others were said to have married Indians and were never retrieved (Chatelain, *Defenses of Spanish Florida,* 128).

41. Eugene Lyon, *Richer Than We Thought: The Material Culture of Sixteenth-Century St. Augustine* (St. Augustine, Fla., 1992).

42. Alférez Alonso Ordóñez to the Crown, Feb. 20, 1577. The Council of the Indies could not have been responding so quickly to Ordóñez's request when three days later it recommended the same plan to the king. There must have been previous requests (Council of the Indies to King Philip II, Feb. 23, 1577, in *Colonial Records of Spanish Florida,* ed. Jeanette Thurber Connor [Deland, Fla., 1930], 120).

43. Patronato 255, AGI, Jeanette Thurber Connor Collection, PKY.

44. Relación de los esclavos forzados que quedaron de la galera San Agustín de la Havana, in *Documentos para la historia colonial de Cuba: Siglos XVI, XVII, XVIII, XIX,* ed. César García del Pino and Alicia Melis Cappa (Havana, 1988), 63–67. Spaniards wishing to take slaves to the Americas were required to obtain licenses for their passage, and these records also document sixteenth-century slaves of diverse ethnic and racial origins.

45. Phillips, *Slavery from Roman Times,* 195; Rout, *African Experience,* 126–61; Bowser, *African Slave in Colonial Peru,* 125–46.

46. "Ordenanzas de Alonso de Cáceres, 1574," cited in Isabel Macías Domínguez, *Cuba en la primera mitad del siglo XVII* (Seville, 1978), 35.

47. Ibid. This plan was never enacted, but it does illustrate contemporary views of St. Augustine as a suburb of Havana, as well as a receptacle for its undesirable.

48. Información promovida para conocer el trato dado a los esclavos por sus amos y las causas por las que aquellos se hacían cimarrones, Mar. 22, 1690, Santo Domingo (hereafter cited as SD) 65, AGI, cited in *Documentos para la historia colonial de Cuba,* 186–99.

49. Kenneth R. Andrews, *The Spanish Caribbean: Trade and Plunder, 1530–1630* (New Haven, Conn., 1978), 136.

50. Información hecha por Diego de Mazariegos sobre la toma de La Habana por Jacques de Sores, 1555, Patronato 267, AGI, cited in *Documentos para la historia colonial de Cuba,* 186–99.

51. Irene Wright, *The Early History of Cuba, 1492–1586* (New York, 1916), 315, 346; Chatelain, *Defenses of Spanish Florida,* 49, 62–63.

52. Chatelain, *Defenses of Spanish Florida,* 49; Bushnell, *Situado and Sabana,* 29–30, 44–46, 136–37, 161–69.

53. Elizabeth also questioned the legality of Spanish territorial claims. "[S]he understood not why her, or any prince's subjects should be debarred from the trade of the Indies, which she could not persuade herself the Spaniards had any just title to by the donation of the Bishop of Rome . . . nor yet by any other claim, than as they that touched here and there upon the coasts, built cottages and gave name to a river or a cape; which things could not entitle them to a propriety" (Queen Elizabeth I to the Spanish Ambassador, 1587, British Museum, Additional Manuscripts, Long Papers, bk. 1, chap. 12, in John Alder Burton, ed., *Archives of British Honduras,* vol. 1 [London, 1931], 48). I am indebted to Kimberly H. Breuer for this reference.

54. Lyon, *Enterprise of Florida,* 191. Memorial of Pedro Menéndez de Avilés, undated (1561–62) in E. Ruidíaz y Caravia, *La Florida* (Madrid, 1893), vol. 2, 322, cited in Woodbury Lowery, *The Spanish Settlements in the Present Limits of the United States, Florida* (New York, 1959), 14–15, 96. This document also appears in the collection of the St. Augustine Foundation and is identified as being from the Archivo del Instituto de Valencia de Don Juan Madrid, Envio 25-H, no. 162, Council of the Indies, n.d. (probably Nov. 1569). Menéndez's demographic estimates appear to be reasonably accurate, for in 1542, after a tour of the island, Hispaniola's archdeacon, Alonso de Castro, estimated the black population at 25,000–30,000, and the white population at only 1,200. Castro also estimated that more than 2,000–3,000 maroons lived on the island. Alonso de Castro to the Council of the Indies, Mar. 26, 1542, cited in José Luis Saez, *La iglesia y el negro esclavo en Santo Domingo: una historia de tres siglos* (Santo Domingo, 1994), 273–74.

55. Andrews, *Spanish Caribbean,* 20–21, 34–35, 136–45. When Menéndez wrote, Spaniards had already battled blacks in Hispaniola (1521), Santa Marta, Colombia (1530), Cuba (1533), Mexico City (1537, 1546) Hispaniola (1545–48), Honduras (1548), and Barquisimeto, Venezuela (1555) (Rout, *African Experience,* 99–125).

56. Rout, *African Experience,* 27–28; Price, *Maroon Societies,* 10–15, 53–54.

57. Cited in *Documents concerning English Voyages to the Spanish Main, 1569–1580,* ed. I. A. Wright (London, 1932), 48–50. When Sir Francis Drake raided Nombre de Dios (Panama) for the third time in 1572, he lost most of his men and was headed for failure, but after maroons (and French corsairs) came to his aid, he managed to seize a fortune in silver (Andrews, *Spanish Caribbean,* 139–41; Irene Wright, *Early History,* 346; Roberto de la Guardia, *Los negros del istmo de Panamá* [Panama, 1977], 90–91).

58. St. Augustine's garrison normally consisted of three hundred *plazas* or positions (Engel Sluiter, *The Florida Situado: Quantifying the First Eighty Years, 1571–1651* [Gainesville, Fla., 1985]).

59. Juan Fernández, a black soldier of the garrison, joined Indians from the neighboring villages in trying to create a diversion at the Drake camp. Various eyewitness testimonies of Drake's raid on St. Augustine are found in Contratación 4802, AGI, St. Augustine Historical Foundation, Flagler College, St. Augustine, Fla.

60. Opinion of the Council, June 4, 1580, in *Colonial Records of Spanish Florida,* 314–17; Juan de Cevadilla to the Crown, Jan. 22, 1581, SD 229, AGI.

61. Fernando Miranda to the Crown, Aug. 20, 1583, cited in Chatelain, *Defenses of Spanish Florida,* 138. The Crown first established a regular annual subsidy for Florida in 1570, to be paid from the royal treasuries of Tierra Firme (Panama) and later Vera Cruz, Mexico City, and finally Puebla (Sluiter, *Florida Situado,* 2–3).

62. A major revolt by the Guale Indians erupted in Santa Elena in 1576 and was only ended in 1580 after the Spaniards put nineteen towns and many granaries and fields to the torch. The black labor force sent from St. Augustine would have witnessed the aftermath of that tragedy (Eugene Lyon, *Santa Elena: A Brief History of the Colony, 1566–1587* [Columbia, S.C., 1984]).

63. Miguel de Ybarra to the Crown, 1603, 54-5-9/47, SC, AGI.

64. Peter H. Wood, "The Changing Population of the Colonial South: An Overview by Race and Region, 1685–1790," in *Powhatan's Mantle: Indians in the Colonial Southeast,* ed. Peter H. Wood, Gregory A. Waselkov, and M. Thomas Hatley (Lincoln, Nebr., 1989), 35–103, esp. 38, 51–56.

65. Ibid., 51–56; Philip III to Sancho de Alquía, captain general of Cuba, Apr. 9, 1618, SD 225, AGI. Florida's governor complained in 1624 that this order had still not been carried out and he repeated the request for blacks from Havana. The Council of the Indies reprimanded Cuba's captain general and again ordered him to comply (Don Luis de Rojas y Borja to Philip IV, May 7, 1624, and Order of the Council of the Indies, May 9, 1624, SD 225, AGI). In the first half of the seventeenth century, blacks made up 45 percent of the population of Cuba, so scarcity was not the problem (Macías Domínguez, *Cuba en la primera mitad del siglo XVII,* 34).

66. Amy Bushnell, "The Menéndez Márquez Cattle Barony at La Chua and the Determinants of Economic Expansion in Seventeenth-Century Florida," *Florida Historical Quarterly* 56 (Apr. 1978): 419.

67. "Documentation Pertaining to the Asile Farm," manuscript translated and annotated by John H. Hann, on file at the San Luis Archaeological and Historical Site, Tallahassee, Fla., 4–5, 67. This information derives from Governor Diego de Rebolledo's 1651 review of his predecessor, Governor Benito Ruiz de Salazar Vallecilla's term of office. On San Luis see Bonnie G. McEwan, "Hispanic Life on the Seventeenth-Century Florida Frontier," in *The Spanish Missions of La Florida,* ed. Bonnie G. McEwan (Gainesville, Fla., 1993), 295–321.

68. Bushnell, "Menéndez Márquez Cattle Barony," 407–31; Lolita Gutiérrez Brockington found that 60 to 80 percent of the permanent ranch hands on Hernando Cortés's cattle ranches were black and mulatto slaves. See *The Leverage of Labor: Managing the Cortés Haciendas in Tehuantepec, 1588–1688* (Durham, N.C., 1989), 126–58, 171–72.

69. For a good overview of seventeenth-century developments in Spain, see J. H. Elliott, "Self-Perception and Decline in Early Seventeenth-Century Spain," *Past and Present* 74 (1977):41–61, and *Imperial Spain,* 317–69.

70. Violet Barbour, "Privateers and Pirates of the West Indies," *American Historical Review* 16 (Apr. 1911): 538–39.

71. From Jamaica, the English pirate Robert Searles led a devastating raid on St. Augustine in 1668 (Bushnell, *Situado and Sabana,* 136–37).

72. Documentos relacionado con el ofrecimiento del Capitán Diego Martín, Diego El Mulato, de pasar al servicio de España, in *Documentos para la historia colonial de Cuba,* 139–40. Diego was also known as Diego de los Reyes and "Diego Lucifer" (David F. Marley, *Pirates and Privateers of the Americas* [Santa Barbara, Calif., 1994], 170).

73. Interrogation of the black corsair Diego by Governor Don Juan Márquez de Cabrera, St. Augustine, Fla., 1686, in the John Tate Lanning Papers, Thomas Jefferson Library, University of Missouri, St. Louis, Mo., 13–18. The mulatto translator Thomas had also participated in the 1683 attack on St. Augustine. I am indebted to John H. Hann, of the San Luis Archaeological and Historical Site, in Tallahassee, Fla., for this reference and for his generosity. For more on the later raid of Monsieur Agramón (Nicholas Grammont) see Luis Arana, "Grammont's Landing at Little Matanzas Inlet, 1686," *El Escribano* 9, no. 3 (1972): 107–13, and Marley, *Pirates and Privateers,* 162–68.

74. The same year another epidemic decimated the Indian laborers (Bushnell, *Situado and Sabana,* 136–42; Luis Rafael Arana and Albert Manucy, *The Building of Castillo de San Marcos* [St. Augustine, Fla., 1977]).

75. Regulations technically forbade any black from remaining in an Indian village longer than three days, but this rule, like many others, was more often breached than observed.

76. Paul E. Hoffman, *The Spanish Crown and the Defense of the Caribbean, 1535–1585: Precedent, Patrimonialism and Royal Parsimony* (Baton Rouge, La., 1980), 40.

77. Información hecha por Diego de Mazariegos sobre la toma de La Habana por Jacques de Sores, 1555, Patronato 267, AGI, cited in *Documentos para la historia colonial de Cuba,* 8–40; Irene Wright, *Early History,* 315.

78. Stephen Weber, "Las compañías de milicia y la defensa del istmo centroamericano en el siglo XVII: el alistamiento general de 1673," *Mesoamérica* 14 (Dec. 1987): 511–28.

79. Herbert S. Klein, "The Colored Militia of Cuba, 1568–1868," *Caribbean Studies* 6 (July 1966): 17–27; Allan J. Kuethe, "The Status of the Free Pardo in the Disciplined Militia of New Granada," *Journal of Negro History* 56 (Apr. 1971): 105–15.

80. The Crown granted Captain Gutierre de Miranda a license to take his mulatto slave, Sebastián de Miranda, from Spain with him to serve as a drummer at the fort at Santa Elena (royal decree of Philip II, Feb. 9, 1580). Sebastián later served as a member of the crew of the *San Juan* (Data de Sueldos, June 21, 1580, Contaduría 232, AGI; see also Roster of Black and Mulatto Militia for St. Augustine, Sept. 20, 1683, SD 266, AGI).

81. De Tapia testified about his occupation in a trial of two Indian counterfeiters (SD 226, AGI, legajo 157A, John B. Stetson Collection [hereafter cited as SC], PKY).

82. Luis Arana, "Military Manpower in Florida, 1670–1703," *El Escribano* 8, no. 2 (1971): 40–63.

83. Herbert E. Bolton and Mary Ross, *The Debatable Land: A Sketch of the Anglo-Spanish Contest for the Georgia Country* (1925; reprint, New York, 1968); J. Leitch Wright, Jr., *Only Land,* chaps. 5 and 6; Verner W. Crane, *The Southern Frontier, 1670–1732* (New York, 1981), 6–10. The abortive Spanish expedition of 1670, under the command of Juan Menéndez Márquez, involved a small flotilla of three ships and fourteen *piraguas* (large canoes), but it was undone by a storm (John E. Worth, *The Struggle for the Georgia Coast: An Eighteenth-Century Spanish Retrospective on Guale and Mocama* [Athens, Ga., 1995], 181).

84. David Hurst Thomas, "The Archaeology of Mission Santa Catalina de Guale: Our First 15 Years," in *The Spanish Missions of La Florida,* ed. Bonnie G. McEwan (Gainesville, Fla., 1993), 1–34.

85. Rebecca Saunders, "Architecture of the Missions of Santa María and Santa Catalina de Amelia," in *The Spanish Missions of La Florida,* ed. Bonnie G. McEwan (Gainesville, Fla., 1993), 35–61.

86. Wood, *Black Majority,* 95–130.

87. Morton's stolen slaves included Peter, Scipio, Doctor, Cushi, Arro, Emo, Caesar, and Sambo. The women were Frank, Bess, and Mammy (J. G. Dunlop, "William Dunlop's Mission to St. Augustine in 1688," *South Carolina Historical and Genealogical Magazine* 34 [Jan. 1933]: 1–30). Two of the thirteen captured slaves escaped the Spaniards and returned to their English masters (Crane, *Southern Frontier,* 31–33; Wood, *Black Majority,* 50; Worth, *Struggle for the Georgia Coast,* 146–71; Edward Randolph to the Board of Trade, Mar. 16, 1699, *Records of the British Public Record Office Relating to South Carolina, 1663–1782,* ed. A. S. Salley [Atlanta, Ga., and Columbia, S.C., 1928–47] [hereafter cited as BPRO Trans.], vol. 4, 88–95).

88. Craven et al. to James Colleton, Mar. 3, 1686, BPRO Trans., vol. 4, 184–88.

89. Although Colleton authorized William Dunlop's mission to St. Augustine and his "demand" for the recovery of Landgrave Morton's eleven slaves, he also sent the new Spanish governor a conciliatory message welcoming him to service and detailing his determination to "extirpate, abolish, and destroy" pirates and "other Sea Robbers" operating out of Carolina (James Colleton to Major William Dunlop, June 15, 1688, William Dunlop Papers, National Library of Scotland, Edinburgh, no. 8456). I am indebted to Joyce Chaplin for this reference.

90. Craven et al to the Grand Council, Oct. 10, 1687, BPRO Trans., vol. 4, 221–28.

91. Crane, *Southern Frontier,* 24–33.

92. Helen Hornbeck Tanner, "The Land and Water Communications Systems of the Southeastern Indians," in *Powhatan's Mantle: Indians in the Colonial Southeast,* ed. Peter H. Wood, Gregory A. Waselkov, and M. Thomas Hatley (Lincoln, Nebr., 1989), 6–20.

93. The men who stole the canoe were named Conano, Jessie, Jacque, Gran Domingo (Big Sunday), Cambo, Mingo, Dicque, and Robi. Names of the females were not given. The owners of the fugitives were Samuel de Bordieu, who owned Mingo and his wife

and daughter; John Bird, two men; Joab Howe, one man; John Berresford, one woman; Christopher Smith, one man; Robert Cuthbert, three men ("William Dunlop's Mission," 4, 26, 28).

94. Among the acts of charity that a good Catholic was urged to perform were to offer protection to the miserable and to shelter fugitives (Maureen Flynn, "Charitable Ritual in Late Medieval and Early Modern Spain," *Sixteenth-Century Journal* 16, no. 3 [1985]: 335–48).

95. Royal officials to Charles II, Mar. 3, 1699, cited in Irene Wright, "Dispatches of Spanish Officials Bearing on the Free Negro Settlement of Gracia Real de Santa Teresa de Mose," *Journal of Negro History* 9 (1924): 151–52.

96. "William Dunlop's Mission."

97. Royal decree, Nov. 7, 1693, SD 58-1-26, SC, PKY.

98. Despite the royal decree of 1693, in 1697 Governor Laureano de Torres y Ayala returned six newly arrived blacks and an Indian "to avoid conflicts and ruptures between the two governments" (Joseph de Zúñiga to Charles II, Oct. 10, 1699, SD 844, microfilm reel 15, PKY).

99. On *repoblación* see Ministerio de Cultura, *Documentación Indiana en Simancas* (Valladolid, 1990): 250–57.

100. McAlister, *Spain and Portugal,* 3–8, 32, 133–52.

101. On the function and significance of godparents, see George M. Foster, "Cofradía and Compadrazgo in Spain and Spanish America," *Southwestern Journal of Anthropology* 9 (1953): 1–28.

102. The Spanish force defending St. Augustine in 1702 consisted of 174 army men, 44 white militiamen, 123 Indians from the Apalachee, Guale, and Timucuan doctrinas, and 57 blacks (Charles W. Arnade, *The Siege of St. Augustine in 1702* [Gainesville, Fla., 1959]: 35). See also John J. TePaske, *The Governorship of Spanish Florida, 1700–1763* (Durham, N.C., 1964), 110–13, 130–32, 196–97.

103. TePaske, *Governorship,* 116–22.

104. Report of Governor Robert Johnson, Jan. 12, 1719, cited in *The Colonial South Carolina Scene, Contemporary Views, 1697–1774,* ed. H. Roy Merrens (Columbia, S.C., 1977), 57–66.

105. Wood, *Black Majority,* 127–30; *The Carolina Chronicle of Dr. Francis Le Jau, 1706–1717,* ed. Frank W. Klingberg (Berkeley, 1956), 60–137.

106. In the aftermath of the Yamasee War Coweta's paramount chief ordered his subjects to switch their allegiance to the Spaniards and he sent four envoys to relay this offer to the Governor Francisco Córcoles in St. Augustine. A literate and Christian Ibaja, Antonio Pérez Campaña (alias Chuchumeco), translated. One chief, Perro Bravo (Mad Dog), who identified himself as an "infidel" and a war captain from Salquicha (elsewhere spelled Salaquiliche) laid before the Spanish governor eight chamois cords full of knots, each of which denoted a town promising to switch allegiance to the Spaniards (a total of 161 towns). Perro Bravo stated that towns of fewer than two hundred persons were not even represented and the chiefs asked that the cords be sent to the king of Spain (Testi-

mony of the four caciques, May 28, 1715, and subsequent report by Governor Francisco de Córcoles y Martínez, Jan. 25, 1716, SD 58–1–30, AGI, SC, PKY). See also Mark F. Boyd, "Diego Peña's Expedition to Apalachee and Apalachicola in 1716," *Florida Historical Quarterly* 28 (July 1949): 1–27; John H. Hann, "St. Augustine's Fallout from the Yamasee War," *Florida Historical Quarterly* 68 (Oct. 1989): 180–200.

107. The following year Carolina enacted a new and harsher slave code (Wood, *Black Majority*, 298–99, 304).

108. Memorial of the Fugitives, 1724, SD 844, microfilm reel 15, PKY.

109. One of the Spanish delegates was the royal accountant, Don Francisco Menéndez Márquez, who was probably already by then the owner of the Mandinga slave who would be his namesake and the future leader of Florida's first free black town. For the exchange on this mission see the letters of Governors Arthur Middleton (Carolina) and Antonio de Benavides (Florida) in *Documentos históricos de la Florida y la Luisiana Siglos XVI al XVII* (Madrid, 1912), 252–60.

110. Consulta by the Council of the Indies, Apr. 12, 1731, cited in Irene Wright, "Dispatches," 166–72.

111. Among the leading citizens purchasing these slaves were St. Augustine's royal accountant, the royal treasurer, several military officers, and even some religious officials (Antonio de Benavides to Philip V, Nov. 11, 1725, cited in ibid., 164–66).

112. Accord, June 27, 1730, SD 844, microfilm reel 15, PKY; Wood, *Black Majority*, 305. Some of the slaves sold at the 1729 auction were taken to Havana by their new owners. Nine years later Governor Manuel de Montiano would try to retrieve them (Decree of Manuel de Montiano, Mar. 3, 1738, SD 844, microfilm reel 15, PKY).

113. June 13, 1728, BPRO Trans., vol. 12, 61–67, cited in Wood, *Black Majority*, 305.

114. Four blacks taken from a plantation near Port Royal in 1726 were later spotted in St. Augustine (Arthur Middleton, June 13, 1728, BPRO Trans., vol. 13, 61–67, and John Pearson, Oct. 20, 1727, BPRO Trans., vol. 19, 127–28, cited in Wood, *Black Majority*, 305).

115. Wood, *Black Majority*, 305.

116. Antonio de Benavides to Philip V, Apr. 27, 1733, SD 833, AGI.

117. The Crown actually issued two separate edicts in 1733. The first, on Oct. 4, 1733, forbade any future compensation to the British, reiterated the royal offer of freedom, and specifically prohibited the sale of fugitives to private citizens (no doubt in response to the auction of 1729). The second, on Oct. 29, 1733, commended the blacks for their bravery against the British in 1728 but also stipulated that they would be required to complete four years of royal service as an indenture prior to being freed (Royal decree, Oct. 4, 1733, SD 58-1-24, SC, PKY; Royal decree, Oct. 29, 1733, SD 58-1-24, SC, PKY).

118. Memorial of the Fugitives, included in Manuel de Montiano to Philip V, Mar. 3, 1738, SD 844, microfilm reel 15, PKY.

119. This may be the same Perro Bravo, also known as Yfallaquisca, whom the paramount chief of Coweta (in the Apalachicola province 180 leagues northwest of St. Augustine) sent to pledge loyalty to the Spaniards in the aftermath of the Yamasee War. In 1717 Perro Bravo appeared in household #8 on the census of Pocotalaca.

120. Jorge claimed to be the chief who had led the Yamasee uprising against the British and stated that he and the other Yamasee chiefs "commonly" made treaties with the slaves (Memorial of Chief Jorge, included in Manuel de Montiano to Philip V, Mar. 3, 1738, SD 844, microfilm reel 15, PKY). It is possible that this Jorge was Chief George, father of the Yamasee youth educated in England to be a native missionary for the Society for the Gospel in Foreign Parts. The young Prince George returned with Commissary Gideon Johnston in 1715 in the midst of the Yamasee War and later wrote, "I have had noos that my Father as gone in Santaugustena and all my Friends." A later account reporting that the father had been killed proved untrue, and another report that he had been captured, returned to Charles Town, and then sold with the rest of his family as slaves was unconfirmed. Nor are there further reports about the young Prince George after Commissary Johnston's death in 1716 (Frank J. Klingberg, "The Mystery of the Lost Yamasee Prince," *South Carolina Historical and Genealogical Magazine* 63 [1962]: 18–32).

121. Petition of Diego Espinosa and reply by Manuel de Montiano, May 5, 1738, SD 845, microfilm reel 16, PKY. Diego de Espinosa was a successful mulatto cattle rancher. At his own expense, he fortified his ranch twenty miles north of St. Augustine on the Diego Plains, and it served as an important outpost guarding the Spanish city.

122. Philip V to Manuel de Montiano, July 15, 1741, AGI 58-1-25, SC 5943, PKY.

Chapter 2
The Origins of a Florida Sanctuary

1. The town's name was a composite of the old Indian placename (Mose), the phrase indicating that the town was established with the king's permission (Gracia Real), and the name of the town's patron saint (Teresa of Avila, who was also the patroness of Spain).

2. Manuel de Montiano to Philip V, Sept. 16, 1740, SD 2658, AGI. On Spanish recognition of natural lords and the autonomy they enjoyed, see Amy Turner Bushnell, "Ruling the 'Republic of Indians' in Seventeenth-Century Florida," in *Powhatan's Mantle: Indians in the Colonial Southeast,* ed. Peter H. Wood, Gregory A. Waselkov, and M. Thomas Hatley (Lincoln, Nebr., 1989), 134–50.

3. Colin A. Palmer describes an analogous relationship between Yanga and Francisco Angola, leaders of the maroon community in the Orizaba region of Vera Cruz, Mexico, of which the free black town San Lorenzo de los Negros de Cerralvo was created in 1618 (*Slaves of the White God: Blacks in Mexico, 1570–1650* [Cambridge, Mass., 1976], 128–30).

4. The names of Menéndez and Eligio de la Puente appear in first and second place on all official Spanish reports on Mose, including those generated after their evacuation to Cuba in 1763 (Evacuation report of Juan Joseph Eligio de la Puente, Jan. 22, 1764, SD 2595, AGI; Price, *Maroon Societies,* 29–30).

5. Juan, slave of the Englishman Captain Davis, was baptized in a case of necessity by Don Antonio de Herrera on Aug. 3, 1737. Francisco Chino died on Mar. 25, 1738, with absolution but no other sacraments due to the acceleration of his illness, and his infant

daughter followed him on Aug. 22, 1738. Another of Davis's former slaves, Josepha, died in 1739 (Burial of Juan, Aug. 3, 1737; burial of Francisco Chino, Mar. 25, 1738; burial of infant daughter of Francisco Chino, Aug. 22, 1738; burial of Josepha, Jan. 17, 1739 (Black Burials, Cathedral Parish Records, Diocese of St. Augustine Catholic Center, Jacksonville, Fla. [hereafter cited as CPR], microfilm reel 284 D, PKY).

6. Decree of Manuel de Montiano, Mar. 3, 1738, SD 844, microfilm reel 15, PKY.

7. Manuel de Montiano to Philip V, Feb. 16, 1739, SD 844, microfilm reel 15, PKY. Mose's population was larger than any of the eight Indian villages still surrounding St. Augustine, the largest of which, San Nicolás de Casapullas (north of St. Augustine), held seventy-one persons (Manuel de Montiano to Juan Francisco de Güemes y Horcasitas, Mar. 3, 1738, Buckingham Smith Collection, PKY).

8. An eyewitness English account from the sixteenth century tells how the maroons of Panama built similar structures. They "fell to cutting of forkes or posts, and poles or rafters, and Palmito boughs, or Plantain leaves, and with great speed set up, to the number of six houses. For everie of which, they first fastned deepe into the ground three or foure great posts with forkes; upon them they layd one Transome, which was commonly about twentie foot, and made the sides in the manner of the roofes of our Country houses, thatching it close with those aforesayd leaves, which keeps out water a long time, observing alwayes that in the lower ground, where greater heat was, they left some three or foure foot open unthatcht below, and made the houses, or rather roofes, so many foot the higher. But in the hils, wher the aire was more peircing and the nights colder, they made our roomes alwayes lower, and thatched them close to the ground, leaving only one doore to enter at, and a lover-hole [louvre] for a vent, in the midst of the roofe. In everie one of these they made foure severall lodgings, and three fires, one in the middest, and one at each end of everie house, so that the roome was most temperately warme, and nothing annoyed with smoake, partly by reason of the wood which they use to burne, yielding verie little smoake, partly by reason of their artificial making of it, as firing the wood (cut in length like our billets) at the ends, and joyning them together so close, that though no flame or fire did appeare, yet the heat continued without intermission" (*Documents concerning English Voyages to the Spanish Main,* 296–97).

9. *St. Augustine Expedition of 1740: A Report to the South Carolina General Assembly. Reprinted from the Colonial Records of South Carolina, with an introduction by John Tate Lanning* (Columbia, S.C., 1954), 25.

10. Antonio de Benavides (former governor of St. Augustine and governor of Vera Cruz) to Philip V, Apr. 28, 1738, AGI, 58-2-16 45, Joseph B. Lockey Collection, PKY.

11. Purchases and Payments for 1739, Cuba 446, AGI.

12. Fugitive Blacks of the English plantations to Philip V, June 10, 1738, SD 844, microfilm reel 15, PKY.

13. Council of the Indies, Oct. 2, 1739, cited in Irene Wright, "Dispatches," 178–80; Council of the Indies, Sept. 28, 1740, SD 845, microfilm reel 16, PKY.

14. Viceroys in seventeenth-century Mexico also used the term Republica de Negros to describe free black towns such as San Miguel de Soyaltepeque (Indios 32, microfilm

reel 12) and San Lorenzo de Cerralvo (Indios 1741, Archivo General de la Nación, Mexico City). This older terminology fell out of use by the eighteenth century.

15. Richard Morse, "Framework for Latin American Urban History," in *Urbanization in Latin America: Approaches and Issues,* ed. Jorge Hardoy (Garden City, N.Y., 1975), 57–107.

16. De la Guardia, *Negros del istmo de Panamá,* 96; Miguel Acosta Saignes, *Vida de los esclavos negros en Venezuela* (Caracas, 1967), chaps. 13 and 14; Palmer, *Slaves of the White God,* 129–30; Arrom and Arévalo, *Cimarrón,* 84.

17. Manuel de Montiano to Philip V, Feb. 16, 1739, SD 845, microfilm reel 16, PKY. The regular branch of the clergy (priests belonging to religious orders such as the Jesuits and the Franciscans) usually served as frontier missionaries to the Indians, while secular priests ministered to the Christians living in Spanish cities.

18. It is lucky for historians that some villagers chose to hold these ceremonies in St. Augustine for none of the Franciscan books from Mose, or any of St. Augustine's satellite Indian villages, have ever been located.

19. Accounts of Sebastián Sánchez, royal treasurer, Mar. 1739–Dec. 1739, Jan. 17, 1740, Cuba 446, AGI; Accounts of Juan Estévan de Peña, royal treasurer, Feb. 27, 1759, SD 2604, AGI. On ritual celebrations in Mexico City, see Curcio-Nagy, "Giants and Gypsies."

20. *Journal of the Commons House of Assembly,* vol. 3, *May 18, 1741–July 10, 1742,* ed. J. H. Easterby (Columbia, S.C., 1951), 83.

21. *Stephens' Journal, 1737–1740,* ed. Allen D. Candler, vol. 4 of *The Colonial Records of the State of Georgia* (Atlanta, 1906), 248. If eight of Davis's nineteen slaves were "workmen," perhaps the other eleven were their wives and children (Manuel de Montiano to Juan Francisco de Güemes y Horcasitas, Feb. 16, 1739, SD 845, microfilm reel 16, PKY). Davis told Montiano that he knew through an informant in Barbados that General Oglethorpe planned to send one thousand men in twenty war ships against St. Augustine (Manuel de Montiano to Juan Francisco de Güemes y Horcasitas, Aug. 31, 1738, *Letters of Montiano; Siege of St. Agustine* [*sic*], vol. 7, pt. 1 of Collections of the Georgia Historical Society [Savannah, 1909] [hereafter cited as *Letters of Montiano*], 27). In a later letter Montiano wrote, "I have had a thorough understanding with Devis [*sic*] and succeeded in making him reveal the present state of these colonies, their news and plans" (Montiano to Juan Francisco de Güemes y Horcasitas, Jan. 3, 1739, ibid.). Davis was apparently playing both sides and also informing General Oglethorpe about St. Augustine (*Stephens' Journal,* 247).

22. Claim of Captain Caleb Davis, Sept. 17, 1751, SD 2584, AGI; *Journal of the Commons House of Assembly,* vol. 1, *Nov. 10, 1736–June 7, 1739,* ed. J. H. Easterby (Columbia, S.C., 1951), 595–97. There is no evidence that Davis ever recouped his losses.

23. Some of these men were "Cattel-hunters" belonging to Captain Macpherson, whose horses they stole, and the runaways would have had opportunity to know the terrain. Although a large posse failed to recapture them, Indian allies of the English did kill one slave ("Account of the Negroe Insurrection," 232–33, cited in Wood, *Black Majority,* 310–11).

24. Lt. Gov. Bull to the duke of Newcastle, May, 1739, BPRO Trans., vol. 20, 40–41, cited in Wood, *Black Majority,* 311–12. Also see Representation of President William Bull, May 25, 1738, *Calendar of State Papers, Colonial Series, America and West Indies,* vol. 44, ed. K. G. Davies (London), 243–45.

25. *Journal of the Commons House of Assembly,* vol. 1, *Nov. 10, 1736–June 7, 1739,* 680–81.

26. Manuel de Montiano to Juan Francisco de Güemes y Horcasitas, Aug. 19, 1739, *Letters of Montiano,* 32.

27. *Journal of the Commons House of Assembly,* vol. 2, *Sept. 12, 1739–May 10, 1740,* 63–67. The most complete analysis of Stono is offered by Peter H. Wood in *Black Majority.* A more traditional account of the rebellion is found in Eugene Sirmans, *Colonial South Carolina: A Political History, 1663–1763* (Chapel Hill, N.C., 1966).

28. According to Thornton, the rebels, who stopped along the road and "set to dancing, Singing and beating the Drums to draw more Negroes to them," were performing dances that were a central element of military training and war preparations in the Kongo (John K. Thornton, "African Dimensions of the Stono Rebellion," *American Historical Review* 96 [Oct. 1991]: 1101–13). For more on Congo war techniques see John K. Thornton, "African Soldiers in the Haitian Revolution," *Journal of Caribbean History* 25 (1991): 58–80. (Throughout this book I have followed the common practice among historians of the region of using *Congo* for the people and *Kongo* for the place.)

The slaves decapitated their first two victims—shopkeepers whose heads they placed on the stairs for maximum shock value. In turn, the Carolinians decapitated many more (some accounts say fifty) of the captured slaves and set their heads on the mile posts along the road ("A Ranger's Report of Travels with General Oglethorpe, 1739–1742," *Travels in the American Colonies,* ed. Newton D. Mereness [New York, 1916], 222–23; Wood, *Black Majority,* chap. 12). Robin Law shows that ritual decapitation of enemies was an important feature of warfare in contemporary Dahomey and that warriors valued heads as trophies of war. Castration of enemies was also common, but later in the eighteenth century these practices were forbidden by Dahomean leaders (Robin Law, "'My Head Belongs to the King': On the Political and Ritual Significance of Decapitation in Pre-Colonial Dahomey," *Journal of African History* 30 (1989): 399–415).

29. Sirmans, *Colonial South Carolina,* 208.

30. "Extract of a Letter from South Carolina Dated October 2," *Gentleman's Magazine* (London), n.s. 10 (1740): 127–29, in *American Negro Slavery: A Documentary History,* ed. Michael Mullin (Columbia, S.C., 1976), 84–87.

31. Wood, *Black Majority,* 326; *Stephens' Journal,* 592.

32. This document complained about lost labor but did not anticipate the more serious danger of the Stono Rebellion, which broke out later that year (Harvey H. Jackson, "The Darien Antislavery Petition of 1739 and the Georgia Plan," *William and Mary Quarterly,* 3d ser., 34 [1977]: 618–19).

33. TePaske, *Governorship,* 139–46; Ricardo Torres-Reyes, *The British Siege of St. Augustine, 1740* (Denver, 1972). One of Oglethorpe's valued scouts, whom he named Captain

Jack, was a black who deserted from St. Augustine (Deposition of William Palmer, Feb. 19, 1740, *St. Augustine Expedition of 1740,* 125). The Georgia accounts of the siege and its aftermath can be followed in *General Oglethorpe's Georgia: Colonial Letters, 1738–1743,* vol. 2, ed. Mills Lane (Savannah, 1975), 422–510. On estimates of Indian allies and black pioneers see *Journal of the Commons House of Assembly,* vol. 3, *May 18, 1741–July 10, 1742,* 168–76. The same volume includes a narrative of the expedition by the Carolinians and Oglethorpe's account (ibid., 93–248). Montiano's account of the same time period can be found in *Letters of Montiano.*

34. On Jan. 8, 1740, Captain Pedro Lamberto Horruytiner commanded a group of twenty-five Florida cavalrymen, twenty-five Spanish infantrymen, and thirty Indians and free blacks (Manuel de Montiano to Juan Francisco de Güemes y Horcasitas, Jan. 31, 1740, SD 2658, AGI). On Jan. 27, 1740, Montiano sent Don Romualdo Ruiz del Moral out on a similar mission with "twenty-five horsemen, twenty-five Indians, and twenty-five free blacks." Montiano lamented, "The difficulty of getting information in our numerous thickets, lagoons, and swamps, is so great as to make the thing almost impossible" (Manuel de Montiano to Juan Francisco de Güemes y Horcasitas, Jan. 31, 1740, *Letters of Montiano,* 36).

35. *General Oglethorpe's Georgia: Colonial Letters,* 447, 507. One of the captured blacks had escaped from a Mrs. Parker in Carolina, and the other said he had been stolen from Colonel Gibbs by Indians. Their houses were apparently well-built, for Oglethorpe refused to allow the Carolinians to burn them, saying they would house the inhabitants he planned to introduce into Florida (*St. Augustine Expedition of 1740,* 23).

36. Zora Neale Hurston, "Communications," *Journal of Negro History* 12 (Oct. 1927): 666.

37. Manuel de Montiano to Juan Francisco de Güemes y Horcasitas, Jan. 31, 1740, *Letters of Montiano,* 40–42.

38. Manuel de Montiano to Juan Francisco de Güemes y Horcasitas, Jan. 17, 1740, SD 2658, AGI; Manuel de Montiano to Juan Francisco de Güemes y Horcasitas, July 6, 1740, *Letters of Montiano,* 56–58; Manuel de Montiano to Juan Francisco de Güemes y Horcasitas, Aug. 9, 1740, SD 845, microfilm reel 16, PKY.

39. *General Oglethorpe's Georgia: Colonial Letters,* 447; *St. Augustine Expedition of 1740,* 47; TePaske, *Governorship,* 143.

40. [James Killpatrick], *An Impartial Account of the Late Expedition against St. Augustine under General Oglethorpe,* facsimile reproduction of the 1742 edition, ed. Aileen Moore Topping (Gainesville, Fla., 1978). After carefully analyzing Oglethorpe's effort, Phinizy Spalding wrote, "In the final analysis the fate of the expedition was sealed at the breached walls of the Negro fort, Mosa" (*Oglethorpe in America* [Athens, Ga., 1984], 115–16, 124).

41. Phinizy Spalding describes the "pamphlet war" that broke out in London as supporters of Oglethorpe countered, and supporters of the Carolinians responded in kind. For an Oglethorpe apologist see "A Ranger's Report of Travels with General Oglethorpe, 1739–1742." Spalding argues that all these accounts focus on Anglo leaders and ignore the "careful and effective defense" mounted by Governor Montiano and the "stubborn and intelligent opposition" of his forces (*Oglethorpe in America,* 118–19, 122).

42. B. R. Carroll, *Historical Collection of South Carolina, Embracing Many Rare and Valuable Pamphlets and Other Documents Relating to the History of the State from Its First Discovery to Its Independence in the Year of 1776,* vol. 2 (New York, 1836), 354. The Carolinians obviously knew these characterizations of idle, mischievous blacks to be untrue, for they had seen firsthand and described the carefully tilled fields and well-built houses and fort at Mose.

43. Lyle N. McAlister, "Social Structure and Social Change in New Spain," *Hispanic American Historical Review* 43 (Apr. 1963): 349–70; John K. Chance, *Race and Class in Colonial Oaxaca* (Stanford, 1978); Robert McCaa, "*Calidad, Clase,* and Marriage in Colonial Mexico: The Case of Parral, 1788–90," *Hispanic American Historical Review* 64 (Aug. 1984): 477–501.

44. Manuel de Montiano to Juan Francisco de Güemes y Horcasitas, Jan. 17, 1740, SD 2658, AGI; Manuel de Montiano to Juan Francisco de Güemes y Horcasitas, Aug. 9, 1740, SD 845, microfilm reel 18, PKY; *Letters of Montiano,* 54–62.

45. The first permanent militia units of free mulattoes and blacks were organized in Cuba as early as 1600 and these were preserved during the extensive military reforms of Charles III (1759–88). Unlike provincial or urban militias which were supported by individual or corporate sponsors and active only during emergencies, the disciplined units were a part of the Spanish army, with standardized battalions and regiments, regular officers, systematic training, and state provisioning and pay (Pedro Deschamps Chapeaux, *Los batallones de pardos y morenos libres* [Havana, 1976], 20–33; Klein, "Colored Militia of Cuba").

46. Manuel de Montiano to Juan Francisco de Güemes y Horcasitas, Mar. 13, 1742, SD 2593. The captain general's response is found in "The Spanish Official Account of the Attack on the Colony of Georgia, in America, and of Its Defeat on St. Simon's Island by General James Oglethorpe," *Collections of the Georgia Historical Society,* vol. 7, pt. 3 (Savannah, Ga., 1913), 32–35.

47. General Oglethorpe to the duke of Newcastle, July 30, 1742, in *Historical Collections of Georgia* (New York, 1854), 463–67; Spalding, *Oglethorpe in America,* chap. 9. I am indebted to Daniel Deans for referring me to a contemporary report by an English participant that inflated Montiano's force to "fifty-six sails" and "seven thousand to eight thousand men" (Patrick Sutherland, "An Account of the Late Invasion of Georgia," *London Gazette,* Dec. 25, 1742). For a Spanish account see the Journal of Antonio de Arredondo, chief engineer, June 5, 1742, in "Spanish Official Account of the Attack on the Colony of Georgia," 52–71.

48. *Boston Weekly Magazine,* Mar. 9, 1743, no. 2, 16. I am indebted to Peter H. Wood for this reference.

49. [Edward Kimber], *A Relation or Journal of a Late Expedition,* facsimile reproduction of the 1744 edition, ed. John Jay TePaske (Gainesville, Fla., 1976), 15.

50. Ibid., 30.

51. Memorial of Francisco Menéndez, Nov. 21, 1740, SD 2658, AGI.

52. Ibid. Spanish notarial practice required illiterates to sign official documents with

an X and for a notary or two witnesses to write underneath, "for ———, who does not know how to write." Menéndez may have been literate in several of the languages he spoke and may have learned his good Spanish while he was a slave of the royal accountant, his godfather, Don Francisco Menéndez Márquez.

53. Manuel de Montiano to Philip V, Sept. 16, 1740, SD 2658, AGI.

54. "Account of the *Revenge*," in *Privateering and Piracy in the Colonial Period: Illustrative Documents*, ed. John Franklin Jameson (New York, 1923), 378–473, esp. 399–403. My thanks to Charles Tingley for this reference.

55. In 1744 the *South Carolina Gazette* estimated that 113 well-manned and well-supplied privateering vessels raided from the British colonies and that many comparable Spanish vessels were based in Havana (Joyce Elizabeth Harmon, *Trade and Privateering in Spanish Florida, 1732–1763* [St. Augustine, Fla., 1969], 35; TePaske, *Governorship*, 100–105).

56. *Between the Devil and the Deep Blue Sea: Merchant Seamen, Pirates and the Anglo-American Maritime World* (Cambridge, 1987), 286; W. Jeffrey Bolster, "'To Feel like a Man': Black Seamen in the Northern States, 1800–1860," *Journal of American History* 76 (Mar. 1990): 1179, 1183. For a firsthand account of a New England slave's maritime adventures in the same period see *A Narrative of the Uncommon Sufferings and Surprizing Deliverance of Briton Hammond, a Negro Man, Servant to General Winslow of Marshfield, in New England; Who returned to Boston, after having been absent almost Thirteen Years* (Boston, 1760), reprinted in *The Garland Library of Narratives of North American Indian Captivities*, vol. 8 (New York, 1978).

57. Manuel de Montiano to Juan Francisco de Güemes y Horcasitas, Jan. 2, 1741 (*Letters of Montiano*, 68–70).

58. Blacks captured in one of the Spanish ships were "disposed of to several Persons in Town [Charleston]," but with the assistance of slaves, they made it to the harbor, stole a longboat, and escaped (*Boston Weekly News Ledger*, Sept. 24–Oct. 10, 1741). I am indebted to Peter H. Wood for this reference. Later that summer the rest of Estrada's crewmen captured two other English sloops and a ship loaded with lumber that was bound for South Carolina. Montiano's reports also identified Don Juan Trujillo, Don Agustín Gallardo, Domingo de la Cruz, and Don Joseph Sánchez Rodríguez as corsairs (Manuel de Montiano to Joseph de la Quintana, Oct. 10, 1741, SD 2584, AGI).

59. Estrada's second raid on Ocracoke took place in July 1741, and his prizes included three sloops and a ship loaded with lumber bound for South Carolina ("Account of the *Revenge*," 399, 402–11).

60. Ibid., 399–403.

61. Ibid., 402–3, 408–11. Norton made no reference to, and may not have known of, the English offer of $50.00 to Indian allies for every scalp taken among the Spaniards (Manuel de Montiano to Juan Francisco de Güemes y Horcasitas, Aug. 31, 1738, *Letters of Montiano*, 25–27).

62. T. J. Davis, *A Rumor of Revolt: The "Great Negro Plot" in Colonial New York* (New York, 1985), 18–19, 79, 81, 98–99, 117, 119–24, 131–37.

63. Ibid., 225–26; "Journal of a Privateersman," *Atlantic Monthly* 8 (1861): 354.

64. "Account of the *Revenge.*"

65. Norton used more hyperbolic invective in describing a captured Frenchman who swore on a cross, "blest and Sanctyfyd by the poluted words and hands of a wretched priest, a Spawn of the whore of Babylon, who is a Monster of Nature and a Servant to the Devill, Who for a Riall will pretend to absolve them from perjury, Incest and parricide" ("Account of the *Revenge,*" 409–10).

66. Menéndez, whom Norton described as "the old Negro Capt.," was sold for only thirty-four pesos, when a prime hand would sell for no less than two hundred pesos. If he fought as a young man in the Yamasee War (1715), he was probably under fifty years old in 1741, but his dangerous reputation may have also lowered his value. The court ruled Augustine was a also a slave and thus could be sold, but it decided Pedro Sancho and And'w Estavie were prisoners of war to be held until ransomed. Augustine was not sold and remained on the *Revenge* as a prisoner when it once again set sail ("Account of the *Revenge,*" 410–11, 414, 416). Among the fifty-five men claiming shares in the prize were three black crewmen from the *Revenge:* the drummer, Richard Norton, the cook, Daniel Walker, and a sailor, Samuel Kerby. Richard Norton earned one full share, the same earned by the company quartermaster, the gunner's mate, and some of the sailors. Most of the sailors earned a three-quarters share, as did Samuel Kerby and Daniel Walker (ibid., 384, 395).

67. "Ex Parte Seventeen Indians Molattos & Negroes," in *Report of Cases in the Vice Admiralty of the Province of New York and in the Court of Admiralty of the State of New York, 1715–1788,* ed. Charles Merrill Hough (New Haven, Conn., 1925), 29–31. Captain Joseph de Espinosa testified and provided documentation from Havana for seventeen men, but the New York court recognized only Anthony de Torres, Fernando Bernal, Anthony Aguilar, and Manuel Servantes [*sic*] (a mulatto) as free.

68. As an incentive to undertake this mission and in order to recover his costs, the governor also allowed Captain Laguna to sell a cargo in New York. Laguna returned to St. Augustine with a shipment of flour, butter, wax, window glass, china, and milling stones (Report of Captain Fernando Laguna, Oct. 7, 1752, SD 846, microfilm reel 17, PKY).

69. Of the forty-five captives, twenty were members of the Batallones de Pardos y Morenos Libres de Havana and carried certificates from their commander (Melchor de Navarrete to Francisco Cagigal, July 7, 1750, SD 2584, AGI).

70. Fulgencio García de Solís to Ferdinand VI, Aug. 25, 1752, SD 845, microfilm reel 17, PKY. The Spanish privateer captained by Francisco Loranzano and captured by the *Revenge* in 1741 had a crew of forty-eight sailors, eleven of whom were of African descent ("Account of the *Revenge,*" 427).

71. Certifications of freedom by Don Simon Básquez, Royal Notary of St. Augustine, July 4, 1750, SD 2584, AGI; Fulgencio García de Solís to Francisco Cagigal, Aug. 25, 1752, SD 846, microfilm reel 17, PKY. Both of the liberated men were mulattoes, and the English may have been more willing to consider them as free men than their darker-skinned fellows, although the Spanish officials provided the same types of documentation for all. Francisco Pérez, who was in the possession of William Walton, may have been freed as a

goodwill gesture because Walton's merchant company did business with St. Augustine. Walton also was "the largest slave importer [into New York] during the years 1715–1764" (James G. Lydon, "New York and the Slave Trade, 1700–1714," *William and Mary Quarterly,* 3d ser. 35 [Apr. 1978]: 389–90).

72. Census of Ginés Sánchez, Feb. 12, 1759, SD 2604, AGI.

73. Manuel de Montiano to Juan Francisco de Güemes y Horcasitas, Aug. 7, 1740, *Letters of Montiano,* 65–67. The Crown did not provide the black troops/laborers Montiano asked for. Three years later the royal engineer complained he only had fifty-seven *forzados* (convict laborers) on hand for all the fortification work, and of that number some were "useless on account of old age" (Report of Antonio de Arredondo, Mar. 3, 1743, Brooks Transcripts, PKY).

74. Francisco Cagigal to Melchor de Navarrete, May 18, 1749, SD 2584, AGI.

75. Lucas de Palacio to Julian de Arriaga, June 1, 1759, SD 2584, AGI. Governor Palacio reported that a total of 175 Canary Islanders had arrived by then, in addition to "diverse family groups, whites as well as blacks, with abilities appropriate to agricultural labor."

76. "A Review of Economic Conditions," in *Colonial South Carolina Scene,* 173–74.

77. On the multi-ethnic nature of the eighteenth-century city see the essays in *Spanish St. Augustine: The Archaeology of a Colonial Creole Community,* ed. Kathleen A. Deagan (New York, 1983).

78. Melchor de Navarrete to Francisco Cagigal, Apr. 2, 1752, cited in Irene Wright, "Dispatches," 184–86. Navarrete asked that he be awarded some title or his family some distinction for his efforts to evangelize the escaped slaves.

79. *Against the Odds;* Jorge Juan and Antonio de Ulloa, "Eighteenth-Century Spanish American Towns: African and Afro-Hispanic Life and Labor in Cities and Suburbs," in *The African in Latin America,* ed. Anne Pescatello (New York, 1975), 106–11; *Neither Slave nor Free.*

80. Historians have commonly assumed that *mestizaje* (racial mixing) involved concubinage and, less frequently, marriage, between Spanish men and Native American women, but Parker has documented Indian men marrying Spanish women, even in one case, the kinswoman of the governor (Susan R. Parker, "Spanish St. Augustine's 'Urban' Indians," *El Escribano* 32 [1993]: 1–15).

81. Pedro Sánchez de Griñan to Julian de Arriaga, July 7, 1756, cited in Michael C. Scardaville and Jesús María Belmonte, "Florida in the Late First Spanish Period: The Griñan Report," *El Escribano* 16 (1979): 1–24.

82. Fulgencio García de Solís to Ferdinand VI, Nov. 29, 1752, SD 844, microfilm reel 17, PKY.

83. He also called the Indians living in St. Augustine "Indios ladinos," a term also used for persons of African descent who had learned Spanish and were Christians (Testimonios y autos . . . entre el cura . . . y el guardian del convento, 1745, SD 864, AGI).

84. Baptism of Domingo, Dec. 10, 1744; Baptism of Miguel, Sept. 29, 1746; Baptism of Francisco, Oct. 14, 1746; Baptism of Miguel Domingo, Jan. 26, 1748, Black Baptisms, CPR, microfilm reel 284 F, PKY.

85. Because town formation was considered critical to territorial control, Spanish governors who established (or reestablished) towns could later claim that as an important service to the Crown (Fulgencio García de Solís to Ferdinand VI, Dec. 7, 1752, AGI 58-1-33/25, cited in Irene Wright, "Dispatches," 187).

86. Deagan and Landers, "Excavating Fort Mose."

87. Report of Father Juan de Solana, Apr. 22, 1759, SD 2584, AGI.

88. Because the St. Augustine church had never formally incorporated the Mose church to itself, Bishop Morell of Cuba advised Father Solana that there were no grounds to fight the appointment of the Franciscans (Julian de Arriaga to Alonso Fernández de Heredia, enclosing royal order approving the Franciscan jurisdiction, Oct. 13, 1756, SD 846, microfilm reel 18, PKY; Pedro Agustín Morell to Julian de Arriaga, Sept. 9, 1757, ibid.; Juan Joseph de Solana to Juan Francisco de Güemes y Horcasitas, Sept. 15, 1757, ibid).

89. Andrés de Vilches's request to retire, Dec. 8, 1757, SD 864, AGI.

90. List of Franciscan Missionaries in Florida, June 23, 1738, ST 5743, PKY; Maynard Geiger, *Biographical Dictionary of the Franciscans in Spanish Florida and Cuba (1528–1841)* (Patterson, N.J., 1940), 52, 104, 116.

91. Vía was a native of Florida who had earlier ministered to the Tamasee in Apalachee (Geiger, *Biographical Dictionary,* 115).

92. Evacuation report of Juan Joseph Eligio de la Puente, Jan. 22, 1764, SD 2595, AGI.

93. Census of Father Ginés Sánchez, Feb. 12, 1759, SD 2604, AGI. Contemporary censuses at the remaining Indian villages recorded only eight households of thirty-two people at Nuestra Señora de Guadalupe de Tolomato. They were the last remnants of many diverse nations; fifteen identified as Chiluque, thirteen as Ibaja, two as Yamasee, one as Chaschis, and one as Uchise. Nuestra Señora de la Leche, north of St. Augustine, had only eleven similarly mixed households (Census of Father Alonso Ruiz, Feb. 10, 1759, ibid.; Hann, "Fallout from the Yamasee War").

94. Census of Father Ginés Sánchez, Feb. 12, 1759, SD 2604, AGI. At the time of the census, Francisco Roso, Tomás Chrisóstomo, Francisco Xavier de Torres and his son, Juan de Arranzate, Pedro Graxales, Joseph de Peña, Juan Francisco de Torres, Joseph Fernández, and Juan Baptista all had slave wives in St. Augustine. The frequency of children born to these unions is testimony that conjugal rights were honored by the slaveowners, as required by the Church.

95. Black Baptisms, CPR, microfilm reel 284 F; Black Marriages, CPR, microfilm reel 284 C; Black Burials, CPR, microfilm reel 284 D, PKY.

96. Francisco and Ana were on the list of Carolinians petitioning for freedom in 1738 (SD 844, microfilm reel 15, PKY). Baptism of Francisca Xaviera, Aug. 30, 1736, and Baptism of Calisto, Oct. 23, 1738, Black Baptisms, CPR, microfilm reel 284 F, PKY. Marriage of the widowed Ana García Pedroso to Diego, the slave of Don Juan Joseph Eligio de la Puente, Jan. 14, 1759, Black Marriages, CPR, microfilm reel 284 C, PKY. Mose militia list, included in the evacuation report of Juan Joseph Eligio de la Puente, Jan. 22, 1764, SD 2595, AGI.

97. In 1738 Juan Jacinto Rodríguez and Ana María Menéndez petitioned for their free-

dom and were listed as the slaves of Petronila Pérez (SD 844, fol. 594, PKY). They were married while enslaved on Oct. 9, 1735 (Black Marriages, CPR, microfilm reel 284 C, PKY). After Juan Jacinto died, Ana María married the free black Antonio de Urisa, of the Lara nation, on Apr. 26, 1740 (ibid.). Juan Jacinto and Ana María's daughter, María Francisca, was baptized on Oct. 11, 1736, while she was still the slave of Petronila Pérez (Black Baptisms, CPR, microfilm reel 284 F, PKY). See also Baptism of Cecilia, Sept. 9, 1737, Black Baptisms, CPR, microfilm reel 284 F, PKY. Juan Lamberto Horruytiner married Cecilia Horruytiner on July 12, 1739 (Black Marriages, CPR, microfilm reel 284 C, PKY); see also Marriage of María Francisca to Marcos de Torres, Aug. 20, 1742, ibid. (The designation "legitimate" denoted someone born to married parents and reflected higher status than a person born of unmarried parents, who would be only a "natural" child.) See the baptism of the daughter of María Francisca and Marcos de Torres, María, May 20, 1743, and of their son, Nicolás de la Concepción, Jan. 10, 1746 (Black Baptisms, CPR, microfilm reel 284 F, PKY). See also the marriage of Tomás Chrisóstomo and María Francisca, Dec. 15, 1760 (Black Marriages, CPR, microfilm reel 284 C, PKY).

98. Marriage of Tomás Chrisóstomo and Ana María Ronquillo, Feb. 28, 1745, Black Marriages, CPR, microfilm reel 284 C, PKY. Baptism of Pedro Graxales, Dec. 9, 1738, Black Baptisms, CPR, microfilm reel 284 F, PKY. Marriage of Pedro Graxales and María de la Concepción Hita, Jan. 19, 1744, Black Marriages, CPR, microfilm reel 284 C, PKY. Baptisms of their children, María, Nov. 8, 1744; Manuela de los Angeles, Jan. 6, 1747; Ysidora de los Angeles, Dec. 22, 1748; Joseph Ynisario, Apr. 4, 1755; Juana Feliciana, July 13, 1757; Pantaleona, Aug. 1, 1758; and María de los Dolores, Aug. 16, 1761, Black Baptisms, CPR, microfilm reel 284 F, PKY.

99. When Mose was first established, Palica held eleven families and forty-eight persons (Report of Manuel de Montiano, Dec. 31, 1738, cited in Geiger, *Biographical Dictionary,* 139).

100. Punta held fourteen families and fifty-one individuals in 1738 (ibid., 139).

101. Marriage of Manuel (Juan Manuel) Chrisóstomo and Antonia Chrisóstomo, Jan. 10, 1744, Black Marriages, CPR, microfilm reel 284 C, PKY. Marriage of Pablo Prezilla and María Magdalena, June 17, 1743, ibid.; Marriage of Phelipe Gutiérres and María Magdalena, Oct. 25, 1745, ibid. Marriage of Juan Manuel Manressa (of Punta) and Joseph Candelaria, May 26, 1747, ibid. Baptism of Manuel Rutiner, legitimate son of Juan Chrisóstomo and María Antonia Espinosa, born Jan. 30, 1744 and baptized Feb. 4, 1744 (Black Baptisms, CPR, microfilm reel 284 F, PKY) and Manuel Rutiner's marriage to Felipa Urisa, June 19, 1756 (Black Marriages, CPR, microfilm reel 284 C, PKY). Because his mother was still a slave, Manuel was a slave, as was his wife. One of the couple's marriage sponsors was Ignacio Roso, of Mose. For the locations of Indian villages near St. Augustine see Howard F. Cline, *Florida Indians II: Provisional Historical Gazeteer with Locational Notes on Florida Colonial Communities* (New York, 1974), map no. 3.

102. Representative Bill Clark of Fort Lauderdale spearheaded efforts of the Florida Black Caucus to secure state funding for historical and archaeological research on Mose and I was contracted as historian on the project. The Fort Mose site has since been acquired by the National Park Service and designated a National Historic Landmark.

103. Deagan and Landers, "Excavating Fort Mose." For a review of other archaeology at African and African American sites on the southeastern Atlantic coast, see Ferguson, *Uncommon Ground;* and for slave sites see Theresa A. Singleton, "The Archaeology of Slave Life," in *Before Freedom Came: African-American Life in the Antebellum South,* ed. Edward D. C. Campbell and Kym S. Rice (Richmond, 1991), 155–75.

104. Another reading may reflect the common West and Central African belief that upon death the deceased would be transported again across the waters to their homeland (Georgia Writers' Project, *Drums and Shadows: Survival Studies among the Georgia Coastal Negroes* [Athens, Ga., 1986], 195–96, 220–22).

105. Descriptions of the black and Indian villages can be found in Father Juan de Solana to Don Pedro Agustín Morell de Santa Cruz, Apr. 22, 1759, SD 516, microfilm reel 28 K, PKY. Gopher tortoises appear in all other known faunal collections from St. Augustine, with the exception of the Indian and African villages (Elizabeth J. Reitz, "Zooarchaeological Analysis of a Free African American Community: Gracia Real de Santa Teresa de Mose," *Historical Archaeology* 28 [1994]:23–40). For comparable analysis of Spanish, criollo, and mestizo household sites see Elizabeth J. Reitz and Stephen L. Cumbaa, "Diet and Foodways of Eighteenth-Century Spanish St. Augustine," in *Spanish St. Augustine: The Archaeology of a Colonial Creole Community,* ed. Kathleen A. Deagan (New York, 1983), 151–85.

106. Father Juan Joseph de Solana to Bishop Pedro Agustín Morell de Santa Cruz, Apr. 22, 1759, SD 516, microfilm reel 28 K, PKY.

107. Protest of the Canary Islanders, Dec. 10, 1758, SD 2660, AGI.

108. Francisco Cagigal to Lucas de Palacio, Apr. 22, 1759, SD 2584, AGI.

109. TePaske, *Governorship,* 227–29. Havana Company officials reported English corsairs seized a company ship which was taking food supplies from Puerto Principe to St. Augustine (Fernando Treviño to Martín de Arostegui, Apr. 8, 1744, ST 55-6-35/12, SD 500, AGI, PKY). Two other company ships that left Cádiz with supplies destined for Florida were seized two months later by English corsairs; the *Conde de Chincho* was taken off Tortuga, and the *Peregrina* was taken at the Cayo de Confites (Martín de Arostegui to Fernando Treviño, June 10, 1744, ST 55-6-35/14, SD 500, AGI, PKY; Father Juan Joseph de Solana to Bishop Pedro Agustín Morell de Santa Cruz, Apr. 22, 1759, SD 516, microfilm reel 28 K, PKY).

110. This is not an isolated example of Indians making political statements by destroying animals or crops they could have well used.

111. Salacaliche does not appear on any contemporary or modern maps, so its precise location is unknown, but the reference to Apalachee indicates it must have been west of St. Augustine. The Indians told the courier that if they had one among them who had hurt so many they would kill him themselves and suggested that solution to the Spaniard, who answered he could not kill an appointee of the king. Father Solana also accused Governor Palacio of irreverence and insults toward the church and of corruption, specifically with regard to the sale of offices and illicit trade with the English (Report of Father Juan de Solana, Apr. 22, 1759, SD 2584, AGI; TePaske, *Governorship,* 37–38).

112. Although the report does not specifically state this, the regular army men posted at Mose may have included members of the Disciplined Militia of Free Pardos and Morenos from Havana (Report of Father Juan de Solana, Apr. 22, 1759, SD 2584, AGI).

113. Díaz, Gallardo, and Roso owned stone homes. De Castilla had a home made partially of stone and partially of plank, and Eligio, Chrisóstomo, and Escovedo had plank homes (Juan Joseph Eligio de la Puente, city map and key, Jan. 22, 1764, PKY). Pedro de Léon, of the Mose militia, and Sergeant Marcos de Ortega, commander of the Disciplined Militia of Pardos and Morenos of Havana, each owned a *solar,* or lot, in St. Augustine, according to this map, and it is possible, but not certain, that the owner of the stone house at L 170, listed as Francisco Mendez, was Francisco Menéndez.

114. Governor Antonio de Benavides had also remarked on the lush terrain and good hardwoods near Mose which could provide building materials (Report of Antonio de Benavides, SD 58-2-16/4 bundle 5725, SC, PKY). Maps drawn by the British show Mose after the trees had been felled. Feliú's ambitious revitalization measures were viewed with great favor by the royal officials of St. Augustine. Feliú also addressed the hunger in the province by arranging for two canoe loads of oysters to be gathered daily for the neediest settlers (Royal Officials of St. Augustine to Julian de Arriaga, Feb. 20, 1763, SD 2542 B, microfilm reel 20, PKY). On Feliú's success with the Indians see TePaske, *Governorship,* 224–25.

115. Captain Manuel Asención Soto commanded the troops of the Disciplined Militia of Free Pardos and Morenos of Havana assigned to St. Augustine, assisted by an adjutant, Juan Fermín de Quixas, a sergeant, Antonio Horrutinier, and seven soldiers (Cuba 1667, AGI).

116. Manuel de Montiano to Juan Francisco de Güemes y Horcasitas, Aug. 7, 1740, *Letters of Montiano,* 66.

117. Evacuation report of Juan Joseph Eligio de la Puente, Jan. 22, 1764, SD 2595, AGI.

118. Fugitive blacks of the English Plantations to Philip V, June 10, 1738, SD 844, microfilm reel 15, PKY. Sergeant Fermín de Quixas's military career in the disciplined pardo militia of Havana began in 1730 and lasted almost a half century. He served ten years as a soldier and then began a slow ascent to finally achieve the rank of captain. In St. Augustine he served as adjutant of the company under the command of his brother-in-law, Manuel Asención Soto, and supervised the Mose militia in military construction projects, including the provisional fort on the San Sebastián River, which was almost completed at the time of the cession to the British. After leaving St. Augustine de Quixas served a period at sea and finally settled in Havana where he applied twice, once in 1801 and again in 1811, for the position of captain in the disciplined pardo militia of that plaza (Cuba 1667, AGI).

119. Instructions concerning the evacuation, July 6 and Nov. 24, 1763, documents 14–24 and 60–63, Archivo General de la Nación, SC, PKY, and cited in Robert L. Gold, "The Settlement of the Pensacola Indians in New Spain, 1763–1770," *Hispanic American Historical Review* 45 (Nov. 1965): 567–76.

120. For many examples of fugitive slaves receiving sanctuary in Spanish colonies, see

Documents relating to fugitive slaves, Indiferente General 1787, AGI. The creation of free black towns in the circum-Caribbean is the subject of my next book.

Chapter 3
Transitions

1. Also on board the same ship was Manuel Asención Soto and seven members of the disciplined pardo militia and their families, totaling eighteen individuals. Other members of the Mose community sailed on different days and ships (Juan Joseph Eligio de la Puente, List of Families Transported to Havana, Feb. 20, 1764, SD 2660, AGI).

2. While smaller groups from the outlying posts of San Marcos de Apalache and San Miguel de Pensacola sailed for Vera Cruz and Campeche in New Spain, most of the Spanish residents from the capital of St. Augustine went to Havana (Evacuation report of Juan Joseph Eligio de la Puente, Jan. 22, 1764, SD 2595, AGI). See also Jane Landers, "An Eighteenth-Century Community in Exile: The Floridanos of Cuba," *New West Indian Guide* 70, nos. 1 and 2 (1996): 37–58. For more on the Florida immigrants in Cuba see M. Sherry Johnson, "'Honor Is Life': Military Reform and the Transformation of Cuban Society, 1753–1796" (Ph.D. diss. Univ. of Florida, 1995), chap. 6.

3. Klein, "Colored Militia of Cuba," 17–27; Allan J. Kuethe, *Cuba, 1753–1815: Crown, Military, and Society* (Knoxville, Tenn., 1986).

4. Sherry Johnson, "'La Guerra contra los Habitantes de los Arrabales': Changing Patterns of Land Use and Land Tenancy in and around Havana, 1763–1800," *Hispanic American Historical Review* 77 (May 1997): 181–209.

5. The freedmen of Mose were skilled carpenters, masons, and ironsmiths who had worked building fortifications and repairing the Castillo de San Marcos and St. Augustine's church in addition to building all their own structures at Mose (Manuel de Montiano to Philip V, Feb. 16, 1739, SD 845, microfilm reel 16, PKY); Petition of Francisco Menéndez, Jan. 31, 1740, SD 2658, AGI; Landers, "Gracia Real," 15–20, 31. All were baptized Catholics, a condition of their sanctuary (Black Baptisms, CPR, microfilm reel 284 F, PKY; Black Marriages, microfilm reel 284 C, PKY).

6. Manuel Rivera was born in St. Augustine, probably of slave parents, but in 1763 he was free and serving in the Mose militia (Evacuation report of Juan Joseph Eligio de la Puente, Jan. 22 1764, SD 2595, AGI). Rivera's accidental death on Jan. 4, 1766, is recorded in Pardo Burials of the archives of the Church of Nuestra Señora de la Asunción, in Guanabacoa, Cuba.

7. Marriage of Bernardo Joseph and Ana María de León, Apr. 24, 1770 (Marriages of Indians, Pardos, and Morenos, vol. 1, fol. 7v, no. 22, Yglesia Auxiliar del Santíssimo Christo de Potosí, de la jurisdicción de San Miguel del Padrón, Regla, Cuba); baptism of Ysidro Silverio, June 22, 1771 (Baptisms of Indians, Pardos and Morenos, vol. 1, fol. 23, no. 131, ibid.).

8. Instructions to Don Simon Rodríguez on the establishment of the Florida families in Matanzas, 1764, SD 2595, AGI.

9. Regarding the arrival of Canary Island families, Aug. 21 1757, Floridas, legajo 21, no. 60, Archivo Nacional, Havana, Cuba (hereafter cited as ANC).

10. Cuentas de Real Hacienda de Matanzas, 1761–82, año de 1764, no. 5 and no. 7, SD 1882, AGI. The slaves were assessed at 150 pesos each, which combined with the stipend of 60 pesos, left each settler responsible for a debt of 210 pesos, to be repaid in nine years, although no payment was required the first year. The relationship between former slaves and their own slaves is unclear.

11. Report of Juan Joseph Eligio de la Puente, Sept. 22, 1766, SD 2595, AGI.

12. Gabino La Rosa Corzo, *Los palenques del oriente de Cuba, resistencia y acoso* (Havana, 1988).

13. Petition of María de Jesus de Justíz, Actas de Cabildo de Matanzas, vol. 5, fol. 145, Municipal Archive, Matanzas, Cuba. Justíz specified that she wanted a piece of land in the area called la Sabana, "behind the one given to Domingo Gonzalez."

14. Marriage of Captain Manuel de Soto and María Agustina Gonzales, "blanca, natural de Tacorente de las Yslas Canarias," Apr. 8, 1764, Black Marriages, Cathedral Archive, Matanzas, Cuba. Baptism of María Josepha Catarina, legitimate daughter of Manuel de Soto and María Agustina Gonzalez, Nov. 25, 1768, Black Baptisms, Cathedral Archive, Matanzas, Cuba. Baptism of the adult Carabalí slave of Captain de Soto, named Juan de la Luz, Apr. 2, 1788, ibid.

15. Rentas de la Real Hacienda de Matanzas, 1764–82, 1782, no. 10, SD 1882, AGI. Despite their poverty, Antonio Eligio donated a peso and Tomás Chrisóstomo donated two pesos toward the construction of a badly needed new bridge in Matanzas. Other free blacks also contributed (List of Donations, Mar. 6, 1775, Cuba 1197, AGI).

16. Burial of Tomás Chrisóstomo, Feb. 23, 1798 (Black Burials, 1797–1823, Parish Archives, Nuestra Señora de la Candelaria, San Agustín de la Nueva Florida de Seiba [*sic*] Mocha, Cuba).

17. Report of Juan Joseph Eligio de la Puente, Sept. 22, 1764, SD 2595, AGI, and Rentas de la Real Hacienda de Matanzas, años 1762–82, SD 1882, AGI.

18. Modern residents of Ceiba Mocha, as it is popularly called, had no knowledge of the town's multiracial history. They believed it was settled exclusively by Canary Islanders and were proud of the distinction. The church at Ceiba Mocha contains images of St. Augustine and of the patron saint of the Canary Islands, la Candelaria (interviews in Ceiba Mocha, Aug. 1991). Official versions of the town's history also identify it as a Canary Island settlement and do not mention its multiracial origins (Pedro Carmona Martín, *Proyecto de grado las fiestas tradicionales en Ceiba Mocha* [Matanzas, 1987], 200).

19. Instancia of María Gertrudis Roso, Sept. 24, 1792, SD 2577, AGI. The family's baptism and marriage records are in the St. Augustine parish registers and Ignacio Roso appears on the militia lists for Mose and on the list of men evacuating from Mose.

20. Daniel L. Schafer, "'Yellow Silk Ferret Tied round Their Wrists': African Americans in British East Florida, 1763–1784," in *The African American Heritage of Florida,* ed. David R. Colburn and Jane L. Landers (Gainesville, Fla., 1995), 71–103.

21. The Bissetts' main plantation comprised ninty-five hundred acres and held a "Ne-

gro Town of good houses for seventy Negroes" (Wilbur Henry Siebert, *Loyalists in East Florida, 1783–1785: The Most Important Documents Pertaining Thereto, Edited With an Accompanying Narrative,* 2 vols., [Deland, Fla., 1929], vol. 2, 92–99, 250–56).

22. Schafer documented acts of resistance by African slaves which included drowning a white overseer, poisoning skilled creole slaves brought from South Carolina, and escapes to the Seminole nation west of the St. Johns River ("Yellow Silk Ferret," 81–82, 88, 93).

23. Daniel L. Schafer, "'Settling a Colony over a Bottle of Claret': Early Plantation Development in British East Florida," *El Escribano* 19 (1982): 47–50, and "Yellow Silk Ferret," 74.

24. J. Leitch Wright, Jr., "Blacks in British East Florida," *Florida Historical Quarterly* 54 (July 1995–Apr. 1976): 425–42.

25. Ibid.

26. J. Leitch Wright, Jr., *Florida in the American Revolution* (Gainesville, Fla., 1975), 108–9.

27. John K. Mahon and Brent R. Weisman, "Florida's Seminole and Miccosukee Peoples," in *The New History of Florida,* ed. Michael Gannon (Gainesville, Fla., 1996), 183–206; Brent R. Weisman, *Like Beads on a String: A Culture History of the Seminole Indians in North Peninsular Florida* (Tuscaloosa, Ala., 1989).

28. *Travels of William Bartram,* ed. Mark Van Doren (New York, 1928), 164–65; *William Bartram on the Southeastern Indians,* ed. Gregory A. Waselkov and Kathryn E. Holland Braund (Lincoln, Nebr., 1995).

29. Joshua R. Giddings, *The Exiles of Florida* (Columbus, Ohio, 1858); Kenneth Wiggins Porter, *The Negro on the American Frontier* (New York, 1971); George Klos, "Blacks and the Seminole Indian Removal Debate, 1821–1835," in *The African American Heritage of Florida,* ed. David R. Colburn and Jane L. Landers (Gainesville, Fla., 1995), 128–56.

30. Treaty of Paris, May 3, 1783, cited in Joseph Byrne Lockey, *East Florida, 1783–1785: A File of Documents Assembled and Many of Them Translated* (Berkeley, 1949), 91.

31. Zéspedes served in the military at Pensacola and Louisiana, and was interim governor of Santiago de Cuba and secretary to the captain general of Cuba (José de Gálvez to Vicente Manuel de Zéspedes, Oct. 31, 1783, Floridas, legajo 10, ANC; cited in Lockey, *East Florida,* 174).

32. Vicente Manuel de Zéspedes to Bernardo de Gálvez, July 16, 1784 (SD 2660, AGI, cited in Lockey, *East Florida,* 223), contains the governor's account of the expedition to St. Augustine, the transfer ceremony, and his first impressions of the province and its inhabitants.

33. Royal decree, 1789.

34. Pensions were approved on an individual basis until several royal decrees formalized the process in 1791. Thereafter, if pensioners got one real in Cuba, they would get one and a half in Florida. There would also be a new penalty of a half real for those who refused to go back, unless they were too old or sick, in which case they would be subsidized as before. Cuban-born children of Floridano parents were also encouraged to go to Florida by the promise of a daily subsidy of two reales for unmarried women and one

real for a married woman. Floridanos who had enjoyed governmental support in Florida but had not received assistance in Cuba would get what they previously received (Royal decree, Mar. 18, 1791, SD 2577, AGI, and Floridas, legajo 9, no. 22, ANC; Royal decree, June 27 1793, Floridas, legajo 14, no. 54, ANC). Petitions on the cessions of lands in the Floridas 1781–1813 (Floridas, legajo 10, no. 7, ANC).

35. Catalina de Porras was able to reclaim the St. Augustine house her mother received as a dowry many years earlier. Ursula and Antonia de Avero also did. However, many others, like the widow of Estévan de Peña, were unsuccessful. After much litigation, authorities ruled that the 1763 sale of her homestead to British agents had been valid (Susan R. Parker, "In My Mother's House: Female Property Ownership in Spanish St. Augustine," paper delivered at the American Society for Ethnohistory, Salt Lake City, Nov. 1992).

36. Diego Eligio de la Puente died on Sept. 25, 1790, at about age seventy and was buried the next day in the Tolomato cemetery by Father Hassett. His name, his free status, and the fact that he had been born in North America make it possible that he was related to Lt. Antonio Eligio de la Puente, of Mose (Burial of Diego Eligio de la Puente, Sept. 25, 1790, Black Burials, vol. 2, CPR, microfilm reel 284 L, PKY).

37. James Cusick, "Across the Border: Commodity Flow and Merchant Networks in Second Spanish Period St. Augustine," *Florida Historical Quarterly* 69 (Jan. 1991): 277–99; Daniel L. Schafer, "'A Class of People neither Freemen nor Slaves': From Spanish to American Race Relations in Florida, 1821–1861," *Journal of Social History* 26 (Spring 1993): 587–609.

38. Carlos Howard to Luis de Las Casas, July 2, 1791, Cuba 1439, AGI.

39. Deagan, *Spanish St. Augustine,* 45–46.

40. Governor Zéspedes complained, "it contains not a single room or apartment not completely inundated when it rains, which is very frequently in this country" (Vicente Manuel de Zéspedes to Juan Ignacio de Urriza, Sept. 16, 1784, cited in Lockey, *East Florida,* 278).

41. Susan R. Parker, "Men without God or King: Rural Settlers of East Florida, 1784–1790," *Florida Historical Quarterly* 64 (Oct. 1990): 135–55; Report of Nicolás Grenier, Nov. 10, 1784, cited in Lockey, *East Florida,* 307.

42. Only three roads connected the province, including the Camino Real, another from St. Augustine to the mouth of Pablo Creek, and a third from St. Augustine to the landing at Six Mile Creek (Report of Nicolás Grenier, Nov. 10, 1784, cited in Lockey, *East Florida,* 305–11).

43. The Georgians charged, and they were probably correct, that even more of their legally owned slaves were harbored by the Spaniards. For examples of the complaints and countercharges see Jane Landers, "Spanish Sanctuary: Fugitives in Florida, 1687–1790," *Florida Historical Quarterly* 62 (Sept. 1984): 296–313.

44. Petition of Richard Lang, Nov. 14, 1789, Correspondence between the Governor and Subordinates on the St. Johns and St. Marys Rivers, 1784–1820, EFP, microfilm reel 46, PKY, cited in Parker, "Men without God," 154.

45. Residents of St. Marys to Vicente Manuel de Zéspedes, Oct. 24, 1787, Correspondence between the Governor and Subordinates on the St. Johns and St. Marys Rivers, 1784–1820, EFP, microfilm reel 45, and Residents of the St. Johns River, Oct. 8, 1789, Correspondence between the Governor and Subordinates on the St. Johns and St. Marys Rivers, 1784–1820, EFP, microfilm reel 46, PKY, cited in Parker, "Men without God," 151.

46. Carlos Howard to Luis de Las Casas, July 2, 1791, Cuba 1439, AGI.

47. Governor Zéspedes granted permission for the merchant house of Panton, Leslie and Company to continue the Indian trade it had conducted under the British regime and later assigned the government Indian trade contract to Don Fernando de la Maza y Arredondo. Cimarrones visited St. Augustine on Jan. 4, 1786, on Feb. 28 and July 31, 1787, and on Aug. 31, 1788 (Caleb Finnegan, "Notes and Commentary on the East Florida Papers: Lists of Gifts to Indians, 1785–1788," unpublished research notes drawn from Accounts of Presents to Indians, 1785–1788, EFP, microfilm reel 167, PKY).

48. Giddings, *Exiles of Florida;* Porter, *Negro on the American Frontier.* See also Klos, "Blacks and the Seminole Indian Removal Debate."

49. Vicente Manuel de Zéspedes to Joseph de Ezpeleta, Nov. 9, 1787, Cuba 1395, AGI.

50. Vicente Manuel de Zéspedes to Bernardo de Gálvez, July 29, 1785, cited in Lockey, *East Florida,* 570–73; Francis Philip Fatio's description of East Florida, Mar. 18, 1785, cited in Lockey, *East Florida,* 479–82; and Accounts of the Royal Treasury, 1784–95, SD 2635, and 1796–1819, SD 2636, AGI.

51. Vicente Manuel de Zéspedes to Arturo O'Neill, Sept. 12, 1784, Cuba 40, AGI; and Zéspedes to Bernardo de Gálvez, July 29, 1785, cited in Lockey, *East Florida,* 570–73.

52. Vicente Manuel de Zéspedes to Arturo O'Neill, Sept. 12, 1784, Cuba 40, AGI, cited in Lockey, *East Florida,* 572.

53. Ibid., and Accounts of the Royal Treasury, 1784–95, SD 2635, AGI. Among the prominent "foreigners" loaning money to the government were Don Francis Phelipe Fatio, Don Juan Leslie, and Don Claudio Guillard. They loaned the money at 6 percent interest, to be paid on arrival of the situado. In later years the destitute Spanish Crown paid no interest on such loans.

54. Pirates captured the situado in 1798. The 1799 situado did not reach Florida until 1803, and it was the last full subsidy received. By 1809 the situado was 750,000 pesos in arrears. Government employees had not been paid in three years, and the troops had not been paid for two years. Governor White at last resorted to scrip on the Havana and Vera Cruz treasuries, which in turn created inflation (Rogers C. Harlan, "A Military History of Florida during the Governorship of Enrique White, 1796–1811" [M.A. thesis, Florida State University, 1971], microfilm reel 118, PKY, 193, 208).

55. Ramón Romero-Cabot, "La defensa de Florida en el segundo período Español" (thesis, University of Seville, 1982) PKY, 39–44.

56. Accounts of the Royal Treasury, 1784–95, SD 2635, and 1796–1819, SD 2636, AGI.

57. Juan Nepomuceno de Quesada to Conde de Lerena, Nov. 15, 1791, cited in Arthur Preston Whitaker, *Documents Relating to the Commercial Policy of Spain in the Floridas* (Deland, Fla., 1931), 157.

58. Romero-Cabot, "Defensa de Florida," 42–44.

59. Historical Records Survey, *Spanish Land Grants in Florida,* 5 vols. (Tallahassee, Fla., 1940–41) (hereafter cited as *SLGF*), vol. 2, xix–xxvi.

60. Carlos Howard to Luis de la Casas, July 2, 1791, Cuba 1439, AGI.

61. James Cusick, transcriber, "Oaths of Allegiance, East Florida Papers, 1793–1804" (unpublished manuscript based on Oaths of Allegiance, 1790–1821, EFP, microfilm reel 163, PKY). Charles Ash brought with him 100 slaves; John Fraser, 370; John Kelsall, 222; Zephaniah Kingsley, Jr., 100; Santiago Main, 190; Daniel McNeill, 400; and Daniel O'Hara, 300. As their names indicate more than 80 percent of the newcomers were born either in a British North America colony, England, Scotland, or Ireland (Schafer, "'Class of People neither Freemen nor Slaves'").

62. For a graphic description of the cruel effort involved in breaking in new plantations in British Florida (just twenty years earlier) see Schafer, "Yellow Silk Ferret."

63. Francis Philip Fatio, Description of East Florida, Mar. 18, 1785, cited in Lockey, *East Florida,* 479–82; Accounts of the Royal Treasury, 1784–95, SD 2635, and 1796–1819, SD 2636, AGI.

64. Carlos Howard to Luis de Las Casas, July 2, 1791, Cuba 1439, AGI; Robert Francis Crider, "The Borderland Floridas, 1815–1821: Spanish Sovereignty under Siege" (Ph.D. diss., Florida State University, 1979), 9–10.

65. Memorial of the Italians, Greeks, and Minorcans, July 12, 1784, and July 13, 1784, cited in Lockey, *East Florida,* 232–33; Vicente Manuel de Zéspedes to José de Gálvez, Oct. 20, 1784, cited in ibid., 285–86. For the history of this community see Patricia C. Griffin, *Mullet on the Beach: The Minorcans of Florida, 1768–1788* (Jacksonville, Fla., 1991). Susan R. Parker describes the coastal estuaries north and south of St. Augustine as a "Minorcan littoral" ("Men without God," 138).

66. Governor Zéspedes ordered all non-Spaniards to present themselves and declare their intentions (Memorials of Francis Philip Fatio, Feb. 23, 1785, and James Clarke, Feb. 26, 1785, cited in Lockey, *East Florida,* 464–65).

67. Twenty-eight of Alexander Patterson's slaves "eloped" during the evacuation. Robert Robinson's slave, Jack, ran away on the day of Robinson's departure for Halifax "for his dread of encountering so cold a climate" (Siebert, *Loyalists in East Florida,* vol. 2, 125, 140).

68. Landers, "Spanish Sanctuary."

69. Vicente Manuel de Zéspedes to Joseph de Ezpeleta, Oct. 2, 1788, Cuba 1395, AGI.

70. Proclamation of Vicente Manuel de Zéspedes, July 26, 1784, cited in Lockey, *East Florida,* 240–41.

71. Patrick Tonyn to Lord Sydney, Dec. 6, 1784, cited in Lockey, *East Florida,* 339.

72. General Archibald MacArthur, commander of the Southern District after the evacuation of Charleston, signed eighty-eight of the documents, Governor Patrick Tonyn signed twenty-one, and Tonyn's aide-de-camp, Lt. Col. William Brown, and Major Samuel Bosworth each signed one (Census Returns, 1784–1814, EFP, microfilm reel 148, PKY).

73. Statement of Bacchus in ibid.

74. Census Returns, 1784–1814, EFP, microfilm reel 148, PKY. The family may have been in St. Augustine for several years before being required to register.

75. Quotations from the runaway notice are included in Letter of Alexander Semple to Commander McFernan, Dec. 16, 1786, To and from the United States, 1784–1821, EFP, microfilm reel 41, PKY. Semple operated a dry goods store on Cumberland Island which was frequented by Floridians living along the St. Marys River (Parker, "Men without God," 154).

76. Statement of Prince, Jan. 9, 1789, Census Returns, 1784–1814, EFP, microfilm reel 148, PKY.

77. Ira Berlin, Steven F. Miller, and Leslie S. Rowland, "Afro-American Families in the Transition from Slavery to Freedom," *Radical History Review* 42 (1988): 89.

78. McAlister, *Spain and Portugal,* 39–40.

79. Census of 1793, Census Returns, 1784–1814, EFP, microfilm reel 148, PKY. Witten's neighbors were Don Juan Leslie, head of the Panton, Leslie and Company Indian trading house, and Don Juan McQueen, of American revolutionary fame, a major landholder and later judge in Spanish Florida.

80. Runaway notice by Henry Williams, May 5, 1785, Papers on Negro Titles, Runaways, etc., 1737–1805, EFP, microfilm reel 167, PKY.

81. Statements of Sam and Hector, Census Returns, 1784–1814, EFP, microfilm reel 148, PKY.

82. Memorial of William Williams, Mar. 5, 1788, Census Returns, 1784–1814, EFP, microfilm reel 148, PKY; Landers, "Spanish Sanctuary," 309–10. Unable to get satisfaction from the Spanish governor, Major Williams finally submitted a claim to the British government for a "Negro woman slave," valued at forty pounds sterling and his brother, William, submitted a claim for Sam, a carpenter, valued at fifty pounds (Siebert, *Loyalists in East Florida,* vol. 2, 277, 281).

83. Josef Taso to Vicente Manuel de Zéspedes, July 12, 1788, Correspondence between the Governor and Subordinates on the St. Johns and St. Marys Rivers, 1784–1820, EFP, microfilm reel 45; and Pedro Carne to the governor, July 2, 1789, ibid., microfilm reel 46, PKY.

84. There is no way to know if this was the same Sharper, but many of the claimants for freedom came from the Savannah region (Herbert Aptheker, "Maroons within the Present Limits of the United States," *Journal of Negro History* 24 [Apr. 1939]: 167–84; *Independent Journal or the General Advertiser* [New York], June 20, 1787; Census Returns, 1784–1814, EFP, microfilm reel 148, PKY).

85. Royal decree included in letter from Luís de Las Casas to Governor Zéspedes, July 21, 1790, Letters from the Captain General, 1784–1821, EFP, microfilm reel 1, PKY. Also see J. Leitch Wright, Jr., *Florida in the American Revolution,* and Landers, "Spanish Sanctuary."

86. Thomas Jefferson to Juan Nepomuceno de Quesada, Mar. 10, 1791, To and from the United States, 1784–1821, EFP, microfilm reel 41, PKY.

87. James Seagrove to Juan Nepomuceno de Quesada, Dec. 17, 1790, and Aug. 9, 1791, To and from the United States, 1784–1821, EFP, microfilm reel 41, PKY.

88. Relations of Missing Slaves, May 1797, EFP, To and from the United States, 1784–1821, EFP, microfilm reel 41, PKY.

89. List of Fugitive Negroes Who Have Come into the Province . . . since Sept. 2, 1790, May 1797, To and from the United States, 1784–1821, EFP, microfilm reel 41, PKY.

90. James Seagrove to Governor Enrique White, July 4, 1797, To and from the United States, 1784–1821, EFP, microfilm reel 42, PKY.

91. Ibid.

92. Franklin W. Knight demonstrated the multiple effects of conflict, ideology, and economic dislocation on the Caribbean in "The American Revolution and the Caribbean," in *Slavery and Freedom in the Age of the American Revolution,* ed. Ira Berlin and Ronald Hoffman (Urbana, Ill., 1986), 237–61. On effects in Florida, see J. Leitch Wright, Jr., *Florida in the American Revolution.*

93. C. L. R. James, *The Black Jacobins: Toussaint L'Ouverture and the San Domingo Revolution* (New York, 1963); David Geggus, *Slavery, War, and Revolution: The British Occupation of Saint Domingue, 1793–1798* (Oxford, 1982); Alfred N. Hunt, *Haiti's Influence on Antebellum America: Slumbering Volcano in the Caribbean* (Baton Rouge, La., 1988); Eugene D. Genovese, *From Rebellion to Revolution: Afro-American Slave Revolts in the Making of the Modern World* (Baton Rouge, La. 1979); Julius S. Scott, "The Common Wind: Currents of Afro-American Communication in the Era of the Haitian Revolution" (Ph.D. diss., Duke University, 1986).

94. Richard K. Murdoch, *The Georgia-Florida Frontier 1793–1796: Spanish Reactions to French Intrigue and American Designs* (Berkeley, 1951). As its title indicates, this is primarily a diplomatic history of the era.

95. Accounts of the Royal Treasury, 1796–1814, Account of 1796, SD 2636, AGI. Members of Biassou's immediate family included his wife, Romana; her mother, Ana Gran Pres; her sisters, Barbara and Cecilia Gran Pres; and her brother, Juan Jorge Jacobo, Biassou's military successor. All were free blacks from Guarico. In the "extended" family were Juan Luis Menar, a free mulatto from Guarico, who married Barbara Gran Pres; Placido Asil, a free black from San Miguel on the coast of Guinea, who married Biassou's slave Isabel, a black from Villa de Granada; Jorge Brus, a free mulatto from Marmelade, and his wife, María Carlota, a free black from Guarico; Pedro Miguel, a free black; Benjamín Seguí, a free mulatto; Peter Yon Frances, ethnicity not given; León Duvigneau, a free mulatto, and his black slave wife, Simonett. This group was identified by searching the black baptisms, marriages, and burials for the post-1796 period (CPR, microfilm reels 284 J, K, and L, PKY). This represents only a partial accounting of the refugees, since many may not have been recorded in these registers.

96. White fears of such men and their "notions" are described in Michel-Rolph Trouillot, "From Planters' Journals to Academia: The Haitian Revolution as Unthinkable History," *Journal of Caribbean History* 25 (1991): 81–99. See also David Geggus, "Racial Equality, Slavery, and Colonial Secession during the Constituent Assembly," *American Historical Review* 94 (Dec. 1989): 1290–1308; Jane Landers, "Rebellion and Royalism in Spanish Florida: The French Revolution on Spain's Northern Colonial Frontier," in *A Turbulent*

Time: The French Revolution and the Greater Caribbean, ed. David Barry Gaspar and David Patrick Geggus (Bloomington, Ind., 1997), 156–77.

97. Herbert Klein points out that approximately one-fourth of the reorganized Cuban army of the late eighteenth century was of African descent. Other Spanish posts in the Caribbean were similarly structured ("Colored Militia of Cuba," 17–27).

98. Licenses on Slaves Imported into East Florida, 1762–63, Cuba 472, AGI.

99. Some counts include the garrison population, which ranged between five hundred men in 1784 to a little over two hundred in 1814 (Census of 1784, Census Returns, 1784–1814, EFP, microfilm reel 148, PKY; Census of 1814, ibid.).

Chapter 4
Black Entrepreneurs and Property-Holders

1. Phillips, *Slavery from Roman Times,* 28, 50.

2. Cortés López, *Orígenes de la esclavitud,* 141–42.

3. Franco Silva, *Regesto documental.* Ruth Pike contends that the surplus of unskilled labor and discriminatory guild regulations, combined with depressed economic conditions in Seville, drove many freed persons to the Americas (*Aristocrats and Traders,* 189).

4. McAlister, *Spain and Portugal,* 3–8, 32, 133–52. Even conquered people might be acceptable settlers, provided that they accepted the superiority of Christianity, swore allegiance to the Crown, and paid tribute (Seed, *Ceremonies of Possession,* chap. 3).

5. Gerhard, "Black Conquistador in Mexico."

6. Numerous examples of homesteading and repopulation plans can be found documented in Ministerio de Cultura, *Documentación Indiana en Simancas,* 250–57.

7. Lyon, *Enterprise of Spanish Florida.* Around 1648, the mulatto Francisco Galindo, former overseer of the Asile ranch, was freed in old age by Governor Horruitiner ("Documentation Pertaining to the Asile Farm," 67). For more on the Spanish development of the region see John H. Hann, *Apalachee: The Land between the Rivers* (Gainesville, Fla., 1988) and Bushnell, "Menéndez Márquez Cattle Barony," 407–31.

8. Governor Zúñiga described Espinosa's San Diego homestead as a small ranch or *hato* in recounting South Carolina governor James Moore's invasion of 1702 (Arnade, *Siege of St. Augustine in 1702,* 60). Over the years the establishment grew in size and importance, was fortified, and became known as Fort San Diego (TePaske, *Governorship,* 135–54).

9. John H. Hann, "Apalachee Counterfeiters in St. Augustine," *Florida Historical Quarterly* 62 (1988): 54–55.

10. Drake's raid is described in Contratación 4802, AGI, ST, PKY. The later raid of pirate Robert Searles is described in Francisco de la Guerra y de la Vega to King Charles II, Aug. 8, 1668, 54-5-18, AGI, transcription in J. T. Connor Collection, Library of Congress, Washington, D.C. On the burning of St. Augustine by Francis Drake in 1586 and Indian wars and uprisings of the sixteenth and seventeenth centuries see Amy Bushnell, *The King's Coffer: Proprietors of the Spanish Florida Treasury, 1565–1702* (Gainesville, Fla., 1981), 4, 12–14.

11. Worth, *Struggle for the Georgia Coast;* Crane, *Southern Frontier;* TePaske, *Governorship,* 108–32.

12. Royal decree, Nov. 7, 1693, AGI 58-1-2/74, ST, PKY.

13. Landers, "Gracia Real," 16; Hann, "Fallout from the Yamasee War," 193.

14. Descendants of Spanish townspeople did make such claims and at least some were successful in retrieving old homesteads or securing comparable grants (Parker, "In My Mother's House").

15. Decree of Vicente Manuel de Zéspedes, July, 14, 1784, in Lockey, *East Florida,* 233–35; James A. Lewis, "*Cracker*—Spanish Florida Style," *Florida Historical Quarterly* 63 (1984): 202.

16. Proclamation of Vicente Manuel de Zéspedes, July 26, 1784 and Zéspedes to Patrick Tonyn, Aug. 6, 1784, cited in Lockey, *East Florida,* 240–41, 333–42.

17. Census Returns, 1784–1814, EFP, microfilm reel 148, PKY.

18. Statements of Small and Morris, July 7, 1788, Census Returns, 1784–1814, EFP, microfilm reel 148, PKY.

19. Petition of Ambrosio Nelson, Apr. 20, 1787, Memorials, 1784–1821, EFP, microfilm reel 77, PKY.

20. Petition of Prince, Nov. 12, 1789, Memorials, 1784–1821, EFP, microfilm reel 77, PKY.

21. Census Returns, 1784–1814, EFP, microfilm reel 148, PKY.

22. Vicente Manuel de Zéspedes to Captain General José de Ezpeleta, Feb. 14, 1789, Cuba 1395, AGI.

23. Memorial of Juan Villalonga, 1797, Memorials, 1784–1821, EFP, microfilm reel 79, no. 74, PKY.

24. Petition of Antonio Coleman, Jan. 9, 1794, Records of Civil Proceedings, 1785–1821, EFP, microfilm reel 152, PKY.

25. Petition of Felipe Edimboro, July 6, 1794, Records of Civil Proceedings, 1785–1821, EFP, microfilm reel 152, PKY.

26. Testimony of Juan Baptista and Manuel Alzendorf, Aug. 8, 1799, Papers on Negro Titles, Runaways, etc., 1787–1805, EFP, microfilm reel 167, PKY.

27. "The Story of Uncle Jack," Buckingham Smith Collection, New York Historical Society, New York. I am grateful to Patricia C. Griffin for sharing her transcription of this document.

28. Relaciones de Jornales, 1805–12, Cuba 417, AGI.

29. Payments to Antonio, June 30, Nov. 29, Dec. 30, 1794, July 1, Dec. 31, 1795, Accounts of the Royal Treasury, 1784–95, SD 2635, AGI; and Payments to Antonio, Jan. 30, May 31, Aug. 31, 1796, Jan. 31, 1797, Accounts of the Royal Treasury, 1796–1819, SD 2636, AGI.

30. Payment to Juan Wright, Nov. 25, 1788, Accounts of the Royal Treasury, 1784–95, SD 2635, AGI. Wright had immigrated from New Providence in the Bahamas, leaving behind a slave woman and her child whose wages paid his passage (Panton, Leslie and Company versus Juan Wright, Oct. 29, 1787, Memorials, 1784–1821, EFP, microfilm reel 77, PKY).

31. Payment to Juan Wright, Nov. 25, 1788, and payment to José Bonom, Dec. 30, 1795,

Accounts of the Royal Treasury, 1784–95, SD 2635, AGI. Payment to Carlos Hall, July 31, 1797, Payments to Felipe Edimboro, July 10 and Sept. 18, 1818, Apr. 26, 1819, Accounts of the Royal Treasury, 1796–1819, SD 2636, AGI. Statement of Pedro Berta, Oct. 9, 1806, Testamentary Records of Bentura Boix, Records of Testamentary Proceedings, 1756–1821, EFP, microfilm reel 134, PKY.

32. Apprenticeship of Nicolás Mañé, Escrituras (Notarized Instruments), 1784–1821, EFP, microfilm reel 168, PKY; and Apprenticeship of Andrés Baccus, May 8, 1801, Escrituras (Notarized Instruments), 1784–1821, EFP, microfilm reel 171, PKY.

33. Petition of Juan Bautista Collins, Aug. 6, 1791, U.S. Board of Land Commissioners, Miscellaneous Spanish Florida Land Records 1808–49, Florida State Archives, Tallahassee, Fla. (hereafter cited as SFLR), record group 599, series 992, Memorials and Concessions, 1786–1821, box 3, folder 18. Suits by Juan Bautista Collins, Mar. 22, 1798, May 9, 1799, Records of Civil Proceedings, 1785–1821, EFP, microfilm reel 154, PKY; Sales by Juan Bautista Collins, Jan. 8 and June 23, 1800, Jan. 16, 1810, Escrituras (Notarized Instruments), 1784–1821, EFP, microfilm reel 171, PKY.

34. Request for a passport by Juan Bautista Collins, Dec. 12, 1792, Memorials, 1784–1821, EFP, microfilm reel 78, PKY.

35. Census of 1793, Census Returns, 1784–1814, EFP, microfilm reel 148, PKY.

36. Baptism of María Rosa Collins, July 2, 1790, Black Baptisms, vol. 1, CPR, microfilm reel 284 J, PKY.

37. Marriage of Juan Bautista Collins and María de la Concepción Tunno, Nov. 18, 1798, Black Marriages, CPR, microfilm reel 284 L, PKY; Baptism of Tomás Felipe Collins, Sept. 30, 1800, Black Baptisms, vol. 2, CPR, microfilm reel 284 J, PKY.

38. Slave Purchase by Juan Bautista Collins, June 23, 1800, and Slave Sales by Juan Bautista Collins, Jan. 8, 1800, Jan. 31, 1801, Escrituras (Notarized Instruments), 1784–1821, EFP, microfilm reel 171, PKY. List of Donations, May 24, 1798, Miscellaneous Legal Instruments and Proceedings, 1784–1819, EFP, microfilm reel 113, PKY.

Collins's natural daughter, María Rosa, followed her father's example of propriety and perhaps his aspirations to status when she legally married the free mulatto militiaman Juan Antonio Florencia (Marriage of María Rosa Collins and Juan Antonio Florencia, Nov. 22, 1806, Black Marriages, CPR, microfilm reel 284 L, PKY).

39. Suits brought by Juan Bautista Collins against Job Wiggins, Mar. 22, 1798, and against Margarita Ryan, May 9, 1799, Records of Civil Proceedings, 1785–1821, EFP, microfilm reel 154, PKY. Collins recovered 147 pesos from the shopkeeper Margarita Ryan. Collins filed numerous other suits to recover debts from an assortment of business associates.

40. Investigations in consequence of the absence of Juan Bautista Collins, May 28, 1801, Records of Civil Proceedings, 1785–1821, EFP, microfilm reel 156, PKY.

41. In one example, Collins sued Don Juan McClery to recover 140 pesos (ibid.).

42. Suit by Juan Bautista Collins against Don José Antonio Yguíniz, Jan. 16, 1810, Records of Civil Proceedings, 1785–1821, EFP, microfilm reel 160, PKY.

43. "The Panton Leslie Papers, Letters of Edmund Doyle to John Innerarity," *Florida Historical Quarterly* 17 (1938): 54.

44. Report of celebrations on the royal accession of Don Carlos IV, Dec. 9, 1789, SD 2588, AGI; Griffin, *Mullet on the Beach,* 174–75.

45. Travel accounts and contemporary descriptions document the popularity of black dances and balls in other circum-Caribbean locations (Howard Johnson, "Slave Life and Leisure in Nassau, Bahamas, 1783–1838," a paper delivered at the Association of Caribbean Historians, San Germán, Mar. 1994; Hanger, *Bounded Lives, Bounded Places,* 132–33, 144–47; *A Voyage to South America: Jorge Juan and Antonio de Ulloa,* trans. John Adams [New York, 1964], 35).

46. Judicial Proceedings Made against . . . Don Juan Villalonga, St. Augustine Historical Society, Vertical File, Blacks, Judicial Proceedings, 1813, typescript, translation by E. W. Lawson, Jan. 1940, original documents in Webb Memorial Museum, St. Augustine Historical Society and Institute of Science.

47. Fernando Ortiz, *Cabildos y fiesta afrocubana,* 4, 6–7.

48. Escrituras (Notarized Instruments), 1784–1821, EFP, microfilm reel 167, PKY. Santiago was part of a shipment of slaves imported on the *Topacio.*

49. Jorge Sanco versus Nansi Wiggins, June 4, 1810, Records of Civil Proceedings, 1785–1821, EFP, microfilm reel 160, PKY.

50. The notarized loan was dated Jan. 12, 1810 (Juan Zamorano versus Felipe Edimboro, Oct. 4, 1810, Records of Civil Proceedings, 1785–1821, EFP, microfilm reel 160, PKY).

51. Felipe Edimboro denied knowing of Zamorano's original loan to Holbran and produced his signed and notarized instrument dated Jan. 30, 1810, acknowledging receipt of fifty pesos from Holbran, as partial payment for his freedom (ibid.).

52. Francis Fatio to Enrique White, June 25, 1800, Correspondence between the Governor and Subordinates on the St. Johns and St. Marys Rivers, 1784–1820, EFP, microfilm reel 55, PKY.

53. Original petitions and government responses are found in SFLR, record group 599, series 992, Memorials and Concessions, 1786–1821. See also SFLR, record group 599, series 997, Concessions for New Settlers, 1791–1821. To demonstrate improvements, a settler had to build a house with a suitable chimney, erect fences, and maintain a prescribed number of livestock on the land. When tenure and improvements were proved by the sworn testimony of witnesses, the homesteader would receive title (*SLGF,* vol. 1, xviii–xxiii).

54. "Land Claims in East Florida," *American State Papers. Documents, Legislative and Executive, of the Congress of the United States . . . Selected and Edited under the Authority of Congress,* 38 vols. (Washington, D.C., 1832–61), Class 8: *Public Lands,* vol. 6, 59, 70–71, 88.

55. *SLGF,* vol. 5, 223–24. Governor Enrique White amended the original headrights system, reducing grants to fifty acres for the head of the family, twenty-five for every child or servant over the age of sixteen, and fifteen acres for every child or servant between the ages of eight and sixteen years (ibid., xxii).

56. "Claim of John Moore," *SLGF,* vol. 1, 238.

57. Grant of Thomas Primus, Survey by Jorge J. F. Clarke, July 5, 1821, SFLR, record group 599, series 1232, Surveys of Land Grants.

58. Thomas Primus versus Lucia Braddock Fitzgerald, Aug. 11, 1798, Records of Civil Proceedings, 1785–1821, EFP, microfilm reel 154, PKY.

59. Census of 1793, Census Returns, 1784–1814, EFP, microfilm reel 148, PKY.

60. Landers, "Rebellion and Royalism"; Murdoch, *Georgia-Florida Frontier,* Carlos Howard to Luis de Las Casas, May 4, 1796, SD 2590, AGI.

61. Petition of Juan Bautista Wiet [*sic*], SFLR, record group 599, series 992, Memorials and Concessions, 1786–1821, box 12, folder 35.

62. Relation of the Free Blacks, July 27, 1807, Miscellaneous Papers, 1784–1858, EFP, microfilm reel 174, PKY; Memorial of Benjamín Seguí, July 5, 1798, Memorials, 1784–1821, EFP, microfilm reel 79, PKY.

63. Petition of Juan [*sic*] Buissou [*sic*], July, 7, 1797, SFLR, record group 599, series 992, Memorials and Concessions, 1786–1821, box 1, folder 32. After Biassou's death in 1806, his brother-in-law and military heir Juan Jorge Jacobo laid claim to Biassou's lands (Landers, "Rebellion and Royalism"). Jacobo must have abandoned the claim, for Governor Coppinger later granted the acreage as a service grant to Estéban Arnau (Claim of Joseph F. White, *SLGF,* vol. 1, 339).

64. Memorial of Felipe Edimboro, May 25, 1799, Memorials, 1784–1821, EFP, microfilm reel 79, PKY.

65. Hill, "George J. F. Clarke," 208–13; United States v. Wiggins, 14 Peters, 334, cited in *SLGF,* vol. 5, 209.

66. Report of Tomás Llorente, Nov. 26, 1813, Correspondence between the Governor and Subordinates on the St. Johns and St. Marys Rivers, 1784–1820, EFP, microfilm reel 62, PKY, cited in Daniel L. Schafer, "Shades of Freedom: Anna Kingsley in Senegal, Florida, and Haiti," in *Against the Odds: Free Blacks in the Slave Societies of the Americas,* ed. Jane G. Landers (London, 1996), 130–54, esp. 141.

67. Anna was literate and signed this petition and others. Patriot War Papers, St. Augustine Historical Society (hereafter cited as SAHS), manuscript collection 31, folder 96, claim 14.

68. Ibid.

69. St. Johns County Deed Book I–J, 389 (Dec. 21, 1832), cited in Schafer, "Shades of Freedom," 145.

70. Landers, "Rebellion and Royalism"; Murdoch, *Georgia-Florida Frontier.* On the State of Muskogee's war against Spain, see J. Leitch Wright, Jr., *William Augustus Bowles, Director General of the Creek Nation* (Athens, Ga., 1967), and on the Patriot Rebellion, see Rembert W. Patrick, *Florida Fiasco: Rampant Rebels on the Georgia-Florida Frontier, 1810–1815* (Athens, Ga., 1954). See also James W. Covington, "The Negro Fort," *Gulf Coast Historical Review* 5 (Spring 1980): 78–91, and Canter Brown, Jr., "The 'Sarrazota,' or Runaway Negro Plantations: Tampa Bay's First Black Community, 1812–1821," *Tampa Bay History* 12 (1990): 5–19.

71. J. H. Alexander, "The Ambush of Captain John Williams, U.S.M.C.: Failure of the East Florida Invasion," *Florida Historical Quarterly* 56 (1977): 286; Patrick, *Florida Fiasco,* 179–344.

72. Review Lists for the Free Black Militia of St. Augustine, 1812, Cuba 357, AGI.

73. Orders to Jorge Jacobo, Prince (Juan Bautista) Witten, and Benjamín Seguí, July 19, 1812, To and from Military Commanders and Other Officers, 1784–1821, EFP, microfilm reel 68, PKY.

74. *SLGF,* vol. 1, xxiv–xxvi.

75. Patriot War Papers, manuscript collection 31, folder 96, 3, SAHS. At least twenty-six free black claimants are recorded in this collection.

76. After having already paid 174 pesos, Sánchez paid his owner's widow twenty-six pesos and bought his freedom for a total price of 200 pesos. He acquired the money by working on the jornal system and he earned seventy-six pesos four reales (slightly over six pesos monthly) in 1808 (Testamentary Proceedings of F. X. Sánchez, 1808, Records of Testamentary Proceedings, 1756–1821, EFP, microfilm reel 141, PKY).

77. Claim of Susannah Sánchez, Sept. 9, 1834 (Patriot War Papers, manuscript collection 31, folder 69, SAHS).

78. Benjamín's English father, Job Wiggins, for many years held the government contract to operate the Indian ferry across the St. Johns River, and his son no doubt learned his piloting skills from his father (Helen Hornbeck Tanner, *Zéspedes in East Florida, 1784–1790* [Jacksonville, Fla., 1989], 130, 133).

79. Wiggins could manage all these employments because, although noted for the good care of stock, he "would go among them once a week, or once a month or more seldom" (Patriot War Papers, Claim of Benjamín Wiggins, Testimony of Carlos W. Clarke, manuscript collection 31, folder 75, SAHS).

80. When Carlos Clarke testified in 1834, Benjamín Wiggins was a stock keeper for Farmer and Ferris near Palatka (ibid.).

81. Memorial of Felipe Edimboro, SFLR, record group 599, series 990, Confirmed Spanish Land Grant Claims, box 11, folder E-4; Sánchez Papers, vault, manuscript box 12, miscellaneous undated papers, PKY.

82. Marriage of José Sánchez and Lucía Ysnardy, Feb. 2, 1805 (Black Marriages, CPR, microfilm reel 284 L, PKY); Testament of Miguel Ysnardy, Mar. 2, 1803, Escrituras (Notarized Instruments), 1784–1821, EFP, reel 171 A, PKY; Testamentary Proceedings of F. X. Sánchez, Nov. 31, 1807, Records of Testamentary Proceedings, 1756–1821, EFP, microfilm reel 141, PKY. Also see Landers, "Traditions of African American Freedom," and Schafer, "Shades of Freedom."

83. In 1796 General Jorge Biassou led a group of former Black Auxiliaries of Charles IV from Santo Domingo to Florida, where many became propertied (Landers, "Rebellion and Royalism").

Chapter 5
Black Religious Life

1. Phillips, *Slavery from Roman Times,* 162–63; Pike, *Aristocrats and Traders,* 173, 180, 186–89.

2. McAlister, *Spain and Portugal,* 18.

3. Larrazábal Blanco, *Negros y la esclavitud en Santo Domingo,* 143–46. Wolof slaves alleged to be Muslims led the first major slave revolt recorded in the Americas (1521) from Diego Colón's sugar plantation in Hispaniola. Thereafter the Crown suspended African imports and only permitted the import of acculturated slaves from Spain, but this limitation was never practicable and was soon dropped.

4. Saez, *Iglesia y el negro esclavo,* 24–32; Bowser, *African Slave in Colonial Peru,* 232–57. Individual members of the Dominican and Jesuit orders sometimes devoted themselves to the evangelization and defense of Africans. After almost a half century working among the Africans of Cartagena (1606–52), a Jesuit, Alonso de Sandoval, wrote an important ethnohistorical treatise on Africans, their capacity for conversion, and the mechanics to be followed to accomplish this desired end (Alonso de Sandoval, *Un tratado sobre la esclavitud,* trans. Enriqueta Vila Vilár [Madrid, 1987], 363–503). His fellow Jesuit, Pedro Claver, continued Sandoval's work among the Africans of Cartagena, and the church eventually canonized him and named him apostle of the slaves (Thornton, *Africa and Africans,* 160–62).

5. Pike, *Aristocrats and Traders,* 188–89; Ortiz, *Cabildos y fiesta afrocubana,* 6.

6. The terms *cofradía* and *cabildo* are often used interchangeably to refer to such lay associations, but cabildo was more commonly used in the circum-Caribbean (Saez, *Iglesia y el negro,* 51–52).

7. Request of Joseph Antonio Carmelita and Agustín Chamiso to reauthorize the Carabalí Ungua cabildo of San Agustín, Sept. 22, 1769, and Request of Antonio Ramos to authorize the fourth Carabalí cabildo of Nuestra Señora del Carmen, Feb. 20, 1772, Cuba 1197, AGI. Fernando Ortiz and earlier authors working in Cuba assumed that the cabildo records had all disappeared but at least some still exist in the Archivo General de Indias *(Cabildos y fiesta afrocubana,* 6–10).

8. John Thornton, "African Nations in the New World Experience," paper presented at Vanderbilt University, Oct. 10, 1992.

9. Request of Juan Bautista Arensibe [*sic*] for authorization of the second Carabalí cabildo, Feb. 16, 1771, Cuba 1197, AGI.

10. In addition to the main house at 46 Calle Florida, the Congos owned several other properties in 1796 (Fernando Ortiz, *Cabildos y fiesta afrocubana,* 7–8, 14).

11. Richard C. Trexler has demonstrated the "plasticity of the magi theme" and traced how different ethnicities and colors were assigned to the three kings in different places and times. As noted above, in eighteenth-century Cuba Melchior was the black king, but in the early seventeeth century Guaman Poma de Ayalla, the noted mestizo chronicler of Peru, made Melchior an Indian, Balthazar a Spaniard, and Gaspar a black *(The Journey of the Magi: Meanings in History of a Christian Story* [Princeton, 1997], 102–7 and 140).

12. Ortiz, *Cabildos y fiesta afrocubana,* 25–64. See also Ortiz's original article, "La Fiesta Afro-Cubana del 'Día de Reyes,'" *Revista Bimestre Cubana* 15 (Jan.–June 1920): 5–17, annotated and translated by Jean Stubbs as "The Afro-Cuban Festival 'Day of Kings,'" in *Cuban Festivals: An Illustrated Anthology,* ed. Judith Bettelheim (New York, 1993), 3–

47; "Los cabildos Afrocubanos," in *Orbita de Fernando Ortiz,* ed. Julio Le Riverand (Havana, 1973), 121–34. Ortiz compares these inversion and license celebrations to similar winter festivities among various African groups.

13. Lydia Cabrera, "Babalú Ayé-San Lazaro," in *La enciclopedia de Cuba,* 14 vols. (San Juan, P.R., 1975–77), 8:162–76. Robert Farris Thompson compares nineteenth-century Cuban costuming to contemporary costumes from Nigeria and Calabar and demonstrates the continuities of form and design *(Flash of the Spirit: African and Afro-American Art and Philosophy* [New York, 1984], 260–67). Scholars have also found similar cultural persistence in British colonies (Thornton, *Africa and Africans*).

14. Fernando Ortiz claims the last cabildo procession was made in 1884, but cabildos existed in a modernized form of associations in Regla through the 1950s at least.

15. Florida had at least one Indian cofradía in the seventeenth century, Nuestra Señora de la Leche (Wilbur H. Siebert, "Some Church History of St. Augustine during the Spanish Regime," *Florida Historical Quarterly* 9 [Oct. 1980]: 118).

16. McEwan, "Hispanic Life"; Bushnell, *Situado and Sabana;* Hann, *Missions to the Calusa* and *Apalachee.*

17. Bushnell, *Situado and Sabana,* 82–94; Michael V. Gannon, *The Cross in the Sand: The Early Catholic Church in Florida, 1518–1870* (Gainesville, Fla., 1965), 27–76; TePaske, *Governorship,* 160–61.

18. CPR. Other studies that analyze black Catholic parish registers in Mexico City include Edgar F. Love, "Marriage Patterns of Persons of African Descent in a Colonial Mexico City Parish," *Hispanic American Historical Review* 51 (1971): 79–91, and Cope, *Limits of Racial Domination.*

19. Insights into behaviors that Florida's Franciscan missionaries considered sinful and sought to eliminate can be found in contemporary manuals for confessors. Among other questions, the Franciscans asked Timucuan chiefs if they had had any black female slaves or servants as mistresses *(Francisco Pareja's 1613 Confesionario: A Documentary Source for Timucuan Ethnography,* ed. Jerald T. Milanich [Tallahassee, Fla., 1972], 34). See also Amy Turner Bushnell, "'That Demonic Game': The Campaign to Stop *Pelota* Playing in Spanish Florida, 1675–1684," *Americas* 35 (July 1978): 1–19; Hann, *Apalachee,* 43, 73–74, 88–91, 341–53.

African rituals and beliefs still survive in many other areas of the Americas. See Isabel Castellanos and Jaime Atencio, "Raíces Hispanas en las Fiestas Religiosas de los Negros del Norte del Cauca, Colombia," *Latin American Research Review* 19, no. 3 (1984): 118–42; Klein, *African Slavery in Latin America,* 182–87; Thompson, *Flash of the Spirit,* and William D. Piersen, *Black Legacy: America's Hidden Heritage* (Amherst, Mass., 1993).

20. If denounced, African "sorcery" and "witchcraft" were prosecuted by officials of the Holy Office, as were bigamy and blasphemy (Noemí Quezada, "The Inquisition's Repression of *Curanderos,*" in *Cultural Encounters: The Impact of the Inquisition in Spain and the New World,* ed. Mary Elizabeth Perry and Anne J. Cruz [Berkeley, 1991], 37–57). See also Gonzalo Aguirre Beltrán, *Medicina y magia: el proceso de aculturación en México* (Mexico City, 1963); Palmer, *Slaves of the White God,* 148–66; Richard Boyer, *Lives of the Bigamists: Marriage, Family and Community in Colonial Mexico* (Albuquerque, N.Mex., 1995), 9.

21. Lyon, *Enterprise of Florida,* 100–130.

22. Although Charles II also urged the conversion of indigenes and slaves, neither England's institutional efforts nor conversion rates ever matched Spain's (Albert J. Raboteau, *Slave Religion: The Invisible Institution in the Antebellum South* [Oxford, 1978], 97–150). The Church of England sent missionaries to Carolina under the auspices of the Society for the Propagation of the Gospel in Foreign Parts, but many planters feared that baptism might lead to emancipation, pretensions of social equality, or rebellion. The missionaries complained that planters impeded their access to the slaves and that few slaves were, therefore, instructed or converted (Wood, *Black Majority,* 133–42). On the other hand, it is entirely possible that some of the fugitives had been exposed to Catholicism, either in Africa or in the Spanish Caribbean (John Thornton, "The Development of an African Catholic Church in the Kingdom of Kongo, 1491–1750," *Journal of African History* 25 [1984]: 147–67).

23. Council of the Indies to the king, Apr. 4, 1731, SD 2530, AGI.

24. Royal decree, Nov. 6, 1693, SD 58-1-26, SC, PKY.

25. These raids also destroyed the physical infrastructure of the church in St. Augustine, including the church, convent, and library (Bushnell, *Situado and Sabana,* 190–98; Lyon, *Enterprise of Florida,* 100–130; TePaske, *Governorship,* 110–16, 130–32, 159).

26. Bushnell, *Situado and Sabana,* 190–98; Worth, *Struggle for the Georgia Coast;* Hann, "Fallout from the Yamasee War."

27. Report of the Visita of Bishop Francisco de San Buenaventura, Apr. 29, 1736, SC 5543, PKY; TePaske, *Governorship,* 167–69.

28. Wood, *Black Majority,* 308–26; Harvey H. Jackson, "Hugh Bryan and the Evangelical Movement in Colonial South Carolina," *William and Mary Quarterly,* 3d ser., 43 (1986): 594–614; Raboteau, *Slave Religion,* 128–50. On the continuing connection see Mullin, *Africa in America,* 241–67.

29. Elizabeth Donnan, *Documents Illustrative of the History of the Slave Trade to America,* vol. 4 (Washington, D.C., 1935), 296–97, 301, 303.

30. Robert Higgins, "Charleston: Terminus and Entrepot of the Colonial Slave Trade," in *The African Diaspora: Interpretive Essays,* ed. Martin L. Kilson and Robert I. Rothberg (Cambridge, 1976), 114–31, esp. 129; Converse D. Clowse, *Measuring Charleston's Overseas Commerce, 1717–1767: Statistics from the Port's Naval Lists,* 31, table A-21; Donnan, *Documents Illustrative of the History of the Slave Trade,* 608–25.

31. Baptism of the Carabalí Domingo, 1744, and Baptism of the Congo Miguel Domingo, Jan. 26, 1748, Black Baptisms, CPR, microfilm reel 284 F, PKY.

32. Landers, "Gracia Real," 30; CPR.

33. Schafer, "Yellow Silk Ferret."

34. More than half of the twelve thousand Loyalist immigrants who entered Florida in 1782 and 1783 were black slaves (J. Leitch Wright, Jr., *Florida in the American Revolution,* 126–27, 133).

35. Albert J. Raboteau, "The Slave Church in the Era of the American Revolution," in *Slavery and Freedom in the Age of the American Revolution,* ed. Ira Berlin and Ronald Hoffman (Urbana, Ill., 1986), 193–213, esp. 208–13.

36. Johann Schoepf, *Travels in the Confederation, 1783–1784* (Philadelphia, 1911), 230.

37. Statement of Jacob Steward, Census Returns, 1784–1814, EFP, microfilm reel 148, PKY. Steward was a free black who emigrated to New Providence at the British cession. Whether these "rites" continued to be practiced at another location after his departure is unknown. The Treaty of Paris allowed British citizens to choose whether they would emigrate or remain when Florida was retroceded to Spain. British planters removed more than six thousand black slaves from Florida, most of whom went to the Bahamas (2,214) and to the United States (2,561) (Report of William Brown, enclosed in Tonyn to Nepean, May 2, 1786 [PRO:CO 5/561], cited in Lockey, *East Florida,* 11).

38. In addition to the main church building on the plaza, the church infrastructure included a chapel in the Castillo de San Marcos for the use of the troops (Relación by Joseph Manuel de López, Nov. 15, 1787, To and from the Bishop and Curate, 1786–1824, EFP, microfilm reel 38, PKY).

39. The Crown sent funds to support the work, which took five years to complete. Citizens, black or white, who could not afford to give money, donated labor, firewood, chickens, corn, or other goods (Donations to Build the New Church, May 24, 1798, Miscellaneous Legal Instruments and Proceedings, 1784–1819, EFP, microfilm reel 113, PKY).

40. The edifice, which cost an estimated 16,905 pesos, rose twenty-four feet into the air and was large enough to accommodate five hundred worshipers (Charles S. Coomes, "The Basilica-Cathedral of St. Augustine, Florida and its History," *El Escribano* 20 [1983]: 32–34).

41. On religion as a mechanism of social integration see McAlister, *Spain and Portugal,* 408; and Bushnell, *Situado and Sabana,* 192. On the centrality of the church in second-Spanish-period Florida see Griffin, *Mullet on the Beach,* 173–75.

42. The list of required "feast days of obligation" included every Sunday, the feasts of Christmas, Epiphany (popularly celebrated as the Día de Reyes), the Circumcision, Easter, the Ascension, Pentecost, and Corpus Christi; the Marian feasts of the Nativity of Our Lady, the Annunciation, the Purification, the Assumption; and the feasts of the apostles Saint Peter and Saint Paul and All Saints Day. Required fast days included the Fridays of Lent, Holy Saturday, and Christmas Eve. The bishop of Cuba might also add special feast days at will, as could the governor (Bushnell, *Situado and Sabana,* 84–92).

43. Hassett was vicar of East Florida and pastor of St. Augustine, and O'Reilly was the assistant pastor with the right of succession. Bishop Cyril de Barcelona complained that neither was initially proficient in Castilian (Bishop Cyril de Barcelona to Don Antonio Porlier, Oct. 24, 1788, SD 2673, AGI). Camps ministered to the Minorcan flock in Menorquín, a dialect of Catalán, until his death in 1790, by which time presumably most Minorcans had become fluent in Castilian (Griffin, *Mullet on the Beach,* 19–24, 110).

In 1791 three new priests, Miguel Crosby, Michael Wallis, and Constantine McCaffrey, also of Irish origin, came to work in Spanish Florida, but Wallis and McCaffrey returned to Cuba within five years. Hassett was promoted to vicar general of the new diocese of Louisiana in 1795 and, thereafter, O'Reilly served as vicar of East Florida and pastor of St. Augustine. When O'Reilly died in 1812, Miguel Crosby succeeded him and Juan Nepomuceno Gómez, who had come to St. Augustine in 1802, became Crosby's assistant pastor (Gannon, *Cross in the Sand,* 89–116).

44. Since the Seminoles were not converting to Catholicism themselves, it is possible that they were having their black slaves baptized to please the Spaniards with whom they were allied. Given the relative, or actual, autonomy of many black "slaves" of the Seminoles, it is also entirely possible that these baptisms were initiated by the blacks themselves (Black Baptisms, vols. 1–3, CPR, microfilm reel 284 J, PKY).

45. Rules and Instructions to Be Observed by the Government in the Direction of Schools, 1786, SD 2588, AGI. On July 24, 1805, Governor Enrique White approved Edmund Walsh's request to open an English-language school, under the supervision of Father Miguel O'Reilly, but those unable to read and write Spanish would not be allowed to attend (To and from the Bishop and Curate, 1786–1824, EFP, microfilm reel 38, PKY). A schoolhouse for free blacks appears to have been built on the lot of the Old Powder House at the southern end of town sometime near the end of the second Spanish period ("Story of Uncle Jack," 24).

46. Gannon, *Cross in the Sand,* 99.

47. Roster of School Boys by Josef Monasterio, Mar. 25, 1796, SD 2531, AGI. Other boys on the list may also have been of African descent, especially Juan Clemente and José Rafael, whose surnames were missing—often an indication of slave origins. Biographical data culled by the author primarily from a combination of parish, military, and land grant records is combined in a First Choice database called Militia.

48. This seems to indicate that until he reiterated the requirement the Anglo planters (who owned all but thirteen of the slaves he counted in the countryside) were not allowing their slaves "church time" (Bishop Cyril de Barcelona to the king, Aug. 6, 1788, SD 2588, AGI). Despite the bishop's effort at reform, the king and council believed his visit had had "little, if any, effect," and they recommended a separate new bishopric for Louisiana and the Floridas (Don Joseph Nicolás de Azara to the minister plenipotentiary of the king in Rome, Mar. 11, 1793, SD 2674, AGI).

49. Some prominent residents like Juan McQueen and María Evans converted to Catholicism, and their slaves often followed suit (Richard K. Murdoch, "Governor Zéspedes and the Religious Problems in East Florida, 1786–1787," *Florida Historical Quarterly* 26 [Apr. 1948]: 487). For numerous examples of Protestant, English-speaking slaves see Records of Criminal Proceedings, 1785–1821, EFP, microfilm reels 124, 125, 126, PKY. Most slaves did not specify which variant of Protestantism they practiced, but the slave Juana, from New York, said she had been baptized in the New Light sect (Auto seguidos . . . contra Juana, Miscellaneous Legal Instruments and Proceedings, 1784–1819, EFP, microfilm reel 110, no. 33, PKY).

50. *Doctrina para Negros,* trans. and ed. Javier Laviña (Barcelona, 1989).

51. Baptisms of Governor Zéspedes's slaves, on pages 14, 42, 50 and 53; of Governor Quesada's slaves, 132–33; of Don Francisco Sánchez's slaves, 26, 100, 108, and of his son, 50; of Commandant Salcedo's slaves, 132; of Colonel de Torres's slaves, 111, 132; of Don

Juan Leslie's slaves, 91, 109, 169; Father Hassett's slaves, 130; of Father Troconis's slaves, 31, 111; and of Bishop Cyril's slaves, 46 (Black Baptisms, vol. 1, CPR, microfilm reel 284 J, PKY). All black baptismal, marriage, and burial records from 1784 to 1821 are in an SPSS database compiled by the author.

52. Seventeenth-century synods in Hispaniola decreed that newborn children should be baptized within twenty days of their birth (Saez, *Iglesia y el negro esclavo,* 44). White Baptisms, vols. 1–4, CPR, microfilm reel 284 I, PKY; and Black Baptisms, CPR, vols. 1–3, microfilm reel 284 J, PKY.

53. Baptisms of the children of Prince Paten and Flora Spole appear on pages 56, 90, 91, 116; of the children of Juan and Mila Right, 34, 62, 119, 120; of the children of Antonio and Ester Capo (Rivas), 27, 36, 95, 130; of the children of Antonio and Anna Overstreet, 57, 58, 117; of the children of Prince Witten and Judy Kenty, 41; Prince's and Judy's baptisms on Jan. 11, 1792, 118 (Black Baptisms, vol. 1, CPR, microfilm reel 284 J, PKY). Prince and Judy took new names on their conversion and became Juan Bautista Witten and María Rafaela Kenty.

54. Thomas Hassett to Vicente Manuel de Zéspedes, Apr. 8, 1790, To and from the Bishop and Curate, 1786–1824, EFP, microfilm reel 38, PKY.

55. Black Baptisms, vol. 1, CPR, microfilm reel 284 J, 74–89, PKY.

56. Baptisms of Fatio slaves, Black Baptisms, vol. 1, CPR, microfilm reel 284 J, 67–72 and 89, PKY.

57. Thomas Hassett to Juan Nepomuceno de Quesada, Apr. 31, 1792 and Apr. 5, 1793, To and from the Bishop and Curate, 1786–1824, EFP, microfilm reel 38, PKY.

58. Baptisms of the McQueen slaves, Apr. 27, 1793, Black Baptisms, vol. 1, CPR, microfilm reel 284 J, PKY.

59. Baptisms of Felipe and Filis Edimboro on July 15 and July 29, 1794, Black Baptisms, vol. 2, CPR, microfilm reel 284 J, PKY. The couple petitioned for *coartación* on July 10, 1794, and achieved freedom on Sept. 4, 1794. See Records of Civil Proceedings, 1785–1821, EFP, microfilm reel 152, PKY.

60. Sidney Mintz, Eric Wolfe, George Foster, Betty Bell, and Hugo Nutini, among others, have studied the mechanism of *compadrazgo* or godparenthood in Latin America, and while noting the flexibility of the institution and regional variations, they agree that in Latin America the relationship between the *compadres* is more significant than that between godparents and godchild, the primary relationship in Spain. None of these studies, however, dealt specifically with *compadrazgo* among blacks (Sidney W. Mintz and Eric R. Wolfe, "An Analysis of Ritual Co-Parenthood (Compadrazgo)," *Southwestern Journal of Anthropology* 6 [Winter 1950]: 341–67; Foster, "Cofradía and Compadrazgo in Spain and Spanish America"; Hugo G. Nutini and Betty Bell, *Ritual Kinship, the Structure and Historical Development of the Compadrazgo System in Rural Tlaxcala* [Princeton, 1980]). Stephen Gudeman and Stuart B. Schwartz found that Brazilian owners were reluctant to promote baptism and avoided sponsoring their own slaves, fearing that the act might somehow threaten slave control. They did not find slaves sponsoring free blacks at baptism as in Spanish Florida ("Cleansing Original Sin: Godparenthood and the Baptism of

Slaves in Eighteenth-Century Bahia," in *Kinship Ideology and Practice in Latin America,* ed. Raymond Smith [Chapel Hill, N.C., 1984], 35–58).

61. Black Baptisms, CPR, microfilm reel 284 J, PKY. Conditional baptisms of the Fatio slaves (Apr. 15, 1790) appear in vol. 1 on pp. 67–72, and the subsequent church baptisms (Oct. 10, 1791, and Dec. 15, 1792) appear in vol. 1 on pp. 112–14 and 128–29. Baptisms of the Cummings y Clarke slaves (Nov. 29, 1785) appear in vol. 1 on p. 7, of the Hijuelos slaves (June 6, 1789) in vol. 1 on p. 54, and of the Perpal slaves (Nov. 16, 1790) in vol. 1 on p. 96.

62. The Wittens had important white baptismal sponsors in their next-door neighbors, Don Manuel Fernández Bendicho and his wife, Doña Rafaela Rodríguez. The children's baptismal sponsors were of a somewhat lower class, who did not earn the status marker of Don. Domingo Martineli and his wife Mariana Cavedo served for Glasgow, and Pedro Cosifacio for Polly. See Baptisms of Prince Witten and Judith Kenty, Jan. 11, 1792, of Glasgow and Polly, Aug. 16, 1788, Black Baptisms, vol. 1, CPR, microfilm reel 284 J, PKY.

Edimboro's children had a lower class of sponsors, including black slaves, free blacks and mulattoes, and free whites (none of whom bore the titles Don or Doña).

63. Ibid. For examples of African-born godparents sponsoring other Africans, see Josefa Fernández sponsoring a *bozal* slave on page 133, and Luis Almansa and María de Belem sponsoring Guinea-born slaves on pages 126, 133, and 135.

64. Stuart B. Schwartz, "Indian Labor and New World Plantations: European Demands and Indian Responses in Northeastern Brazil," *American Historical Review* 83 (Feb. 1978): 69–72.

65. Francisco Xavier Sánchez died intestate on Nov. 31, 1807. For the settlement of his estate see Records of Testamentary Proceedings, 1756–1821, EFP, microfilm reel 141, 1–364, PKY.

66. Black Marriages, CPR, microfilm reel 284 L, PKY.

67. Report of Bishop Cyril de Barcelona, Oct. 24, 1788, SD 2673, AGI. Cyril reported 281 blacks living in St. Augustine and 367 in the countryside in 1788. The numbers grew rapidly after 1790, when changes in Spanish land policy attracted more Anglo planters who, in turn, introduced many more slaves into the province.

68. Susan Socolow, "Love and Marriage in Colonial Latin America," paper delivered at the Conference on Latin American History, Washington, D.C., Dec. 1991. Also see Kathy Waldron, "The Sinners and the Bishop in Colonial Venezuela: The *Visita* of Bishop Mariano Martí, 1771–1784," and Thomas Calvo, "The Warmth of the Hearth: Seventeenth-Century Guadalajara Families," in *Sexuality and Marriage in Colonial Latin America,* ed. Asunción Lavrin (Lincoln, Nebr., 1989), 156–77, 287–312.

69. James Lockhart finds many of the same patterns for free blacks in colonial Peru (*Spanish Peru, 1532–1560* [Madison, Wis., 1994], 217).

70. The Carabalí slave Josefa Fernández was a sponsor at the marriage of Luis Almansa (a.k.a. Pérez) from Guinea and María de Belem of the Carabalí nation (Marriage of Luis Pérez and María Belem Zayas, Aug. 4, 1790, Black Marriages, CPR, microfilm reel 284 L, PKY). Luis Almansa and María de Belem in turn sponsored the marriages of

Guinea-born slaves (see Black Marriages, pp. 10, 16, 32, 33, 36, 41, 43, and 45, CPR, microfilm reel 284 L, PKY).

71. José Rivas and María de la Luz also sponsored marriages (see Black Marriages, pp. 12, 14, 15, 21, 28, 42, and 48, CPR, microfilm reel 284 L, PKY).

72. Whites also served as marriage sponsors for persons of African descent (see Black Marriages, pp. 1, 2, 4, 5, 8, 13, 23, 26, 49, and 51, CPR, microfilm reel 284 L, PKY).

73. Marriage of Francisco Sánchez and Catalina Mariana Morales, Dec. 6, 1800 (Black Marriages, CPR, microfilm reel 284 L, PKY). Francisco Sánchez's petition and the responses by Morales and Francisco Xavier Sánchez, Oct. 23, 1802, Records of Civil Proceedings, 1785–1821, EFP, microfilm reel 156, PKY.

74. See Sánchez's petition and the responses. An added irony, which surely escaped no one in the community, was that the sponsors at Francisco and Catalina's marriage had been none other than Felipe and Filis Edimboro, who had also successfully sued Sánchez to allow their self-purchase.

75. For more on slave marriages see Christine Hunefeldt, *Paying the Price of Freedom: Family and Labor among Lima's Slaves, 1800–1854* (Berkeley, 1994), 149–66; Palmer, *Slaves of the White God,* 106–12; and Bowser, *African Slave in Colonial Peru,* 254–71.

76. Petition of Moses Travers, Jan. 16, 1811, and Governors' Tribunal, Records of Civil Proceedings, 1785–1821, EFP, microfilm reel 160, PKY.

77. Lockhart, *Spanish Peru,* 217.

78. Marriage of Benjamín Wiggins and Nicolasa Edimboro, Jan. 14, 1812, Black Marriages, CPR, microfilm reel 284 L, PKY. Both Benjamín Wiggins and Nicolasa Edimboro later formed unions with and had children with other partners. What happened to their union is unknown. Nicolasa's child with Don Francisco Díaz had as godparents Don Martín Canobas and Doña Manuela Bravo.

79. Black Baptisms, vol. 3, entry 400 B, CPR, microfilm reel 284 J, PKY. Antonio later served as an Indian translator for the United States military. His son, George Proctor, became a master builder in territorial Tallahassee and his grandson, John Proctor, became a Republican senator in Florida's Reconstruction government (Lee H. Warner, *Free Men in an Age of Servitude: Three Generations of a Black Family* [Lexington, Ky., 1992]).

80. Black Baptisms, vol. 3, entry 498, CPR, microfilm reel 284 J, PKY.

81. Black Baptisms, vol. 3, entry 466, CPR, microfilm reel 284 J, PKY.

82. Black Baptisms, CPR, microfilm reel 284 J, PKY. For the Camel children, vol. 1, p. 93; for the Cheves baptism, see vol. 1, p. 159; for the Thompson children, vol. 2, p. 8. For baptisms of persons from South Carolina for whom the Wittens served as godparents see vol. 1, pp. 99, 127, 135, 158, 159, 170, and 172. María Witten was also the godmother for the child of her slave, Isabel Plouden. See vol. 2, p. 34.

83. Jane Landers, "Rebellion and Royalism."

84. Marriage of Jorge Jacobo and Rafaela Huiten [*sic*], Apr. 12, 1786 (Black Marriages, CPR, microfilm reel 284 L, PKY). For another study on black marriage strategies and alliances see Hunefeldt, *Paying the Price of Freedom,* 144–48.

85. The baptismal sponsors of the children of Jorge Jacobo and María Rafaela Witten

were free blacks and mulattoes with links to the family or to the free black militia. María Rafaela's father, Juan Bautista Witten, and Jorge's mother, Ana Gran Pres, sponsored their child María del Carmen. María Rafaela's brother, Francisco Witten, and Jorge's sister, Barbara Gran Pres, sponsored Julian, who died the next day. Marcelino Espinosa, a free mulatto militia member from Havana, sponsored their child Joseph Baltasar, and Benjamín Seguí, a mulatto from Guarico, who was an officer of the black militia, sponsored their child Catalina Melchora. See Black Baptisms, vol. 2, entries 176, 563, 670, and vol. 3, entry 31, CPR, microfilm reel 284 J, PKY.

86. Marriage of Juan Bautista and María Rafaela July 7, 1798, and Marriage of Francisco Weeten [*sic*] and María Francisca (Fatio), Jan. 26, 1799 (Black Marriages, CPR, microfilm reel 284 L, PKY).

87. Requests of Josef de Arrivas, June 10, 1786, and Antonio Huertas, Apr. 27, 1787, Matrimonial Licenses, 1785–1803, EFP, microfilm reel 132, PKY.

88. Request of Francisco Pérez, Jan. 28, 1795, Matrimonial Licenses, 1785–1803, EFP, microfilm reel 132, PKY. On the ideals of Spanish womanhood, see Mary Elizabeth Perry, *Gender and Disorder in Early Modern Seville* (Princeton, 1990). Also see Susan M. Socolow, "Acceptable Partners: Marriage Choice in Colonial Argentina, 1778–1810," in *Sexuality and Marriage in Colonial Latin America,* ed. Asunción Lavrin (Lincoln, Nebr., 1989), 209–51.

89. Matrimonial Licenses, 1785–1803, EFP, microfilm reel 132, PKY.

90. Request of José Manuel Fernández to wed Ana Sánchez, May 10, 1795, ibid.

91. Request of Francisco Sánchez to wed Catalina Sánchez, Jan. 4, 1802, ibid.

92. Matrimonial Licenses, 1785–1803, EFP, microfilm reel 132, PKY. For mixed race marriages see entries 1, 22, 53, 81, 82, 83, and 142.

93. Marriage of José Sánchez and Lucía Ysnardy, Feb. 2, 1805, Black Marriages, CPR, microfilm reel 284 L, PKY. At their wedding, José's sister Catalina and his Spanish brother-in-law, Francisco Sánchez, were wedding sponsors.

94. First-Spanish-period burial records for blacks extend over a longer range of years (1594–1763) and are more complete, although gaps appear in the final turbulent years prior to evacuation.

95. Black Burials, CPR, microfilm reel 284 L, PKY.

96. A number of Spanish confraternities were devoted to the imprisoned, arising out of the medieval obligation to redeem captives, and they offered a range of services to prisoners. Other confraternities, like the Misericordia, offered funeral services to the dead. According to Maureen Flynn, "Of all the merciful acts, the burial of the dead was considered the holiest" *(Sacred Charity: Confraternities and Social Welfare in Spain, 1400–1700* [Ithaca, N.Y., 1989], 62–69).

97. Black Burials, CPR, microfilm reel 284 L, PKY.

98. Drawing and Notes on the Cemetery by Don Manuel de la Piedra, June 28, 1811, To and from the Bishop and Curate, 1786–1824, EFP, microfilm reel 38, PKY.

99. The significance of water sources for African burials is noted elsewhere in this chapter. It would appear that planters such as Fatio practiced religious toleration, just as Spanish

authorities did (Criminal Case against Liberty, Jan. 23, 1796, Records of Criminal Proceedings, 1785–1821, EFP, microfilm reel 124, PKY).

100. Kevin Mulroy, *Freedom on the Border: The Seminole Maroons in Florida, the Indian Territory, Coahuila, and Texas* (Lubbock, Tex., 1993).

101. Georgia Writers' Project, *Drums and Shadows;* Wood, *Black Majority;* Daniel Littlefield, *Rice and Slaves: Ethnicity and the Slave Trade in Colonial South Carolina* (Urbana, Ill., 1991); Charles Joyner, *Down by the Riverside: A South Carolina Slave Community* (Urbana, Ill., 1984); Patricia Jones-Jackson, *When Roots Die: Endangered Traditions on the Sea Islands* (Athens, Ga., 1987); Zora Neale Hurston, *Mules and Men* (Philadelphia, 1935); Thompson, *Flash of the Spirit;* Lorenzo Dow Turner, *Africanisms in the Gullah Dialect* (Chicago, 1949); Ian Hancock, "Creole Features in the Afro-Seminole Speech of Brackettville, Texas," *Society for Caribbean Linguistics Occasional Papers* 3 (1975).

102. Thompson, *Flash of the Spirit,* 132–45, and Robert Farris Thompson, *Face of the Gods: Art and Altars of Africa and the African Americas* (New York, 1993). Also see Georgia Writers' Project, *Drums and Shadows.*

103. Gomez, "Muslims in Early America," and *Exchanging Our Country Marks: The Transformation of African Identities in the Colonial and Antebellum South* (Chapel Hill, N.C., 1998); B. G. Martin, "Sapelo Island's Arabic Document: The 'Bilali Diary' in Context," *Georgia Historical Quarterly* 78 (Fall 1994): 589–601.

104. Thomas Madiou, *Histoire d'Haiti* (Port-au-Prince, 1922–23).

105. Trouillot, "From Planters' Journals to Academia: The Haitian Revolution as Unthinkable History"; Hunt, *Haiti's Influence on Antebellum America.*

106. Testamentary Proceedings of Jorge Viassou [*sic*], July 15, 1801, Records of Testamentary Proceedings, 1756–1821, entry 2, EFP, microfilm reel 138, PKY.

107. Thornton, "African Nations."

108. Thornton, "African Soldiers in the Haitian Revolution," 59.

109. Although he was given an impressive military funeral, Biassou died deeply in debt, and his many creditors began clamoring to be paid. Biassou's greatest asset was his pension and that had been heavily borrowed against. There was far from enough to pay the bakers, tailors, storekeepers, and landlords who had allowed him credit so the governor ordered Biassou's gold medal melted and the proceeds applied toward his debts (Testamentary Proceedings of Jorge Biassou, Records of Testamentary Proceedings, 1756–1821, entry 2, EFP, microfilm reel 138, PKY).

Biassou's widow, Romana, remained in Havana. Ill and destitute after Biassou's death, she requested a widow's pension, or half of his monthly salary of 250 pesos. She received considerably less—a pension equal to that of a captain's widow (Petition of Romana Jacobo, Oct. 12, 1801, SD 1268, AGI and Marques de Someruelos to Cavallero, Oct. 22, 1801, ibid.). Thanks to Julius S. Scott for Jacobo reference.

110. Don Roberto McHardy complains of the conduct of the free black Antonio Williams, July 13, 1815, Records of Criminal Proceedings, 1785–1821, no. 5, EFP, microfilm reel 126, PKY.

111. Zephaniah Kingsley, *A Treatise on the Patriarchal or Cooperative System of Society as*

It Exists in Some Governments and Colonies in America, and in the United States, under the Name of Slavery, with Its Necessity and Advantages (1829; reprint, Freeport, N.Y., 1971), 13.

112. Ibid.

113. Ibid.

114. In the final years of the regime, worried parents recorded a number of baptisms for children born years earlier. For example see the entries of Ana Juana Hannahan Kingsley and Josefa Ana Kingsley, baptized on Oct. 17, 1819. Their birth dates are not given, but they were the children of the Wolof Sophia Chidigene Kingsley and of Abraham Hannahan, a mulatto from Charleston, both former slaves of Zephaniah Kingsley (Black Baptisms, vol. 3, CPR, microfilm reel 284 K, PKY).

Chapter 6
The Lives of Black Women

1. Jacqueline Jones, *Labor of Love, Labor of Sorrow: Black Women, Work, and the Family from Slavery to the Present* (New York, 1985), chap. 1; Deborah Gray White, *Ar'n't I a Woman? Female Slaves in the Plantation South* (New York, 1985).

2. Jane Landers, "African and African American Women and Their Pursuit of Rights through Eighteenth-Century Spanish Texts," in *Haunted Bodies: Gender and Southern Texts,* ed. Anne Goodwyn Jones and Susan V. Donaldson (Charlottesville, Va., 1998), 56–76. For comparable findings in Louisiana see Hall, *Africans in Colonial Louisiana,* and Kimberly S. Hanger, "'The Fortunes of Women': Spanish New Orleans's Free Women of African Descent and Their Relations with Slave Women," in *Discovering the Women in Slavery: Emancipating Perspectives on the American Past,* ed. Patricia Morton (Athens, Ga., 1996), 153–78.

3. Landers,"Traditions of African American Freedom," 17–41.

4. These patterns are similar to those Suzanne Lebsock found for free women of color in Petersburg, Va. (*The Free Women of Petersburg: Status and Culture in a Southern Town, 1784–1860* [New York, 1985], chap. 4).

5. Heath Dillard, *Daughters of the Reconquest: Women in Castilian Town Society, 1100–1300* (Cambridge, 1984), 12–35. On the legal and social position of women in Spain and the Spanish colonies see Eugene H. Korth, S.J., and Della M. Flusche, "Dowry and Inheritance in Colonial Spanish America: Peninsular Law and Chilean Practice," *Americas* 43 (Apr. 1987): 395–410; Asunción Lavrin, "Introduction" and "In Search of the Colonial Woman in Mexico: The Seventeenth and Eighteenth Centuries," in *Latin American Women: Historical Perspectives,* ed. Asunción Lavrin (Westport, Conn., 1978), 3–22, 23–59.

6. Dillard, *Daughters of the Reconquest,* 35–67, 96–126. In colonial Latin America, unmarried women over the age of twenty-five and widows enjoyed even more freedom than their married counterparts (Lavrin, "In Search of the Colonial Woman," 30, 41). Also see Patricia Seed, *To Love, Honor, and Obey in Colonial Mexico: Conflicts over Marriage Choice, 1574–1821* (Stanford, 1988); Socolow, "Love and Marriage," and Ramón A. Gutiérrez,

"From Honor to Love: Transformations of the Meaning of Sexuality in Colonial New Mexico," in *Kinship Ideology and Practice in Latin America,* ed. Raymond T. Smith (Chapel Hill, N.C., 1984), 237–63.

7. Fernando de Rojas, *La Celestina,* trans. Lesley Byrd Simpson (Berkeley, 1955), 5–8. *Celestina* draws heavily on the earlier classic by Alfonso Martínez de Toledo, *Little Sermons on Sin: The Archpriest of Talavera,* trans. Lesley Byrd Simpson (Berkeley, 1959).

8. Mary Elizabeth Perry has argued that Spain's patriarchal society became most obsessed with controlling female sexual behavior during times of rapid change or crisis—during plague or famine years, for example, and especially during the period of high mobility and migration that followed the discovery of the Americas. During these periods, society worked to enclose women in the home, the convent, and the brothel. Anxiety over social order might also lead to punitive actions against other "minorities" such as Jews, Muslims, or slaves (Perry, *Gender and Disorder,* 3–13).

9. Ibid., 38–44, 56. For examples of the disadvantages faced by women in Latin America, see the essays in *Sexuality and Marriage in Colonial Latin America.*

10. Dillard, *Daughters of the Reconquest,* 26–30; Asunción Lavrin and Edith Couturier, "Dowries and Wills: A View of Women's Socioeconomic Role in Colonial Guadalajara and Puebla, 1640–1790," *Hispanic American Historical Review* 59 (1979): 280–304; Edith Couturier, "Women and the Family in Eighteenth-Century Mexico: Law and Practice," *Journal of Family History* 10 (Fall, 1985): 294–304.

11. Phillips, *Slavery from Roman Times,* 154–70; Pike, *Aristocrats and Traders,* 170–92; Klein, *African Slavery in Latin America,* 217–41.

12. McAlister, *Spain and Portugal,* 24–26; Charles R. Cutter, *The Legal Culture of Northern New Spain, 1700–1810* (Albuquerque, N.Mex., 1995).

13. Another standard closing might be "The humble petitioner fully expects to be graced with the charity and justice for which your esteemed Majesty is well-known. I kiss your hand and pray that God grant you many years."

On treatment of the "miserable classes" and Christian obligations see Flynn, "Charitable Ritual in Late Medieval and Early Modern Spain."

14. Landers, "Traditions of African American Freedom."

15. Ibid.

16. Hubert H. S. Aimes, "Coartación: A Spanish Institution for the Advancement of Slaves into Freedmen," *Yale Review* 17 (Feb. 1909): 412–31.

17. Manumissions of Catarina, Cecilia, and Catalina Tunno, May 29 and Nov. 3, 1789, Escrituras (Notarized Instruments), 1784–1821, EFP, microfilm reel 169, PKY; Baptisms of Cecilia Francisca Tunno and Catalina Joaquina Tunno, Mar. 4, 1796, Black Baptisms, vol. 2, CPR, microfilm reel 284 J, PKY.

18. Manumission of Mary Beard, Nov. 20, 1818, Notarized Public Instruments from Fernandina, 1813–21, EFP, microfilm reel 166, PKY.

19. Aimes, "Coartación"; Rebecca Scott, *Slave Emancipation in Cuba,* 13–14.

20. The poverty of the colony made uncompensated manumissions a rarity in Florida. Most owners received reimbursements of between two hundred and three hundred

pesos for the freedom of adult slaves, and usually less than one hundred pesos for children (Memorials, 1784–1821, EFP, microfilm reels 76–82, and Records of Civil Proceedings, 1785–1821, EFP, microfilm reels 150–63, PKY).

21. Margarita "Peggy" Saunders was the daughter of Alejandro Saunders, a white South Carolinian, and his black slave, Isabel, and it is possible that she was actually Juan Saunders's half-sister (Frank Marotti, Jr., "Edward Wanton and the Settling of Micanopy," *Florida Historical Quarterly* 73 [Apr. 1995]: 456–77, esp. 460).

22. Petition of Margarita Saunders, Oct. 15, 1794, Records of Civil Proceedings, 1785–1821, EFP, microfilm reel 152, PKY; Will of Edward Wanton, Apr. 5, 1820, Escrituras (Notarized Instruments), 1784–1821, EFP, microfilm reel 168, PKY, cited in Marotti, "Edward Wanton and the Settling of Micanopy," 460, 466. Margaret's children with Eduardo Wanton included Luiz Guillermo Wanton, born Apr. 13, 1795; Juan Zeferino Wanton, born Aug. 26, 1798; María Ysabel Wanton, born Sept. 20, 1800; Carlos Josef Wanton, born May 31, 1802; Enrique Manuel Wanton, born Jan. 15, 1805; Manuela Wanton, born Aug. 24, 1809; Jaime Wanton, born Apr. 22, 1811; Felipe Antonio Manuel Wanton, born Aug. 12, 1819 (Black Baptisms, CPR, vols. 2 and 3, microfilm reels 284 J and K, PKY).

23. Petition of Lucia Saunders, Oct. 5, 1795, Records of Civil Proceedings, 1785–1821, EFP, microfilm reel 152, PKY.

24. Andaina was born in Baltimore and was therefore probably literate in English as well as in Spanish (Petition of Andaina, Feb. 13, 1793, Memorials, 1784–1821, EFP, microfilm reel 78, PKY).

25. The attention to her clothing is significant for several reasons. The Siete Partidas obligated owners to clothe slaves and a slave's charge that they failed to do so might lead to court intervention. Anecdotal references from Spanish sources suggest that free and enslaved Africans, like Spaniards, greatly appreciated fine clothing. Moreover, a slave had property rights in Spanish societies and slaves in St. Augustine sought legal remedy against owners who attempted to alienate animals, tools, clothing, or other forms of slave property.

26. Response of Catalina Cantar (alias Acosta), Dec. 12, 1797, Memorials, 1784–1821, EFP, microfilm reel 79, PKY.

27. Spanish society customarily attached status to clothing and tried unsuccessfully to maintain social boundaries with sumptuary legislation. Andaina described the clothing she bought herself as "cotton cloth with a white background and stripes," so possibly Osnaburg. Catalina described Andaina's ball attire as "yellowish-brown shoes and full dress" (Statement of Catalina Acosta, Feb. 27, 1793, Memorials, 1784–1821, EFP, microfilm reel 78, PKY).

28. Petition of Andaina, Feb. 13, 1793, ibid.

29. Response of Catalina Cantar (Acosta), Dec. 12, 1797, Memorials, 1784–1821, EFP, microfilm reel 79, PKY.

30. Memorial of Andaina, Dec. 2, 1797, and Response of Catalina Cantar (Acosta), Dec. 12, 1797, Memorials, 1784–1821, EFP, microfilm reel 79, PKY.

31. Ibid. Apparently Don Domingo Reyes never purchased his daughter's freedom as planned.

32. This claim indicates that Nancy knew others had successfully been designated free and been granted homesteads (Petition of Nancy, Sept. 19, 1792, Records of Civil Proceedings, 1785–1821, EFP, microfilm reel 151, PKY). For more on Juan McQueen see *The Letters of Don Juan McQueen to His Family, Written from Spanish East Florida, 1791–1807,* ed. Walter Charlton Hartridge (Columbia, S.C., 1943).

33. Petition of Nancy, Sept. 19, 1792, Records of Civil Proceedings, 1785–1821, EFP, microfilm reel 151, PKY.

34. Ibid.

35. Ibid.

36. Investigations consequent to the unauthorized absence of Juan Bautista Collins, May 21, 1801, Records of Civil Proceedings, 1785–1821, EFP, microfilm reel 156, PKY. Collins later returned to Florida to satisfy his debts and resume his business.

37. Memorial of María Witten, Aug. 27, 1798, Memorials, 1784–1821, EFP, microfilm reel 79, PKY.

38. Ibid., and response by Dons José and Bernardino Sánchez. For a discussion of Spanish interrogatories and the relative weight assigned to witnesses of different status, see Alexandra Parma Cook and Noble David Cook, *Good Faith and Truthful Ignorance: A Case of Transatlantic Bigamy* (Durham, N.C., 1991), 87–89, 91–103, 112–14.

39. Payments to Antonio, June 30, Nov. 29, Dec. 30, 1794, Accounts of the Royal Treasury, 1784–95, SD 2635, AGI; Payment to Juan Wright, Nov. 25, 1788, to Carlos Hall, July 31, 1797, and to Felipe Edimboro, July 13, 1818, Accounts of the Royal Treasury, 1796–1819, SD 2636, AGI.

40. Petition of Felipe Edimboro, July 6, 1794, Records of Civil Proceedings, 1785–1821, EFP, microfilm reel 152, PKY. In order to improve their chances in the courts, Felipe and Filis Edimboro were baptized and married in the Catholic church. The couple was baptized on July 15, 1794 (Black Baptisms, vol. 2, CPR, microfilm reel 284 J, PKY), and married on July 29, 1794 (Black Marriages, CPR, microfilm reel 284 L, PKY). The free black couple María de la Luz and Joseph de Arrivas served as their baptismal and marriage sponsors and also were godparents for five of their twelve children.

41. Cecilia also complained that Lasaga had insulted her (Memorials of Cecilia Tunno, Mar. 20, 1794, and of Rafaela, Aug. 2, 1796, Memorials, 1784–1821, EFP, microfilm reel 79, PKY).

42. Memorial of Mariana Tudory, Dec. 12, 1793, Memorials, 1784–1821, EFP, microfilm reel 78, PKY. Mariana Tudory was illiterate, so her daughter Margarita wrote her petition for her.

43. Rafaela asked the court to order Vara to return her pig, which had not yet been impregnated after two months. Vara wanted eight pesos for the pig's care, which Rafaela found exorbitant. With the court's arbitration, the women agreed that Vara would accept four pesos and two piglets from a future litter (Memorial of Rafaela, Aug. 4, 1796, Memorials, 1784–1821, EFP, microfilm reel 79, PKY.

44. Robert Olwell, "'Loose, Idle and Disorderly': Slave Women in the Eighteenth-Century Charleston Marketplace," in *More Than Chattel: Black Women and Slavery in the*

Americas, ed. David Barry Gaspar and Darlene Clark Hines (Indianapolis, Ind., 1996), 97–110. On basketry see Ferguson, *Uncommon Ground,* chap. 1; John Michael Vlach, *The Afro-American Tradition in Decorative Arts* (Athens, Ga., 1990), chap. 1; Dale Rosengarten, *Row upon Row: Sea Grass Baskets of the South Carolina Lowcountry* (Columbia, S.C., 1987).

45. The couple's six children inherited the other half of Juan's "fortune" (Testament of Juan Fernández, 1821, Escrituras [Notarized Instruments], 1784–1821, EFP, microfilm reel 168, PKY).

46. Testamentary Proceedings of F. X. Sánchez, fol. 93, Records of Testamentary Proceedings, 1756–1821, EFP, microfilm reel 141, PKY.

47. Jornales que pagan al mes los negros pertenecientes a los menores hijos de Don Juan Saunders, July 31, 1800, Records of Civil Proceedings, 1785–1821, EFP, microfilm reel 155, PKY. Richel is probably a Spanish spelling of Rachel.

48. Spanish officials conducted detailed inventories of the property of rebels, debtors, persons leaving the province, and persons charged with serious crimes, or in cases where a propertied person died intestate. These extensive slave lists show names and ages of the individuals, with family groupings identified, and often give information about special skills, infirmities, and even which mothers were nursing children. See the multiple inventories of planters charged with rebellion in 1795 (Proceedings on the Seizures Relevant to the Rebellion of 1795, 1795–99, EFP, microfilm reels 129–30, PKY). Also see List of the San Pablo Plantation Slaves, belonging to the Panton, Leslie and Company, Feb. 8, 1815, Cuba 419 A, AGI, and the inventories and probates of Francisco Xavier Sánchez, Nov. 31, 1807, Records of Testamentary Proceedings, 1756 1821, EFP, microfilm reel 141, PKY, and Diego Espinosa, Sept. 3, 1756, Records of Testamentary Proceedings, 1756–1821, EFP, microfilm reel 134, PKY. María Evans's debts led to the inventory of her New Waterford estate, which includes three generations of slave families, on Oct. 19, 1792. See Patricia C. Griffin, "Mary Evans: A Woman of Substance," *El Escribano* 14 (1977): 57–76. Slaveowners also produced their own lists to report thefts by Indians or invaders, for example, see lists of slaves stolen by Indians from Francis Phelipe Fatio, July 16, 1802, and from Mrs. Susan Cashen Murphy, May 18, 1837, in Glunt Papers and those of Zephaniah Kingsley, Patriot War Papers, Claims 1812–13, manuscript collection 31, claim no. 57, SAHS.

49. The enslaved Nora obviously cared for her charge because she sent small gifts of clothing to Clarissa in St. Augustine (Testimony of Diane McGirtt [also Saunders], in Investigations of Alix, free black, Nov. 13, 1791, Records of Criminal Proceedings, 1785–1821, EFP, microfilm reel 123, PKY).

50. Tannenbaum, *Slave and Citizen.* See Landers, "Traditions of African American Freedom"; Schafer, "Shades of Freedom"; and Marotti, "Edward M. Wanton and the Settling of Micanopy." Kimberly Hanger finds many similar cases of cross-racial inheritance in Spanish New Orleans. See *Bounded Lives, Bounded Places.*

51. McAlister, *Spain and Portugal,* 133–52. For an excellent look at how these systems actually operated see Stephanie Blank, "Patrons, Clients and Kin in Seventeenth-Century

Caracas: A Methodological Essay in Colonial Spanish American History," *Hispanic American Historical Review* 54, no. 2 (1974): 260–83. An older but still useful study is by Foster, "Cofradía and Compadrazgo."

52. Baptism of María Beatriz Stone, Feb. 17, 1788, Black Baptisms, vol. 1, CPR, microfilm reel 284 J, PKY. Beatriz was the free mulatto daughter of John Stone of South Carolina and of his slave Regina. She was approximately thirty-nine years old when she converted to the Catholic faith and, after examination by the priest, was baptized. Baptism of Joseph (b. 1771), Nov. 12, 1773; Beatriz María (b. Mar. 15, 1776), Dec. 21, 1779; Anna María (b. Jan. 18, 1777), Dec. 21, 1779; Catalina Rosa María (b. Sept. 16, 1779), Dec. 21, 1779; María de la Concepción and María del Carmen (b. June 19, 1784), July 24, 1784; and Francisco Mateo, July 12, 1787, Black Baptisms, vol. 1, CPR, microfilm reel 284 J, PKY. Copies of these baptismal records also appear in Testamentary Proceedings of F. X. Sánchez, 1808, Records of Testamentary Proceedings, 1756–1821, EFP, microfilm reel 141, PKY. The baptismal record of Antonio José, who was born in 1782, cannot be located.

53. A two-story stone structure on San Carlos (Charlotte) Street housed the family on the top floor and the general store on the street level. Sánchez's second town house was located on Marina Street. See Inventory and appraisal of the estate of Francisco Xavier Sánchez, Oct. 1808, Records of Testamentary Proceedings, 1756–1821, EFP, microfilm reel 141, PKY.

54. Accounts of F. X. Sánchez in *Florida Plantation Records,* ed. U. B. Phillips and J. D. Glunt (St. Louis, Mo., 1927). For Florida shipping records for 1795 and 1796 see Accounts of the Royal Treasury, 1784–95, SD 2635, and 1796–1819, SD 2636, AGI.

55. The family of eight children and five slaves appears as household no. 55 on San Carlos Street (Census of 1793, Census Returns, 1784–1814, EFP, microfilm reel 148, PKY). Antonio and Mateo Sánchez appear on the Roster of School Boys, Mar. 25, 1796, SD 2531, AGI. Both died suddenly on June 19, 1804, Antonio at age 22, and Mateo at age 18. The cause may have been accidental since there was no mention of illness. They were buried the following day in the church cemetery (Black Burials, CPR, microfilm reel 284 L, PKY).

56. Beatriz María Sánchez married Francisco Pérez of Castile, Anna María Sánchez married José Manuel Fernández of Galicia, and Catalina married Francisco Sánchez of Granada (Matrimonial Licenses, 1785–1803, EFP, microfilm reel 132, PKY; Black Marriages, CPR, microfilm reel 284 L, PKY).

57. Census of 1793, Census Returns, 1784–1814, EFP, microfilm reel 148, PKY.

58. Marriage sponsors were the groom's siblings Francisco Sánchez and Catalina Sánchez (Marriage of José Sánchez and Lucía Ysnardy, Feb. 20, 1805, Black Marriages, CPR, microfilm reel 284 L, PKY). Lucía Ysnardy inherited a wooden house from her father, perhaps as a dowry (Testament of Miguel Ysnardy, Mar. 2, 1803, Escrituras (Notarized Instruments), 1784–1821, EFP, microfilm reel 171 A, PKY).

59. Burial of María Beatriz de Piedra (Stone), Nov. 30, 1791, Black Burials, CPR, microfilm reel 284 L, PKY. Among the families for whom Beatriz served as godmother were Filis and Felipe Edimboro Sánchez, when they were still her slaves. She was the godmother of their son Tiburcio, who was baptized on Aug. 17, 1788 (Black Baptisms, vol. 1, CPR, microfilm reel 284 J, PKY).

60. The baptisms of Sánchez's eleven legitimate children are recorded in White Baptisms, CPR, vols. 1–4, microfilm reel 284 I, PKY. Francisco Xavier Sánchez and his wife María del Carmen Hill served as godparents for Fulgencio Pérez, the son of Sánchez's quadroon daughter Beatriz María and her Spanish husband Francisco Pérez on Jan. 16, 1802; Francisco Xavier Sánchez's legitimate children Manuel Sánchez and Teresa Sánchez served as godparents for Juan Rafael Ulatia Fernández, the son of Sánchez's quadroon daughter Ana and her Spanish husband, José Fernández, on Jan. 14, 1802; and Sánchez's legitimate children Domingo Sánchez and Rafaela Sánchez served as godparents for another of that couple's children, Estanislao Manuel Basilio Fernández, on May 7, 1804 (Black Baptisms, vol. 2, CPR, microfilm reel 284 J, PKY).

61. Testamentary proceedings ordered on the death of Don Francisco Xavier Sánchez, Nov. 31, 1807 (Records of Testamentary Proceedings, 1756–1821, EFP, microfilm reel 141, PKY). Two unmarried daughters and their brother lived in the house. The other three sisters married Spaniards and had homes of their own.

62. Will of Zephaniah Kingsley, Duval County Probates, 1203, cited in Schafer, "Shades of Freedom," 138.

63. The ruins of Munsilna McGundo's large two-story tabby house still stand on Fort George Island, Fla., down the road from the plantation complex where Kingsley and Anna Magigine Jai presided (Schafer, "Shades of Freedom," 137–39, 144–45).

64. Testamentary Proceedings of Jacob Wiggins, Nov. 14, 1797, Records of Testamentary Proceedings, 1756–1821, EFP, microfilm reel 134, PKY. Declaration of Ana Gallum, Oct. 3, 1799, ibid.

Baptisms of Patricia Wiggins (b. 1782), María Wiggins (b. 1785), Benjamín Wiggins (b. 1788), and Abigail Juana Wiggins (b. 1789) all on Feb. 13, 1795, Black Baptisms, vol. 2, CPR, microfilm reel 284 J, PKY; Baptisms of Ana María Wiggins (b. May, 15, 1792) and Jorge José Wiggins (b. July 10, 1795) both on Nov. 8, 1797, ibid.

65. The free black militiaman Jorge Sanco brought suit against Ana (alias Nansi) Wiggins to try to force the manumission of his wife, Rosa, which Ana contested (Petition of Jorge Sanco, June 4, 1810, Records of Civil Proceedings, 1785–1821, EFP, microfilm reel 160, PKY).

66. Testamentary Proceedings of Jacob Wiggins, Nov. 14, 1797, Records of Testamentary Proceedings, 1756–1821, EFP, microfilm reel 134, PKY; Declaration of Ana Gallum, Oct. 3, 1799, ibid.; Baptism of Pedro Casaly, (b. Sept. 18, 1799) on Sept. 5, 1800. The child is listed as the natural son of Pedro Casaly and Ana Wiggins, free black from Senegal (Black Baptisms, vol. 2, CPR, microfilm reel 284 J, PKY).

67. Petition of Nancy Wiggins, July 3, 1811, and reply by Governor Juan José de Estrada, July 9, 1811, SFLR, record group 599, series 992, Memorials and Concessions, 1786–1821, box 12, folder 41.

68. Ana (Nansi) Wiggins owned lots 6 and 8 in square 16 and half-lots 3 and 4 in square 14 (Census of Fernandina and Amelia Island, 1814, Census Returns, 1784–1814, EFP, microfilm reel 148, PKY). Ana's daughter Isabella (also known as Eliza, Elizabeth, Beatriz and Patty) and her four children lived as a family with the white militia officer Don Carlos

Clarke, in Fernandina. Isabella Wiggins held lot 14, square 8, and the half-lot 12, on the same square. She built a house on the latter. The United States government voided her claim to three hundred acres on the east side of Lake George on the basis that she failed to comply with the conditions of the Spanish grant (The United States v. Wiggins, 14 Peters, 334; *SLGF,* vol. 1, 339–40).

69. Jacqueline Jones, *Labor of Love,* chap. 1; White, *Ar'n't I a Woman?* chap. 1; Melton A. McLaurin, *Celia, a Slave* (Athens, Ga., 1991).

70. Investigations of . . . Tony, July 19, 1786, Miscellaneous Legal Instruments and Proceedings, 1784–1819, EFP, microfilm reel 110, PKY.

71. Petition of Luzia [*sic*], Sept. 6, 1796, Memorials, 1784–1821, EFP, microfilm reel 79, PKY.

72. Thomas was approximately thirty-three years of age and was a sawyer. He and Sara and another slave named Juan escaped from the plantation of Isaac Wied. The fourth member of the party, Diego, escaped from another unnamed owner, and all the runaways left spouses behind (Criminal Case against Thomas, 1789, Records of Criminal Proceedings, 1785–1821, EFP, microfilm reel 122, PKY).

73. Witnesses who testified at Thomas's hearing were Fernando Falany, who had given Sara refuge, the free black, Ysaias, a white visitor to Falany's named Juan Taylor, and Don Jorge J. F. Clarke, Thomas's employer who spoke on his behalf (ibid.).

74. *Narrative of A Voyage to the Spanish Main in the Ship "Two Friends"; The Occupation of Amelia island, by M'Gregor, &c.—Sketches of the Province of East Florida; and Anecdotes Illustrative of the Habits and Manners of the Seminole Indians,* ed. John W. Griffin (Gainesville, Fla., 1978), 142.

75. Accounts of Don Juan Saunders, July 3, 1800, Records of Civil Proceedings, 1785–1821, EFP, microfilm reel 155, PKY. The same practitioner, Francisco Pérez, bled Saunders's slaves and his daughter and extracted the daughter's molar.

76. Statement of Don Juan Joseph Bousquet, May 9, 1789, Records of Criminal Proceedings, 1785–1821, EFP, microfilm reel 122, PKY.

Chapter 7
Slaves and the Slave Trade

1. Fish had traded with St. Augustine since the 1730s (J. Leitch Wright, Jr., *Florida in the American Revolution,* 107). Gordon paid duties on three cargoes of African slaves in 1764–65 (William S. Coker and Thomas D. Watson, *Indian Traders of the Southeastern Spanish Borderlands: Panton, Leslie & Company and John Forbes and Company, 1783–1847* [Pensacola, Fla., 1986], 16). Kip's connections to St. Augustine also date to the 1730s when his brother, Abraham, piloted William Walton's provision-laden sloops from New York to Florida. Abraham Kip also owned a brewhouse in New York City patronized by some of the conspirators in the "Great Negro Plot" of 1741 (*Calendar of State Papers, Colonial Series, America and West Indies,* vol. 44, 136–37; Harmon, *Trade and Privateering in Spanish Florida,* 89–90; T. J. Davis, *Rumor of Revolt,* 87).

2. Books of Slave Duties, 1752–63, Cuba 472, AGI.

3. Manuel Moreno Fraginals points out that the British slavers introduced as many slaves into Cuba in eleven months as the Spaniards would have in twelve to fifteen years, at their previous rates (*The Sugarmill: The Socioeconomic Complex of Sugar in Cuba* [New York, 1976], 17).

4. Fish and his partner, John Gordon, served as sales agents for Spaniards evacuating Florida. Estimates of their acquisitions of prime Florida properties range from 4,000,000 to 10,000,000 acres. Fish probably employed some of his young African slaves on the plantation he built on Anastasia Island (Coker and Watson, *Indian Traders of the Southeastern Spanish Borderlands,* 16).

5. Schafer, "Yellow Silk Ferret." David Hancock describes the international nature of Oswald's contacts and diverse enterprises and how they enabled him to "integrate backward" into agriculture in Florida (*Citizens of the World: London Merchants and the Integration of the British Atlantic Community, 1735–1785* [Cambridge, 1995], chap. 5, and chap. 6, 203–4).

6. Schafer, "Yellow Silk Ferret," 76–78, 82–85.

7. One author claims that most of the slaves that New York traders acquired on the Guinea Coast were sold in "the West Indies, Charleston, or in Florida after the British occupation" (Virginia Harrington, *The New York Merchants on the Eve of the Revolution* [New York, 1935], 202). For the Africanization of Louisiana see Hall, *Africans in Colonial Louisiana.*

8. More than half of the twelve thousand immigrants who entered Florida in 1782 and 1783 were black slaves (J. Leitch Wright, Jr., *Florida in the American Revolution,* 126–27, 133, and "Blacks in British East Florida."

9. Siebert, *Loyalists in East Florida,* vol. 2, 15–17, 37–41, 71–82.

10. Schafer, "Yellow Silk Ferret," 93–97.

11. Siebert, *Loyalists in East Florida,* vol. 2, 125, 140.

12. Governor Zéspedes constantly complained that he had insufficient manpower and even asked to import one hundred Guachinango Indians from New Spain for paid labor in Florida, but this plan came to naught (Vicente Manuel de Zéspedes to Joseph de Ezpeleta, Nov. 9, 1787, Cuba 1395, AGI).

13. Taxes on the Introduction of Slaves, Accounts of the Royal Treasury, 1784–95, SD 2635, and 1796–1819, SD 2636, AGI.

14. Memorials of Gonzalo Zamorano, Mar. 14, 1787, and Apr. 1, 1789, SD 2576, AGI; Royal decree permitting the free commerce of slaves, Feb. 28, 1789, SD 2207, AGI.

15. Notarized purchase of a slave woman by Sebastián Berazaluze for 230 pesos, Feb. 22, 1796, Cuba 419, AGI.

16. Census of 1793, Nov. 30, 1793, Cuba 1436, AGI.

17. Taxes on the Introduction of Slaves, 1793, Accounts of the Royal Treasury, 1784–95, SD 2635, AGI.

18. Report of Vicente Manuel de Zéspedes, Oct. 20, 1784, SD 2587, AGI; Census of Father Thomas Hassett, 1786, Census Returns, 1784–1814, EFP, microfilm reel 148, PKY;

Report of Vicente Manuel de Zéspedes, Oct. 2, 1788, Cuba 1395, AGI; Report of Juan Nepomuceno de Quesada, Nov. 30, 1793, Cuba 1437, AGI; Report of Sebastián Kindelán, Oct. 5, 1814, Inspection Returns of the Third Battalion of Cuba, 1785–1814, EFP, microfilm reel 76, PKY.

19. That year, census takers recorded a total of seventy-nine whites (forty males and thirty-nine females) and 319 slaves (172 males and 147 females) living along the banks of the St. Johns River (Census for St. Johns River, June 1, 1813, Correspondence between the Governor and Subordinates on the St. Johns and St. Marys Rivers, 1784–1820, EFP, microfilm reel 55 A, PKY).

20. The free white population on Amelia Island totaled 428 (217 males and 211 females) while the enslaved population totalled 861 (524 males and 337 females) (Fernandina Census, June 1, 1813, Correspondence between the Governor and Subordinates on the St. Johns and St. Marys Rivers, 1784–1820, EFP, microfilm reel 55 A, PKY).

21. Accounts of the Royal Treasury, 1784–95, SD 2635, and 1796–1819, SD 2636, AGI.

22. Schafer, "Yellow Silk Ferret." For a comparison to Anglo-Caribbean, lowcountry, and Chesapeake plantations see Mullin, *Africa in America,* chaps. 4 and 6.

23. Susan R. Parker, "'I Am neither Your Subject nor Your Subordinate,'" *El Escribano* (1988): 44–60. Fatio requested and received permission to ship lumber, tar, resin, and turpentine to Guarico on Apr. 13, 1787 (Memorials, 1784–1821, EFP, microfilm reel 77, PKY; Claims of F. J. Fatio and Francis P. Fatio, *SLGF,* vol. 3, 67–71).

24. Francis Phelipe Fatio's List of Slaves Stolen, July 16, 1802, cited in James David Glunt, "Plantation and Frontier Records of East and Middle Florida, 1789–1868" (Ph.D. diss., University of Michigan, 1930), 15–19.

25. Patrick Tonyn to Vicente Manuel de Zéspedes, July 5, 1784, in Lockey, *East Florida,* 215.

26. Census of Father Thomas Hassett, 1786, Census Returns, 1784–1814, EFP, microfilm reel 148, PKY.

27. Testamentary Proceedings, Estate of Francisco Xavier Sánchez, 1807, Records of Testamentary Proceedings, 1756–1821, EFP, microfilm reel 141, PKY; Claims of Heirs of Francis Xavier Sánchez, *SLGF,* vol. 5, 25–32.

28. Governor Benjamin Guerard of South Carolina charged that Sánchez and his partners, Daniel McGirtt and Luciano Herrera, purchased the condemned schooner, *Flying Fish,* in Havana and then returned to the St. Johns River to load "upwards of one hundred Negroes from the St. Johns River . . . the property of the gentlemen of South Carolina and Georgia" for sale in Havana (Benjamin Guerard to Luis de Unzaga, Aug. 2, 1783, manuscript box 45, PKY). Despite Guerard's complaint, the *Flying Fish* carried seventy-six slaves into Havana in July 1799, eight-one slaves in Feb. 1800, and ninety slaves in Nov. 1800 (Registration of Blacks Introduced into Havana, SD 2207, AGI).

29. Petition of Felipe Edimboro, Mar. 6, 1794, Records of Civil Proceedings, 1785–1821, EFP, microfilm reel 152, PKY.

30. Commission of Don Juan McQueen as Captain of Militia, Dec. 20, 1798; Appoint-

ment of Don Juan McQueen as Judge, Nov. 13, 1801 *(Letters of Don Juan McQueen,* 49–50, 57–58); Claims of Heirs of John McQueen, *SLGF,* vol. 4, 109–12.

31. John McQueen's License to Admit Slaves, Oct. 15, 1798, Papers on Negro Titles, Runaways, etc., 1787–1805, EFP, microfilm reel 167, PKY.

32. *Letters of Don Juan McQueen,* 19.

33. John McQueen to Eliza Anne McQueen, Apr. 24, 1792, and John McQueen to Liza Anne McQueen, Jan. 20, 1801, ibid., 18, 56.

34. John McQueen, Junior, to Eliza Anne McQueen, Aug. 25, 1797, ibid., 41–42.

35. McQueen complained that he was forced to discharge the previous overseer, William Hollinsworth, for being a "worthless idle fellow" who "attended more to his own interests than to my affairs" (ibid., 72–73).

36. Testamentary Proceedings of Don Juan McQueen, Oct. 14, 1807, Records of Testamentary Proceedings, 1756–1821, EFP, microfilm reel 141, PKY.

37. John McQueen to Eliza Anne McQueen, Dec. 1, 1793, *Letters of Don Juan McQueen,* 19–20.

38. Juan McQueen died on the evening of Oct. 11, 1807, before the arrival of a physician. Under Harry's supervision, his slaves buried him the next day. The following day Spanish officials arrived and ordered the slaves to dig up McQueen's casket and open it. After inspecting McQueen's body, they took it to St. Augustine for burial in "holy ground" (Testamentary Proceedings of Don Juan McQueen, Testimony of Enrique Harry, Oct. 14, 1807, Records of Testamentary Proceedings, 1756–1821, EFP, microfilm reel 141, PKY; Claim of Harry McQueen, Patriot War Papers, Claim no. 269, manuscript collection 31, SAHS).

39. John Houston McIntosh later became embroiled in the Patriot Rebellion of 1812 and, when he was forced to leave the colony, sold the Fort George Island estate to Zephaniah Kingsley (John McQueen to John McQueen, Jr., Jan. 5, 1804, *Letters of Don Juan McQueen,* 62–64).

40. Schafer, "Shades of Freedom."

41. Claims of Anna and Zephaniah Kingsley, *SLGF,* vol. 4, 6–37.

42. Petition of Zephaniah Kingsley to Robert Reid, Judge of the Superior Court for the District of East Florida, Claims 1812–13, ms box 131, SAHS; Schafer, "Shades of Freedom," 140–42.

43. There is no way to know Morton's reasoning (Kingsley, *Treatise,* 14).

44. Ibid., 8–10.

45. Schafer, "Shades of Freedom," 145–48.

46. After raiders ruined his interior plantations Kingsley purchased Juan McQueen's old plantation on Fort George Island from the failed Patriot, John Houston McIntosh, and transferred his family and slaves there in 1814 (Claims of Zephaniah Kingsley, *SLGF,* vol 4., 24–25; Schafer, "Shades of Freedom," 141). It is clear that, although Kingsley allowed his slaves free time and some autonomy, he still regulated them by disallowing visiting and screening visitors *(Treatise,* 14).

47. For a detailed discussion of the advantages to slaves of the Caribbean management style see Mullin, *Africa in America,* chap. 6.

48. Daniel L. Schafer is preparing a manuscript on Zephaniah Kingsley and places Jack Tinguebari and his family among the sixteen slaves Kingsley shipped to Florida with Captain Joel Dunn. See appendix 9 (Personal communication, Daniel L. Schafer, Oct. 20, 1996).

49. On the importance of the *minkisi* bags see Thompson, *Flash of the Spirit,* 117–19, and *Face of the Gods,* 56–60. Such Congo charms were raffia bags on cords that contained medicines (clay, powdered wood, seeds, sticks, stones, claws) and a soul that directed the power of the charm. Jack distributed crab claws among the conspirators of the Vesey plot and said that they would prevent the bearer from being wounded *(Denmark Vesey: The Slave Conspiracy of 1822,* ed. Robert S. Starobin [Englewood Cliffs, N.J., 1970], 3, 41–42). One of famed bluesman Robert Johnson's versions of "Come on in My Kitchen" includes a line "I've taken the last nickel out of her nation sack."

50. Although most scholars of the Vesey rebellion describe Jack as a "conjurer," or religious leader, in fact, Kingsley described him as a skilled carpenter, "very prime" *(Treatise,* 13–14). Kingsley commended several Muslim "drivers, or influential negroes, whose integrity to their masters and influence over their slaves prevented it [deserting to the enemy]" and he added, "what is still more remarkable, in both instances the influential negroes were Africans, and professors of the Mahomedan religion." Kingsley may have been referring to the Muslim slave drivers Bilali, Thomas Spalding's slave driver on Sapelo Island, and his countryman, Salih Bilali, on St. Simon's (Interview with Cornelia Walker Bailey, Aug. 2–3, 1990, Hog Hammock, Sapelo Island, Ga.). Mrs. Bailey is the great-great-great granddaughter of Bilali (B. G. Martin, "Sapelo Island's Arabic Document: The 'Bilali Diary' in Context," *Georgia Historical Quarterly* 78 (Fall 1994): 589–601). See too Gomez, "Muslims in Early America."

51. Kingsley, *Treatise,* 14.

52. Charles H. Fairbanks, "The Kingsley Slave Cabins in Duval County, Florida, 1968," *Conference on Historic Sites Archaeology Papers,* vol. 7 (Columbia, S.C., 1972), 62–93; Karen Jo Walker, "Kingsley and His Slaves: Anthropological Interpretation and Evaluation," *Volumes in Historical Archaeology,* vol. 5 (Columbia, S.C., 1989).

53. Claims of John Fraser, *SLGF,* vol. 3, 141–45; *Guinea Journals: Journeys into Guinea-Conakry during the Sierra Leone Phase, 1800–1821,* ed. Bruce L. Mouser (Washington, D.C., 1979), 128–30.

54. Fraser's executors presented claims against the United States for the considerable damages to his Greenfield plantation during the Patriot War. The claim was eventually settled for $157,146 (Patriot War Papers, Claims of John Fraser, manuscript collection 31, claim no. 54, SAHS).

55. Schafer, "Shades of Freedom," 137, n. 152. Fraser's agent at Bangra, Charles Hickson, probably facilitated this process *(SLGF,* vol. 3, 145).

56. Fenda and John Fraser had five children—James, Margal (Margaret), Mary Lyn (Mary Ann), Eleanor, and Elizabeth. Although their daughters remained in Africa with

Fenda, Fraser took James to South Carolina with him, presumably to learn his father's business. Trusting him to pursue the best interests of his children in Africa, Fraser named Kingsley as an executor of his will. Fraser instructed his executors to sell his property, including all but a few favored slaves whom he freed, and to invest the proceeds in the United States to fund English educations for the children and to care for them until age twenty-one (Testamentary Proceedings of John Fraser, 1814, Records of Testamentary Proceedings, 1756–1821, EFP, reel 134, PKY; and Jan. 24, 1816, Escrituras [Notarized Instruments], 1784–1821, EFP, microfilm reel 173, PKY). See also Daniel L. Schafer, "Family Ties That Bind: Anglo-African Slave Traders in Africa and Florida, John Fraser and His Descendants," unpublished manuscript.

Fraser's daughter Eleanor died at Sinburria in Rio Pongo on Sept. 1, 1824, and James and Margaret were also dead by 1826, when the surviving daughters and their husbands made claims on Fraser's estate. Daughter Elizabeth Frazer [*sic*] and William Skelton were "lawfully married according to the customs of this Country," on May 20, 1825, according to the signed statements of Mongo Barky, chief of Bashia Branch, Rio Pongo, and Mongo Besenty, chief of Bahia, Rio Pongo. On July 2, 1826, "by special license," the Reverend G. H. E. Metgen of St. Patrick married the couple a second time in Sierra Leone. Fraser's other surviving daughter, Mary Ann, married another native of Africa, Thomas Gaffrey Curtis. Skelton and Curtis, like their wives, may have had European fathers (Claims of John Fraser, *SLGF,* vol. 3, 141–45).

57. Coker and Watson, *Indian Traders of the Southeastern Spanish Borderlands,* 34. Payments to Langueste, Oct. 5 and Dec. 29, 1784, Accounts of the Royal Treasury, 1784–95, SD 2635, AGI.

58. Census Returns, 1784–1814, EFP, microfilm reel 148, PKY.

59. John Forbes's List of Property at the San Pablo Plantation, Feb. 8, 1815, Cuba 417 A, AGI.

60. Governor Guerard charged that Francisco Xavier Sánchez stole more than one hundred slaves from South Carolina and Georgia and sold them in Havana in June of 1783 (Benjamin Guerard to Luis de Unzaga, Aug. 2, 1783, manuscript box 45, PKY).

61. Domingo de Ferrariz to Pedro de Lerena, Nov. 29, 1790, SD 2207, AGI.

62. Judicial Sales of the Estates of Juan Hudson, Oct. 4, 1790, Escrituras (Notarized Instruments), EFP, microfilm reel 169, PKY; and of Jesse Fish, Apr. 30, 1792, ibid., microfilm reel 170.

63. Officials conducted a complete inventory of the seized estates in July and August of 1795 (Proceedings on the Seizures Relevant to the Rebellion of 1795, 1795–99, EFP, microfilm reels 129–30, PKY; Sale of the Slaves of Jorge Knolls [Paris, Waley and her child, and Waley's mother, Paty] to Francis Xavier Sánchez, Dec. 20, 1789, ibid.).

64. Judicial Sale of the Property of Carlos Seton, May 17, 1819, Escrituras (Notarized Instruments), 1784–1821, EFP, microfilm reel 168, PKY.

65. Escrituras (Notarized Instruments), 1819, EFP, microfilm reel 168, PKY.

66. The royal interpreter of Indian languages, Antonio Huertas, translated and signed for Pincali, Simancy, and Pafosafacho (Sales to Don Manuel Solana, May 13 and July 12,

1819, Escrituras [Notarized Instruments], 1784–1821, EFP, microfilm reel 168, PKY). The later notarial records also include other sales to Solana and to other Spaniards in 1820 and 1821.

Indians of the Argentine frontier developed an economy based on capture and ransom of Spanish settlers (primarily women), and the Spanish government eventually budgeted annual allotments to pay these ransoms (Susan Migden Socolow, "Spanish Captives in Indian Societies: Cultural Contact Along the Argentine Frontier, 1600–1835," *Hispanic American Historical Review* 72 [Feb. 1992]: 73–99).

67. Sale of slaves brought in the brigantine *Ida,* Oct. 30, 1800, Escrituras (Notarized Instruments), 1784–1821, EFP, microfilm reel 171, PKY.

68. The cargo consisted of 168 adult males, or *piezas,* twenty-seven adult females, seven male and eleven female adolescents, and fourteen male and eleven female children. Given Kingsley's association with John Fraser, these slaves may have come from the Rio Pongo coast (Data on Slaves Introduced into Havana on the Frigate *Superior,* by Zephaniah Kingsley, Mar. 31, 1802, SD 2207, AGI). Kingsley imported sixteen slaves from Mozambique in 1806 (Miscellaneous Legal Instruments and Proceedings, 1784–1819, EFP, microfilm reel 114, PKY).

69. Sales by William Lawrence, July 29, 1802, Escrituras (Notarized Instruments), 1784–1821, EFP, microfilm reel 171 A, PKY. Arredondo appears in Spanish Florida records by at least 1800 and registered a bilander in the province in 1802. Sometime thereafter, his son Juan became the company's factor in Spanish Florida.

70. Cook's slaves said that after leaving Guinea they landed at another port (possibly Havana) and were loaded onto the ship in which they were interviewed, the schooner *Cristiana.* The two cargo inspections are found in William Cook, Feb. 1802, and William Northrup, July 20, 1802, Miscellaneous Legal Instruments and Proceedings, 1784–1819, EFP, microfilm reel 113, PKY.

John Thornton argues that African nations were recognized ethnolinguistically, and that many nations subsumed smaller states or groups by which Africans primarily identified. While recognizing the complexity, he warns that the degree of diversity can be, and has been, exaggerated. This shipment may have been anomalous, yet it seems surprising that the black translators did not command any of the lingua francas such as Mandinga or Yoruba by that time (Thornton, *Africa and Africans,* 185–91).

71. John McQueen to Robert Mackay, Feb. 4, 1807, Hartridge, *Letters of Don Juan McQueen,* 72–73.

72. Registration of the *Cirila* by Don Tadeo de Arribas, Jan. 19, 1810, and registration of the *Don Alonso,* Jan. 25, 1810, Cuba 419, AGI.

73. On Mar. 1, 1810, Hurlbert declared that he had ten *piezas* or adult males, eight *muleques* or adolescent males, seventeen adult females, including two nursing mothers, and four adolescent females (Miscellaneous Legal Instruments and Proceedings, 1784–1819, EFP, microfilm reel 115, PKY).

74. John Fraser to Governor Enrique White, Apr. 28, 1810, Exechequer Proceedings, 1787–1819, EFP, microfilm reel 133, PKY, cited in Schafer, "Family Ties That Bind." Fraser owned the *Aguila,* which was also known as the *Eagle of Charleston,* ibid.

75. Puerto Rican officials impounded ninety-two slaves from the Rio Pongo on June 8, 1810, twelve of whom belonged to James Cashen and Gaspar Hernandez, but Cashen successfully imported twenty-eight slaves from the coast of Africa to Fernandina on July 9, 1810. Cashen kept twelve of the bozales for his own plantation and sold the remaining sixteen (Cuba 419 A, AGI; SD 2533, AGI).

76. Fernando de la Maza y Arredondo to Governor Enrique White, Dec. 20, 1810, Exechequer Proceedings, 1787–1819, EFP, microfilm reel 133, PKY, cited in Schafer, "Family Ties That Bind."

77. In exchange for the land grant Hibberson and Yonge agreed to free entry for all government ships and a peso duty to the state on all other ships (Claims of Hibberson and Yonge, *SLGF,* vol. 3, 254–56).

78. Laird W. Bergad, Fe Iglesias García, and María del Carmen Barcia, *The Cuban Slave Market, 1790–1880* (Cambridge, 1995), 21. Cuba's national entry into the African slave trade was relatively late, the "first successful Cuban" slaving expedition returning from Senegal with 123 slaves in 1798. Prior to that year, official traders from elite Cuban families and English traders conducted the trade (Fraginals, *Sugarmill,* 19).

79. An annual royal subsidy of 10,000 pesos, up from the original 6,000 allotment, covered the costs of the Indian gifts and Arredondo's expenses (Harlan, "Military History of Florida," 119–20).

80. The captain, pilot, and sixteen-man crew of the *Sevilla* collected wages for a ten-month round trip voyage. The slave mortality rate on the *Sevilla* was 20 percent (Relation of the Expenses of the Frigate *Sevilla,* Aug. 12, 1800, and Relation of the Sale of the Cargo of the Frigate, *Sevilla,* Aug. 6, 1810, Cuba 419 A, AGI; Relation of the Expenses of the Frigate, *Doña Juana,* Mar. 20, 1811, and Relation of the Sales of the Cargo of the Frigate *Doña Juana,* Mar. 15, 1811, Cuba 419 A, AGI). Thirty percent of the slaves loaded onto the *Juana* died en route.

81. Relation of the Expenses of the Frigate *Sevilla,* Aug. 12, 1810, Cuba 419 A, AGI; Relation of the Sales of the Cargo of the Frigate *Sevilla,* Aug. 6, 1810, Cuba 419 A, AGI. For a discussion of the shipboard causes of mortality see Kenneth F. Kiple and Brian T. Higgins, "Mortality Caused by Dehydration during the Middle Passage," in *The Atlantic Slave Trade: Effects on Economics, Societies, and Peoples in Africa, the Americas, and Europe,* ed. Joseph E. Inikori and Stanley L. Engerman (Durham, N.C., 1992), 321–37. Also see Herbert S. Klein, "Profits and the Causes of Mortality," in *The Rise of the Merchant Empires,* ed. James D. Tracy (Cambridge, 1990), 287–308.

82. Expenses included 9,536 pesos for salaries for the captain and crew for fifteen months. Included in this sum was the cost of clothing for the slaves. A medic and medicines cost an additional 438 pesos. Herbert Klein found that nineteenth-century slavers made profits of slightly less than 20 percent or almost double the profits made by eighteenth-century French and English slavers (Klein, "Profits and the Causes of Mortality"). A simple subtraction of expenses from sales receipts renders a 45 percent gross profit on the *Doña Juana*'s shipment. Although undetermined other expenses would reduce this profit level, it was still significant (Relation of the Expenses of the Frigate *Doña Juana,* Mar. 20, 1811, Cuba 419 A, AGI).

83. After extensive litigation and investigations, the United States Supreme Court upheld the huge Arredondo grant in 1837 (Claims of F. M. Arredondo, Jr., *SLGF*, vol. 2, 37–112).

One of the other developers of the grant that was to become Micanopy, Fla., was Edward Mills Wanton, assisted by his quadroon son, Billy (Marotti, "Edward M. Wanton and the Settling of Micanopy," 470–77).

84. In addition to selling slaves to Spanish citizens, Dexter and Hurlbert sold African imports to Thomas Fitch of Georgia and to men who held United States citizenship but were residents of Florida, such as Winslow Forbes and James Oliver (Escrituras [Notarized Instruments], 1784–1821, EFP, microfilm reels 167–68, PKY).

85. Claims of Abbey Dexter and Horatio S. Dexter, *SLGF*, vol. 3, 26–28, and Claims of Daniel Hurlbert, ibid., 296–98; Claims of Horatio S. Dexter, ibid., vol. 1, 68–76.

86. Two years later the matter was still being reviewed in the courts in Havana (Testimony on the Investigation on the Introduction of Bozales on the Schooner *Florida*, 1819, Cuba 470, AGI). The case review is also found in Exchequer Proceedings, 1787–1819, EFP, microfilm reel 134, PKY.

87. Governor Cornelius Coppinger awarded Darley the 500-acre grant on June 15, 1817. A native of Great Britain, Darley also petitioned for and received a large saw mill grant of 23,000 acres on the west side of Dunn's Lake, a grant by Coppinger on Nov. 11, 1817 (Unconfirmed claims of James Darley, *SLGF*, vol. 1, 52–57).

88. Since none of the men could produce proof of their free status, the government auctioned them off and the proceeds went to the royal coffers. The two criollos were skilled carpenters and all the men were prime hands so the government profited by 1465 pesos (Inquiry, July 13, 1799, Papers on Negro Titles, Runaways, etc., 1787–1805, EFP, microfilm reel 167, PKY).

89. The slaves were Jane, age 25; Dolly, age 23; María, age 19; Amelia, age 22; Ana, age 22; and Florido, age 19 (Sale by Felipe Yonge to Juan Atkinson, May 24, 1819, Escrituras [Notarized Instruments], 1784–1821, EFP, microfilm reel 168, PKY). Other sales describing persons sold as having entered on specific ships can be found throughout reel 168. Michael Mullin documents the same strength of shipboard associations in the Anglo Caribbean (*Africa in America*, 32, 83, 161).

90. W. E. B. Du Bois, *The Suppression of the African Slave Trade to the United States, 1638–1870* (London, 1896), 118–23; Philip D. Curtain, *The Atlantic Slave Trade: A Census* (Madison, Wis., 1969); Edwin L. Williams, "Negro Slavery in Florida," *Florida Historical Quarterly* 28 (July 1949–Apr. 1950): 93–110; Frances J. Stafford, "Illegal Importations: Enforcement of the Slave Trade Laws along the Florida Coast, 1810–1824," *Florida Historical Quarterly* 46 (Oct. 1967): 124–40; Kenneth F. Kiple, "The Case against a Nineteenth-Century Cuba-Florida Slave Trade," *Florida Historical Quarterly* 49 (Apr. 1971): 346–55.

91. *Nile's Weekly Register*, Nov. 29, 1817.

92. Belton A. Copp, Collector of Port of St. Marys, Ga., cited in T. Frederick Davis, "MacGregor's Invasion of Florida, 1817," *Florida Historical Quarterly* 7 (July 1928): 3–71, quotation on 45.

93. War Department Orders, Nov. 12, 1817, and Navy Department Orders, Nov. 14, 1817, cited in ibid., 39–42.

94. Letters of Captain John H. Elton to the secretary of the navy, Oct. 19, 1817, and Jan. 3, 1818, cited in *Nile's Weekly Register,* Nov. 29, 1817. Elton described the filthy conditions on the *Jupiter,* which he intercepted and sent to Savannah and he described its captain as "an old offender, by the name of Austin" (John H. Elton to the secretary of the navy, Nov. 15, 1817, ibid.).

95. Elton reported that the Spanish captain was also ill of the "coast fever which in all probability, will terminate his mortal career" (Captain John H. Elton, cited in *Nile's Weekly Register,* Feb. 21, 1818).

96. *Savannah Republican,* May 2, 1818.

97. The *Antelope* carried a commission from José Artigas, father of the as yet unsecured nation of Uruguay, a commission the Portuguese spokesman said was no better than one issued by the Seminoles (John T. Noonan, Jr., *The Antelope: The Ordeal of the Recaptured Africans in the Administrations of James Monroe and John Quincy Adams* [Berkeley, 1977], 4, 135–38, 145, 152).

98. John Quincy Adams to the Senate and House of Representatives, Apr. 30, 1828, "Africans at Key West," doc. no. 262, 20th Cong., 1st sess., 3.

99. Noonan, *Antelope.*

100. Marshal Waters Smith to the secretary of the treasury, Richard Rush, Papers relating to the introduction of slaves into the port of St. Augustine, "Africans at Key West," doc. no. 262, 20th Cong., 1st sess., 9–10. Three men were said to have run away, but Marshal Smith suspected Kingsley knew their whereabouts (Jean B. Stephens, "Zephaniah Kingsley and the Recaptured Africans," *El Escribano* 15 [1978]: 71–76).

Chapter 8
Crime and Punishment

1. Cutter contends that "Honed to the essentials, judicial administration in these extensive marginal areas nevertheless squared unmistakably with the Spanish legal tradition" *(Legal Culture of Northern New Spain,* 5, 36).

2. An anonymous British visitor to Amelia Island found this noteworthy and wrote "The slave may demand compliance with the laws, an infraction of which incurs the penalty of release of service" *(Narrative of A Voyage to the Spanish Main,* 127).

3. One difference between what Cutter finds on the frontier of northern New Spain and Spanish Florida is that Florida enjoyed the services of highly trained Scottish and French physicians to conduct their medical investigations and autopsies *(Legal Culture of Northern New Spain,* chap. 5).

4. Bowser, *African Slave in Colonial Peru,* 172.

5. Cesar kept the gun loaded "since the past war" (the French-inspired invasion of 1795). All material related to this case is located in Criminales contra el negro Liberty, Records of Criminal Proceedings, 1785–1821, EFP, microfilm reel 124, no. 1, PKY.

6. On Fatio's influence see Parker, "I Am neither Your Subject nor Your Subordinate." White's predecessor, Governor Juan Nepomuceno de Quesada, delivered much harder sentences. He sentenced the Guinea-born free black Prince Patens to two years of hard labor when his wife sold two squashes to a runaway slave (under duress). See Diligencias obradas contra Alix, Records of Criminal Proceedings, 1785–1821, EFP, microfilm reel 123, no. 6, PKY.

7. Two surgeons, Don Tomás Sterling and Don Juan Bousquet of the Royal Hospital, examined Benito's corpse and found an eight-inch wound from which some of the victim's intestines extruded. All material related to this case is found in Criminales seguidos contra el negro Bob o Roberto, Records of Criminal Proceedings, 1785–1821, EFP, microfilm reel 124, no. 2, PKY.

8. Roberto's employer, Yguíniz, served as his godfather at the condemned man's baptism in the Castillo, and the brothers of the Misericordia escorted him to his death (Baptism of Roberto Jones, Jan. 7, 1802, Black Baptisms, vol. 2, CPR, microfilm reel 284 J, PKY).

9. Juana had run west to the ferry, where she found a black man willing to transport her across the San Sebastián River in his canoe. Before she could escape, however, a white man captured Juana and took her back to town. All of the material on the case is found in Autos seguidos . . . contra Juana, esclava de Juan Salom, por haver ahogados dos niños suyos en un pozo de su casa, Miscellaneous Legal Instruments and Proceedings, 1784–1819, EFP, microfilm reel 110, no. 33, PKY.

Father Thomas Hassett presided over the Christian burial of Juana's children in the town's Catholic cemetery (Burials of Juan Baptista Salom and Isabel Anna Salom, Oct. 7, 1787, Black Burials, CPR, microfilm reel 284 L, PKY). The five-year-old Juan Baptista Salom had been baptized only three months earlier, with the Minorcans Lorenzo Capo and María Mestre serving as his godparents (Baptism of Juan Baptista Salom, July 23, 1787, Black Baptisms, vol. 1, CPR, microfilm reel 284 J, PKY).

10. Cutter, *Legal Culture of Northern New Spain,* chap. 2; McAlister, *Spain and Portugal,* 24–26.

11. Dillard, *Daughters of the Reconquest,* 208–10. Because children were highly valued in the Reconquest era, when colonizing an ever-advancing frontier was critical, infanticide was harshly punished, and men and women were usually executed for this crime. Women convicted of such a grave crime were usually burned alive. In other parts of early modern Europe, women were more often drowned for this crime, and more women were executed for this crime than for any other, except witchcraft. See Merry E. Weisner, *Women and Gender in Early Modern Europe* (Cambridge, 1993), 51–52.

12. In many African cosmologies, bodies of water are seen as the boundary between this world and the next, and African slaves commonly believed that after death they would be carried across the Atlantic to be reborn in their homeland. There are many colonial accounts of slave suicides by drowning, but water also held sacred meanings associated with purification (Thompson, *Flash of the Spirit,* 134–38, and *Face of the Gods*).

13. This would indicate that Juana was still nursing her own two-year-old, Isabel Anna.

14. I am indebted to Patricia Griffin for a reference to the Salom family from the 1786 Hassett census, which records Juan Salom, age 35, a native of Alayor (Minorca), his wife Margarita Neto, age 30, from San Felipe (Minorca), their children Juan, 7, and Clara, 4, and two male and two female slaves, unnamed and not baptized (Census Returns, 1784–1814, EFP, microfilm reel 148, PKY).

15. Slaves who asked the court for changes of owners or who were asking to initiate self-purchase often charged that their owners had not properly clothed or fed them (as required by the Siete Partidas). This seems to have been an effective argument and it was used repeatedly. Slaves also charged they had been denied access to church and that, too, was an effective complaint (Landers, "Traditions of African American Freedom," 29).

16. Slaves living in St. Augustine had often mastered at least three languages and sometimes more, and many were commonly bilingual. Just as slaves learned new languages, they also adapted to a variety of new legal and social systems. On Minorcan households see Griffin, *Mullet on the Beach.*

17. Cook and Cook, *Good Faith and Truthful Ignorance,* 87–89, 91–103, 112–14.

18. Salom signed the Minorcan declaration of loyalty to Governor Vicente Manuel de Zéspedes on July 13, 1784 (Lockey, *East Florida,* 233).

19. Autos seguidos . . . contra Juana, esclava de Juan Salom, por haver ahogados dos niños suyos en un pozo de su casa, Miscellaneous Legal Instruments and Proceedings, 1784–1819, EFP, microfilm reel 110, no. 33, PKY.

20. Ibid.

21. These are the only cases of the murder of slaves that I have located in the East Florida Papers; however, some crimes may have escaped detection if slaves failed to report them to the authorities.

22. Ironically, James "Santiago" Cashen began his career in Florida as a slave trader. He moved to Spanish Florida in 1800 as a new homesteader and received lands based on headrights. Indian raids drove his family to Amelia Island, where he opened a store in Fernandina and served as a cavalry captain in the local militia. For that service the government named him a justice of the peace in 1812 and in 1816 granted him a 1,050-acre tract on the St. Marys River. Over the years he purchased many other large tracts *(SLGF,* vol. 2, 259–72).

23. All three steps were required procedure (Cutter, *Legal Culture of Northern New Spain,* chap. 5). All material related to this case is found in Criminales contra Don Domingo Fernández sobre la muerte de un negro de su propiedad nombrado Yare, Mar. 12, 1811, Records of Criminal Proceedings, 1785–1821, EFP, microfilm reel 126, PKY. In 1817 Fernández owned more than sixteen thousand acres of prime acreage and thirty slaves, as well as several town lots in Fernandina *(SLGF,* vol. 3, 80–99).

24. Although the physician felt that the slaves who watched the procedure were satisfied that physical blows did not kill Yare, what they actually thought the autopsy signified is unknown.

25. Criminales contra Don Domingo Fernández sobre la muerte de un negro de su

propiedad nombrado Yare, Mar. 12, 1811, Records of Criminal Proceedings, 1785–1821, EFP, microfilm reel 126, PKY.

26. Henry "Enrique" Yonge was a partner in Hibberson and Yonge and owned town lots, a warehouse, and a dry goods store in Fernandina. In 1815 Governor Enrique White granted him 980 acres in parcels on the St. Johns and St. Marys River, and Amelia Island for military service. He then owned thirty-seven slaves *(SLGF,* vol. 5, 227–34).

27. Planters who testified as to Braddock's good character included Luis Mattair, Guillermo O'Neill, and Roberto Andrew.

28. O'Neill's 550-acre plantation was located near Langford (Lanceford) Creek on the St. Marys River *(SLGF,* vol. 4, 149–52).

29. Gantt came to Florida from Warrington, Md., and the more terrible damage to slaves he referred to must have been witnessed there. Don Enrique (Henry) Yonge, who had first reported the "inhuman" and "abominable" crime, witnessed Gantt's autopsy and reported the same congealed blood, but was unable to say that the blows Duncan suffered caused his death.

30. *SLGF,* vol. 2, 202.

31. Memorial by Samuel Rumford, Mar. 1, 1787, and Response by Father Miguel O'Reilly, Mar. 3, 1787, Memorials, 1784–1821, EFP, microfilm reel 77, PKY.

32. Memorial by Sam (Rumford) and Response by Eduardo Nugent, May 7, 1787, Memorials, 1784–1821, EFP, microfilm reel 77, PKY.

33. Rumford was alleged to have given Wright pieces of meat which killed the dog that ate them (Vicente Manuel de Zéspedes to José de Ezpeleta, Feb. 2 and Apr. 22, 1789, Cuba 1395).

34. The phrase is a standard one employed in cases where blacks have challenged whites (Auditor de Guerra Joseph de Ortega to Governor Enrique White, Apr. 4, 1805, To and from Military Commanders and Other Officers, 1784–1821, EFP, microfilm reel 68, PKY).

35. On Nov. 10, 1803, Governor Enrique White granted Aysick Travers 115 acres on the Matanzas River, south of St. Augustine. Governor José Coppinger confirmed this claim on Apr. 9, 1821 *(SLGF,* vol. 2, 134–36).

36. The original complainant was Don Samuel Betts, a factor for Arredondo and Sons, a major mercantile house and slave trading firm. The military inquiry was conducted by Benito de Paniagua, a captain of the Cuban Infantry Regiment. Anglo accusers included Don Thomas Backhouse, of London; Don José Gaunt, of Maryland; Don Santiago Cashen, of Dublin; and Don Carlos Sibbald, of the United States (Sumario promovido por Don Samuel Betts, June 15, 1815, Records of Criminal Proceedings, 17851–1821, EFP, microfilm reel 126, PKY).

37. On June 19, 1816, Travers received absolute title for "himself and his heirs and successors" to a military service grant on the North River in an area known as Colonel Braun's Savannah (SFLR, record group 599, series 997, Concessions for New Settlers, 1791–1821, box 1, 50–51). The Spanish government later granted Travers property in Fernandina (lot 4, square 12, and lot 2, square 8) which he reclaimed on Oct. 30, 1827, but the U.S. Board of Commissioners did not confirm his title to those properties *(SLGF,* vol. 1, 309).

38. Relación de los oficiales, sargentos, cabos, y soldados de pardos y morenos . . . que . . . han emigrado, Nov. 13, 1823, Cuba 358, AGI.

39. Ruth Pike, *Penal Servitude in Early Modern Spain* (Madison, Wis., 1983). On the Caribbean presidios see chap. 8. Also see Ruth Pike, "Penal Servitude in the Spanish Empire: Presidio Labor in the Eighteenth Century," *Hispanic American Historical Review* 58 (1978): 21–40.

40. Sentence of Joseph Gallovera, Dec. 6, 1785; Sentence of Antonio Escobar, Mar. 4, 1786; Sentence of Manuel Josef de la Luz, Mar. 4, 1786, Letters from the Captain General, 1784–1821, EFP, microfilm reel 1, PKY.

41. Once their terms expired, convicts requested and received a license certifying their free status and permitting them to go home, unless they had been exiled for conspiracy or other serious crimes (Vicente Manuel de Zéspedes to Joseph de Ezpeleta, Nov. 9, 1787, Cuba 1395, AGI). In 1799, Governor Enrique White also appealed to Havana for convict laborers, but that year there were none to be had.

42. Roster of Prisoners, 1784–96, Cuba 365 A, AGI. Lists of convict laborers for 1813 appear in Cuba 460, AGI.

43. Manuel de Hita to Enrique White, Oct. 25, 1804, and Response by Josef de Ortega, Nov. 2, 1804, To and from the Engineering Department, 1784–1821, EFP, microfilm reel 74, PKY.

44. After appraising their value, Florida officials held a public auction on Nov. 16, 1817, and sold the freed prisoners as slaves (Proceedings on the Sale of José María Balmaceda and José Joaquín Placeres, 1817, Exchequer Proceedings, 1787–1819, EFP, microfilm reel 134, PKY). Aline Helg discusses the deterioration of Cuban race relations resulting from the furor of the famed "conspiracy" of La Escalera in 1844, but the change is visible even earlier ("Race and Black Mobilization in Colonial and Early Independent Cuba: A Comparative Perspective," *Ethnohistory* 44 [1997]: 53–74).

45. Proclamation by Vicente Manuel de Zéspedes, Aug. 29, 1787, and Proclamation by Enrique White, Sept. 26, 1807, Proclamations and Edicts, 1786–1821, EFP, microfilm reel 118, PKY.

46. Juan Nepomuceno de Quesada, Bando de Buen Gobierno, Sept. 2, 1790, Proclamations and Edicts, 1786–1821, EFP, microfilm reel 118, PKY.

47. Census Returns, 1784–1814, EFP, microfilm reel 148, PKY; Relación de los negros libres que se han presentado, 1792, Selected Papers, 1784–1821, EFP, microfilm reel 174, PKY.

48. Spaniards drafted free black laborers on demand in other colonies as well (Thomas Fiehrer, "Slaves and Freedmen in Colonial Central America: Rediscovering a Forgotten Black Past," *Journal of Negro History* 64 [1979]: 39–57).

49. Criminales contra los negros Santiago y Benjamín, May 29, 1801, and sentence, June 20, 1801, Records of Criminal Proceedings, 1785–1821, EFP, microfilm reel 125, PKY.

50. Charles Cutter finds that Pueblo Indians and persons of mixed descent in New Mexico learned how to negotiate their interests in Spanish courts and insisted that the Spaniards play by the "rules of the game" *(Legal Culture of Northern New Spain,* 38–43).

Chapter 9
Black Military Service

1. Leon Campbell called these areas the "Negroid littoral" ("The Changing Racial and Administrative Structure of the Peruvian Military under the Later Bourbons," *Americas* 32 (1975): 117–33. See too Peter M. Voelz, *Slave and Soldier: The Military Impact of Blacks in the Colonial Americas* (New York, 1993), chap. 2; Stephen Webre, "Las compañías de milicia y la defensa del istmos centroamericano en el siglo XVII: el alistamiento general de 1763," *Mesoamérica* 14 (1987): 511–29.

2. Klein, "Colored Militia of Cuba," 17; Campbell, "Changing Racial and Administrative Structure," 131.

3. On reforms in other Spanish colonies see W. James Miller, "The Militia System of Spanish Louisiana," in *The Military Presence on the Gulf Coast,* ed. William S. Coker (Pensacola, Fla., 1975), 36–63; Roland C. McConnell, *Negro Troops of Antebellum Louisiana* (Baton Rouge, La., 1968), chap. 2; Margarita Gascón, "The Military of Santo Domingo, 1720–1764," *Hispanic American Historical Review* 73 (1993): 431–52; Joseph P. Sánchez, "African Freedmen and the Fuero Militar: A Historical Overview of Pardo and Moreno Militiamen in the Late Spanish Empire," *Colonial Latin American Historical Review* 3 (1994): 165–84.

4. "I have resolved that the men of these unites should be given the good treatment that their operations merit, considering them as my vassals, in whom I have complete satisfaction for the [service] that they have always rendered in my royal service; and I therefore order the governor and captain general of the island of Cuba, and of the city of San Cristobal of Havana, the sergeant major, and other military officials of that island and city, and the [civil] officials, council members, and other judges and justices of the said city to take special care to see that the free pardos of the said companies be treated well as they deserve to be, without allowing anyone to hatefully call them indecorous names or to make insulting references to their nation [race], rather, they should use their given names, because it is my royal will that they be treated well and with love and that they not suffer the least outrage or insult" (Philip V to the royal officials of Havana, May 20, 1714, SD 337, AGI, cited in Klein, "Colored Militia of Cuba," 18).

5. Military reforms were codified in the *Reglamento para las milicias de infantería y caballería de la Isla de Cuba.* Florida's military reorganization served as a model for subsequent militia reforms in Puerto Rico, Louisiana, Cartagena, and Panama, where blacks also enlisted in large numbers (Lyle N. McAlister, "The Reorganization of the Army of New Spain, 1763–1767," *Hispanic American Historical Review* 33 [1953]: 1–32; Allan J. Kuethe, *Military Reform and Society in New Granada, 1773–1808* [Gainesville, Fla., 1978], 8–27, 38–39; Christon I. Archer, *The Army in Bourbon Mexico, 1760–1810* [Albuquerque, N.Mex., 1977], 4, 224–31; Klein, "Colored Militia of Cuba").

For more on blacks and the *fuero* see Lyle N. McAlister, *El fuero militar en la Nueva España (1764–1800)* (Mexico City, 1982); Kuethe, "Status of the Free Pardo in the Disciplined Militia of New Granada"; Deschamps Chapeaux, *Batallones de pardos y morenos libres;* and Sánchez, "African Freedmen and the Fuero Militar."

6. Scholars who rely almost exclusively on Spanish sources have missed this point. Juan Marchena chronicles the steady decline of troop strength over the second Spanish period but contends, incorrectly, that militia units existed "only on paper" (Juan Marchena Fernández, "Guarnaciones y población militar en Florida oriental [1700–1820]," *Revista de Indias* 163–64 [1981]: 103–4). Romero-Cabot follows Marchena's lead ("Defensa de Florida").

7. Disputes with Georgians about contested slave property involved diplomatic negotiations of the highest order. More than 250 former slaves were freed by the Spanish before pressure from United States Secretary of State Thomas Jefferson forced Spain to abrogate the sanctuary provision in 1790. The lists of freed slaves appear in Census Returns, 1784–1814, EFP, microfilm reel 148, PKY. Also see Landers, "Spanish Sanctuary."

8. Letters of Vicente Manuel de Zéspedes, included in Miró to Caballo, May 12, 1790, and cited in Derek Noel Kerr, "Petty Felony, Slave Defiance, and Frontier Villainy: Crime and Criminal Justice in Spanish Louisiana, 1770–1803" (Ph.D. diss., Tulane University, 1983), 194.

9. Kerr, "Petty Felony," 193; Harlan, "Military History of Florida," 34–40.

10. The Third Battalion arrived in Florida in 1789 and remained active until it was disbanded in 1815 (Marchena Fernández, "Guarnaciones y población militar," 103–4).

11. Letter of Vicente Manuel de Zéspedes, included in Miró to Cabello, May 12, 1790, and cited in Kerr, "Petty Felony," 194.

12. Murdoch, *Georgia-Florida Frontier.*

13. Juan Nepomuceno de Quesada to Luis de Las Casas, Dec. 10, 1792, Cuba 1439, AGI. Gwendolyn Midlo Hall has described the caliber of the French troops in Louisiana in almost identical terms in *Africans in Colonial Louisiana.* Kerr has done the same for the Spanish troops in Louisiana ("Petty Felony"). This distrust led Governor Quesada repeatedly to deny land grants to black applicants; he even failed to honor the grants made by his predecessor (Memorials of Villy Villen, Oct. 5, 1790, and Prince Witten, July 14, 1791, Memorials, 1784–1821, EFP, microfilm reel 77, PKY).

14. Carlos Howard to Luis de Las Casas, May 4, 1796, SD 2590, AGI. Also see Records of Criminal Proceedings: Rebellion of 1795, EFP, microfilm reels 128–29, PKY.

15. As in other parts of the empire the officers were community leaders—in the main, plantation owners and merchants—and they contributed to outfitting the units. The first unit of twenty-four men and horses was commanded by Don Andres Atkinson, the second, with thirty men and horses, by Don Nathaniel Hall, and the third, by Don Timoteo Hollingsworth (Roster of the Urban Cavalry Militia, Dec. 23, 1795, Cuba 357, AGI).

16. Junta de Guerra, Jan. 14, 1794, Records of Criminal Proceedings: Rebellion of 1795, EFP, microfilm reels 128–29, PKY.

17. Don Juan Leslie, one of the commanders of the free black militia, was a partner in the important southeastern trading company of Panton, Leslie and Company. Like many other elite members of the Spanish community, he had mulatto children, whom he recognized and provided for (J. Leitch Wright, "Blacks in St. Augustine, 1763–1845," typescript available at the Historic St. Augustine Preservation Board). For further examples

of interracial unions in Spanish Florida, see Jane G. Landers, "Acquisition and Loss on a Spanish Frontier," in *Against the Odds: Free Blacks in the Slave Societies of the Americas,* ed. Jane G. Landers (London, 1996), 85–101, and Schafer, "Shades of Freedom."

18. David Geggus, "The Enigma of Jamaica in the 1790s: New Light on the Causes of Slave Rebellion," *William and Mary Quarterly* 44 (Apr. 1987), 274–99.

19. Account of 1794, Accounts of the Royal Treasury, 1784–96, SD 2635, AGI.

20. Juan Nepomuceno de Quesada to Luis de Las Casas, Apr. 21, 1794, Cuba 1439, AGI.

21. Bando of Juan Nepomuceno de Quesada, Jan. 22, 1794, Proclamations and Edicts, 1786–1821 EFP, microfilm reel 118, PKY. Slaves and free blacks and white troops all worked together constructing new fortifications at Dos Hermanas, Quesada, San Juan, San Nicolás, and Santa Ysabel (Juan Nepomuceno de Quesada to Luis de Las Casas, Apr. 12, 1794, Cuba 1439, AGI).

22. As discussed in chapter 4, Collins was the son of a white planter from Louisiana, which may have also made him suspect. He became a merchant and beef contractor in St. Augustine and traveled to Havana, Pensacola, Charleston, and the Indian nations on business. On one such occasion, Quesada approved his license for travel to Havana when Collins presented a letter from his creditors attesting to his "well-known good character" (Memorial of J. B. Collins, Oct. 24, 1792, Memorials, 1784–1821, EFP, microfilm reel 78, PKY).

23. Account of 1795, Accounts of the Royal Treasury, 1784–96, SD 2635, AGI.

24. Juan Nepomuceno de Quesada to Luis de Las Casas, Apr. 21, 1794, Cuba 1439, AGI. Recognizing the weakness of St. Augustine's defenses, Havana finally ordered reinforcements from the Infantry Regiment of Mexico to assist Quesada. The group of approximately two hundred men was commanded by Colonel Sebastián Kindelán, who later became governor of East Florida and an advocate of its black militia. Additional troops from Catalonia also added force.

25. Another schooner carried Don Juan McQueen and thirty Cuban soldiers, and a third gunboat carried the rest of the regular troops, including a small contingent of Catalan light infantrymen (Juan Nepomuceno de Quesada to Luis de Las Casas, July 23, 1795, Letters to the Captain General, 1784–1821, EFP, microfilm reel 10, PKY; Inventory by Don Bernardo Seguí, July 29, 1795, Records of Criminal Proceedings: Rebellion of 1795, EFP, microfilm reel 128, PKY).

26. Only some of those revolts were directly inspired by the French Revolution—others had more local roots (Geggus, "Enigma of Jamaica," 279, and "Slavery, War, and Revolution in the Greater Caribbean, 1789–1815," in *A Turbulent Time: The French Revolution and the Greater Caribbean,* ed. David Barry Gaspar and David Patrick Geggus [Bloomington, Ind., 1997], 1–50; Carey Robinson, *The Fighting Maroons of Jamaica* [Jamaica, 1971]; Hall, *Africans in Colonial Louisiana,* chap. 11; Edward L. Cox, "Fedon's Rebellion 1795–96: Causes and Consequences," *Journal of Negro History* 68 [1982]: 7–33; Federico Brito Figueroa, *Las insurrecciones de los esclavos negros en la sociedad colonial Venezolana* [Caracas, 1961]; Emilia Viotta da Costa, *Crowns of Glory, Tears of Blood: The Demerara Slave Rebellion of 1823* [New York, 1994]).

27. Account of 1795, Accounts of the Royal Treasury, SD 2635, AGI.

28. Juan Nepomuceno de Quesada to Luis de Las Casas, Oct. 26, 1795, Letters to the Captain General, 1784–1821, EFP, microfilm reel 10, PKY.

29. Records of Criminal Proceedings: Rebellion of 1795, EFP, microfilm reels 128–29, PKY; Proclamation of the Governor, Dec. 31, 1801, Records of Criminal Proceedings: Rebellion of 1795, EFP, microfilm reel 129, PKY.

30. Morales asked for assistance in deciding the punishment for recidivist deserters (Bartolomé Morales to Luis de Las Casas, May 5, 1796, Cuba 1439, AGI).

31. Ibid.

32. Account of 1796, Accounts of the Royal Treasury, 1796–1814, SD 2636, AGI. Biassou's immediate family included his wife, Romana, her mother, Ana Gran Pres, her sisters, Barbara and Cecilia Gran Pres, and her brother, Juan Jorge Jacobo, Biassou's military successor. All were free blacks from Guarico. "Extended" family members were Juan Luis Menar, a free mulatto from Guarico who married Biassou's sister Barbara Gran Pres on Apr. 24, 1797; Placido Asil, a free black from San Miguel on the coast of Guinea who married Biassou's slave Isabel, a black from Villa de Granada, on Oct. 6, 1798; Jorge Brus, a free mulatto from Marmelade who married María Carlota, a free black from Guarico, on June 8, 1797; Pedro Miguel, a free black; Benjamín Seguí, a free mulatto; Peter Yon Frances, ethnicity not given; León Duvigneau, a free mulatto, and his black slave wife, Simonett. To identify this group I searched the black baptisms, marriages, and burials for the post-1796 period (CPR, microfilm reels 284 J, K, and L, PKY). This represents only a partial accounting of the refugees.

33. James describes Biassou as "a fire-eater, always drunk, always ready for the fiercest and most dangerous exploits" (*Black Jacobins,* 93–94, 106). Carolyn E. Fick agrees with these characterizations and goes so far as to assert that "among the prominent leaders, it was now Biassou, the fiery and impassioned voodoo adept who, in his more impulsive moments, best incarnated the aspirations and mentality of the insurgent slaves" (*The Making of Haiti: The Saint Domingue Revolution from Below* [Knoxville, Tenn., 1990], 115). To say that Biassou might "incarnate" the "mentality" of the slaves would be a leap in any case, but certainly not because of his impulsive and fiery nature. One might equally argue that Biassou's actions exhibit pragmatic and assiduous pursuit of self-interest.

34. The more moderate Toussaint stayed his superior's order (James, *Black Jacobins,* 106).

35. Robert Debs Heinl, Jr., and Nancy Gordon Heinl, *Written in Blood: The Story of the Haitian People, 1492–1971* (Boston, 1978), 63; Twelve other subchiefs received medals of silver and documents attesting to their meritorious service (Captain General Joaquín García to the Duque de la Alcudia, Feb. 18, 1794, ES 14, doc. 86, AGI).

36. James, *Black Jacobins,* 124, 155.

37. Thomas O. Ott asserts that Toussaint's defection from the Spaniards was in part motivated by his own ambition and that he felt his advancement within the Spanish camp was blocked by Biassou and Jean-François. He describes Toussaint's "power struggle" with Biassou and Toussaint's military victories over his former superior (*The Haitian Revolution, 1789–1804* [Knoxville, Tenn., 1973], 83–84). Carolyn Fick agrees; see *Making of Hai-*

ti, 184. Biassou's forces were with the Spaniards at Saint-Raphael when Toussaint surprised and defeated them on May 6, 1794. For more on the slave revolt see Geggus, "Slavery, War, and Revolution"; Genovese, *From Rebellion to Revolution;* Julius Scott, "Common Wind."

38. On July 7, 1794, the Spaniards and their black auxiliaries massacred more than one thousand French men, women, and children who had accepted Spanish offers of protection to return from the United States. Although the Spanish authorities and most historians place the blame for the Bayajá massacre on Jean-François, Jean-François accused Biassou and his men of the atrocities (James, *Black Jacobins,* 123–51; Memorial of Jean-François, Jan. 14, 1796, ES V-A, doc. 28, AGI).

39. The Marquis of Casa Calvo to Luis de Las Casas, Dec. 31, 1795, ES 5-A, doc. 23, AGI. Although Spaniards were also involved in the killings at Bayajá, in the cited document Casa Calvo refers to the incident as a "cruel crime" which "inspired in the sanguinary hearts and entrails [of the blacks] the reckless belief that they had reconquered the town and saved the Spanish garrison from a plot against them by the French emigres."

40. Ibid.

41. Joaquín García to the Duque de la Alcudia, Feb. 18, 1794, ES 14, doc. 86, AGI; Petition of Romana Jacobo, Oct. 12, 1801, SD 1268, AGI. The governor of Bayajá wrote disparagingly that some of the black auxiliaries thought the abandonment of their property would excuse their crimes and be proof of fidelity but that their sacrifices were only "illusions" and were made in their own self-interest (Marquis de Casa Calvo to Luis de Las Casas, Dec. 31, 1795, ES 5-A, doc. 23, AGI).

42. Complaint of Jorge Biassou, May 31, 1794, ES 13, doc. 11, AGI.

43. Luis de Las Casas to the Duque de Alcudia, Jan. 18, 1796, ES 5-A, doc. 24, AGI.

44. Petition of Jorge Biassou, Sept. 14, 1796, Cuba 1439, AGI. In one account, during his mother's rescue from the Hospital of the Holy Fathers in Le Cap, Biassou murdered all the patients in their beds; see Heinl and Heinl, *Written in Blood,* 54.

45. Enrique White to Luis de las Casas, Oct. 1, 1796, Cuba 1439, AGI.

46. Criminal Proceedings against Louis Boeff, Dec. 24, 1796, Cuba 169, AGI.

47. Juan Nepomuceno de Quesada to Luis de Las Casas, Jan. 25, 1796, Cuba 1439, AGI.

48. Juan Nepomuceno de Quesada to Luis de Las Casas, Mar. 5, 1796, Cuba 1439, AGI.

49. Ibid.

50. Jorge Biassou to Luis de Las Casas, Jan. 31, 1796, Cuba 1439, AGI. The governor assigned Biassou an interpreter from the Cuban Third Battalion who translated Biassou's French dictation into Spanish, which a Spanish amanuensis in turn wrote down for Biassou. Because Biassou could not write in any language, he customarily marked his correspondence with a specially made black stamp.

51. Juan Nepomuceno de Quesada to Luis de Las Casas, Mar. 5, 1796, Cuba 1439, AGI; Enrique White to Luis de Las Casas, July 15, 1796, ibid.

52. Juan Nepomuceno de Quesada to Luis de Las Casas, Mar. 5, 1796, Letters to the Captain General, 1784–1821, EFP, microfilm reel 10, PKY. Biassou had proof of having received 320 pesos monthly through Feb. 1796, but other documents indicated he had

once been paid 250 pesos monthly. Treasury officials seized this excuse to pay the lower rate (Gonzalo Zamorano to Interim Governor Bartolomé Morales, Jan. 25, 1796, Cuba 1439, AGI; Accounts of the Royal Treasury, 1784–95, SD 2635, and 1796–1819, SD 2636, AGI).

53. Enrique White to Luis de Las Casas, Mar. 15 and July 15, 1796, Cuba 1439, AGI.

54. Jorge recounted his service at battles at the towns of Prus, Plegarias, San Rafael, Plaza Chica de San Miguel, and Barica. This man was probably Jorge Jacobo, Biassou's brother-in-law and heir apparent (Petition of Jorge, Nov. 20, 1798, Letters to the Captain General, 1784–1821, EFP, microfilm reel 10, PKY).

55. Memorial of Juan Bautista, June 25, 1798, Memorials, 1784–1821, EFP, microfilm reel 79, PKY. Juan Bautista alleged that English-speaking black militiamen always wanted to fight with him because they knew him to be valiant. Those men replied that Bautista was the instigator of the fights. These charges seem to indicate some division among St. Augustine's black community along language lines. Memorial of Jorge Biassou, June 26, 1798, ibid. It is interesting to note that Biassou accuses Juan Bautista of chronic drunkenness, a charge Spanish officials leveled against Biassou. Perhaps the charge against Juan Bautista was true, but Biassou may also have been using a standard European slur to discredit the soldier.

56. Witnesses at the marriage of Jorge Jacobo and María Rafaela Kenty (a.k.a. Polly Witten) included the groom's sister and Biassou's wife, Romana, and Rafaela's brother, Francisco (a.k.a. Glasgow Witten) (Marriage of Jorge Jacobo and María Rafaela Kenty, Apr. 12, 1796, Black Marriages, CPR, microfilm reel 284 L, PKY). When the couple's children were born, the maternal grandfather, Juan Bautista (Prince) Witten, and the paternal grandmother, Ana Gran Pres, served as godparents for María del Carmen and the maternal uncle, Francisco Witten, and the paternal aunt, Barbara Gran Pres, served as godparents for the next child, Julian. Another member of the black militia, Marcelino Espinosa, was godfather to the couple's third child, Joseph Baltasar, and yet another militiaman, Benjamín Seguí, was Catalina Melchora Jacobo's godfather (Black Baptisms, vol. 2, entries no. 176, 563, 670, 799, and vol. 3, entry no. 31, CPR, microfilm reel 284 J, PKY).

57. Black Marriages, CPR, microfilm reel 284 L, PKY. Scholars working on other Spanish colonies have found similar patterns of social advancement, family linkages, and multigenerational patterns of service among free black militiamen. See George Reid Andrews, "The Afro-Argentine Officers of Buenos Aires Province, 1800–1860," *Journal of Negro History* 64 (1979): 85–100, and Deschamps Chapeaux, *Batallones de pardos y morenos libres,* 56–62.

58. Marriage of Tomás Herrera and María de los Dolores, July 30, 1796; Marriage of Francisco Witten and María Francisca Fatio, Jan. 26, 1799; Marriage of Juan Bautista Witten and María Rafaela Kenty, July 7, 1798, all in Black Marriages, CPR, microfilm reel 284 L, PKY. Felipe Edimboro's daughter, Nicolasa, married Benjamín Wiggins, who was a translator of Indian languages in his father-in-law's militia unit, and when the couple's son was born, his maternal grandparents were the godparents. Another of Felipe Edimboro's daughters, Isabel, married Pedro Casaly, Benjamín Wiggins's half-brother, and

the godfather of their son was another militiaman, Fermín Fernández (Black Baptisms, vol. 3, entries 400, 466, 498, CPR, microfilm reel 284 J, PKY).

59. In one example, correspondence to General Biassou was addressed with the honorific "Don." An unknown hand scratched out "Don" and wrote instead "Señor" (Orders to General Biassou, 1801, Correspondence between the Governor and Subordinates on the St. Johns and St. Marys Rivers, 1784–1820, EFP, microfilm reel 55, PKY).

60. Enrique White to Conde de Santa Clara, May 24, 1799, Guerra Moderna, 6921, Archivo General de Simancas, Spain.

61. Memorials of Jorge Biassou, Nov. 2 and Dec. 6, 1799, Letters from the Captain General, 1784–1821, EFP, microfilm reel 2, PKY; Marques de Someruelos to Enrique White, Mar. 15, 1800, and May 28, 1801, ibid. The request to divide the unit along color lines may seem incongruous since Biassou was black, but disciplined units throughout the Spanish Caribbean were similarly divided.

62. One of Bowles's Bahamian supporters was Lord Dunmore, who had also effectively used black troops in the Southeast during the American Revolution (J. Leitch Wright, Jr., *William Augustus Bowles;* Lyle N. McAlister, "William Augustus Bowles and the State of Muskogee," *Florida Historical Quarterly* 40 [1962]: 317–28; David H. White, "The Spaniards and William Augustus Bowles in Florida, 1799–1803," *Florida Historical Quarterly* 54 [1975]: 145–55; James Seagrove to Juan McQueen, June 24, 1800, To and from the United States, 1784–1821, EFP, microfilm reel 41, PKY).

63. The raiders did not respect international borders and also raided into Georgia (United States Commissioner James Seagrove to John McQueen, June 24, 1800, Letters to and from the United States, 1784–1821, EFP, microfilm reel 41, PKY).

64. Francis Phelipe Fatio to Enrique White, June 25, 1800, Correspondence between the Governor and Subordinates on the St. Johns and St. Marys Rivers, 1784–1820, EFP, microfilm reel 55, PKY; Fernando de la Puente to Enrique White, June 24, 1800, ibid.

65. Cited in Lyle N. McAlister, "The Marine Forces of William Augustus Bowles and His 'State of Muskogee,'" *Florida Historical Quarterly* 32 (July 1953): 3–27, esp. 10–11.

66. Enrique White, War Orders for Picolata, July 1, 1800, Correspondence between the Governor and Subordinates on the St. Johns and St. Marys Rivers, 1784–1820, EFP, microfilm reel 55, PKY; Instructions for General Biassou, Matanzas, July 1, 1800, ibid.; Petition of Jorge Jacobo, Feb. 9, 1802, Cuba 357, AGI.

67. Council of War, June 30, 1800, Papers of the Councils of War, 1777–1817, EFP, microfilm reel 117, PKY. Orders of General Jorge Biassou, 1801, Correspondence between the Governor and Subordinates on the St. Johns and St. Marys Rivers, 17841–1820, EFP, microfilm reel 55, PKY. Biassou's burial entry noted he was a native of Guarico and the son of the blacks Carlos and Diana. He received no sacraments "due to the unexpectedly rapid death which overtook him" (Burial of Jorge Biassou, July 14, 1801, Black Burials, CPR, microfilm reel 284 L, PKY). The account of Biassou's death has been garbled. Some accounts follow James's erroneous story that Biassou was murdered and that Toussaint awarded a pension to his widow *(Black Jacobins,* 254). Others say that Biassou died in a drunken brawl in St. Augustine (Heinl and Heinl, *Written in Blood,* 70).

68. Though his funeral was conducted with military splendor, Biassou was deeply in debt when he died. His greatest asset was his pension and that had been heavily borrowed against. Because there was far from enough to pay the bakers, tailors, storekeepers, and landlords who had allowed him credit, the governor ordered Biassou's gold medal melted and the proceeds applied toward his debts (Testamentary Proceedings of Jorge Biassou, Records of Testamentary Proceedings, 1756–1821, EFP, microfilm reel 138, PKY). Romana Jacobo, Biassou's widow, remained in Havana. Ill and destitute after Biassou's death, she requested a widow's pension, or half of his monthly salary of 250 pesos. She received considerably less—a pension equal to that of a captain's widow (Petition of Romana Jacobo, Oct. 12, 1801, SD 1268, AGI, and Marques de Someruelos to Cavallero, Oct. 22, 1801, ibid.). I am indebted to Julius S. Scott for the reference on Romana Jacobo.

69. Trouillot, "From Planters' Journals to Academia"; Hunt, *Haiti's Influence on Antebellum America.* See also Landers, "Rebellion and Royalism."

70. Junta de Guerra, Jan. 29, 1802, Cuba 357, AGI.

71. The group included the carpenters Juan Bautista Witten, Prince Paten, and Estévan Cheves, the butcher Felipe Edimboro, hostelers Jorge Clark and Hary Box, and the skilled guides and pilots Pedro Miguel and Prins Leslie (Report of Fernando de la Puente, Aug. 19, 1809, To and from Military Commanders and Other Officers, 1784–1821, EFP, microfilm reel 68, PKY).

72. Black Marriages, CPR, microfilm reel 284 L, PKY, and Black Baptisms, vols. 1–3, CPR, microfilm reel 284 J, PKY.

73. Expenses of the Free Black Militias, Aug. 4 and Sept. 24, 1802, Cuba 433, AGI.

74. The white urban militia garrisoned the safer posts closer to the city (Review Lists for the Free Black Militia of St. Augustine, 1802, Cuba 357, AGI).

75. The men of the black militia did not hesitate to appeal when they considered their rights had been violated. However, they understood that they owed their freedom to royal favor, and couched their petitions in respectful terms designed to elicit a sense of obligation in their king (Petition of Jorge Jacobo, Feb. 9, 1802, Cuba 357, AGI).

76. The Spaniards had arrested Bowles before—in 1788—but that time he managed to escape while en route from the Philippines to Madrid and resumed his southeastern intrigues. This time Bowles was not so lucky, and he died in the Morro Castle in Cuba (McAlister, "William Augustus Bowles," 327).

77. Harlan, "Military History of Florida," 168. Despite the shortages a force of between fifty-one and sixty free blacks still reported during emergencies (Reviews of the Garrison, 1807 and 1809, To and from Military Commanders and Other Officers, 1784–1821, EFP, microfilm reel 68, PKY).

78. In 1809 the pardo or mulatto unit was comprised of one first sergeant, one second, one corporal, and fourteen soldiers, while the moreno or black unit had one first sergeant, two second sergeants, two corporals, and forty-six soldiers (Milicia Urbana de la Plaza de San Agustin de la Florida, Aug. 19, 1809, Hacienda 1211, Archivo General de la Nación, Mexico City).

79. Napoleon Bonaparte's invasion of Spain in 1808, the subsequent abdication of King Ferdinand in favor of his son Charles, who also abdicated, the Spanish war of resistance against Napoleon's brother, Joseph, and the weakness of the peripatetic Central Junta created a crisis of legitimacy with imperial ramifications. Many foreign governments, including that of the United States, did not recognize the Junta, although government officials in Spanish Florida did. They erected a stone obelisk (which still stands) in St. Augustine's central plaza honoring the promulgation of Spain's liberal Constitution of 1812. A Washington newspaper editorial described Spain's political crisis as a "golden opportunity" and urged the seizure of Spain's American colonies *(National Intelligencer* 13 [Aug. 24, 1813]).

80. On Jan. 25, 1811, at President James Madison's urging, Congress passed a secret joint resolution approving a "temporary" occupation of East Florida. Madison then authorized General George Matthews to treat with Spanish authorities and sanctioned the seizure of Florida only if the Spanish governor chose to cede the province or if it were in danger of being taken by another foreign nation (Britain). Madison was encouraged by the fact that Spain's governor for West Florida, Vicente Folch, had in desperation offered in 1810 to cede his province to the United States, only to quickly renege when he finally got assistance from his superiors (Rufus Kay Wyllys, "The East Florida Revolution of 1812–1814," *Hispanic American Historical Review* 9 [1929]: 415–45).

81. Lieut. Col. Smith to U.S. Adjutant and Inspector, June 4, 1812, cited in T. Frederick Davis, ed., "United States Troops in Spanish East Florida, 1812–13, I," *Florida Historical Quarterly* 9 (July 1930): 3–23.

82. Rembert W. Patrick, ed., "Letters of the Invaders of East Florida, 1812," *Florida Historical Quarterly* 28 (July 1949): 53–65. For more complete coverage of this "Contra-like" operation, see Patrick, *Florida Fiasco.*

83. Sebastián Kindelán to Juan Ruiz de Apodaca, Sept. 30, 1813, Cuba 1790, AGI. Despite these negative assessments, Kindelán incorporated black convicts from Havana into the unit once they completed their sentences in St. Augustine. The literate free black José Menéndez was sentenced to one year's banishment in St. Augustine for planning an uprising in Havana but wanted to return to his "beloved country" when his time was served. While he awaited a decision on his future, Menéndez offered his services to the Havana militia in Florida and because he had behaved well while in the province, Kindelán accepted him. Due to the nature of his crime, Cuba's captain general refused to readmit Menéndez and he remained in St. Augustine (Memorial of José Menéndez, Sept. 6, 1813; Sebastián Kindelán to Juan Ruiz de Apodaca, Oct. 15, 1813; Juan Ruiz de Apodaca to Sebastián Kindelán, Nov. 1, 1813, Cuba 1790, AGI).

84. Porter, *Negro on the American Frontier,* 186–94.

85. David Mitchell to Secretary of State James Monroe, July 17, 1812, cited in Alexander, "Ambush of Captain John Williams," 286.

86. Ludovick Ashley to the commandant of Amelia Island, Mar. 6, 1812, Cuba 1789, AGI; Lieut. Col. Smith to the secretary of war, Mar. 18, 1812, in Patrick, "Letters of the Invaders of East Florida"; Davis, "United States Troops in Spanish East Florida, I"; T.

Frederick Davis, ed., "United States Troops in Spanish East Florida, IV," *Florida Historical Quarterly* 9 (Apr. 1931): 259–78.

87. David Mitchell to Sebastián Kindelán, July 6, 1812, Patriot War Papers, manuscript collection 31, folder 30, SAHS.

88. Ibid.

89. Sebastián Kindelán to Juan Ruiz de Apodaca, Sept. 31, 1813, Cuba 1790, AGI.

90. Orders to Jorge Jacobo, Juan Bautista Witten, and Benjamín Seguí, July 19, 1812, To and from Military Commanders and Other Officers, 1784–1821, EFP, microfilm reel 68, PKY.

91. The Patriot captain, Fielder Ridgeway, wrote his brother that on some days he had as many as fifty-three sick soldiers to care for, and that many of them suffered dangerous illnesses. He also described the frequent Indian raids and the horror of seeing his friends scalped before his eyes (Fielder Ridgeway to his brother, Sept. 5, 1812, Cuba 1789, AGI).

92. With horror, Kinnear described how, after murdering the unlucky mail carrier, the Indian and black guerrillas cut off his nose, ears, and genitals (William Kinnear to his mother and brother, Sept. 11, 1812, in Patrick, "Letters of the Invaders of East Florida," 61–63). The Georgians also employed psychological warfare when they used ventriloquists to warn the Seminoles at La Chua that if they took arms against them or aided the Spaniards their pigs and other animals would turn into snakes that would devour them. Kindelán reported the Seminoles believed that invisible beings had given this advice (Sebastián Kindelán to Juan Ruiz de Apodaca, Sept. 30, 1813, Cuba 1790, AGI).

93. Sergeant Felipe Edimboro and fourteen men served among the Seminoles. Among Edimboro's troops were his son-in-law, Corporal Second Class Benjamín Wiggins (the mulatto son of Job Wiggins and the Senegalese Ana Gallum), who served as an interpreter (Review Lists for the Free Black Militia of St. Augustine, Oct. 12, 1812, Cuba 357, AGI). The Spanish/Seminole alliance held despite the fact that Kindelán had not been able to present them with gifts in over three years (Sebastián Kindelán to Juan Ruiz de Apodaca, July 29, 1812, Cuba 1789, AGI).

94. Sebastián Kindelán to Juan Ruiz de Apodaca, Aug. 12, 1812, Cuba 1789, AGI; Kenneth Wiggins Porter, "Negroes and the East Florida Annexation Plot," *Journal of Negro History* 30 (1945): 11–16.

95. On the important role of black linguists in the Seminole Wars see Klos, "Blacks and the Seminole Indian Removal Debate." Even after the Spaniards left Florida, Seminoles and blacks among them maintained trade and contacts with Spanish Cuba.

96. Edward Wanton to Sebastián Kindelán, July 3, 1812, Correspondence between the Governor and Subordinates on the St. Johns and St. Marys Rivers, 1784–1820, EFP, microfilm reel 61, PKY; Sebastián Kindelán to Juan Ruiz de Apodaca, Aug. 13, 1812, Cuba 1789, AGI. Four years later, on Mar. 8, 1816, Governor José Coppinger also awarded Tony Proctor a military service grant of 185 acres *(SLGF,* vol. 4, 226–27).

97. Sebastián Kindelán to Juan Ruiz de Apodaca, Aug. 19, 1812, Cuba 1789, AGI.

98. Review Lists for the Free Black Militia of St. Augustine, 1812, Cuba 357, AGI.

99. Nominations for Promotions, Sept. 30, 1812, Cuba 357, AGI. Company review lists

state that Duvigneau "makes a donation of his entire salary earned in favor of his mother country" and Duvigneau signed with a flourish (Review Lists for the Free Black Militia of St. Augustine, Mar. 16 and Apr. 30, 1812, Cuba 357, and Jan. 1813, Cuba 433, AGI).

100. Parties of the free black militias brought in ninety-five head of cattle in July 1812. In three separate forays in August they brought in seventy, forty, and ninety-three head and the following month they brought in 162 head. The governor wrote that the seventy head collected in August would only feed the townspeople for two weeks (Sebastián Kindelán to Juan Ruiz de Apodaca, July 2, Aug. 12, Aug. 15, and Sept. 15, 1812, Cuba 1789, AGI). Sebastián Kindelán to Juan Ruiz de Apodaca, Jan. 12, Aug. 8, Sept. 30, Sept. 31, and Oct. 22, 1813, Cuba 1790, AGI.

101. Sebastián Kindelán to Juan Ruiz de Apodaca, Aug. 2, 1812, Cuba 1789, AGI. Although mortally wounded by eight bullets, Marine captain John Williams lived long enough to describe the night battle and the death and scalping of his sergeant (Captain John Williams to Lieut. Samuel Miller, Adjutant, Sept. 15, 1812, Letters Received, #44, Marine Corps 1812 Archives, National Archives).

102. The Spaniards captured and translated rebel letters detailing the toll Indian raids were taking, and Kindelán annotated the letters to remark that the so-called Indians were actually black. Other accounts of the blacks living among the Seminoles remark that they adopted Indian dress, but perhaps Witten and the urban black militia who fought alongside them also did so for battle—for psychological impact (Sebastián Kindelán to Juan Ruiz de Apodaca, Sept. 13, 1812, Cuba 1789, AGI).

103. Alexander, "Ambush of Captain John Williams"; T. Frederick Davis, ed., "United States Troops in Spanish East Florida, 1812–13, III," *Florida Historical Quarterly* 9 (Jan. 1931): 135–55.

104. Major General Thomas Pinckney to Sebastián Kindelán, Mar. 20, 1813, and Kindelán to Pinckney, Mar. 31, 1813, cited in T. Frederick Davis, ed., "United States Troops in Spanish East Florida, 1812–13, V," *Florida Historical Quarterly* 10 (July 1931): 24–34.

105. Orders to Jorge Jacobo, Juan Bautista Witten, and Benjamín Seguí, July 19, 1812, To and from Military Commanders and Other Officers, 1784–1821, EFP, microfilm reel 68, PKY.

106. Testimony of Zephaniah Kingsley, Sen. Misc. Doc., no. 55, 36th Cong., 1 sess., 24, cited in Wyllys, "East Florida Revolution," 444.

107. Decree of Sebastián Kindelán, Apr. 1, 1813, Cuba 1790, AGI.

108. The governor noted that no foodstuffs from the St. Johns River plantations ever made it to St. Augustine—either because of the distance involved or because Amelia Island consumed them all (Sebastián Kindelán to Juan Ruiz de Apodaca, June 4, 1813, Cuba 1790, AGI).

Chapter 10

Racial Geopolitics and the Demise of Spanish Florida

1. During the Creek War (1813–14), Americans under the command of Andrew Jackson waged a series of pitched battles against the nativist Creeks or Red Sticks. On Mar.

27, 1814, at Horseshoe Bend, the already decimated Red Sticks lost approximately another eight hundred warriors, or half their remaining force. Survivors, including the Prophet Francis, fled to Spanish Florida, where some made a final stand at Prospect Bluff (Gregory Evans Dowd, *A Spirited Resistance: The North American Indian Struggle for Unity, 1745–1815* [Baltimore, Md., 1992], 185–90).

2. Covington, "Negro Fort," 79; Coker and Watson, *Indian Traders of the Southeastern Spanish Borderlands,* 309.

3. Cockburn to Cochran, Jan. 26, 1815, cited in Mary R. Bullard, *Black Liberation on Cumberland Island in 1815* (DeLeon Springs, Fla., 1983), 56–57.

4. The captain general for Cuba and the Floridas, Juan Ruiz de Apodaca, forwarded the petitions of Spanish slaveowners to the Audiencia of Santo Domingo, which, in turn, sent them to the Council of the Indies for royal review (Representations of Juan Ruiz de Apodaca, May 6, July 13, and Aug. 9, 1815, SD 2580, AGI).

5. Kingsley, *Treatise,* 11.

6. Coker and Watson, *Indian Traders of the Southeastern Spanish Borderlands,* chap. 14; Thomas P. Abernethy, "Florida and the Spanish Frontier, 1811–1819," in *The Americanization of the Gulf Coast, 1803–1850,* ed. Lucius F. Ellsworth (Pensacola, Fla., 1972), 88–120, esp. 108–9; Bullard, *Black Liberation,* 54–61.

7. Covington, "Negro Fort," 72–91; John D. Milligan, "Slave Rebelliousness and the Florida Maroon," *Prologue: The Journal of the National Archives* 6 (Spring 1974): 5–18.

8. To protect Georgia settlers, Jackson ordered Fort Scott built at the juncture of the Flint and Chattahoochee Rivers. Vessels supplying the fort from New Orleans had to pass by the Negro Fort (Milligan, "Slave Rebelliousness," 11).

9. List of the Slaves Belonging to Owners in Pensacola, Dec. 30, 1814, and Mar. 4 and May 6, 1815, SD 2580, AGI.

10. John Innerarity to Commander Gonzalo Manrique, May 16, 1814, cited in "Documents Relating to Colonel Edward Nicolls and Captain George Woodlune in Pensacola, 1814," *Florida Historical Quarterly* 10 (July 1931): 51–54. Pintado's list identifies Billy as a cowboy and identifies his wife and children as Dolly, Crepy, Flora, Beck, Cimpthia and Neron. It identifies the eleventh missing slave as Paris, a field hand (List of the Slaves Belonging to Owners in Pensacola, Dec. 30, 1814, Mar. 4 and May 6, 1815, SD 2580, AGI). Edmund Doyle to John Innerarity, Apr. 6, 1815, cited in "The Panton, Leslie Papers, Letters of Edmund Doyle," *Florida Historical Quarterly* 17 (Jan. 1939): 237–42.

11. List of the Slaves Belonging to Owners in Pensacola, Mar. 4 and May 6, 1815, SD 2580, AGI.

12. Ibid.; Herbert Aptheker, "Maroons within the Present Limits of the United States," *Journal of Negro History* 24 (Apr. 1939): 167–84.

13. Doyle signed his letter "In hopes that you may yet hang the Scoundrel" (Edmund Doyle to Captain R. C. Spencer [of the Royal Navy], undated, "Panton, Leslie Papers, Letters of Edmund Doyle," 242). Despite Doyle's negative assessment, which was shared by the United States Indian agent, Benjamin Hawkins, Nicolls and Woodbine demonstrated concern for their black and Indian allies on a number of occasions. For instance, Nicolls of-

fered to pay the remaining two hundred pesos that the mulatto Carlos owed his owner for his freedom, but Pintado felt he had no authority to accept it (List of the Slaves Belonging to Owners in Pensacola, Dec. 30, 1814, and Mar. 4 and May 6, 1815, SD 2580, AGI).

14. Nicolls complained that Americans attacked Seminole chief Bowlegs's town on two separate occasions in March and May of 1815, killing warriors and stealing cattle (Colonel Edward Nicolls to Colonel Benjamin Hawkins, Apr. 28, and May 12, 1815; Colonel Benjamin Hawkins to Colonel Edward Nicolls, May 28, 1815; *Niles Weekly Register,* June 10, 1815).

15. Admiral Alexander Cochrane's offer of freedom was issued in Bermuda on Apr. 2, 1814 (Vicente Sebastián Pintado to José de Soto, Apr. 29, 1815, SD 2580, AGI; List of the Slaves Belonging to Owners in Pensacola, May 6, 1815, SD 2580, AGI).

16. Vicente Sebastián Pintado to José de Soto, Apr. 29, 1815, SD 2580, AGI.

17. Colonel D. L. Clinch to Colonel R. Butler, Aug. 2, 1816 cited in James Grant Forbes, *Sketches Historical and Topographical, of the Floridas; More Particularly of East Florida* (New York, 1821), 202.

18. Report by a Gentleman from New Orleans, *Niles Weekly Register,* Sept. 14, 1816; Report of the Attack of Major M'Intosh, *Niles Weekly Register,* Aug. 31, 1816.

19. Colonel D. L. Clinch to Colonel R. Butler, Aug. 2, 1816, record group 45, U.S. Navy 1775–1910, subject file J, box 181, National Archives.

20. Ibid. Colonel Clinch's letter describing the events at the Negro Fort was reprinted in the *National Intelligencer,* Nov. 15, 1819. I am indebted to Stephanie Cole for this reference. Covington, "Negro Fort," 87.

21. Alexander Arbuthnot to John Arbuthnot, Apr. 2, 1818, cited in *Narrative of A Voyage to the Spanish Main,* 216–18.

22. Hachy was also known as Hijah, and in fact he did have blacks among his people (General Edmund P. Gaines to the Seminoly Chief, and King Hachy to General Gaines, Aug. 1818, cited in ibid., 221–22).

23. Robert Ambrister to Edward Nicolls, 1818, cited in ibid., 260.

24. J. Leitch Wright, Jr., "A Note on the First Seminole War, as Seen by the Indians, Negroes, and Their British Advisors," *Journal of Southern History* 34 (Nov. 1968): 565–75. Coker and Watson, *Indian Traders of the Southeastern Spanish Borderlands,* chap. 15. From Bowlegs Town, Jackson exulted prematurely, "I have reached and destroyed this and the other town in its vicinity, and having captured the principal exciters of the war I think I may safely say, that the Indian war, for the present, is terminated" (Andrew Jackson to Governor Rabun of Georgia, Apr. 20, 1818, cited in *Niles Weekly Register,* May 23, 1818).

25. From the Suwannee, Jackson marched westward and seized Spanish Pensacola, concluding the so-called First Seminole War (Canter Brown, Jr., *Florida's Peace River Frontier* [Orlando, Fla., 1991], 9–10; Brown, "'Sarrazota,' or Runaway Negro Plantations"). Arbuthnot had warned "Tell my friend Bowlegs, that it is throwing away his people to attempt to resist such a powerful force as will be down on Sahwahnee" (Alexander Arbuthnot to John Arbuthnot, Apr. 2, 1818, cited in *Narrative of A Voyage to the Spanish Main,* 217).

26. "The Defences of the Floridas: A Report of Captain James Gadsden, Aide-de-Camp to General Andrew Jackson," *Florida Historical Quarterly* 15 (Apr. 1937): 248. Creeks and Seminoles traditionally migrated to hunting grounds in southern Florida from November to March of each year, and because the Seminole hunters traveled with their families, they established permanent villages around Tampa Bay (Brown, *Florida's Peace River Frontier,* 4–5).

27. Brown, "'Sarrazota,' or Runaway Negro Plantations"; Department of Archives, *The Bahamas in the Age of Revolution, 1775–1848* (Nassau, 1989), 16.

28. United States Secretary of War John C. Calhoun denounced the raid and blamed it on the Creek nation (Nassau *Royal Gazette and Bahama Advertiser,* Mar. 20, 1822, cited in Brown, "'Sarrazota,' or Runaway Negro Plantations'").

29. Department of Archives, *Bahamas in the Age of Revolution,* 16.

30. Thomas W. Call to Francisco de Ribera, commandant at Amelia, Sept. 23, 1813, Papers on Fernandina, 1813–17, EFP, microfilm reel 86, PKY.

31. José Hibberson to Charles Harris, Nov. 19, 1813, and Charles Harris to Governor Peter Early, Nov. 29, 1813, in "East Florida Documents," *Georgia Historical Quarterly* 13 (Mar. 1929): 154–58. On charm bags see Thompson, *Flash of the Spirit,* 117–19, and *Face of the Gods,* 56–59; and Georgia Writers' Project, *Drums and Shadows.*

32. Sen. Misc. Doc., no. 55, 36th Cong., 1 sess., 17–18; *United States v. Ferreira,* cited in Wyllys, "East Florida Revolution," 424.

33. Census of Fernandina and Amelia Island, 1814, Census Returns, 1784–1814, EFP, microfilm reel 148, PKY.

34. Forbes, *Sketches Historical and Topographical, of the Floridas,* 74. Forty percent of Florida's total population (3,729) lived on Amelia Island by 1815 (David Bushnell, "The Florida Republic: An Overview," in *La República de las Floridas: Texts and Documents,* ed. David Bushnell [Mexico City, 1986], 7–18, esp. 10).

35. Map of Fernandina and Key, State Archives, Tallahassee, Fla..

36. Susan R. Parker has traced similar residential patterning for Spanish mothers and daughters in St. Augustine and argues that because Castilian law allowed women to hold and dispose of property, mothers bequeathed to daughters rather than to husbands or sons, thus maintaining control of homesites over the generations. This made them attractive marriage partners and was a source of economic and social power. Some of the female property owners received their properties as dowries, which Spanish courts assiduously protected (Parker, "In My Mother's House").

37. "Land Claims in East Florida," *American State Papers: Public Lands,* vol. 6, 113.

38. Like other white storekeepers, Jacobo paid three pesos per trimester for a store license (Relation of Payments by Persons Maintaining Stores in Fernandina, Mar. 6, 1811, Papers on Military Posts on the St. Johns River and Amelia Island, 1740–1815, EFP, microfilm reel 86, PKY; a second mention of Jacobo's store occurs on Sept. 25, 1811, Correspondence between the Governor and Subordinates on the St. Johns and St. Marys Rivers, 1784–1820, EFP, microfilm reel 61, PKY; List of Free Morenos, Aug. 12, 1811, ibid.,

microfilm reel 61, PKY; Census of Fernandina and Amelia Island, 1814, Census Returns, 1784–1814, EFP, microfilm reel 148, PKY).

39. The unit consisted of Lieutenant Juan Jorge Jacobo, Jorge Brus, José Bont, José (Richo also Simmons?), Manuel Holsendorf, Sandi Embara (Edimboro), Bob Rivas, Jorge Ribas, Sanco, Miguel Sanco, Jorge Sanco, Estévan Cheves, Francisco Cheves, Simon Cheves, Ebran, Geronimo Travers, Juan Moses, Jary (Harry) McQueen, Thomas Mor (Moore), Eman, Pedro Botella, Antonio Mose, Juan Bautista, Jayme Clarke, Thomas Clarke, José García, Jayme Ros (List of the Black Militia of Fernandina, Aug. 12, 1811, Correspondence between the Governor and Subordinates on the St. Johns and St. Marys Rivers, 1784–1820, EFP, microfilm reel 61, PKY).

40. Other black donors were José Richo, José Brus, and Manuel Holsendolf. Jacobo, Brus, and Holsendolf were all French-speaking veterans of Santo Domingo (List of Contributors, June 25, 1810, Miscellaneous Legal Instruments and Proceedings, 1784–1819, EFP, microfilm reel 115, PKY). Many generations of Richo family members are buried in the Fernandina cemetery.

41. Clarke's will, dated Aug. 28, 1834, identified his other children by Flora as James F. Clarke, Thomas L. Clarke, Daniel L. A. Clarke, George P. Clarke, Joseph L. Clarke, John D. Clarke and William R. Clarke (Louise Biles Hill, "George J. F. Clarke," *Florida Historical Quarterly* 21 [Jan. 1943]: 199–200, 209–13, 234, 246).

Baptismal records have been located for Josef Luis Clarke, born Aug. 25, 1802, and baptized Sept. 12, 1802; Juan Nepomuceno Diego Clarke, born May 16, 1806, and baptized June 26, 1806; Guillermo Roman Clarke, born Mar. 5, 1808, and baptized Mar. 27, 1808; and Jorge Felipe Clarke, born June 6, 1814, and baptized June 20, 1814. The free mulatto Juana Fish, like Flora an ex-slave from South Carolina, was godmother to Josef Luis and Guillermo Roman, and Jorge Felipe's godparents were the free black couple Felipe and Filis Edimboro (Black Baptisms, vol. 2, CPR, microfilm reel 284 J, and vol. 3, CPR, microfilm reels 284 J and K, PKY).

42. In his 1834 will, Clarke listed his and Hannah's children as Thomas Hilario, under eight; Philip Demetrius, above five; and Eligio, about three; their fourth child was not yet born. In 1835, Clarke's claims against the United States were settled in the amount of $13,320 (Hill, "George J. F. Clarke," 200–202, 244).

43. The six natural children of Carlos Clarke and Isabella Wiggins were Ana Josefa Clarke, born Jan. 12, 1799, and baptized Oct. 31, 1799; Carlos Manuel Clarke, born Jan. 24, 1802, and baptized Feb. 20, 1802; María Leonór Clarke, born Apr. 7, 1804, and baptized Apr. 9, 1804; José Clarke, born Aug. 25, 1805, and baptized Jan. 30, 1807; Ysabel Josefa Leona María Wiggins, born Apr. 11, 1809, and baptized Apr. 22, 1809; and Jayme Francisco Clarke, born July 16, 1812, and baptized Nov. 6, 1812 (Black Baptisms, vol. 2, CPR, microfilm reel 284 J, and vol. 3, CPR, microfilm reels 284 J and K, PKY; Hill, "George J. F. Clarke," 208).

44. Clarke's district comprised Amelia, Tiger, and Talbot islands, both banks of the Nassau River, and the right bank of the St. Marys. The other elected magistrates were Zephaniah Kingsley and Henry (Enrique) Yonge (Hill, "George J. F. Clarke," 228–30;

George J. F. Clarke to Captain John R. Bell, July 25, 1821, cited in C. Seton Fleming, "George I. *[sic]* F. Clarke," *Florida Historical Quarterly* 4 [July 1925]; D. C. Corbitt, "The Return of Spanish Rule to the St. Marys and the St. Johns, 1813–1821," *Florida Historical Quarterly* 20 [July 1941]: 47–71).

45. Tomás Llorente to José Coppinger, Sept. 17, 1817, Correspondence between the Governor and Subordinates on the St. Johns and St. Marys Rivers, 1784–1820, EFP, microfilm reel 63, PKY.

46. Hill, "George J. F. Clarke"; *SLGF,* vols. 1–4.

47. List of the Black Militia of Fernandina, Aug. 12, 1811, Correspondence between the Governor and Subordinates on the St. Johns and St. Marys Rivers, 1784–1820, EFP, microfilm reel 61, PKY. Sergeant Jorge Jacobo and others of his men were veterans of the slave revolt of Santo Domingo and may have faced off against some of their erstwhile countrymen. Monthly review lists for Fernandina's black militia for 1813–15 are found in Cuba 353, AGI.

48. Tomás Llorente to Juan José de Estrada, Sept. 13, 1815, To and from Military Commanders and Other Officers, 1784–1821, EFP, microfilm reel 68, PKY.

49. *Niles Weekly Register,* Sept. 22, 1817; David Bushnell, "Florida Republic," 7–18; T. Frederick Davis, "MacGregor's Invasion"; Rufus Kay Wyllys, "The Filibusters of Amelia Island," *Georgia Historical Quarterly* 12 (Dec. 1928): 297–325. Representatives of the "republics of Mexico, Buenos Ayres, New Grenada, and Venezuela" (in Philadelphia) commissioned MacGregor to seize Amelia on his way to liberate the South American continent (Abernethy, "Florida and the Spanish Frontier," 110–14).

With MacGregor's invasion, Jorge J. F. Clarke temporarily moved his family to safety in St. Marys, Georgia, and Governor Coppinger appointed him vice consul to that state and South Carolina (Hill, "George J. F. Clarke," 230).

50. In the midst of the fighting, a small Spanish schooner loaded with slaves from the African coast sailed into view, and the insurgent privateer *Morgiana* promptly seized it (*Niles Weekly Register,* Sept. 22, 1817; Abernethy, "Florida and the Spanish Frontier," 114; *Narrative of A Voyage to the Spanish Main,* 94).

51. Jorge J. F. Clarke to José Coppinger, July 6, 1817, Correspondence between the Governor and Subordinates on the St. Johns and St. Marys Rivers, 1784–1820, EFP, microfilm reel 63, PKY.

52. Tomás de Llorente to José Coppinger, July 6, 1817, Correspondence between the Governor and Subordinates on the St. Johns and St. Marys Rivers, 1784–1820, EFP, microfilm reel 63, PKY.

53. Bando of Governor José Coppinger, July 10, 1817, Proclamations and Edicts, 1786–1821, EFP, microfilm reel 118, PKY. Members of the extended Clarke families who received these military service grants included Jorge J. F. Clarke, his sons James, Thomas, and Daniel, and his son-in-law William Garvin, husband of Felicia, Carlos Clarke, and his son Carlos W. Clarke (Hill, "George J. F. Clarke," 217, 222–23).

54. Since many of his own forces included freed blacks, this offer might have actually added to black property holdings in Florida, but Aury never had a chance to deliver on

his promises (David Bushnell, "Florida Republic," 13–17; Abernethy, "Florida and the Spanish Frontier," 114).

55. William R. Rein, "Filibustering Expeditions of Sir Gregor MacGregor and Luis Aury against Spanish East Florida" (M.A. thesis, Auburn University, 1971), 61, cited in David Bushnell, "Florida Republic," 15; Thomas Wayne to Benjamin Homans, Sept. 27, 1817, cited in *Niles Weekly Register,* Jan. 3, 1818.

56. *Niles Weekly Register,* Nov. 29, 1817.

57. Letters of Captain John H. Elton to the secretary of the navy, Oct. 19, 1817, and Jan. 3, 1818, cited in *Niles Weekly Register,* Nov. 29, 1817; Belton A. Copp, collector of Port of St. Marys, Ga., cited in T. Frederick Davis, "MacGregor's Invasion," 45.

58. John Houston McIntosh to Secretary of the Treasury William H. Crawford, July 30, 1817, *American State Papers. Documents, Legislative and Executive, of the Congress of the United States . . . Selected and Edited under the Authority of Congress,* 38 vols. (Washington, D.C., 1832–61), Class 1: *Foreign Relations,* vol. 4, 128, cited in T. Frederick Davis, "MacGregor's Invasion," 39. The same letter appeared in the *Savannah Republican,* Nov. 8, 1817, cited in David Bushnell, "Florida Republic," 25, and in the *Niles Weekly Register,* Jan. 3, 1818; *Savannah Republican,* Jan. 3, 1818.

59. Wyllys, "Filibusters of Amelia Island"; President James Monroe to Congress, Dec. 2, 1817, *American State Papers: Foreign Relations,* vol. 4, 130, cited in T. Frederick Davis, "MacGregor's Invasion," 59–60; Abernethy, "Florida and the Spanish Frontier," 116; Hill, "George J. F. Clarke," 234.

60. L. David Norris, "The Squeeze: Spain Cedes Florida to the United States," in *Clash between Cultures: Spanish East Florida, 1784–1821,* ed. Jacqueline K. Fretwell and Susan R. Parker (St. Augustine, Fla., 1988), 103–33, esp. 124–25.

61. Proclamation of José Coppinger, July 7, 1821, cited in ibid., 127.

62. Relation of the Florida Exiles, Aug. 22, 1821, Cuba 357 and 358, AGI.

63. David Geggus describes the conservative approach of the slave rebels of Saint Domingue and their use of "church-and-king" rhetoric ("Racial Equality, Slavery, and Colonial Secession during the Constituent Assembly"). Other scholars agree on the use of the rhetoric, if not on its sincerity.

64. List of the Officials . . . Emigrated, Nov. 13, 1823, Cuba 358, AGI.

65. Landers, "Traditions of African American Freedom"; Schafer, "Shades of Freedom"; Anna Ruth B. Barr and Modeste Hargis, "The Voluntary Exile of Free Negroes of Pensacola," *Florida Historical Quarterly* 17 (1938): 3–14.

Afterword

1. Jane Gilmer Landers, *The World around Us: Florida* (New York, 1995).

2. Even the important and pioneering work of Kenneth W. Porter, to whom we are all indebted, suffers from this defect. A revised edition of Porter's work attempts some inclusion of Spanish language sources from Mexico, but none from Florida (Kenneth W.

Porter, *The Black Seminoles,* rev. and ed. Alcione M. Amos and Thomas P. Senter [Gainesville, Fla., 1996]).

3. *A Guide to African Villages in New Providence,* comp. Patrice Williams (Nassau, Bahamas, 1979); Department of Archives, *Bahamas in the Age of Revolution,* 16.

4. Canter Brown, Jr. "The Florida Crisis of 1826–1827 and the Second Seminole War," *Florida Historical Quarterly* 73 (1995): 419–42. Although more distant, the Denmark Vesey (1822) and Nat Turner (1831) Revolts heightened fears of slave insurrection throughout the South.

5. Klos, "Blacks and the Seminole Indian Removal Debate"; Mulroy, *Freedom on the Border;* Brown, "Florida Crisis."

6. Canter Brown, Jr., "Race Relations in Territorial Florida, 1821–1845," *Florida Historical Quarterly* 73 (Jan. 1995): 287–307; Schafer, "'Class of People neither Freemen nor Slaves.'" In 1824 James Clarke, the quadroon son of Jorge J. F. Clarke, contested a discriminatory race-based tax and, agreeing that the tax was unconstitutional, Superior Court Justice Smith prohibited its collection *(East Florida Herald,* Nov. 20, 1824). I am indebted to Charles Tingley for this reference.

7. *St. Augustine News,* Sept. 13, 1839, SAHS; Reward offered by John L'Engle for return of a slave, Primus, Apr. 6, 1839, and reward offered by John Hamlet for return of Mosea, Apr. 27, 1839, *St. Augustine News,* SAHS; *St. Augustine News,* July 29, Aug. 5, Oct. 7, Oct. 20, 1843, SAHS.

Index

JANE LANDERS is an assistant professor of history and a member of the Center for Latin American and Iberian Studies at Vanderbilt University. Her interest in the Caribbean and in the historical study of race relations dates to her childhood in the Dominican Republic. She received her M.A. in inter-American studies from the Center for Advanced International Studies at the University of Miami and her Ph.D. in colonial Latin American history at the University of Florida. Landers's earlier publications include two edited volumes, *Against the Odds: Free Blacks in the Slave Societies of the Americas* (London, 1996) and *The African American Heritage of Florida,* which she coedited with David R. Colburn. She has also published essays on the African history of the Hispanic Southeast and of the circum-Caribbean in the *American Historical Review, The New West Indian Guide, Colonial Latin American Historical Review,* and *Slavery and Abolition.*

Blacks in the New World

Before the Ghetto: Black Detroit in the Nineteenth Century *David M. Katzman*

Black Business in the New South: A Social History of the North Carolina Mutual Life Insurance Company *Walter B. Weare*

The Search for a Black Nationality: Black Colonization and Emigration, 1787–1863 *Floyd J. Miller*

Black Americans and the White Man's Burden, 1898–1903 *Willard B. Gatewood, Jr.*

Slavery and the Numbers Game: A Critique of *Time on the Cross* *Herbert G. Gutman*

A Ghetto Takes Shape: Black Cleveland, 1870–1930 *Kenneth L. Kusmer*

Freedmen, Philanthropy, and Fraud: A History of the Freedman's Savings Bank *Carl R. Osthaus*

The Democratic Party and the Negro: Northern and National Politics, 1868–92 *Lawrence Grossman*

Black Ohio and the Color Line, 1860–1915 *David A. Gerber*

Along the Color Line: Explorations in the Black Experience *August Meier and Elliott Rudwick*

Black over White: Negro Political Leadership in South Carolina during Reconstruction *Thomas Holt*

Keeping the Faith: A. Philip Randolph, Milton P. Webster, and the Brotherhood of Sleeping Car Porters, 1925–37 *William H. Harris*

Abolitionism: The Brazilian Antislavery Struggle *Joaquim Nabuco; translated and edited by Robert Conrad*

Black Georgia in the Progressive Era, 1900–1920 *John Dittmer*

Medicine and Slavery: Health Care of Blacks in Antebellum Virginia *Todd L. Savitt*

Alley Life in Washington: Family, Community, Religion, and Folklife in the City, 1850–1970 *James Borchert*

Human Cargoes: The British Slave Trade to Spanish America, 1700–1739 *Colin A. Palmer*

Southern Black Leaders of the Reconstruction Era *Edited by Howard N. Rabinowitz*

Black Leaders of the Twentieth Century *Edited by John Hope Franklin and August Meier*

Slaves and Missionaries: The Disintegration of Jamaican Slave Society, 1787–1834 *Mary Turner*

Father Divine and the Struggle for Racial Equality *Robert Weisbrot*

Communists in Harlem during the Depression *Mark Naison*

Down from Equality: Black Chicagoans and the Public Schools, 1920–41 *Michael W. Homel*

Race and Kinship in a Midwestern Town: The Black Experience in Monroe, Michigan, 1900–1915 *James E. DeVries*

Down by the Riverside: A South Carolina Slave Community *Charles Joyner*

Black Milwaukee: The Making of an Industrial Proletariat, 1915–45 *Joe William Trotter, Jr.*

Religious Philanthropy and Colonial Slavery: The American Correspondence of the Associates of Dr. Bray, 1717–77 *Edited by John C. Van Horne*

Black History and the Historical Profession, 1915–80 *August Meier and Elliott Rudwick*
Paul Cuffe: Black Entrepreneur and Pan-Africanist (formerly Rise to Be a People: A Biography of Paul Cuffe) *Lamont D. Thomas*
Making Their Own Way: Southern Blacks' Migration to Pittsburgh, 1916–30 *Peter Gottlieb*
My Bondage and My Freedom *Frederick Douglass; edited by William L. Andrews*
Black Leaders of the Nineteenth Century *Edited by Leon Litwack and August Meier*
Charles Richard Drew: The Man and the Myth *Charles E. Wynes*
John Mercer Langston and the Fight for Black Freedom, 1829–65 *William Cheek and Aimee Lee Cheek*
The Old Village and the Great House: An Archaeological and Historical Examination of Drax Hall Plantation, St. Ann's Bay, Jamaica *Douglas V. Armstrong*
Black Property Owners in the South, 1790–1915 *Loren Schweninger*
The Sociogenesis of a Race Riot: Springfield, Illinois, in 1908 *Roberta Senechal*
Coal, Class, and Color: Blacks in Southern West Virginia, 1915–32 *Joe William Trotter, Jr.*
No Crooked Death: Coatesville, Pennsylvania, and the Lynching of Zachariah Walker *Dennis B. Downey and Raymond M. Hyser*
Black Towns and Profit: Promotion and Development in the Trans-Appalachian West, 1877–1915 *Kenneth Marvin Hamilton*
Slaves, Peasants, and Rebels: Reconsidering Brazilian Slavery *Stuart B. Schwartz*
Africa in America: Slave Acculturation and Resistance in the American South and the British Caribbean, 1736–1831 *Michael Mullin*
The Creation of Jazz: Music, Race, and Culture in Urban America *Burton W. Peretti*
Kenneth and John B. Rayner and the Limits of Southern Dissent *Gregg Cantrell*
Lynching in the New South: Georgia and Virginia, 1880–1930 *W. Fitzhugh Brundage*
Local People: The Struggle for Civil Rights in Mississippi *John Dittmer*
Indians at Hampton Institute, 1877–1923 *Donal F. Lindsey*
A Voice of Thunder: A Black Soldier's Civil War (formerly A Voice of Thunder: The Civil War Letters of George E. Stephens) *Edited by Donald Yacovone*
Freedom's Port: The African American Community of Baltimore, 1790–1860 *Christopher Phillips*
Black Society in Spanish Florida *Jane Landers*

Reprint Editions

King: A Biography (2d ed.) *David Levering Lewis*
The Death and Life of Malcolm X (2d ed.) *Peter Goldman*
Race Relations in the Urban South, 1865–1890 *Howard N. Rabinowitz; foreword by C. Vann Woodward*
Race Riot at East St. Louis, July 2, 1917 *Elliott Rudwick*
W. E. B. Du Bois: Voice of the Black Protest Movement *Elliott Rudwick*

The Negro's Civil War: How American Negroes Felt and Acted during the War for the Union *James M. McPherson*

Lincoln and Black Freedom: A Study in Presidential Leadership *LaWanda Cox*

Slavery and Freedom in the Age of the American Revolution *Edited by Ira Berlin and Ronald Hoffman*

Diary of a Sit-In (2d ed.) *Merrill Proudfoot; introduction by Michael S. Mayer*

They Who Would Be Free: Blacks' Search for Freedom, 1830–61 *Jane H. Pease and William H. Pease*

The Reshaping of Plantation Society: The Natchez District, 1860–80 *Michael Wayne*

Rice and Slaves: Ethnicity and the Slave Trade in Colonial South Carolina *Daniel C. Littlefield*

Race Riot: Chicago in the Red Summer of 1919 *William M. Tuttle, Jr.*

Typeset in 10.5/13 Adobe Garamond
with Adobe Garamond display
Designed by Dennis Roberts
Composed at the University of Illinois Press

University of Illinois Press
1325 South Oak Street
Champaign, IL 61820-6903
www.press.uillinois.edu